— *Asian Law Center* —

UNIVERSITY OF WASHINGTON

SCHOOL OF LAW

ASIAN LAW SERIES

NUMBER 19

The Asian Law Series was initiated in 1969, with thc cooperation of the University of Washington Press and the Institute for Comparative and Foreign Area Studies (now the Henry M. Jackson School of International Studies). A complete listing of the books in the series appears at the end of the book.

LAW
IN JAPAN

A Turning Point

Edited by
DANIEL H. FOOTE

UNIVERSITY OF WASHINGTON PRESS
Seattle and London

This book was funded by a generous grant from Nagashima Ohno & Tsunematsu through the cooperation of the Japan Foundation.

Printed in United States of America
Designed by Pam Canell
12 11 10 09 08 07 5 4 3 2 1

University of Washington Press
PO Box 50096, Seattle, WA 98145
www.washington.edu/uwpress

Library of Congress Cataloging-in-Publication Data
Law in Japan : a turning point / /Edited by Daniel H. Foote.
p. cm. — (Asian law series ; no. 19)
ISBN–13: 978-0-295-98731-6 (hardback : alk. paper)
ISBN–10: 0-295-98731-6 (hardback : alk. paper)
1. Law—Japan—History. 2. Justice, Administration of—Japan—History.
I. Foote, Daniel H. (Daniel Harrington), 1954–
KNX120.L39 2007 349.52—dc22 2007025511

The paper used in this publication is acid-free and meets the minimum requirements of American National Standard for Information Sciences—Permanence of Paper for Printed Library Materials, ANSI Z39.48–1984.∞

DEDICATED TO THE MEMORY OF DAN FENNO HENDERSON

Contents

Preface and Acknowledgments

DANIEL H. FOOTE

In September 1961, a historic conference took place at Harvard Law School. Twelve of Japan's leading legal authorities presented papers discussing fundamental issues in their respective fields of expertise. Over the course of the conference, they explored those and many other issues together with some thirty U.S. scholars, as well as three Japanese legal scholars then beginning their graduate studies at Harvard. Those twelve essays, along with five additional papers exploring other major fields of Japanese law, were ably edited by Professor Arthur Taylor von Mehren and published two years later in the classic work *Law in Japan: The Legal Order in a Changing Society.*

The current project is modeled on the 1961 conference and resulting book. Building on that foundation, the current project seeks to look back—by exploring the major developments that have taken place in Japanese law over the intervening four decades—and to look ahead—by examining prospects for Japanese law in the coming years of the twenty-first century.

At a conference in August 2002 in Seattle, Washington, sponsored by the Law Offices of Nagashima Ohno & Tsunematsu and held under the auspices of the Asian Law Center of the University of Washington School of Law, seventeen of Japan's leading legal experts gave presentations in their fields of expertise. In a reflection of the vast expansion in the field of Japanese law since 1961, this time the Japanese participants were joined by an equal number of foreign experts on Japanese law, with seventeen non-Japanese scholars making presentations as well. (In a further reflection of the growth of interest in Japanese law, nearly one hundred people attended the 2002 conference, from Europe and other parts of Asia as well as the United States and Japan, and from the worlds of government and practice as well as academia.) Twenty-five of the essays, exploring most of the major fields of Japanese law, were developed into the chapters of this volume.

The 1961 conference and book represented the culmination of the Japanese American Program for Cooperation in Legal Studies, a program that began in 1954, enabled by support from the Ford Foundation. The Cooperative Program, including the conference and book, played a vital role in the development of the field of Japanese legal studies in the United States. It is scarcely an exaggeration to say that the Cooperative Program led to the very recognition of Japanese legal studies as a field worthy of study in its own right. *Law in Japan: The Legal Order in a Changing Society* became an instant classic (and remains a valuable reference work to this day). The essays contained in that volume revealed the richness and the intellectual excitement offered by the field of Japanese law. Many of those essays spurred interest among scholars in the United States, Japan, and elsewhere, which in turn generated further waves of scholarship. The impetus generated by the Cooperative Program also fostered greater interest in Japanese law at several law schools in the United States. That interest, along with additional funding from the Ford Foundation, led to the establishment of Japanese legal studies programs at the University of Washington School of Law (which later became the Asian Law Center) and the University of Michigan School of Law, as well as the East Asian Legal Studies program at Harvard Law School. In addition, the Cooperative Program helped provide the impetus for the establishment, in 1964, of the Japanese American Society for Legal Studies, an organization devoted to the mutual understanding of American and Japanese law. One of the undertakings of that society was the publication, from 1967 through 2002, of the journal *Law in Japan: An Annual*. As its title reflects, the roots of that journal lie in the 1963 book, and for many years *Law in Japan: An Annual* was the only consistent source for articles in English concerning Japanese law.

As of 1961, the major postwar legal reforms were still fresh in people's minds. As indicated by the subtitle, *The Legal Order in a Changing Society*, many of the chapters for that conference explored the manner in which fundamental reforms patterned on U.S. law, such as the adversary system and constitutional review powers, had developed in Japan. Today, Japan is in the midst of another period of fundamental reform. As the subtitle of this book suggests, Japanese law is at "a turning point." The chapters of this book capture the extent of the change in this, another watershed period for Japanese law and society.

The structure of this conference and volume reflects two sets of developments during the intervening four decades. First, inevitably, some fields of law declined in importance while others expanded, thereby warranting shifts in coverage. Thus, this volume contains chapters on environmental law, health law, intellectual property, and insolvency, all fields that have increased dramatically in importance in the interim.

A second major development is the great rise in the study of Japanese law by non-Japanese scholars, brought about in part by the very success of the original conference and the other activities of the Japanese American Program for Cooperation in Legal Studies. For the 1961 conference, each of the Japanese participants was paired with an American "editorial assistant." Reflecting the vast increase in the number of non-Japanese scholars who specialize in Japanese law, the collaboration for the 2002 conference was taken one step further. For each of the fields included, a leading Japanese scholar was paired with a non-Japanese scholar whose research has focused on the same field of Japanese law. (The sole exception was the field of intellectual property, where Professors Toshiko Takenaka and Naoki Koizumi, both native Japanese, were paired. As Professor Takenaka has taught at the University of Washington since 1993 and has conducted extensive research in Germany, she brings a strong international perspective to the field.) Notably, the study of Japanese law has expanded greatly not just in the United States but in Europe and Asia as well. That growth is made apparent by the fact that the non-Japanese participants included scholars from Germany and Australia, as well as the United States. Indeed, the growth in the field of Japanese legal studies outside Japan posed two enviable problems with regard to organizing the project. There are so many excellent scholars that it was not possible to include them all; many outstanding scholars had to be left out. Moreover, many scholars have conducted in-depth research in several different fields of Japanese law; deciding which field they should be asked to focus on posed a bit of a dilemma. (In organizing the conference, though, I was grateful that virtually all those invited to participate willingly agreed to do so, without questioning the fields or pairings I had suggested.)

Notwithstanding the great expansion in the Japanese legal studies field over the past four decades, the number of specialists in Japanese law in the United States (and elsewhere outside Japan) still pales in comparison to the number of law professors who focus on Europe. As the chapters of this volume demonstrate, however, the range of scholarship on Japanese law is truly impressive.

In addition to comparative perspectives, the chapters offer a variety of theoretical approaches, including law and economics perspectives and a wide range of historical and socio-legal perspectives.

As with the 1961 conference, the key to success for this project lay in achieving the participation of top scholars in the various fields, rather than in seeking to micromanage the specific contents of their contributions. To that end the form of collaboration was left entirely to the discretion of the two scholars. As the chapters of this volume show, the chosen approaches varied. In some cases the two scholars worked closely together in preparing a single joint paper; seven of the chapters in this book follow that pattern. In others, such as constitutional law, the two scholars coordinated their efforts in preparing separate chapters exploring different aspects of the same field. In still others, one of the scholars prepared the main paper and the other prepared a written response (that being the pattern for the chapters on administrative law, criminal law, and taxation in this volume). Finally, in a few cases, one of the collaborators prepared a chapter, with the collaborator offering comments and suggestions in advance of the conference, along with oral remarks at the conference. Whatever the approach taken, the chapters reflect outstanding scholarship in the respective fields. The chapters were prepared for the 2002 conference. Some subsequent developments have been incorporated, but not all. Rather, the primary focus of this work is on the major themes that have animated Japanese law over the past four decades and ongoing trends. Just as the themes explored in 1961 have continued to resonate over the intervening four decades, the themes explored in this volume seem certain to continue to resonate for many years to come.

In addition to serving as an opportunity to consider developments since the first Law in Japan conference and to look ahead to future prospects for Japanese law and society, this project serves two other major purposes. First, it serves as a celebration of the merger, in 2000, of the law firm Nagashima & Ohno with the law firm Tsunematsu Yanase & Sekine, to form the Law Offices of Nagashima Ohno & Tsunematsu, Japan's largest full-service law firm. To commemorate the merger in a manner that would have a lasting impact, Nagashima Ohno & Tsunematsu graciously offered to sponsor the 2002 conference. Without that support, this project would not have been possible. This volume serves as testament to the commitment of Nagashima Ohno & Tsunematsu to broadened understanding and appreciation of Japanese law.

Second, this volume also serves to honor the late Professor Dan Fenno Henderson, a true giant in the field of Japanese legal studies. Professor Henderson expressed enthusiasm about the concept for this project and was actively involved in the initial planning efforts. By all rights, he would have offered a keynote address at the conference. Tragically, Professor Henderson passed away in March 2001, at the age of seventy-nine. It is my fond hope that this volume may serve as a fitting tribute to his legacy.

The list of people and organizations to acknowledge is long. First, I am grateful to Professor von Mehren (who, in another great loss, passed away in 2006) and everyone else involved in the original Law in Japan conference and book for providing such a fine model to follow. In adjusting that model to today's circumstances, I benefited from advice from many people, including Professors John O. Haley, J. Mark Ramseyer, Veronica L. Taylor, and Masahito Inouye. I deeply appreciate the support of the Japanese Ministry of Justice for this project, and I am grateful for the kind advice and support of Prosecutor General Akio Harada, who participated actively in discussions at the conference (in addition to providing advice both before and since the conference), and for the support of Mitsuhiro Katsumaru, Kazumi Okamura, and many others from the Ministry of Justice.

I extend my sincere appreciation to everyone who participated in or attended the conference. In addition to those whose chapters appear in this volume (to whom I extend special thanks), I am deeply grateful to the following scholars who submitted essays or made presentations at the conference: Professors Misao Tatsuta, Doshisha University (and Professor Emeritus, Kyoto University); Richard O. Kummert, the University of Washington School of Law; Masahito Inouye, the University of Tokyo; Shigeaki Tanaka, then of Kyoto University (and now of Kwansei Gakuin University); and Takeshi Kojima, Chuo University; and Mr. Alan Miller, the World Bank. I extend special thanks to Mr. Eugene Lee, Mr. Paul Clarke, Mr. Yasuhiro Fujita, and Professor Haley for moving tributes to Professor Henderson at a conference dinner. I would also like to express my appreciation for the Ministry of Education, Culture, Sports, Science and Technology, Grant-in-Aid for Scientific Research (B)(2), No. 13420012, 2001–2005, which helped provide support for my own work on this project.

I express my deep appreciation to my former employer, the University of Washington, for its continued support for this project even though I had moved to the University of Tokyo before the conference actually took place. Among the many people and organizations at the University of Washington that provided support for this project, I am grateful to the then-president, Richard McCormick, who hosted a reception for the participants at the president's official residence; to the School of Law and Dean Joe Knight, who hosted a dinner and supported the project in many ways (as well as former dean Roland Hjorth, who provided support during the planning stage); to the Asian Law Center at the School of Law; to Dana Raigrodski, assistant director of the Asian Law Center; to the many staff members who assisted in this project, including Kathy Kline, Margaret Reynolds, and Frances Scott; to research assistants, including Bryan Brown, Toshitaka Kudo, Kyoko Ishida, and Scot Ritchey; and, especially, to Professor Veronica L. Taylor, director of the Asian Law Center, who has provided invaluable advice and support, and who has expended tremendous time and effort, at all stages of this project. I am also grateful to Lorri Hagman, Mary Ribesky, and the University of Washington Press for their assistance.

In closing, I would like to express my special gratitude to one organization, the Law Offices of Nagashima Ohno & Tsunematsu, and two individuals, Mr. Yasuharu Nagashima and Professor Dan Fenno Henderson.

All those connected with the conference and this volume are deeply indebted to the Law Offices of Nagashima Ohno & Tsunematsu for its support. Without that support, this project would not have been possible.

I am personally grateful to Mr. Nagashima in many ways. Most people familiar with Japanese law know Mr. Nagashima as an outstanding lawyer, the guiding force behind Japan's flagship law firm. To me, he is also a mentor. When he was a visiting professor at Harvard Law School in 1978, he taught the first course in Japanese law I ever took. Sixteen years later, when we were both visiting professors at Harvard Law School, I was delighted and honored to have the opportunity to co-teach a class with him. Throughout his entire professional career, Mr. Nagashima has dedicated himself to the mutual understanding of Japanese and U.S. law. For forty years, from the founding of the Japanese American Society for Legal Studies in 1964 through 2004, he served as a director of that society (including four years as representative director). In fact, Mr. Nagashima's connection to the original Law in Japan conference is even more direct; in the fall of 1961, he was one of the three Japanese legal scholars then beginning their graduate studies at Harvard, and thus he himself attended the original conference. (Incidentally, another of those three young scholars was Professor Hiroshi Kaneko, who contributed the chapter on taxation in this volume.) A few years ago, when I mentioned my idea for a follow-up Law in Japan conference to Mr. Nagashima and described the difficulty I was experiencing in locating financial support for the project, I was oblivious to his personal involvement in the original conference and had no thought whatsoever that he or his firm might sponsor the follow-up conference. It thus came as a great—and very pleasant—surprise when he later contacted me to inquire whether the Law Offices of Nagashima Ohno & Tsunematsu might sponsor the project. For that sponsorship, for his lifelong commitment to mutual understanding of Japanese and U.S. law, and for all I have learned from him over the past twenty-nine years, I am deeply grateful to Mr. Yasuharu Nagashima.

Above all, I am grateful to Professor Dan Fenno Henderson, my mentor, colleague, and friend.

Introduction and Overview

Japanese Law at a Turning Point

DANIEL H. FOOTE

Japanese law is in the midst of a period of major change. It truly does stand at a turning point. From 1961, when the first Law in Japan conference was held, through the 1980s, the situation in most of the major fields of Japanese law might best be summed up by the term *gradualism*. That term is often associated with the field of employment discrimination,[1] but, as the chapters contained in this volume reflect, it might equally be applied to any number of other fields of law.

There are exceptions, of course. Pollution and environmental law did not even merit a mention in the 1963 volume *Law in Japan: The Legal Order in a Changing Society*.[2] In the decade after that book appeared, as discussed in the chapter on environmental law by Professor Kōichirō Fujikura in this volume,[3] Minamata and other environmental disasters precipitated what, by any measure, rank as far-reaching reforms—reforms that extended to the judicial, administrative, and legislative realms. As of the early 1960s, motor-vehicle accidents had become a sufficiently serious problem to warrant a full chapter in the 1963 volume, by Professor Ichirō Katō.[4] As mentioned in the chapter on dispute resolution by Professor Eric A. Feldman in this volume,[5] in the 1960s major reforms were undertaken in the handling of traffic accident disputes, mainly at the judicial level (but, notably, with significant involvement in relevant discussions by Professor Katō himself). Although coming relatively late in the 1980s, the tax reforms of 1986–88 discussed by Professor Hiroshi Kaneko[6] warrant special note. Anger over one of those reforms, the introduction of the Consumption Tax, energized the electorate, which in turn played at least an indirect role in laying the groundwork for some of the subsequent major reforms.

In field after field, however, from the 1960s through the 1980s change was incremental. One need only glance through the chapters in this volume to find numerous prominent examples of gradual, incremental change, including in the fields of civil procedure, constitutional law, administrative law, criminal law and procedure, and legal education. One might add to that list the subjects to which Professor Dan Fenno Henderson devoted an entire 574–page book, foreign investment and regulation of foreign enterprise.[7]

In sharp contrast, the 1990s and the first few years of the twenty-first century have witnessed pathbreaking change. The changes are not simply isolated changes to individual statutes, but rather extend to fundamental reform of the justice system. Indeed, in many ways these changes represent a reshaping of Japanese society itself. The chapters in this volume explore the major changes admirably. There is no need to catalog all of them here; a few examples will suffice. As discussed by Professor Kazuyuki Takahashi,[8] electoral and other reforms have aimed at strengthening political leadership, centered on a strong prime minister and Cabinet. In the administrative law realm, the Administrative Procedure Act of 1993 and the Information Disclosure Act of 1999, discussed by Professors Katsuya Uga[9] and Tom Ginsburg,[10] have altered the landscape of relations between, respectively, bureaucrats and regulated parties and bureaucrats and the general public. Another major development, the push for deregulation, is a central theme of the chapter by Professors Yoshirō Miwa and J. Mark Ramseyer[11] and is raised in numerous other chapters as well. And Professor Kahei Rokumoto examines in detail the sweeping reform in the system of legal education.[12]

I. JUSTICE SYSTEM REFORM COUNCIL

The extent of change in the legal realm is exemplified, above all, by one set of events: the Justice System Reform Council of 1999–2001 (hereinafter, the Reform Council or simply the council) and the reforms resulting from that council's recommendations. Several chapters in this volume describe specific aspects of the Reform Council's recommendations and resulting reforms. To give some sense of the scope of the recent changes in Japanese law, however, it may be useful here at the outset of this volume to provide a brief overview of the Reform Council's activities and recommendations and the resulting reforms.

The Justice System Reform Council was established through legislation enacted by the Diet in July 1999, at the behest of Prime Minister Keizō Obuchi. According to the Justice System Reform Council Establishment Act, the Reform Council was established for the following purposes:

> to clarify the role to be played by justice in Japanese society in the 21st century; and to examine and deliberate fundamental measures necessary for the realization of a justice system that is easy for the people to utilize, measures necessary for participation by the people in the justice system, measures necessary for . . . strengthening the functions of the legal profession, and other reforms of the justice system, as well as improvements in the infrastructure of that system.[13]

As that list reflects, the Reform Council's mandate was broad, extending to all aspects of the justice system. And the Reform Council pursued that mandate vigorously.

A. THE REFORM COUNCIL'S COMPOSITION AND ACTIVITIES

Of the Reform Council's thirteen members, only three—a practicing attorney, a former judge, and a former prosecutor—came from the legal profession per se. Three more were legal academics. The other seven, constituting a majority of the council, came from fields other than law, with two professors from non-law fields, two business leaders, a labor leader, a consumer advocate, and a well-known novelist. Each of the members was nominated by name, and all were approved by the Diet.

The composition of the Reform Council was important. In the past, decisions about matters directly related to the justice system had been left largely to the so-called *hōsō sansha*—the "three branches" of the legal profession, that is, the practicing bar, the judiciary, and the procuracy, with consensus by all three branches usually required before significant action could be undertaken. Under those circumstances, there had been a marked tendency to maintain the status quo; fundamental reform had proven difficult to achieve. By limiting representation of the *hōsō sansha* to just three members, and by insuring added legitimacy through Diet approval of each of the members, the structure of the Reform Council was instrumental in enabling fundamental reexamination of the justice system.

The Reform Council was assisted by a secretariat of approximately a dozen members. The executive director of the secretariat was seconded from the

Ministry of Justice, and the staff of the secretariat included members drawn from all three branches of the legal profession, as well as other ministries and business. The Reform Council was wary of the danger that its agenda or recommendations might be dominated by the *hōsō sansha* indirectly, through the influence of the secretariat. To reduce that possibility, in the early stages of its deliberations the Reform Council proceeded by dividing up the major topics and having individual council members report on those topics; the full council then discussed those topics collectively in setting its future agenda.[14]

The Reform Council was impaneled for a two-year term. During those two years, the council undertook extensive investigation into many aspects of the entire justice system. It held over sixty meetings, including several all-day sessions. Among other activities, it also held public hearings at four locations around Japan; conducted fact-finding visits to justice-related organizations; commissioned a survey of court users, focused on litigants in civil cases; and undertook visits to Europe and the United States to examine other justice systems. In addition to the public hearings and user survey, the Reform Council solicited public comment in various other ways. The meetings themselves were not open to the general public but were open to the press (via video-camera link to an adjoining room), and a number of the sessions received considerable publicity. Moreover, the minutes of the meetings were released and posted on the Internet.[15] The Reform Council also issued an extensive interim report,[16] setting forth basic principles for the reforms along with a wide range of tentative recommendations, on which it solicited public comment.

B. THE "THREE PILLARS" OF JUSTICE SYSTEM REFORM

On June 12, 2001, the Reform Council issued a comprehensive set of recommendations, in a final report bearing the subtitle *A Justice System to Support Japan in the 21st Century*.[17] That report was well over one hundred pages long, and the recommendations extended to a vast range of aspects of the justice system.

At the outset of its final report, the Reform Council announced three basic principles underlying the reforms, the so-called three pillars of the reforms. These three pillars, which closely paralleled the reform goals set forth by the Diet in the law establishing the Reform Council, were as follows:

First, achieving "a justice system that meets public expectations." In the words of the council, "in order to achieve 'a justice system that meets public expectations,' the justice system shall be made easier to use, easier to understand, and more reliable."

Second, strengthening "the legal profession supporting the justice system."

By reforming the legal profession, the council concluded, "a legal profession that . . . is rich both in quality and quantity shall be secured."

Third, "establishing a popular base for the justice system." In explaining this third pillar, the council stated, "Public trust in the justice system shall be enhanced by introducing systems for popular participation in legal proceedings and other measures."[18]

In the view of the Reform Council, all three pillars were closely interrelated. As a prominent example, one of the concerns underlying many of the council's recommendations was the perception that the justice system—not only the courts and judges, but all three branches of the legal profession—were too insulated and did not sufficiently respond to or reflect the views of the public. One part of the solution to this perceived shortcoming lay in the first pillar, in the form of recommendations for measures to enhance access to and understanding of the justice system by the general public. Yet, while such measures might "respond to popular expectations," they would still in essence emanate from the top down. To ensure that the views of the public would be directly reflected in the justice system in the future, the third pillar, popular participation, also was vital. In connection with popular participation, the so-called *saiban'in* system—the Japanese-style jury system (discussed in more detail below)—has received the lion's share of the publicity, but the Reform Council recommended expansion of existing systems and establishment of new systems for popular participation in many other settings as well, so as to ensure that the views of the public would be reflected throughout the justice system.

In the view of the Reform Council, the second pillar—strengthening the legal profession—also was crucial to each of the other pillars. A strengthened legal profession was seen as vital not only for expanding access to and understanding of the justice system but for enabling meaningful popular participation in the justice system. Accordingly, both of the other pillars envisioned an expanded role for the legal profession, and thus depended heavily on a legal profession strengthened both in terms of quantity and quality. Indeed, in a reflection of how important this second pillar was to successful achievement of the other reforms, strengthening the legal profession was placed first on the agenda at the implementation stage.

C. PRIOR PROPOSALS FOR JUSTICE SYSTEM REFORM

The deliberations of the Reform Council were not the first time many of the same concerns had been raised. The Reform Council was not even the first official body to investigate the justice system as a whole and offer recommendations for fundamental reform. That distinction belongs to the Provisional Justice System Investigation Committee (hereinafter, the Investigation Committee), a twenty-member committee (consisting of seven Diet members, three judges, three prosecutors, three attorneys, and four scholars and chaired by leading legal scholar Professor Sakae Wagatsuma), which was established in 1962.

Like the Reform Council, the Investigation Committee met for two years. Its investigation was narrower in scope than that of the Reform Council, focusing primarily on the legal profession and the court system. Within that more limited range, the Investigation Committee's final recommendations,[19] issued in 1964, bear a number of striking similarities to the Reform Council's recommendations, issued thirty-seven years later. Just as with the Reform Council, for example, the Investigation Committee called for increasing the number of judges, recruiting more judges from among practicing lawyers and prosecutors, increasing legal aid, placing greater emphasis on legal ethics, and taking steps to encourage lawyers to practice in areas other than the large cities. Most notably, the Investigation Committee also emphasized the need for substantial increases in the size of the bar.

The recommendation for increasing the size of the bar may have had a slight impact. The year the Investigation Committee issued its recommendations, 1964, the number of successful passers of the bar examination exceeded 500 for the first time. The increase was only 12 from the year before, however, from 496 to 508. Moreover, despite a 30 percent increase in Japan's population and a dramatic expansion in economic activity over the subsequent twenty-five years, the number of passers remained virtually unchanged, at approximately 500 per year, until 1990, followed by only gradual increases thereafter. Most of the Investigation Committee's other recommendations languished for a number of years and then disappeared from view—doomed in large part by failure to achieve consensus among the *hōsō sansha*. As the experiences of the Investigation Committee reflect, in the past, wide-ranging proposals for justice system reform typically had withered on the vine.

D. RAPID IMPLEMENTATION OF REFORM COUNCIL RECOMMENDATIONS

In sharp contrast, the reforms proposed by the Reform Council have taken shape at a remarkable pace. As mentioned above, the council issued its recommendations in June 2001. In November of that year, the Diet, with a view toward assuring the implementation of key recommendations, enacted the Act for Promotion of Justice System Reform.[20] Pursuant to that act, the following month, December 2001, the Headquarters for Promotion of Justice System Reform (hereinafter, the Headquarters) was established for a three-year term. By law, the Headquarters was to be located "within the Cabinet." In fact, the Headquarters comprised the entire Cabinet itself, with the prime minister serving as the chair (and with the Reform Council's chair, Professor Kōji Satō, appointed as one of the special advisors to the Headquarters). The composition of the Headquarters reflected and, at the same time, offered a potent symbol of the importance accorded to the reforms in political circles. Its composition also presumably aided in overcoming differences of opinion among ministries.

In March 2002, the Headquarters issued, in the form of a Cabinet resolution, the Plan for Promotion of Justice System Reform (hereinafter, the Promotion Plan).[21] It also established eleven Expert Advisory Committees (*kentōkai*), responsible for the following subject areas: labor, access to justice, alternative dispute resolution (ADR), arbitration, administrative litigation, *saiban'in* system / criminal justice, publicly provided defense counsel system, internationalization, legal training, legal profession (*hōsō seido*), and intellectual property. The Headquarters set forth rather specific mandates for each of the Expert Advisory Committees and also established a clear timetable for implementation of specific elements of the reforms.

The reforms moved forward rapidly. More than twenty significant pieces of legislation implementing proposed reforms were enacted; by the time the three-year term of the Headquarters expired in November 2004, nearly all of the major legislative measures included in the Promotion Plan were passed. In addition, many other reforms that did not require legislative action were implemented. In sum, sweeping reform of the justice system has occurred at a speed that would have been unthinkable even a decade ago.

E. WHY SO FAR AND SO FAST?

Leaving for later an examination of some of the major reforms, an obvious initial question is what accounts for the breadth and speed of reform on this occasion. Two interrelated factors have already been mentioned. First, unlike earlier efforts at justice system reform, reform was not left to the *hōsō sansha* but instead was treated as a matter of wide public concern. Second, the political branch accorded high priority to the reform efforts. Prime Minister

Obuchi, who first pushed for establishment of the Reform Council, passed away suddenly less than a year after the Reform Council had begun its deliberations. By the time the Reform Council issued its recommendations in June 2001, the post of prime minister had been assumed by Jun'ichirō Koizumi. Koizumi, who already had achieved a reputation as a reformer, quickly embraced the reform efforts. His support undoubtedly played an important role in the rapid implementation of the reform proposals.

Yet why was it that, after decades of having been left largely to the *hōsō sansha*, on this occasion justice system reform was treated as a matter for public debate and political action? The reasons are complex; and any attempt to answer that question concisely is bound to miss important elements. Many of the chapters contained in this volume address relevant factors. Let me offer a few additional speculative comments of my own.

One reason for the success of the reform efforts this time is simply that certain problems with the justice system had festered for so long they could no longer be ignored. The most prominent examples are the size of the legal profession and access to legal services in areas of lawyer scarcity. As far back as 1964, the Investigation Committee had highlighted both concerns. Despite modest increases in the number of new entrants to the legal profession in the 1990s, as of 2001 there were still fewer than nineteen thousand practicing lawyers in the entire nation of over 130 million—far too few to meet the growing demand for legal services. And, if anything, the problem of lawyer scarcity had gotten even worse over the intervening four decades. As of 1964, 65 percent of all practicing lawyers were members of the local bar associations in just four cities: Tokyo, Yokohama, Osaka, and Nagoya.[22] By 2001, that proportion had risen to over 70 percent.[23] For people living in many other areas, lack of access to legal services had become an acute problem. The Reform Council captured the concern over lawyer scarcity well with the phrase "zero-one regions," using that phrase as shorthand for regions having either no lawyers at all or just one lawyer. As of 2000, of the 253 court districts in Japan, 72 were zero-one districts. More striking, out of 3,371 registered cities and towns in Japan, 3,023, or nearly 90 percent, were zero-one regions.[24] In sum, the inadequate size of the legal profession and the issue of lawyer scarcity had persisted for so long and become so acute they demanded attention. Many of the other reforms proposed by the Reform Council also addressed longstanding problems that had become increasingly difficult to ignore.

As Professor Kōya Matsuo observes in his chapter on criminal law in this volume,[25] two symbolic factors also may have played a role in the speed and scope of reform: the shift from the Shōwa to the Heisei era and the advent of the twenty-first century. Both of these events carried psychological overtones of a new beginning. And the fact that most of the key figures in the reform movement grew up and were educated in the postwar era likely contributed to their desire to embrace the opportunity for a new beginning.

Another important factor underlying the reforms is internationalization. By this, I do not mean foreign pressure (or *gaiatsu*). One of the striking aspects of the justice system reform process is how little direct foreign pressure there was. As the chapters in this volume by Professor Joseph L. Hoffmann[26] and by Professors Hideki Kanda and Curtis J. Milhaupt[27] highlight, however, the impact of internationalization extends far beyond foreign pressure and manifests itself in many ways. Increasing internationalization, for example, brought greater demand for legal services and demand for new types of legal services (in areas such as arbitration and intellectual property, for example). And, as the chapter in this volume by Messrs. Yasuharu Nagashima and E. Anthony Zaloom[28] reveals, the growing presence of foreign law firms in Japan increased competitive pressure on Japanese business law firms to expand and develop greater specialization.

More significant for placing justice system reform on the political agenda, internationalization played an important role in generating business support for reform. Throughout much of the 1980s, Japanese business leaders viewed the United States as a nation with too many lawyers, leading to excessive litigation, which in turn hampered the competitiveness of U.S. businesses. In contrast, according to that view, the limited number of lawyers in Japan was one reason for Japan's economic success. (Notably, many U.S. business leaders—and even Derek Bok, former president of Harvard University[29]—expressed similar views.) Accordingly, in the past many Japanese business leaders sided with the bar in opposing substantial increases in the number of lawyers in Japan.

In large part as a result of internationalization, though, business views shifted. Through their own experiences after their companies had become involved in disputes in the United States and elsewhere, business leaders developed a greater appreciation for the valuable roles played by lawyers in resolving disputes and, through advance planning, heading off potential future disputes. Moreover, business leaders came to recognize the broader roles served by the legal profession. In the past, businesses tended to view lawyers primarily as litigators, who would seek only to divide the pie (and take a cut for themselves at the same time). Over the years, however, many Japanese businesses utilized U.S. and other foreign lawyers, as well as an increasing number of Japanese lawyers, to provide general business advice, negotiate, or otherwise facilitate business transactions, or to advise on regulatory matters or handle other non-dispute matters. Through these experiences, business leaders came to realize that lawyers not only divide the pie through litigation but also often help to expand the pie through other activities. Accordingly, many Japanese business leaders came to support an increase in the size of the legal profession, coupled with an expansion in the legal profession's role. This growing business support for justice system reform in turn served as one factor underlying the increased support by the ruling Liberal Democratic Party (LDP).

A further reason for support for reform by the business community and the LDP related to the broad issues of deregulation and administrative reform. A fundamental goal embraced by the Reform Council was "to transform the excessive advance-control/adjustment type society to an after-the-fact review/remedy type society." This goal in turn tied to the final recommendations of the Administrative Reform Council (on which Prof. Satō, who chaired the Justice System Reform Council, also served). As discussed by Professor Takahashi in his chapter in this volume, the recommendations of the Administrative Reform Council, issued in late 1997, helped bring about a reorganization of the central government ministries and agencies and a strengthening of political control and the functions of the Cabinet. In addition, the Administrative Reform Council advocated reinforcing "the rule of law," as "an essential base for promoting deregulation, aimed at abolishing unclear advance administrative control and converting to an after-the-fact review/remedy type society."[30] In other words, the Administrative Reform Council supported the goal of replacing vague, ambiguous, and highly discretionary administrative guidance with a system of clear, enforceable rules. The Justice System Reform Council endorsed the same objective.

Many business leaders and politicians welcomed that shift. Over the years, a number of business leaders have voiced frustration at instances of administrative guidance by bureaucrats. Those leaders would have welcomed the prospect of reducing the seemingly unreviewable discretion of bureaucrats. In the case of the LDP, as Professor Ginsburg discusses, support for this "transformation" in turn related to the fact that the party no longer could count on the absolute majority it had enjoyed for so much of the postwar era. By moving to an after-the-fact review system, the politicians presumably could entrust the courts to enforce policy preferences embodied in legislation supported by the LDP, even in the event of a subsequent shift in control of the Cabinet. For both the business community and the LDP, moreover, a major factor in support for reform undoubtedly was the seemingly never-ending recession that began in the early 1990s and continued well into the twenty-first century. Administrative guidance—the "advance-control/adjustment" approach—was seen as having failed. Perhaps deregulation would hold the answer to Japan's economic doldrums.

In turn, in the view of the Reform Council, an essential precondition to deregulation and the shift to an "after-the-fact review/remedy type society" was raising the quantity and quality of the legal profession. As the Reform Council emphasized, the legal profession would need to play a vital role both in shaping and in implementing the rules underpinning the review/remedy approach. A strengthened legal profession was indispensable for doing so.

Granted, the business community and politicians may have supported the broad goals of deregulation and a strengthened legal profession, along with many of the more specific reforms, such as reforms relating to arbitration and intellectual property litigation, but it is hard to imagine great business support for many of the other reforms, including the establishment of the *saiban'in* system and other reforms relating to criminal justice. Yet business support helped break through the mindset that justice system reform was a matter reserved for decision by the *hōsō sansha*, and once the justice system became an object for debate among a broad range of constituencies, the door was opened for wide-reaching reforms.

F. CONCRETE REFORMS

To give some sense of just how wide reaching the resulting reforms have been, the following is a *partial* list:

- Sweeping reform of the legal education system, including establishment of a new tier of graduate-level law schools and substantial increases in the number of new entrants into the legal profession. (These reforms are described in detail by Professor Rokumoto.)
- Establishment of the *saiban'in* system, a new system for lay participation in the judging of serious criminal cases, which is to commence by the year 2009.[31]
- Enactment of the Comprehensive Legal Assistance Act,[32] which, as its centerpiece, establishes a new nationwide legal assistance network, the so-called *Hō Terasu* (Law Terrace). This network, which began operations in late 2006, consists of a centrally administered system, with branches throughout the nation staffed by full-time attorneys. It is designed to provide expanded legal assistance in civil cases, a strengthened public defense system for criminal cases,

assistance to victims of crime, and a variety of other legal consultation services, with especial attention to overcoming problems with access to legal services in the regions of lawyer scarcity.[33] This new network is of such potential importance in expanding access to legal services that Professor Satō, who chaired the Reform Council, has referred to it in public remarks as the "hidden fourth pillar" of justice reform.

- Enactment of the Act concerning Speeding Up of Trials,[34] pledging efforts to achieve the goal of completing all first-instance trials (civil and criminal alike) in no more than two years.
- Establishment of an appeals court specializing in intellectual property matters, to ensure greater expertise in handling of intellectual property cases.[35]
- Establishment of a new system for judging individual labor disputes, with a three-member panel composed of two lay members knowledgeable about labor matters sitting together with one professional judge.[36]
- Expansion in ADR mechanisms.
- Enactment of a new Arbitration Act,[37] designed to embody prevailing international arbitration standards.
- Various reforms to civil procedure, including expanded pretrial procedures to expedite trials and some expansion in discovery mechanisms.[38]
- Various reforms to the administrative litigation system, including some expansion in standing, increased access to evidence, and expanded rights to preliminary relief.[39]
- Various reforms to criminal procedure, including expanded pretrial procedures to expedite trials, expanded discovery, and steps to effectuate concentrated trials.[40]
- Expansion of the right to publicly provided counsel in criminal cases, with publicly provided counsel to be made available from the point at which an order for detention is issued to a suspect (as opposed to upon indictment, as in the past), initially limited to a specified range of relatively serious cases.[41]
- Strengthening of inquest of prosecution (*kensatsu shinsakai*) functions, by providing the inquests (committees composed of members drawn from the general public) with authority to demand explanations for decisions not to prosecute and, in certain cases, to insist on institution of prosecution.[42]
- Various reforms to the Attorneys (*Bengoshi*) Act, Foreign Attorneys (*Gaikokuhō jimu bengoshi*) Act, Patent Attorneys (*Benrishi*) Act, Tax Attorneys (*Zeirishi*) Act, and other laws and rules relating to the legal profession, including reforms permitting attorneys (*bengoshi*) to work freely in public institutions and private companies; reforms allowing foreign law firms to hire *bengoshi* and to enter into partnerships with *bengoshi*; and reforms permitting patent attorneys and

tax attorneys to handle litigation matters in their respective areas of expertise, in association with *bengoshi*.

- Establishment of a committee, the Advisory Committee on Appointment of Lower Court Judges,[43] containing a majority of members from outside the judiciary, to screen candidates for initial appointments to the judiciary and to screen judges being considered for reappointment. (In Japan's career judiciary, as discussed in detail by Professor John O. Haley in his chapter on the judiciary in this volume,[44] each new entrant to the judiciary normally is appointed for a ten-year term as assistant judge upon completion of the Legal Training and Research Institute, followed by reappointment as judge, again for a ten-year term, and reappointment every ten years thereafter until retirement.)
- Efforts to invigorate the system for recruiting judges from among the ranks of practicing attorneys.
- Enactment of a law permitting assistant judges and prosecutors to work in private law firms for up to two years, then return to the judiciary or procuracy.[45]

II. REFLECTIONS ON THE *SAIBAN'IN* SYSTEM AND POPULAR PARTICIPATION

With the possible exception of the new law school system, the reform that has received the most publicity is the *saiban'in* system. Under this system, which is to commence operation by the year 2009, mixed panels of lay judges (*saiban'in*) and professional judges will in principle judge all criminal cases involving potential penalties above specified levels. In contested cases, the panel is to consist of nine members: six lay members and three professional judges. Mixed panels are to be convened even in uncontested cases; in those cases, the panel is to consist of five members: four lay members and one professional judge. In contrast to juries in the United States, these mixed panels will be responsible not only for fact-finding but for determining sentences.[46]

The *saiban'in* system represents one of the centerpieces of the reform efforts. Yet, at least initially, public reaction to the new system has been at best lukewarm. According to a survey conducted by Yomiuri Shinbun in May 2004, slightly over half of those surveyed voiced approval for the *saiban'in* system. When asked whether they themselves would want to serve as *saiban'in*, however, 69 percent said no. Furthermore, 33 percent said they had "no confidence" they would be able to judge cases properly, and another 38 percent said they had "little confidence" they could do so.[47] A transition period of five years was established for implementation of the new system. The primary purpose of the transition period presumably was to afford sufficient time to construct facilities and to introduce and fine-tune all of the necessary changes in procedures; but another major task for the transition period is a public relations campaign to generate greater public understanding of and support for the new system.

Notwithstanding the lukewarm public reaction, the *saiban'in* system carries fundamental importance in two major respects, quite apart from its significance for the fact-finding process. First, it serves as the linchpin that holds together a set of interrelated criminal justice reforms. In theory, in Japan: (1) criminal justice is governed by the adversary system, (2) concentrated trials are the goal, and (3) trials are to be conducted in accordance with the basic principles of "directness" and "orality." Those two principles in turn signify, respectively, that trials are to be decided based on direct evaluation by the judges of evidence and witness testimony, and that trials are to be centered on oral testimony of witnesses and oral arguments of the parties in open court. The reality, however, has been quite different from these ideals.

While in form the criminal justice system is an adversary system, in practice prosecutors have played such a central role that many respected observers characterize Japan's system as one of "prosecutorial justice" (*kensatsukan shihō*).[48] In a 1991 article, leading criminal procedure scholar Professor Masahito Inouye (who was a member of the Reform Council and later served as chair of the Expert Advisory Committee on the *saiban'in* system and criminal justice) suggested that the dominance of the prosecutors had left such a limited role for defense counsel that criminal defense was losing its appeal for practicing lawyers.[49] He stated that, unless defense counsel were afforded a more meaningful role, "skilled and zealous lawyers may lose the will to handle criminal matters. . . . If things go on as they are, truly conscientious, top-notch lawyers may move away from criminal practice. This, in my view, is where the true crisis [in Japan's criminal justice system] lies."[50] To avoid that crisis, he argued in that article, the role of defense counsel should be invigorated.

With respect to concentrated trials and the principles of directness and orality, as well, the reality has been far different from the theory. While minor or uncontested cases often are disposed of in a single court session or in two or three sessions held on consecutive days, most other trials are not conducted in a concentrated fashion, but rather are spread out over months or in some cases even years, with court sessions scheduled every few weeks. As to the principles of directness and orality, in practice many trials, even in contested cases, consist of so-called *chōsho saiban* (written record trials), in which virtually all evidence is introduced in the form of written statements of witnesses (and written statements of the defendant), prepared by prosecutors and submitted as evidence either with the consent of defense counsel or pursuant to exceptions to the hearsay rule. Indeed, in a telling reflection of how little weight is currently placed on the principles of directness and orality, it is not uncommon for judges to switch midway through trials. Given the practice of transferring judges every three or four years, in some long-running trials not one of the three judges involved in the final judgment has heard the case from beginning to end.

The Reform Council sought to conform actual practice to the stated ideals in all three of the above respects. "The basic direction for this reform," the Reform Council declared in its recommendations, "is to realize efficient and effective trial proceedings for truly contested cases through active allegation and presentation of evidence by the parties, . . . in concentrated proceedings. . . , premised on sufficient advance preparation by both parties." Among its specific recommendations, the council called for (1) realization of concentrated trials, (2) realization of the principles of directness and orality, and (3) invigoration of the defense counsel system (with steps to that end including expansion of the public criminal defense system and expanded discovery).

However much the Reform Council might have advocated realization of the above ideals, in the absence of fundamental structural reform it seems likely that such calls would have ended up as little more than empty rhetoric. The *saiban'in* system is the glue that binds together these other reforms. Introduction of the *saiban'in* system will necessitate concentrated trials; the participation of lay members will entail much greater reliance on live, in-court testimony (in other words, realization of the principles of directness and orality) than in the past, thereby presumably breaking the pattern of *chōsho saiban*. In turn, achieving concentrated trials with live testimony will require advance preparation by defense counsel as well as prosecutors. Expanded discovery is important for facilitating advance preparation, and invigoration of the criminal defense system is vital to the success of the reforms. Viewed in this manner, it is the *saiban'in* system that ties together the entire set of criminal justice reforms.

The *saiban'in* system carries fundamental importance at an even broader level as well. It serves as the most concrete symbol of the third "pillar" of justice system reform: popular participation. As mentioned above, the Reform Council's recommendations called for establishment of a wide range of other mechanisms for popular participation in the justice system, and many of those mechanisms have been adopted, some through legislation and others that have not required legislation. Thus, for example, the inquest of prosecution system was strengthened through legislation; without the need for new legislation, the judiciary, the procuracy, and the bar all have established advisory councils, composed of members from outside the legal profession, designed to provide input from the public on the administration of those institutions. In keeping with another recommendation by the Reform Council, all three branches of the legal profession have greatly expanded the range of information about their operations available to the public, with much of that information readily accessible through the Internet.

Particularly noteworthy are the steps that have been taken to overcome the perception that judges and prosecutors are too insulated from society and at times are out of touch with the concerns of the public. The final three reforms on the list introduced earlier all seek to address that issue, from different directions. The new committee to screen lower-court judges is intended to ensure that the views of the public are reflected in judicial selection. The efforts to invigorate the systems for appointing judges and prosecutors from among practicing lawyers seek to reduce the insulated nature of the career judiciary and career procuracy by hiring more people with broad societal experience at the mid-career stage. That reform seeks to increase mobility among the three branches of the legal profession, thereby reducing the relatively closed nature of the existing career system. The third reform, the new system for seconding assistant judges and young prosecutors to law firms, approaches the issue of the insulated nature of the judiciary and procuracy from the opposite direction. Within the context of the prevailing career system, that reform aims at overcoming the perceived insulation by exposing career judges and career prosecutors to experiences outside the judiciary and procuracy.

At least in the criminal setting, however, it is the *saiban'in* system that is viewed as having the greatest potential for overcoming the perceived insulation of judges and prosecutors and for ensuring that the views of the public are reflected in the justice system. Through the *saiban'in* system, professional judges in criminal cases will be exposed directly to views of members of the general public, and prosecutors handling the cases presumably will need to be more sensitive to those views than in the past. At the same time, members of the general public will themselves directly participate in the justice system. Through that experience, they are expected to develop a deeper understanding of the system and a greater capacity for identifying problems with the system. In this connection, one additional aspect of the *saiban'in* system bears note. As mentioned above, the three branches of the legal profession have established various committees and advisory councils designed to reflect the views of "the public." True, all or a majority of the members of those committees and advisory councils come from outside the legal profession; but nearly all of the members still are drawn from rather elite segments of society. In contrast, the *saiban'in* are to be selected by lot from among the general public. Accordingly, participation in the justice system will extend to a much broader swath of society.

III. FROM "POPULAR PARTICIPATION" TO "POPULAR SOVEREIGNTY"

The fundamental philosophy of the Reform Council recommendations does not stop at popular participation. Rather, the council's ultimate aim is to strengthen popular sovereignty. In the words of the council: "[These] various reforms assume as a basic premise the people's transformation from governed objects to governing subjects and at the same time seek to promote such transformation. This is a transformation in which the people will break out of viewing the government as the ruler (the authority) and instead will take heavy responsibility for governance themselves, and in which the government will convert itself into one that responds to such people."[51]

The three pillars of justice system reform—a justice system that meets public expectations, a strengthened legal profession, and a strengthened popular base for the justice system—all are closely related to this ultimate goal of enhanced popular sovereignty. So, too, are three other major trends referred to earlier and discussed in more detail in other chapters in this volume: political reform, deregulation (the shift from an "advance-control/adjustment type society" to a "review/remedy" type society), and various reforms designed to promote transparency and accountability. All represent fundamental philosophical shifts. Perhaps another volume of *Law in Japan* forty years hence will reveal just how successful these reforms ultimately prove to be in transforming Japanese society.

NOTES

1. See Note (Loraine Parkinson), "The Japanese Equal Employment Opportunity Law: An Alternative Approach to Social Change," *Columbia Law Review* 89 (1989): 604.

2. Arthur Taylor von Mehren, ed., *Law in Japan: The Legal Order in a Changing Society* (Cambridge, MA: Harvard University Press, 1963).

3. Kōichirō Fujikura, "Litigation, Administrative Relief, and Political Settlement for Pollution Victim Compensation: Minamata Mercury Poisoning after Fifty Years" (this volume).

4. Ichirō Katō, "The Treatment of Motor-Vehicle Accidents: The Impact of Technological Change on Legal Relations," in von Mehren, ed., *Law in Japan*, 399.

5. Eric A. Feldman, "Law, Culture, and Conflict: Dispute Resolution in Postwar Japan" (this volume).

6. Hiroshi Kaneko, "The Reform of the Japanese Tax System in the Latter Half of the Twentieth Century and into the Twenty-first Century" (this volume).

7. Dan Fenno Henderson, *Foreign Enterprise in Japan: Laws and Policies* (Chapel Hill: University of North Carolina Press, 1973).

8. Kazuyuki Takahashi, "Ongoing Changes in the Infrastructure of a Constitutional System: From 'Bureaucracy' to Democracy" (this volume).

9. Katsuya Uga, "Development of the Concepts of Transparency and Accountability in Japanese Administrative Law" (this volume).

10. Tom Ginsburg, "The Politics of Transparency in Japanese Administrative Law" (this volume).

11. Yoshirō Miwa and J. Mark Ramseyer, "The Legislative Dynamic: Evidence from the Deregulation of Financial Services in Japan" (this volume).

12. Kahei Rokumoto, "Legal Education" (this volume).

13. Shihō seido kaikaku shingikai setchihō [Justice System Reform Council Establishment Act], Law No. 68 of 1999, art. 2.

14. See Masahito Inouye, "Nihon ni okeru shihō seido kaikaku no keii to gaiyō" [Background and Overview of Justice System Reform in Japan] (paper prepared for presentation at the International Seminar on Judicial Reform, Taipei, Taiwan, September 23, 2004), copy on file with author.

15. As of mid-2007, the minutes still may be viewed at (http://www.kantei.go.jp/jp/sihouseido/).

16. Shihō seido kaikaku shingikai [Justice System Reform Council], "Chūkan hōkoku" [Interim Report] (November 20, 2000), available at (http://www.kantei.go.jp/jp/sihouseido/report/naka_pdfdex.html).

17. *Shihō seido kaikaku shingikai ikensho—21 seiki no Nihon o sasaeru shihō seido* [Recommendations of the Justice System Reform Council—a Justice System to Support Japan in the Twenty-first Century] (June 12, 2001), available at (http://www.kantei.go.jp/jp/sihouseido/report/ikensyo/pdf-dex.html); English translation available at (http://www.kantei.go.jp/foreign/judiciary/2001/0612report.html).

18. Ibid., 9.

19. See "Rinji shihō seido chōsakai, Ketsugi yōmoku" [Provisional Justice Sys-

tem Investigation Committee, Main Points] (August 28, 1964), reprinted in "Sankō shiryō" [Reference Materials] for Meeting No. 2 of the Justice System Reform Council (September 2, 1999), available at (http://www.kantei.go.jp/jp/sihouseido/dai2kai-append/husamura3.html).

20. Shihō seido kaikaku suishinhō [Act for Promotion of Justice System Reform], Law No. 119 of 2001.

21. Shihō seido kaikaku suishin keikaku [Plan for Promotion of Justice System Reform], Cabinet Resolution of March 19, 2002, available at (http://www.kantei.go.jp/jp/singi/sihou/keikaku/020319keikaku.html).

22. See Shiryō 14 [Material 14], Sankō shiryō [Reference Materials] for August 8–9, 2000, session of the Justice System Reform Council.

23. See Nihon bengoshi rengōkai [Japan Federation of Bar Associations], ed., *Bengoshi hakusho* [White Paper on Bengoshi], 2003 ed. (2003), 21.

24. See Inouye, "Nihon ni okeru shihō seido kaikaku no keii to gaiyō."

25. Kōya Matsuo, "The Development of Criminal Law in Japan since 1961" (this volume).

26. Joseph L. Hoffmann, "Globalization and Japanese Criminal Law" (this volume).

27. Hideki Kanda and Curtis J. Milhaupt, "Reexamining Legal Transplants: The Director's Fiduciary Duty in Japanese Corporate Law" (this volume).

28. Yasuharu Nagashima and E. Anthony Zaloom, "The Rise of the Large Japanese Business Law Firm and Its Prospects for the Future" (this volume).

29. See Derek Bok, "A Flawed System of Law Practice and Training," *Journal of Legal Education* 33 (1983): 570.

30. Gyōsei kaikaku kaigi [Administrative Reform Council], "Saishū hōkoku" [Final Report] (December 3, 1997), available at (http://www.kantei.go.jp/jp/gyokaku/report-final/).

31. See Saiban'in no sanka suru keiji saiban ni kansuru hōritsu [Act concerning Criminal Trials in Which Saiban'in Participate], Law No. 63 of 2004.

32. Sōgō hōritsu shienhō [Comprehensive Legal Assistance Act], Law No. 74 of 2004.

33. An overview of and commentary on the legal assistance network (initially called Shihō Netto, or Justice Network) are contained in "Tokushū, Shihō netto no seibi" [Special Topic, Preparation of Shihō Netto], *Jurisuto*, no. 1262 (2004): 6–77.

34. Saiban no jinsokuka ni kansuru hōritsu [Act concerning Speeding Up of Trials], Law No. 107 of 2003.

35. Chiteki zaisan kōtō saibansho setchihō [Intellectual Property Appeals Court Establishment Act], Law No. 119 of 2004.

36. Rōdō shinpanhō [Labor Judgment Act], Law No. 45 of 2004.

37. Chūsaihō [Arbitration Act], Law No. 138 of 2003.

38. See Minji soshōhō tō no ichibu o kaisei suru hōritsu [Act Partially Amending the Civil Procedure Code, etc.], Law No. 108 of 2003.

39. Gyōsei jiken soshōhō no ichibu o kaisei suru hōritsu [Act Partially Amending the Administrative Case Litigation Act], Law No. 84 of 2004.

40. See Keiji soshōhō tō no ichibu o kaisei suru hōritsu [Act Partially Amending the Criminal Procedure Code, etc.], Law No. 62 of 2004.

41. See ibid.

42. See ibid.

43. See Kakyū saibansho saibankan shimei shimon iinkai no setchi ni kansuru kisoku [Rule concerning Establishment of the Advisory Committee on Appointment of Lower Court Judges], Supreme Court Rule No. 6 of 2003. Under the new system, which commenced operation in 2003, a central advisory committee screens candidates and forwards recommendations to the General Secretariat of the Supreme Court. That central committee is assisted by eight regional committees, which assemble information on the candidates. Initially, the central committee comprised eleven members: two judges, one professor who formerly was a Supreme Court justice, one prosecutor, two practicing attorneys, two other professors, and three members from other fields. In its first year of operation, the committee screened 109 recent graduates from the Legal Training and Research Institute who sought initial appointment as assistant judges, of whom eight were not recommended (and not appointed). In its first year the committee also reviewed 181 assistant judges and judges being considered for reappointment. Of those 181, 6 were not recommended (and those 6 evidently were not reappointed). This was by far the largest number of judges in history to be denied reappointment. Another noteworthy feature of the new system is that those denied appointment or reappointment have the right to receive an explanation of the reasons for the decision.

44. John O. Haley, "The Japanese Judiciary: Maintaining Integrity, Autonomy, and the Public Trust" (this volume).

45. See Hanjiho oyobi kenji no bengoshi shokumu keiken ni kansuru hōritsu [Act concerning Assistant Judges' and Prosecutors' Experience in the Work of Practicing Attorneys], Law No. 121 of 2004.

46. See Saiban'in no sanka suru keiji saiban ni kansuru hōritsu, art. 6.

47. Survey results available at (http://www.yomiuri.co.jp/yoron/p_total01.htm).

48. See David T. Johnson, *The Japanese Way of Justice: Prosecuting Crime in Japan* (New York: Oxford University Press, 2002); and Malcolm M. Feeley and Setsuo Miyazawa, eds., *The Japanese Adversary System in Context: Controversies and Comparisons* (Hampshire, UK: Palgrave Macmillan, 2002).

49. Masahito Inouye, "Keiji saiban ni taisuru teigen" [Suggestions for Improving the Administration of Criminal Justice], in *Shihō kenshūjo ronshū* [Collection of Works for the Legal Training and Research Institute], 1991-I (1991): 93.

50. Ibid., 111.

51. *Shihō seido kaikaku shingikai ikensho*, 4.

LAW IN JAPAN

PART I

The Legal System and the Law's Processes

THIS VOLUME BEGINS with the chapter "New Knowledge Concerning Japan's Legal System before 1868, Acquired from Japanese Sources by Western Writers since 1963," in which Carl Steenstrup tackles head-on the question of what possible relevance the study of legal history might have to practicing lawyers today. In answering that question (in the affirmative, of course), Steenstrup offers lessons relating to law and legal institutions, legal mentality, and legal philosophy, drawn from a synthesis and distillation of a lifetime of study of Japanese law from its earliest origins down to the present. The chapter also summarizes the key ways in which Western knowledge of pre-Meiji law has grown and changed over the past forty years and closes with a careful examination of one specific issue: the reforms in civil litigation procedure that took place in the courts of the warrior regime in the thirteenth century.

The second chapter, "Criminal Trials in the Early Meiji Era—with Particular Reference to the *Ukagai/Shirei* System," by Nobuhiko Kasumi, focuses on legal history from a different perspective. In contrast to the sweeping scope of Steenstrup's chapter, Kasumi takes a detailed look at one set of key developments in the field of criminal justice at a single point of great change. Focusing on the four-year period of Meiji 4–8 (1871–75), he explores the questions of when and how a uniform system of criminal trials came to be established throughout Japan. The chapter offers a fascinating look at a formative period of Japanese law and introduces several important themes, including the concern for uniformity in interpretation and application of law, devices to achieve uniformity and accuracy of judgments (including criminal punishment for judges who issued erroneous judgments), the role of precedent, and the shift from a dual system of jurisdiction with considerable local autonomy to a centralized system in which the Ministry of Justice occupied a dominant position.

Many of the essays in the 1963 volume, *Law in Japan: The Legal Order in a Changing Society*, had lasting impact; but one in particular stands out in that regard: Takeyoshi Kawashima's "Dispute Resolution in Contemporary Japan." In "Law, Culture, and Conflict: Dispute Resolution in Postwar Japan," Eric A. Feldman explores the original Kawashima essay and its legacy. As Feldman states, "Kawashima's work has powerfully influenced the entire corpus of scholarship on dispute resolution in Japan." Feldman examines four major schools of thought on Japanese dispute resolution: culturalist, institutional, law and economics, and case study–based approaches. He concludes with a discussion of the recent justice system reforms, as those reforms relate to dispute resolution.

Another important theme explored in the 1963 volume was Japan's "experiment with the adversary system." In "The Development of an Adversary System in Japanese Civil Procedure," Yasuhei Taniguchi explores the manner in which the adversary system has developed over the intervening four decades. As Taniguchi explains, in some respects Japanese civil procedure has remained relatively unchanged not only since 1963 but ever since the inception of the modern civil procedure system in 1890. In other important respects, however, civil procedure has changed. Taniguchi concludes that, through these changes, Japanese civil procedure at present occupies a "middle" ground between the Civil Law and Common Law approaches, nearing the ideal set forth by Kohji Tanabe in his essay in the 1963 volume.

In "The Japanese Judiciary: Maintaining Integrity, Autonomy, and the Public Trust," John O. Haley presents a detailed analysis of the distinctive features of the Japanese judiciary, its structure, and its administration by senior career judges assigned to the General Secretariat of the Supreme Court. He argues that Japanese judicial organization, the mentoring and monitoring role of senior judges, and the decisions on promotion and assignment by judicial administrators have resulted in an extraordinary record of judicial integrity and an equally remarkable level of institutional autonomy. In turn, Haley suggests, these features of the Japanese judiciary help to explain the high level of public trust in the integrity and competence of the judiciary.

One of the great changes affecting the Japanese legal profession is the rise of the large business law firm. It is simply impossible to imagine two people better qualified to discuss that subject than the eminent lawyers Yasuharu Nagashima and E. Anthony Zaloom. In their aptly titled chapter, "The Rise of the Large Japanese Business Law Firm and Its Prospects for the Future," they examine the reasons for and implications of that change. In doing so, they explore the changing role played by the Japanese legal profession. They also offer their views on the impact of foreign competition and their assessment of the prediction that, as with the Japanese securities industry, only one of the large law firms will survive as an independent entity.

According to Yoshirō Miwa and J. Mark Ramseyer, in their chapter "The Legislative Dynamic: Evidence from the Deregulation of Financial Services in Japan," the recent financial distress in Japan in many ways traces itself to the limited range of nonbank financial intermediaries available. That limited availability is itself a creature of regulation. By examining the deregulation of commercial paper issues by financial intermediaries, they explore the dynamics of the regulatory process that originally contributed to—if not caused—the recent distress. They also use this case study to explore the dynamics of the Japanese legislative and regulatory process more generally. As they explain, at a specific level, the dynamics illustrate the classic Stiglerian theory of regulation; at a more general level, they illustrate the transnational economic logic to the Japanese legislative and regulatory process.

The final chapter in this part, "Legal Education" by Kahei Rokumoto, provides a detailed examination of the profound recent changes in Japan's legal training system. After reviewing the existing legal education system and its perceived shortcomings, Rokumoto describes and critiques the recent reforms. While recognizing the value of the goals of the reforms, he raises doubts regarding whether those goals will be achieved.

1 New Knowledge Concerning Japan's Legal System before 1868, Acquired from Japanese Sources by Western Writers since 1963

CARL STEENSTRUP

I. WHY PRE-MEIJI LAW IS LESS DEAD THAN THE DODO

The practice of law consists of predicting future decisions by judges. As counsel, this skill allows one to advise clients properly, and on the bench, this skill allows a judge to see his or her decisions confirmed by judges of courts of appeal. In contrast, the history of law is the knowledge of legal rules that are no longer applied by courts. Seen in this manner, the history of law is of little value to lawyers except when, as is sometimes the case in British common law, the *ratio decidendi* of a decision that is still valid as precedent is found embedded in a set of circumstances that belong to a state of society now past.

In Japan, the Meiji modernizations of the law implied a deliberate break with the past. Thus, knowledge of the genesis of an article in the Japanese Civil Code can inform us about the aims of the legislators, and, since much of the institutional framework of Meiji law is still standing, this knowledge is valuable to the lawyer. On the other hand, knowledge of the contents of or the reasons for a piece of Tokugawa or even older legislation has antiquarian value only. Even when, as in commercial law, some customs of trade were kept alive until new statutes changed them, the practical validity of such customs depended on their being noted and used by Meiji judges; if not, the new codes applied. Thus it is reasonable that in most universities in Japan, books on pre-Meiji law are found under the heading "history" rather than under the heading "law."

Why, then, did eminently practical lawyers such as John Henry Wigmore and Dan Fenno Henderson spend years of their lives studying pre-Meiji law?[1] They had at least four good reasons for doing so.

First, Japan never had a true revolution. Japan's institutions changed their names but kept much of their substance. Research tracing pre-Meiji roots of modern institutions was therefore of great value to modern law. Dan Fenno Henderson's *Conciliation and Japanese Law*[2] is a prime and brilliant example.

Second, slowly developing institutions formed mentalities that survived centuries and still influence the ways in which the Japanese judiciary thinks. In his book *Rechtsdenken und Rechtsauffassung in Japan*, Guntram Rahn showed that Japanese judges often make decisions in civil cases more acceptable to the parties by first finding in Japanese custom a solution both parties can live with, and afterward quoting a provision from a Western-inspired code that somehow justifies that solution. Rahn also showed that such ways of dispensing justice more according to the circumstances of the individual case than according to abstract rules conform to traditional Japanese thinking and are therefore welcomed, though the predictability of judgments is somewhat diminished.[3]

Third, Western efforts to understand the way in which law is administered in Japan are aided by a strange parallelism, which is ancient and pervasive: namely, that statutory law has been used in Japan at least since Nara times as a tool of social engineering and not primarily, as in most other non-Western civilizations, as a means to enforce an ideology.[4] It was this pragmatic use of statutory law that made the reception of foreign law possible, even from nations that the Japanese politically distrusted, such as T'ang China in the Taika and Nara eras and the Western imperialistic nations in Meiji times.[5] In Japan as in the Western world, the early growth of interest in law as an intellectual challenge, even when the law in question was no longer in actual use, went hand in hand with the use of statutory law as a tool of social engineering. Exegesis of the no longer applied Justinian codes started in Bologna in the eleventh century; in the ninth century the exegesis of the eighth-century codes began in Japan, though these had by now been superseded by customary administrative law.[6] In the same way, Tokugawa scholars showed an abiding interest in Chinese legal and paralegal norm systems though these scholars were, politically, increasingly focused on Japan.[7]

This interest in norm systems as such, apart from their actual usefulness, was paralleled by the intensive studies of Indian logic among Nara-period Buddhist intellectuals. These studies sharpened the wits of the intellectual class and made dialectics possible. Ultimately, the mastery of logic helped Japanese lawyers grasp and use the utterly alien Roman law in its French and

German guises; first came the moderately difficult reception of foreign law rules, and then the intensely difficult reception of the ways in which these rules have to be interpreted in order to form a consistent system.[8] The idea that the norms of a society can have different sources and must, through interpretation, be "bent" to form a consistent system came easily to Western and Japanese lawyers steeped in feudal diversity, but was much harder to grasp for their colleagues in "monolithic" systems such as those of China and Islam. Through most of the premodern period, Japanese law was anything but monolithic. From late Heian through Muromachi times there were, each in its own sphere, manorial law, warrior law, and the law of the emperor's bureaucrats;[9] in Sengoku and Tokugawa times, the law was different not only for each daimiate but also for each village and for each status class.[10] The persistent necessity of having to determine, before the substance of litigation could be solved, which court was competent and which norm system applied, sharpened the law users' minds and engendered ways of jurisprudential thinking in form and substance not too different from those of medieval and early modern European law.[11] In short, the third reason why even pre-Meiji Japanese law can sometimes be helpful for the modern Western lawyer operating in a Japanese setting is the fact that the legal traditions of Japan—of which Japanese judges and attorneys are now the carriers—are somehow more akin to the Western lawyer's own traditions than, say, those of Chinese, Islamic, or Hindu law.[12] For instance, Chinese law was generally hostile to associations of citizens, whereas premodern Japanese law accepted and even used such associations for social control, in spite of the potential challenges to the all-pervasiveness of state power inherent in them.[13]

Japanese law lost most of its religious roots with the end of the state governed by the Nara codes, whereas Islamic and Hindu law remained grounded in metaphysical worldviews. Yet the status of the law expert in Japan was as high as in these cultures, and higher than in China, whose law was also increasingly secular, because the "knower of the law" in Japan was, bearing Japan's insular situation in mind, a potential vehicle for new recipes of social engineering from abroad. In the same way, the Western European legal expert was, at least outside the Common Law area, regarded as a carrier of ideas from the idealized world of ancient, but sophisticated Rome. The importance of parallels between traditional Western and traditional Japanese approaches to the function of law in society for modernization theory is obvious; in case the lawyer is concerned with economics—and who is not?—he should know something about them, because the sphere of business in Japan contains at least as many links with the past as the sphere of law does.[14]

The fourth reason why knowledge of pre-Meiji law sometimes helps to predict legal decisions in present-day Japan is, paradoxically enough, a historically grounded and fundamental difference in legal philosophy between the United States and Japan. The United States is still heir to the doctrine of British eighteenth-century Enlightenment ideologues who thought that law, being rooted in human nature, legitimizes the state. On the other hand, the Japanese, despite their present U.S.-inspired constitution, are heirs to the Chinese idea, reinforced through the late Roman belief conveyed to Japan in Meiji times through imperial Germany, that the state antedates, engenders, and legitimizes the legal system. Practically, this latter view implies that it is up to the rulers to decide when to use the tool called "law" and when not to do so, and that the higher one's rank within the system of power, the more arbitrarily one can rule over those in the lower ranks. Japan is, however, not unusual in its "vertical" organization: most views of legal history show that vertical organization is the statistical norm, which in some few parts of the globe, and in some particular periods, has been challenged by the preference for the supremacy of law over historically grown power. The claim that sly pundits of authoritarianism somehow "diverted" the Meiji government from a democratic future through their roles as advisers is not the whole truth. Legislation from Taika through Tokugawa already had firmly established an authoritarian, vertical pattern in Japanese society, which could, by the Meiji period, be transformed by fiat from rule by status into rule "by" law. Only after 1945, and only partially so, was this system transformed into a rule "of" law.[15]

Premodern human relationships and mentalities tend to survive changes "from above." The Western lawyer who works in Japan understands these relationships and mentalities better, therefore, if he has some knowledge of the legislative measures through which they came to be. To state this point bluntly, bureaucratism, militarism, the suppression of women and juniors, and so-called groupishness are not standard traits in the old Chinese descriptions of the Japanese, but seem to have been deliberately inculcated through the Nara codes as a means of strengthening the social unit against possible attacks from the Asian continent. Likewise, fierce loyalty to non-kin superiors is not prevalent in the oldest layers of the oldest chronicles. It seems to have developed in medieval war bands, and from there to have filtered down to the commoners when mass armies grew in the Sengoku era. In criminal law, the insistence on confession, and the abuses that tend to accompany this insistence, can be traced to Chinese law by way of Tokugawa law. It is possible, then, that most of what makes Japanese behavior seem "strange" to

Western observers can be explained more easily by the influence of old statutes than by ethnic, religious, climatic, or linguistic peculiarities.[16]

While some legal traditions—in Japan as elsewhere—have been genuinely transmitted from one age to the next, other traditions that simply look "old" are in fact invented traditions. For the legal historian, distinguishing the two is as important as the task of tracing the antecedents of present-day institutions.[17]

II. HOW THE VIEW OF PRE-MEIJI LAW AND INSTITUTIONS HAS CHANGED SINCE 1963

Looking back over these forty years since 1963, what do we know now about these matters that we did not know then? Most of the new knowledge, of course, came from Japanese scholars; it was the publication of the enormous collections of Nara, Heian, and Kamakura documents in 1944–91 that triggered this research.[18] These are some of the more important findings:

As early as the first century A.D., villages were vertically ruled, strictly organized, and collectively structured "rice factories." From about A.D. 400, Japan was a major military power. Less than a century later there existed a bureaucratic machinery with hereditary officials at the top, whose rule was supported by equally hereditary corporations of commoners who supplied grain, raw materials, and civil and military labor services. The basic self-strengthening decisions of the government were taken in A.D. 540, that is, 105 years before the Taika Reform. The A.D. 540 decisions established household registers and a system of direct supervisors appointed by the central government. The large-scale use of Buddhism as a tool of government started before A.D. 600. The so-called Seventeen-Article Constitution of 604 mentions institutions that were not established until considerably later. It was formerly believed, therefore, that this document was deliberately antedated by Nara or later scholars. It now seems, however, that most of the institutions mentioned in the document actually existed in 604, though under other names.[19] Japan's growth from tribalism into a bureaucratic state is now seen to have developed slowly under the impact of legislative measures that, step-by-step, strengthened the hand of the central government. Likewise, most former suggestions that the Nara and pre-Nara statutes existed on paper only have proved premature. Between about A.D. 700 and about A.D. 800 they actually worked and provided subsequent regimes, including the medieval ones, with a carapace of law, order, taxes, and paperwork, which prevented Japanese society from disintegrating under the onslaught of later internal wars between factions of the ruling classes.

As for Heian laws and institutions, we have tended to see them through the spectacles of literature, focusing on the poetizing, feasting, religious qualms, and lovemaking of the noble bureaucrats rather than on what they and their assistants were doing in their offices. We now realize that for the most part of almost four hundred years the Heian officialdom, with limited bloodshed and considerable acumen and success, carried on entrepreneurial endeavors of exploiting the actual and potential wealth of the provinces, built an administrative system that fitted Japanese realities better than the T'ang system borrowed in Nara times, and—a point often overlooked—initiated countless military operations large and small against guerrillas on the northern frontier, criminal gangs, and tax-evading fugitive commoners. In the process, the noble bureaucrats amassed enormous wealth in the capital, which allowed their ladies the time needed for writing great literature, and their artists to create great art.[20] Heian society was not, as often maintained, matriarchal, in spite of many uxorilocal marriage arrangements. It was for most practical purposes dominated by males.[21] And most successful efforts of the noble bureaucrats to privatize the rice land and the commoners tilling it were, we now know, legal.[22]

What we call "feudalism" in Japan was fully developed before 1100 and was no product of the so-called rise of the warriors. On the contrary, the warriors tended to disturb and ultimately to wreck the intricate vertical order of tenures.[23] The process was slower than formerly thought. In the Kamakura era, the typical warrior offices for security (*shugo*) and land exploitation (*jitō*) were established later than previously assumed,[24] and administration and jurisdiction by Kyoto nobles and their representatives remained in place in many regions later than warrior chronicles would have us believe.[25] The development from the Heian age through the Kamakura age was thus no revolution, but an incremental change from a civil bureaucratic state into a military bureaucratic state. The outcome was a return to military dominance, as in the late fifth century, but strengthened by the Chinese administrative techniques imported in the seventh and eighth centuries.

Japan did not experience the kind of general decline in jurisprudential standards suffered by the former Western Roman Empire from about 500 to about 1100.[26] About 1320, just after a period of strict self-strengthening measures against a third Mongol onslaught that never came, but which transformed the Kamakura regime into a sort of military dictatorship, we find the first Japanese manual for laymen about civil litigation. This manual depicts a civil litigation system more just and careful than that found in Western Europe at the time and no decay in standards as compared to the heyday of the warrior regime seven decades before.[27] I shall return to this matter in the last part of this chapter. When, in 1333, the Kamakura government fell, the resurgent imperial government, which held sway in the capital for three years, produced reams of innovative legislation, recently the subject of investigation.[28] The basic idea that statutory law is the best tool of social engineering did not change. We see the same thing when the warriors in 1336 had reestablished their rule in the capital and then issued a political program with the force of law, called, after the historical era, the *Kenmu* Formulary. Most of the officials who signed it had served the warrior government until it fell in 1333, then worked for the short-lived imperial restoration government from 1333 to 1336, and now served the resurgent warrior government of the Ashikaga.[29] The formulary stresses the necessity of retaining useful institutions of former regimes. Likewise, there is little difference in content between late Kamakura and early Ashikaga legislative measures. The former view of the Ashikaga age as one of institutional decay has been proved wrong. In the field of case handling, authoritarianism returned. But there were well-developed customary rules even for changing sides in civil wars;[30] though the destructive battles of 1467–77 had left Kyoto in shambles, the officialdom of the shogunate operated according to bureaucratic routines of almost Weberian rationality.[31] The more the warlords fought among themselves, the more efficiently did towns and villages organize their own defense, administration, and jurisdiction and develop institutions of self-government to meet these needs. Even peasant leagues against the exactions by the elites were, to some extent, bureaucratically organized.[32]

The widespread ability to handle paperwork was a late legacy of the Nara Penal and Administrative Laws (*Ritsuryō*) and was not forgotten during the bloody and colorful political and military history of the fifteenth and sixteenth centuries. Another such legacy was the trend to subject "outsiders" of all kinds to discrimination by law.[33] Even in the heyday of warlordism, the Sengoku era (1467–1573), legislation prevailed, if only inside each warlord's territory, over the alternative "arbitrary use of power." The traditional theory that Sengoku daimiates were ruled through such use of power has been proven wrong. What happened was that the warlords usurped the shogun's legislative competences and established their own territorial law system, in which the warlord, now called *daimyō*, reserved to himself direct control over every person in his realm, irrespective of that person's clan and family allegiances. One can call it an "anti-feudal reform"—the logical outcome of a development from tribe to state that had begun in 540.[34] The *daimyōs*' laws for their respective domains were, on the whole, extremely cruel only in matters of internal and external security—otherwise, economic exploitation of all resources of the domain was the tenor of these laws, rather than terrorizing the civilians.[35]

The greatest strides in the exploration of premodern law were made in the field of Tokugawa law. The traditional notion of an immobile society ruled by a four-estate regime has given way to the picture of a politically repressive but institutionally vibrant and complicated polity, which left many ideas to Meiji Japan, if only for the reason that the Meiji reformers all had their formative years in the Tokugawa era. For strong-minded persons, also when they were peasants or women, Tokugawa society *did* have channels to assert private interests.[36] Civil litigation was common, and there were enough officials to handle the caseload.[37] In the big towns, the beginnings of a free labor market existed;[38] in Osaka there was an exchange dealing in futures;[39] and in Edo and Osaka, one could find the rudiments of a bar that assisted litigants in civil suits.[40] It was also easier for commoners to travel in Japan, in spite of the samurai-guarded barriers, than hitherto believed.[41] The idea that local shogunal administrators, the *daikan*, all inherited their posts has also been proved wrong; two-thirds of the *daikan* rose by ability, through a system not too different from a modern civil service system.[42] The view that the Tokugawa polity—the so-called *bakuhan* system—lacked the elements of centralization that could have eventually brought about a modern unified state is now in doubt. In reality, the *daimyō*, in spite of their feudal trappings and immunities, were, since the central government in Edo could transfer and dismiss them, on the way to civil service status. The "constitutional trend" pointed toward a unitary state long before Matthew Perry and his black ships reached Japan.[43]

Tokugawa Japan had also, by trial and error, developed a fairly workable system of transmitting letters, cash, and goods that "streamlined" business transactions.[44] We also now understand another very real reason for samurai discontent quite apart from dwindling income: if attacked, samurai could be punished both if they fought and if they ran away.[45] In short, at many levels we have today a much clearer picture of what it was like, in fact and in law, to be a samurai, a villager, or a town dweller in Tokugawa Japan than we had forty years ago.[46]

However, there are still considerable gaps in Western knowledge of premodern Japanese society. The amount of books and articles produced in Japan on premodern society and law is overwhelming, but Western students of these matters must depend on the Japanese scholar who guides their research in Japan, and they may out of loyalty perpetuate his views when they return to academe in the Western world. Given the difficulty of the Japanese language, particularly in document form, this can hardly be otherwise; working in Japan as a PhD student is still the most efficient bridge to new Japanese research. But it sometimes takes years until such research is reflected in Western works. Also, there is little money and few career opportunities in the study of premodern law. To the average Japanologist, the texts are difficult and often forbiddingly "dry." To legally trained Japanologists, dealing with past law is a waste of time that could have been spent profitably in the study of modern law. Scholars like Dan Fenno Henderson will be increasingly rare in the future, and the gaps in Western knowledge will only be filled slowly.

Some important lacunae still exist. There is a Russian translation of the *Ritsuryō* 702–18, but in other Western languages we have only fragments.[47] A German translation was finished in 1944 but was burned during an air raid.[48] As for Kamakura law, the basic compilation of 1232, the so-called *Go-seibai* or *Jōei shikimoku*, exists in a somewhat dated English, and in a more modern German, translation.[49] The Kamakura statutes before and after 1232 are not available in a Western translation. The most important legislation of the Imperial Restoration period 1333–36 has now been translated,[50] as have some important *daimyō* codes of the medieval and Sengoku eras.[51] However, there are no systematic translations of the statutes of Oda Nobunaga and of Toyotomi Hideyoshi into a Western language.[52] English translations are available for the following Tokugawa bakufu statutes: for the imperial courtiers (*Kuge shohatto*), for the *daimyō* (*Buke shohatto*), for ordinary Tokugawa samurai (*Shoshi hatto*), for commoners (*Edo kōsatsu*), and the Civil and Penal Law Codification of 1742 (*O-sadamegaki hyakkajō*) with some supplements.[53] But there was much more bakufu legislation than is covered by these now-dated translations, or by modern translations. The Tokugawa laws were voluminous, very detailed in economic matters, and often repetitive.[54] Because of this, they may never be translated; and there is even less prospect for translation of the bulk of daimiate statutory law. Western interest during the past few decades has focused on documents rather than on statutes, because documents are "safer" sources; even when false, they show the problems people struggled with, whereas a statute may reflect only what the rulers *wanted* to be done, or even an ideal that was never enforced.

The key period of pre-Meiji law was that of Heian. The Nara laws went out of use and were supplanted by customary law of the various offices of the imperial government and, in the countryside, by the enactments of the great landed families of Kyoto, which acted as hereditary bureaucrats through their deputies on the land. We have good secondary works for this period,[55] but, since, as noted in the first part of this chapter, this was an era in which the investigation of law became a task for scholars, future translations of Heian statutes and exegetical works will be of great interest.

III. THE THIRTEENTH-CENTURY CULMINATION OF INDIGENOUS JURISPRUDENCE: WHY?

Japan seems to be the only country in Asia that once brought, without influences from the West, the handling of civil cases—which is, according to Gaius, the core of jurisprudence—to such a level of quality that even the loser could leave the court convinced that it had heard him carefully, weighed all the arguments, and decided his case impartially. It happened in the period from about 1220 to about 1320, and only in the courts of the bakufu in Kamakura and its branch office in Rokuhara in Kyoto.[56] Only a tiny fraction of Japan's population could sue in these courts: the bakufu's own men, and—in practice—also temples and civilian landowners. All others needed a letter of recommendation from their local *jitō*; those who could be sued were the shogun's men, not the shogunate itself.[57] The commoners were adjudicated in criminal cases by their local lords, civilian or military; their venue in civil cases was normally the court of the deputy of the Kyoto noble who owned the land. Yet, once the case had been admitted in a bakufu court, the procedures were astonishingly "modern": The parties themselves determined the object of litigation, which steps to take during litigation, and when to stop it; each party had access to all the arguments of the other party and could contest them in court; not the courts, but the parties, sought out the facts; the court decided what was proved or not proved, not by mechanical rules, but according to experience; the court was neutral to the parties and heard them impartially; the court could award a party no more than that party had claimed; there were efficient guarantees against corrupt or sloppy decisions, in particular the method of decision by lot as to which chamber of the court was to hear a particular case; there were also ample provisions for rehearings and appeals.[58] These principles were fully developed in cases concerning real property, and somewhat less so in cases concerning chattels, torts, and debts. Documents and witnesses gradually replaced the previous fact-finding methods of oaths and ordeals, and even criminal cases were processed in an adversarial manner and without the torture commonly used in the courts of the Kyoto bureaucracy and in the courts of the civilian landowners.[59]

The Kamakura / Rokuhara court system grew in response to the flood of complaints of violence brought before the warrior leaders after their victories over the Kyoto power holders in 1185 and 1221. The warrior leaders left considerable areas of jurisdiction to the emperor's bureaucrats, in particular, litigation between civilian landowners including temples, shrines, and monasteries; among Kyoto businessmen; and criminal cases in the Kyoto area involving no bakufu men. From the early thirteenth century, the imperial authorities copied some of the "progressive" features of the bakufu courts.[60] What the warrior leaders wanted was to carve out their own state in northern Japan without antagonizing too blatantly the landholding interests that upheld the imperial system. Civil and military power holders (*kenmon*) had many interests in common.

That, however, does not answer the question why the Hōjō clan, which ruled in Kamakura from 1203 to 1333, and which was deeply conservative in its economic policies, systematically improved the system of civil litigation from about 1220 until about 1320. Deciding civil cases arbitrarily would have been faster and cheaper and would have met with little or no resistance among the military. The standard explanations—to which I also once subscribed—are that the Hōjō, whose rule lacked a legal basis, wanted to stand out as Confucian upholders of moral norms, and in particular that they wanted other warrior clans to spend time and resources on litigation rather than on feuding. Also, inducing such clans to litigate in bakufu courts was a way to make these clans all show their allegiance to the bakufu.[61] This explanation is ingenious, but is weakened by the following considerations: (a) the Confucian ideas common to most thirteenth-century Hōjō leaders required rule by moral suasion rather than by furthering litigation; and (b) since there is no evidence showing the existence of barristers, courts' fees, and similar risks of litigation, the Hōjō could not weaken their potential rivals by letting them litigate until they went broke. However fairly treated, the loser might feel more resentment toward the Hōjō judges than against his adversary; therefore, as a political instrument to enhance loyalty, a court system such as this was, after all, no safe bet.[62]

If we want to find a plausible reason for the court reforms—which proceeded from about 1220 until about 1320, under moral and immoral warrior leaders, during peace as well as during war conditions—there must have been some other continuous factor at work. The reform edicts of the bakufu were piecemeal, and the typical reason given for a new statute is just the concrete abuse to be abolished.[63] But perhaps the underlying reason for the court modernization drive may be found in the dominance in Japan's economic life from about 1200 of a new class of men, namely, capital-owning traders, moneylenders, and shipowners. They were neither warriors nor titleholders of civil nobility, but were mostly monks or lay commoners.[64] In spite of bakufu resistance, they often, because of their business skills, acted as advisors or agents for warriors and civil nobles, even in matters of litigation. And when they were forbidden to appear in court, they wrote the briefs. This new capitalist class could not wait years for a decision, for they had to reinvest their capital; they wanted foreseeable decisions, based on documents, hearings, and witnesses, rather than on ordeals. If the judges felt "outsmarted" by these men skilled in business, they could easily obtain new rules of court procedure, because the High Court, or *Hyōjōshū*, was also the Council of State.[65] The pressure on the courts in the direction of speedier and more rational procedures might also explain the existence of a great many documents containing pleas before courts, but written informally on folded paper (*origami*) rather than on the paper prescribed for such documents, namely, long, unfolded reams, or *tategami*. Pleas on *origami* are not dated, whereas pleas on *tategami* are dated.[66] Could it be that pleas on *origami* were memos that summarized what the party said in court, and which the party afterward handed to the court clerk as an aid to protocollation? The memo could be left undated because the clerk had already noted the date when the oral plea was presented. This is admittedly speculative. But it fits in well with the description of litigation in Article 12 of the *Sata mirensho*, where it is pointed out that what a party writes to the court on *origami* is something other—and, in the context, less—than a plea that initiates a trial.[67]

If we add these three features, namely, the advance of a money and credit economy, more oral presentation of evidence and arguments to the court, and a constant rationalization of court procedures, we may arrive at the following mechanism: The bakufu courts tried to keep up with the ever more businesslike *users* of the courts; documents, witnesses, and confrontation of the parties' statements accordingly supplanted the reliance on affidavits, oaths, and ordeals. Likewise, oral argument as such became more important than the time-honored but also time-consuming exchange of litigation documents.[68] Thus, the pressure for reform of litigation techniques may have come from the users below rather than from the government above.

This line of thought may also explain why most of the reforms were rescinded in the Ashikaga age.[69] The shogun had now become the largest merchant of the realm, living off currency manipulation, money lending, and the China trade. He had to, because he held only a few provinces and could not live on landed wealth alone. Private traders were no longer challengers to the system, but competitors, even enemies. The guarantees for fair trials disappeared, and the Ashikaga shogun or his deputy, presiding as supreme judge, made political decisions from the bench of judges.[70] The Sengoku and

Tokugawa rulers preferred the Ashikaga model to the Kamakura model: to have one's case adjudicated was a grace, not a right. Also, there was the ever-present risk that the judge would switch to the brutal methods of the criminal procedure when confronted with "contempt" in the form of a party who would not compromise.[71]

When, at the end of the nineteenth century, modernization of the litigation system became necessary, the indigenous achievements of the thirteenth century had long since been forgotten. A reform even partially based on these achievements would not have been tolerated by the Western powers, which demanded the adoption of a European system in exchange for even negotiating the abolition of unequal treaties.[72] Yet it should not be forgotten that seven centuries ago, Japan was in the absolute forefront of the march of litigation techniques from arbitrariness and intimidation toward "rule of law" and fairness.

There is reason to believe that those who implemented the procedural reforms of the Hōjō bakufu courts were the scions of those Heian jurists who had taken service in Kamakura when the bakufu was founded, and who had transmitted their legal skills to their own descendants.[73] Thus reform could gain momentum so to speak "unseen." There is a strange parallel here. It was believed until recently that in Japan the study of Western law began in the 1870s. It was difficult to understand how the Japanese legal experts came to understand first French and English and eventually Roman and German law with such amazing speed, even allowing for the efforts of the *Hōmushō* (Ministry of Justice), the pressure from the *Gaimushō* (Ministry of Foreign Affairs), and the work of the foreign advisors. Then one scholar of Japanese law undertook to investigate whether the studies of Western law in Japan may have started *earlier* than commonly believed. He discovered that these studies had begun as early as *1841*, with regard to Dutch statutes, particularly in the area of civil procedure. May I therefore end with a deserved tribute to Dr. F. B. Verwayen of Leiden University, who had the necessary curiosity, guts, and grit to devote years of his busy life as an attorney and university don to learning Tokugawa Japanese and Classical Chinese in order to investigate when Japanese studies of Western law began, and how they were pursued.[74] His findings help to answer the question of how Meiji law reformers and their assistants could have grasped the essentials of Western law as rapidly as they did.

No case can be won, and no fees earned, through such discoveries. They just add to our understanding. And though we now live in an age in which only what is useful counts, the goal of understanding may still be an aim worthwhile in itself.[75]

POSTSCRIPT

Among major new findings between the Seattle Conference in 2002 and Spring 2007, when preparation for publication was completed, the following warrant especial mention.

(1) The traditional idea that archaic Japan (5th through 7th) centuries lacked the concept of "sin" may be wrong. So too may be the idea that the concept of *tsumi* (guilt) grew in "folk law," without governmental intervention. See Yoko Williams, *Tsumi—Offence and Retribution in Early Japan* (London: Routledge, 2003); and, with some doubts about the new theory, Joan R. Piggott's review of Williams, *Journal of Japanese Studies* 33(1) (2007): 116–70.

(2) The traditional idea that the worsening of woman's status and rights in late medieval Japan was due to the prevalence of the *ie* type of extended family may be wrong. On the contrary, when the *ie* decayed, women got less to hold and to say. See Noriko Kurushima, "Marriage and Female Inheritance in Medieval Japan," in *The International Journal of Asian Studies* 1 (2004): 223–45.

(3) The traditional idea that Tokugawa samurai families lived according to Confucian principles and rarely divorced is wrong. See Harald Fuess, *Divorce in Japan: Family, Gender, and the State 1600–2000* (Stanford: Stanford University Press, 2004); and, on the whole agreeing, Anne E. Imamura's review of Fuess, *Journal of Japanese Studies* 32(1) (2006): 212–15.

(4) The traditional idea that the cruel discriminatory laws against Tokugawa outcastes came about because the shogunate and the daimyo just went along with the prejudices of the commoners may be wrong. On the contrary, the rulers aided and abetted these prejudices. See Gerald Groemer, "The Creation of the Edo Outcaste Order," *Journal of Japanese Studies* 27(2) (2001): 263–93.

(5) The traditional idea that the cruel penal practices of the Tokugawa era were abolished in Meiji times under the combined pressures of internal reformers and foreign demands is only partially correct. The internal reformers—whose first voices were heard already in the 18th century—achieved little. And the Meiji government instrumentalized foreign demands for penal reforms in order to create new ways of oppression, often cruel ones. See Daniel V. Botsman, *Punishment and Power in the Making of Modern Japan* (Princeton: Princeton University Press, 2005); and, agreeing, Philip Brown's review of Botsman, *Journal of Japanese Studies* 33(1) (2007): 175–79.

NOTES

1. John Henry Wigmore, *Law and Justice in Tokugawa Japan: Materials for the History of Japanese Law and Justice under the Tokugawa Shogunate 1603–1867*, 20 vols. (Tokyo: University of Tokyo Press, 1967–83). For a list of Dan Fenno Henderson's most important works on Tokugawa law, and for some by his friend and collaborator, the late Yoshirō Hiramatsu, see Carl Steenstrup, *A History of Law in Japan until 1868*, 2nd ed. (Leiden: Brill, 1996), 181.

2. Dan Fenno Henderson, *Conciliation and Japanese Law: Tokugawa and Modern*, 2 vols. (Seattle: Association for Asian Studies / University of Washington Press, 1965).

3. Guntram Rahn, *Rechtsdenken und Rechtsauffassung in Japan: Dargestellt an der Entwicklung der modernen Zivilrechtsmethodik* [Legal Thought and Views of Law in Japan, as Seen through the Development of the Ways to Interpret the Law in Civil Cases] (Munich: Beck, 1990); Hans Peter Marutschke, *Einführung in das japanische Recht* [Introduction to Japanese Law] (Munich: Beck, 1999), 15–17; and Ronald Frank, "Traditional Legal Thought and Present-Day Law," in Josef Kreiner, ed., *The Impact of Traditional Thought on Present-Day Japan* (Munich: Iudicium, 1996), 209–35, esp. 226–31.

4. See Ogyū Sorai, *Discourse on Government (Seidan)*, trans. and ed. Olof Lidin (Wiesbaden: Harrassowitz, 1999), 324–25.

5. See Zentarō Kitagawa, *Rezeption und Fortbildung des europäischen Zivilrechts in Japan* [How European Law on Civil Cases Was Introduced and Developed in Japan] (Frankfurt am Main: Metzner, 1970), 44–53.

6. See Ryōsuke Ishii, *Nihon hōseishi gaisetsu* [An Outline of the History of Law in Japan] (Tokyo: Sōbunsha 1976), 64–65, 69; and Cornelius J. Kiley, "The Imperial Court as a Legal Authority in the Kamakura Age," in Jeffrey P. Mass, ed., *Court and Bakufu in Japan—Essays in Kamakura History* (New Haven, CT: Yale University Press, 1982), 29–44, esp. 34.

7. See Dan Fenno Henderson, "Chinese Legal Studies in Early 18th Century Japan—Scholars and Sources," *Journal of Asian Studies* 30(1) (1970): 21–56; and Henderson, "Chinese Influence on 18th Century Tokugawa Codes," in Jerome Alan Cohen, R. Randle Edwards, and Fu-mei Chang Chen, eds., *Essays on China's Legal Tradition* (Princeton, NJ: Princeton University Press, 1980), 270–301.

8. See Gregor Paul, *Philosophie in Japan—von den Anfängen bis zur Heian-Zeit* [Philosophy in Japan—from the Beginnings until (and including) the Heian Era] (Munich: Iudicium, 1993), 185–93, 349–65; and Kitagawa, *Rezeption und Fortbildung*, chap. 2, secs. 4–7.

9. See Norihiko Haga, "Ryōshūshihai to hō" [The Lordship of Warrior Land

Developers and the Law], in *Iwanami kōza Nihon rekishi* [The Iwanami Symposium on the History of Japan] (Tokyo: Iwanami Shoten, 1975), 5:169–210; and Astrid Brochlos, *Grundherrschaft in Japan—Entstehung und Struktur des Minase no shō* [Lordship over Land in Japan—the Origins and Structure of the Latifundium "Minase"] (Wiesbaden: Harrassowitz, 2001), chaps. 3.2, 3.3. The book contains, inter alia, a lexicon of medieval terms of land law and tax law.

10. On pre-Tokugawa times, see Markus Rüttermann, *Das Dorf Suganoura und seine historischen Quellen—Untersuchungen zur Genese einer japanischen Dorfgemeinde im späten Mittelalter* [The Village Suganoura and Its Historical Sources—Investigations into the Beginnings of a Japanese Village Community in the Late Medieval Era] (Hamburg: Gesellschaft für Natur-und Völkerkunde Ostasiens PTO, 1996), chaps. 3.5, 3.9. Rüttermann's footnotes and bibliography contain, among other things, references to important—and too little used—works in *French* on medieval Japanese law. On Tokugawa times, see Yoshirō Hiramatsu, "Tokugawa Law," *Law in Japan: An Annual* 14 (1981): 1–48.

11. See Makoto Takeuchi, "Festivals and Fights—Urban Life and the State in the Early Modern Era," in James McClain et al., eds., *Edo and Paris—Urban Life and the State in the Early Modern Era* (Ithaca, NY: Cornell University Press, 1994), 384–406.

12. See Konrad Zweigert and Hein Kötz, *Einführung in die Rechtsvergleichung auf dem Gebiete des Privatrechts* [Introduction to Comparative Law in the Field of the Law of Civil Cases], 2 vols. (Tübingen: J. C. B. Mohr, 1984), 1:404–38.

13. On China, see Oskar Weggel, *Chinesische Rechtsgeschichte* [History of Law in China] (Leiden: Brill, 1980), 125–28. For Japan, see Kristina Kade Troost, "Peasants, Elites, and Villages in the Fourteenth Century," in Jeffrey P. Mass, ed., *The Origins of Japan's Medieval World—Courtiers, Clerics, Warriors, and Peasants in the Fourteenth Century* (Stanford, CA: Stanford University Press, 1997), 91–109; and Klaus Vollmer, *Professionen und ihre "Wege" im mittelalterlichen Japan—eine Einführung in ihre Sozialgeschichte und literarische Repräsentation am Beispiel des Tōhoku'in-shokunin-utaawase* [The (Artisanal) Professions and Their Ideals in Medieval Japan—an Introduction to Their Social History and How They Were Presented in Literature, as Seen in the *Tōhoku'in* Collection of the Song Contests of Artisans] (Hamburg: Gesellschaft für Natur-und Völkerkunde Ostasiens, 1995). See also Ryōsuke Ishii, *A History of Political Institutions in Japan* (Tokyo: Japan Foundation, 1980), 56–57.

14. See Yōtarō Sakudō, "The Management Practices of Family Business," in Chie Nakane et al., eds., *Tokugawa Japan—the Social and Economic Antecedents of Modern Japan* (Tokyo: University of Tokyo Press, 1990), 147–66.

15. See John O. Haley, *Authority without Power—Law and the Japanese Paradox* (New York: Oxford University Press, 1991), 168–83.

16. See Ryūsaku Tsunoda and C. Carrington Goodrich, *Japan in the Chinese Dynastic Histories* (South Pasadena, CA: P. D. and Ione Perkins, 1951), 1–2, 13–16, 22–24, 30; Akio Yoshie, "Bushidan" [Warrior Bands], in Keiji Nagahara et al., eds., *Chūseishi handobukku* [Manual of Medieval History] (Tokyo: Kintō shuppan, 1974), 39–41; Yasuo Watanabe, *Keiji handan monogatari* [The Story of the Judge for Penal Cases] (Tokyo: Chōshutsu shuppan), 114–16; Kiyoyoshi Kanai, "Jihaku wa kō shite tsukurareta" [How Confessions Were Brought About], in Masao Ono and Yasuo Watanabe, eds., *Keiji saiban no hikari to kage* [Light and Shadows of Judge(s) for Penal Cases] (Tokyo: Yūhikaku, 1989), chap. 3; John M. Maki, ed., *Court and Constitution in Japan—Selected Supreme Court Decisions 1948–1960* (Seattle: University of Washington Press, 1964), 191–206; Petra Schmidt, *Die Todesstrafe in Japan* [The Death Penalty in Japan] (Hamburg: Deutsch-Japanische Juristenvereinigung, 1996), 38–59; Amnesty International Japan, *The Death Penalty and the Need for More Safeguards against Ill-Treatment of Detainees* (London: Amnesty International, 1991); Lawrence Repeta, "Special Issue on Civil Liberties in Japan," *Law in Japan: An Annual* 20 (1987): 14–23, 54–73. *Law in Japan: An Annual* was one of the few law journals consistently championing suspects' human rights in Japan. For the—unsuccessful—efforts of some premodern Japanese intellectuals to develop—on Buddhist or Confucian fundaments—an indigenous ideology of "Human Rights," see Carl Steenstrup, "Grund und Grenzen der Menschenrechte im japanischen Verständnis" [How the Basis and Limits of "Human Rights" Are Understood in Japan], in Walter Schweidler, ed., *Menschenrechte und Gemeinsinn—westlicher und östlicher Weg?* [Human Rights and the Agreement on Public Values—(Is There) a "Western" and an "Eastern" Approach?] (Sankt Augustin: Academia Verlag, 1998), 307–35.

17. See Wilhelm Röhl, "Rechtsgeschichtliches zu jōri" ["Jōri" (Natural Justice) (in the Light of) Legal History], in Heinrich Menkhaus, ed., *Das Japanische im japanischen Recht* [The Japanese (Elements) in the Law of Japan] (Munich: Iudicium, 1994), 39–49; and Shirō Ishii, "Bemerkungen zu jōri bzw. dōri" in Menkhaus, *Das Japanische im japanischen Recht*, 51–58. See also Taryō Ōbayashi, "Der Ursprung der shintoistischen Hochzeit" [The Origins of the Shinto'istic Marriage (Rite)], in Klaus Antoni, ed., *Rituale und ihre Urheber—Invented Traditions in der japanischen Religionsgeschichte* [Rituals and Their Makers—Invented Traditions in the History of Religion in Japan] (Hamburg: LIT Verlag, 1997), 39–48; and Yōtarō Sakudō, "Traditional Labor Management in Japan, 1710–1890," in Keiichirō Nakagawa et al., eds., *The International Conference on Business History (Proceedings of the 4th Fuji Conference)*, 7 vols. (Tokyo: University of Tokyo Press, 1979), 4:127–40.

18. Rizō Takeuchi, ed., *Nara ibun* [Documents Remaining from the Nara Era] (Tokyo: Tōkyōdō shuppan, 1944); Takeuchi, ed., *Heian ibun* [Documents Remain-

ing from the Heian Era], 15 vols. (Tokyo: Tōkyōdō shuppan, 1974–80); and Takeuchi, ed., *Kamakura ibun* [Documents Remaining from the Kamakura Era], 42 vols. (Tokyo: Tōkyōdō shuppan, 1973–91).

19. See Mitsusada Inoue, "The Century of Reform," in Delmer M. Brown, ed., *The Cambridge History of Japan* (Cambridge: Cambridge University Press, 1993), 1:163–220, esp. 180–81. For the economic proficiency of wet rice agriculture and village organization two thousand years ago, see J. Edward Kidder Jr., "The Earliest Societies in Japan," in Brown, *The Cambridge History of Japan*, 1:48–107, esp. 90–92. For pre-Nara growth of political institutions, see Delmer M. Brown, "The Yamato Kingdom," in Brown, *The Cambridge History of Japan*, 1:108–62; and Gina L. Barnes, *Protohistoric Yamato—Archaeology of the First Japanese State* (Ann Arbor: University of Michigan Center for Japanese Studies, 1988), 261–77. On pre-Taika criminal law, and how echoes of it have survived in Shinto mythology (the prevailing opinion had it the other way around!), see Nelly Naumann, "Zur ursprünglichen Bedeutung des *harahe*" [On the Original Meaning of (the Word) *Harahe* ("Cleansing")], in *Festgabe Herbert Zachert 70 Jahre* [Writings in Honor of the Seventieth Anniversary of Herbert Zachert], 3 vols. (Bonn: Bonner Zeitschrift für Japanologie, 1979), 1:169–87.

20. For the military organization of the Nara and the Heian state, see Karl Friday, *Hired Swords—the Rise of Private Warrior Power in Early Japan* (Stanford, CA: Stanford University Press, 1992), chap. 4. For the administrative framework in the century in which the *Ritsuryō* system actually worked, see Toshiya Terao, "Nara Economic and Social Institutions," in Brown, *The Cambridge History of Japan*, 1:415–52, esp. 430–48. For the unique ways in which the late seventh-century government made a "service nobility" out of the autochthonous warrior clans, see Richard J. Miller, *Ancient Japanese Nobility—The* Kabane *Ranking System* (Berkeley: University of California Press, 1974). For the government offices and their functions, see William Wayne Farris, "Trade Money and Merchants in Nara Japan," in *Monumenta Nipponica* 53(3) (Fall 1998): 303–34, esp. 320–34 on the entrepreneurial role of officialdom; and Richard J. Miller, *Japan's First Bureaucracy—a Study of Eighth-Century Government*, East Asia Papers, vol. 19 (Ithaca, NY: Cornell University Press, 1978). Miller's work was edited, completed, and published after his death by Prof. Felicia G. Bock. Her annotated translation of the *Engishiki: Procedures of the Engi Era*, 2 vols. (Tokyo: Sophia University Press, 1970–72), starts with a lucid summary of Japanese legal history until the middle of the tenth century. For the administrative organization of the next century, see Françine Hérail, *Fonctions et fonctionnaires japonais au début du XIe siècle* [Public Posts and Their Holders at the Beginning of Eleventh Century Japan] (Paris: Publications Orientalistes de France, 1977). For the rationalization of the central administration that took

place under the rule of the retired emperors, see G. Cameron Hurst III, *Insei—Abdicated Sovereigns in the Politics of Late Heian Japan, 1086–1185* (New York: Columbia University Press, 1976), 217–36, 279–84. In the countryside, both on public land (*kokugaryō*) and on privatized land (*shōen*), new and ingenious ways of administering, exploiting, and increasing agricultural wealth were developed. See Elizabeth Sato, "The Early Development of the Shōen," in John W. Hall and Jeffrey P. Mass, eds., *Medieval Japan—Essays in Institutional History* (New Haven, CT: Yale University Press, 1974), 91–108; and Cornelius J. Kiley, "Estate and Property in the Late Heian Period," in Hall and Mass, *Medieval Japan*, 109–24. Just as the Kamakura era was the high point of the development of private and procedural law, the Heian era was the high point of the development of administrative law. This is a point often overlooked.

21. See Peter Nickerson, "The Meaning of Matrilocality—Kinship, Property, and Politics in Mid-Heian," *Monumenta Nipponica* 48(4) (Winter 1993): 429–67. The dominant males were not the eldest ones, but the active mid-age ones; old age often meant status loss. See Susanne Formanek, *Denn dem Alter kann keiner entfliehen—Altern und Alter in Japan der Nara und Heian-Zeit* [For Nobody Can Escape (the Decay Going with) Aging—Growing Old and Being Old in Nara and Heian Japan] (Vienna: Österreichische Akademie der Wissenschaflen, 1994), 403, 407–9, 419–22, 439–49.

22. See Cornelius J. Kiley, "Provincial Administration and Land Tenure," in Donald H. Shively and William H. McCullough, eds., *The Cambridge History of Japan* (Cambridge: Cambridge University Press, 1999), 2:236–40; and Dana Morris, "Land and Society," in Shively and McCullough, *The Cambridge History of Japan*, 1:183–235. In the middle of the ninth century, however, central and local privatizers of land "reinterpreted" the land laws of the central government on a grand scale, often with the connivance of the high officials themselves; see Michael Charlier, *Das Dairi-Shiki—Eine Studie zu seiner Entstehung und Wirkung* [The Palace (Ceremony) Rule (of A.D. 821, with Later Modifications)—a Study of Its Origin and Effects] (Wiesbaden: Harrassowitz, 1975), 26–28.

23. See Jeffrey P. Mass, *The Development of Kamakura Rule, 1180–1250—a History with Documents* (Stanford, CA: Stanford University Press, 1979), 48–55, 154–59.

24. See Jeffrey P. Mass, *Yoritomo and the Founding of the First Bakufu—the Origins of Dual Government in Japan* (Stanford, CA: Stanford University Press, 2000), 121–28, 196–218.

25. See Jeffrey P. Mass, *Antiquity and Anachronism in Japanese History* (Stanford, CA: Stanford University Press, 1992), chaps. 2, 3.

26. The reason is simple: in Japan there was no "collapse of culture" (literacy, sanitation, urbanism, trade, police, armed forces, schools, religious tolerance)

between "antiquity" and the "medieval age." The use of these terms with respect to Japan is—even in legal history—a Eurocentric construct. See Susumu Ishii, "Der Charakter des japanischen Mittelalters" [The (Basic) Feature(s) of the Medieval Era of Japan], *Bochumer Jahrbuch zur Ostasienforschung* 11 (1979): 326–38.

27. See Mass, *Antiquity and Anachronism*, 191.

28. See Carolin Reimers, "*Kemmuki*—Aufzeichnungen aus der ära Kemmu" ["Kemmuki"—Records of the Kemmu Era], *Nachrichten der Gesellschaft für Natur- und Völkerkunde Ostasiens* 149–150 (1991): 85–164. For the *Kenmu* "reform laws" in general, see Andrew Goble, *Kenmu—Go Daigo's Revolution* (Cambridge, MA: Council on East Asian Studies, 1997).

29. See Kenneth A. Grossberg and Kanamoto Nobuhisa, trans. and eds., *The Laws of the Muromachi Bakufu* (Tokyo: Sophia University Press, 1981), 15–22.

30. See Thomas Conlan, "Largesse and the Limits of Loyalty in the Fourteenth Century," in Mass, *The Origins of Japan's Medieval World*, 39–64.

31. Carl Steenstrup with Hyun-ki Shin, "*Busei kihan*—eine Quelle zu Justiz und Verwaltung der Ashikaga-Zeit" [*Busei kihan*—a Source (Document) for Judicial and Administrative (Practices) in the Ashikaga Era], in Ulrich Apel et al., eds., *Referate des 10. Deutschen Japanologentages vom 9. bis 12. Oktober 1996* [Report of the Tenth Meeting of German(-Speaking) Japanologists, October 9–12, 1996] (Munich: Center for Japan Studies of the University of Munich, 1997), published as CD-ROM, 73-91.

32. See Rüttermann, *Das Dorf Suganoura*, 77–78.

33. See Klaus Vollmer, "Die Begriffswelt des Marginalen im mittelalterlichen Japan—Zum Problem der Klassifizierung gesellschaftlicher Randgruppen und ihrer Bezeichnungen" [The Field of the Concept "Outsider" in Medieval Japan—How the Various Classes of Outsiders Were Defined and Named], *Oriens Extremus* 37(1) (1994): 5–44. "Non-Marginals" were those who held homesteads (*zaike*) and their kin. For the *zaike* concept, see Detlev Taranczewski, *Lokale Grundherrschaft und Ackerbau in der Kamakura-Zeit—dargestellt anhand der Nitta no shō in der Provinz Kōzuke* [Lordship and Agriculture in the Kamakura Era, as Seen in the Latifundium "Nitta" in Kōzuke Province], *Bonner Zeitschrift für Japanologie*, vol. 10 (Bonn: Förderverein Bonner Zeitschrift für Japanologie, 1988). The status law—written and customary—was at the center of the premodern legal order, also before the Tokugawa age, but is often difficult to disentangle in the sources, because contemporaries took knowledge of the status law for granted. Yoshihiko Amino and his school of historians have found that even in medieval Japan, many people made a living at occupations other than farming. On the term *hyakushō*, see Thomas Keirstead, *The Geography of Power in Medieval Japan* (Princeton, NJ: Princeton University Press, 1992), chap. 2. They made out the bulk of taxpaying,

resident tillers of the soil. On temple and shrine servants, armed and civilian, see Mikael S. Adolphson, *The Gates of Power—Monks, Courtiers, and Warriors in Premodern Japan* (Honolulu: University of Hawai'i Press, 2000), esp. 53–62, 291, 328. On traders, see Rüttermann, *Das Dorf Suganoura*; and Hitomi Tonomura, *Community and Commerce in Late Medieval Japan—the Corporate Villages of Tokuchin-ho* (Stanford, CA: Stanford University Press, 1992), chap. 5. On nuns, artisans, fishermen, peddlers, actors, jugglers, shamans, and female entertainers, see Barbara Ruch, "The Other Side of Culture in Medieval Japan," in Kōzō Yamamura, ed., *The Cambridge History of Japan* (Cambridge: Cambridge University Press, 1990), 3:500–543. On outcasts, see Keiji Nagahara, "The Medieval Origins of the Eta-Hinin," *Journal of Japanese Studies* 5 (1979): 385–403. On the handicapped, see Ingrid Fritsch, *Japans blinde Sänger* [The Blind Bards of Japan] (Munich: Iudicium, 1996). On the courtesans, see Michael Stein, *Japans Kurtisanen* [The Courtesans of Japan] (Munich: Iudicium; Tokyo: Deutsche Gesellschaft für Natur-und Völkerkunde Ostasiens, 1997). What mattered legally was the application of outcast status, which depended on one's proximity to blood and death; see Klaus Vollmer, "Buddhism and the Killing of Animals in Pre-modern Japan," in Michael Zimmermann, ed., *Buddhism and Violence* (Kathmandu: Lumbini International Research Institute, 2006), 195–211; and Vollmer, "Ordnungen des Unreinen. Zur Typologie von 'Kegare' in der japanischen Kultur der Vormoderne" [The Taxonomies of Pollution. On the Typology of "Kegare" (Ritual Uncleanness) in the Culture of Premodern Japan], in *Nachrichten der Gesellschaft für Natur-und Völkerkunde Ostasiens*, vol. 76, Heft [Fascicle] 179–80 (Hamburg 2006): 197–208. In addition to outcast status, many other status differences among various occupational classes became, as is well known, stricter under the Tokugawa.

34. See John W. Hall, "Foundations of the Modern Japanese Daimyō," in John W. Hall and Marius B. Jansen, eds., *Studies in the Institutional History of Early Modern Japan* (Princeton, NJ: Princeton University Press, 1968), 65–77.

35. See Shizuo Katsumata and Martin Collcutt, "The Development of Sengoku Law," in John W. Hall et al., eds., *Japan before Tokugawa—Political Consolidation and Economic Growth, 1500—1650* (Princeton, NJ: Princeton University Press, 1981), 101–24. See also Reinhard Zöllner, *The Ludowinger and the Takeda—Feudale Herrschaft in Thüringen und Kai no Kuni* [The "Ludovingians" and the Takeda—Feudal Rule in Thuringia (Germany) and Kai Province (Japan)] (Bonn: Dieter Born, 1995), 199, 222–25, 240–43, 262–67. The more important provincial codes (*bunkokuhō*) have been translated and annotated by Wilhelm Röhl: the provincial code of the Takeda in *Oriens Extremus* 6 (1959): 210–35; that of the Miyoshi in *Oriens Extremus* 7 (1960): 51–67; that of the Imagawa in *Nachrichten der Gesellschaft für Natur-und Völkerkunde Ostasiens* 85–86 (1959): 60–72; and that of

the Date in *Mitteilungen der Ostasiatischen Gesellschaft* 41 A (1960): 1–122. The provincial code of the Uesugi was translated and annotated by Ronald Frank; see Apel et al. *Referate des 10. Deutschen Japanologentages*, 33–43. An annotated translation of the provincial code of the Chōsokabe, by Marius B. Jansen, is found in Nakane et al., *Tokugawa Japan*, 83–108; and the code of the Munakata clan, translated by the present author, in *Japonica Humboldtiana* 7 (2003): 93–122. Many warrior clans also had secret instructions on how to keep power (*kakun*). On *kakun*, see Carl Steenstrup, *Hōjō Shigetoki (1198–1261) and His Role in the History of Political and Ethical Ideas in Japan*, Scandinavian Institute of Asian Studies, Monograph Series no. 41 (London: Curzon Press, 1979), chap. 2. *Kakun* may be the ancestors of the modern company codes for employees. The standard notion that the warlords cowed the imperial court into political silence was disproved by Lee Butler in his *Emperor and Aristocracy in Japan, 1467–1680: Resilience and Renewal* (Cambridge, MA: Harvard University Asia Center, 2002), esp. chap. 4.

36. See Herman Ooms, *Tokugawa Village Practice—Class, Status, Power, Law* (Berkeley: University of California Press, 1996), esp. chaps. 1, 4; and Peter Kornicki, *The Book in Japan—a Cultural History from the Beginnings to the Nineteenth Century* (Leiden: Brill, 1998), 244–50 and 349–52.

37. See Christian Wöllschläger, "Historical Trends of Civil Litigation in Japan, Arizona, Sweden, and Germany: Japanese Legal Culture in the Light of Judicial Statistics," in Harald Baum, ed., *Japan—Economic Success and Legal System* (New York: Walter de Gruyter, 1997), 89–142, esp. 111–13. The Wöllschläger article strengthens the findings of John O. Haley, in "The Myth of the Reluctant Litigant," *Journal of Japanese Studies* 4(2) (1978): 359–90: How much people litigate depends on whether institutional arrangements favor litigation, rather than on the ethics prevalent in that particular society.

38. See Gary P. Leupp, *Servants, Shophands, and Laborers in the Cities of Tokugawa Japan* (Princeton, NJ: Princeton University Press, 1992), 17, 23, 33, 69–72, 75, 85, 100–106, 118–20, 126, 147.

39. See Ulrike Schaede, *Forwards and Futures in Tokugawa-Period in Japan: A New Perspective on the Dojima Rice Market* (Occasional Paper no. 2 of the Center for Japanese Studies of Marburg University, 1988), 20–21, 27–29, 36–37; and Schaede, "Die Vergangenheit der Futures. Was die findigen Tokugawa-Kaufleute 'im voraus' taten" ["Futures" in the Past; How Ingenious Tokugawa Merchants Managed (Their) Future(s)], in Peter Pörtner, ed., *Japan-Lesebuch II* (Tübingen: Konkursbuch-Verlag, 1990), 241–59.

40. See Richard W. Rabinowitz, "The Historical Development of the Japanese Bar," *Harvard Law Review* 70 (1956): 61–81. This article has withstood the test of time.

41. See Constantine Nomikos Vaporis, *Breaking Barriers—Travel and the State in Early Modern Japan* (Cambridge, MA: Harvard University Press, 1994), chap. 1, 5.

42. See Ulrich Goch, "Zur Amtslaufbahn der Lokalverwalter des Shogunats in Japan des 18. and 19. Jahrhunderts" [On the Careers of Local Governors of Shogunal (Lands) in Eighteenth- and Nineteenth-Century Japan], *Bochumer Jahrbuch für Ostasienforschung* 17 (1993): 27–75; and for the censors of the bakufu, the *metsuke*, see Ann Behrens, "Interview with a Bakumatsu Official," in *Monumenta Nipponica* 55(3) (Fall 2000): 369–98.

43. See Shirō Ishii, "Recht und Verfassung in Japan während der Tokugawa-Zeit" [Law and Constitution in Japan during the Tokugawa Era], in Knut Schulz, ed., *Beiträge zur Wirtschafts-und Sozialgeschichte des Mittelalters—Festschrift für Herbert Helbig zum 65. Geburtstag* [Contributions to Medieval Economic and Social History in Honor of Herbert Helbig on the Occasion of His Sixty-fifth Anniversary] (Vienna: Böhlau Verlag, 1976), 323–38. The "classical" idea is that the *bakuhan* system could be transformed into a modern nation-state only through a push from the outside, thus Mark Ravina, *Land and Lordship in Early Modern Japan* (Stanford, CA: Stanford University Press, 1999), 27–31, 192–201. But see the review article by Ronald P. Toby, "Rescuing the Nation from History," *Monumenta Nipponica* 56(2) (Summer 2001): 197–237. The Meiji reformers of the legal system held the view that the *bakuhan* system was irreparably outmoded. See Ryōsuke Ishii, *Hōseishi* [History of Law], *Taikei Nihonshi sōsho* [A Systematic Collection of (Texts on) Japanese History] (Tokyo: Yamakawa, 1969), 4:257–62, 271–74, 305–8; and Paul-Christian Schenck, *Der deutsche Anteil an der Gestaltung des modernen japanischen Rechts-und Verfassungswesens* [The German Contribution to the Development of Law and Constitution in Modern Japan] (Stuttgart: Steiner, 1997), 52–58, 89–101. The greatest obstacle to unification was probably *not* the *bakuhan* system in itself, but the interest of the *shōgun* and each *daimyō* to hang on to his right to tax the tillers of his domain for the benefit of himself or his vassals; see Patricia Sippel, "Abandoned Fields: Negotiating Taxes in the Bakufu Domain," in *Monumenta Nipponica* 53(2) (Summer 1998): 197–223.

44. See Shiro Kohsaka and Johannes Laube, eds., *Informationssystem und Kulturelles Leben in den Städten der Edo-Zeit* [The Informational System and Cultural Life in the Towns of the Edo Era] (Wiesbaden: Harrassowitz, 2000), esp. pt. 1; and Katsuhisa Moriya, "Urban Networks and Information Networks," in Nakane et al., *Tokugawa Japan*, 97–123, esp. 109–14. Most of the tools and practices of the credit and banking business had been developed long *before* the Tokugawa era; see Suzanne Gay, *The Money Lenders of Late Medieval Kyoto* (Honolulu: University of Hawai'i Press, 2001), esp. chaps. 2–3.

45. See Eiko Ikegami, *The Taming of the Samurai—Honorific Idealism and the*

Making of Modern Japan (Cambridge, MA: Harvard University Press, 1995), chaps. 11, 16.

46. See, in particular, Susan B. Hanley, *Everyday Things in Pre-modern Japan—the Hidden Legacy of Material Culture* (Berkeley: University of California Press, 1997). The worst barrier against the exploration of Japan's legal past is, obviously, that most sources are written in *Kanbun*. Two self-study textbooks are now available, namely, Astrid Brochlos, *Kanbun—Grundlagen der klassischen sino-japanischen Schriftsprache* [Kanbun—Fundaments of the Classical Sino-Japanese Written Language] (Wiesbaden: Harrassowitz, 2004), and Inge-Lore Kluge, *Kanbun—Ein Lehr- und Übungsbuch; Überarbeite und herausgegeben von Hannelore Eisenhofer-Halim* [Kanbun—a Textbook with Exercises. Revised and published (after the death of Prof. Kluge) by Hannelore Eisenhofer-Halim] (Frankfurt am Main: Peter Lang, 1977). Both books have an Annex, containing solutions to their exercises. Akira Komai and Thomas H. Rohlich, *An Introduction to Japanese Kanbun* (Nagoya: The University of Nagoya Press, 1999), has no such Annex, but provides easier access for English-speaking students.

47. See K. A. Popov, *Svod zakonov Taihōryō 702–718 gg.* [The Taihōryō Collection of Statutes (from) the Years 702–718], 4 vols. (Moscow: Nauka, 1985–89), of which vol. 4 translates and annotates the most important pre-*Ritsuryō* edicts. George Appert, C. J. Tarring, George B. Sansom, Richard J. Miller, and, more recently, Hans-Adalbert Dettmer in particular have translated important *Ritsuryō* chapters. See the bibliography in Steenstrup, *A History of Law in Japan until 1868*, 168–69. The following books by Hans-Adalbert Dettmer contain large chunks of annotated Ritsuryō translations: *Die Steuergesetzgebung der Nara-Zeit* [The Tax Legislation of the Nara Era] (Wiesbaden: Harrassowitz, 1959); and *Die Urkunden Japans vom 8. bis ins 10. Jahrhundert* [Basic Documents of Eighth- through Tenth-Century Japan], *Die Ränge—Zum Dienstverhältnis der Urkundsbeamten, Band 1* [Vol. 1, Official Ranks—the Service Relations of the (Imperially) Appointed Civil Servants] (Wiesbaden: Harrassowitz, 1972). For Felicia G. Bock's translation of the *Engishiki*, see note 20 above.

48. Parts of this lost translation are found in the footnotes of volume 2 of Oskar Nachod, *Geschichte von Japan* [A History of Japan], 2 vols. (Leipzig: Friedrich Andreas Perthes, 1906). A thorough analysis of land legislation in the Nara era is found in Harro von Senger, *Chinesische Bodeninstitutionen im Taihō-Verwaltungskodex: Niida Noboru's Beitrag zur Rekonstruktion der Bodeninstitutionen der T'ang-Zeit* [Institutions of Chinese Land Law (Found) in the Taihō Administrative Code: The Contribution of Noboru Niida to the Reconstruction of the Land (Law) Institutions of T'ang China] (Wiesbaden: Harrassowitz, 1983).

49. The pioneer translation first appeared in John Carey Hall, *Transactions of*

the Asiatic Society of Japan 34 (1906): 1–44, and has been reprinted in John Carey Hall, *Japanese Feudal Law* (Washington, DC: University Publications of America, 1979), 19–46. The modern translation by Wilhelm Röhl is found in *Oriens Extremus* 5 (1958): 228–45.

50. Relevant translations are cited in note 28 above.

51. Relevant translations are cited in note 35 above.

52. For good summaries of their legislative activities, see Jeroen Lamers, *Japonius Tyrannus—The Japanese Warlord Oda Nobunaga Reconsidered* (Leiden: Hotei, 2000); and Mary Elizabeth Berry, *Hideyoshi* (Cambridge, MA: Harvard University Press, 1982).

53. John Carey Hall's pioneer translations are to be found in *Transactions of the Asiatic Society of Japan* 38(3) (1911): 269–331. They have been reprinted in Hall, *Japanese Feudal Law* (see n. 49 above).

54. See Ooms, *Tokugawa Village Practice*, chap. 6; and Carolin Reimers, *Gesetzgebung im vormodernen Japan—Rechtsgebote und die Ideen der Konfuzianer in der Edo-Zeit (1603–1868)* [Legislation in Premodern Japan—Law Decrees and the Ideas of the Confucians in the Edo Era (1603–1868)] (Munich: Iudicium, 2000). In the crucial field of status law, bakufu legislation did not simply reinforce but actually created social realities; see, in particular, Gerald Groemer, "The Creation of the Edo Outcast Order," in *Journal of Japanese Studies* 27(2) (Summer 2001): 263–93.

55. Relevant works are cited in note 20 above.

56. See Jeffrey P. Mass, "The Kamakura Bakufu—Bakufu Governance," in Yamamura, *The Cambridge History of Japan*, 3:74–80; and Carl Steenstrup, "The Principles of Civil Litigation in Thirteenth-Century Japan," *Journal of Intercultural Studies* 14 (1987): 52–60.

57. See Mass, "The Kamakura Bakufu," 74–80; and Carl Steenstrup, "The Legal System of Kamakura Japan at the End of the Kamakura Period from the Litigants' Point of View," in Brian E. McKnight, ed., *Law and the State in Traditional East Asia—Six Studies in the Sources of East Asian Law* (Honolulu: University of Hawai'i Press, 1987), 72–110, esp. 90–91. On the origins and functions of the system, see Mass, *The Development of Kamakura Rule, 1180–1250*, pt. 2, esp. chap. 5.

58. See Carl Steenstrup, "Sata Mirensho: A Fourteenth Century Law Primer," *Monumenta Nipponica* 35(4) (1980): 405–35, esp. arts. 14, 21, 23, 29–32, 37, 149–50. The courts could operate with reasonable speed, because they probably took decisions by majority vote. Markus Rüttermann has found that monks were not the only ones to use majority voting: many lay authorities in premodern Japan used it, too. See Markus Rüttermann, "Das Prinzip der Majorität (*tabun*) im Japanischen Mittelalter" [The Principle of Majority (*Tabun*) (Decision Making) in the Japanese Medieval Era], *Saeculum* 48(1) (1997): 21–71, esp. n. 38.

59. Steenstrup, "The Legal System of Kamakura Japan at the End of the Kamakura Period from the Litigants' Point of View," 93.

60. See Kiley, "The Imperial Court as a Legal Authority in the Kamakura Age."

61. See Steenstrup, "The Legal System of Kamakura Japan at the End of the Kamakura Period from the Litigants' Point of View," 75–76.

62. See J. Mark Ramseyer's criticism in *Monumenta Nipponica* 42 (1987): 504–5; and *Monumenta Nipponica* 43 (1988): 231.

63. See Susumu Ishii et al., eds., *Chūsei seiji—shakai shisō, jō* [Medieval Political and Social Thought, Part 1], *Nihon shisō taikei* [Japanese Thought in Systematical (Arrangement)] (Tokyo: Iwanami Shoten, 1994), 21:123–37.

64. See Yoshihiko Amino, "Commerce and Finance in the Middle Ages: The Beginnings of 'Capitalism,'" *Acta Asiatica*, ed. Tōhō Gakkai, 81 (2001): 1–19.

65. See Motohisa Yasuda, "Shikken-seiji" [The Policy of (Having) the Shōgun's Deputy (Rule)], in Kunihiko Fujiki and Mitsusada Inoue, eds., *Seijishi* [Political History], vol. 1 of *Taikei Nihonshi sōsho* [A Systematic Collection of (Texts on) Japanese History] (Tokyo: Yamakawa, 1976), chap. 5, 277, 281.

66. See Hiroshi Kasamatsu, "Undated Statements of Accusation and Rebuttal," *Acta Asiatica* 81 (2001): 31–52.

67. Steenstrup, "Sata Mirensho: A Fourteenth Century Law Primer," art. 12.

68. Ibid., arts. 22, 23. If pleas on *origami* paper were among the *gusho* (enclosures) handed to the *Hikitsuke* chamber chairman *before* the confrontation of the parties (*taiketsu*), dating the *gusho* would not have been necessary, since the plea itself was dated.

69. See R. Ishii, *Nihon hōseishi gaisetsu*, 292–93; and Steenstrup with Hyun-ki Shin, "Busei kihan," arts. 2, 3, 20, 36.

70. Steenstrup with Hyun-ki Shin, "Busei kihan," art. 12.

71. See Rüttermann, *Das Dorf Suganoura*, 277–83; and Henderson, *Conciliation and Japanese Law*, 1:176.

72. See Schenck, *Der deutsche Anteil an der Gestaltung des modernen japanischen Rechts-und Verfassungswesens*, 171. On the Japanese " rediscovery" of their own legal history, see, e.g., Carl Steenstrup, "Rechtsgeschichte" [History of Law], in Klaus Kracht and Markus Rüttermann, eds., *Grundriss der Japanologie (Izumi, Quellen, Studien und Materialien zur Kultur Japans)* [An Outline of Japanology (*Izumi*, Sources, Researches and Materials concerning the Culture of Japan)] (Wiesbaden: Harrassowitz, 2001), 7:233–62, esp. 240–43.

73. The Heian/Kamakura jurisprudential tradition achieved a considerable level of conceptual abstraction. See Kiley, "The Imperial Court as a Legal Authority in the Kamakura Age"; and for practical examples, Jeffrey P. Mass, *Lordship and Inheritance in Early Medieval Japan—a Study of the Kamakura Sōryō System* (Stan-

ford, CA: Stanford University Press, 1989), chap. 1, and 134–35, 142–44, 149–52, 160–61, 179–87, 227–28, 234–41, 247–50, 253–55, 260–61, 270–71, and 279–81. But not all Japanese experts share this view. See Wilhelm Röhl, "Begriffe aus dem Grundstücksrecht Japans im Mittelalter" [Some Concepts of the Land Law of Medieval Japan], in Hans G. Leser and Tamotsu Isomura, eds., *Wege zum japanischen Recht—Festschrift für Kitagawa Zentarō* [Ways (to Understand) Japanese Law—Articles in Honor of Kitagawa Zentarō] (Berlin: Duncker and Humblot, 1992), 575–99, esp. 583.

74. See F. B. Verwayen, "Tokugawa Translations of Dutch Legal Texts," *Monumenta Nipponica* 53(3) (Autumn 1998): 335–58. The entire history of Japanese law, from the end of Tokugawa until today, is now told by ten specialists, each covering his or her area of the law, and edited by Wilhelm Röhl, who also contributed several chapters on his own: *A History of Law in Japan since 1868* (Leiden: Brill, 2005).

75. A final word regarding resources: It takes, on average, three to five years for a major Japanese new finding in the field of premodern Japanese law to reach a Western publication. Year by year, the time lag decreases, but it is still there. For those who want to keep abreast of Japanese research in this field the best medium is the journal *Hōseishi kenkyū* [Studies on Legal History] published by the Hōseishi Gakkai [Legal History Research Society], whose secretariat is now with the Law Faculty of Keiō University. Unfortunately, few Japanological libraries in the West subscribe to this excellent journal. The next best choice is, of course, the *Shigaku zasshi* [Journal of Historical Studies] with its annual bibliographies. Finally, it should not be forgotten that Japanese researchers now currently publish their findings in English in the *Acta Asiatica*, ed. Tōhō Gakkai, which most orientalist libraries subscribe to. Important volumes for premodern Japanese law are, in particular, the following: 35 (1978), for the daimiate laws from the sixteenth through the nineteenth centuries; 39 (1980), for the money economy of the Nara, Heian, and Tokugawa eras; 44 (1983), for the social and economic institutions in medieval Japan (Kamakura and Muromachi eras); 49 (1985), for the warriors as "state builders" from the Kamakura through the Tokugawa eras; 69 (1995), for the state and its law codes from pre-Nara through the Nara era; and 81 (2001), for the beginnings of "capitalism" in the Kamakura era and the civil litigation documents of that time.

2 Criminal Trials in the Early Meiji Era—with Particular Reference to the *Ukagai/Shirei* System

NOBUHIKO KASUMI

Translated by Daniel H. Foote

I. INTRODUCTION

Precisely when, following the Meiji Restoration, did criminal trials in Japan come to be conducted on a national scale, broadly throughout the entire country? In seeking to answer that question, an observation by Yutaka Tezuka[1] is of great significance. As he noted, the abolition of the *han* and establishment of prefectures on July 14, 1871 (Meiji 4), which were made possible by the rise in "political power" of the new Meiji government, and the nationwide putting into force of the first post-Restoration uniform penal code, the *Shinritsu kōryō* (Outline of the New Criminal Code), promulgated in late December of the prior year, were mutually related. That is because the existence of a uniform penal code is essential in establishing the milieu for achieving a national system of criminal trials.

The so-called *fu-han-ken sanchisei* (*fu-han-ken* tripartite governance system) was the approach to regional governance followed by the new Meiji government immediately prior to the abolition of the *han* and establishment of prefectures. This tripartite governance system continued to retain the system of *han*, fiefs under local control, as a remnant of the Tokugawa *bakuhan* structure. This was a far cry from overall command of the regions by the new government. Accordingly, whatever the case may have been for the prefectures under direct control (*fu* and *ken*), in the *han*, matters of "justice" (*shihō*) continued to be subsumed within the *han* administration, in a manner essentially unchanged from the Edo era. Thus, there was no scope for establishment of a uniform system of criminal trials by the state.

With the abolition of the *han*, however, the above structure met its demise; while it is undeniable that there were differences in degree among the various areas of Japan, the "regions" were placed under the direct control of the Meiji government through the establishment of a system of regional governance centered on the prefectures. In that context, the Prefecture Establishment Ordinance (*Kenchi jōrei*), promulgated on November 27, 1871, recognized that each prefecture held authority not only over administrative matters but over matters of justice, as well. Through that ordinance, civil and criminal trials alike, which were referred to as *chōshō* and *dangoku*, respectively, were recognized as matters under the exclusive jurisdiction of the prefectures. (Hereafter in this chapter, unless specified otherwise, consideration of "trials" will be confined to "criminal trials.") Viewing these developments together with the observations of Tezuka set forth above, we may conclude that this period marked the exact turning point at which the responsibility for conducting criminal trials passed to the prefectures and developed on a nationwide basis.

However, the criminal trials conducted by the prefectures were subjected to a major reform with the assumption of office by Shimpei Etō on April 25, 1872, as the first minister of justice. (The Ministry of Justice had been established on July 9 of the prior year.) As much prior scholarship has already observed, Etō, who desired thorough reform of the justice system, sought, as the centerpiece of that reform, to establish a sole monopoly for the central government, namely, the Ministry of Justice, over the authority for matters of justice (*shihōken*) that previously had belonged exclusively to the prefectures. As measures for legal adjustment to achieve those aims, on August 3 of that year, through a Notice of the Great Council of State, Etō established the 108-article *Shihō shokumu teisei* (Standing Regulations concerning the Functions of the Judiciary), which was the first comprehensive set of regulations concerning the administration of justice and the trial system following the Restoration. Chapter 15, Articles 56 *et sequens* of those Standing Regulations established the prefectural courts (*fuken saibansho*), which were under the Ministry of Justice. And it was precisely the establishment of those prefectural courts that represented the advance guard in the effort to bring under the control of the Ministry of Justice the authority for matters of justice that had been monopolized by regional officials since the abolition of the *han*.

Yet Etō's objective of developing prefectural courts as quickly as possible throughout the entire nation could not necessarily be achieved easily, with one important obstacle being the fact that it involved financial implications that placed the Ministry of Justice and the Ministry of Finance at odds. As of April 19, 1873, when Etō left the Ministry of Justice, prefectural courts had been established in only three *fu* and thirteen *ken* (and that includes the Tokyo Court, which had been established within the Ministry of Justice on December 26, 1872, prior to and separately from the justice system reforms). The process of establishment of prefectural courts remained slow and gradual thereafter as well. As a result, criminal trials were conducted by two different sets of institutions, the prefectures themselves and the prefectural courts under the Ministry of Justice. As Masaaki Kikuyama has observed,[2] this situation continued until 1876.

As noted above, following the abolition of the *han* and the establishment of the prefectures, criminal trials came to be conducted on a national scale. For the past few years, one of the major areas of interest of this author has been elucidating the actual circumstances of the structure of criminal trials in that era. That structure developed in the context of the existence of the two sets of judicial institutions described above, those of the prefectures and the prefectural courts under the Ministry of Justice. Moreover, that structure was promoted in close association with the Meihōryō (Institute for Legal Studies), a body of legal professionals established in the Ministry of Justice on September 27, 1871, which may be said to be the first think tank in Japan.

Referring to the observations of prior scholarship, this author has named the above structure the "*ukagai/shirei* trial structure." This term may be defined as follows:

> A criminal trial system that operated for a period, albeit brief, in the early Meiji era, centered on the Meihōryō, which was directly under the Ministry of Justice. As the fundamental basis of this system, those in charge of trials in the respective prefectures (to which the effectuation of criminal trials had been entrusted in the process of abolition of *han* and establishment of prefectures following the Restoration) and the judges of the prefectural courts (established by the Ministry of Justice after August 1872 pursuant to the Standing Regulations concerning the Functions of the Judiciary) raised all sorts of doubts (*ukagai*) concerning the interpretation and application of law. The Ministry of Justice (in actuality the Meihōryō) responded to these inquiries (*ukagai*) by issuing responses (*shirei*). In this manner the law was applied and punishments meted out.

In various writings to date, this author has given especial attention, within matters concerning the *ukagai/shirei* trial structure, to two matters: first, how those in charge of trials within the prefectures and the Ministry of Justice judges (*Shihōshō hanji*) in the prefectural courts[3] respectively actually carried out their own solemn duties to apply the law and mete out punishments during the period in which the *Shinritsu kōryō* alone was in effect,[4] which may be said to be the Period of Enlightenment for criminal trials in Japan; and second, the role played in that process by reports published in the Ministry of Justice's first official publication, *Shihōshō nisshi* (Ministry of Justice Journal), which commenced publication in January 1873. In this chapter, the author seeks to organize his accumulated research to date and to provide an overview of the *ukagai/shirei* trial structure, in the sincere hope that this may shed a small light on one corner of the history of criminal trials in the early Meiji era.

II. OPERATION OF THE *UKAGAI/SHIREI* SYSTEM

A. CONCERN: HOW TO APPLY THE LAW PROPERLY, WITHOUT MISTAKES

At present, two collections of *ukagai*, the *Fuken ukagai dome* and the *Kakusaibansho ukagai dome*, may be found in the Ministry of Justice library. The first person to focus on these publications was Masaya Numa. In a detailed historical investigation,[5] he characterized these collections of *ukagai* as "Records of the Section on Preparation of *Shirei* of the Institute for Legal Studies [Meihōryō]." To sum up, the two *ukagai dome* contain a tremendous number of inquiries—*ukagai*—concerning the conduct of criminal trials, submitted by the prefectures and by the prefectural courts, respectively, together with the responses—*shirei*—issued by the Ministry of Justice (in actuality, the Meihōryō) that were exchanged between 1871 and 1875. Considering the contents in more detail, the majority of inquiries consist of those seeking to clarify doubts concerning proper interpretation in connection with the application of the *Shinritsu kōryō* and *Kaitei ritsurei*. In contrast, inquiries merely concerning the handling of specific concrete matters are scarcely to be found.

These two collections of *ukagai* truly constitute essential historical sources for learning about the legal knowledge (to adopt a term in vogue these days, the "legal mind") possessed by those involved in the conduct of trials in the *ukagai/shirei* trial structure, their understanding of the laws then in effect, and their stance toward the conduct of criminal trials. Below I will seek to explore more closely the issues set forth in the introduction, by focusing on the *ukagai* issued by the respective institutions that are collected in the two *ukagai dome* and analyzing the contents of those *ukagai*.

During the period in which the *Shinritsu kōryō* alone was in effect, the matter that troubled those involved in the conduct of trials, in making their decisions, was the *Kōryō* itself. As Tezuka has made clear in his detailed study,[6] the *Kōryō* was applied pursuant to a complex set of amendments and additions unique to the criminal law. In short, in applying the various provisions of the *Kōryō* to specific concrete cases, the most important first step was to grasp precisely what the applicable standards were under existing law, exercising great care in doing so. If, notwithstanding this care, those involved in the conduct of trials made mistakes in applying the law that resulted in erroneous judgments, they themselves were subject to criminal punishment.[7]

Given these circumstances, how might those involved in the conduct of criminal trials ensure that they were conducting trials properly while at the same time avoiding responsibility for erroneous judgments? Answering that question is an important step in revealing both the stance those officials took toward their duties and the actual constitution of the *ukagai / shirei* trial structure.

B. SITUATION FOR THOSE RESPONSIBLE FOR TRIALS IN THE PREFECTURES

First, let us consider those responsible for trials in the prefectures. In a recent publication, Hiromichi Fujita has examined the backgrounds of those who constituted the Trial Section of Ashigara Prefecture (*Ashigaraken chōshōka*), who are assumed to have been responsible for conducting criminal trials prior to the establishment of the Ashigara [Prefectural] Court;[8] in a prior work,[9] I have discussed the eight people who moved from positions with Saitama Prefecture to become officials of the Ministry of Justice in the Saitama Prefectural Court at the time of its establishment on August 17, 1872.

These "transfers" of personnel to the newly established prefectural courts presumably reflect the fact that those involved had been engaged in civil and criminal trials within the prefectures and had been recognized for their experience and ability. From these circumstances, one can easily surmise that they possessed sufficient ability to understand the contents of the *Shinritsu kōryō* and to point out inconsistencies and questionable points therein. At the same time, as I have observed previously,[10] the provisions on fugitives in the laws on the family register of the *Shinritsu kōryō* contain no express provision on point, and, based on the existence of *ukagai* from various prefectures concerning the proper treatment under criminal law of "surrendering fugitives who had escaped from the family register," one finds clear differences in form between the *ukagai* from the prefectures and the *ukagai* on the same topic from the prefectural courts.

As I will discuss further below, during the period in which the *Shinritsu kōryō* alone was in effect, the *ukagai* from judges serving in the various prefectural courts took the form of raising doubts, with regard to the proper treatment, by referring to and citing materials other than the existing law itself as providing the "basis" (*yoridokoro*) thereof (this author has referred to these materials as "decisional materials" [*handanjō no shiryō*]). In contrast, when one examines the *ukagai* contained in the *Fuken ukagai dome* for roughly the same period, including *ukagai* relating to confessing fugitives dropped from the family register, in my view, one can find no examples whatsoever of *ukagai* following this form.

From this, one can conclude that those responsible for trials in the prefectures viewed the "basis" for judgments in criminal cases as being limited to the *Kōryō* as distributed at the time, decrees and circulars of the Great Council of State and the Ministry of Justice amending or changing the contents thereof, and the responses (*shirei*) issued in response to their own inquiries (*ukagai*). As I have explained elsewhere, one cannot help but to conclude that "apart from decrees, circulars, and discrete responses (*shirei*), the Ministry of Justice did not actively provide information to the various prefectures regarding how to put into effect the abstruse *Kōryō*."[11]

To add a brief note, in accordance with the provisions on prefectural affairs in the aforementioned Prefecture Establishment Ordinance, those responsible for trials were required to request permission in advance from the Ministry of Justice for the execution of death sentences; they also bore responsibility for making after-the-fact reports to the ministry with respect to lesser sentences. When one also considers that they were subject to punishment for erroneous judgments, one can easily surmise that those officials were subject to rather strict scrutiny by the ministry. Accordingly, especially in the period up to the publication of the *Ministry of Justice Journal* (*Shihōshō nisshi*) in early 1873, one may say that the sole and most effective means that those in charge of trials in the various prefectures had, in order to avoid erroneous judgments and at the same avoid criminal punishment for themselves when faced with specific issues, was to consider the application of the laws carefully, utilizing their aforementioned ability and legal knowledge to the utmost, and, as necessary, obtaining the most up-to-date information by not hesitating to submit *ukagai* diligently and receive *shirei* in response. The staggering number of *ukagai* contained in the *Fuken ukagai dome* provides emblematic evidence clearly revealing this stance toward handling of criminal trials of those responsible for trials in the prefectures.

C. SITUATION FOR JUDGES SENT FROM THE MINISTRY OF JUSTICE TO THE PREFECTURAL COURTS

As mentioned earlier, the centerpiece of Minister of Justice Etō's aggressive policy for justice reform was the establishment of prefectural courts, albeit initially in a limited number of regions, and the sending out of Ministry of Justice judges—judges who were under the direct authority of the Ministry of Justice—for postings as judges in those courts. In most cases, those judges assumed posts as the chief judges in charge of the courts and served as the frontline troops in the battle to establish a sole monopoly for the central government (the Ministry of Justice) over the authority for matters of justice, which Etō sought.

That being the case, what was the stance of those judges toward criminal trials in the *ukagai/shirei* trial structure during the period in which the *Shinritsu kōryō* alone was in effect? In a series of studies published previously, this author has sought to analyze *ukagai* concerning the application of law and meting out of punishment, submitted by the prefectural courts that were established by early 1873, and the responses to those *ukagai*, as contained in the *Kakusaibansho ukagai dome*. In that process, very important facts have been discovered relevant to the question posed above, and materials have been provided that help make clear the actual stance adopted by the judges in the prefectural courts toward the handling of criminal trials.

First, during the period in which the *Shinritsu kōryō* alone was in effect, a substantial number of the *ukagai* submitted by the several prefectural courts cite the document *Monkei jōrei* and raise doubts concerning the application of law and meting out of punishment. Upon investigating the relationship between that *Monkei jōrei* and a document by the same name contained in the collection of the Ministry of Justice library,[12] the *Monkei jōrei* referred to in the *ukagai* "cannot be assumed to have possessed binding authority as a 'legal source' that always applies to matters of interpretation and application." Nonetheless, it was a document that was already widely known both by the Ministry of Justice judges submitting the *ukagai* and the Meihōryō issuing the *shirei* in response, and one can surmise that "it was recognized as a 'basis' (*yoridokoro*) that could be applied to matters of interpretation and application following approval through the *ukagai* process, in the *Shinritsu kōryō* period when there were repeated revisions and additions to the laws."

Moreover, upon examining the *ukagai* from the prefectural courts concerning the proper treatment under criminal law of "surrendering fugitives who had escaped from the family register," as to which the *Shinritsu kōryō* contained no express provision on point, one finds that those *ukagai* all contained either the term *Monkei jōrei* or just the word *jōrei* and took the form in common of inquiring with respect to treatment of said confessing fugitives, taking into account the contents of the "provision on confessing fugitives dropped from the family register"[13] contained in that *jōrei*. From this, one may surmise—although it remains only a hypothesis—that the copying and keeping in possession of "decisional materials" such as the *Monkei jōrei* and the Ordinance concerning the New Criminal Code (*Shinritsu jōrei*) "can be regarded as a common practice for all Ministry of Justice officials moving directly from the Ministry to assume posts in the Prefectural Courts."[14]

Finally, in order to reconsider comprehensively such matters as whether judges assuming office in the prefectural courts in 1872 and 1873 always carried "decisional materials" with them and kept them close at hand, and whether the "decisional materials" contained other documents, in addition to the previously confirmed *Monkei jōrei* and *Shinritsu jōrei*, this author has undertaken a sampling and analysis of the *ukagai* (submitted during the period in which the *Shinritsu kōryō* alone was in effect) contained in the *Kakusaibansho ukagai dome*.[15] As a result, I have slightly modified the above hypothesis and have concluded that, from a relatively early date following the establishment of prefectural courts in August 1872, for the Ministry of Justice judges assuming office in those courts, there was a "high probability" that they would carry the "decisional materials" with them, and the "decisional materials" consisted only of the *Monkei jōrei* and the *Shinritsu jōrei*.

Next, based on the above reflections, let me turn to the stance of judges in the prefectural courts toward criminal trials. It is not hard to imagine that most judges who assumed office in the prefectural courts during the period in which the *Shinritsu kōryō* alone was in effect, and more precisely through the end of 1872, were fully aware of the complexity and difficulty of ascertaining exactly what the law was at any given time, in the context of the repeated complex revisions and additions to the *Kōryō*. This would be especially true given the fact that, from the nature of their work, prior to assuming office as judges they would have had ample opportunity to experience the reality of application of law and meting out of punishment at the Ministry of Justice. Accordingly, when they left the Ministry of Justice, they would have shared in common with those in charge of the conduct of trials the consciousness of avoiding erroneous judgments and thereby avoiding criminal punishment themselves; it is also evident that they would have made every effort to obtain the most up-to-date information regarding then-current law and that they would have carried along the most effective "decisional materials" as they set out for their posts.

In the *ukagai* of these prefectural court judges who arrived at their posts with *Monkei jōrei* in hand, one finds numerous examples of *ukagai* that set forth provisions from that *jōrei* and then seek to confirm whether the contents remained valid as of the date of the inquiry, with no error to result from application thereof. From these *ukagai*, one gets the sense of just how difficult the application of the *Kōryō* was in practice, making it necessary always to obtain confirmation of the existing law. In addition, one may also get a sense that the judges' lot was one of placing caution upon caution.

D. THE *MINISTRY OF JUSTICE JOURNAL*

As discussed above, in the *ukagai / shirei* trial structure during the period in which the *Shinritsu kōryō* alone was in effect, while the circumstances of the two sets of courts differed somewhat, those involved in the conduct of trials took great pains to grasp accurately the law then in effect. For them, there can be no question that January 1873 was a special month. The reason is that in that month the Ministry of Justice commenced publication of the *Ministry of Justice Journal* (*Shihōshō nisshi*, sometimes referred to hereinafter as the *Journal*).

The *Journal* was the Ministry of Justice's first regularly issued publication. With two breaks early on, it was published for a total of three periods over three years, from January 1873 through May 1876. Details of the *Journal* have been provided by Numa.[16] The ultimate concern of this author has been to investigate the role the *Journal* played in the *ukagai / shirei* trial structure. To that end, to date I have published six essays on this topic. Reflecting on my studies to date, I will begin by considering what I meant by saying that "January 1873 was a special month."

One may conjecture without a doubt that the common consciousness of those involved in the conduct of trials at the prefectures themselves and the judges of the prefectural courts, upon their first contact with the contents of the *Ministry of Justice Journal* after publication and distribution began, must have been a sense that they had finally been freed from the most troublesome task in the process of applying law and meting out punishment utilizing the *Shinritsu kōryō* in criminal trials—namely, the task of ascertaining what the existing law was. As noted above, at the time they assumed their posts, the Ministry of Justice judges would have carried along with them the "decisional materials," consisting of the *Monkei jōrei* and the *Shinritsu jōrei*. Yet even they, after assuming their posts, submitted *ukagai* relating to cases before them, inquiring whether the provisions contained in those "decisional materials" continued to represent existing law—in short, whether they were still "good law." From this, it is apparent just how heavy the burden must have been for those handling criminal trials in the prefectures themselves, for whom it was impossible up until that time to obtain information from the Ministry of Justice in an active manner. Given this situation, for those involved in the conduct of trials, who ceaselessly sought error-free criminal trials, the chance to read the *ukagai* submitted by others and to obtain the most up-to-date information through the Ministry of Justice's responses to those *ukagai* must have seemed like blessed rain in the midst of a drought. This, then, is what made January 1873 such a special month.

That those involved in the conduct of trials watched carefully and closely the *ukagai* and *shirei* published in the *Journal*, and that they promptly sought to utilize the information received thereby in cases they handled themselves, can easily be seen by reference to matters contained in the six essays mentioned earlier. For example, in one essay[17] I consider an *ukagai* from the Yamanashi Court, which was published in the third issue of the *Ministry of Justice Journal*, for January 8, 1873. That *ukagai* concerned whether a confessing fugitive who had been dropped from the family register but who had been restored to the register and then confessed, in a case in which the period on the run exceeded fifty days, could be granted the privilege of *shumen* (acquittal of punishment from surrendering oneself). The Ministry of Justice's response was that *shumen* should be recognized. As explained previously, the *Shinritsu kōryō* contained no provision regarding the treatment of confessing fugitives dropped from the family register; this *shirei*, setting forth an official declaration of the proper treatment of such fugitives, must have received great attention from those involved in the conduct of trials. It is not difficult to surmise that this *shirei* must have occasioned deep concern by Ministry of Justice judges especially, since the contents of this *shirei* differed from the existing treatment set forth in their "decisional materials." As though to reflect this level of concern, various *ukagai* were submitted inquiring into the propriety of this *shirei* or confirming that it represented a change in policy.

Among these *ukagai*, one that is very valuable for understanding the attitude of those involved in the conduct of trials toward the *Journal* is an *ukagai* of February 1873 submitted by the Saitama Court. That *ukagai* was an after-the-fact treatment of a case in which, relying on the *shirei* published in the third issue of the *Journal*, the court had immediately relieved the party of responsibility. With regard to the circumstances of this granting of relief, in another essay[18] I have offered the speculation that the judges in the Saitama Court came into contact with the above-mentioned *shirei* and without hesitation granted an acquittal, in the form of the *hōmen* (release from punishment), in accordance with the Ministry of Justice *shirei* published in the *Journal*. This, as it were, "overly prompt reaction" by the Saitama Court may be regarded as conduct that is emblematic of the great weight accorded to the *Journal* by those involved in the conduct of trials in the prefectures and by the judges of the prefectural courts, who paid close attention to the *ukagai* and *shirei* published in the *Journal* and sought to comply without delay to the guidance from the Ministry of Justice.

For those involved in the conduct of trials, who had greeted the *ukagai* and *shirei* published in the *Ministry of Justice Journal* with such great anticipation and interest, the next thing they desired and focused on was whether the contents of the *shirei* could be applied as is to the handling of similar criminal cases or to legal interpretation. If this use were officially recognized and became possible, how greatly it would aid in achieving prompt and fair trials and in avoiding erroneous judgments and the responsibility for such erroneous judgments. As though to demonstrate the existence of this desire, *ukagai* submitted in April 1873 and thereafter, from Wakayama, Meito, and Yamaguchi prefectures, respectively, expressed the wish that *shirei* published in the *Journal* might be treated as "matters tantamount to new statutes," made by the Ministry of Justice, and accordingly might be applied directly to other cases.[19] Indeed, these *ukagai* might even be taken as requests. These various *ukagai*, which were submitted one after another, could be said to have advocated the heartfelt desire of those responsible for trials in the prefectures, who up until that time had not even possessed any effective "decisional materials," that they be relieved of the very heavy load they had been bearing by means of treating the *shirei* published in the *Journal* as a source of law.

The Ministry of Justice rejected this desire, however. Not only that, on August 3, 1873, at about the same time that the *Kaitei ritsurei* went into effect and the temporarily suspended *Journal* recommenced publication, the Ministry of Justice issued Notice No. 124 of 1873, addressed to "the prefectures" (*fu-ken*). The object of Notice No. 124 was limited to the prefectures; it provided that *shirei* in response to *ukagai* from the prefectures published in the *Journal*, dealing with matters as to which no express provision was contained in the *Kōryō*, were not to be cited and relied on. However, this notice did not contain any special restriction on such acts by judges of the prefectural courts, nor did it address the use of *shirei* published in the *Journal* in connection with questions concerning interpretation of laws. Therefore, this notice did not represent a comprehensive directive indicating whether or not effect should be given to *shirei* in the *Journal* as a source of law for criminal trials in general. Rather, it was sparked by the *ukagai* from the three prefectures mentioned above and sought to generalize the discrete *shirei* issued in each of those individual cases and officially extend the Ministry of Justice's views to all the prefectures.

Next, in October 1873, in the name of judges serving on the prefectural courts in Chiba and Niihari, *ukagai* were submitted requesting the citation and reliance on *shirei* published in the *Journal* in criminal cases. Both were submitted with full knowledge of Notice No. 124, and the Ministry of Justice *shirei* in response stated that the prior *shirei* "might be used for reference (*sankō*)." There can be no doubt that the thrust of this *shirei* differs not only from the *shirei* issued in response to the *ukagai* from the three prefectures but even to some extent from Notice No. 124.

Then, on January 20, 1874, the Ministry of Justice issued Ministry of Justice Notice No. 1 of 1874, addressed to "each court" and "each prefecture." In this notice the ministry proclaimed that, with regard to the *shirei* portion of law-related *ukagai*/*shirei* published in the *Journal*, "citation and application" was permitted to the extent that "the text of the law, the *ukagai* and the *shirei* all are included in the publication." In other words, this notice made clear that the contents of *shirei* that satisfy the preceding conditions could be applied directly to criminal matters, as the latest views of the Ministry of Justice, without the need to submit a new *ukagai*. This was the instant, in early 1874, at which the reports in the *Journal* ceased to be mere "reports" and instead came to be recognized as having effect as "sources of law" in the *ukagai*/*shirei* trial structure. That moment came as the publication of the *Journal* entered its second year, and just as the publication recommenced for the third time, with its steady continued publication expected.

When they assumed their duties for conducting criminal trials in November 1871, and thereafter during the period in which the *Shinritsu kōryō* alone was in effect, those responsible for trials in the prefectures had had to struggle to determine what the "existing law" was and to deal with the complex issues of applying the law, virtually alone and unaided. After making it through that period, next came the period in which the *Shinritsu kōryō* was in effect jointly with the *Kaitei ritsurei*, which was drafted and put into effect in order to remedy the incompleteness of the *Kōryō*. Then, finally, they were able to obtain official "decisional materials."

Of course, the Ministry of Justice judges also must have desired that the *shirei* in the *Journal* be made a source of law. For example, as I observe in an essay regarding Judge Takeshi Mishima of the Niihari Prefectural Court,[20] from the time of his posting to that court he had focused on the utility of the *Journal*

In February 1874, in the name of the "criminal section of the Niihari Court," he collected the *ukagai* and *shirei* related to the *Kōryō* and *Ritsurei* from the second period of the *Journal*'s publication, which commenced from July 1873, and from the third period of publication, which commenced in January 1874, together with the *ukagai* he himself had submitted and the *shirei* in response thereto. From these, he created a publication, in three volumes, titled *Keihō shirei zuiroku* (Record of Criminal *Shirei*). In the explanatory notes at the start of this record, he notes that the compilation of this record was occasioned by the conditional recognition of reliance on the *shirei* published in the *Journal*, set forth in Notice No. 1, and he also stated that there was a need for the record to be updated continuously in the future. Plainly evident from these explanatory notes are Mishima's strong interest in the fact that the *shirei* in the *Journal* had been given effect as a source of law, together with the even greater weight accorded to the *shirei* than in the past. Even though others may not have left the evidence in such concrete form, there can be little doubt that this consciousness was shared by the Ministry of Justice judges serving in all of the prefectural courts.

Whatever the case may be, by means of the Ministry of Justice's recognition, albeit with conditions attached, of reliance on the *shirei* published in the *Journal*, through the ministry's promulgation of Notice No. 1, the basic situation changed in an important way. From the early days of the Meiji era, criminal trials had been conducted under the dual structure of the prefectures themselves and the prefectural courts—in other words, through the *ukagai/shirei* trial structure. With the Ministry of Justice's conditional recognition of reliance on the *shirei* published in the *Journal*, the system shifted to the establishment of a structure whereby the views of the Ministry of Justice regarding the application of law and meting out of punishment were disseminated uniformly.

III. CONCLUSION

In this chapter I have sought to organize my accumulated research, centered on the period during which the *Shinritsu kōryō* alone was in effect. In so doing, I have sought to reflect on what the circumstances were for those responsible for trials in the prefectures and for the judges of the prefectural courts, in the criminal trials of the early Meiji era that are known as the *ukagai/shirei* trial structure, and what their stance was regarding the performance of their duties. In closing, let me offer a few thoughts regarding the overall significance of this study.

As explained above, the difference in whether or not officials possessed "decisional materials" placed a very heavy burden on those responsible for trials in the prefectures, in connection with their conduct of criminal trials.

That being the case, why did that situation continue to persist? I believe that this fact, along with the heartless rejection of the *ukagai* from the three prefectures seeking to rely on the *shirei* published in the *Journal*, and the subsequent twists and turns regarding reliance on the *shirei*, are all of a piece, reflecting a certain "design" on the part of the Ministry of Justice. In short, that design lay in the achievement of the aim, strongly promoted by Minister of Justice Etō, of wresting authority for matters of justice away from the regional officials. To that end, the prefectures were provided with as little information as possible. When information was necessary, it was provided by means of having those involved submit *ukagai* and receive instructions in response. This in turn required the regional officials to come under the aegis of the ministry, and one can understand this as a strategy in the "design" of effectively achieving overall control over the conduct of trials.

However, with the conditional recognition of reliance on *shirei* published in the *Journal*, there was a sudden shift in direction. Yet one should by no means assume that this was a simple reform of the system in order to suit the convenience of those responsible for trials. Rather, this appears to have been part of a shift in power relations, both within the Ministry of Justice and between that ministry and other organs, originating in Etō's retirement from public life and the resignation of high-ranking Ministry of Justice officials from the Etō faction in the latter half of 1873. In considering these developments one must take into account factors residing in the "twisted" structure of the Japanese "justice" circle in its Period of Enlightenment. As but one example, the Ministry of Justice itself shelved the above "design," and, in an effort to reduce the authority of the Meihōryō and the officials associated with it (who, as the persons effectively in charge of the *shirei*, had engaged in multifaceted activities), replaced as much as possible the role played by the Meihōryō with the *shirei* published in the *Journal*.

In any event, viewed objectively, the stance toward criminal trials of those involved in the conduct of trials at the time was sincere and should be evaluated highly. In particular, those responsible for trials in the prefectures, if not superior to the judges of the prefectural courts, were at least their equals. From four *ukagai* submitted by Shiga Prefecture in September 1873 and thereafter,[21] in the debate sparked by matters of interpretation of laws relating to the effect of old and new laws before and after the *Kaitei ritsurei* took effect, one catches sight of an official responsible for trials in that prefecture who asserts the propriety of his own judgment and dignifiedly makes out the case for his views. This is a fine example reflecting the pride of these officials, who bore responsibility for one wing of the criminal trials in the early Meiji era.

The final volumes of the *Fuken ukagai dome* and the *Kakusaibansho ukagai dome*, which contain a huge number of *ukagai* and *shirei* from this period, carry *shirei* drafts dated from early June of 1875. However, the *ukagai/shirei* trial structure discussed herein, which had the Meihōryō as its motive force, met its end as a system with the abolition of the Meihōryō on May 4, 1875.

NOTES

1. Yutaka Tezuka, "Kokkateki keibatsuken to hikokkateki keibatsuken" [National Penal Authority and Nonnational Penal Authority], in Yutaka Tezuka, *Meiji keihōshi no kenkyū (jō)* [Research on the History of Meiji Penal Law, vol. 1] (Tokyo: Keiō tsūshin, 1984), 197.

2. Masaaki Kikuyama, "Daiyonshō: Meiji hachi-nen no shihō kaikaku" [Chapter 4: Justice Reform of 1875 (Meiji 8)], in Masaaki Kikuyama, *Meiji kokka no keisei to shihō seido* [The Formation of the Meiji State and the Justice System] (Tokyo: Ochanomizu shobō, 1993), 191.

3. These judges also sometimes are referred to as Prefectural Court judges (*Fukensaibansho saibankan*). Moreover, those in charge of trials in the prefectures and the Prefectural Court judges sometimes are referred to collectively as "those involved in the conduct of trials" (*saiban jitsumu kankeisha*) in this essay.

4. The *Kaitei ritsurei* [The Amended Criminal Regulations] took effect on July 10, 1873, and thereafter was applied together with the *Shinritsu kōryō*. In this essay the *Kaitei ritsurei* sometimes is referred to as *Ritsurei*.

5. This historical investigation is set forth in essays contained in Masaya Numa, *Zaisanhō no genri to kazokuhō no genri (shinpan)* [Principles of Property Law and Principles of Family Law (new edition)] (Kyoto: Sanwa shobō, 1980).

6. Yutaka Tezuka, "Meiji rokunen dajōkan fukoku dai rokujūgogō no kōryoku—saikōsaibansho hanketsu ni taisuru ichi-iken" [The Effect of Decree No. 65 of 1873 of the Great Council of State—One Differing View regarding Supreme Court Judgments], in Tezuka, *Meiji keihōshi no kenkyū (jō)*, 117.

7. The liability to punishment for erroneous judgments was set forth in the Provisions on Punishments for Erroneous Judgments by Officials involved in the Conduct of Criminal Trials under the Laws on Trial and Imprisonment of the Outline of the New Criminal Code (*Shinritsu kōryō dangokuritsu shutsunyūjinzai-jō*) (abrogated in April 1876).

8. Hiromichi Fujita, "Fuken saibansho setchi no hitokoma—Ashigara saibansho no baai" [One Episode in the Establishment of Prefectural Courts—the Case of the Ashigara Court], in Hiromichi Fujita, *Shinritsu kōryō/kaitei ritsurei hensanshi*

[History of the Compilation of the *Shinritsu Kōryō* and *Kaitei Ritsurei*] (Tokyo: Keio University Press, 2001), 297.

9. Nobuhiko Kasumi, "Futatsu no Saitama saibansho ukagai o megutte" [Concerning Two *Ukagai* from the Saitama Court], *Hōgaku Kenkyū* 64(10) (1994): 1.

10. Nobuhiko Kasumi and Yoshitsugu Hara, "Dasseki tōbō jishusha no shobun o meguru jakkan no kōsatsu" [A Few Reflections on the Treatment of Surrendering Fugitives Who Had Escaped from the Family Register], *Hōgaku Kenkyū* 64(1) (1991): 233.

11. Ibid.

12. That investigation is set forth in Nobuhiko Kasumi, "Monkei jōrei o meguru jakkan no kōsatsu" [Reflections on the *Monkei jōrei*], *Biburosu* 41(7) (1990): 1.

13. Provisional name adopted by the author.

14. See Kasumi, "Futatsu no Saitama saibansho ukagai o megutte," 1.

15. See Nobuhiko Kasumi, "Fukensaibansho sōsetsuki ni miru ukagai/shirei saiban taisei no ichi danmen" [One Aspect of the *Ukagai/Shirei* Trial Structure as Seen in the Period of Establishment of Prefectural Courts], *Kenshū* 608 (1999): 3.

16. See Masaya Numa, "Kazoku kankeihō ni okeru kindaiteki shii no kakuritsu katei (sono ichi)" [The Process of Establishment of Modern Thinking in Family Relations Law (1)], 206, and "Shihōshō shirei no keisei o meguru Meihōryō no yakuwari" [The Role of the Meihōryō in the Formulation of *Shirei* by the Ministry of Justice], 662, in Numa, *Zaisanhō no genri to kazokuhō no genri.*

17. Nobuhiko Kasumi, "Shihōshō nisshi kiji o meguru ichishiron" [An Exploration of Reports in the *Ministry of Justice Journal*], in *Keiō daigaku hōgakubu hōritsugakka kaisetsu hyakunen kinen ronbunshū (hōritsugakka hen)* [Collection of Works to Commemorate the One-Hundredth Anniversary of the Founding of the Legal Department of the Keio University Faculty of Law (Legal Department Volume)] (Tokyo: Keiō tsūshin, 1990), 353.

18. Kasumi, "Futatsu no Saitama saibansho ukagai o megutte," 1.

19. See Nobuhiko Kasumi, "'Shihōshō nisshi' tōsai shirei no en'in o meguru ichi kōsatsu" [Reflections on the Origins of *Shirei* Appearing in the *Ministry of Justice Journal*], *Kenshū* 565 (1995): 3.

20. See Nobuhiko Kasumi, "Niihari saibansho zaikin—Shihō gon no shohanji Mishima Takeshi no ichi sokumen" [One Aspect of Ministry of Justice Judge Mishima, Stationed in Niihari Court], in Yoshirō Togawa, ed., *Mishima Chūshū no gakugei to sono shōgai* [The Achievements and Life of Mishima Chūshū] (Tokyo: Yūzankaku, 1999), 275.

21. See Nobuhiko Kasumi, "Kaiteiritsurei shikō to shinkyūhō no kōryoku o megutte" [Concerning the Taking Effect of the *Kaitei ritsurei* and the Effect of Old and New Law], *Kenshū* 585 (1997): 4.

3 Law, Culture, and Conflict

Dispute Resolution in Postwar Japan

ERIC A. FELDMAN

I. INTRODUCTION

The 1963 publication of Takeyoshi Kawashima's "Dispute Resolution in Contemporary Japan" has indelibly influenced the study of law and conflict in postwar Japan. A mere nineteen text pages of Arthur Taylor von Mehren's seven hundred–page volume, *Law in Japan: The Legal Order in a Changing Society*,[1] Kawashima's observations about the infrequency of litigation in Japan, and his emphasis on the sociocultural context of conflict, continue to resonate. As a noted scholar of Japanese law has succinctly written, "Virtually every scholarly work [about Japanese law] in the last thirty-five years has been framed in some way or another by the conceptual construct Professor Kawashima offered."[2]

Kawashima was appointed as a professor of civil law at Japan's preeminent legal academy, the Faculty of Law at the University of Tokyo, before the outbreak of World War II. He held that institution's first chair of legal sociology, and during his career he published scores of books and articles. But "Dispute Resolution in Contemporary Japan" was Kawashima's first article to be translated into English, and it remains the most complete access to his work for English-language readers unable to tackle the vernacular Japanese text.[3]

It is a matter of speculation as to why "Dispute Resolution in Contemporary Japan" fell on such receptive ears. Perhaps it spoke to concerns about American litigiousness that were on the minds of legal academics and policy makers, who were looking for ways to rein in the use of the courts in the United

States. Maybe it fit well with the stereotypes of Japan developed in the preceding years by English speakers, many of whom had been schooled on the work of Ruth Benedict and others who emphasized the uniqueness of Japanese culture.[4] Possibly it filled a void—there was very little work on Japanese law available in English in 1963, and even less that was well written, interesting, and relatively free of jargon. Surely Kawashima's article and much of his other work articulated a point of view that resonated with Japanese scholars and students, who continue to read and emulate his work. At least in part, Kawashima's appeal to both foreign and Japanese readers was that his article was rich with insight and had identified a challenging puzzle—why was litigation uncommon in Japan?—whatever one may think of the solution he offers.[5]

"Dispute Resolution in Contemporary Japan" has served as a Rorschach test for succeeding generations of Japanese and American legal scholars.[6] For those seeking a normative statement about the role of law in Japanese society, Kawashima's article appears to supply an answer. His portrayal of the importance of informal mechanisms of dispute resolution, and the sidelining of litigation as a last resort in intractable conflicts involving "pugnacious, litigious fellows," has been read to imply the desirability, indeed superiority, of solving conflict without resort to the formal mechanisms of law. In contrast to a society in which lawyers and courts depersonalize disputes and destroy the social fabric, Japan is described as a place where a powerful social glue can be stretched, but not snapped, by conflict.

As a theoretical exercise, Kawashima also stimulated debate. Legal theorists interested in the relationship between law and society found food for thought in Kawashima's account of Japan, which seems to present an ideal case for tracing the allegedly powerful links between industrialization, urbanization, and a modern legal system.[7] Like his contemporary, political theorist Masao Maruyama, Kawashima was deeply interested in the mechanisms through which Japan would modernize, and he was particularly concerned with how new, democratic institutions would arise and develop.[8] Surely Kawashima's prediction that law and litigation would come to occupy an increasingly important role in Japan *had* to be correct; the very best theories of his day emphasized the increasing similarity between Japan and other economically developed nations, and many were convinced that their "convergence" was inevitable.[9]

Descriptively, "Dispute Resolution in Contemporary Japan" struck a resonant chord. For Japanese readers, Kawashima seemed to have uncovered a deep and compelling truth. Scholars and laypeople alike knew that the Japanese sought ways to manage conflict that kept disputes informal. Kawashima claimed to have identified the underlying explanation for this behavior: a set of values deeply embedded in Japanese culture that shaped the way individuals handled conflict. Western readers were similarly impressed. They saw in Kawashima an elegant confirmation of exactly what they had always suspected. The Japanese were close-knit, inward looking, inscrutable; they were part of a culture that honored a set of values anathema to Western rationalism.[10]

It is tempting to write off Kawashima as being whatever one wants him to be, and no more. But his esteemed position in the pantheon of Japanese legal scholars counsels against a facile dismissal. His writings are still read by many law students in Japan; scholars in and out of Japan continue to cite him, challenge him, reify him, and feel irritated by him; in American classes about Japanese law his writings are generally on the syllabus, and many students find them compelling.

This chapter first identifies the central claims of Kawashima's article and evaluates their strengths and weaknesses. Next, it examines four types of scholarship on Japanese law that owe a significant debt to Kawashima: culturalist views of Japanese law, institutional analyses of the Japanese legal system, law and economics approaches to legal behavior in Japan, and case studies of Japanese law and society. In doing so, it further explores Kawashima's most significant contributions as well as his oversights. The article concludes with a brief discussion of the recent movement to reform the legal system, which seems likely to bring about at least some of the changes to dispute resolution that Kawashima predicted. Both too much and too little have been read into Kawashima's work. Its elegant simplicity hides a complex set of observations. At the same time, those observations can be clearly stated and evaluated.

II. KAWASHIMA'S THEORY OF DISPUTE RESOLUTION

Aside from a requisite citation to Arthur Taylor von Mehren, a distinguished Harvard Law School professor and the editor of *Law in Japan: The Legal Order in a Changing Society*, Kawashima's essay referenced only one non-Japanese scholar's work on Japanese law. That distinction belongs to Dan Fenno Henderson, whose magisterial work on conciliation in the Tokugawa era is one of the most intellectually rich studies of the Japanese legal system in any language.[11] Henderson's work detailed the process of extrajudicial dispute resolution in premodern and modern Japan, and in so doing revealed the state's direct involvement in Japanese conflict management. Disputants were often required by government decree to submit to conciliation before bringing their claims to court and found themselves obligated to follow a set of procedures that made it difficult, often impossible, to file a lawsuit. The power of Henderson's work came from its careful analysis of the mechanism of conciliation, with its attention to the interplay between institutional design and social practice.

Kawashima was familiar with at least some of Henderson's writings; he cites a 1952 article, "Some Aspects of Tokugawa Law," in his discussion of conciliation after the Meiji Restoration.[12] Moreover, nothing in Kawashima's article suggests that he rejects Henderson's emphasis on the involvement of the state in promoting the extrajudicial dispute resolution process. To the contrary, he appears to fully embrace Henderson's perspective. In his discussion of Japanese industrialization and urbanization during World War I, for example, Kawashima notes that the traditional social structure was becoming unhinged. Litigation increased, and "those who had been in an inferior position began to assert their legal rights."[13] By requiring conciliation, the government was able to "wash away" (*mizu ni nagasu*) disputes. "[T]he emerging individualistic interests of lessees, tenants, and employees," Kawashima writes, "were to be kept from being converted into firmly established vested interests independent of the will of their superiors."[14]

Kawashima's embrace of Henderson's perspective would not be particularly notable if it simply reflected the seriousness with which one prominent academic took the work of a peer. What makes it surprising is that Henderson's emphasis on the coercive nature of conciliation flatly contradicts the standard interpretation of Kawashima. According to that interpretation, Kawashima is devoted to monolithic cultural explanations of Japanese legal behavior. In fact, that view finds some support in "Dispute Resolution in Contemporary Japan." Kawashima claims, for example, that of the "several possible explanations for [the] relative lack of litigation [in Japan]," the most important can be "found in the socio-cultural background of the problem," particularly in "the nature of the traditional social groups in Japan."[15] Those groups, he says, "may be epitomized by two characteristics. First, they are hierarchical in the sense that social status is differentiated in terms of deference and authority . . . Second, . . . social roles are defined in general and very flexible terms . . . [T]his definition of social roles can be, and commonly is, characterized by the term 'harmony.'"[16]

To be sure, these claims are overgeneralized, which makes Kawashima particularly vulnerable to the charge of being too enamored by the influence of culture while neglecting to say what culture means. One need only go back to the beginning of his essay, however, to contextualize his claims about law, culture, and dispute resolution. In the very first paragraph, he states:

> There is probably no society in which litigation is the normal means of resolving disputes. Rarely will both parties press their claims so far as to require resort to a court; instead, one of the disputants will probably offer a satisfactory settlement or propose the use of some extrajudicial, informal procedure. Although direct evidence of this tendency is difficult to obtain, the phenomena described below offer indirect support for the existence of these attitudes among the Japanese people.[17]

In other words, Kawashima's argument is that the vast majority of Japanese legal attitudes and practices are fundamentally similar to those in other nations. His essay is not explicitly rooted in a view of Japanese uniqueness; to the contrary, Kawashima is pressing for an understanding of dispute resolution in Japan that strongly resembles dispute resolution in every other society. And while he does not overly emphasize the role of the state in forging and framing approaches to dispute resolution, Kawashima's invocation of Henderson makes clear that his devotion to cultural explanations is bounded. Nonetheless, he does see a crucial role for culture: to the extent that nations develop generalizable cultural practices and values, Kawashima suggests that those practices and values can help us to understand how people resolve their disputes.

Kawashima's claim that Japanese disputants generally resolve their conflicts without going to court is not merely a theoretical formulation. Much of the power of Kawashima's analysis comes from his use of data. The text of Kawashima's article is followed by fourteen tables, documenting the number of civil cases filed from 1925 and 1934, litigation over traffic accidents from 1953 to 1960, the percentage of administrative cases appealed to high courts, the amount of time it took for district courts to resolve cases from 1916 to 1959, and many other issues. Based on these data, he argues that mediation prevailed even when one might predict that the dams would break and the courts would be flooded with claims. An acute housing shortage following World War II, for example, led to conflict over housing, but not much litigation. The economic depression after 1927 caused a large number of bankruptcies, but no surge of lawsuits. In the quotidian world of common public transportation, few cases were brought involving taxi or train accidents. In short, Kawashima argues that despite certain social changes, litigation rates in Japan did not increase.

Culture is neither the first nor the only explanation Kawashima provides to explain the data. First, he notes that litigation takes time and costs money, so many are dissuaded. Second, he observes that those who are willing to expend time and money are poorly rewarded because litigation results in minimal compensation. Together, these explanations at least to some extent anticipate a rational actor perspective on litigation, as will be discussed below. Third, Kawashima asserts that there is an underlying incompatibility between the universalistic standards of litigation (by which he seems to mean black-letter legal rules applied by an objective judge without regard to the status or characteristics of the parties) and certain sociocultural currents in Japan, such as a tradition of deferring to authority and the contingency of social roles. It is crucial to remember that all three of these responses remain tightly contained. They do not assert that the reluctance to litigate is a particularly Japanese characteristic. Instead, they take as a given that litigation is uncommon everywhere and provide an explanation for the Japanese experience: distinctive perhaps, but not unique.[18]

Nonetheless, Kawashima complicates (and ultimately weakens) his argument by focusing on what he considers Japan's most distinctive element of dispute resolution, its low litigation rate, which he thinks is the consequence of a limited number of lawyers and a lack of industrialization. The result, in his view, is that in comparison to the West "demand for lawyers' services is not great" in Japan. Had he remembered Henderson's emphasis on government, Kawashima could have speculated that the lack of lawyers' services resulted from a limited supply, not simply a low demand. By asserting that in contrast to the West the Japanese do not demand the service of lawyers, however, he implies an innate cultural or psychological preference for non-lawyer-driven dispute resolution.[19]

Kawashima predicted that as Japan industrialized, entrenched social relationships inhibiting overt forms of conflict would weaken, "traditional" Japanese values such as deference to authority would change, and litigation would increase. In doing so, he is clearly reflecting the academic climate of his times. Of the various intellectual currents that captivated scholars in the 1950s and 1960s, modernization and convergence were perhaps the most compelling. Kawashima did not simply catch the wave; he was at the forefront of Japanese modernization theorists who were consumed by the notion that Japan was "behind" the West and ought to, had to, "catch up." Closing the gap with the West was not a simple matter of exchanging tatami for tile and kimono for khaki. It involved the retooling of a broad array of social and political practices, including law and legal behavior. Some could be transformed, or at least changed, by design; others would change less consciously, a result of fundamental shifts such as industrialization that had an ever-widening circle of influence. In either case, modernization theorists saw a clear relationship between macro changes in social and economic structure and changes in individual behavior.

True to modernization theory, the contrast Kawashima draws between Japan and the West is neither sharp nor absolute. In his view, litigation is the exception, not the rule, in the resolution of conflicts everywhere. If litigation is more common in the United States than Japan, this phenomenon is as likely to be a consequence of their different political economies, which strongly influence (and, although Kawashima was not explicit about this, are undoubtedly influenced by) cultural preferences and individual behavior. For Kawashima and others, therefore, understanding the relationship between social, economic, and political structure and law became a core area of inquiry; exploring individual attitudes and beliefs about law, what came to be called "legal culture," was an important part of their effort.[20]

A stepchild to literature on political culture that sought to correlate political attitudes and beliefs with democratic practices and economic development, analysts of legal culture were particularly interested in the connection between law and modernization.[21] To better understand legal culture, they relied on opinion polls, questionnaires, and survey research that sought to identify individual attitudes about law and conflict. Kawashima's writings on legal consciousness influenced many of those who studied Japanese legal culture, who often forgot that sociocultural dispositions were only one aspect of Kawashima's explanation of the Japanese legal system.

Many studies of legal culture were methodologically unsophisticated, and little consensus emerged about the meaning of legal culture generally or the specifics of legal culture in any particular setting.[22] Nonetheless, to specialists and casual observers, often armed with no more than anecdotal data, Japan provided an interesting contrast to their vision of American legal culture. If modern societies required modern legal systems (an assumption of those studying legal culture in the United States),[23] and one quality of a modern legal system is its use by citizens to resolve disputes, then how should one understand Japan? Litigation rates in Japan were far lower than those in the United States; various aspects of Japan's legal system seemed out of step with the requirements of modernity.[24] Yet Japan enjoyed the benefits of modern law—most importantly, industrialization and a vibrant economy. The attraction of studying Japanese legal culture was that it offered a possible solution to a puzzle; by exploring attitudes and beliefs about law in Japan, perhaps it would be possible to better understand how, when, and why people turned to the formal legal system, and which features of that system were critical to the growth of political and economic institutions. Such high expectations help to explain why the study of Japanese legal culture captured the imagination of so many scholars.

In a recent "hermeneutic, interpretive" essay in which he notes that "it is no exaggeration to say that all Japanese studies have as their starting point a discussion of Japanese culture," Takao Tanase offers a thoughtful view of the relationship between law, culture, and modernization.[25] Taking as his starting point Japan's reception of foreign legal codes in the late nineteenth century, Tanase accepts neither that such laws were anathema to Japanese culture nor that they faced no cultural barriers. Instead, he claims that Japanese society integrated and accommodated foreign legal codes in its own particular manner. Arguing that "the low mobilization of the law among the general public facilitated rather than hindered modernization in Japan," Tanase rejects Kawashima's claims about the necessary connection between law, culture, and modernization. In place of the assumption that Japan would inevitably "progress" toward a modern, rational, Western legal system, Tanase posits that Japan's historical conditions make Japan unique in its experience of modernity and its development of a legal system.[26] Perhaps the different conclusions reached by Kawashima and Tanase are simply a consequence of the decades that divide them. Whatever the explanation, it is a testament to the enduring influence of Kawashima's work that Tanase, one of contemporary Japan's most respected legal sociologists, continues to grapple with an issue raised in Kawashima's 1963 essay.

Before further examining Kawashima's influence, it may be useful to recap the key features of his essay. Kawashima invoked Japanese culture, particularly values such as deference to authority and harmony, to explain the infrequency with which disputes end up in Japanese courts. His turn to culture takes places within the context of a complex (and sometimes contradictory) argument that the state can exercise its authority by controlling formal conflict, and that disputes in every society are likely to be resolved informally. In Japan (as elsewhere), he indicates that there are many reasons why people keep their distance from courts, including the monetary costs of litigation and the limited compensation awarded by Japanese judges. Looking to the future, he predicts that Japan will change as a consequence of industrialization and urbanization, making courts, lawyers, and litigation a more central part of the system of dispute resolution. But that change will be subtle; litigation will not spiral out of control, and alternative means of resolving disputes will survive, as they do everywhere, and will continue to offer disputants a faster, less expensive, and more responsive way to handle conflict.

III. KAWASHIMA'S INFLUENCE ON THE POSTWAR STUDY OF JAPANESE LAW

Kawashima's work has powerfully influenced the entire corpus of scholarship on dispute resolution in Japan. Strong convictions have been developed about its merits and flaws by scholars and students (even those who have not read much or any of Kawashima's writing) who cut their critical teeth by attacking or extolling Kawashima's central claims and proposing alternative (and allegedly more sound) theories of Japanese conflict. A multitude of follow-up studies pursue both his core themes and more tangential issues. He is widely considered one of the most influential minds (often *the* single most influential mind) of Japan's postwar legal academy.[27] Why Kawashima has struck such an extraordinarily resonant chord is a question about which one can speculate. That he did so is beyond dispute.[28]

Four types of research and writing about Japanese law and disputing are particularly identifiable as Kawashima's progeny. First are culturalist approaches, which assert or assume that the study of Japanese dispute resolution is primarily a subset of the study of Japanese culture. Second are analyses that focus on social and political structure as the explanatory engine of Japanese conflict. Third is research in law and economics that applies a set of assumptions about rational behavior to the study of Japanese disputing. Fourth are case studies of law and society in Japan that make use of and extend the insights of cultural, institutional, and law and economics perspectives by examining concrete legal disputes. In what follows, I will highlight what I consider to be the writings that best exemplify each of these approaches to the analysis of Japanese dispute resolution. Together, they constitute a large body of work that emerges from Kawashima's analysis in "Dispute Resolution in Contemporary Japan" but pushes it in new and important directions.

A. CULTURALIST APPROACHES

Kawashima's most fundamental contribution has been to stimulate research and writing on the link between Japanese law and Japanese culture. Indeed, many have read Kawashima narrowly, as if his only insight was that Japanese law is an outgrowth of Japanese culture. One example is the 1979 article by Chin Kim and Craig M. Lawson, "The Law of the Subtle Mind: The Traditional Japanese Conception of Law."[29] Kim and Lawson argue that, at root, the Japanese simply do not "like" law. As they put it:

> The resolution of disputes [in Japan] . . . requires the restoration of harmony and mutual understanding. Lawsuits, on the other hand, pit one party against the other and determine which one shall win, thereby further straining the relationship and further injuring the delicate spirit of *wa*. The spirit of harmony and the social tie (*en*) that binds all relationships act together on the Japanese mind, which therefore tends not to view a dispute in terms of personal rights and duties. The harmonious settlement of disputes through mutual understanding is virtuous; the fight to finish in the courtroom is shameful.[30]

A more recent example can be found in Yasunobu Sato's *Commercial Dispute Processing and Japan*, where he writes: "Japan, together with China and other East Asian countries influenced by Confucian philosophy, has a conciliation culture where mediation or conciliation has long been a preferred mechanism for dispute processing. This culture is in sharp contrast to the Western adversarial culture based on individuals, which views conflict and dispute positively."[31]

In these and many other writings that acknowledge a debt to Kawashima, much of the nuance and complexity that characterize "Dispute Resolution in Contemporary Japan" is lost, replaced by the uninspiring claim that the influence of Japanese culture on Japanese law is unmitigated. To the question of why the Japanese do not sue, Kawashima's supposed answer is culture. To the question of why Japan has so few lawyers comes his answer, culture. To the question of why informal mechanisms of dispute resolution are well utilized in Japan, again, culture. Never mind that Kawashima makes clear in his writing that culture is only one of many factors that shape legal behavior; forget his insistence that litigation is disfavored everywhere, regardless of culture. The conventional wisdom is simply that Kawashima was a champion of culturalist views of Japanese law.[32] For the past four decades, scholars in Japan and the United States who are interested in shedding light on law in Japan have taken that view as their starting point. From their efforts has emerged a set of articles about legal behavior in Japan that generally exaggerate and oversimplify what they assert to be Kawashima's basic premise.

Summarizing fifty years of comparative scholarship on dispute resolution in the United States and Japan in 1975, for example, Roger Benjamin writes:

> [T]he Japanese are held to be group-oriented, structure their individual and collective relationships in vertical combinations for social control purposes,

> and emphasize consensus in conflict resolution. By contrast, Americans are thought to be individualistic, stress equality in individual and collective relationships to structure social control, and prefer an adversarial, bargaining style of conflict resolution. Fundamentally, these differences are attributed to value systems in the two societies which emphasize individualistic versus group-oriented decision-making styles. And it is axiomatic that, at the base of these decision-making styles, are very different value systems of conflict resolution and social control.[33]

Others have pursued more specific aspects of the nexus between law and culture. Richard Parker, for example, accepts the view that Japanese values of trust, interdependence, and group harmony create a general antipathy to law.[34] In his view, one important but overlooked reason for the relatively marginal place of law in Japanese society is that, unlike in the West, Japanese society is not structured around language. Because law, according to Parker, controls behavior through the use of a written language, and written language occupies a less central place in Japan than in the West, law is less vital in Japan. J. C. Smith also reads Kawashima as positing that the Japanese have a unique distaste for law.[35] Instead of tracing the source of that distaste to language, he posits that the key difference between the role of law in Japan and the West can best be understood by exploring psychology and ethics, particularly conceptions of self, that lead people in Japan to privilege emotions over reason. Similar claims have been turned into political arguments. Former government official Naohiro Amaya believes that cultural differences between Japan and the United States cause U.S. antimonopoly laws to clash with Japanese values and argues that those laws therefore should not be adopted. Minister Toranosuke Katayama of the Ministry of Public Management, Home Affairs, Posts and Telecommunications, criticizing a lawsuit brought against his ministry by five telecom companies, states: "Resorting to legal action (over this kind of case) has been popular in the United States . . . But such means are not harmonious with Japan's (legal) culture."[36]

There have been some more serious attempts to examine the relationship between law and culture. Setsuo Miyazawa, in a review essay that discusses the legacy of Kawashima, describes a number of empirical studies of legal culture and legal consciousness.[37] One of them, by Kawashima's successor at the University of Tokyo, Kahei Rokumoto, relied on a particularly sophisticated group of empirical and theoretical studies.[38] Despite the research of Rokumoto and a few others, however, Miyazawa concludes that "since Kawashima's works appeared, the dominant form of analysis of Japanese legal consciousness has been anecdotal." Miyazawa describes as "ambiguous" and "contradictory" several national surveys of law and culture conducted in the 1970s and 1980s by the *Nippon Bunka Kaigi*, *Nihon Bengoshi Rengokai*, and others, and he argues that surveys on Japanese legal culture contain weak questions and obtain unreliable answers.

There are, of course, studies of dispute resolution that acknowledge a debt to Kawashima's claims about Japanese legal culture but are not overly constrained by them. In an article that examines the role of courts and judges in dispute resolution in Japan, for example, Tetsuya Obuchi challenges Kawashima's claim that the Japanese regard law like an heirloom samurai sword, something to be treasured but not used.[39] Instead, he argues that while people may first seek negotiated settlements to their disputes, they will also resort to litigation. Legal culture, in his view, can accommodate a variety of different approaches to conflict. And, notwithstanding his criticism of the literature on Japanese legal culture, Miyazawa himself did not abandon culture as a variable in understanding differences between legal behavior in the United States and Japan, as his work on international conflict resolution makes clear.[40] Nonetheless, the study of Japanese legal culture has not gone much beyond the insights contained in Kawashima's 1963 article. Indeed, many studies have ignored the context in which Kawashima embedded his cultural analysis and have instead argued for a vision of law and dispute resolution in Japan that is entirely shaped by culture. The narrow scope of such views has invited ridicule, and many scholars have turned away from culture and sought other explanations for Japanese legal behavior. One of them, presented as a direct challenge to culture, is a structural analysis that focuses on the configuration of legal institutions.

B. INSTITUTIONAL APPROACHES

Cultural explanations of Japanese disputing behavior owe much to Kawashima's analysis of why individuals allegedly prefer to resolve conflicts outside of formal legal channels. Individual preferences, however, are neither simple to identify nor easy to generalize, and whether culture or something else is the source of individual law-related behavior is difficult to establish. Not only are individuals members of and participants in cultural practices and rituals; they are also influenced by a variety of political and economic forces that give shape to social practices.

In his landmark article on Japanese law, "The Myth of the Reluctant Litigant," John Owen Haley countered what he saw as Kawashima's overemphasis on culture in explaining Japanese dispute resolution.[41] Haley expresses skepticism about claims that the Japanese have a "deeply rooted cultural preference" for informal, mediated settlements; an aversion to formal adjudication; a penchant for compromise; a distrust of all-or-none solutions; and a dislike of public quarrels.[42] To evaluate what he sees as Kawashima's overreliance on cultural causes of legal behavior, Haley seeks to answer a decisive question: Are the Japanese so strongly oriented by their culture to informally resolve disputes that they are willing to settle for less than they would be awarded if they litigated?[43] If the answer is yes, then Haley will concede that the Japanese are averse to litigation. No concession is necessary; he answers his query in the negative.

At the heart of Haley's argument is an examination of litigation rates between 1890 and 1974.[44] Noting that litigation was more frequent before 1937 than in more recent decades, Haley labels as "myth" the view that the Japanese are reluctant to resolve their grievances in court. The reality, he suggests, is that litigation was offensive to "those who wished to maintain a paternalistic order based on a hierarchical submission to authority."[45] Because governing elites viewed litigation as destructive of a social order based on personal relationships (which, not coincidentally, is exactly the type of social order that enabled the elites to govern), they sought to limit litigation by creating other avenues for the resolution of disputes.

Japanese elites, in Haley's view, used a number of mechanisms to suppress litigation. They controlled the number of judges and attorneys by using an examination system that artificially limited entry to the legal profession.[46] Caseloads were made high and the legal process was crafted to operate slowly, results of a conscious decision to dissuade people from utilizing the formal legal process. Courts were denied contempt powers and possessed few remedies, which made it difficult to enforce judicial decisions. These and other features of the Japanese legal system made going to court expensive, time-consuming, frustrating, and unrewarding and resulted in many people foregoing their day in court. Like Kawashima, therefore, Haley did more than simply assert the importance of his claims. He turned to the data and argued that the Japanese government carefully controlled the process of dispute resolution. By forcing people to use informal mechanisms to resolve disputes and promoting the belief that they do so because they are harmonious and shun overt conflict, the government succeeded in minimizing challenges to its legitimacy and authority.

The brilliance of Haley's argument was his presentation of a seemingly clear and plausible causal alternative to the idea that traditional values were the primary shaper of legal behavior. Institutions also have a powerful influence on behavior, he argued; then he demonstrated how institutions themselves were manipulated to keep people from the courts. His dichotomy between culture and institutions was crucial to his project. Without spelling out whether he meant to bring attention to institutions as organizational units or social practices, and never offering a solution to the chicken-and-egg problem of how to disentangle institutions from their cultural context, Haley made it easy for readers to feel that there was now an alternative paradigm to culture as a window on Japanese law.

Haley's emphasis on institutional configuration in the analysis of Japanese conflict has been pursued by a number of other specialists of Japanese law and society. Although he is a keen observer of culture, David Johnson's study of Japanese criminal justice, for example, concentrates on factors such as the training and promotion of prosecutors to explain conviction rates and sentencing.[47] And Toshiko Takenaka, in her evaluation of Japan's legal regime controlling intellectual property, rejects a cultural approach and instead argues that intellectual property law in Japan is the result of conscious political choices aimed at crafting a particular set of legal doctrines and practices.[48]

Although the arguments presented by Kawashima and Haley may appear to be powerfully contradictory, they can be read as simply differing in emphasis rather than as mutually exclusive formulations. Kawashima is attentive to issues of political and social structure, but they are not his primary interest. His discussion of how the government instituted *chōtei* (mediation) practices suggests an appreciation of the influence of institutional configuration on the behavior of disputants, and his claim that citizens "preferred" mediation to litigation leaves room for an explanation that such preferences are created by institutional design. Similarly, Haley does not explicitly address the question of why (or whether) the particular institutions he highlights are more prominent in Japan than elsewhere. The context and origin of Haley's institutions go largely unexplored, but the individuals who constitute institutions and the time and place in which those institutions arose are connected to a particular society, which suggests a crucial role for culture.[49] Unfortunately, the subtlety of Kawashima's and Haley's disagreement has been regularly ignored, with the result that much scholarship about law and dispute resolution in Japan asks whether it is best understood through the lens of culture *or* institutions, as if these were concepts that did not almost always intersect.[50]

The oft-noted tension between Kawashima's emphasis on cultural explanations of Japanese disputing behavior and the primacy Haley gives to institutions, therefore, is far less acute than one might initially suppose. As already stated, Kawashima is well aware of the power of mutable (and manipulable) institutions, even though he chooses to focus much of his writing on culture. Likewise, there is ample room in Haley's thesis to insert culture; at the very least, it is the context in which the elite create and mutate various institutions, and must therefore exert some influence on both the shapers of institutions and institutions themselves. More fundamental, the issue at stake in the differing interpretations set forth by Kawashima and Haley—whether cultural or institutional factors have a greater influence on legal behavior and therefore on the resolution of disputes—may ultimately resist a compelling conclusion. Disentangling culture from institutions has shown itself to be an extraordinarily difficult, if not impossible, task. Culture is dynamic, shaped and transformed over time by changes in technology, new forms of social organization, and a variety of other factors.[51] Institutions are similarly malleable. Since culture is both a product of and the genesis of institutions, and institutions both create and are created by culture, convincingly demonstrating which one of them is responsible for certain aspects of the legal system is likely to elude even the most able minds.

C. LAW AND ECONOMICS APPROACHES

It should come as no surprise that a third approach to disputing behavior in Japan, most closely identified with Harvard Law School's J. Mark Ramseyer, exhibits both great originality and a deep debt to previous scholarship. Rooted in a view of individual behavior that emphasizes rational decision making, this perspective examines the choices of those engaged in conflict, particularly their decisions about whether and when to settle or sue. Although a rational choice approach to the analysis of disputes does not explicitly reject the potential relevance of cultural or institutional perspectives (indeed, it incorporates elements of both), it takes a somewhat different path in seeking to understand the contours of disputing behavior. At its core is the claim that the measure of a successful legal system is predictability. A predictable system makes it easier for potential litigants to settle their disputes "in the shadow of the law," thereby achieving results that are similar to those that would result from litigation but without the high transaction costs.

Whereas culturalists posit that disputing behavior is primarily a consequence of psychosocial values and influences, and structuralists emphasize the shaping power of institutions, those working within the assumptions of law and economics highlight the intellectual, rational bases of decisions about the resolution of conflict that enable litigants to maximize their wealth in light of expected litigated outcomes. These different emphases should not obscure important similarities. Litigants may make rational, wealth-maximizing decisions about whether to settle or sue, but they make those decisions within a cultural and institutional context that determines the legal rules, the availability of dispute resolution procedures, the norms that govern relationships between people and groups, and the definition of rationality. As Ramseyer puts it, "Through culture, people make sense of what they experience; through culture, they decide what it is that they most value. As a result, one cannot properly understand the empirical world without a sense of culture."[52] Ramseyer's emphasis on rational decision making and wealth maximization clearly differs from Kawashima's focus. But Kawashima certainly would have embraced (and did to some extent anticipate) one aspect of the law and economics analysis, arguing that "parties in dispute usually find that resort to a lawsuit is less profitable than resort to other means of settlement."[53] Haley's focus on the costs imposed by institutional barriers to litigation also complements Ramseyer's analysis. As Ramseyer approvingly notes, "Haley's first and central proposition [in "The Myth of the Reluctant Litigant" is that] Japanese do not sue because suing does not pay."[54]

The connection between approaches to law and dispute resolution that focus on institutions per Haley and individual rationality per Ramseyer is most apparent with regard to predictability. The predictability of judicial decisions depends on a number of factors. A legal system without rules of stare decisis and dependent on juries, for example, would in most cases be less predictable than one that emphasized the importance of following precedent and gave judges a monopoly on decision making. In Japan, Ramseyer emphasizes, there are no juries; judges can (and do) communicate their leanings to litigants; trials unfold slowly over many months or years; and a highly ordered judicial structure emphasizes the standardization of judgments.[55] Haley might regard these features of the Japanese legal system as institutional impediments that are manipulated to dissuade people from litigating; Ramseyer emphasizes their economic, communicative function, which enables litigants rationally to decide whether to pursue their disputes in court or to seek a resolution through other means. Ramseyer and Haley may agree about the rationality of disputants, who evaluate the cost of litigation when deciding whether to sue. But where Haley sees institutional barriers that make using the courts prohibitively expensive, Ramseyer sees a legal system that is so transparent that litigants can resolve their differences with reference to their expected litigated outcomes.

Like approaches to disputing grounded in culture and institutions, a rational choice perspective offers an explanation of Japanese dispute-resolving behavior that cannot stand alone. If rationality means that individuals will refuse to settle for an amount less than a court is likely to award—that is, that people in Japan will "avoid" a judicial determination only if they think that the determination is no more lucrative than an out-of-court settlement—then data become essential. What do people and/or their legal representatives know, and think they know, about how courts will resolve particular disputes? Are they similarly well (or poorly) informed about extrajudicial processes? Can potential litigants and their counsel obtain sufficient information about how a particular conflict is likely to be handled by different dispute resolvers when they are actually facing a dispute? As Ramseyer acknowledges, his thesis and the issues it raises "don't lend themselves to testable hypotheses."[56]

Consequently, one can use the basic framework he proposes while reshaping the theory in various ways. Rather than associate rational behavior with actions that are exclusively influenced by financial incentives, for example, the definition of rationality can be broadened. Research on courts and litigation reveals a mix of incentives for why people go to court; winning is one of them, but so too is the opportunity to have one's day in court, to be heard by a neutral third party, to exercise one's rights.[57] There may be equally strong reasons why people choose not to litigate; it takes time, can exact a reputational cost, and can conclusively sever a relationship, among others.[58] In addition, people may have a particular self-image—as strong-willed and assertive, or perhaps harmonious and consensual—and make decisions about which method of dispute resolution to utilize that are not primarily motivated by an assessment of their likelihood of victory. This does not mean that such litigants are irrational, but that different people in similar circumstances may take into consideration different conditions in their rational calculations. Understanding those differences may lead one back to a consideration of cultural and institutional variation.[59]

The economic perspective on dispute resolution in Japan includes a normative claim that conflicts with Haley's emphasis on institutional design. In Ramseyer's view, Japan's system of dispute resolution (indeed, *any* system of dispute resolution) is laudable if it is highly predictable and thereby encourages disputants to settle their claims informally. As he puts it, "Litigation is scarce in Japan not because the system is bankrupt. It is scarce because the system works."[60] That conclusion clashes with a normative implication of Haley's work—that Japan's scarcity of litigation is an indication that people are being inappropriately kept from the courts and are unable to seek justice.

Ramseyer may be correct in arguing that it is desirable for a legal system to minimize transaction costs and maximize individual advantage by finding ways for disputants to resolve conflicts without the time and expense associated with litigation. But his position takes as a given the content of legal rules, and it therefore has little to say about the degree to which the resolution of conflict "in the shadow of the law" achieves a normatively desirable result in a given case. Similarly, his approach does not address the role that litigation may play in changing legal rules. Judicial decisions often reshape or at least adjust particular rules as a consequence of new cases that challenge existing legal interpretations and practices. In simple and highly standardized areas of law the rules may be relatively impermeable. But in many situations new cases bring novel issues, and if they are not litigated then legal rules will fossilize and the "shadow" of the law will cease to shift.

D. CASE STUDIES

Studies that focus on the evolution and resolution of particular legal conflicts also owe a debt to Kawashima. In "Dispute Resolution in Contemporary Japan" and many of his later writings, Kawashima made elegant use of particular legal conflicts to illustrate his theoretical concerns. In fact, many of Kawashima's generalizations about Japanese law and culture appear to have emerged from his study of specific types of conflicts, particularly disputes between contracting parties.[61] Some have followed a similar path and sought to examine concrete legal conflicts in order to develop and test theories of Japanese dispute resolution. Such studies tend to be conceptually rooted in one of the approaches discussed above—cultural, institutional, and law and economics. But they differ from the writings highlighted under those headings because they ground their analyses in detailed case studies of discrete conflicts and are therefore more inductive than many (but not all) of the previously discussed works.

The resolution of disputes over traffic accidents, for example, has attracted the attention of a number of scholars. It was Kawashima who first used traffic accidents to generalize about dispute resolution. He noticed that although there were numerous railroad and taxi accidents in 1960, very few were brought to court.[62] His explanation for this, like his explanation for low levels of litigation more generally, highlighted what he called "the social-cultural background."[63] By using traffic accident data as a window on Japanese dispute resolution, Kawashima triggered an ongoing debate.

In both an article and a book chapter, Ramseyer argues that the behavior of heirs of victims of fatal traffic accidents calls into question claims that the Japanese do not assert their legal rights because of cultural barriers and also contradicts the assumptions of institutional approaches. Instead, he argues, heirs settle their claims for amounts that are close to what a court would award, which strongly suggests that legal rules structure out-of-court settlements.[64] Tanase offers a somewhat different analysis, proposing a "management model" for Japanese non-litigiousness.[65] Using data about compensation for automobile accidents (a broader category than the fatal accidents that Ramseyer examines), he claims that the Japanese government creates a non-litigious society by successfully managing both the supply of judicial resources and the demand for litigation. It does so by providing free consultation to accident victims, creating a standard system of compensation, and offering extrajudicial methods of dispute resolution. Tanase's model borrows aspects of the cultural, institutional, and economic approaches, but combines them in a novel way. Other studies of traffic accident disputes, like those of Shozo Ota and Daniel Foote, add further nuance to the interpretation of how best to understand the disposition of such conflicts.[66] These studies provide valuable insight into how a certain type of conflict—one that is routine, addresses harms that range from minor to fatal, and brings together random parties—is handled. But there are many other forms of conflict that do not fit such a pattern; since the mid-1980s, a number of studies have focused on disputes that bring to the table a variety of other issues.

A case-based approach—and one that also investigates quotidian conflicts—animates Mark West's work on karaoke, lost objects, love hotels, and other issues. In "The Resolution of Karaoke Disputes: The Calculus of Institutions and Social Capital," for example, West frames his work with references to Kawashima, Haley, and Ramseyer.[67] Like them, he is interested in explaining the cause of Japanese non-litigiousness; to do so, he highlights the interplay of individual decision making, economics, and culture. Picking up on Frank Upham's work on environmental pollution (discussed below) but narrowing the focus to private disputes over noisy karaoke bars, West argues that the decision to pursue complaints over karaoke noise through litigation, extralegal dispute resolution mechanisms, or settlement reflects a mix of pressures—financial, institutional, and cultural. Which factor is most relevant will depend largely on the type and context of the dispute and on the available dispute resolution options. Rather than offer support for a single approach to dispute resolution, West suggests that the best explanation is likely to be eclectic.

In *Law and Social Change in Postwar Japan*, the most well-known example of a case-based approach to Japanese dispute resolution, Frank Upham tackles issues far more complex than traffic accidents.[68] Upham roots his book in the study of four legal conflicts that involve the state: environmental pollution, minority rights, gender discrimination, and industrial policy. Each section of the book unravels a complex dispute, which enables the reader to gain an understanding of the personalities, politics, and particularities of the specific issue being presented. But the conflicts are not simply described; they are couched in the context of a more general argument about the operation of Japanese law.

Upham's chapter on environmental pollution illustrates his argument. It tells the tragic story of mercury poisoning caused by industrial effluents released by the Chisso company and the response of those who suffered as a consequence of the pollution. We learn that some of those affected by the mercury were reluctant to sue, in part because they worried about being known as people who would use the legal system to vindicate their rights.[69] Ultimately, the victims were split into three groups; those who asked the government's Ministry of Health and Welfare to mediate their dispute with Chisso, those who directly negotiated with Chisso, and those who sued. It is here that Upham turns his lens to the interests of the government and makes his most original contribution. He argues that the state's primary concern is with the process through which the conflict between Chisso and the victims of mercury contamination is resolved, not the content of the resolution. The government worried that the victims and their growing political movement would seize control of the dispute resolution process, and it therefore moved to placate those who sought justice. It did so in three ways: by working to solve the underlying problem of industrial pollution, disempowering the antipollution movement by creating an extrajudicial process through which disputes over pollution could be resolved, and "settling the moral accounts" resulting from government and business involvement in industrial pollution by compensating victims.[70] Upham's argument does not champion a particular version of Japanese culture, but it does locate the victims of Chisso's pollution in a social context, in which their actions are embedded in values that reflect Japanese village life. Likewise, he emphasizes the institutions that facilitate and/or inhibit the resolution of conflict.

The core cases discussed in *Law and Social Change in Postwar Japan* revolve around conflicts between groups of the aggrieved and the state. Moreover, the victims in three of the four cases are relatively powerless and traditionally disadvantaged; that may explain, at least in part, their willingness to litigate. It is therefore difficult to generalize from these cases to more individually focused resolution of conflict, as well as to disputes that arise between those of relatively equal social status. Nonetheless, Upham has extended Kawashima's emphasis on specific, individual conflicts to a consideration of disputes that are political, moral, and socially disruptive. More than disputes over barking dogs and bad brakes, such conflicts may reveal the fundamental values and workings of a society.

Others have also examined broad-based social conflict as a means of better understanding dispute resolution in Japan. In *The Ritual of Rights in Japan: Law, Society, and Health Policy*, for example, I highlight two disputes that involve both legislation and litigation—brain death / organ transplantation, and HIV/AIDS—to draw attention to how the explicit assertion of legal rights has become a common feature of Japanese dispute resolution.[71] Rather than seek to explain *why* there is so little litigation in Japan, my concern is to better understand the many dimensions of Japanese conflict—cultural, economic, and political—and how it is resolved. The disputes I investigate are not the everyday conflicts between neighbors; they involve broad issues of policy, large groups of people, and highly politicized struggles.

Contentious public disputes over policy are not the only, or necessarily the last, vantage point from which to understand the role of law in the resolution of disputes, as I discuss in my study of the tuna auction at Tokyo's Tsukiji wholesale market.[72] At Tsukiji, dealers make use of an ingenious government-operated tuna court to manage conflicts over the quality of auctioned fish. In contrast to studies in the United States that highlight the efficiency of informal norms for resolving disputes among close-knit actors, and the corrosive impact of formal legal conflict on continuing relationships, I argue that Japan's tuna merchants are heavily dependent on formal legal rules to resolve their conflicts. In the Tokyo tuna auction, the invocation of law and the embrace of formal methods to resolve conflict bind tuna traders, strengthen their relationships, and are extremely fast and effective. Setsuo Miyazawa, Robert Kidder, David Apter, Susan Pharr, John Campbell, Chalmers Johnson, Mark Levin, Robert Leflar, and other scholars of law and politics have also moved beyond Kawashima's focus on individual conflict resolution and examined aggregated claims and politicized disputes.[73] Many of their studies examine issues that emerged in late twentieth-century Japan, such as gender equality, industrial pollution, and patients' rights, among others. Because such conflicts are less likely to be shaped by interpersonal pressures or community norms than those highlighted by Kawashima, they may more frequently end up in court.[74] Indeed, certain factors that Kawashima identified as affecting the future of dispute resolution—urbanization, industrialization, greater equality of citizens, more universalistic standards, and greater assertion of legal rights—appear to have had an impact on the types of disputes that arise and the process through which they are resolved. Were he alive today, Kawashima might counsel legal scholars to develop a taxonomy of conflict, from the mundane to the far-reaching, from those involving exclusively private disputes to group-oriented policy controversies, and seek to disentangle the relative influences of culture, costs, institutions, and political power that have an impact on how they are managed, both in Japan and comparatively. Without such guidance, scholars may continue to examine discrete areas of conflict without the benefit of a general framework that distinguishes different types of conflicts and links them to a particular approach to dispute resolution.

IV. CONCLUSION: THE FUTURE OF DISPUTE RESOLUTION IN JAPAN

Looking back at the forty years of scholarship on Japanese law and conflict inspired by Kawashima's "Dispute Resolution in Contemporary Japan," it is extraordinary that one paper (followed, of course, by his many other publications) has played such a central role in delineating the questions that continue to animate the study of Japanese law and society. Even today, almost every important contribution to the literature on disputing in Japan, and most general writings on the Japanese legal system, directly or indirectly pay homage to Kawashima. Kawashima's work is the reference point from which all others—young and not so young, Japanese and non-Japanese, lawyers, sociologists, and political scientists—begin.

Kawashima's predictions about the future of law and dispute resolution in Japan are also regularly revisited. For every article that claims Kawashima's expectations have proved true, one can find contrary assertions that history has exposed his errors.[75] It is therefore particularly interesting that the movement to reform the Japanese legal system that began in the mid-1990s may be poised to bring about, by conscious institutional manipulation, a variety of the changes that Kawashima thought would inevitably arise from modernization.[76] Organizations and institutions such as Keidanren, the Japan Federation of Bar Associations, the Supreme Court, the Ministry of Justice, the Liberal Democratic Party, and others have at least superficially embraced the "rule of law" as an essential component of Japan's future success.[77] For a variety of often conflicting reasons, these groups have agreed (with varying degrees of enthusiasm) to expand the population of legal professionals in

Japan, speed up the workings of the civil courts, introduce lay opinion into determinations of criminal wrongdoing, decrease the financial costs imposed on those who want to sue, make legal expertise more readily available to those who previously could not afford it, change the system of legal education, and allow law firms more flexibility to operate in a competitive domestic and international environment, among other things.

The overall impact of these changes is unclear, at least for now, but it is possible that they will push the system in the direction that Kawashima predicted—a greater reliance on universalistic rules, more individual rights assertion, more litigation, and less reliance on social norms as the glue that orders social relations. Ironically—but perhaps not surprisingly, given that many reformers graduated from the University of Tokyo's Faculty of Law when Kawashima's influence was at its peak—the reformers retain a strong allegiance to a culturalist view of Japanese law, despite their conscious manipulation of institutions to facilitate change. For example, the June 2001 report of the Justice System Reform Council, the government's key legal reform body, states:

> [T]he Council has determined that the fundamental task for reform of the justice system is to define clearly "what we must do to transform both the spirit of the law and the rule of law into the flesh and blood of this country, so that they become 'the shape of our country'". . . In other words, how should those mechanisms [of the justice system] and the legal profession be reformed so as to make the law (order), which serves as the core of freedom and fairness on which "our country" should be based, broadly penetrate the entire state and all of society and become alive in the people's daily life?[78]

It is impossible to know whether or to what extent such efforts to revamp Japan's legal culture will succeed, or how the changes that are now occurring will ultimately affect the process of dispute resolution or the substantive outcome of particular conflicts. Significant political differences have surfaced among those involved in the conceptualization and implementation of judicial reform, and some parties would like to create an expanded role for alternative methods of dispute resolution that could limit the number of cases that end up in the courts. Regardless of whose interests prevail in the current legal reform debate, it is clear that the framework Kawashima provided for examining the interweaving of law and culture in Japan will continue to shape the analysis and discussion of dispute resolution for decades to come.

NOTES

I am grateful to the University of Pennsylvania Law School for summer funding that supported the research and writing of this chapter, and to a number of colleagues for their thoughtful comments on an earlier draft, particularly Steven Burbank, Daniel Foote, David Johnson, Setsuo Miyazawa, Mark Ramseyer, Frank Upham, and Mark West.

1. Takeyoshi Kawashima, "Dispute Resolution in Contemporary Japan," in Arthur Taylor von Mehren, ed., *Law in Japan: The Legal Order in a Changing Society* (Cambridge, MA: Harvard University Press, 1963), 41.

2. Michael K. Young, Masanobu Kato, and Akira Fujimoto, "Japanese Attitudes towards Contracts: An Empirical Wrinkle in the Debate," *George Washington International Law Review* 34 (2003): 789, 790.

3. Kawashima published a book that further explored many of the issues raised in the article. See Takeyoshi Kawashima, *Nihonjin no hō ishiki* [The Legal Consciousness of the Japanese] (Tokyo: Iwanami, 1967).

4. Ruth Benedict, *The Chrysanthemum and the Sword: Patterns of Japanese Culture* (Boston: Houghton Mifflin, 1946). It is a sign of changed times in the legal academy that in 1997 Frank Upham argued that American scholars of Japanese law find cultural explanations "anathema." See Frank K. Upham, "The Place of Japanese Legal Studies in American Comparative Law," *Utah Law Review* 1997 (1997): 639.

5. Kawashima does not, however, explain how one can determine what counts as "frequent," "infrequent," or "normal" amounts of litigation. He uses little comparative data, does not defend his various comparative references to the United States, and does not present criteria for evaluating the relative frequency of litigation in one or a number of locales. Still, many scholars who have followed Kawashima share his assumption that litigation is uncommon in Japan, and their research is aimed at finding an explanation for that phenomenon.

6. Young, for example, says that he "remains a bit mystified about Professor Kawashima's precise point in his many writings" and goes on to offer one partial version of Kawashima's thesis. Young, Kato, and Fujimoto, "Japanese Attitudes towards Contracts," 790–91.

7. Marc Galanter, "The Modernization of Law," in Lawrence M. Friedman and Stewart Macaulay, eds., *Law and the Behavioral Sciences* (Indianapolis: Bobbs-Merrill, 1977), 1046–55.

8. Some of Maruyama's work has been collected in Masao Maruyama, *Thought and Behavior in Modern Japanese Politics*, ed. Ivan Morris (New York: Oxford University Press, 1963).

9. See, e.g., Reinhard Bendix, *Nation-Building and Citizenship: Studies in Our Changing Social Order* (Berkeley: University of California Press, 1964).

10. For a variety of perspectives on Japanese culture, see Benedict, *The Chrysanthemum and the Sword*; Peter Dale, *The Myth of Japanese Uniqueness* (New York: St. Martin's Press, 1986); and Ross Mouer and Yoshio Sugimoto, *Images of Japanese Society* (New York: Kegan Paul International, 1990).

11. Dan Fenno Henderson, *Conciliation and Japanese Law: Tokugawa and Modern*, 2 vols. (Seattle: Association for Asian Studies / University of Washington Press, 1965).

12. Dan Fenno Henderson, "Some Aspects of Tokugawa Law," *Washington Law Review* 27(1) (1952): 85.

13. Kawashima, "Dispute Resolution in Contemporary Japan," 53.

14. Ibid., 54.

15. Ibid., 43.

16. Ibid., 45.

17. Ibid., 41.

18. Christian Wöllschläger, who examined civil case filings in Japan between 1875 and 1994, claims that his "findings confirm the traditionalist explanation of the avoidance of litigation as it was laid down in Kawashima's historical studies . . . Social attitudes towards law which continue from an agrarian feudal state are indeed the only basis for explaining the stable secular development of litigation in Japan as well as the wide distance from Western nations. The low demand for civil justice is a genuine element of legal culture insofar as it distinguishes the practical operation of law from Western nations. It is the Japanese aspect of Japanese law which otherwise comprises many foreign imports." Christian Wöllschläger, "Historical Trends of Civil Litigation in Japan, Arizona, Sweden, and Germany: Japanese Legal Culture in the Light of Judicial Statistics," in Harald Baum, ed., *Japan: Economic Success and Legal System* (New York: Walter de Gruyter, 1997), 89–142, 134. Wöllschläger qualifies these finding by notifying readers that he is unable to make use of Japanese-language materials. In addition, he too quickly discounts other possible explanations for litigation rates in Japan; see the discussion in this chapter, below.

19. See, e.g., Kawashima, *Nihonjin no hō ishiki*, 166–78, where he relies on cultural preferences rather than political or institutional factors to explain Japanese legal behavior.

20. For a more complete discussion of research on Japanese legal culture, see Eric A. Feldman, *The Ritual of Rights in Japan: Law, Society, and Health Policy* (New York: Cambridge University Press, 2000), chap. 7, 141–65.

21. Galanter, "The Modernization of Law," 1046–55.

22. See generally David Nelkin, ed., *Comparing Legal Cultures* (Brookfield, VT: Dartmouth Publishing Company, 1997).

23. Galanter, "The Modernization of Law," 1046–55.

24. See ibid.

25. Takao Tanase, "The Empty Space of the Modern in Japanese Law Discourse," in David Nelken and Johannes Feest, eds., *Adapting Legal Cultures* (Portland, OR: Hart Publishing, 2001): 187, 188.

26. An analysis of the rule of law, and its relationship to economic development, can be found in Frank Upham, "Mythmaking in the Rule of Law Orthodoxy," Carnegie Endowment for International Peace, September 2002, downloaded from (http://www.ceip.org/files/pdf/wp30.pdf).

27. See, e.g., Young, Kato, and Fujimoto, "Japanese Attitudes towards Contracts," 789.

28. Yoshiyuki Matsumura, "The Works of Takeyoshi Kawashima," *Law and Society Review* 22 (1988): 1037 ("all subsequent scholarship dealing with Japanese attitudes toward law and the legal system have had to take into account Kawashima's hypothesis").

29. Chin Kim and Craig M. Lawson, "The Law of the Subtle Mind: The Traditional Japanese Conception of Law," *International and Comparative Law Quarterly* 28 (July 1979): 491.

30. Ibid., 502.

31. Yasunobu Sato, *Commercial Dispute Processing and Japan* (New York: Kluwer Law International, 2001), 330.

32. Kawashima himself was clearly intrigued with the part of his explanation that focused on culture. He followed "Dispute Resolution in Contemporary Japan" with a book, *Nihonjin no hō ishiki* [The Legal Consciousness of the Japanese], which introduced the concept of legal consciousness into the study of Japanese law, and much of his writing was particularly aimed at exploring the relationship between law and culture.

33. Roger W. Benjamin, "Images of Conflict Resolution and Social Control: American and Japanese Attitudes toward the Adversary System," *Journal of Conflict Resolution* 19(1) (March 1975): 123–37.

34. Richard B. Parker, "Law and Language in Japan and the United States," *Osaka University Law Review* 34 (1987): 47.

35. Joseph Carman Smith, "Ajase and Oedipus: Ideas of the Self in Japanese and Western Legal Consciousness," *Osaka University Law Review* 34 (1987): 1. Another psychological approach to Kawashima is Yoshiyuki Matsumura, "Procedural Justice in Dispute Resolution—Japan and the West" (paper presented at the Annual Meeting of the Law and Society Association, University of Amster-

dam, June 26–29, 1991), on file with author. Matsumura was Kawashima's last student (*joshu*), and his focus on American social psychology reflects Kawashima's interest in that field.

36. Naohiro Amaya, "Harmony and the Antimonopoly Law," *Japan Echo* 8 (1981): 85; "Gov't to Maintain Competition Policy on Connection Fees," *Kyodo News Online*, July 18, 2003, at (http://www.findarticles.com/p/articles/mi_g01973/is_200307/ai_n9007646).

37. Setsuo Miyazawa, "Taking Kawashima Seriously: A Review of Japanese Research on Japanese Legal Consciousness and Disputing Behavior," *Law and Society Review* 21(2) (1987): 219–41.

38. Kahei Rokumoto, "Nihonjin no hō ishiki no chōsa" [A Survey of the Legal Consciousness of the Japanese], in *Hōgaku kyōshitsu* 109 (October 1989): 94–100, 97; Rokumoto, *Hōshakaigaku* [Sociology of Law] (Tokyo: Yūhikaku, 1986), chap. 5, 189–232.

39. Tetsuya Obuchi, "Role of the Court in the Process of Informal Dispute Resolution in Japan: Traditional and Modern Aspects, with Special Emphasis on In-Court Compromise," *Law in Japan: An Annual* 20 (1987): 74, 81.

40. Setsuo Miyazawa, "How Does Culture Count? A Discussion on International Conflicts as Conflicts of Legal Cultures" (paper from 13th World Congress on Philosophy of Law and Social Philosophy, Kobe, Japan, August 25, 1987); published in Japanese as "Bunka wa ikanaru imi ni oite jūyō ka? Bunka-teki setsumei to kōriteki setsumei," in Kōichirō Fujikura and Ryūichi Nagao, *Kokusai masatsu: sono hōbunka-teki haikei* [International Friction: Its Background in Legal Culture] (Tokyo: Nihon Hyōronsha, 1989), 274–97.

41. John O. Haley, "The Myth of the Reluctant Litigant," *Journal of Japanese Studies* 4(2) (1978): 359–89.

42. Ibid., 359.

43. Ibid., 365.

44. Ibid., 368. Haley measures litigation rates by calculating the number of filed/disposed civil suits per capita. On that basis, he concludes that there is less litigation in Japan than in Australia, Denmark, and the United Kingdom, for example, but more than in Norway, Sweden, and Finland (364).

45. Ibid., 371.

46. Ibid., 385.

47. David T. Johnson, *The Japanese Way of Justice: Prosecuting Crime in Japan* (New York: Oxford University Press, 2002).

48. Toshiko Takenaka, "Does a Cultural Barrier to Intellectual Property Trade Exist? The Japanese Example," *NYU Journal of International Law and Politics* 29 (Fall 1996–Winter 1997): 153.

49. On the difficulty of decoupling culture and institutions, see Michael Thompson, Richard Ellis, and Aaron Wildavsky, *Cultural Theory* (Boulder, CO: Westview Press, 1990); and Mary Douglas, *How Institutions Think* (Syracuse, NY: Syracuse University Press, 1986).

50. In fact, Haley appears to have gradually revised what was arguably the most radical implication of "The Myth of the Reluctant Litigant"—that elites consciously manipulated institutions to keep people from resolving their disputes in court. In his later work, Haley appears to be suggesting something less than the conscious, intentional shaping of institutions. He also makes more room for sociocultural variables in his explanation of Japanese dispute resolution. See generally John O. Haley, *Authority without Power: Law and the Japanese Paradox* (New York: Oxford University Press, 1991); David T. Johnson, "Authority with Power: John Haley on Japan's Law and Politics," *Law and Society Review* 27 (1993): 619; and John O. Haley, "Litigation in Japan: A New Look at Old Problems," *Willamette Journal of International Law and Dispute Resolution* 10 (2002): 7.

51. See, e.g., Stephen Vlastos, ed., *Mirror of Modernity: Invented Traditions of Modern Japan* (Berkeley: University of California Press, 1998).

52. J. Mark Ramseyer and Minoru Nakazato, "The Rational Litigant: Settlement Amounts and Verdict Rates in Japan," *Journal of Legal Studies* 18 (June 1989): 263, 290.

53. Kawashima, "Dispute Resolution in Contemporary Japan," 49.

54. J. Mark Ramseyer, "Reluctant Litigant Revisited: Rationality and Disputes in Japan," *Journal of Japanese Studies* 14(2) (1988): 111, 112.

55. Ibid., 113.

56. Ibid., 120.

57. See, e.g., Tom R. Tyler, *Why People Obey the Law* (New Haven, CT: Yale University Press, 1990); and E. Alan Lind and Tom R. Tyler, *The Social Psychology of Procedural Justice* (New York: Plenum Press, 1988).

58. For an insightful discussion of the "costs" of litigation in an American community, see David Engel, "The Oven Bird's Song: Insiders, Outsiders, and Personal Injuries in an American Community," *Law and Society Review* 18 (1984): 551.

59. At some point, the definition of rationality becomes so broad as to be meaningless. If an individual's actions are deemed rational because the individual did what he or she intends and wants to do, then rationality becomes tautological, and it no longer provides a useful explanation of particular behavioral choices.

60. Ramseyer and Nakazato, "The Rational Litigant," 290.

61. I will not discuss Kawashima's work on contracts, although it does represent another important part of his influence. See Takeyoshi Kawashima, "The Legal Consciousness of Contract in Japan," *Law in Japan: An Annual* 7 (1974): 1 (a

translation of chapter 4 of *Nihonjin no hō ishiki*). See also Young, Kato, and Fujimoto, "Japanese Attitudes towards Contracts"; Willem M. Visser 't Hooft, *Japanese Contract and Anti-trust Law: A Sociological and Comparative Study* (New York: RoutledgeCurzon, 2002); and Curtis J. Milhaupt, "A Relational Theory of Japanese Corporate Governance: Contract, Culture, and the Rule of Law," *Harvard International Law Journal* 37 (Winter 1996): 3–64.

62. An unusual aspect of tort law in Japan is that railroad companies can often be plaintiffs in train accidents because trains are forced to run on tracks according to fixed schedules. Those who are hit by trains because they are on the tracks are legally liable for the train delay and other damages. In fact, railroad companies rarely (if ever) bring such claims. I am indebted to Setsuo Miyazawa for this point.

63. Kawashima, "Dispute Resolution in Contemporary Japan," 43. After the publication of Kawashima's paper, the Traffic Department of the Tokyo District Court established guidelines for the resolution of traffic disputes in order to prevent an increase in traffic accident cases. Police, insurance companies, and lawyers have been using those standards, which has served to limit traffic accident litigation.

64. J. Mark Ramseyer and Minoru Nakazato, *Japanese Law: An Economic Approach* (Chicago: University of Chicago Press, 1999), 99.

65. Takao Tanase, "The Management of Disputes: Automobile Accident Compensation in Japan," *Law and Society Review* 24 (1990): 651.

66. Shozo Ota, "Traffic Accidents in Japan: Law and Civil Dispute Resolution," in E. Hondius, ed., *Modern Trends in Tort Law* (Netherlands: Kluwer Law International, 1999), 79–93; Daniel Foote, "Resolution of Traffic Accident Disputes and Judicial Activism in Japan," *Law in Japan: An Annual* 25 (1995): 19.

67. Mark D. West, "The Resolution of Karaoke Disputes: The Calculus of Institutions and Social Capital," *Journal of Japanese Studies* 28 (2002): 301–37.

68. Frank Upham, *Law and Social Change in Postwar Japan* (Cambridge, MA: Harvard University Press, 1987).

69. Ibid., 37.

70. Ibid., 56.

71. Feldman, *The Ritual of Rights in Japan*. I also make use of a case-based approach in two international, comparative studies of conflict. See Eric A. Feldman and Ronald Bayer, eds., *Blood Feuds: AIDS, Blood, and the Politics of Medical Disaster* (New York: Oxford University Press, 1999); and Eric A. Feldman and Ronald Bayer, eds., *Unfiltered: Conflicts over Tobacco Policy and Public Health* (Cambridge, MA: Harvard University Press, 2004).

72. Eric A. Feldman, "The Tuna Court: Law and Norms in the World's Premier Fish Auction," *California Law Review* 94 (2006): 313.

73. See, e.g., Robert L. Kidder and Setsuo Miyazawa, "Long-Term Strategies

in Japanese Environmental Litigation," *Law and Social Inquiry* 18 (1993): 605; Susan Pharr, *Losing Face: Status Politics in Japan* (Berkeley: University of California Press, 1990); David Apter and Nagayo Sawa, *Against the State: Politics and Social Protest in Japan* (Cambridge, MA: Harvard University Press, 1984); Mark Levin, "Smoke around the Rising Sun: An American Look at Tobacco Regulation in Japan," *Stanford Journal of Law and Policy* 8 (1997): 99; Robert Leflar, "Informed Consent and Patients' Rights in Japan," *Houston Law Review* 33 (1996): 1; John Creighton Campbell, *How Policies Change: The Japanese Government and the Aging Society* (Princeton, NJ: Princeton University Press, 1992); and Chalmers Johnson, *Conspiracy at Matsukawa* (Berkeley: University of California Press, 1972).

74. In "Dispute Resolution in Contemporary Japan," Kawashima mentioned disputes between different social groups as not triggering the sociocultural concerns about hierarchy and harmony that inhibited much individual litigation. But he believed that the preference for conciliation would spill over from individual to group disputes and would therefore limit litigation in such areas as well.

75. See Wöllschläger, "Historical Trends of Civil Litigation in Japan, Arizona, Sweden, and Germany." Basing his claim on evidence that litigation rates, both civil and administrative, remain lower in Japan than in other places, Wöllschläger rejects Kawashima's prediction that as Japanese law modernized people would become more conscious of their rights and use the courts more frequently. See also Takao Tanase, "Soshō riyō to kindaika kasetsu" [Litigation Utilization and the Modernization Thesis], *Minji soshōhō riron no arata na kōchiku: Shindō Kōji Sensei koki shukuga* [A New Construction of Civil Procedure Theory: A Tribute to Professor Kōji Shindō on His Seventieth Birthday] (Tokyo: Yūhikaku, 2001), 288; and Seigo Hirowatari, "Post-war Japan and the Law: Mapping Discourses of Legalization and Modernization," *Social Science Japan Journal* 3 (2000): 155.

76. An interesting discussion of recent legal changes and cultural change is Kahei Rokumoto, "Law and Culture in Transition" (paper presented at symposium "Legal Reform and Socio-Legal Change in Japan," Boalt Hall School of Law, University of California, Berkeley, November 4–5, 1999), on file with author.

77. For a detailed account of the debate over legal reform in Japan, see Setsuo Miyazawa, "The Politics of Judicial Reform in Japan: The Rule of Law at Last?" in "Reform in Japanese Legal Education," special issue, *Asian Pacific Law and Policy Journal*, 2001 (online); 2003 updated version on file with author.

78. Justice System Reform Council, Final Report, June 12, 2001, at (http://www.kantei.go.jp/foreign/judiciary/2001/0612report.html).

4 The Development of an Adversary System in Japanese Civil Procedure

YASUHEI TANIGUCHI

I. INTRODUCTION

When the late Judge Kohji Tanabe wrote his much-acclaimed article, "The Processes of Litigation: An Experiment with the Adversary System," which was published in 1963 in the original volume of *Law in Japan: The Legal Order in a Changing Society*, Japanese civil procedure was still in the course of recovery from the shock of postwar reform and looking for a way to settle in. As Judge Tanabe described, the postwar legal reform posed a nearly impossible task for judges and practitioners, let alone parties who had to represent themselves pro se.

The postwar reform in civil procedure was embodied in only a couple of changes to the Code of Civil Procedure as amended in 1948. Probably the most significant postwar provision was the new Article 294, which required examination of witnesses to be conducted first by the parties and only secondarily by the judge. Another change was the repeal of Article 261, which had allowed the judge to examine ex officio any evidence at almost any time he deemed it necessary.

These two changes in the code expressed the legislative intention to shift the driving force of proceedings from the judge to the parties. The repeal of Article 261 signified to judges that it was not only unnecessary but also prohibited to assist parties whose presentation of evidence was insufficient to support their case. The philosophy underlying these changes led judges to ignore the still-existing Article 127, which allowed them to address questions to the parties and to make suggestions for the parties to adduce further evidence. This power of the judge, called "the power of clarification" (*shaku-meiken*) was considered in prewar time so fundamental that the justice system could not have been accomplished without it. In fact, it was not just a right but also rather a heavy duty of the judge, in accordance with its original German concept of *Aufklärungspflicht* meaning the duty of clarification. The prewar highest court, the Grand Court of Judicature (*Daishin'in*), firmly held that a failure to exercise the clarification power constituted reversible error, despite the fact that the 1926 amendment to the code changed the relevant word from *duty* to *power*.

The postwar Supreme Court under the amended code was ready to lend itself to the new procedural philosophy. It held that clarification was a power and not a duty and therefore a failure to exercise it was no longer reversible error. Judge Tanabe explained how much confusion and dissatisfaction resulted from the new practice and how the Supreme Court rather quickly (several years later) changed its view back to the prewar interpretation that the judge was obliged to exercise the clarification power in appropriate cases.

The later development of case law up until today has been a history of the strengthening of the same position. Today, as it was before the war, clarification is firmly established not just as a power but also as an important duty of the judge. Emphasis on the clarification duty has much mitigated the importance of the repeal of Article 261, abolition of ex officio evidence taking, because the judge can and must invite a party to produce needed evidence and such an invitation is normally accepted readily. But how much did this change limit the adversary system introduced by the postwar reform?

What happened, for example, to another aspect of the adversary procedure also introduced in 1948, namely, the examination of witnesses by the parties? Judge Tanabe did not give any definite answer about its fate, because it was not yet clear how things would develop thereafter. But he concluded his article by saying, "[T]he gravitation from an exaggerated and extreme version of the adversary concept to what I have labeled a midway position probably suggests the pattern of the future in the District Courts . . . The midway position is in a real sense a fusion of the Continental and the Anglo-American philosophies."[1]

The period of some forty years that has followed since Judge Tanabe wrote his article has seen a development culminating in the new Code of Civil Procedure of 1996 (enforced from January 1 of 1998) and the practice under it, which seems to have given us certain answers to the questions that Judge Tanabe would have liked to ask. Even now, what Judge Tanabe described as the "midway" position can still be seen. This essay will explicate the events that have occurred during these intervening forty years. From the author's point of view, several key factors have led Japanese civil procedure to its present state. Some factors have remained relatively unchanged throughout not only these forty years, but in fact have not changed even since the inception of the modern Japanese civil procedure system in 1890. Other factors were added at some point of the development with impacts of varying degrees of importance.

II. OVERVIEW OF THE BASIC SCHEME OF JAPANESE CIVIL PROCEDURE

Let me first underscore an unchanged feature of the Japanese civil procedure. It is often asserted from the Common Law camp that the continental European civil procedure is characterized by the so-called inquisitorial system. The Civil Law camp rebuts this by saying that the Civil Law civil procedure adopts the so-called principle of party control and not an inquisitorial system at all. Without going too much into the details of this discussion, the German and therefore Japanese civil procedure can be said to have been "adversary" in the sense that it is the parties that lay a binding framework within which the court is allowed to make a decision.[2]

The principle of party control was introduced to Japanese civil procedure from Germany with a German-styled Code of Civil Procedure in 1890 and has since remained unchanged in principle until today. The principle of party control is that presentations made by the parties will have a binding effect on the court. Thus, this principle binds the judge's power within the scope of (a) a claim (cause of action and quantum) proposed by the plaintiff and (b) the factual allegation of the parties in support of such a claim.

For example, where a plaintiff asks for a judgment for payment of damages of five million yen for breach of a contract, the court is not allowed to grant a judgment for specific performance nor damages of ten million yen, because the underlying cause of action is different or the granted quantum exceeds the prayed-for relief. The plaintiff must always state a prayer for a specific relief in the complaint. So-called general relief is not permitted. This is an application of the so-called principle of free disposition, a branch of the principle of party control. (The principle of free disposition, *dispositionsmaxime*, expresses itself also in the freedom to withdraw an action, freedom to settle an action, etc.)

Next, the plaintiff must substantiate his or her claim by factual allegations. The same applies to a defense raised by the defendant. An important implication of this is that the factual allegation cannot be replaced by presentation of evidence. For example, in an action for loan collection, the defendant who did not allege payment of the debt must lose even if the evidence has clearly shown a payment. Thus, the unfolding of a civil case totally depends on the parties' initiative. If a party fails to present a factual allegation, the court is not allowed to find such a fact because no issue of fact has been formed about such fact. Thus, the "burden of pleading" is borne by the plaintiff for factual substantiation of a claim and by the defendant for a defense. This branch of the principle of party control is called the "principle of argumentation" (*Verhandlungsmaxime*). Some Japanese commentators seem to think that, by adopting such a principle of autonomy of the parties, the Japanese civil procedure adopted some sort of adversary system. As discussed later, this understanding is not accurate in my view when applied to the stage of proof.

The principle of argumentation, and accordingly the burden of pleading, were not enforced in their pure form from the beginning but were attenuated by the judge's "power of clarification." We distinguish two types of power of clarification: The first type simply enables the judge to understand more fully a party's assertion. When exercised properly, this does not add anything to the principle of argumentation. It only assures that a party's assertion is fully understood by the court. When we discuss the clarification power, however, we usually think of something more. It is the second function of the clarification power that really changes the nature of the principle of argumentation and lessens the party's burden of pleading. The court cannot supply a missing factual allegation, but it can suggest what is missing. Upon such suggestion, the party who bears the burden of assertion will most likely supply such a factual allegation. Thus, the Japanese version of "adversary system," if it is such, is not enforced in a pure form because, as said before, the exercise of the power is considered to be a duty of the judge.

III. ADVERSARINESS IN PROOF

Let us now turn to the phase of proof and see how adversarial it was in the original form of the code and how it was changed after the war. In my view, one of the basic differences between the German-styled party presentation and the Common Law adversary system can be found in the approach to the party's role in proving the disputed facts. In order to clarify the difference, it is convenient to distinguish between two meanings of "evidence." Evidence may mean a piece of paper or a witness that is examined. Evidence can also mean the information contained in the piece of paper in the form of meaningful letters or the statement (testimony) made by the witness in the form of spoken language.

The evidence in the former meaning can be better called the "evidential medium" because it carries with it certain information yet to be elicited. In the latter meaning, it can be called the "evidential information" which may or may not be useful for deciding a case. When certain evidential information is useful, it can be called "effective evidential information." Under the original Japanese Code of Civil Procedure borrowed from Germany, there was a degree of party control over the proof as far as evidential media were concerned. It was primarily the role of the parties to propose evidential media to the court, which had discretion to decide which evidential medium to adopt for examination.[3] In addition, however, the court could decide to examine "supplemental evidence" whenever the court considered that the case before it was "not yet ripe for a final decision."[4] The 1926 amendment not only continued to adopt the same scheme but also made the judge's initiative more explicit than before.[5]

The new Article 261 of 1926 now provided, "The court may examine any evidence *ex officio* when it is not convinced by the evidence submitted by the parties or when it otherwise deems it necessary." In practice, however, the court's power to adopt an evidential medium not proposed by a party was exercised sparingly. When necessary, the court rather resorted to the power of clarification to suggest to a party to propose a new evidential medium, and the party most likely presented such new medium whenever possible. Thus, the degree of a party's control over an evidential medium was almost as high as, or as low as, that over the factual allegation because the party's control over the factual allegations might be similarly attenuated by exercise of the court's clarification power as explained before. We can say, therefore, that the party's control over the evidential medium was, at least as a matter of principle, well preserved.

However, when we observe the level of evidential information, a party's control was much more restricted or almost nil as to certain evidential media, such as witnesses and experts. In the case of documentary evidence, evidential media and evidential information are inseparably combined because the medium is itself the information it contains. In other words, the production of a document (medium) is also a presentation of the information it conveys. However, in the case of testimonial evidence, different versions of evidential information may be elicited from an identical evidential medium, a particular witness.

In this respect, the pre-1948 code recognized little control by the parties.

When a witness was adopted, it was the presiding judge who was primarily supposed to question the witness and to decide how to question (by way of a continuous narrative or by question and answer). Even the associate judges had to obtain from the presiding judge permission to ask questions. The law expressly stated, "The parties cannot ask questions of a witness. However, a party may apply for permission of the presiding judge to ask in order to clarify the statement of a witness." Therefore, the scope of a party's questioning was limited to that already laid down by the presiding judge. In practice, the party's questioning was not active at all. Moreover, as a matter of legal ethics, as common in all Civil Law jurisdictions, the party and the attorney were not supposed to have contact with a prospective witness in advance. Under such circumstances, it was difficult for a party (attorney) to ask intelligent questions even when allowed to do so.

The postwar reform tried to change this situation as described earlier. In other words, greater party control over evidential information was introduced by changing the main actor of witness questioning from the presiding judge to the party who proposed the witness and by then giving an opportunity to the adversary to cross-examine.[6] The presiding judge had to wait until both parties had finished their questioning. The respective roles of the presiding judge and the parties were completely reversed. In order to make the parties' questioning as effective as possible, the new rules promulgated by the Supreme Court now officially encouraged the parties to interview prospective witnesses.[7]

Thus, a party in Japanese civil litigation was given, at least in theory, complete control over the making of a case, from the presentation of a claim, to factual allegations, and through the elicitation of relevant evidential information from adopted witnesses. This last point is particularly significant in Japan in view of the predominant importance of testimonial evidence in civil litigation there. Precise documentation of commercial or noncommercial transactions is not legally required as in some other Civil Law systems and often such documentation may not even exist. When a dispute arises, therefore, firm documentary evidence is usually scant and the court must rely heavily on testimonial evidence.

IV. INSTITUTIONAL BACKGROUND

Judge Tanabe pointed out how Japanese courts reacted to elements of an adversary system introduced by the postwar procedural reform. As far as the clarification power was concerned, the court was rather quick to return to the prewar solution. I believe that it was inevitable for a conscientious judiciary to do so in view of the two conditions prevailing in the 1950s—first, a large percentage of pro se representation even at the district court level and, second, a bar that had not changed radically from its prewar character. In addition, of course, there was also the strong willingness of judges to give a just solution to each case irrespective of the parties' or their lawyers' performance.

The Japanese Code of Civil Procedure of 1890 was borrowed from the German code of 1877 but the two codes differ on some important points. Chief among these is the fact that the Japanese version did not adopt a system of compulsory representation by a lawyer (*Anwaltszwang*) even at the district court level and above, though this was an integral part of the German code of the time. When a lawyer was retained in Japan, no special license was required for appearing before a higher court including the then-highest court, the Great Court of Judicature (*Daishin'in*). This is the situation still prevailing today in Japan. Litigation involving at least one party without a lawyer, usually the defendant, or even two parties without lawyers was common and can still be seen today. In these circumstances, a conscientious judge would feel compelled to intervene to clarify the factual and legal situation of the dispute in order to determine a just solution. The need to do so would be intense even when only one of the parties was without legal representation.

Even where both parties were represented, judges wanted to intervene and were expected to do so whenever a lawyer's performance was not satisfactory in their eyes. Before the war, judges and lawyers were trained separately and differently. Generally speaking, the qualification and the training of the lawyers were inferior to those of judges. A judge often looked on lawyers with a paternalistic bias.

The postwar professional education reform unified the training of the three branches of legal professions, the judge, prosecutor, and lawyer, and elevated the educational background of all three professions to the same standard. However, as of the 1950s, the lawyers who received the postwar unified training were still young and did not yet form the mainstream of the practicing bar. The judges at the time did not see any necessity to change their attitude toward these practitioners. This condition has completely changed now. As of 2000, all of the practicing lawyers and judges are the product of the postwar professional training at the Legal Training and Research Institute, and, more importantly, a significant change has taken place in which the judges have come to see the lawyers as on a par with themselves.

One element, however, did not change. The number of lawyers and the rate of pro se lawsuits without any lawyer at all, or with a lawyer on one side only, remained constant. Now, the number of lawyers has increased consid-

TABLE 4.1. Representation in Japanese District Court Cases

Year	*Location of district courts*	*Number of cases with no lawyer at all*	*Number of cases with only plaintiff represented*	*Total number of cases*
1960	All of Japan	17,887	17,476	65,157
	Tokyo	1,083	3,209	12,001
	Miyazaki	460	150	820
1998	All of Japan	32,634	54,312	156,683
	Tokyo	5,176	13,950	36,263
	Miyazaki	307	403	1,090
2000	All of Japan	33,988	52,162	158,779

NOTE: At writing, no data were available by cities for the year 2000.

erably. More than eight hundred new lawyers per year have been appearing recently, and the total number of lawyers has exceeded twenty thousand. But these are mostly in the Tokyo and Osaka areas. There are still many civil cases conducted without the help of a lawyer. Table 4.1 shows statistics comparing the situation in 1960 with that of the late 1990s in all district courts, the first instance court of general jurisdiction.

V. WHAT HAS HAPPENED SINCE 1960?

It is in these conditions—some changing, others unchanging—that Japanese civil procedure has developed since the early 1960s when Judge Tanabe's article was written. Several significant events during the intervening period have directly or indirectly affected the way Japanese civil procedure was conducted and eventually provided some stimulus for legislative change. At this point, it must be emphasized that procedural reform cannot be achieved only by changes in the language of law. Procedure must be supported by a massive infrastructure, both tangible and intangible. The failure of the postwar reform can perhaps best be explained from this point of view.

While the basic theoretical structure of the Japanese civil procedure has not changed at all, there have been several important events since the 1960s, each of which has had and is still having a considerable influence on the way Japanese civil procedure operates today. First, there was a reform in Germany in the 1970s, the so-called Stuttgart Model, and ensuing reform by the Simplification Act (*Vereinfachungsnovelle*), which, considering the German origin of modern Japanese civil procedure, had a considerable impact in Japan. Second, the relative position of the judiciary and the bar began to change in the 1970s. The bar gained more confidence and power and, perhaps with a motivation of its own, became more cooperative with the judiciary's effort to streamline and expedite proceedings. Third, public dissatisfaction with the state of civil litigation mounted and, especially in the 1990s after the demise of the bubble economy, politically influential business groups, such as the *Keizaidōyūkai* and *Keidanren*, became interested, perhaps for the first time in Japanese modern history, in the function of civil justice.

All these factors worked to motivate the successful legislation of the new Code of Civil Procedure of 1996. This political driving force continued to give rise to a larger wave that touched all aspects of the basic justice system. Most scholars understand the creation by the Cabinet of the Justice System Reform Council in 1999 in this context also. I shall deal with the first two factors first and then proceed to the litigation practice that has appeared under the new Code of Civil Procedure enforced since 1998.

VI. IMPACT OF THE STUTTGART MODEL

There was a movement in Stuttgart, Germany, to make civil procedure more efficient. Under the initiative of Judge Rolf Bender of the Stuttgart District Court, an innovative method was developed from the 1960s and became widely known as the *Stuttgarter Modell*. It was eventually adopted by legislation in 1977 (*Vereinfachungsnovelle*). Because of its traditional affinity with German law, Japan showed much interest in the new development in Germany. Scholars studied the model, and the judiciary sent some young judges to Germany. A considerable amount of publications followed.

The main feature of the Stuttgart Model was that the judge took initiative in the early stage of litigation to narrow the issues of the case by holding a conference involving not only the attorneys but also the parties in person. In Japan, the preparatory procedure preliminary to a plenary hearing has long been a central subject of the discussion of how best to achieve the expeditious disposition of civil cases. In fact, the Japanese legislative history has been marked by various—but not fruitful—efforts to introduce a more effective preparatory procedure since the 1926 amendment of the Code of Civil Procedure.

In an attempt to make the procedure more regimented and expeditious, the 1926 law made preparatory procedure mandatory and required all possible allegations and evidence to be presented at this stage.[8] All allegations and evidence not mentioned in the record of preparatory procedure were to be permanently excluded unless a good reason was proven.[9] The effort was a total failure. Parties were not ready to present all available allegations and evidence, and the courts were reluctant to strictly enforce the rule of exclusion. The postwar reform changed this slightly. It made the preparatory procedure elective at the discretion of the court but retained the exclusionary rule when the procedure was adopted.[10] The result was the virtual nonuse of preparatory procedure.

We can see in this development the enduring dilemma in Japanese civil procedure: the legislature clearly intended to encourage and expected the parties to participate actively in the process by presenting necessary allegations and evidence on time. Inactive and unprepared parties, often without professional assistance, were not able to live up to the legislative expectation. Judges who wished to do justice under the constriction of the principle of party presentation had to risk a long duration of the process in favor of a substantively just resolution of the dispute. Thus, the so-called May rain type (*samidare-shiki*) proceedings became the norm, in which a long series of short hearings took place over the span of an extended period.

Typically, the first several sessions served a preparatory purpose with exchanges of briefs and the judge's exercise of the clarification power. Thereafter witnesses were heard only one by one in each session of the oral proceedings. Very often, the cross-examination would occur not immediately after the examination in chief, but in the next session a couple of months later. Yet the process of "preparation" would never end. When a new fact arose from testimony, a party was allowed to amend the complaint or raise a new defense. In a sense, as Professor Dan Fenno Henderson once remarked, the first half of the whole process, often taking as long as a couple of years, could still be described as the "discovery" stage. Problems inherent in this type of procedure are evident. The process tends to take a long time. Moreover, judges were not able to make decisions based on a fresh impression of testimony. Also, the presiding judge would often change because of a regular transfer or retirement, and a new judge would have to decide the case solely on the basis of the written record.

Dissatisfaction with this system was widespread, but achieving a remedy was difficult. The experiment in Stuttgart attracted much attention in Japan because it seemed to succeed in radically expediting the process of litigation in Germany, which was also suffering from a similar procedural malaise, though in a much lesser degree. Willing Japanese judges started their own experiments. They tried to create a kind of preparatory procedure that allowed them to determine the real issues at an early stage of the process and schedule concentrated sessions to take testimonies while avoiding the type of preparatory procedure found in the code. What they created was called "*Benronkenwakai*," literally meaning "pleading (*benron*) and settlement (*wakai*) at the same time." Judges held an informal session with the parties (with their attorneys present) to find out which issues the court must decide and if it was possible to achieve a settlement. Sometimes, the judge would place emphasis on achieving a settlement and at other times, on joining the issues. In all cases, an informal session was held, not in the courtroom, but in a closed room reserved for settlement negotiation or preparatory procedure.

The presumed hybrid nature of the device was controversial. If it was a pure settlement negotiation, there was no problem in conducting it in a closed room; but if it was a session for "*benron*," the Constitution mandated that it be held in open court. Complaints were voiced from the bar that the judges risked the danger of "shaping" a case too prematurely. This reaction is understandable because lawyers were accustomed to wait for a "natural ripening" of a case through the May rain type procedure. The new practice required the lawyers to be better prepared at an early stage of litigation.

Despite lack of authorization in the code, this practice became considerably widespread in urban district courts and proved effective for expeditious disposition of cases. The practice was effective not only for bringing complicated cases to a stage where they were ready for witness examination in a relatively short period of preparation, but it was also very useful in inducing an early settlement and thereby relieving the court's heavy caseload.

VII. CONCENTRATION OF WITNESS EXAMINATION

The next step was how to realize a concentrated and efficient witness examination. This was a more difficult task. Here the German model was not as useful because in Germany the judges examine witnesses, while in Japan the parties must do so, and this takes more time. In large cities, each judge was simultaneously in charge of a few hundred cases. Each case would progress only slowly by way of the May rain method. If some cases were given priority and accorded a greater amount of time than the rest of the cases, other cases would be delayed. Some courts reacted to this problem by creating new teams of judges who would specialize in experimentation with more concentrated treatment of cases.

More importantly, cooperation by participating lawyers was essential for successful concentration of witness examination, but most lawyers were reluctant to cooperate because of the preparation time required, though it was still not so onerous as for an American type of trial. Responding to the court's initiative, however, the organized bar made constructive proposals and conferences, and consultations were held between the court and the bar. Meanwhile, increasing numbers of lawyers became willing to cooperate with the venture. This process was a phenomenon that may have been inconceivable to Judge Tanabe when he wrote his article in the early 1960s.

VIII. CHANGING ATTITUDE OF THE BAR

For a long time after the end of the war, the Japanese organized bar took a strong antiestablishment posture. The mainstream of the bar allied itself with the opposition parties (Socialist Party and Communist Party) and was mostly opposed to proposals by the judiciary collectively or by judges individually. This antagonistic relationship prevented both the judiciary and the bar from making constructive proposals for improvement in the practice of civil litigation.

The situation began to change in the 1980s. In my view, there are several factors behind this change. First, those lawyers who had been trained at the postwar Legal Training and Research Institute came to occupy a majority of the leading positions within the organized bar. Second, starting in the 1960s, the bar increasingly attracted eligible young jurists who would previously have gone to the judiciary. This fostered a mutual respect and spirit of cooperation between the judiciary and the bar. Third, the political environment radically changed in 1993 when the so-called 1955 setup collapsed, and the Liberal Democratic Party lost the hegemony. The political polarization that had spawned mutual mistrust between the judiciary and the bar loosened considerably, if it did not disappear altogether.

Study groups formed within major bar associations and many made public proposals for the rationalization of the litigation process. The court welcomed these constructive proposals and criticisms. It was in such an enthusiastic atmosphere that various experimental practices were adopted by willing judges and lawyers in large district courts in Tokyo and Osaka, and finally the Law Revision Commission of the Ministry of Justice started consideration of a total revision of the Code of Civil Procedure in 1989.

IX. INNOVATIONS WITHIN COURTHOUSES

It is also worth noting that there have been some changes in the infrastructure of the court system. Active participation of the court clerks in case management is noteworthy as a strong support for the new mode of case processing. Court clerks long remained in a subordinate and obscure position, responsible only for preparing the court record. The task of case management was considered to be the judge's responsibility. The postwar establishment of the Training Institute for Court Clerks and a rigorous employment policy raised the standard of court clerks considerably.

However, the relationship between the judges and the clerks was not a friendly one, partly because of the strong unionization of the latter. In the wave of this reform movement in civil litigation, some innovative judges started giving greater responsibility to clerks, within the limit of the law. Willing court clerks responded to this new challenge with enthusiasm. For the smooth progress of the litigation process, good coordination among the parties and the judge is essential and a great deal of labor and time is needed to achieve successful preparatory work and concentrated witness examination. Clerks were redefined as "court managers" and became instrumental to successful experiments for innovation.

Another interesting aspect of reform is found in the physical environment of the courtroom. When the new practice of "pleading-settlement" sessions in a closed room was criticized, a real courtroom that was still suitable for an informal session became necessary. The so-called roundtable courtroom was created and implemented in several large courthouses in the late 1980s. These rooms have a large roundtable around which the judge, the clerk, the lawyers, and witnesses all sit at the same level, side -by side. The spectators' section is in the other half of the room, separated by a bar. This type of courtroom is convenient, not only for generating a cooperative atmosphere among the participants, but also to circulate documents easily among them. Such roundtable courtrooms have increased in number considerably since then.

X. THE NEW CODE OF CIVIL PROCEDURE OF 1996

Work for revision of the Code of Civil Procedure was started under the strong leadership of Akira Mikazuki, professor emeritus of the University of Tokyo and the leading figure in the field of civil procedure scholarship. After an unprecedentedly short period of deliberation and drafting, the new code passed the Diet in June 1996 and was enforced beginning January 1, 1998. It is noteworthy that the Division for Civil Procedure of the Law Revision Commission of the Ministry of Justice included for the first time a few eminent lawyers as official members from the very beginning of deliberations. This practice has become widespread today in the legislative process in general.

An overview of the new code is presented in my article in the *American*

Journal of Comparative Law.[11] I will try not to repeat what I have already written there. I would rather limit myself to the aspects of the new code and the practice under it that relate to the theme of an adversary system in Japanese civil procedure.

The practice of the pleading-settlement was not adopted by the new code. Instead, it created three kinds of preparatory procedure. The first type is the preparatory plenary hearing. As mentioned earlier, under the so-called May rain type of procedure, the first several sessions had to function as a preparatory stage for the next testimony-taking stage. The new code formalized this as one type of preparatory procedure.

The second type is the proceeding preparatory to plenary hearing. This is a direct descendant of the former preparatory proceeding and revamped form of the pleading-settlement session. An important change was that it became possible to introduce and officially examine documentary evidence at that stage. Another change was a loosening of the exclusionary effect on allegations and evidence not presented in the preparatory stage. This change was made in light of the past failure to enforce strict exclusion.

The third type is a preparation by documents only, which is designed to accommodate parties in remote places. Practice has proved that the second method is most preferred. This is understandable because the second type was derived from the successful experiment of the pleading-settlement practice.

The new code does not provide much about the concentration of witness examination. It contains a new provision that the examination of witnesses and the parties in person must be held in a concentrated manner "after conclusion of the arrangement of points at issue and evidence."[12] When witness examination begins, documentary exhibits have already been presented and examined by the court, and all parties know the evidential information contained therein.

Another important change brought about by the new code was a reconsideration of the regime for the examination of witnesses that was introduced by the postwar reform. As mentioned before, the postwar code mandated that the party who presents a witness must conduct the initial examination of that witness, and this must be followed by an opportunity for cross-examination by the adversary. As a rule, the judge can ask questions only after both parties have finished. A famous remark by Professor Tōichirō Kigawa, an eminent proceduralist, criticized this as "the worst error in postwar legal reform."[13] The unsatisfactory result of this procedure is well known. The new code made it possible for the judge to change the order of examination. It is now possible for the judge to start the questioning, with the agreement of the parties.[14]

As I have pointed out, however, even before the amendment, when faced with parties who were not represented by a lawyer, a judge would often question a witness first by relying on the provision that allowed the judge to "ask a question at any time when necessary."[15] It does not seem, however, that judges exercise this initiative under the new code in ordinary cases where both parties are represented by a lawyer. All Japanese lawyers who have trained or practiced in the past fifty years are now more or less accustomed to the art of examining witnesses.

XI. PRACTICE UNDER THE NEW CODE

Now we must ask how much has actually been achieved with this statutory framework during the time since the enforcement of the new code in 1998. As I emphasized in my previous article on the new code, litigation practice is always difficult to change. The history of modern Japanese civil procedure is full of examples of failures to attain an intended objective. The failure of the preparatory procedure of the 1926 amendment, the unsuccessful abolishment of clarification power, and the imposition of the heavy task of witness examination on untrained parties are all examples.

But these mistakes can teach us lessons about how difficult procedural reform is in practice unless both judges and lawyers accept the change. Innovative movements before and during the drafting of the 1996 code gave hope to many that the new code would be successfully enforced as planned. When I wrote my article in 1997 before the actual enforcement of the new code, however, I was not very optimistic. I noted that there was a sort of enthusiasm for reform, but I was apprehensive about how long the enthusiasm could last and whether it would fade away before establishing a new standard. I am glad to report that my experience of these past four years has been encouraging.

Judge Takahisa Fukuda of the Tokyo District Court recently reported on the changes taking place in his court.[16] He served as one of the presiding civil judges of this large court from a year before the enforcement of the code and for four years thereafter. He describes the change as "dramatic," and he notes that the present practice looks as if it were "practice in a foreign country" when compared with the situation before. According to Judge Fukuda, litigation in Tokyo is "becoming among the fastest in the world." The greatest factor accounting for this change, he says, is the changing attitude of the practicing lawyers. They are now better prepared for and more responsive to the need for speedy disposition of cases. A questionnaire survey within the Tokyo District Court in June 2000 showed that concentrated witness exam-

TABLE 4.2. Average Duration, in Months, of Case Litigation in Nationwide District Courts 1991–2000

Year	1991	1992	1993	1994	1995	1996	1997	1998	1999	2000
Months	12.2	10.9	10.1	9.8	10.1	10.2	10.0	9.3	9.2	8.8

ination (at least two witnesses examined on the same day) was practiced in virtually all cases.[17] Remember that examination of only one witness per day was the previous norm. This requires a great amount of preparation on the part of lawyers, but it also greatly reduces the duration of litigation.

Judge Fukuda does not mention the situation in many other courts than in Tokyo, but a similar report was made about the situation in the Osaka District Court after only one year of enforcement of the new code.[18] Table 4.2 presents national statistics showing the considerable shortening of the duration of first-instance litigation in district courts nationwide.

Supposedly, local courts are slower to change because of the traditional attitudes of those in the bar (more aged lawyers), the smaller caseload of the court (less pressure to expedite), and the greater percentage of lawyerless litigation (general inefficiency).

Active participation by the parties in an early stage of litigation becomes possible when the parties have advance access to likely evidence (evidential media). In the previous May rain type of procedure, a long time was spent for the unintended purpose of discovery. Viewed that way, it was not entirely meaningless for a judge to wait until a case had matured, under the principle of party presentation, before giving a just decision.

When the whole process is expedited and witness examination is concentrated, there emerges a variance between the provided evidential information and factual allegation based on specific legal theory developed by pleadings. Under the previous May rain practice, such variance could be readily corrected by an amendment of pleading because the proceedings were supposed to be continuing anyway. How and whether this problem is solved under the typical present practice in Tokyo as just described is an interesting question.

XII. ACCESS TO EVIDENCE

One of the major points emphasized in the legislation of the new code was improvement in the methods of collecting evidence. As a result, the availability of document production orders was expanded, but this is still a far cry from American discovery. In short, what was limited to only three specific categories of document has now been enlarged to include all kinds of documents, with some specific exceptions.[19] Some of these exceptions and their interpretations by the courts are very controversial. But it is a widely accepted view among Japanese lawyers today that the document production order has become much more available under the new code than it was before. In practice, the party holding a document will normally comply with a judge's informal request during the preparatory procedure. This is because the parties know that the judge is ready and able to issue a production order if necessary.

It has also become a common practice to produce statements for all prospective witnesses in advance. When a lawyer is retained, the lawyer normally interviews and assists witnesses for the purpose of drafting such a statement. Lawyers are encouraged to do this at the stage of preparatory procedure in order to agree on the issues and witnesses to be examined. Both the judge and the parties will know of all available documentary evidential media, including those produced by force of a production order, by the close of preparatory procedure. This is because documents may be officially produced and examined by the court during preparatory procedure. Thus, if both parties (i.e., their attorneys) are diligent, the concentrated witness examination that follows will not create much variance.

XIII. CLARIFICATION AND DISCUSSION

An expedited and yet substantively just solution of disputes depends on a successful preparatory procedure. Therefore, the preparatory stage may take longer than before, and the judge's role in this stage will become more important. The judge's power of clarification should be efficiently exercised and a serious and lively discussion should be held between the judge and lawyers on the legal theories and the facts to be proved. This procedure has long been considered ideal in order to reach a just result. In order to expedite the process, a judge's exercise of the clarification power can be made by fax at any time. Previously, this power could be exercised only at a formal meeting.

In the past, when a judge exercised his clarification power, he would be criticized as too authoritarian and imposing. Unprepared and less competent lawyers often voiced this criticism. If well prepared and competent, a lawyer will engage in a debate with the judge in order to correct any misunderstanding on the part of the judge. It is still worth asking how best to realize this ideal situation in the Tokyo District Court today.

I am still not too optimistic. But from what has been written and spoken, I think that the new code has made a good start. In my view, this is the first time in the history of Japanese civil procedure that an elevated general standard of the Japanese bar has played a crucial role in putting the legislative objective into practice. We should also remember that representative members of the bar were included in the drafting of the new code and that their opinions were incorporated here and there in the new code.

XIV. CONCLUSION

The main theme of Judge Tanabe's article forty years ago was how to evaluate the development of the adversary system in Japan. Judge Tanabe suggested that the best direction for the Japanese civil procedure would be a "middle way" between Common Law procedure and Civil Law procedure. I would like to conclude this short essay by saying that his ideal is being realized, at least in part. In order to spread the practices currently found in large cities throughout the entire country, we need more lawyers and more judges. Unless we can minimize pro se litigation, if we allow it to exist at all, the innovation occurring typically in Tokyo will not become the Japanese standard.

A large-scale reform of the justice system is being planned and has already been realized in part along the lines of proposals made by the Justice System Reform Council in June 2001. The future of the Japanese civil procedure can now be considered only in the context of the reforms yet to come.[20]

NOTES

1. Kohji Tanabe, "The Processes of Litigation: An Experiment with the Adversary System," in Arthur Taylor von Mehren, ed., *Law in Japan: The Legal Order in a Changing Society* (Cambridge, MA: Harvard University Press, 1963), 110.

2. For a comparison of these systems, see Yasuhei Taniguchi, "Between Verhandlungsmaxime and Adversary System—in Search for Place of Japanese Civil Procedure," in Peter Gottwald and Hanns Prütting, eds., *Festschrift für Karl Heinz Schwab zum 70. Geburtstag* (Munich: Beck, 1990), 487–501.

3. Minji soshōhō [Code of Civil Procedure (before the 1926 amendment)], art. 274.

4. Minji soshōhō (before the 1926 amendment), art. 285.

5. Minji soshōhō (before 1996), arts. 258, 259; Minji soshōhō (before 1948), art. 261.

6. Minji soshōhō (after 1948), art. 294, ¶¶ 1, 2.

7. Rules for Continuous Hearing in Minji soshō (of 1950), art. 2.

8. Minji soshōhō (of 1926), art. 249.

9. Minji soshōhō (of 1926), art. 255.

10. Minji soshōhō (after 1948), arts. 249, 255.

11. Yasuhei Taniguchi, "The 1996 Code of Civil Procedure of Japan—a Procedure for the Coming Century?" *American Journal of Comparative Law* 45 (1997): 767.

12. Minji soshōhō [New Code of Civil Procedure], art. 182.

13. Tōichirō Kigawa, "Sengo saidai no erā—Kōgo jinmon no dōnyū" [Adoption of Cross-Examination System: The Greatest Post-War Error], *Hanrei taimuzu* 400 (1980): 96.

14. Minji soshōhō (new code), art. 202, ¶ 2.

15. Minji soshōhō (before 1996), art. 294, ¶ 3.

16. Takahisa Fukuda, "Minji soshō no atarashii jitsumu" [New Practice of Civil Litigation], *Hanrei taimuzu* 1077 (2002): 26.

17. *Hanrei jihō* 1735 (2001): 28.

18. Takahisa Fukuda, "Shinpojiumu shinminji soshō no ichinen o furikaette" [Symposium: Looking Back on One Year of the New Code of Civil Procedure], *Hanrei taimuzu* 1007 (1999): 37, 49, 52.

19. Minji soshōhō (new code), art. 220.

20. For developments after 2001, see Yasuhei Taniguchi, "Development of Civil Procedure in Japan: An Experiment to Fuse Civil Law and Common Law," in *Studia in Honorem Németh János* (Budapest, Hungary: ELTE, 2003), 835–54; and Taniguchi, "Japan's Recent Civil Procedure Reform: Its Seeming Success and Left Problems," in Nicolo Trocker and Vincenzo Varano, eds., *The Reforms of Civil Procedure in Comparative Perspective* (Turin, Italy: Giappichelli Editore, 2005), 91–113.

5 The Japanese Judiciary

Maintaining Integrity, Autonomy, and the Public Trust

JOHN O. HALEY

Japanese judges are among the most honest, politically independent, and professionally competent in the world today. Organized as an autonomous national bureaucracy, the judiciary comprises a small, largely self-regulating cadre of elite legal professionals who enjoy with reason an extraordinarily high level of public trust. The vast majority of judges begin their careers in their mid-to-late twenties upon graduation from the court-administered Legal Training and Research Institute (LTRI).[1] Most spend a professional life of thirty to forty years within the nationwide structure of courts that they themselves administer. Assignments and promotions are determined by a central personnel office staffed by peers. (This feature of the judiciary is shared by nearly all public and private organizations of appreciable size in Japan, including all major business enterprises as well as the national ministries and the procuracy.) Coupled with a jurisprudential approach that favors certainty and consistency, the Japanese judiciary is by nearly all accounts cautiously conservative. Yet paradoxically, judges play an activist role in the development of legal norms, filling lacunae left by legislative and administrative inaction.[2] With less irony than may appear at first glance, they have also become a target of criticism for failure to participate more fully in Japanese governance through progressive judicial policy making.

My aim in this chapter is first to describe the judiciary and its exemplary features. I begin with the structure and organization of the courts and the career paths of regular judges. An examination of the Supreme Court follows, focusing on its dual roles at the apex of the judicial hierarchy as a constitutional court as well as the court of last resort for all appeals. The core of this chapter, however, is an evaluation of two of the most significant features of the Japanese judiciary: its extraordinary record of integrity and its equally remarkable record of political independence. I should emphasize at the outset that judicial independence as defined in Japan does not mean the freedom of individual judges from any internal control or influence within the judiciary except through formal processes for judicial review. This sort of "judicial autonomy" cannot exist in Japan. Career judges are, as detailed below, members of a largely self-governing elite bureaucracy in which all are mentored and monitored by seniors and peers.

I. STRUCTURE AND ORGANIZATION OF THE COURTS

Japan has a unitary judicial system. At the first of the four tiers of courts are the 438 summary courts (*kan'i saibansho*), staffed by 806 summary court judges. Summary courts handle civil cases involving claims of nine hundred thousand yen (approximately eight thousand U.S. dollars) or less and minor criminal offenses for which the penalty is limited to a fine or brief imprisonment. Summary court adjudication requires only a single judge. Summary court judges are not career judges. Qualification as a regular judge is not required. Instead, summary court judges are formally nominated for pro forma Cabinet appointment by a special selection committee formally comprising all Supreme Court justices, the president (*chōkan*) of the Tokyo High Court, the deputy procurator general, representatives of the bar, and others "with special knowledge and experience."[3] Most summary court judges are in fact well known to the judiciary. The majority have served previously as administrative secretaries or clerks within the court system or as career judges or prosecutors. After reaching their respective mandatory retirement ages (sixty-five for judges; sixty-three for prosecutors), they have sought to add several more years of judicial service, the mandatory retirement age for summary court judges being seventy.

At the second tier are the district courts (*chihō saibansho*), the principal courts of first instance. There are 50 district courts with an additional 203 branches. Except for minor cases, which account for 80–90 percent of all adjudicated cases, trials require a three-judge panel. There is no civil or criminal jury (although, as of this writing, a system is being planned to include lay judges, along with professional judges, in some criminal cases). Sitting alone or as a panel, judges decide all issues of fact and law and must in all judgments write a full statement of findings of fact and application of law. The district courts also have an appellate function with respect to civil judgments and rulings from summary courts. Criminal judgments are appealed directly to a high court. Because the first, or *kōso*, appeal under Japanese procedure can involve a de novo trial of the facts, the district courts are in effect trial courts in all cases.

Paralleling the district courts is an equal number of family courts (*katei saibansho*) with jurisdiction over domestic relations, succession, and juvenile offenses. Unlike other courts in Japan, the principal actors of the family courts are not judges or other legal professionals but rather lay conciliators (*chōtei'in*) appointed by the Supreme Court. Most are socially prominent members of the community. Many are women. Some are law graduates. A few are distinguished scholars. They generally serve for many years, much longer than any of the career judges assigned to the court. Except for more serious juvenile offenses and contested issues in domestic relations and succession cases, family court proceedings are in effect discussions between the conciliators and the parties intended to produce settlement.

Above the district courts are Japan's eight high courts (*kōtō saibansho*), located from northeast to southwest in Sapporo, Sendai, Tokyo, Nagoya, Osaka, Takamatsu, Hiroshima, and Fukuoka, with six branches in Akita, Kanazawa, Okayama, Matsue, Miyazaki, and Naha. The high courts are appellate courts for either *kōso* appeals from district court judgments, criminal judgments from summary courts, or, in civil cases tried initially in summary courts, second (*jōkoku*) appeals limited to issues of law.

With 953 separate summary, district, family, and high courts (including branch courts), in addition to the 120 plus judges assigned each year to the administrative offices of the Supreme Court in Tokyo,[4] Japan's 1,393 career judges and 621 assistant judges are spread very thinly throughout the nation. Some of the branch court positions are not filled, but no district court has fewer than seven judges. The number assigned to each court varies in relationship to the district caseload. Not surprisingly, the Tokyo District Court is the largest. A third of the Tokyo District Court judges are assigned to the criminal division and two-thirds to the civil division. With less than half the number of judges as Tokyo, the Osaka District Court is still Japan's second largest court. Together, those two courts handle more than half of all civil and criminal cases in the entire nation. However, neither Tokyo nor Osaka has the highest rate of litigation per capita. That honor goes to the Oita District Court in Kyushu, along with Tottori in the southwestern part of Honshu. These two regions have long had the highest litigation rates in Japan and have as a consequence nearly twice the number of judges relative to the districts' population as courts in districts with significantly less litigation per capita, particularly the Tohoku region in northeastern Honshu. In 2002, for example, the Oita District Court had seventeen judges (including those assigned to branch courts) in a district of 1.28 million persons, amounting to one judge for every 75,000 persons. In comparison, the Fukushima District Court had nineteen judges for a district of 2.13 million persons, yielding a ratio of one judge per 112,000 persons. Similarly, the number of judges assigned to branch district courts varies from twenty-eight for the Hachioji branch of the Tokyo District Court (with an additional eight judges assigned to the Hachioji branch family court) to the forty-two branch district courts without a permanently assigned judge and the seventy-seven branches with only one judge.[5]

At the apex of the judicial hierarchy is the fifteen-justice Supreme Court (*Saikō saibansho*). As described in greater detail below, no regular career judge as such sits on the court, but by convention from five to six of the justices are former career judges who have retired or reached retirement age.

The caseload for lower court judges is enormous. On average the 1,700 regular and assistant judges assigned to district courts dispose of over 283 civil, administrative, and criminal first instance trial cases per judge per year.[6] If one includes all civil actions, including bankruptcy, business reorganization, and civil execution, the number of dispositions per judge triples. Three-quarters of all cases are civil suits adjudicated by three-judge panels, meaning that judges assigned to civil cases actually deal with an even greater caseload. No summary judgment procedures exist. Furthermore all lawsuits filed are either settled or pursued through trial to judgment; as mentioned above, all judgments must include both the judges' findings of fact and application of law. Under such circumstances, judicial management and the efficient disposition of cases are given considerable priority over other matters, including the appropriate direction of a particular legal doctrine or nationwide uniformity of judgments in like cases. Judges of course consider such issues, along with the social consequences of the courts' interpretation of particular legal rules and principles, but these are rarely more than minor concerns.

II. CAREER PATHS

A judicial career begins with entry to the LTRI on the basis of Japan's highly competitive national judicial examination (*shihō shiken*). The previously two-year but now year-and-a-half program includes assignment to both the criminal and civil divisions of a district court, a district court prosecutor's office, and a law firm, in addition to two extended periods of classroom lectures and exercises, conducted at the institute in Tokyo. Recruitment of new judges is begun at the institute by career judges who participate in the program as instructors or mentors to the apprentices. Upon graduation those interested in a judicial career apply to the Supreme Court for appointment as assistant judges. Although the Cabinet formally makes appointments from a list of nominees presented by the Supreme Court,[7] selection is actually made by the central personnel bureau of the Court's secretariat, which prepares the list. Assistant judges are appointed to ten-year terms. At the end of those ten years, they are eligible for appointment as full judges, again for another ten-year term. Reappointment is routine. The vast majority continue to serve until they reach retirement age at sixty-five. (Mandatory retirement for both Supreme Court justices and summary court judges is at age seventy.)

To give some sense of the typical career patterns of judges, let us briefly examine the seventy-one judges who were appointed in 1970 (the twenty-second class of the LTRI). In 1996, twenty-six years later, fifty-three of those seventy-one (74.6 percent) were still on the bench, with three of those fifty-three serving as research judges or in nonjudicial administrative posts and one as a summary court judge after having reached mandatory retirement age as a regular judge. Another career judge had reached mandatory retirement age but had not continued to work as a lawyer or summary court judge. One was deceased. All of the remaining career judges who had left the bench before mandatory retirement age had gone into private practice, five having served from one to ten years; five, eleven to twenty years; and four, over twenty years.[8] Incidentally, two judges serving in 1996 had become judges after twenty plus years of active practice as attorneys.

Only two judges have ever been denied reappointment, although a few others may have resigned in anticipation that they would be terminated if they did not. The best-known case involved Assistant Judge Yasuaki Miyamoto, about whom I will have more to say below. The other was a judge who refused for family reasons to accept a routine transfer.[9] In no case did the Cabinet make this decision. In each instance senior judges assigned to the Supreme Court's General Secretariat decided not to include the judge on the list presented to the Cabinet for reappointment.

Japan's career judges staff all of Japan's district and high courts as well as the principal administrative offices necessary for the management of the entire judicial branch, including the senior administrative positions in the General Secretariat. In addition, about thirty research judges (*chōsakan*) are appointed from the senior ranks of the career judiciary to assist the Supreme Court. All career judges are subject to assignment to courts nationwide, usually for a period of three years for each post. When newly appointed as assistant judges, nearly all are assigned for an initial period of two years to either the Tokyo or Osaka District Court or a district court in another large metropolitan area, such as Nagoya, Fukuoka, or Sapporo. As a regular judge the three-year assignments continue to various courts initially throughout the country but often later within a particular region, such as the Kanto region around Tokyo, or Kansai and western Japan. A career judge will typically serve two or three times on a major district court, one or more family courts, and perhaps a rural branch court, as well as a high court. Many will also spend time in Tokyo at the Supreme Court, with an administrative or research assignment, returning as a senior judge to a family or district court or as presiding judge for the court. The position of *chōkan* (chief judge or president) of a high court is the highest post a career judge can hold during a regular judicial career. As noted below, a handful of retired career judges are appointed to the Supreme Court. Nearly all of them have been *chōkan* of either the Tokyo or Osaka High Court at the time of their retirement from the regular judiciary.

The career paths of Japanese judges follow stable patterns. As noted above, Japanese judges do not simply move upward in a hierarchy of courts. Rather, they spiral upward in terms of positions, but they serve multiple times in courts at all levels, from junior positions at the district court level on up. At mid career a judge may already have served not only several times in district and family courts but also on a high court, in an administrative post in Tokyo or in a research position as *chōsakan* at the Supreme Court. Assigned to an administrative post in the General Secretariat, three years later he or she could be assigned back to the district level as head of a civil or criminal division and, following that, perhaps to the position of presiding judge. A favorable career path for an ambitious young judge would include multiple assignments in Tokyo in the General Secretariat. A presiding judgeship toward the end of a career in a more remote family court, followed by a presiding judgeship with a less remote district court, is evidence of a normal but still favorable progression of advancement.

Returning to the sample of judges who graduated from the LTRI in 1970, nearly all began as assistant judges with a two-year district court assignment followed by a three-year family court assignment, this being a standard pattern after 1965. (Until 1966, as a rule, assistant judges served their first term in a family court and then three years later were assigned to a district court.[10]) As of 1995, twenty-five years after their graduation from the LTRI, nearly half of the fifty-three judges who remained active were the presiding judge of a family court (nine) or presided over or headed a division of a district court (fourteen). A year later seven more members of their class had been appointed to similar positions. This pattern of spiraling assignments ensures the continuous and pervasive influence of senior judges as monitors and mentors throughout the judicial system.

The combination of a central personnel office responsible for recruiting, mentoring, assigning, and promoting all career judges with this system of periodic spiraling assignments to courts throughout the country appears to be unique to Japan and South Korea.[11] No judicial system in Europe or North America, not even Japan's closest model, that of Germany,[12] shares either of these two features. In Japan, this organizational structure is typical. The judiciary is by no means exceptional. Nearly all private and public organizations have these organizational features in common. In the United States, at least, the closest equivalent is the military services. Only within such a structure, however, could the autonomy and coherence of Japan's courts be achieved.

III. THE SUPREME COURT

The Supreme Court functions, as do supreme courts in the United States, as both a constitutional court and court of last resort for ordinary appeals. Unlike the United States Supreme Court and most state supreme courts in the United States, however, the Supreme Court of Japan does not exercise any significant discretion over its docket. The losing parties' right to a second *jōkoku* appeal extends to all cases. Thus the right of appeal to the Supreme Court applies in all cases except those that commenced in a summary court, for which a high court would adjudicate a second appeal. Until 1998, the Supreme Court lacked any discretionary control over appeals in civil cases. Not surprisingly, that resulted in a staggering caseload; Japan's justices had to review and decide over four thousand civil, administrative, and criminal cases each year. The new Code of Civil Procedure, which became effective in 1998, does allow the Supreme Court as well as high courts adjudicating *jōkoku* appeals to refuse to hear appeals in cases not involving constitutional issues where, from the record, an appeal is determined to be unfounded.[13] Since 1998 the Court had been able to reduce the number of cases it reviews fully to about 165 civil and a few criminal cases each year. For example, as to civil cases raising only nonconstitutional issues of law, in 2002 the Supreme Court accepted and rendered opinions on the issue of law in only 85 cases; it declined to review 2,286 cases without giving an opinion on the issue of law. Thus, even under the new system, the Supreme Court does at least utter a last word in all cases and on a wide range of issues of law.

Except for constitutional cases the Court rarely decides cases en banc. Most cases are decided by one of the three petty benches, each with five justices, into which the court is divided and to which cases are assigned in sequence.[14] This means that each justice is generally responsible for reviewing about thirteen hundred cases annually. The number of appeals the Court must review remains a major problem that reduces the quality of its decisions.

The Supreme Court is today among the most autonomous constitutional or highest regular courts in the industrial world, despite the enormous potential for at least indirect political or electorate influence. Appointments to the court are formally among Japan's most politically significant. The chief justice is ostensibly nominated by the Cabinet with ceremonial appointment by the emperor and is accorded the same rank and salary as the prime minister. The other fourteen justices have equal rank and salary as ministers of state and are appointed by the Cabinet. The statutory requirements for Supreme Court justices are broadly worded. Article 41 of the 1947 Court Organization Act[15] provides:

> Justices of the Supreme Court shall be appointed from among persons of broad vision and extensive knowledge of law, who are not less than forty years of age. At least ten of them shall be persons who have held one or two of the positions mentioned in item (i) or (ii) for not less than ten years, or one or more positions mentioned in the following items for a total period of twenty years or more:
>
> (i) President (*chōkan*) of a high court
> (ii) Judge
> (iii) Summary court judge
> (iv) Public prosecutor
> (v) Lawyer
> (vi) Professor or assistant professor in law in universities as determined separately by statute.

The pool of qualified persons as defined by statute is extraordinarily large. Hence the potential for political appointments is equally great. Yet not since the first justices were selected have party or Cabinet-level political considerations influenced even the appointment of the chief justice. Rather, just as senior procurators and bar leaders determine who among their respective cohorts will be eligible to be nominated, so too senior career judges who administer the judiciary largely determine who among soon-to-retire career judges will become a Supreme Court justice or which sitting justice will become the chief justice.

Illustrative is the Mainichi Shinbun Social Affairs Bureau account of the appointment of Ryōhachi Kusaba as Japan's twelfth chief justice in February 1990.[16] Two months before the appointment, soon-to-retire Chief Justice Kōichi Yaguchi visited the official residence of the then prime minister Toshiki Kaifu. The purpose was to inform the prime minister of the judiciary's choice for his replacement, a choice made with the participation of the principal administrators of the judicial branch—all of whom were career judges themselves. Kaifu did not object. As one official is quoted to have said (translated into idiomatic English): "We wouldn't have the vaguest idea who anyone they might suggest was, and we wouldn't have any way of finding out whether they would be suitable. The Supreme Court people have researched this. We trust their judgment."[17] A similar procedure has been followed in the appointment of every chief justice since 1962.

To date, all but four of Japan's fifteen chief justices, including all chief justices since 1978, have themselves been career judges.[18] Only one lawyer has held the post of chief justice (Ekizō Fujibayashi, who was appointed in 1976), and only one prosecutor (Masao Okahara, who followed Fujibayashi the next year, in 1977). Two University of Tokyo law professors (Kōtarō Tanaka and Kisaburō Yokota) were appointed back-to-back as the second and third chief justices in 1950 and 1960. The remaining eleven have all been career judges. Moreover, all had previously held high-level administrative posts within the General Secretariat. In fact, two of the past five chief justices previously held the judiciary's highest administrative post, the position of secretary general (*Saikōsai jimu sōchō*).[19]

Well-defined appointment patterns are found not just in the case of chief justices, but all Supreme Court justices. By convention, at least a third of all justices are appointed from the career judiciary, with another third from the practicing bar and up to five of the fifteen from among other persons of "attainment in their profession with knowledge of law." Between 1947 and July 2003, 123 persons had served as justice. Of these, forty-eight had been career judges,[20] thirty-nine practicing lawyers, thirteen prosecutors, twelve other career government officials, and nine (or ten, depending on one's interpretation, as discussed below) legal scholars. These categories are well defined and, with rare exceptions, are followed with respect to successor appointments, with judge replacing judge, for example, and lawyer replacing lawyer.

Within each category, moreover, appointments follow remarkably well-defined patterns. Looking first at the judiciary, of the forty-eight career judges who were appointed to the Supreme Court, forty-three were serving as president of a high court at the time of appointment. Of these, twenty were from the Tokyo High Court, fifteen from the Osaka High Court, four from the Nagoya High Court, and four from the Fukuoka High Court. Excluding the first appointments in 1947, which included three former Great Court of Cassation justices and one former councilor of the Administrative Court, only three career judges have ever been appointed to the Court who were not serving at the time of appointment as the president of one of the four principal high courts. Several in fact were transferred from the presidency of one of the apparently lesser high courts—Hiroshima, Sapporo, Sendai, and Takamatsu—to the Tokyo or Osaka High Court immediately before appointment to the Supreme Court. Many of the career judges also had held major administrative posts within the Supreme Court's General Secretariat.

Just as the careers of justices appointed from the career judiciary follow rather fixed patterns, so too do the careers of those appointed from the practicing bar and even other appointees. Of the thirty-nine lawyers who have served on the Court as of this writing, nineteen were former bar association presidents or vice presidents, with most coming from either the Tokyo or Osaka region. All of the thirteen prosecutors appointed to the Court were serving at the time of their appointment as the chief or superintending prosecutor for a high court (nine) or the deputy chief prosecutor for the Supreme Court (three).[21] Five of the twelve career government officials appointed were former diplomats; all were former ambassadors, who rose through the ranks of the Foreign Affairs Ministry and had held influential and prestigious administrative posts within the ministry. Five more of the government officials held the post of chief of the Cabinet Legislation Bureau (*Naikaku hōsei kyoku*) or similar agency attached to one of the houses of the Diet at the time of their appointment. The remaining two former government officials are both women. The first woman to serve on the Court was Hisako Takahashi, a career Ministry of Labor official. The second was Kazuko Yokoo, a career Health and Welfare Ministry official. (Justice Yokoo is the only justice without a law degree. She is a 1964 graduate of the International Christian University [ICU], an American-styled liberal arts college without a law faculty or law major.)

The final major category of justices is legal scholars. Their prior careers have been almost as predictable as the other justices. All have been members of Japan's academic elite. All but two had spent their academic careers as members of the law faculty of either the University of Tokyo (five) or Kyoto University (two). The two exceptions were Kyushu University professor Matasuke Kawamura, one of the initial appointments to the Court in 1947, and Tohoku University law professor Tokiyasu Fujita, appointed in autumn 2002. Itsuo Sonobe, who served on the Court from 1989 to April 1997 and who was included above among the forty-eight career judges, could also be included in the list of Kyoto University faculty appointments. Sonobe is one of the most interesting and exceptional appointments. After serving on the Kyoto University Law Faculty for fourteen years, he resigned his teaching post to become a judge. After fifteen years as a judge (including positions at the family, district, and high court levels, as well as serving as a research judge [*chōsakan*] at the Supreme Court), he returned to teaching for four years at Seikei University prior to his appointment as justice.

A common feature of all these appointment patterns is the absence of partisan or other political influence on Supreme Court appointments. As noted previously, the presidency of a high court is the highest position a career judge can attain within the regular judiciary. From start to finish—including appointment to the Supreme Court—a judge's career advancement is determined initially by senior judges and at the end by judicial peers, not agencies, political or otherwise, outside of the courts.

The appointments of lawyers, prosecutors, diplomats, even scholars, and the handful of career administrative officials have followed similarly predictable patterns. Most have achieved elite status within their respective career or professional organizations. Only two have had significant career mobility.[22] Sonobe, as noted, was exceptional. Another exception was Shunzō Kobayashi, who, although serving as president of the Tokyo High Court at the time of his appointment, had spent most of his professional life as a practicing attorney. It bears note that Kobayashi also served as president of the Second Tokyo Bar Association; the predominance of former bar officials exemplifies the influence of the bar itself rather than political leaders on which attorneys are selected to become justices.

Even with regard to appointments from the civil and diplomatic bureaucracies, which are among the most political in any other country, in Japan political considerations appear to have been secondary to a purely bureaucratic concern to reward those who have served the institution and themselves well. As noted above, all five of the former diplomats were former ambassadors who also had held important administrative posts within the Ministry of Foreign Affairs. Five of the former administrative officials were at the time of their appointment serving in one of Japan's most politically neutral and prestigious administrative posts, as head of the Cabinet Legislation Bureau or its Diet equivalent. Even the two exceptions adhere to a pattern. Both were women.

In short, for those justices who were career judges, the recommendations to the prime minister have been based on evaluations by their peers within the judiciary; for those justices who were not career judges, the recommendations to the prime minister have been based on consultations with the leaders of the major bar associations and senior levels of the procuracy and other government bureaucracies. There is no evidence of any partisan party consideration, however negligible. Instead, internal competition within each of these separate career organizations has determined the appointment. No evidence exists of any direct political lobbying even with respect to the scholars who have been appointed to the Court.

Nor has political change significantly affected the Court and these patterns of appointment. Nine justices were appointed between 1993 and 1995, following the political upheaval that ended nearly four decades of single-party rule in Japan. The Hosokawa Cabinet (August 1993–April 1994) appointed four—Hideo Chikusa, Shigeharu Negishi, Hisako Takahashi, and Yukinobu Ozaki. The Murayama Cabinet (June 1994–January 1996), the Liberal Democratic Party (LDP)–Social Democratic Party (former Socialist Party) coalition, appointed five—Shin'ichi Kawai, Mitsuo Endō, Kazutomo Ijima, Hiroshi Fukuda, and Masao Fujii. Of the two career judges, one, Chikusa, had been secretary general of the Supreme Court, and the other, Fujii, the president of the Osaka High Court. One of the two prosecutors, Negishi, was superintending prosecutor for the Tokyo High Court at the time of his appointment. The other, Ijima, was deputy procurator general. All three of the practicing attorneys appointed, Ozaki, Kawai, and Endō, had been the president or vice president of their respective bar associations in Tokyo or Osaka as well as directors of the Japan Federation of Bar Associations. Fukuda, a diplomat, had held a series of influential administrative posts within the Ministry of Foreign Affairs. The only apparent change in the composition of the court and pattern of appointments was the appointment, as noted, of Japan's first woman justice—Hisako Takahashi. Socialist prime ministers too, it appears, appoint those recommended by senior judges and the legal and bureaucratic establishments. Indeed, the Murayama Cabinet also elevated Justice Tōru Miyoshi, one of the most conservative members of the Court, from associate justice to chief justice.

Predictability in the pattern of Court appointments is furthered by another pattern. A balance between the two leading national law faculties is attempted, albeit not always perfectly maintained. In 2002, for example, six justices were

Kyoto University law graduates and six were University of Tokyo law graduates. One was a Chuo University law graduate, and one a Nagoya University law graduate. (As noted, Justice Yokoo is an ICU liberal arts college graduate.) A year later five justices had retired. All were Kyoto graduates. They were replaced by two Kyoto graduates, two Tokyo graduates, and one Chuo graduate—still a perfect balance in appointments, although regrettably not outcome.

The age of the justices and thus their brief tenure on the Court is another striking feature of the composition of the Court. Since 1952 only two persons under sixty years of age have ever been appointed to the Court, Jirō Tanaka and Ken'ichi Okuno, both of whom were fifty-eight. Only two were sixty. Thus only four of the 123 postwar justices will have served ten or more years. No one has served more than a dozen years, and, as of this writing, no person born after December 7, 1941, has ever been a member of Japan's highest court. Nor until 1990 was anyone appointed who received his or her legal education in postwar Japan. Among the fifteen justices on the Court today (June 2003) only one, Hiroshi Fukuda, was on the Court before 1997. This short tenure also necessarily implies rapid turnover. Between March and November 2002 five justices reached seventy and were required to retire. Thus a turnover of over a third of the Court occurred within just nine months.

In sum, appointments to the Supreme Court reflect persistent adherence to well-established patterns of selection in which leadership—especially an influential administrative post—in one of five or six career organizations has become in effect a customary prerequisite. As such Supreme Court appointments evidence an extraordinary degree of insulation from partisan political influence. Senior judges, senior prosecutors, and bar association leaders, as officials and leading administrators in their respective professional organizations—not politicians—determine who from their respective organizations will become eligible for appointment. One can predict with remarkable certainly the composition of the tiny pool of potential nominees. Judges will replace judges and thus if a former career judge on the Court retires, his or her most likely replacement will be a recently appointed president to the Tokyo or Osaka High Court. If the retiring justice was a practicing attorney when appointed, look to the officers of the Japan Federation of Bar Associations for his or her replacement. And, if the retiring justice was from Osaka, then bet on the president or vice president of the Osaka Bar Association, or if from Tokyo, then an officer in one of the three Tokyo bar associations.

One recent study, by David O'Brien and Yasuo Ohkoshi,[23] emphasizes the influence of the chief justice and Court's secretary general. Neither the chief justice nor the secretary general has any voice, however, in the careers of prosecutors, attorneys, civil bureaucrats, legal scholars, or diplomats. Although those holding the posts of chief justice and secretary general may, as O'Brien and Ohkoshi argue, determine who from among retiring career judges will be appointed, their influence on the total composition of the Court is more limited; the number of retired career judges on the fifteen-justice Court has never exceeded six at one time. It is possible that, by forwarding recommendations to the prime minister with regard to appointments from among practicing lawyers, the chief justice and secretary general could play a significant role in the appointments of lawyers from the practicing bar. As O'Brien and Ohkoshi note,[24] a third of the members of the Court (32.2 percent between 1947 and 1995) were appointed from the bar, making that category second only to former career judges in number and percentage. The number of contending candidates is larger, the bar does not have the organizational cohesion of either the procuracy or the judiciary, and thus there is greater room for choice in the selection of the candidates proposed by the bar. Moreover, given the fact that the Japanese bar has a long history of progressive political activity, the potential for politically motivated appointments to prevent progressive ideological influence is quite great.

Nevertheless, in these, potentially the most politically charged of all Cabinet appointments, politics appear to have had no place. No politician or political leader has ever been appointed to the Court. Indeed no evidence of any partisan political consideration seems to exist. Party simply does not seem to matter. Former chief justice Tōru Miyoshi, initially appointed to the Court as an associate justice under an allegedly conservative LDP Cabinet, was elevated to the post of chief justice three and a half years later by Japan's first Socialist prime minister in a half century. This lack of active involvement by politicians in the appointment process may have no parallel. At least, as in the case of career judges, the Japanese pattern of appointments to its highest court appears to be unique in comparison with every other in the world.[25]

IV. INTEGRITY

Japanese courts are unique in other respects as well. Judicial corruption is virtually unknown. Judges do not take bribes. A combination of factors helps to explain this extraordinary integrity. Even what might be considered relatively minor infractions in other highly respected legal systems including the United States' can be and are swiftly and severely punished. Both formal process and informal means apply.

A rather elaborate formal structure for discipline and removal of judges exists. Separate statutes provide for disciplinary action and removal by impeachment and conviction of judges.[26] The judiciary administers disciplinary proceedings to preserve judicial independence from the political branches of government.[27] However, for impeachment and removal, by statute a special Impeachment Committee and Removal Court comprising members of the Diet have been established. Disciplinary actions commence with a charge brought by motion of the court with supervisory authority over the judge accused of the infraction. A five-judge bench of the high court for the relevant district hears disciplinary actions against district, family, and summary court judges; the Supreme Court, sitting en banc, adjudicates cases against a high court judge or justice charged. In the case of impeachment and removal proceedings, a special Judges Indictment Committee (*Saibankan sotsui iinkai*) comprising members of both houses of the Diet initiates the proceeding by impeachment. Any person may file a charge and thereby initiate a proceeding. The committee also has authority to commence an investigation on its own. In addition, the chief justice is required by law to initiate a proceeding if he or she determines that there is cause for impeachment and removal. Either on request or on its own authority, the committee investigates the grounds for impeachment. Impeachment—as an indictment for removal—requires a two-thirds vote of the committee. At that point, a special Judges Impeachment Court (*Saibankan dangai saibansho*), comprising seven member of each house of the Diet, is convened to adjudicate the case. A two-thirds majority is also needed for conviction and removal. The two grounds for removal are (1) conduct in grave contravention of official duties, and (2) other misconduct impeaching the integrity of the judge.

The number of petitions for investigation filed with the Indictment Committee each year is surprisingly high. In 2000, for example, the committee reviewed 493 complaints. Between 1948 and 2002 the number of cases totaled 8,928. However, in only twelve cases did the committee find any grounds for impeachment. Most petitions are filed, it appears, against trial judges by a losing party, in many cases involving protracted or politically charged litigation. Rarely if ever is the personal integrity of the judge challenged. Since 1948 only four judges have been impeached and removed in connection with a criminal conviction. Two of the cases—one in 1982 and the other in 2001—involved sexual scandals, the first involving a prostitute and the second sexual relations with a minor. A judge was removed in 1978 for having made a telephone call to the prime minister impersonating the procurator general. (He was convicted in 1983 for the misconduct as an offense under the Public

Employees Act.) Only one case involved conviction of a judge for receiving unlawful pecuniary benefit in return for an official favor—a case in which a judge had been treated to a golf game by a lawyer who was subsequently appointed a trustee in bankruptcy.

The number of judges removed after criminal conviction does not of course determine the number of judges who may actually be disciplined for misconduct. At least with respect to core personnel, most private enterprises and public agencies in Japan are closely knit, cohesive organizations. Nearly all hire core personnel only at the entry level and have a centralized personnel office—staffed by core personnel themselves subject to routine periodic reassignment—responsible for hiring, assigning, promoting, and generally administering nearly all career employees. These offices enable pervasive mentoring and monitoring throughout the organization. Misconduct—even criminal misconduct—can be and commonly is dealt with internally without resort to formal proceedings. Thus in most organizations, including the judiciary, less formal means of discipline are available. Compared to an enterprise or agency with many thousand employees, monitoring judicial behavior is quite easy. With fewer than three thousand judges and a system of regularly scheduled nationwide transfers to courts at all levels, the senior judges assigned to the judiciary's personnel office have a much easier task in monitoring the behavior of their peers. As members of a close-knit elite bureaucracy, career judges are subject to an institutional system of formal and informal peer control familiar only to the military in the United States. Any judge guilty of misconduct is readily subject to various peer and institutional sanctions and usually can be effectively encouraged to resign. Whatever the cause, by all accounts, judicial corruption is simply unheard of in Japan.

V. JUDICIAL AUTONOMY AND THE PUBLIC TRUST

As mentioned earlier, individual judges in Japan do not share the breadth of individual autonomy taken for granted by judges in the United States and many other legal systems. They do, however, enjoy a greater degree of independence from political intrusion than in any other industrial democracy, both with respect to individual cases as well as the composition of the judiciary, even, as discussed above, at the level of the highest and most politically significant court, the Supreme Court.

Popular belief and scholarly claims to the contrary notwithstanding, judicial independence has in fact long been an established norm of Japanese governance. In terms of separation of powers, freedom from intervention in the adjudication of particular cases, and the personal security of judges, judicial independence was secured in the late nineteenth century by constitution and statute. Judicial independence from the political branches was emphatically established as a fundamental principle of governance in Article 57 of the 1889 Constitution. Of all branches of government only the courts exercised authority "in the name of the emperor" (*tennō no na ni oite*). This exclusive reservation of authority to act in the emperor's name exceeded even the military's prewar claim that the "supreme command" of the emperor precluded legislative or executive civilian control. It thereby insulated the courts from any direct political intervention in the adjudication of cases by either legislative or administrative organs. Placed prominently in all courtrooms was the inscription "in the name of the emperor" as a meaningful reminder to imperial officials and subjects alike that the emperor's judges were not subject to political control or direction.

Express provisions of Japan's first comprehensive court law[28] also guaranteed the security of judges. Under Article 58 of the Court Organization Act of 1890, judges were to be appointed by the emperor with life tenure. Unless physically or mentally unable to carry out their duties or by virtue of a criminal conviction or disciplinary sanction, no judges could against their will be removed to a different office or court, nor could they be suspended or dismissed or have their salary reduced.[29] The statute did delegate authority over judicial appointments, promotions, and assignments to the minister of justice, and judges were made subject to mandatory retirement from active judicial service at age sixty-three for all judges except those serving on the Great Court of Cassation (*Daishin'in*).[30] Nevertheless, judges did enjoy a significant degree of formal security.

Nor in practice does the independence of Japan's prewar judiciary from direct political control appear to be in doubt.[31] Institutionally judicial independence from political intervention was secured by means of the construction of the judiciary and the procuracy as elite professional bureaucracies. By the end of the nineteenth century all judges and procurators in Japan were selected by examination. The 1890 Court Organization Act provided that judges and prosecutors had to pass two successive tests. Between the two tests, a three-year period of practical training in the courts was required.[32] Graduates of an imperial university were exempted from the first but not the second examination.[33] Imperial university professors were eligible after three years without examination.[34] By 1900 Japan's judiciary comprised 1,244 career judges, nearly all of whom had been selected through this process. Initially, it appears, a significant degree of mobility between the judiciary and procuracy existed. Japanese procurators had acquired the functions of the French *juge d'instruction* in preliminary criminal proceedings prior to trial. Several of Japan's leading prewar procurators—including Kiichirō Hiranuma and his protégé, Kisaburō Suzuki—had begun their careers at the turn of the century in the Ministry of Justice as judges. By the 1930s, however, the two career paths diverged, as two separate bureaucracies developed within the Ministry of Justice.

The separation of judges from procurators as separate career organizations with different privileges and legal protections was evident in the budgetary crisis sparked by the Great Depression. The Depression had reached its peak in Japan between 1930 and 1933. By 1934 the country had begun to recover. In the early 1930s, however, governments under both political parties—the *Minseitō* Hamaguchi (1929–31) and Watatsuki (1931) Cabinets and the *Seiyūkai* Inukai (1931–32) Cabinet—were embroiled in a prolonged controversy over the effect on the judiciary of measures designed to reduce costs generally.[35] Because the tenure and salary of judges but not procurators was secured under the 1890 Court Organization Act, judges' salaries could not be reduced without amending the statute. Prosecutors, who, like other officials, were required to take a cut, objected to what they argued was unfair, discriminatory treatment favoring judges. In the end, the judges were pressured to take "voluntary" pay cuts.

Judicial independence also required that judges refrain from public political activity. Political neutrality and professional integrity were considered fundamental to judicial independence. Judges were not allowed to participate in any public political activity. Needless to say, they could not join or be affiliated with any political party. The 1890 Court Organization Act prohibited judges "on the active list of the judicial service" "to interest themselves in any public involvement in political affairs" or "to become members of any political party or association or of any local, municipal, or district assembly."

The preservation of judicial independence underwent the greatest strains in prewar Japan from the late 1920s through the 1930s. During these years judges were, like other government officials, subject to increasingly strident ideological forces of all extremes. Some judges held moderate to extreme progressive views. A few were prosecuted under the Peace Preservation Act or induced to resign because of suspected communist views.[36] Others shared prevailing conservative nationalist views.[37] Most presumably kept their ideological beliefs private and avoided both extremes.

The prewar concern over judicial independence centered not on either political intervention in the judiciary or political activity by judges but on the independence of judges from the procuracy and administrative oversight of the judiciary. The Japanese bar was especially critical of the Ministry of Justice's supervision over both judges and procurators.[38] The bar's concern was not any potential political intervention but the close identification of judges with the procuracy. Criminal defense attorneys were especially critical. They considered this identification especially inappropriate. They and other lawyers, all members of the trial bar, also resented their inferior status relative to both procurator and judge.[39]

For judges as well, Ministry of Justice control involved concern over status, lack of full autonomy, and career separation of judicial and prosecutorial offices. The judges of the Great Court of Cassation, including the chief justice, were ranked inferior in status to the minister of justice.[40] The administrative authority of the Ministry of Justice also meant that the procuracy had an often determinative voice in the assignment of judges, including appointment of the chief justice of Japan's highest court,[41] and also could and did claim equality of status.[42] Since judges were equals within the ministry bureaucracy, it should be emphasized, they did exercise a significant degree of influence over the administration of justice in general and predominant influence over the administration of the courts. Nonetheless, conflicts were bound to occur, and when they did the potential for prosecutorial influence was unavoidable. Thus it is not surprising that among the postwar reforms desired by the judiciary itself was to gain as much institutional autonomy as possible.

The prewar record contains nothing to suggest, however, that political intervention in judicial affairs was a matter of concern. As exemplified by the careers of both Hiranuma and Suzuki, the problem in the late 1920s and 1930s was the converse—entry into politics after retirement by justice officials at the highest level and their sustained effort to reduce the influence of democratic political forces in Japanese governance.

These concerns found expression within the small group of Japan specialists assembled in the United States Department of State in the early war years, as preparations for a military occupation of a defeated Japan were prepared.[43] Judicial reforms were hardly their first priority, but proposals to transfer administrative control over the judiciary from the Ministry of Justice appear in early planning documents. It was in fact one of the first and most concrete reforms of the legal system suggested in the course of pre-surrender planning. The first mention of any need for judicial reforms in available pre-surrender planning documents appears to be a May 9, 1944, revision of a preliminary memo, "Japan: Abolition of Militarism and Strengthening Democratic Processes," dated five days earlier and drafted by Hugh Borton. The revised version recommended change in the process for appointing judges by the Ministry of Justice.[44] In July 1944 the planning group prepared a separate memo on the judicial reforms. Titled "Japan: Treatment of Courts in Japan during Military Government," the document commended the high professional standards of Japanese judges who received appointment, in the words of the memo, "after rigorous qualifying examinations."[45] The memo suggested no reforms in the existing system except the elimination of the Administrative Court and some provision to ensure the "independence of judges" from the Ministry of Justice.[46]

One of these recommended reforms was also included in Japanese proposals for amendment of the Meiji Constitution during the first months of the Allied Occupation.[47] The constitutional revisions proposed initially by the committee headed by Minister of State Jōji Matsumoto (1877–1954), which the Supreme Commander for the Allied Powers (SCAP) rejected outright, included the abolition of the Administrative Court and transfer to the regular judiciary of competence to adjudicate direct appeals from administrative decisions. The transfer of administrative jurisdiction over the judiciary from the Ministry of Justice to a separate judicial administrative organ would have undoubtedly been high on the list of reforms proposed by postwar Japanese officials as a revision of the Court Organizations Act.

The transfer of administrative authority to administrative organs of the proposed Supreme Court became a point of contention within the SCAP committee chaired by Col. Charles L. Kades, the deputy chief of the Government Section and a lawyer, appointed in February 1946 to draft a model constitution for postwar Japan. The views of the majority coincided with concerns of postwar Japanese progressives who urged the removal of jurisdiction over judicial administration from the Ministry of Justice.[48] Kades repeatedly questioned the powers the committee on the judiciary had proposed for the courts, arguing with perceptive foresight that the "kind of Supreme Court established in this draft might develop into a judicial oligarchy."[49] The solution, which did not fully satisfy Kades,[50] was to provide for Cabinet appointment of all judges and electoral review with potential dismissal of Supreme Court justices.[51] By these means some assurance of political accountability would balance the implicit powers of judicial review. Japan's postwar constitution, as revised by a joint American and Japanese effort and later during deliberations in the Diet, includes nearly all of the provisions and much of the language related to the judiciary of the original SCAP model.[52] The provisions for judicial independence were almost identical. The Constitution of Japan provides:

> Article 76.
>
> . . . . All judges shall be independent in the exercise of their conscience and shall be bound only by this constitution and the laws.[53]
>
> Article 80.
>
> The judges of the inferior courts shall be appointed by the Cabinet from a list of persons nominated by the Supreme Court. All such judges shall hold office for a term of ten (10) years with privilege of reappointment, provided that they shall be retired upon the attainment of the age as fixed by law.
>
> The judges of inferior courts shall receive, at regular fixed intervals, adequate compensation, which shall not be decreased during their terms of office.

Despite the attempt to assure a degree of political accountability, Japan's new constitutional structure has operated in fact to ensure greater not less judicial autonomy and political insulation. The first and only attempt by one of the political branches to the Japanese government to openly influence the courts came in 1948. On May 6, the House of Councilors Judiciary Committee announced that it was opening an investigation of district court decisions in a half-dozen criminal cases, in which the courts had denied detention or otherwise had been too lenient, in the view of the committee, in not applying the full rigor of the law. The Supreme Court protested, charging that the inquiry infringed the constitutionally protected independence of the judiciary. The Legal Affairs Committee responded by formally deciding on October 17 to widen the investigation to include the operations of the procuracy as well as the courts. The *Urawa* case became the focal point. The Supreme Court responded with a strongly worded formal denunciation of the committee's actions:

> The investigatory authority set out in Article 62 of the Constitution is merely a supplementary authority for collecting information required for the exercise of the legislative powers, consideration of the budget, and other powers vested in the Diet and each house by the Constitution. . . .
>
> The judicial power, however, belongs exclusively under the Constitution to the courts; other state organs are absolutely unauthorized under the Constitution to interfere in any way with its exercise. In this sense . . . actions of the Committee in reviewing and criticizing findings of fact or sentencing can only be viewed as violating judicial independence and exceeding the scope of investigatory authority for national administration entrusted in the Diet by the Constitution.[54]

The protest was effective. The affair ended. There has been no repetition. The judiciary effectively established its autonomy from legislative oversight or even formal critique of pending cases. The Supreme Court's unchallenged action also implied an assertion of the judiciary's right to define the limits of the Diet's legislative authority at least as it pertains to the courts.

Formal and structural barriers, coupled with a notable emphasis on institutional autonomy shared by most Japanese organizations, also work to prevent political intervention and manipulation of the courts, including even the composition of the Supreme Court. Despite Cabinet appointment of Supreme Court justices and, at ten-year intervals, all career judges who staff all but one lower court, as detailed below, the judiciary has remained virtually free of any direct political intervention or manipulation. To this extent, Kades's fears of a judicial oligarchy have been realized. Yet Japanese judges do not wield the sort of coercive power that would have given such concerns cause.

Political checks remain and do influence judicial administration. Those who administer the career judiciary are mindful that their autonomy depends on the trust of the public generally and more immediately those who exercise political leadership, who must themselves comply with public demands. The Cabinet's constitutional authority to appoint judges provides the continuous potential for political intervention. This ever-present possibility of active political oversight has been argued to provide a catalyst for self-policing as a form of silent, indirect but quite effective political manipulation and control.[55] As discussed in detail below, the data offered in support suggest a more plausible effect. The potential for partisan or other political intervention motivates the judges assigned to judicial administration to be more vigilant than perhaps they might otherwise be to ensure that the judiciary enjoys the highest levels of public trust. Thus acceptability of judges to politicians has to be viewed in relation to the similar accountability of politicians to the public. Political intervention and control are precluded by that trust. Given the extraordinary degree of public confidence the courts enjoy, the voters do not appear to want political intervention and control. The equally extreme low levels of trust politicians engender suggest, moreover, that the public would not allow it. The result is a set of well-established patterns for appointments and promotion that effectively insulates the selection of judges and justices from any direct political influence. These established conventions also operate within an equally well-established system of judicial oversight with intensive mentoring and monitoring of individual judges to ensure that the judiciary itself maintains a corps of honest, competent judges who adjudicate cases within predictable and generally accepted legal parameters. Individual judges thus function within the shadow of potential political intrusion. They cannot help but be aware that in adjudicating highly publicized, politically sensitive cases, they can be held professionally accountable for their decisions. Judges themselves, however, exercise the oversight, not politicians directly or indirectly.

Some disagree. A series of incidents took place in the 1970s, reflecting the tensions produced by the small group of young judges, many active in the radical student movement, who had entered the judiciary in the 1960s. As senior judges in the General Secretariat became increasingly fearful of their influence, they began to weed the judicial garden. The story of Assistant Judge Yasuaki Miyamoto has been often told.

Purposefully omitted from the 1971 Supreme Court's list of assistant judges who had served for ten years and were recommended to the Cabinet for reappointment and promotion to full judge was the name of Yasuaki Miyamoto. Miyamoto was a member of the Young Jurists League (*Seinen hōritsuka kyōkai*). Formed in the early 1950s, the league's members included lawyers, legal scholars, and judges whose ideological leanings ranged from progressive to radical Left. The league has been described as a Communist Party affiliate.[56] By 1971 an estimated 230 younger judges had joined the league, many in the late 1960s at the peak of radical student activity in Japan. The Cabinet as usual affirmed all of the recommendations. Every assistant judge on the list was promoted. Having not been recommended, Miyamoto was not reappointed and thus, as of April 1972, was no longer a judge. No reason was given, nor was one required. Past and present practice gave the judiciary the determinative voice in deciding who would be promoted. No one questions that senior judges themselves feared the influence of those affiliated with the league and had decided to act. Other judges associated with the league were dealt with less directly but perhaps no less harshly. They simply did not advance professionally. Some, facing remotely located, less significant assignments, often replacing advancing younger judges, quietly resigned. The purge was thus completed.

The Miyamoto and related incidents confirm for some the extent of control over individual judges exercised by their politically conservative seniors assigned to the Supreme Court's secretariat and personnel bureau.[57] They are the ones who exercise control and impose penalties on nonconforming judges. For others the Miyamoto affair, together with other incidents, suggest instead the pernicious influence of politicians on the judiciary. They go well beyond the view that the potential for political intervention in judicial appointments functions to keep judges mindful of the need to maintain public trust in their integrity, competence, and political neutrality and to ensure conscientious self-governance by the judiciary itself. Three highly respected scholars claim instead that political actors in fact aggressively manipulate and control judges in order to direct the development of the law.

Harvard Law School professor J. Mark Ramseyer, joined by his Yale colleague in political science Frances McCall Rosenbluth, initially made the charge in 1993.[58] Subsequently, over the course of a decade, now joined by Professor Eric B. Rasmusen of Indiana University, Ramseyer coauthored a half-dozen articles published in a variety of scholarly and professional journals in which he continued to assert that politicians control the judges. They have now bundled these articles into a single volume titled *Measuring Judicial Independence: The Political Economy of Judging in Japan.*[59] Ramseyer and Rasmusen analyze data detailing the career paths of nearly every one of the 793 persons appointed a career judge between 1959 and 1968.[60] They have tracked judicial posts held by each in relation to educational background, judicial decisions in several potentially "politically charged" categories of cases, and membership in the Young Jurists League.

Their case for political control is barely plausible. As suggested above, one might well be made and evidence found if the selection of members of the practicing bar to serve on the Supreme Court could be examined in detail and depth. But this is not what Ramseyer, Rosenbluth, and Rasmusen are about. They seek to show political control over the career judiciary. Yet, they do not find, or at least do not offer, any evidence of direct or indirect intervention by any politician in any decision made by senior judges assigned to the General Secretariat in appointing, assigning, or promoting any judge during the entire thirty-year period they studied (1959–89). They excuse this lack of proof as unnecessary. Instead they rely on a theory that is almost impossible to prove or disprove, nearly tautological in effect. Because, they argue, of the uninterrupted period of Liberal Democratic Party rule between 1955 to July 1993, senior judges assigned to the General Secretariat of the Supreme Court could discern (as "agents"), without any instruction—like, they say, an accomplished English butler—just what their political "masters" wanted. Hence, according to Ramseyer, Rosenbluth, and Rasmusen, no evidence of actual intervention—direct or indirect—is necessary.

Ramseyer and Rasmusen do not attempt the task of identifying and isolating cases in which LDP politicians had a distinctive interest or preference in the outcome that would have been clearly distinguishable either from the preferences of senior judges making the decisions or from those of the electorate as a whole. Nor do they even consider more narrowly defined personal or partisan interests—such as the appointment of friends, cronies, or political supporters—in the mix. Unless this is done, however, we cannot know for sure without entering the minds of the judges themselves whose preferences mattered. In the selection of decisions and the assumptions regarding LDP preferences, Ramseyer and Rasmusen in effect conflate the policy preferences of LDP politicians with those of Japan's senior judges, which in turn are held, by all accounts, by the majority of Japanese voters. They do not ask whether the preferences they identify were in fact peculiar to the LDP. For example, they identify judicial decisions holding unconstitutional statutory prohibition of door-to-door campaigning as "politically charged" and "antigovernment," inasmuch as such restrictions would presumably favor better-known incumbent LDP politicians. However, one can reasonably surmise that the vast majority of Japanese voters, not wanting to be bothered at home by eager politicians and their advocates, also favored the ban. Moreover, the Supreme Court had repeatedly upheld the prohibition. Thus, the judges who held the ban to be invalid were flouting voter opinion and the courts at least as much as LDP politicians.

The best cases Ramseyer, Rosenbluth, and Rasmusen offer in support of their claim are lower court decisions on the constitutionality of Japanese defense policies under Article 9 of the postwar constitution. No postwar judicial decisions better reflected the views of the league's membership or that of the radical Left. If any decisions "flouted" government policy, these were they. There were only two. The first was the 1959 Tokyo District Court decision in the *Sunakawa* case by Judge Akio Date and his two colleagues, Judge Shunzō Shimizu and Assistant Judge Ichirō Matsumoto. They held unconstitutional the 1951 United States–Japan Security Treaty.[61] The second decision was handed down fourteen years later by the 1973 Sapporo District Court decision in the *Naganuma* case.[62] In that decision, Judge Shigeo Fukushima, joined by Judge Takao Inamori and Assistant Judge Tatsuki Inada, held that the Self-Defense Forces (SDF) were unconstitutional. The Supreme Court subsequently reversed both.[63] Neither decision flatly contradicted Supreme Court precedent. The first case in fact produced the Supreme Court's landmark unanimous en banc decision in the *Sunakawa* case, which authoritatively construed Article 9 to allow Japan to pursue military policies for purposes of self-defense. Although distinguishable, the *Naganuma* decision, however, was certainly inconsistent with the reasoning of the opinions expressed by all fifteen justices in the *Sunakawa* case, and few would argue that the district court judges in either case reasonably believed that the Supreme Court would affirm their decisions.

Six judges participated in these cases. A panel of three judges adjudicated each. All continued on the bench. Not one judge was terminated. In each instance, each judge whose ten-year term had expired before he retired or reached retirement age was reappointed by the Cabinet, his name having been included on the list for renewal submitted by the General Secretariat. Four of the six judges had joined the judiciary after 1947. Thus their careers can easily be tracked using the data Ramseyer and Rasmusen rely on from the *Judges Almanac*.[64] Assistant Judge Matsumoto, only three years out of the LTRI at the time of his participation in the *Sunakawa* case, may have fared the worse. He resigned three years later in 1962 and entered private practice. Whether he agreed with Judge Date is not certain. Nor is it clear that he resigned under pressure. Nonetheless, his vote as one of the three judges *could* have made the difference and he *could* have been encouraged to resign by senior judges who *could* have been critical of his role in the decision. Judge Fukushima and the judge or judges who joined him in the *Naganuma* decision, however, were neither terminated nor forced to resign. All three continued to serve for more than a decade and a half afterward. As Ramseyer and Rasmusen note,[65] Judge Fukushima retired in 1989, at fifty-nine years of age. Judge Inamori retired in 1996, at the age of sixty-two, to become a notary public. He appears to have had good postings since 1973. His last position was the presiding judge of the Nagoya High Court. At age fifty-seven, Judge Inada is still on the bench. He too appears to have had reasonably decent judicial assignments. His current assignment (as of August 2003) is chief judge of the Sapporo Family Court.

The claim made by Ramseyer and his coauthors would not be contested were they to substitute "senior judges and most Japanese" for the LDP. The subsequent reversals by unanimous opinion by the Supreme Court and the Sapporo High Court suggest at least some hostility toward the views expressed by Judges Date and Fukushima and whichever of their colleagues joined them. Moreover, as the most ardent critics of Japan postwar defense policies themselves admit,[66] the Japanese public accepts the legitimacy of the SDF but also overwhelmingly rejects attempts to revise Article 9, a seemingly contradictory viewpoint that the Supreme Court's approach in the *Sunakawa* and *Naganuma* cases allows to prevail. One would thus expect that the careers of judges who were perceived not only to adhere to leftist views but also to be willing to act on those views, deciding cases at variance with judicial precedents as well as widely held public preferences, did indeed suffer.

But this has long been as well established as it has been well known. No one questions the basic proposition that Japan's senior judges reacted in the 1970s to what they perceived to be a serious threat from the Left by attempting to cull actively "radical" judges from the career judiciary. Their fear intensified as they witnessed Far Left student activists of the late 1950s and mid-1960s entering the legal profession and other mainstream occupations. Nor does anyone doubt that conservative politicians shared these concerns.

What is remarkable is that so many of the 140 judges whom Ramseyer and Rasmusen identified as Young Jurists League members did so well. Presumably because league members were among the "best and brightest," on average they had better assignments, better positions, and in the end better pay than their peers.[67] The data show that of these only a handful—no more than fifty—did not fare as well or better than the average judge. In each instance the judge who did not advance as fast or as far as his or her peers had decided cases and authored decisions at variance with well-established Supreme Court precedents and widely accepted norms of judicial restraint. Judges who defied these precedents were more apt subsequently to be denied plum assignments. The Ramseyer, Rosenbluth, and Rasmusen claim rests essentially on the finding that judges who refused to adhere to Supreme Court precedents on malapportionment or on the constitutionality and reviewability of Japan's defense policies or judicial construction of legislative constraints on injunctions against government offices and officials tended to receive less prestigious assignments and positions.[68]

Treat the Ramseyer, Rosenbluth, and Rasmusen claim as the playful overstatement of three gifted scholars overly enthralled by a theory, and the result is a convincing case for the institutional autonomy of the Japanese judiciary. They give us a glimpse of how competently and conscientiously, albeit conservatively and cautiously, Japan's judges govern themselves. They note that in nearly all of the categories of cases they studied—including taxpayer suits—the judges who received the best assignments, the earliest promotions, and the best pay were in fact the most talented, hardest working, and most competent.[69] They even found that high conviction rates in criminal trials appear to be equally related to competence, not political policing and control. Their data thus confirm the conclusions of the most comprehensive study of Japanese prosecutors.[70] High conviction rates are the result of the reluctance of prosecutors to indict defendants where they harbor any doubts concerning guilt or whose guilt they are not certain they can prove. Prosecutors who lose cases tend to suffer. Like judges, prosecutors are rewarded for honesty, hard work, and talent. In the end, *Measuring Judicial Independence*, the most thoroughly researched study on judicial independence in Japan to date, shows how conscientious and competent as well as cautious and conservative the senior judges who administer the judiciary really are. Nor do they act alone. They must take into account the views and preferences of their peers, the opinions and preferences of the judiciary as a whole.

Missing in almost all accounts are the consequences of the Miyamoto affair. The protests from Japan's judges were immediate and widespread. Over a third openly protested in one form or another, and many others quietly made their objections known. The judiciary became the center of a political storm. Miyamoto received nationwide media attention. Articles and books condemning the action poured forth. Since the Miyamoto incident, no judge, as of this writing, has been denied reappointment. Denial of tenure was no longer a viable sanction. Instead, the career judges who persisted in continuing their membership and acted on their ideological convictions as judges became subject to discriminatory treatment in court assignments and promotions. Control in this form, however, has not provoked public outcry.

Miyamoto's dismissal by senior judges did represent an unusually strong public statement that the Japanese judiciary would not tolerate any significant departure from an essentially moderate to conservative approach to legal change and judge-driven social reform. Ramseyer, Rosenbluth, and Rasmusen would thus be quite correct were they to claim that as a result of the Secretariat's actions, Japan's conservative political establishment—and electorate—could continue to place their confidence and trust in an autonomous judiciary. Those who sought a more active and socially responsive judiciary were naturally dismayed. Those who feared a subversive, radical element in the judiciary were relieved. Overlooked—or ignored—by the trio is the trajectory of subsequent landmark decisions in the 1970s by courts at all levels. These were the years of significant judicial activism. Judges determined policy in the pollution cases and revised established precedents in the parricide, malapportionment, and economic freedom cases.[71] The courts in these decisions were not acting as tools for LDP politicians. To the contrary these decisions overturned well-established government policies. One might ask whether the courts could have proceeded as freely without political intervention as they did had the Secretariat not affirmed, by means of the Miyamoto affair, public confidence that the judiciary was free from partisan and ideological control.

The judiciary emerged from the Miyamoto affair by all accounts an even more autonomously governed bureaucracy for which there are few if any parallels in the world. In a perceptive essay written as the events unfolded, Kazuhiko Tokoro analyzed the Japanese judiciary as an amalgam of three separate models—political, professional, and bureaucratic, from each of which separate elements could be detected. Characteristic, however, was the minimal level of popular participation or control. The Japanese judiciary relies less, Tokoro concluded, on legal rules made within administrative bureaucracies with some popular participation, as in "bureaucratic" models; or on outside experts, such as lawyers and other legal specialists, as in "professional" systems; or on the personal values of individual judges, who, if not acceptable to their political principals, can be replaced. Rather, the Japanese judiciary is more insulated from popular control in any of these forms than the courts of almost any other industrial democracy.[72] In other words, the judiciary itself, not any political branch of government, determines the parameters of responsible judicial behavior.

Japan's judges depend for their autonomy on the public's trust. Trust is the judiciary's most significant attribute. It gives judges status and legitimacy. It also operates to contain any threat of intrusive political meddling, or the sort of political control that Ramseyer, Rosenbluth, and Rasmusen claim exists. Trust rests, however, on confidence that resort to court will not result in arbitrary outcomes, a confidence based in turn on the integrity of individual judges and their independence from outside influence. Thus to maintain autonomy the judiciary must also maintain public confidence that the institution is indeed trustworthy.

In this respect the judiciary's success is not disputed. Japan's judges are among the most trusted in the world. Public opinion polls routinely reveal judges, along with the police and prosecutors, to enjoy the highest levels of public trust. The degree of public confidence in the courts in Japan is especially notable in comparison with other civic and government institutions, and with other countries, including the United States. Newspaper polls, for example, routinely show that trust of the courts in Japan is second only to the procuracy and police. In one relatively recent *Yomiuri* newspaper poll, trust in the judiciary was three times as great as trust in religious institutions or the self-defense forces, five times greater than for the Diet, and more than seven times greater than for offices of the national government. The prime minister ranked last. Trust in the courts in the United States, however, was less than half the Japanese level and ranked below all religious institutions and all political branches except national government offices.[73]

To achieve and maintain public trust, the judges assigned the task of administering Japan's judicial bureaucracy must themselves share a deeply felt responsibility to maintain judicial integrity and competence. They cannot but also share concern that the judiciary itself would suffer were the public ever to perceive that judges were freely deciding cases out of partisan preference or any extreme personal ideological bias at odds with what they would themselves consider the "sense of society." For them, little if any threat exists to judicial independence in Japan so long as they control the process for appointment and promotion of career judges. They may be correct, but, one would like to add, only insofar as they have themselves internalized the values of integrity, autonomy, and competence. One lesson of the Miyamoto incident was the necessity of their listening to the voices—expressed and unexpressed—of their colleagues on the bench and the public. By doing so they seemed to have ensured for a generation that, unlike career judiciaries in other industrial democracies in the wake of the worldwide rebellions of the 1960s,[74] the Japanese judiciary would remain obdurately apolitical. The political independence of Japan's judges and, at least as important for the judges themselves, their tenure were secured. Under these conditions the trustworthiness and autonomy of the Japanese judiciary should be secured for many years to come.

NOTES

This chapter is based on an essay originally presented at a conference held in Seattle, Washington, August 22–24, 2002, honoring the late Dan Fenno Henderson. Titled "Law in Japan: A Turning Point," the conference was sponsored by the Tokyo law firm of Nagashima Ohno & Tsunematsu and the University of Washington Asian Law Center. This chapter revises two previously published studies by the author on the Japanese judiciary—"Judicial Independence in Japan Revisited," *Law in Japan: An Annual* 25 (1995): 1, and "Law's Actors II," in John Owen Haley, *The Spirit of Japanese Law* (Athens: University of Georgia Press, 1998), 90–122 (chap. 5). To colleagues and friends who reviewed and provided valuable comments on earlier drafts I would like to express my gratitude. I am especially grateful to J. Mark Ramseyer, Eric Rasmusen, and Judge Masahiro Iseki for their helpful suggestions and corrections.

1. This is the official English translation for *Shihō kenshū sho*, which is sometimes also unofficially, but with respect to the order of Chinese characters, more literally translated into English as Legal Research and Training Institute (LRTI).

2. The activist but predominantly conservative role of judges in Japan has been well documented. See, e.g., Frank K. Upham, *Law and Social Change in Postwar Japan* (Cambridge, MA: Harvard University Press, 1987), esp. chaps. 2–4; Michael K. Young, "Judicial Review of Administrative Guidance: Governmentally Encouraged Consensual Dispute Resolution in Japan," *Columbia Law Review* 84 (1984): 923; Daniel H. Foote, "Judicial Creation of Norms in Japanese Labor Law: Activism in the Service of—Stability?" *UCLA Law Review* 43 (1996): 635; and, most

recently, Andrew M. Pardieck, "The Formation and Transformation of Securities Law in Japan: From the Bubble to the Big Bang," *UCLA Pacific Basin Law Journal* 19 (2001): 1.

3. Kan'i saibansho hanji senkō kisoku [Rules on Selection of Summary Court Judges], Supreme Court Rule No. 2, 1947.

4. As of 1998, 126 judges were assigned to the following administrative, instructional, and research offices of the Supreme Court: General Affairs Bureau (51), Legal Training and Research Institute (29), Office of Court Clerks (11), Family Court Research Bureau (3), Supreme Court Library (1), and research judges (31). Nihon minshu hōritsuka kyōkai shihō seido iinkai [Japan Democratic Jurists Association, Legal System Committee], eds., *Zensaibankan keireki sōran: Kaitei shinpan* [Judges Almanac: Revised New Edition], 3rd ed., 2 vols. (Tokyo: Nihon Minshu Hōritsuka Kyōkai, 1998), 1:256 (hereinafter 1998 *Judges Almanac*).

5. Nihon minshu hōritsuka kyōkai shihō seido iinkai [Japan Democratic Jurists Association, Legal System Committee], eds., *Zensaibankan keireki sōran: Kaitei shinpan* [Judges Almanac: Revised New Edition], 2nd ed. (Tokyo: Nihon Minshu Hōritsuka Kyōkai, 1990), 452–57 (hereinafter 1990 *Judges Almanac*); 1998 *Judges Almanac*, 1:256–61. See Saikō saibansho jimu sōkyoku [Supreme Court General Secretariat], *Shihō tōkei nenpō* [Annual Report of Judicial Statistics] (Tokyo: Saikō saibansho jimu sōkyoku, 2001), vol. 1 (Civil Cases), vol. 2 (Criminal Cases), also available at (http://courts.go.jp/tokei_y.nsf). For purposes of clarity, it might be noted that district court judges assigned to branch courts also serve as family court judges.

6. See Saikō saibansho jimu sōkyoku, *Shihō tōkei nenpō*, vols. 1 and 2.

7. For the best account in any language of the formal processes for the selection of judges, see Takaaki Hattori, "The Role of the Supreme Court of Japan in the Field of Judicial Administration," *Washington Law Review* 60 (1984): 69. Hattori had served as chief justice and had spent much of his career in the administration of the judiciary.

8. 1998 *Judges Almanac*, 1:150–54.

9. See J. Mark Ramseyer and Eric B. Rasmusen, *Measuring Judicial Independence: The Political Economy of Judging in Japan* (Chicago: University of Chicago Press, 2003), 8.

10. See 1998 *Judges Almanac*, vol. 2.

11. See, e.g., Peter H. Russell and David M. O'Brien, eds., *Judicial Independence in the Age of Democracy* (Charlottesville: University of Virginia Press, 2001); Mary L. Volcansek (with Maria Elisabetta de Franciscis and Jaqueline Lucienne Lafon), *Judicial Misconduct: A Cross-National Comparison* (Gainesville: University of Florida Press, 1996); Jerold L. Waltman and Kenneth M. Holland, eds., *The Political Role*

of Law Courts in Modern Democracies (Houndsmill, Hampshire: Macmillan, 1988); and Shimon Shetreet and Jules Deschênes, eds., *Judicial Independence: The Contemporary Debate* (Dordrecht: M. Nijhoff, 1985).

12. See Donald P. Kommers, "Autonomy versus Accountability: The German Judiciary," in Russell and O'Brien, *Judicial Independence in the Age of Democracy*, 131–54.

13. Minji soshō hō [Code of Civil Procedure], art. 312. The losing party on the first appeal can lodge a second, or *jōkoku*, appeal on constitutional grounds (art. 312) but cannot argue on other issues of law. If the court believes the appeal is not founded it can reject the appeal without hearing, but it gives its opinion on the constitutional issue (art. 319). Or the losing party may seek review on non-constitutional issues of law (art. 318). In this event, the Supreme Court has discretion to accept or decline the case. If the Court decides not to accept the case, it merely states, "This *jōkoku* appeal shall not be accepted" [*Honken jōkoku o juri shinai*], and gives no opinion on the issue of law involved in the case.

14. See Lawrence W. Beer and Hiroshi Itoh, *The Constitutional Case Law of Japan, 1970 through 1990* (Seattle: University of Washington Press, 1996), 66.

15. Saibansho hō, Act No. 59 of 1947.

16. Mainichi shinbun shakaibu [Mainichi Newspaper Social Affairs Bureau], ed., *Kenshō—Saikō saibansho: Hōfuku no mukō de* [Verification—Supreme Court: Behind the Judicial Robes] (Tokyo: Mainichi shinbunsha, 1991), 263–65.

17. Ibid., 266.

18. The official Web site for the Supreme Court of Japan (http://courts.go.jp) provides biographical profiles of all justices currently on the Court. The information on the background of Supreme Court justices in the following pages is based on information from these profiles as well as the 1990 and 1998 *Judges Almanacs*.

19. Mainichi shinbun shakaibu, *Kenshō—Saikō saibansho*, 265.

20. In addition to the forty-eight career judges, five other justices began their professional careers as judges but made an early career change, to become prosecutors, administrative officials, or, in one case, an academic. Of the forty-eight, all but one (Itsuo Sonobe, discussed later in this section) had been judges throughout their careers, usually beginning as assistant judges while in their mid-twenties.

21. Tatsuo Kainaka, for example, was appointed deputy prosecutor general in 2001; a year later, in autumn 2002, he was appointed justice after what can only be considered a qualifying appointment as superintending prosecutor for the Tokyo High Court. Another career prosecutor appointed to the Supreme Court in 2005, Yūki Furuta, served briefly as chief of the Criminal Affairs Section of the

Supreme Public Prosecutors Office (2002) and then as Deputy Prosecutor General (2003) before retiring in 2004.

22. As mentioned in note 20 above, five justices, including one of the legal scholars and two of the administrative officials, began their careers as judges but made an early career change. In addition, one of the legal scholars was a former attorney.

23. David M. O'Brien and Yasuo Ohkoshi, "Stifling Judicial Independence from Within: The Japanese Judiciary," in Russell and O'Brien, *Judicial Independence in the Age of Democracy*, 39.

24. Ibid., 53.

25. See, e.g., Russell and O'Brien, *Judicial Independence in the Age of Democracy*; Volcansek, *Judicial Misconduct*; Waltman and Holland, *The Political Role of Law Courts in Modern Democracies*; and Shetreet and Deschênes, *Judicial Independence*.

26. Saibankan bungen hō [Judges Disciplinary Act], Act No. 127 of 1947; Saibankan dangai hō [Judges Impeachment Act], Act No. 137 of 1947.

27. Dan Fenno Henderson and Takaaki Hattori, *Civil Procedure in Japan* (New York: Matthew Bender, 1983), ¶3.02[7], 3–36.

28. Saibansho kōsei hō [Court Organization Act], Act No. 6 of 1890.

29. Ibid., arts. 73 and 74.

30. Ibid., art. 74-2 (added by amendment), Act No. 101 of 1921.

31. For an eloquent argument to the contrary, see J. Mark Ramseyer and Frances M. Rosenbluth, *The Politics of Oligarchy* (Cambridge: Cambridge University Press, 1996), restated but even more abstracted from historical context in Ramseyer and Rasmusen, *Measuring Judicial Independence*, 132–39.

32. Saibansho kōsei hō, art. 58.

33. Ibid., art. 65.

34. Ibid.

35. See *Asahi shinbun* (Tokyo), November 2, 1930, 1 (Ministry of Justice unable to reduce budget by 2.1 million yen [1.5 million U.S. dollars] as requested by government); November 5, 1930, 2 (Judges and procurators oppose reductions in salaries); November 6, 1930, 1 (twenty judges and ten prosecutors will have to be let go to meet budget); January 1, 1931, 2 (eleven upper-level employees of the Justice Ministry to retire during year); March 10, 1931, 2 (Seiyūkai protests government order for "cessation of work" (*jimu teishi*) at sixty-two courts as economizing measure, charging measure amounts to discontinuation of courts in violation of 1890 Court Organization Act); March 31, 1931, 3 (editorial criticizes Hamaguchi Cabinet action as improper means of economizing); May 10, 1931, 2 (judges and procurators strongly oppose proposed salary reductions); May 22,

1931, 2 (Ministry of Justice considers reductions of judges' salaries by imperial ordinance illegal under Court Organization Act); May 28, 1931, 1 (judges' salaries exempt; procurators protest discriminatory treatment; judges unenthusiastic in "voluntarily" accepting cuts); June 1, 1931, 1, (salary reductions for all government officials except judges go into effect); June 10, 1931, 1 (Justice Ministry cuts 700,000 yen [approximately 350,000 U.S. dollars] from budget); July 4, 1931, 1 (Ministry of Finance announces further reductions in government expenditures necessary because of revenue shortfall); August 8, 1931, 1 (government must reduce expenditures by 30 million yen [15 million U.S. dollars] for year; Ministry of Justice considers cuts in sum allocated for jury system to save 1.42 million yen [710,000 U.S. dollars]); October 1, 1931, 1 (Ministry of Finance plans to reduce national budget by 2.2 million yen [1.1 million U.S. dollars]); October 4, 1931, 1 (Ministry of Justice to have difficulty meeting budget); October 28, 1931, 2 (amendment to be introduced in Diet to permit layoff of judges and procurators); November 3, 1931, 2 (Ministry of Justice agrees to lay off employees if other agencies agree to do same; refuses to agree to more layoffs of judges and prosecutors); and December 9, 1931 (last holdout among judges agrees to voluntary reduction in salary; in response government will not introduce legislation or issue imperial ordinance).

36. See, e.g., *Asahi shinbun* (Tokyo), February 10, 1929, 11 (prosecutor seeks ten years imprisonment in Peace Preservation Act trial of "Red Judge" Ozaki; asks for three-year terms for three other judges on trial); February 11, 1931 (Ozaki sentenced to eight years); May 11, 1931, 2 (prosecutor reigns after being seen in company of cafe hostess identified as a communist and mistakenly identified as brother-in-law politician, under attack for communist sympathies).

37. For an example of the attitude of judges in the late 1930s toward stricter penalties for violations of the 1925 Peace Preservation Act (*Chian iji hō*), see Richard H. Mitchell, *Janus-Faced Justice: Political Criminals in Imperial Japan* (Honolulu: University of Hawai'i Press, 1992), 99.

38. See Nihon bengoshi rengōkai [Japan Federation of Bar Associations], ed., *Nihon bengoshi enkakushi* [History of the Development of the Japanese Legal Profession] (Tokyo: Nihon bengoshi rengōkai, 1959), 183–97.

39. See ibid., 183–97. See also Atsushi Satō, "Shihō kanryō to hōsei kanryō" [Judicial Administration and Legal Affairs Administration], in Toshitaka Ushiomi, ed., *Gendai no hōritsuka* [Contemporary Jurists], vol. 6, *Gendai hō* [Contemporary Law] (Tokyo: Iwanami shoten, 1966), 44–60 (discussing activities by bar to seek reform).

40. See comment by former chief justice Kisaburō Yokota in Kisaburō Yokota, *Saiban no hanashi* [Speaking about the Courts] (Tokyo: Kōdansha, 1967), 41.

41. In 1935, for example, procurator Raisaburō Hayashi was appointed chief justice of the Great Court of Cassation over objections by career judges who favored Judge Torajirō Ikeda. *Asahi shinbun* (Tokyo), April 22, 1935, 2; May 8, 1935, 2. A year later however, Hayashi became justice minister and was replaced as chief justice by Ikeda. *Asahi shinbun* (Tokyo), March 13, 1936, 1. Hayashi, it might be noted, was a relatively liberal reformist justice minister.

42. See Masayasu Hasegawa, *Shihōken no dokuritsu* [Independence of Judicial Authority] (Tokyo: Shin Nihon shuppansha, 1971), 85.

43. For general descriptions of pre-surrender planning for a military occupation of Japan, see Makoto Iokibe, *Beikoku no Nihon seisaku* [America's Japan Policy] (Tokyo: Chūō kōronsha, 1985), 2 vols.; Marlene Mayo, "American Wartime Planning for Occupied Japan," in Robert Wolfe, ed., *Americans as Proconsuls: United States Military Government in Germany and Japan, 1944–1952* (Carbondale: Southern Illinois University Press, 1984), 2–51; Robert E. Ward, "Presurrender Planning: Treatment of the Emperor and Constitutional Changes," in Robert E. Ward and Yoshikazu Sakamoto, eds., *Democratizing Japan: The Allied Occupation* (Honolulu: University of Hawai'i Press, 1987), 1–41.

44. National Archives, Diplomatic Section, Notter Files, T-1221 reel 3, CAC 185/185a.

45. Notter Files, T-1221 reel 4, CAC 249, July 7, 1944.

46. Ibid., 2.

47. Dale M. Hellegers, *We the Japanese People: World War II and the Origins of the Japanese Constitution* (Stanford, CA: Stanford University Press, 2002), 2:478, 645.

48. See, e.g., memorandum of Robert A. Fearey, Jr., "Comparative Analysis of the Published Constitutional Revision Plans of the Japanese Progressive, Liberal, Socialist and Communist Parties, Two Private Study Groups [including the Federation of Bar Associations], and Dr. Takano Iwasaburo," in *Foreign Relations of the United States* 8 (1946): 170.

49. Kenzō Takayanagi, Ichirō Ōmoto, and Hideo Tanaka, *Nihon kempō seitei no katei* [Process of Drafting the Constitution of Japan], 3rd ed. (Tokyo: Yūhikaku, 1984), 186, 256.

50. Ibid., 256.

51. Kenpō [Constitution], art. 79(2) and (3).

52. See Kenpō, chap. 6, arts. 76–82.

53. A more accurate translation of this provision would read "judges shall exercise their authority [or function] independently in accordance with their conscience and shall be bound by this constitution and the laws."

54. Materials on House of Councilors Judiciary Committee, Saikō saibansho no ikensho [Supreme Court opinion letter] (May 20, 1949), 1, printed in *Hōsō jihō*

5 (1949): 71–72. See also Nobuo Kumamoto, "Contemporary Reflections on Judicial Independence in Japan," in Shetreet and Deschênes, *Judicial Independence*, 239.

55. See Ramseyer and Rasmusen, *Measuring Judicial Independence*.

56. Ibid., 19; Yasuhei Taniguchi, "Japan," in Shetreet and Deschênes, *Judicial Independence*, 210.

57. See Setsuo Miyazawa, "Administrative Control of Japanese Judges," Joint Annual Meeting of the Law and Society Association and the International Sociological Association Research Committee on the Sociology of Law (Amsterdam, the Netherlands, June 25–29, 1991); O'Brien and Ohkoshi, "Stifling Judicial Independence from Within."

58. Frances McCall Rosenbluth and J. Mark Ramseyer, *Japan's Political Marketplace* (Cambridge, MA: Harvard University Press, 1993).

59. Ramseyer and Rasmusen, *Measuring Judicial Independence*. See also book review (by author), in *Journal of Japanese Studies* 30(1) (Winter 2004).

60. Ramseyer and Rasmusen, *Measuring Judicial Independence*, 177.

61. Japan v. Sakata (Tokyo Dist. Ct., March 30, 1959), *Hanrei jihō* 180 (1959): 2. The case was brought by the Tokyo District Court Prosecutors Office in 1957, charging the defendant Sakata and six others with illegal entry onto an American military base. The case arose out of protests by local residents, landowners, and their supporters protesting the extension of a runway at the Tachikawa Air Base outside of Tokyo.

62. Itō v. Minister of Agriculture and Forestry, *Hanrei jihō* 712 (1973): 24. Filed in 1968, the case was brought by residents of the village of Naganuma in the northernmost island of Hokkaido to block the building of an SDF Nike missile base. In a presage to what was to come, in 1969 Judge Fukushima granted an injunction against construction of the base, a decision that was immediately appealed to the Sapporo High Court and reversed. See discussion of these cases in "Recent Developments," *Law in Japan: An Annual* 6 (1973): 175.

63. To be precise, in the Sunakawa case the Supreme Court on expedited appeal unanimously reversed the Tokyo District Court decision. Japan v. Sakata (Sup. Ct., Grand Bench, Dec. 16, 1959), *Keishū* 13 (1959): 3225. In the Naganuma case, the Court affirmed the Sapporo High Court reversal of the district court decision. Ministry of Agriculture and Forestry v. Itō (Sup. Ct., 1st Petty Bench, Sept. 9, 1982), *Minshū* 36 (1982): 1679.

64. See 1998 *Judges Almanac*.

65. Ramseyer and Rasmusen, *Measuring Judicial Independence*, 20.

66. See, e.g., Glenn D. Hook and Gavan McCormack, *Japan's Contested Constitution: Documents and Analysis* (New York: Routledge, 2001), 14.

67. Ramseyer and Rasmusen, *Measuring Judicial Independence*, 25.

68. Ibid., 67, 70–72, 75–76.

69. Ibid., 95.

70. See David T. Johnson, *The Japanese Way of Justice: Prosecuting Crime in Japan* (Oxford: Oxford University Press, 2002), 214–42.

71. See "Symposium: The Constitution of Japan; The Fifth Decade," *Law and Contemporary Problems* 53(1–2) (1990).

72. Kazuhiko Tokoro, "Saiban no minshu-teki tōsei to dokuritsu" [Democratic Control and Independence of the Courts], Hōshakai gakkai [Association for Sociology of Law], *Saibankanron* [Study of Judges], *Hōshakaigaku* 26 (1973).

73. *Yomiuri* Newspaper Poll, "National Perceptions," *World Surveys*, April–May 1995, 651, cited in John O. Haley, "Litigation in Japan: A New Look at Old Problems," *Willamette Journal of International Law and Dispute Resolution* 10 (2002): 121.

74. See, e.g., observations on the Italian experience in Frederic Spotts and Theodor Wieser, *Italy, a Difficult Democracy: A Survey of Italian Politics* (Cambridge: Cambridge University Press, 1986), 158–61, quoted in John Henry Merryman, David S. Clark, and John O. Haley, eds., *The Civil Law Tradition: Europe, Latin America, and East Asia* (Charlottesville, VA: Michie, 1995), 578–81.

6 The Rise of the Large Japanese Business Law Firm and Its Prospects for the Future

YASUHARU NAGASHIMA & E. ANTHONY ZALOOM

I. JAPAN THROUGH AT LEAST THE 1970s: NO LARGE BUSINESS LAW FIRMS

How can one explain the emergence of the large Japanese business law firm in the late 1990s? When the authors began their practice of law, in the 1950s and 1960s respectively, there were no such firms and all indications showed that there never would be any.

That was of course in stark contrast with the situation in the United States at the time, where the demand for the services of such firms and the supply of professionals to staff them had been strong for a long time. The primary components of a so-called Wall Street big firm practice, then and now, include corporate finance, mergers and acquisitions, general contract work, dealing with government (both to influence prospective legislation through lobbying and to challenge government determinations), and business litigation.

The chief executive officers of major American corporations regularly seek out the senior partners of such firms not just for technical advice but for their judgment in business matters as well. The lawyers who work in these firms are drawn from a very large lawyer population. One might say that their legal education prepares them well to function as advisers to business. Aside from courses such as contracts and property in the first year of law school, all American law schools offer courses in corporations, commercial transactions, securities regulation, antitrust, accounting, corporate finance, and taxation. And the method of instruction is to a great degree the case method, which places a heavy emphasis on factual orientation, "thinking on one's feet," and considering alternative solutions to problems.

Japan's economy in the 1950s, 1960s, and 1970s had neither the demand for such services nor people trained to provide them. Its securities markets, in comparison with those of the United States, were small and undeveloped. Disclosure requirements in those security markets as a practical matter were minimal, because there were not private rights of action under the securities law (although there was a tort-based theory of recovery for securities fraud) nor was there a strong regulatory agency comparable to the Securities and Exchange Commission. Nor was there any class action mechanism in Japan's Code of Civil Procedure. As a result, there was no such thing as a "securities lawyer" in Japan, at least for domestic securities issues. Banks were far more important than the securities markets as a source of external finance. But banks extended credit in accordance with standardized, creditor-favoring documentation rather than bringing in lawyers to negotiate detailed borrower representations, warranties, and covenants on a case-by-case basis in the way that so strongly characterizes bank term lending in the United States. Banks also tended in their extensions of credit to rely on the protection of real estate collateral, another reason not to require credit documentation customized to accord with the borrower's business and cash flow. When companies were in financial distress, rather than going into formal bankruptcy proceedings (and thus generating work for lawyers), they tended to rely on their main banks for "rescue" by means of debt forgiveness and on the seconding of bank officers to senior officer positions, arranging for asset sales, and so on.

Japanese mergers and acquisitions were relatively rare. The Japanese view of companies was not so much as property owned by shareholders that may be bought and sold, but rather as communities with obligations to a wider range of stakeholders, especially employees. (Hence the pejorative term for selling a company, *mi uri*, or to sell one's body, as would a prostitute.) And even when companies were bought or merged, it was often in accordance with arrangements worked out by government agencies, main banks, and top management behind closed doors. The resulting agreements were usually no more than a few pages. Due diligence was minimal if done at all. Nor did Japanese business have much need for detailed contracts in other contexts.

Attempting to influence legislation or bureaucratic determinations through lawyers was also almost unheard of in Japanese society. Those two corners of Japan's well-known "iron triangle," business and the bureaucracy, had a primarily cooperative rather than adversarial relationship. Business itself also tended to be conducted among parties with longstanding relationships. Problems tended to be worked out by informal methods rather than through litigation or formal administrative proceedings.

Japanese business leaders did not ordinarily look to lawyers or any other outside professionals for their judgment on important matters. Japanese management has tended to be intensely consultative within the individual enterprise, making it impractical to tap judgment outside that enterprise.

Japanese management, however, often did tap the judgment of officials in the ministries responsible for regulating the company. The officials' stance toward the company was more of guidance and cooperation when compared with that of the typical American government official. Checking with the management of other companies in the same industry was also common, consistent with often-muted intra-industry competition. But in neither case was the participation of outside counsel required.

The legal work that Japanese corporations did have, other than litigation, was usually done within the corporation. Thus, for instance, labor law matters would be handled by the personnel department (although even from the 1950s, certain important labor law matters were referred to outside counsel); tax matters by the accounting department; securities law matters at the time of issue by the finance department, and afterward by the securities section of the general affairs department; and zoning compliance by the real estate section of the general affairs department. By the 1970s, the general affairs departments of most large companies contained a legal department staffed by nonlawyers with undergraduate legal degrees.

Japan's supply side for the independent legal profession matched well the near nonexistence of business demand for outside legal services. The yearly number of formally qualified legal professionals was for many years limited to only a few hundred by the government (for the twenty-five-year period between 1965 and 1990, for instance, hovering at around five hundred per year).[1] Their undergraduate legal education, consistent with Japan's civil law system, was highly theoretical with little thought to practical application and few business law courses; it was heavily oriented toward mastery of rules and doctrine rather than development of analytic skills. The training that lawyers received in the nation's Legal Training and Research Institute (LTRI) was to a considerable degree aimed at the nuts and bolts of litigation pleading and practice, including the writing of judicial opinions.

And yet, one cannot say that there were absolutely no business lawyers in Japan at this early time. Japan imposed strict limitations on direct foreign participation in the Japanese economy through its foreign-exchange control and foreign investment laws. Many foreign, especially American, companies have long looked to local counsel for advice about such restrictions when venturing outside of their home country, and Japan was no exception. The first lawyers in Japan to provide that advice were a group of expatriate Americans who had come to Japan within the first decade after World War II. At that time they were able to take advantage of a temporary Occupation period regulation whereby foreign lawyer admissions in their home jurisdictions entitled them, with little or no examination, to be admitted in Japan to advise on Japanese law to clients from those jurisdictions.[2] Consequently, very few of them had more than a smattering of knowledge of Japanese law.

Most of these lawyers had not worked in a Wall Street or other large business law firm in the United States, but before long they found themselves counseling such blue chip firms as IBM and JP Morgan about their operations in Japan. In order to acquire the requisite Japanese law knowledge for their practices, they hired Japanese lawyers and eventually took them into partnership. Limitations on foreign investment in Japan correspondingly limited to a degree the types of problems that these lawyers were asked by their clients to address. Most of their practices related to distributorships, licensing agreements, joint ventures, the regulation of foreign bank branches in Japan, and an occasional lawsuit. Conspicuously absent were many of the important staples of the American business practice such as corporate finance and mergers and acquisitions. Contact with Japanese government ministries was an important part of the practice, but it was limited primarily to securing government approval of clients' investments in Japan.

Though they were small and limited, these practices were Japan's first business law firms. Japanese lawyers working in them were required not only to draft and counsel in English but also to work with foreign clients who looked to their lawyers primarily for mixed legal and business advice, as opposed to representation in litigation. To enhance their skills, these firms sent their lawyers in increasing numbers to the United States for a graduate law degree and a year's apprenticeship in an American law firm. They began to leave these firms (sometimes in the 1970s referred to as "Occupation firms" by the young American lawyers working in them) to start their own *shōgai* (foreign matters) firms. Other Japanese lawyers began to establish *shōgai* firms without the apprenticeship in an Occupation firm but with the benefit of the U.S. graduate law degree and time spent in an American law office. But the numbers of lawyers in these firms remained small, usually fewer than twenty or so lawyers in even the largest such firms.

II. PRELUDE TO CHANGE IN THE PROFESSION: JAPAN BEGINS TO CHANGE

The demand for business lawyers in Japan has changed because Japan itself has changed in very fundamental ways. Some of these changes took place in the early 1980s. By that time, Japan had liberalized restrictions on foreign exchange transactions and corporate bond issuance. Many large Japanese corporations took advantage of the resulting opportunity to satisfy their external financing needs in the Eurobond market—and to increase their use of lawyers for the necessary documentation and compliance advice. Japanese companies had already gone abroad for financing in the 1960s and 1970s, but it was only with the 1980 reform of the Foreign Exchange and Trade Control Act—and the much cheaper bond issue costs of the Euro-markets—that such financings became really substantial. By 1983, foreign bond issues of Japanese companies exceeded 50 percent of their total bond issues.[3]

Although Japanese companies did not use outside counsel for domestic offerings, the convention of the Euro-markets that outside counsel of the issuers and underwriters be involved in financings left them no choice to do otherwise. In 1982, Japan also passed additional legislation prohibiting corporate payoffs to the *sōkaiya* in connection with the conduct of annual general meetings.[4] What had previously been an area for private resolution between company and *sōkaiya* now absolutely required sophisticated legal advice. Companies began to use business lawyers to help them "orchestrate" annual general meetings and cope with the strong-arm tactics of the *sōkaiya*. (At least one such lawyer became well known for wearing a bulletproof vest to annual general meetings.)

Throughout the 1980s, Japanese businesses increasingly went abroad, where quite often, especially in the United States, they discovered how convenient it was to use local law firms for guidance on mixed questions of law and business. Japanese computer manufacturers, for instance, used American law firms both to represent them in disputes with IBM over the scope of its copyrights in operating system software and also to counsel them on how to develop their own software to avoid future problems.

Change requiring outside legal advice accelerated in the 1990s. American perceptions that Japan was an unfair competitor led to the so-called Structural Impediments Initiative.[5] One important component of that initiative was the reduction of the required filing fee for shareholder derivative suits to a nominal amount. There immediately resulted a steady increase in such suits against corporate directors, who not only needed lawyers to defend them but also began increasingly to consult with lawyers beforehand so as to minimize the possibility of such suits. A company might think it did not need lawyers to settle a dispute with another company, but it might still very much want to consult lawyers to confirm that the settlement would not create personal liability on the part of its directors.

Public acceptance of the cozy relationships between business and the bureaucracy was shaken by a series of scandals that resulted in legislation prohibiting informal contact between the two.[6] More generally, there was a move away from rule by bureaucrats in an informal, opaque manner toward rule by clear laws and procedures. For the financial services industry this might be said to have culminated in the so-called big bang reforms proposed by then prime minister Ryūtarō Hashimoto.[7] But more and more business-related laws were being amended in an attempt to cope with Japan's increasing economic malaise in the 1990s—the company law many times, especially. All of these developments contributed to the need for more outside legal advice.

Conditions in the mid- and late 1990s particularly led businesses to seek outside legal advice. The poor performance of many Japanese companies in the financial and automotive sectors led to the formation of cooperative arrangements with, or takeover in whole or in part by, foreign firms. This trend could be seen in the cases of Long Term Credit Bank (LTCB), Toho Life Insurance, Japan Lease, Yamaichi Securities, Nikko Securities, Nissan, and Mitsubishi Motors. Not long thereafter, accounting rule changes and continuing poor performance forced many other large Japanese corporations to divest themselves of subsidiaries and divisions that were not part of their core competence. Even when between two Japanese companies, these transactions differed from the intra-Japan deals of the past. They were often with relative strangers, so that at least some due diligence and more careful contracting was required, often to at least some extent based on the models increasingly provided by foreign firms coming into Japan.

The same financial pressures on Japanese companies to improve their balance sheets caused them to shed other assets such as loan receivables and headquarters buildings not just by simple sale but also by means of asset securitization. Japanese banks began to sell billions of dollars worth of nonperforming loans to American "vulture funds" such as Cerberus. The NEC headquarters building and the Ikebukuro Seibu Department Store were securitized, in each case for close to a billion dollars. This new technique of securitization—facilitated greatly by legislative changes that were part of the financial big bang—demanded complicated legal analysis and structuring, voluminous documentation, and a knowledge of both domestic and foreign financial markets. All of these requirements played well to the strengths of

Japanese business lawyers with foreign legal education and work experience. Even simpler, more straightforward sales of assets required extensive legal due diligence. The foreign buyers of the nonperforming loans also have tended to be much more aggressive than the Japanese banks had been in collecting them, generating still more work for lawyers.

Of course, much of this demand for legal advice might have been met by Japanese corporate legal departments. Indeed, those departments continue to grow. But in many cases they have become consumers rather than providers of advice, limiting their role to coordinating the provision of advice to their business departments by outside counsel. The sheer volume of the work, the demand for specialization and sophistication, and the magnitude of risks from any error (and a consequent tendency to rely on the "insurance policy" of an outside opinion) often leave them little choice to do otherwise.

An important factor on the supply side that has helped set the stage for the rise of the large Japanese business law firm is the substantial increase in the annual number of graduates from the LTRI. In 1992 the number increased by almost 20 percent to 594. In 2000 this number had reached 975. There is at least some speculation about what caused these early increases. There was pressure from a combination of Japanese business lawyers, who in the late 1980s felt understaffed and threatened by the arrival of foreign law firms in Tokyo from 1987 (as a result of the first partial liberalization of international practice), and the Ministry of Justice, which wanted to increase its pool of young candidates for prosecutor positions.[8]

By the turn of the century a far more dramatic increase in new lawyers was planned and for more fundamental reasons. In 2001, the prime minister's Judicial System Reform Council published its final report, which states that the council's objective is to "define clearly what we must do to transform both the spirit of the law and the rule of law into the flesh and blood of this country."[9] One such action is a sharp increase in the annual number of new lawyers. Japan's present objective is three thousand per year. Numbers aside, Japan's best and brightest in greater numbers began to opt for a career as a lawyer rather than in the increasingly discredited and less well-compensated bureaucracy.[10]

III. THE RESPONSE OF JAPANESE LAW FIRMS

By 1998, several Japanese firms responding to this surging demand for business legal advice had become very large by traditional Japanese standards. During the period leading up to that year, four of the largest had achieved significant numbers of lawyers, as shown in the following table.

TABLE 6.1. Numbers of Lawyers in the Four Largest Japanese Law Firms from 1985 to 2002

	Year	*1985*	*1990*	*1995*	*1996*	*1997*	*1998*	*1999*	*2000*	*2001*	*2002*
Anderson Mori	Partners	-	16	17	18	21	23	25	26	27	30
	Associates and Others	-	27	28	26	26	29	34	50	64	62
	Total	-	43	45	44	47	52	59	76	91	92
Mori Sogo	Partners	6	13	19	20	25	23	28	31	34	36
	Associates and Others	8	14	34	37	34	40	39	53	64	62
	Total	14	27	53	57	59	63	67	84	98	98
Nagashima Ohno & Tsunematsu	Partners	10	14	17	16	20	24	24	37	42	41
	Associates and Others	22	39	44	48	53	49	54	82	94	105
	Total	32	53	61	64	73	73	78	119	136	146
Nishimura & Partners	Partners	14	14	14	18	17	20	21	20	24	28
	Associates and Others	8	42	40	36	43	47	44	57	76	87
	Total	22	56	54	54	60	67	65	77	100	115

It is not surprising that three of these four firms had from an early date been either representing primarily foreign clients or at least practicing primarily transnational business law—virtually the only practice area in which there had been much demand for so-called business law advice.

Anderson Mori had originally been one of the so-called Occupation firms, established and brought to ascendancy among them by three Americans: James Anderson, Arthur Mori, and Richard Rabinowitz. By the 1990s, it had become an entirely Japanese partnership. The name partner in the Nishimura firm had been a young partner in the Tokyo office of Baker & McKenzie in the 1960s. The Nagashima firm had also started out as a firm concentrating to a large extent on international transactions. Even Mori Sogo, although originating primarily as a domestic litigation firm, had many of its lawyers go abroad over the years for graduate law degrees and practical experience in foreign firms.

Such drastic increases in lawyers were necessary if only to meet the staffing requirements for due diligence, regulatory review, and contract drafting in a single acquisition by a foreign company of an insolvent Japanese target in the heavily regulated financial services sector. And there were several of these. The accelerating amendments and wholesale additions to the company law and other business laws gave a sharp competitive advantage to the larger firms that could organize internally to analyze these new laws and disseminate know-how about them within the office. Within these firms, lawyers also began to develop areas of specialization. Some of them in areas such as securities, mergers and acquisitions, banking, and structured finance became—if not household names—very familiar to businesses active in these fields. Foreign clients began to mobilize Japanese lawyers in these firms to assist them in lobbying for legislative change. The content of Japan's new Soil Contamination Measures Act, passed in 2002, for instance, was heavily influenced by a lobbying combination of the American Chamber of Commerce in Japan and U.S. financial institutions, the latter making extensive use of outside Japanese legal counsel. Lawyers considered authorities in such areas as bankruptcy and venture capital began to appear as members in the consultation committees attached to ministries working on new legislation.

Just hiring more lawyers was not enough, however. Starting in 1999, law firm mergers also began to fuel the growth of the large business firms. In that year, Nagashima & Ohno, strong in general corporate matters, announced its merger, effective January 1, 2000, with the medium-sized firm Tsunematsu Yanase & Sekine, which had developed a strong practice in corporate finance.[11] Over the next two years, two similar such mergers were announced, one between Tokyo Aoyama and Aoki, Christianson and the other between Mori Sogo and Hamada & Matsumoto. Both of these mergers involved the combination of a general corporate practice with a corporate finance practice. In July 2002, the merger of the Asahi Law Office and Komatsu, Koma was announced, resulting in a firm of over one hundred lawyers. By the end of 2002, the two largest firms would be Mori Hamada & Matsumoto and Nagashima Ohno & Tsunematsu—both with about 160 lawyers.

IV. GROWING PAINS

The large Japanese business law firm would seem then to be on the verge of achieving preeminence comparable to that of its counterpart in the United States. And yet at this moment, some are prophesying its early demise. Charles Stevens, a prominent American lawyer in the Tokyo office of Freshfields, likens four of the Japanese law firms to the Japanese securities industry big four of the 1980s—only one of them survives as an independent firm today. He predicts that, similarly, in five years there will be only one surviving large Japanese law firm, the rest all absorbed by multinational firms. He likens the recent Japanese law firm mergers to those of the Japanese banks that have resulted in such behemoths as Mizuho Financial Holdings—resulting in only unmanageable bigness for its own sake.[12]

There are certainly many complaints about the large Japanese firms from foreign lawyers as well as foreign and Japanese clients. The most basic complaint, perhaps the source of all others, is that there are still far fewer lawyers in these firms than are necessary to satisfy clients' needs. GE Capital, for instance, claims that in order to do one major acquisition transaction it had to use a combination of six different law firms in Tokyo, because no single firm had a sufficient number of lawyers to handle the work.[13] Insufficient numbers of lawyers also result in a slowness of service that would not be acceptable in New York or London and is also thought to be the reason for the less-than-thorough analytical memoranda that clients sometimes receive from the large Japanese firms. Experienced business lawyers at these firms are still too few in number to make themselves available for clients for extended periods. It is rare, for instance, for a client to be able to have an experienced partner from one of these firms be the lead negotiator on one of its deals for a period of several days—let alone several weeks.

One often also hears about Japanese business lawyers continuing to indulge themselves in the luxury of being generalists when there is an increasing need for specialization. Notwithstanding how impressive many of the seasoned business lawyers are in their skills, they do not always seem able—or even inclined—to mobilize teams of lawyer specialists effectively at all levels within their own office. And the enormous amount of study necessary to pass the still extremely competitive bar exam makes Japanese lawyers seem "academic" in the eyes of some. They are felt by some clients to be distant, even aloof, or arrogant.[14] They do not have the entrepreneurial drive of the Anglo-American lawyers, who regularly initiate contact with clients about new developments in the law or simply in order to learn from the clients more about their businesses and needs for assistance. The erudition of Japanese lawyers enables them to answer questions put to them about law, but they still tend not to think enough or consider why a question was asked. Therefore, their answers too often tend to be "no" or "you can't" rather than "you can't do it that way, but perhaps this other way is possible."

Many international clients also complain about the relatively poor English of the large Japanese firms. Usually the long and intense preparation for the competitive bar examination has given the Japanese lawyer little time to devote to foreign languages. Yet the large firms, especially with the increased financial strength following from increased demand for their services, should be able to recruit cadres of experienced foreign attorneys and build strong translation groups within their firms. That they have not done so may be indicative of another, more fundamental area of concern: management.

Generally speaking, management in the larger Japanese firms has not kept up with the increase in their number of lawyers. One Japanese interview respondent spoke of "amoeba management," or the pattern where firms acquire more work, then hire more people, which itself generates more work, requiring the hiring of more people, and so on. Perhaps not much attention is paid to practice area selection or management or to giving the younger lawyers in the firm any sense of the vision of the firm's leaders. None of the larger Japanese firms, for instance, is willing to take on the management challenge of recruiting a substantial number of seasoned foreign business lawyers to assist in its international practice, even though many foreign and Japanese clients would like them to do so.

It appears that Japanese companies doing joint ventures of any substantial scale with foreign parties, even when entirely in Japan and with Japanese law governing, will often choose to use the Tokyo office of a foreign law firm because of the absence of U.S. or U.K. partner-level business attorneys in Japanese law firms. That absence similarly prevents Japanese firms from aspiring to play a major role as "regional players" in East Asia the way that the U.K. and U.S. firms do out of their Hong Kong offices.

Many of these firms do not seem at all inclined to use discretionary compensation of partners as a management tool, relying instead on the easier, more impersonal approaches of either lockstep or formula-based compensation.[15] Although there are rigorous standards employed in recruiting decisions, in most of the big firms there is as yet no highly selective and strict "up-or-out" policy with respect to partnership decisions.[16] Once the client's interests have been satisfied, conflict issues are often resolved in accordance with individual lawyers' preferences or a "first-come, first-preferred" approach rather than a consideration of the overall interest of the law firm. None of the larger Japanese firms has yet hired a nonlawyer business manager of equal stature with the law partners to manage the firm as "a business" as has been done in many of the largest firms in the United States.

Yet most of these criticized aspects of the large Japanese firms can be said to arise from the unforeseen suddenness with which the demand for business law services in Japan has grown. It may be many years before the most fundamental problem, insufficient numbers of lawyers, is mitigated by an increasing number of lawyers graduating from the LTRI. The continuing independent streak and sometimes-seen disinclination of the Japanese lawyer to specialize or delegate are not surprising when one considers that, until only some twenty years ago, all Japanese lawyers practiced alone or in small firms. Law firm management has been a neglected, in fact almost nonexistent, discipline for the same reason. Even in the United States, it is a relatively recent phenomenon. It was not so long ago that one American firm's managing partner stated that "professional firms are managed in one of two ways: badly or not at all."[17] It should be noted that the Japanese lawyer's relative "aloofness" and lack of "entrepreneurial drive" are not unique at all; other lawyers in many civil law countries share these characteristics. In this respect, Anglo-American lawyers are the real outliers. Only within the past several years have there been movements to reform Japanese legal education to give it a more practical orientation.

V. THE U.S. AND U.K. FIRMS: A COMPETITIVE THREAT?

Do the large Japanese firms have the luxury of taking their time to address the above concerns? Or will Charles Stevens's prophecy prevail, where most if not all of the large Japanese firms become the Tokyo offices of multinational law firms, "just like what happened in France and Germany"?[18]

Japan is different from France and Germany in ways that decrease but do not necessarily eliminate the likelihood of any similar such outcome. Europe is much closer physically to the home bases of the U.S. and U.K. law firm "invaders," and English is much more the language of everyday business there than it could ever be in Japan. Anglo-Americans find it much easier to live in Europe, and their firms find it much cheaper to have them do so. The new legal environment in Europe (the new set of Euro-law rules and the challenging interplay among them and between individual member countries' national law regimes) plays well to the strengths of the Americans. They are used to operating in multiple jurisdictions at once, having learned in the United States how to exploit the potential of a fifty-state, two-level federal system for the benefit of their clients.[19]

Japan, on the other hand, is not so hospitable an environment to foreign law firms. Not only do foreign entrants have serious language and cost handicaps when coming into the Japanese legal market, but they also face the same difficulty in recruiting Japanese lawyers that confronts Japanese firms: the shortage of graduates coming out of the LTRI. In fact, recruiting is an even more serious problem for foreign firms. First, there is a set of legal restrictions imposed on association between foreign and Japanese attorneys that prevents the Japanese attorneys from aspiring to be partners in the foreign firm, although these restrictions may be relaxed or eliminated sometime in the near future.[20] Another more fundamental problem is the frequent perception among Japanese lawyers that they would be treated as second-class citizens at the foreign firms and delayed in the development of professional skills by the relative absence of senior Japanese practitioners in the foreign firms.

Yet the foreign firms in Tokyo do have some competitive advantages. In contrast to the larger Japanese firms, most do not hesitate to accept the challenge of bringing together Japanese and foreign lawyers on an equal basis under one roof so as to better service clients. Although still few in number, the recruitment of several senior, respected Japanese lawyers by foreign firms is beginning to reduce the young Japanese lawyers' perception that they will not be adequately trained in Japanese law matters at the foreign firms. Foreign firms are also several decades ahead of the Japanese firms in practice management, which shows in such areas as the monitoring of attorney utilization rates, marketing, and information technology. Foreign firms also have easier access, through their home and other offices, to non-Japanese transactional and regulatory know-how that is sometimes highly relevant to even purely domestic Japanese problems, as Japan brings itself closer to U.S. and other foreign economic models. One more potential aid to the recruiting effort of foreign firms is their ability, unmatched by the Japanese firms, to send their young lawyers abroad for training within their own organizations.

VI. THE FUTURE

The most likely outcome of competition between the Japanese and multinational firms in years to come is therefore difficult to judge. Charles Stevens's prediction that most of the large firms will have disappeared or lost their independence in five years nonetheless seems exaggerated. At this writing, the larger Japanese firms have more than enough quality work to keep busy. They are also uniformly perceived to have a decisive advantage in Japanese law expertise over all of the foreign firms in Tokyo. One lawyer at one of the larger Japanese firms stated that his firm does not even think of the foreign firms as competitors, because of their limited capability in Japanese law. This is a sentiment likely shared by most of the lawyers in the larger Japanese firms.

Even within the next five years some of the foreign firms may be able to exploit a significant advantage in recruiting young Japanese lawyers, especially those who want to enter international practice. That advantage would be the foreign firms' perceived superior ability to provide a quality practice experience abroad to the young lawyer. Such an advantage could put pressure on the larger Japanese firms, all of which consider it extremely important to maintain their current ability to recruit from the best young lawyers coming out of the LTRI. That pressure might in turn result in one or more of the larger Japanese firms entering into some exclusive relationship with a foreign firm.

Beyond five years the future of the larger Japanese firms in transnational, English-documented practice becomes even more uncertain. By that time, there will likely be many well-regarded Japanese lawyers working in the foreign firms, giving those firms a much stronger capability in advising on Japanese law than they have now. They will then be able both to field teams of Japanese and foreign lawyers working together and to access transactional and regulatory know-how throughout their global organizations. Clients will likely favor such firms rather than the stand-alone larger Japanese firms in transnational, English-documented work. With the best of this work going to foreign firms, their recruiting advantage will increase, not only at the LTRI, but also when taking experienced lawyers from the larger Japanese firms.

Thus, the first competitive threat from the foreign firms will likely be from an increasing ability to recruit some of the best Japanese lawyers for transnational practice. The larger Japanese firms that are still heavily dependent on transnational practice may lose many of their best lawyers and eventually be pressured into merging or otherwise cooperating exclusively with a foreign firm.

Nonetheless, as Japan's corporate sector becomes more litigious and deal- and contract-oriented, it brings more work that is purely domestic to the larger Japanese firms. Highly visible international mergers and acquisitions such as the Ripplewood acquisition of LTCB and Citigroup's investment in Nikko have obscured the fact that the larger Japanese firms are becoming less and less dependent on transnational practice. One of them, usually thought of as primarily engaged in an international practice, states that its proportion of purely domestic work is now at least two-thirds, a figure that is probably true for most, if not all, of the others as well.

The purely domestic practice is one in which the foreign firms' primary competitive advantages (entrepreneurial foreign lawyers, English-language facility, more businesslike management, and easier access to legal know-how abroad) become far less important, even when combined with high-level Japanese law expertise. The purely domestic practice is also more fee sensitive. There is already a perception among Japanese clients that they are charged more for the same Japanese law advice by foreign firms than by Japanese firms because of their higher cost structures and obsession with profits per partner. Notwithstanding the fact that most of the large Japanese law firms may eventually lose much of the best-quality transnational practice to the multinational firms, they will likely continue to grow and prosper in a domestic business practice that will expand for decades.

NOTES

The authors have written this chapter, in 2001, based primarily on their own first-hand knowledge of large Japanese business law firms together with the results of interviews of lawyers in those firms and their clients.

1. Statistical information received from the Legal Training and Research Institute, on file with the authors.

2. Glen Fukushima et al., "Background," in Richard Wohl et al., eds., *Practice by Foreign Lawyers in Japan* (Chicago: American Bar Association, 1989), 10.

3. Takeo Hoshi and Anil Kashyap, *Corporate Financing and Governance in Japan: The Road to the Future* (Cambridge, MA: MIT Press, 2001), 234.

4. Robert C. Hsu, *The MIT Encyclopedia of the Japanese Economy* (Cambridge,

MA: MIT Press, 1999), defines *sōkaiya* as "shareholder-extortionists who extort money from companies by threatening to disrupt companies' annual shareholders' meetings by revealing companies' internal scandals."

5. The initiative is described generally in Mitsumasa Tanabe, "The Globalization of Japanese Law," in Barry A. K. Rider, Yutaka Tajima, and Fiona Macmillan, eds., *Commercial Law in a Global Context* (New York: Kluwer Law International, 1998), 113–17.

6. Kokka kōmuin rinrihō [Public Official Ethics Act], Act No. 129 of 1999.

7. The announced objective of these reforms was to make Japan's financial markets "free, fair, and global" and to make Tokyo an international financial center on a par with London. Some of the major components of this reform included enabling financial institutions to set up holding companies; permitting banks, trust banks, securities companies, and insurance companies to enter one another's markets; the deregulation of securities trading commissions; and the transition to a transparent, less discretionary, rule-based regulatory system.

8. See Setsuo Miyazawa, "The Politics of Judicial Reform in Japan: Judiciary, Lawyers, Legal Education and Legal Aid," in Curtis J. Milhaupt et al., eds., *Japanese Law in Context: Readings in Society, the Economy, and Politics* (Cambridge, MA: Harvard University Press, 2001), 103.

9. Justice System Reform Council [Shihō Seido Kaikaku Shingikai], *Recommendations of the Justice System Reform Council—for a Justice System to Support Japan in the Twenty-first Century* (June 12, 2001), at: (http://kantei.go.jp/foreign/policy/sihou/singikai/index_e.html).

10. Curtis J. Milhaupt and Mark D. West, "Law's Dominion and the Market for Legal Elites in Japan," *Law and Policy in International Business* 34 (2003): 451.

11. The rationale for the merger is set out in Yasuharu Nagashima, "Nihon no law firm no gappei to daikiboka ni tsuite" [The Merger and Increase in Scale of Japanese Law Firms], *Jiyū to seigi* 50 (1999): 14.

12. Remarks before the Legal Services Committee, Corporate Counsel Subcommittee of the American Chamber of Commerce in Japan, July 3, 2002.

13. Written submission by Larry Bates to the Legal Services Committee, Corporate Counsel Subcommittee of the American Chamber of Commerce in Japan, July 3, 2002, on file with the authors.

14. See, e.g., "Kokusaika kentōkai hōmushō puresen yomiage" [Reading of Ministry of Justice Presentation at Expert Consultation Group on Internationalization] (draft) (included in the explanatory materials submitted by the Ministry of Justice, to the Second Meeting of the Expert Consultation Group on Internationalization, Headquarters for Promotion of Justice System Reform, February 25, 2002), 7.

15. It should also be noted, however, that many well-managed U.S. and U.K. firms have deliberately avoided discretionary compensation of partners—as unnecessarily divisive—in favor of a lockstep system.

16. These days an "up-or-out" policy should be easier for Japanese firms because the professional opportunities for experienced business lawyers are proliferating. In-house positions, especially with foreign-owned business entities, are increasing. Legislation passed in 2000 permits government agencies to hire lawyers for up to five years. And the law schools to be newly established by 2004 are desperately looking for lawyers with practical experience to serve as faculty.

17. Quoted in David H. Maister, *Managing the Professional Firm* (New York: Free Press, 1993), 291.

18. In Germany, for instance, a German lawyer in an American firm describes the following situation: "Almost all first- and second-tier German firms have either merged with a foreign firm, or have entered into some kind of a 'best-friend' arrangement. . . . Many other 'mergers' resulted from foreign firms taking over entire offices or a significant number of lawyers from existing German firms."

19. For an insightful analysis of the impact of U.S. law firms on law and law practice in Europe, see David M. Trubek, Yves Dezalay, Ruth Buchanan, and John R. Davis, "Global Restructuring and the Law," *Case Western Reserve Law Review* 44 (1994): 407, 420–56.

20. Gaikoku bengoshi ni yoru hōritsu jimu no toriatsukai ni kansuru tokubetsu sochi hō [Special Measures Act for Handling Legal Matters by Foreign Lawyers], Act No. 66 of 1986, art. 49, no. 2. [Editors' note: As the authors of this chapter predicted, a 2003 revision to this Special Measures Act (effective from 2005) removed the restrictions that prevented Japanese attorneys as a substantive matter from becoming partners in foreign firms.]

7 The Legislative Dynamic

Evidence from the Deregulation of Financial Services in Japan

YOSHIRŌ MIWA & J. MARK RAMSEYER

A decade into the worst recession since the war, Japanese firms in the late 1990s seemed doomed to more of the same. Most everyone blamed the banks. A decade since asset prices fell, banks still held debt for which their collateral gave scant recourse. To many observers, nothing less than a general financial collapse seemed in store for the future.

United States banks and firms suffered far less severe a recession in the 1990s and showed little risk of collapsing. Much of this contrast traced itself to structural differences in the financial services industry in the two countries. More specifically, it traced itself to differences in the range of nonbank financial institutions that investors and firms could tap. As Merton Miller put it: "Banking is not only basically 19th-century technology, but it is disaster-prone technology. And in the summer of 1997 a banking-driven disaster struck in East Asia. . . . That the U.S. economy did not freeze up into depression in 1989–90, as it had in 1931 and so often before that, can be credited, I believe, to the rich variety of non-bank financial markets and institutions available to American firms and households."[1]

Why the different range of institutions and markets? The quick answer points to regulatory barriers. Yet if the U.S. economy could avoid disaster by having nonbank financial institutions, why did Japanese authorities not permit the same? Institutionally, they readily could have done so. Economically, they surely understood the issues involved. Before 1940, the largest Japanese firms did raise most of their funds through stock and bond markets and relied on banks only secondarily.[2] In the intervening half century, what changed? Why did the Japanese government pursue such ill-advised policies?

The blame for the lack of diversification in Japan lies in the regulatory framework, and in this chapter we explore the political economy behind it. More specifically, we examine the way the Ministry of Finance stymied the development of a commercial paper market for nonbank financial intermediaries. Justifying its role with an idiosyncratic statutory interpretation, the ministry blocked nonbank intermediaries from using commercial paper to raise funds. In the process, it made it harder for those nonbank intermediaries to circumvent the regulatory framework by which it had coddled the banks and securities firms through the postwar decades. In this chapter, we ask why the regime changed in the late 1980s and 1990s, why it had not changed earlier, and why the nonbank intermediaries deferred to the Ministry of Finance's only dubiously based instructions.

This exercise in historical reconstruction raises broader issues in the Japanese legislative process. First, it illustrates the political dynamics behind regulation and legislation. Although many specialists claim that Japan operates by its own political logic, we find the logic consistent with that which governs regulation and legislation in most advanced capitalist democracies. More specifically, the logic illustrates George Stigler's classic observations that (a) most regulation represents an attempt to enforce the terms of a cartel against its internal prisoners' dilemma and (b) as such is a service for which there is both a supply and a demand.[3]

Second, the chapter shows how the Japanese government was sometimes able to induce firms to comply with its informal regulation. Most specialists assert that Japanese firms comply either because of strong social norms dictating compliance or because bureaucrats wield unreviewable power. Elsewhere, we show that bureaucrats seldom had such power and that firms frequently did not comply.[4] In this chapter, we show that those firms that complied did so for more tractable and straightforward reasons.

Last, the chapter illustrates the congenital inability of government to improve outcomes by manipulating the market.[5] As sensible policy, the strategies the Japanese government adopted in the financial services industry failed catastrophically. Given that failure, we have little reason to think it could have manipulated markets to facilitate growth during the high-growth 1950s and 1960s either.

As part of a survey volume on Japanese law, this chapter comprises two distinct parts. In the first, we outline the institutional structure of the Japanese legislative process and summarize the academic debate over it (section

I). In the second part of the chapter, we use the deregulation of the market for nonbank commercial paper as a case study in the dynamics of the regulatory and legislative process (section II).

I. THE PUZZLE OF LEGISLATIVE PROCESS

A. THE FORM OF THE PROCESS

1. *Constitutional Structure*

Formally, the Japanese legislative process is easy enough to describe: to become law, a bill must pass both houses of the democratically elected bicameral parliament (the Diet; Constitution, Article 59).[6] The principal details add some length to the description, but not much: members of the upper house serve for six years, and those of the lower serve four (unless the house is earlier dissolved; Articles 45–46); if the lower house is dissolved, new elections must be called within forty days (Article 54); if the upper house rejects a bill passed by the lower house, it still becomes law if passed again with a two-thirds vote of the lower house (Article 59).

As befits a parliamentary democracy, the executive answers to the legislature. Thus, the lower house elects the prime minister (Article 67) and can fire him through a no-confidence vote (Article 69). In practice, the head of the majority party (provided there is one) in the lower house becomes prime minister. He then picks the Cabinet (Article 68), and the Cabinet runs the bureaucracy. The Cabinet passes the orders necessary to enforce statutes (Article 73), and the orders are enforceable in court if consistent with the constitution and statutes (Article 41).[7]

2. *Electoral Rules*

For most of the postwar period, voters elected lower house legislators from multimember districts through a single nontransferable vote. This required the majority party in many districts to split its supporters among several candidates. Primarily, it did this through candidate-specific support groups. For reasons discussed elsewhere, it cultivated these groups by routing to incumbents cash that they then used to provide private goods with which to tie voters to specific support groups.[8]

In 1994, the Diet changed the electoral rules radically. Henceforth, voters would elect a majority of lower house legislators from single-member districts. Apparently, the majority party leaders reasoned that they could safely capture most of the single-member districts. By using a party list system for a substantial minority of legislators, however, they could also ensure that the other parties not coalesce into a single, more threatening opposition.[9]

3. *Politics*

The Liberal Democratic Party (LDP) kept a majority in the lower house from its founding in 1955 until 1993. That year, intra-party brinkmanship tied to quarrels over the electoral reforms caused many LDP members to defect. Two opposition governments followed, but the LDP resumed power in 1996. As of mid-2006, it continues to control the Cabinet.

4. *Judicial Review*

Japanese courts review both the constitutionality of legislation and the legality of orders and regulations (Article 81). They also interpret and apply the constitution, laws, orders, and regulations as necessary. They retain full jurisdiction over private disputes, criminal disputes, and disputes involving the government. They hold the government subject both to injunctions and to damage claims and control a wide panoply of enforcement mechanisms.[10]

The Cabinet appoints the judges. Those on the Supreme Court serve until mandatory retirement at age seventy. Those on the district and high courts serve ten-year terms, but virtually all are reappointed.[11]

B. THE SUBSTANCE OF THE PROCESS

1. *Introduction*

If the formal legislative structure is straightforward, its import is not. As with so much in Western Japan-oriented scholarship, the scholarly divide turns on the extent to which economic theory explains Japanese phenomena. By standard theory, structure matters crucially: structure determines which players have a role in making policy, what endowments they bring to the process, and what deals they can cut.

By contrast, Japan specialists traditionally claimed that formal structure mattered little: notwithstanding the structure, bureaucrats dominated politicians; notwithstanding the unenforceability of bureaucratic preferences, citizens did as they were told; notwithstanding the failure of bureaucratic planning elsewhere, Japanese bureaucrats masterminded growth with aplomb.

These "facts," they then claimed, were explicable only in idiosyncratically Japanese terms.

More recently, scholars have looked harder both at economic theory and at the "facts" the theory supposedly fails to explain. On doing so, they find that the dominant patterns of government-firm interaction do embody social-scientifically predictable responses to institutional structures. That earlier scholars failed to notice this sometimes reflected their failure to think hard enough about the theory. Other times it reflected their failure to look critically enough at the "facts."[12]

2. *The Japan-Specific Story*

a. Bureaucrats and Politicians

For decades, area specialists claimed Japanese bureaucrats dictated policy independently of politicians. Kiyoaki Tsuji had already made the point a staple within Japan by 1952.[13] T. J. Pempel helped bring the claim to the United States, and Chalmers Johnson transformed it into the orthodoxy.[14] Indeed, he made it central to his master claim that Japanese bureaucrats masterminded Japanese economic growth. In potentially the most oft-quoted line by an American scholar on Japanese political structure, he forthrightly declared that "the elite bureaucracy of Japan makes most major decisions, drafts virtually all legislation, controls the national budget, and is the source of all major policy innovations in the system."[15]

The claim persists. To be sure, observers today routinely report a decline in bureaucratic power. Yet as a benchmark from which to measure decline, they posit a bureaucratically hegemonic past. "The declining role of industrial policy as an engine of growth is much discussed and well-documented," explained Ronald Dore.[16] What observers document, though, are the current bureaucratic flailings—easy enough to do. They do not document the decline. Instead, they simply posit a past Valhalla of bureaucratic hegemony. Bureaucrats do not currently enjoy much power. According to these accounts, however, they lack it because they lost it—not because they never had it.

b. Bureaucrats and Business

Japanese bureaucrats obtain their control through voluntary compliance. According to the Japan-specific accounts, Japanese bureaucrats rule (or at least used to rule) informally in such a way that regulatory practice remains both unreviewable and unenforceable.[17] Nonetheless, firms and individuals comply voluntarily.

Conventionally, all this went by the phrase "administrative guidance." Joseph Sanders, for example, wrote that "MITI's [Ministry of International Trade and Industry] core activity is administrative guidance—advice or direction by government officials carried out voluntarily by the recipient."[18] Karel van Wolferen claimed that courts have "almost totally insulat[ed] bureaucratic activity from judicial review."[19] Ulrike Schaede asserted that "there is effectively no legal recourse" for firms that would contest the administrative guidance.[20] And Frank Upham declared that "the doctrines governing judicial review of administrative action" left MITI "virtually unrestrained legally."[21]

Why firms comply, in these Japan-specific circles, remains something of a puzzle. Some attribute the compliance to raw, unreviewable power. Schaede, for instance, described what she saw as a "carrot-and-stick" logic. Ministries can approve or deny approvals and licenses "on entirely discretionary grounds," she explained. For the denied firms, no "administrative or legal appeal [is] available."[22] Henry Rosovsky wrote that "no Japanese would dare ask" a MITI bureaucrat what legal authority he had for the administrative guidance.[23]

Others turn to Japanese culture. "The more familiar you become with Japanese customs," wrote James Fallows, "the more you are impressed with the virtue of doing *the expected thing*."[24] Culturalist if ever there was one, Wolfgang Pape declared that the "extremely effective" practice of administrative guidance "has deep roots in the sociocultural foundations of Japanese society. . . . The recipient of administrative guidance is conscious of the necessity of understanding and harmony with government agencies that can override interests held in common with peers that possibly contravene it."[25] Indeed, explained Dore, "an almost universal assumption" in Japan has been the notion that "government should, and in the proper hands could, be a repository of virtuous and benevolent leadership."[26]

c. Bureaucrats and the "Public Interest"

Having posited informal yet omnipotent bureaucrats, the Japan myth proceeds to a virtuous climax: through this informal power, bureaucrats masterminded, indeed created, Japan's "miraculous growth" and triumphant transformation. Sector by successful sector, their role was to Fallows "familiar and obvious."[27] By economic logic they should never have succeeded, or even tried. Yet to Fallows as to so many in Japanese studies, Japan is the case that proves universalistic economic theory wrong. To Fallows the journalist, Japan operates by a "noncapitalistic market economy."[28] To Johnson the political scientist, the U.S. economy operates by a "market rational" logic, while Japan runs by a radically contrasting "plan-rational" one. To Dore the sociologist, the United States is a "Goldilocks economy," while Japan keeps a "sense of belonging to a national community which sustains cooperation within industries, and makes possible inclusive, and redistributive, educational and social welfare systems."[29]

Romeo comes in many guises, of course, and Stalinism by any other name would smell as sweet.[30] Traditional economists did not just repeat this legend; some helped create it. Back in 1972, Henry Rosovsky declared Japan to "be the only capitalist country in the world in which the Government decides how many firms should be in a given industry, and sets about to arrange the desired number."[31] Twenty years later, Paul Krugman could claim that there was "no question" that "before the early 1970s the Japanese system was heavily directed from the top, with the MITI and the Ministry of Finance influencing the allocation of credit and foreign exchange."[32]

Japanese economists have been no less enamored of the government-grew-the-economy hypothesis. According to University of Tokyo economists Tetsuji Okazaki and Masahiro Okuno-Fujiwara, through its "industrial policy" the Japanese government uses "administrative guidance and other discretionary measures to achieve 'development' and establish 'order' in the industry." In the process, it covers three steps:

> First comes the "discovery" of an industry for development, using forecasts of future trends in technology or demand. . . . At the second stage, industries selected for development and sectors earmarked for growth have to be nurtured and given support. . . . The third stage requires co-ordination of the allocation of funds and other resources between industries through inducive means. The allocation of the necessary facilities, and the selection and co-ordination of firms is carried out through discretionary administrative guidance against a backdrop of regulatory and financial measures.
>
> The result of this is that all firms in the sector have access to the same information on new business opportunities, and have a strong incentive to get ahead of others and quickly establish a foothold in the new business. This leads to excess competition, circumstances where investment and facilities are expanded beyond the individual firm's means, and to business plans that target market share rather than profits.[33]

To prevent the resulting "systemic risk," the government in Okazaki and Okuno Fujiwara's account then coordinates cartels and subsidies.

3. *The Myth Reexamined*

a. Bureaucrats and Politicians

By economic theory, none of these points should be true. Given the Japanese institutional framework, politicians should control bureaucrats. If administrative guidance is truly unenforceable, recalcitrant firms should not comply. And given the incentives and informational problems they face, bureaucrats should not improve on market outcomes. Consider each point in turn.

Most basically, institutions should matter. As explained earlier, they will matter because they determine who the players in the game will be, what relative endowments they will bring, and what enforceable bargains they will make. Suppose, for example, that bureaucrats hold information not available to politicians, set the agenda by which legislators can act, and face no risk of retaliation from politicians. Suppose further that they choose to pursue goals they know majority politicians do not support. In some cases, politicians will lack the information necessary to stop them. Even where politicians know of their ploy, they will not be able to place reform on the agenda. When bureaucrats flout their political preferences, they will have no way to punish the miscreant bureaucrats.[34]

Suppose, however, that those conditions do not hold. The possibility is crucial, because in Japan they emphatically do not hold. In Japan, most bureaucratic action involves little technical expertise, and when it does the politicians can independently acquire (by hiring staff) the necessary information with ease. In Japan, politicians control the legislative agenda and can readily repeal regulations by statute. And in Japan, politicians can easily derail bureaucratic careers.

Under such circumstances, in equilibrium we still would rarely see political intervention. We would rarely see it because, as several prominent political scientists explained, "the process of policy administration by autonomous agencies is observationally equivalent to that under strict [legislative] control."[35] The observational equivalence reflects the fact that in neither a bureaucratic-dominant nor in the politician-dominant world will legislators intervene. To be sure, if bureaucrats are independent, they will do as they please, and legislators will leave them alone. Yet if legislators strictly control bureaucrats they will still leave the bureaucrats alone. They will leave them alone because (a) bureaucrats will know that legislators could potentially intervene, both to change policy and to ruin their careers; (b) bureaucrats will know that legislators will indeed intervene if they do flout legislative preferences; and (c) rational bureaucrats will avoid that outcome by giving legislators what they want from the start.

Indeed, in equilibrium bureaucrats will want what legislators want anyway. Reasoning that administering policies they do not like is no fun, potential bureaucrats who do not share the political preferences of the legislative majority will self-select out of bureaucratic careers. In the end, those who choose to become bureaucrats will disproportionately include those who want what majority legislators want.

b. Bureaucrats and Business

By standard theory, rational bureaucrats will also act informally whenever possible. They will do so because informality is cheaper than formality. An agency that must formalize its action both incurs costs itself and imposes costs on the regulated firms—costs that both could otherwise avoid. In splitting the gains that accrue to informality, they potentially both gain.

Perhaps the analogy to litigation would help. Whether in Japan or anywhere else, disputants do not litigate most quarrels. Instead, they settle them out of court. In doing so, however, they do not render the law irrelevant. Instead, they settle by reference to the expected litigated outcome. Given that they would both incur substantial litigation fees if they took the dispute to court, they both gain by negotiating an out-of-court settlement that reflects the expected litigated outcome.[36]

Crucially, however, even when bureaucrats act informally, they will obtain compliance only if they can credibly threaten to formalize their instructions. In litigation, defendants will pay plaintiffs large sums out of court only when plaintiffs can credibly threaten to sue. In regulation, reluctant firms will comply with informal instructions only when they know bureaucrats could formalize those instructions and force them to comply if they did anything else. Absent an agency's power to formalize its instructions, firms that object to the instructions will not comply.

c. Bureaucrats and the "Public Interest"

More than to anyone else, the modern theory of policy making owes its genesis to George J. Stigler. According to Stigler, "as a rule, regulation is acquired by the industry and is designed and operated primarily for its benefit."[37] Disproportionately, regulation will occur when firms demand it strongly, and they will demand it when they need the government to keep prices high.

As prisoners' dilemmas, cartels are necessarily unstable. Consequently, as Fred S. McChesney put it, "as a long-run source of rents" they "are notoriously unreliable." Potentially, regulation solves this problem. "With its ability to legalize price fixing, to police cartelizing agreements with taxpayer funds, and especially to restrict entry into markets," continued McChesney, "regulation can often perform rent-creating functions more efficaciously than private parties themselves can."[38]

Even when regulation does not transfer wealth to all firms in the industry, it will usually transfer wealth to some. Most commonly, it will prevent a competitive fringe in an industry from competing away the profits of all. Again, in McChesney's words: "[A]n entire industry of producers does not seek regulation to benefit itself at the expense of purchasers. Instead, some relatively homogeneous subgroup of producers lobbies for and obtains regulation that benefits itself at the expense of another subgroup of producers."[39]

What politicians and bureaucrats will not do, by this theory, is promote growth by manipulating the market. They will not do so, both because they gain little from doing so and because they would not know how. They lack the incentives because growth is a "public good." Because it benefits the public at large, few firms or voters have reason to lobby or campaign actively for it. By contrast, cartels are a "private good." Because they benefit small groups intensely, those groups will often have reason to demand them vociferously. As a result, firms and voters who use their votes and cash to bid for private goods (like cartel enforcement) will generally outbid those that bid for public goods (like growth).

Politicians and bureaucrats lack the information to promote growth by manipulating the market because market outcomes already embody the collective judgment of the investing community. Investors have a simple reason to buy into firms they think present the best growth potential: if right, they get rich. Given that incentive, they devote enormous resources to acquiring the information they need to identify the right projects. Bureaucrats and politicians could promote growth by manipulating the market only with better information still—better information than the investing community about the relative prospects of various products, services, and technologies. Absent a reason to think sinecured generalists on the government payroll can routinely outguess investors with millions of their own at stake, theory gives us no reason to think either politicians or bureaucrats will outguess the market.[40]

d. The Japan-Specific Claims

In truth, most of the Japan-specific "facts" at issue are dead wrong. Bureaucrats do not, for example, work independently of their political masters. Instead, they generally pursue (and since 1955 have consistently pursued) goals that further the electoral interests of the ruling LDP. Controversial to be sure, some evidence shows that political considerations do indeed shape the careers of senior government employees, and other evidence suggests policy outcomes reflect even the factional composition of the LDP itself.[41]

Similarly, administrative guidance has always been reviewable. Suppose a regulator "interprets" a statute in a way that bans firm A from taking a given action. If A wants to contest the interpretation, it need simply ignore it. By so doing, it forces the regulator to formalize its interpretation and sue. When it does, the court will face a justiciable controversy. From time to time Japanese firms have indeed done just that. From time to time courts have indeed declared administrative guidance invalid.[42]

Neither does the administrative guidance necessarily induce firms to comply. Even when government power and ideological pressure were the strongest—at the height of World War II—the Japanese government could not obtain the compliance it wanted.[43] The postwar Ministry of Finance has done little better. Already in the 1950s, the ministry had adopted a policy of requiring city banks to divest their trust businesses. The Daiwa Bank refused. After a decade's worth of Daiwa intransigence, in 1965 the Ministry of Finance publicly told the bank to divest. Desperate to induce compliance, it even offered the bank regulatory favors if it did. The bank still refused—with banking industry representatives publicly noting to the press the ministry's lack of a statutory basis for its instructions—and has kept its trust business to this day.[44]

The Ministry of Finance was not powerless. Rather, it had the power the legislators and courts chose to allocate it. This power stemmed precisely from the fact that its formal regulatory actions *were* reviewable. Precisely because it could formalize its informal policy, when a court would enforce its formalized regulation firms would comply with the informal analogues independently. Concomitantly, however, when a court would not enforce the ministry's formalized version, neither would firms necessarily comply informally. Instead, as the Daiwa Bank showed, they could choose to stay intransigent to the end.

More generally, most of the famous tales about bureaucrats who forced renegade firms to comply with informal directives are no more than so many urban legends. As we explain in detail elsewhere, the best known of them are simply false. The ministries involved had no power to coerce, and the firms did not comply. When firms apparently did comply, in most cases the ministry was doing no more than sanctioning a private cartel.[45]

Japanese bureaucratic action has never been about promoting economic growth anyway, much less about "plan-rational" guidance. Again in keeping with Stigler's explanation, usually it has reflected the economic self-interest of the firms at stake. Usually, it has involved simply the use of state power to enforce cartels.[46]

II. THE COMMERCIAL PAPER DISPUTE

A. INTRODUCTION

To explore the Japanese legislative and regulatory process in more detail, we turn to a case study: the opening of the commercial paper market to nonbank financial intermediaries. We first summarize the history of the liberalization (section B), then review the literature (section C) and clarify the law on which the government claimed to rely (section D). We conclude by explaining the political economy of the deregulation: the bargain involved in the opening of the market, and the timing of the event (section E).

Through this case study, we explore some of the issues raised in section I, but we do not explore all. First and most obviously, we ask why the nonbank intermediaries complied with the informal Ministry of Finance directives for so long. Although firms generally flouted formally unenforceable directives, in this case they did not. Our study lets us ask why they did not. Second, we ask why the Ministry of Finance pursued the policies that it did. The policies baldly contravened the public interest, and we ask what the ministry might have been doing.[47] Last, we do not address the relative power of politicians and bureaucrats. We do not address it, because it does not arise. It does not arise, because on the issues at stake the politicians and bureaucrats held largely congruent preferences.

B. THE STORY IN BRIEF

1. *Commercial Paper*

Established U.S. firms often raise a large portion of their funds through commercial paper. The paper, as several prominent scholars described it, "is a short-term, unsecured obligation of the corporation, issued for a fixed amount and bearing a fixed rate of interest. Commercial paper occupies a middle ground between stocks and bonds, on the one hand, and commercial loans on the other; it is sold in a market like stocks and bonds, rather than being individually negotiated like commercial loans, but the sales generally occur by private placement, rather than through public offerings."[48]

In a world (such as postwar Japan and the United States) of bifurcated commercial and investment banking, this put commercial paper in a legislative free-fire zone. Because it was short-term, it was relatively safe and could cost-effectively substitute for direct bank loans. Because it was readily tradable, it could also substitute for stocks and bonds. Effectively, it thus threatened both commercial banks and securities firms. What it effectively threatened, of course, it also potentially promised. Precisely because it substituted for loans and securities, it potentially offered entrepreneurial bankers and brokers a means to steal clients.

2. *The Bureaucratic Role*

In Japan, the Ministry of Finance regulates both banks and securities firms. Whether it would regulate commercial paper, however, was unclear. If the paper were a security, the Japanese analogue to Glass-Steagall would have placed it out of bounds to the banks and inbounds for the securities firms.[49] Yet it was not clearly a security; the ministry had no formal regulatory jurisdiction over nonbank, non-securities-firm intermediaries; and in the abstract the ministry had no power to decide what commercial paper was anyway. Yet who could issue and trade in the paper depended crucially on what the paper was.

Tax law only complicated matters. Under the postwar tax regime, traders in securities paid a transactions tax. The rate depended on the transferor and the type of security. As of the early 1980s, a private investor who sold a bond paid a tax of 0.045 percent on its gross sales proceeds (not net profits, and payable with every turnover).[50] By contrast, makers of promissory notes (but not later transferors) paid a less burdensome stamp tax.[51] For a market realistically to develop, qualifying as a promissory note for tax purposes was crucial.

Importantly, the Ministry of Finance not only regulated banks and brokers, it also helped enforce the tax code. Not only did it make preliminary decisions (subject to judicial review, of course) about what businesses banks and securities firms could undertake legally.[52] It also had administrative responsibility over the taxes they and other firms owed.[53]

3. The Deregulation

By the mid-1980s, the Ministry of Finance decided to create the market (table for the moment its authority and incentives to do so) for commercial paper. In the process, however, it decided to ban direct paper (commercial paper sold directly to investors), but to allow dealer paper (paper underwritten by a bank or securities firm).[54] Subject to a variety of constraints, the market began in November 1987.

The market flourished. From its start in November 1987, the commercial paper market grew rapidly: 13.07 trillion yen's worth outstanding at the close of 1989, to 15.76 trillion by 1990 when the ministry lowered the stamp tax on the paper to 5000 yen.[55] That year it also opened the market to issues by securities firms. Central to this case study, in 1993 it opened the market to issues by nonbank intermediaries.[56]

To justify its role in controlling access to the new market by the nonbank intermediaries, the Ministry of Finance had first to argue that the intermediaries could not have issued the paper on their own. For the ministry, this claim involved two steps. First, it treated the firms as members of the lending industry for purposes of Section 2(c) of the Capital Funding Act (see section II.D., below).[57] Second, it called commercial paper a bond. Because the act banned lending companies from using bond proceeds in their loans, it could then argue that the firms could not have issued the paper for loan capital. Relatedly, it could also justify letting them issue paper on the pretext that they not route the proceeds to their loans.

As the leasing firms expanded the market, they continued to push for further deregulation. With due deliberation to be sure, the government responded positively. It relaxed the limits on the amount of funds the firms could raise. It allowed direct placements. And by the end of 1998, it repealed Section 2(c) outright.[58] Thereafter, licensed (but only licensed) nonbank intermediaries could use commercial paper proceeds for their loans. Including major leasing firms like ORIX, by early 2002 over sixty such firms had received a license.[59]

C. THE LITERATURE

On the deregulation of the Japanese commercial paper market, the fullest study in English remains the 1990 essay by David G. Litt, Jonathan R. Macey, Geoffrey P. Miller, and Edward L. Rubin.[60] Focusing on the conflict between the banks and securities firms, Litt et al. called the process a "political battle" between "powerful and well-organized special interest groups."[61] The dynamics through which the government let banks enter the commercial paper market in the United States and Japan were "remarkably similar," they wrote. In both countries the banks fought to protect their "core banking business of extending short term credit to large business firms."

Despite that similarity, Litt et al. claimed that the participants in the "political battle" adopted different strategies in the two countries. In Japan, they explained, the participants showed a predisposition toward "preclearance," a tendency to negotiate potential regulatory conflict in advance.[62] In the United States, they did nothing of the sort. "Open conflict is anathema" to Japanese, they reasoned, but not to Americans. In Japan "public displays of disaffection are assiduously avoided."[63]

As carefully as they analyzed the process, Litt et al. unwittingly raised several issues. First, do we need these cultural characterizations to explain the dynamics in Japan? That the liberalization of commercial paper pitted banks against securities firms we do not contest. That it reflected a peculiarly Japanese antipathy to open conflict we do.

Second—and relatedly—by positing a cultural proclivity not to cross the Ministry of Finance, Litt et al. glossed over the financial dynamics of doing so. Why did the banks and securities firms not create the market on their own? Ministry bureaucrats may not have wanted them to create the market, but no statute clearly banned one. Why did they care what the bureaucrats wanted? Litt et al. wrote that a "number of the people we interviewed stated that it would simply be inconceivable for a bank to begin issuing commercial paper without regulatory approval."[64] Yet if ever there were a nonanswer that is surely one.

Third—and centrally for this essay—what of the nonbank financial intermediaries? Banks and securities firms were not the only firms interested in the commercial paper market. In the United States neither group dominates the market. Instead, the nonbank financial intermediaries do.[65] Why did the Japanese nonbanks not create the commercial paper market on their own? Would Litt et al. have us attribute this to a Japanese proclivity for "preclearance" too? They would apparently have us believe that the firms forsook substantial profits from a commercial paper market simply to avoid a public clash. Yet what financial incentives did the parties actually face?[66]

D. THE CAPITAL FUNDING ACT

1. *Why Firms Complied*

To begin to ask why the nonbank intermediaries acquiesced to the Ministry of Finance's preferences for so long, consider the explanation given by one of the intermediaries itself. Part of the puzzle is why banks and securities firms acquiesced, but another concerns these nonbanks. At least the banks and securities firms were under the general regulatory jurisdiction of the ministry. The nonbanks were not, yet they refrained from starting a commercial paper market before 1993 anyway. Even after 1993, they refused to expand their role beyond that authorized by the Ministry of Finance. Why were the leasing firms so docile?

By the 1990s, the Deregulation Subcommittee of the Administrative Reform Committee began to explore the prospect of deregulating the field. By statute, the committee reported to the prime minister, and he in turn was required to weigh its conclusions heavily. As part of the work of producing that report, in November 1995 one of us (Miwa) asked a representative from the ORIX leasing firm (Hironao Fukushima) why the firm was so docile.[67] The colloquy occurred at a public hearing with a Ministry of Finance representative present and concerned the rules by which the ministry had decided to let nonbank intermediaries like ORIX issue commercial paper:

Miwa: Currently, leasing companies too can issue commercial paper, right?

Fukushima: Restrictions aside, we've been able to issue commercial paper since June 1993. There are lots of those restrictions, though: limits on what we can do with the funds, reporting requirements, rules about putting part of the funds in capital surplus, rules about organizing and retaining documents, demands that we keep special accounts, limits on how much we can raise through commercial paper, and so on. What we're asking today is that these restrictions be reconsidered and abolished.

Miwa: Do you issue a substantial amount?

Fukushima: [By March 1996 we had 252 billion yen's worth outstanding.] That's a substantial amount. Still, relative to the total funds we raise, it's trivial. [Again as of March 1996, we had total debt of 2.99 trillion yen.][68]

Miwa: The rules about what you can do with the funds you raise, and about allocating amounts to capital surplus are ineffective? A waste?

Fukushima: Neither rule has any substantive effect. This is just regulation for the sake of regulation. Money can't be traced. So what if you demand reports to ensure that the firms don't use the funds for loan capital? So what if you make them maintain special bank accounts for the funds? So what if you limit the use they can make of the funds? Substantively, none of that makes a bit of difference.

Miwa: It sounds as if you've got quite a few complaints: that leasing companies face restrictions on what they can do with the funds they raise through commercial paper, that the reasons for the restrictions are inappropriate, that the basis for them is unclear and inappropriate.

If you're so unhappy with this, why don't you just violate it? All you're complaining about is an interpretation of Section 2(c) of the Capital Funding Act [discussed below], after all. And that interpretation is just an "administrative communication" from an MoF [Ministry of Finance] section chief. Right? It's not even a circular.

I don't know if these administrative communications are called "administrative guidance," but why should a communication like that bind a leasing company on such an important issue? Suppose ORIX, as a representative firm, ignored it. What would happen? It's not as if MoF could sue for "violations of an administrative communication." Are there sanctions? Why is commercial paper a "bond" within Section 2(c)? Why is ORIX a "corporation having as its principal business the lending of money" within Section 2(c)?

If commercial paper isn't a bond, then none of this matters, right? And if ORIX isn't a "corporation having as its principal business the lending of money," then Section 2(a) doesn't apply, right? You have a section chief's "administrative communication" about MoF's "interpretation," and you're complying with it? Quietly? Without even trying to contest it?

Fukushima: Well, we could ignore it. But commercial paper is dealer paper. If we ignored it, banks and securities firms wouldn't handle our paper. And if they didn't handle it, that'd be their own choice. Suppose we sued 'em. It'd be a private civil dispute, we'd probably lose, and even if we did win the decision wouldn't govern the meaning of Section 2(c). Even if MoF's preferences were behind it all, we'd never be able to prove it.

Miwa: Why don't you place the commercial paper directly? Does it have to be dealer paper?

Fukushima: . . .

Miwa: What if you tried?

Fukushima: It's hard to say. But if it got harder to issue dealer paper, the costs would be huge. If the securities firms and banks will line up behind MoF, we can't experiment very easily. We don't want to jeopardize large dealer-paper issues with a small direct-placement issue.

Miwa: Then there's the stamp-tax question. Commercial paper is treated as a promissory note, right? What are the implications of all this?

Fukushima: Under an amendment to the Special Tax Measures Act, commercial paper is subject to a flat five thousand yen per note stamp tax, provided it meets certain conditions. If it doesn't meet them, it incurs a tax that varies by the amount of funds raised—and the offering's not going to be attractive. MoF's tax office administers the Special Tax Measures Act. So if the commercial paper isn't dealer paper, it's not going to qualify for this tax preference.

Miwa: So you comply because of the stamp tax, and because banks and securities firms do what MoF wants?

Fukushima: That's right.

If ever Japanese bureaucratic power were overdetermined, it was overdetermined here. The Ministry of Finance regulates banks and securities companies. Through the National Tax Office it collects taxes. And whatever the limits to the ministry's regulatory discretion and interpretive authority (crucially, neither is boundless), banks and securities firms had a collective self-interest in keeping commercial paper inaccessible to the nonbank financial intermediaries anyway. As a result, the Ministry of Finance did not need the power to force an entire industry to comply against interest. It needed only to prevent renegade banks and securities firms from cheating on the industry cartel. That much power it apparently had.

2. *The Statute*

As the colloquy suggests, the only statute on which the Ministry of Finance based its claim that it could ban nonbank financial intermediaries from issuing commercial paper was the 1954 Capital Funding Act. Had the act's drafters designed it to transfer monopoly rents to banks, they could not have done so more baldly. The act banned firms not licensed as banks from taking deposits as a business (Section 2[a]). Crucially for nonbanks that hoped to issue commercial paper, it also provided (Section 2[c]): "A corporation having as its principal business the lending of money . . . which borrows money from a large, unspecified number of people through the issuance of bonds will be treated as a firm taking deposits as a business." Section 8 then imposed fines and prison time on those who violated Section 2.

3. *Its Genesis*

a. The Early Consumer Credit Industry

If the design of the Capital Funding Act suggests legislators hoped to transfer rents to banks, its drafters justified it as an antifraud statute.[69] In the chaotic early postwar years, entrepreneurs concocted a bewildering array of ways to induce savers to entrust their money with them. By some estimates, they formed tens of thousands of firms to collect and lend such savings. Many of these firms were straightforward savings associations. Others are hard to decipher a half century after the fact, but probably functioned more as pyramid schemes.

As eventually enacted, the Capital Funding Act targeted one of the less-than-respectable finance firms: the joint-stock mutual finance firm. Critics accused the operators of these firms of collecting savings by promising investors distributions larger than what the firms could plausibly pay. They proposed either to police the marketing claims or to ban the firms outright.

Some critics hoped initially to control the joint-stock mutuals through the Securities Exchange Act. When that proposal proved problematic, they turned to the Capital Funding Act. The drafters of the Capital Funding Act had not originally envisioned it as a way to regulate joint-stock mutuals and had seen no reason to treat bond issues as "deposits" within the act's Section 2(a) ban. The mutuals' critics, however, argued that they needed a measure that would prevent the mutuals from raising capital through bond issues. To stop such a ploy, they induced the drafters to include bond finance within Section 2(c).[70]

This eleventh-hour switch left technically inclined observers unhappy. Although the Capital Funding Act fell under the joint jurisdiction of the ministries of both justice and finance, it pleased bureaucrats at neither. "On a variety of details, the bill leaves theoretical issues unresolved," complained one official from the Justice Ministry.[71] "You can't say the language is crystal clear," agreed a Ministry of Finance bureau chief. "I talked about it with the Justice Ministry and studied how to write it. In the end, though, we just couldn't come up with anything better."[72]

b. Other Statutes

Other than the Capital Funding Act, few postwar statutes regulated nonbank intermediaries. In 1983, the Diet did pass a Finance Industry Act that mandated licenses, imposed disclosure requirements, and banned what Americans call "predatory lending."[73] Until then, however, the nonbanks had faced only minimal restrictions. The Interest Regulation Act and the Temporary Interest Adjustment Act capped interest rates at the 15–20 percent range, but the caps were easy to evade and carried no criminal penalties anyway.[74]

Even the Capital Funding Act did very little. It imposed criminal sanctions for usury, but only if a lender charged over 109.5 percent a year.[75] It did stop the intermediaries from either taking deposits or selling bonds, but not from borrowing at a bank. Other than ban interest charges over 109 percent, in short, it did almost nothing to regulate how the firms lent money. It merely limited how they raised the money they did lend. Even in recent years, the application of the act has primarily involved schemes to sell investment opportunities fraudulently.[76]

4. *Its Application to Commercial Paper*

Come mid-1993, The Ministry of Finance announced that nonbank intermediaries could raise funds through commercial paper. It is not as though the Diet amended a statute or repealed a ban. It is not as though the Diet passed anything at all. It is not even as though the ministry had general regulatory authority over nonbank intermediaries in the first place. Instead, the ministry merely amended its internal circular "Regarding the Handling of Commercial Paper," added an accompanying set of explanations and conditions, and thereby apparently settled the matter.[77]

Circulars are not "law." As the Supreme Court put it, a "circular is an instruction to a subordinate administrative unit regarding the exercise of administrative power. It is not law that binds the citizens."[78] Consequently, circulars do not bind the parties with whom the agency deals—though to the extent they reflect what an agency is likely to do, they obviously affect such parties. Neither do they bind courts—though to the extent judges want either to minimize effort or to defer to specialists, they obviously affect judicial outcomes.

In its amended 1993 circular, the Ministry of Finance announced the conditions under which nonbanks could issue the paper. They could issue only dealer paper, only in denominations of at least 100 million yen, and only with maturities of under a year. They would need to maintain special bank accounts to handle the funds raised through the commercial paper, to use the funds only for restricted purposes, and to certify that they did not use the funds as loan capital.

The Ministry of Finance said nothing in the circular or the attachments about its statutory authority for doing this: why nonbanks could not legally issue commercial paper before, and why they could now. Given that no statute or regulation had changed, logically the legal status of commercial paper should not have changed either. If nonbanks could not legally issue it before, they could not legally issue it now. If they could legally issue it now, they could legally have done so before.

Presumably, if pressed the Ministry of Finance would have claimed that commercial paper was a "bond" within the scope of Section 2(c) and that the nonbanks had as their "principal business the lending of money." If so, then Section 2(c) prevented them from issuing that paper before and subjected them to criminal sanctions if they did so now. Although the act fell within the joint jurisdiction of the ministries of justice and finance, finance had the initial regulatory authority. Presumably, the Ministry of Finance could claim that the circular lowered the risk (though hardly to zero, given the instability in the Cabinet) that it would recommend the prosecution of a nonbank that issued commercial paper.

The question, however, is whether the Ministry of Finance was right. As of 1987, one securities law treatise could declare that there was no statutory ban on commercial paper in Japan.[79] The senior University of Tokyo corporate law scholar could flatly announce that "if a firm wants to issue commercial paper, under current law it should be able freely to do so."[80] Was commercial paper a bond? On the one hand, it was a debt, and so was a bond; it was transferable, and so was a bond. On the other hand, the paper came in much larger denominations, was offered only to large institutional investors, and bore a much shorter term.

And did a leasing company have as its "principal business the lending of money"? Was a lease a loan? Formally, no. The parties negotiated contractual terms that coupled a transfer of the right to use equipment with a promise to pay periodic fees for that right. Formally, that made it a different contract from one that coupled the transfer of funds with a promise to pay fees for the right to use those funds to buy the equipment. Substantively, however, the leasing firm might as well be lending money. In substance, the firm and the lessee could negotiate contractual terms that accomplished the same result as if the lessor had lent the money and the lessee then used that money to buy the equipment from the manufacturer.[81]

Arguably the Ministry of Finance just allowed firms to issue the paper under conditions that insured that a court would treat it as a promissory note rather than a bond. Yet if so, the parties hardly needed the ministry's help.

They knew the market, and they could read the law. If they wanted to issue notes rather than bonds, they did not need the ministry to tell them how to do so. Indeed, the ministry's requirements were not economically binding anyway. In the mid-1990s, when the Ministry of Finance demanded maturities of under a year for the paper, ORIX issued most of its paper with three-month terms; when the ministry demanded face amounts of at least 100 million yen, ORIX typically issued it at face amounts of 5–30 billion yen.[82]

E. THE BARGAIN

1. *The Deal*

At the same time it announced that nonbank intermediaries could issue commercial paper, the Ministry of Finance also asserted regulatory jurisdiction over the intermediaries. That it coupled the two matters captures the bargain and explains the dynamic behind both the earlier ban and its repeal: in exchange for access to the commercial paper market, the nonbank intermediaries agreed to submit to the ministry's regulatory jurisdiction. In the process, they also agreed to abide by the terms of the cartel in the banking industry.

For the essence of Ministry of Finance regulation lay in the cartel. Since the war, the ministry had regulated the banks in classic Stiglerian fashion: against firms that would try to cheat on the terms of the industry cartel, it enforced the cartel's terms. Given the fungibility of money and the alternative ways to raise it, the cartel had never generated large rents.[83] Of the major threats to the cartel, the nonbank financial intermediaries simply represented the most recent. By bringing them within its jurisdiction as well, the ministry mitigated their corrosive potential.

2. *The Banking Cartel*

a. Bonds

The postwar history of the bond market illustrates the way banks had earlier fought to preserve their cartel. If for industrial firms an active bond market represented a financing opportunity, for banks it represented a threat. Precisely because it gave their best customers a way to raise debt capital without them, it was an institution banks worked to cripple.

Primarily, banks reduced the threat the bond market posed by imposing a toll charge on those who would use it. They charged the toll by requiring most issuers to post collateral.[84] They imposed the requirement through a "bond issue committee," which they in turn dominated. Because by law only banks could manage the collateral,[85] the collateralization rule routed fees to the banking industry even when firms turned elsewhere.[86] In exchange for letting a few firms raise their debt on the bond market, in other words, it used the collateralization requirement to route banks a toll charge when they did.

By the 1980s, things changed. The government loosened foreign exchange controls, and technological change eased communication and trade.[87] In the process, many of the larger manufacturing firms discovered increased access to the far less regulated European financial market. In 1980, Japanese firms raised only 680 billion yen through overseas bonds. By 1984, they were raising 2.8 trillion yen, and by 1989 11.1 trillion.[88]

As Euro-issues grew, the domestic market languished. From 1981 to 1985, the amount that manufacturing firms raised through domestic straight bond issues fell from 1,269 billion yen to 944 billion. By 1989 it had fallen to 729 billion. Even these numbers exaggerate domestic issues, for most were utility company issues: 73.4, 59.1, and 95.1 percent of all private-sector domestic straight bond issues by nonfinancial firms in 1981, 1985, and 1989, respectively. Other than NTT and KDD (the telephone companies), nonfinancial firms simply did not issue domestic straight bonds.[89]

b. Commercial Paper

Similarly the commercial paper market represented a threat to the banking cartel, and it too the banks sought to stifle. To be sure, the two alternatives threatened different sectors of the banking industry. As long-term debt, bonds threatened the profitability of the banks specializing in longer-term loans, disproportionately banks like the Industrial Bank of Japan and the trust banks. As short-term debt, commercial paper threatened those specializing in shorter-term loans, disproportionately the large money-center banks.[90] The nonbank intermediaries borrowed heavily from the latter, though they also borrowed from the trust banks.

Lest there be any doubt, note that the earlier ban on commercial paper had nothing to do with "investor protection." Several years before it allowed a market for domestically issued commercial paper, the Ministry of Finance had already allowed domestic trading in overseas issues.[91] Fundamentally, it was the issuing of the paper by Japanese firms that concerned the government, not the purchase of the instruments by Japanese investors. Where it had allowed domestic investors to trade in the paper of foreign firms by 1984, it did not allow them to trade the paper of foreign affiliates of Japanese firms until later.

By the mid-1990s, deregulation hit both the bond and the commercial paper markets. After two decades of gradual liberalization, the bond market was completely deregulated by 1996.[92] With the repeal of the Capital Funding Act in 1998, the final restrictions on commercial paper issues by the nonbanks disappeared as well.

c. The Waning Cartel

Never secure in the first place, by the close of the 1980s the banking cartel had atrophied badly. Internationally, the few preeminent institutions like the Mizuho (Daiichi Kangyo) Bank and Nomura Securities obscure the highly competitive character of the Japanese financial services industry. As of the early 1990s, Japanese firms chose from among 140-plus banks.[93] To be sure, traditionally only three could issue debentures and primarily only trust banks managed client trusts. Otherwise, however, the market was for banks a free-for-all.

In this competitive market, banks loaned funds at rates that reflected borrower risk.[94] Throughout the postwar period, the government and industry purported to regulate the interest rates banks could charge their lenders. As we explain elsewhere, the rates did not bind. Firms that needed funds, after all, had access not only to the highly competitive banking world but to a wide variety of sources other than banks besides. The large Japanese trading firms routinely provided capital. Contractual partners provided trade credit. The agricultural cooperatives lent funds, and (as the discussion above indicates) as technological change lowered the costs of tapping sources overseas so did foreign institutions.[95]

Although the government regulated the rates banks could pay depositors, banks were not the only place investors could park their money. Instead, they could choose from among a variety of investments, including trusts, life insurance contracts, and securities funds.[96] Given this competition, insiders would necessarily have earned few rents.

Low to begin with, come international competition the rents to cartelization fell even further. As they fell, so did the support that Japanese banks—especially the more efficient banks—were willing to offer it. Increasingly, they eyed the gains to be had from dismantling the status quo. Increasingly, the other banks found it harder to maintain the financial order unchanged.

d. The Rising Nonbank Intermediaries

Although deregulation followed, the nonbank financial intermediaries were among the last to reap its benefits. Several reasons account for this. First, ostensibly the key to access lay in Section 2(c) repeal. Yet facially Section 2(c) merely prevented money-lending firms from issuing bonds, and until the 1980s the banks had kept the bond market crippled anyway. Absent much of a bond market, Section 2(c) would have seemed a nonissue. Second, to issue commercial paper cost-effectively, the nonbanks also had to convince either the Ministry of Finance or the Diet to levy only a low tax on the paper. Until it did, Section 2(c) made little difference.

Third, before the 1990s, the nonbank intermediaries had neither the ability nor the incentive to lobby for either Section 2(c) repeal or the prerequisite tax change. They lacked the ability because they lacked political substance. ORIX was the largest of the leasing firms, but as of 1980 even it had only 506 employees. Only by 1990 did it grow to two thousand employees. By the year 2000 it had grown to over three thousand. Only with such scope did the industry obtain the political influence it needed. Before the 1990s, the nonbank intermediaries also lacked the incentive to lobby. Because commercial paper is unsecured, even in the United States only the biggest and safest firms can use it to raise funds.[97] Until the leasing firms acquired that stability, they simply could not have issued paper—until then, legal license was a nonissue.

3. *Why the Ministry of Finance Banned the Issues, Then Relented*

Eventually, the bargain came to pass: the Ministry of Finance agreed to let the nonbank intermediaries issue commercial paper, and the intermediaries agreed to submit to its regulatory jurisdiction. A 1991 committee report from the ministry hinted at what would become the bargain. The ministry should consider letting nonbanks issue commercial paper, it declared, if but only "if the place of the non-bank financial intermediaries were clarified within the financial system, and if an appropriate supervisory and regulatory system were established."[98] Maybe the nonbank intermediaries could some day issue the paper, but only if they first agreed to be regulated.

As of the early 1990s, the Ministry of Finance (and the banks whose interests it largely represented) and the nonbank intermediaries had not yet made the bargain. Already, however, the government was starting to try to pull them within the ministry's regulatory orb. In December 1990, the Financial Issues

Research Committee of the LDP reported that "the non-bank intermediaries were channeling massive loans into real estate." They must, it cautioned, "conduct their loan business in an appropriate and healthy manner." Notwithstanding, a subcommittee concluded a few months later, the government still "was not able to supervise investments in a way that would let it address the current real-estate loan problems."[99]

Soon the government did begin to assert that regulatory jurisdiction. It did pass legislation imposing on the nonbank financial intermediaries reporting requirements for real estate loans, for example.[100] What it had not yet done was to subject the nonbanks to general regulatory jurisdiction. Obviously, the banks could have tried to induce the government to do so by legislative fiat—and the nonbanks might or might not have successfully blocked them. Just as obviously, the nonbanks might have tried to obtain the legislation necessary cost-effectively to issue commercial paper (including the lower tax rates and a general authorization for direct paper)—and the banks might or might not have successfully blocked them. The banks and nonbanks might have combined to lobby for a legislative package that did both.

Instead, the banks and nonbanks negotiated through administrative forums. The Ministry of Finance had organized a "nonbank study committee." After a series of meetings, the committee in April 1991 detailed the potential deal to be made. On the one hand, banks and nonbanks competed, and banks were regulated while the nonbank intermediaries were not. On the other hand, nonbanks could not issue commercial paper. Couple the issues, and make the deal: give nonbanks the right to issue the paper, and "clarify the role of nonbank intermediaries in the financial world and institute an appropriate system for guiding and instructing" the nonbanks.[101]

A year later, another Ministry of Finance committee repeated the potential deal. "Given the current circumstances of the nonbanks," it noted, it would be good if "the administrative offices had a better grasp of the general situation and a better ability to monitor." While the nonbank intermediaries ought to be able to "issue commercial paper for raising capital other than loan funds," they should be able to do so only if "there were in place an institutional apparatus for guiding and directing the nonbanks."[102]

The pretext for the deal lay in the Capital Funding Act requirement (if that indeed is what it was) that lenders segregate bond proceeds from loan capital. Never mind that money is fungible and that intra-firm segregation rarely accomplishes anything. By equating leasing firms with moneylenders and commercial paper with bonds, the banks and nonbanks could use the Capital Funding Act requirement to justify coupling commercial-paper access with regulatory jurisdiction. As the ministry committee above noted in its 1992 report, it purported to want to insure that nonbanks did not loan out the commercial paper proceeds. The ministry should allow nonbanks into the commercial paper market—but only if "measures could be put in place to insure that the commercial paper proceeds not be used to fund loans."[103]

III. CONCLUSIONS

Much of the recent financial distress in Japan traces itself to the limited range of nonbank financial intermediaries that investors and firms can tap. That limited range, in turn, is a creature of regulation. If the regulation seems bad policy, it is. Yet as a means to the public good, the postwar regulatory regime in the financial services industry never made sense anyway. The regime crippled the market for bonds. It squelched the market for commercial paper. It stifled firms that might threaten the banks. It capped interest rates. It stopped most new branches. For several years (think "Robot Protection Act") it even shut down ATMs over evenings and weekends.

Yet while the details differ, the more fundamental point is hardly specific to Japan. As a means to the public good, regulation seldom makes sense anywhere. As Ronald Coase put it in 1964: "What the regulatory commissions are trying to do is difficult to discover; what effect these commissions actually have is, to a larger extent, unknown; when it can be discovered, it is often absurd."[104] The U.S. financial services industry had its Glass-Steagall, its bans on branch banks, its interest rate caps. Other countries and other industries have had their own equivalents.

At root, regulation is not about the public good, and never has been—not in the West, and not in Japan. It has been about redistribution. Sometimes the redistribution is explicit: think dairy cows in the American Midwest, silkworms in central Japan. And sometimes the redistribution takes the form of cartel enforcement. Because they are so unstable, as a long-term source of rents cartels can be notoriously unreliable. Sometimes, the government can help the industry preserve those rents by preserving that stability.

In the Japanese financial sector, the government helped preserve cartel stability by stifling competition. For years, that entailed crippling nonbank intermediaries and the markets for corporate bonds and commercial paper. By the late 1980s, it entailed liberalizing the commercial paper market, but only by simultaneously bringing the nonbanks within its cartel-enforcing regulatory jurisdiction.

All this is a story one could tell about most any democracy. Yet such is the very nature of social scientific theory: it applies across nations, across cultures, across time. We do not claim the vicissitudes of nonbank intermediaries, and commercial paper issues in Japan prove that universality. No case study ever could. We do claim the case study illustrates the dynamic involved: both the dynamics of the Japanese legislative and regulatory process, and the dynamics of political economy more generally.

NOTES

We gratefully acknowledge the assistance of Hironao Fukushima, Satoru Miura, Yoshihiko Miyauchi, and Masahiko Taumi of ORIX, K. K. We received helpful comments from Hideki Kanda, Curtis Milhaupt, Mark West, and the participants at the August 2002 conference at the University of Washington. We received generous financial assistance from the Center for International Research on the Japanese Economy at the University of Tokyo, the John M. Olin Program in Law, Economics and Business at the Harvard Law School, and the Sloan Foundation.

1. Merton H. Miller, "Financial Markets and Economic Growth," *Bank of America Journal of Applied Corporate Finance* 11(3) (Fall 1998): 8.

2. See Yoshiro Miwa and J. Mark Ramseyer, "Banks and Economic Growth: Implications from Japanese History," *Journal of Law and Economics* 45 (2002): 127. Smaller Japanese firms had relied heavily on trade credit. See Yoshiro Miwa and J. Mark Ramseyer, "Japanese Industrial Finance at the Close of the Nineteenth Century: Trade Credit and Financial Intermediation," *Explorations in Economic History* 43 (2006): 94.

3. See generally George J. Stigler, "The Theory of Economic Regulation," *Bell Journal of Economics and Management Science* 2 (1970): 3; and Sam Peltzman, "Toward a More General Theory of Regulation," *Journal of Law and Economics* 19 (1976): 211. On the political economy of the Japanese financial services industry, see Yoshirō Miwa, *Kin'yū gyōsei kaikaku* [Financial Administration Reform] (Tokyo: Nihon keizai shimbun, 1993); and Frances McCall Rosenbluth, *Financial Politics in Contemporary Japan* (Ithaca, NY: Cornell University Press, 1989).

4. Yoshirō Miwa and J. Mark Ramseyer, "The Multiple Roles of Banks? Convenient Tales from Modern Japan," in Klaus J. Hopt, Eddy Wymeersch, Hideki Kanda, and Harald Baum, eds., *Corporate Governance in Context: Corporations, States, and Markets in Europe, Japan, and the U.S.* (Oxford: Oxford University Press, 2005), 527–66; Miwa and Ramseyer, "Asking the Wrong Question: Changes of Governance in Historical Perspective?" in Hopt et al., *Corporate Governance in Context*, 73–84; Miwa and Ramseyer, *Sangyō seisaku ron no gokai: Kōdō seichō no shinjitsu*

[Misunderstandings about Industrial Policy: The Truth about High Growth] (Tokyo: Tōyō keizai shimpō sha, 2002); Miwa and Ramseyer, "Directed Credit? The Loan Market in High-Growth Japan," *Journal of Economics and Management Strategy* 13 (2003): 171; Miwa and Ramseyer, "Capitalist Politicians, Socialist Bureaucrats? Tales We Tell of Japan," *Antitrust Bulletin* 48 (2003): 595; Miwa and Ramseyer, "Nihon no keizai seisaku to seisaku kenkyū" [Japanese Economic Policy and Policy Research], *Keizai kenkyū* 52 (2001): 193; Yoshirō Miwa, *State Competence and Economic Growth in Japan* (London: RoutledgeCurzon, 2004).

5. Miwa, *State Competence and Economic Growth in Japan.*

6. Nihon koku kempō [Constitution of Japan], effective 1947.

7. See generally J. Mark Ramseyer and Minoru Nakazato, *Japanese Law: An Economic Approach* (Chicago: University of Chicago Press, 1999), chap. 8.

8. See generally J. Mark Ramseyer and Frances McCall Rosenbluth, *Japan's Political Marketplace*, rev. ed. (Cambridge, MA: Harvard University Press, 1997), chap. 2.

9. See ibid., "Preface, 1997."

10. See Ramseyer and Nakazato, *Japanese Law*, 147–50.

11. We leave for other forums questions about how independent judges are in what sorts of cases. See generally J. Mark Ramseyer and Eric B. Rasmusen, *Measuring Judicial Independence: The Political Economy of Judging in Japan* (Chicago: University of Chicago Press, 2003).

12. For an amusing if idiosyncratic take on the debate in political science, see John C. Campbell, "Hedgehogs and Foxes: The Divisive Rational Choice Debate in the Study of Japanese Politics," *Social Science Japan* 8 (1997): 36.

For evidence that similar failings plague the literature on the Japanese economy, see Miwa and Ramseyer, *Sangyō seisaku ron no gokai*; Yoshirō Miwa and J. Mark Ramseyer, *Nihon keizai ron no gokai: "Keiretsu" no jūbaku kara no kaihō* [Misunderstandings in the Theory of the Japanese Economy: Liberation from the Spell of the "Keiretsu"] (Tokyo: Tōyō keizai shimpō sha, 2001); Miwa and Ramseyer, "The Fable of the Keiretsu," *Journal of Economics and Management Strategy* 11 (2002): 169; Miwa and Ramseyer, "The Myth of the Main Bank: Japan and Comparative Corporate Governance," *Law and Social Inquiry* 27 (2002): 401; Miwa and Ramseyer, "'Keiretsu no kenkyū' no keiretsu no kenkyū" [Research on the Keiretsu in "Research on the Keiretsu"], *Keizaigaku ronshū* 67(2) (2001): 36, *Keizaigaku ronshū* 67(3) (2001): 68; Miwa and Ramseyer, "Does Relationship Banking Matter? The Myth of the Japanese Main Bank," *Journal of Empirical Legal Studies* 2 (2005): 261–302; Miwa and Ramseyer, "Who Appoints Them, What Do They Do? Evidence on Outside Directors from Japan," *Journal of Economics and Management Strategy* 14 (2005): 299–337; and Miwa and Ramseyer, "Conflicts of Interest in

Japanese Insolvencies: The Problem of Bank Rescues," *Theoretical Inquiries in Law* 6 (2005): 301–39.

13. See Kiyoaki Tsuji, *Nihon kanryōsei no kenkyū* [New Edition: A Study of the Japanese Bureaucratic System] (Tokyo: Kōbundō, 1952).

14. See T. J. Pempel, "The Bureaucratization of Policymaking in Postwar Japan," *American Journal of Political Science* 18 (1974): 647; and Chalmers Johnson, MITI *and the Japanese Miracle* (Stanford, CA: Stanford University Press, 1982).

15. Johnson, *MITI and the Japanese Miracle*, 20–21.

16. Ronald Dore, *Stock Market Capitalism: Welfare Capitalism* (Oxford: Oxford University Press, 2000), 157; see also, e.g., Curtis J. Milhaupt and Mark D. West, "Law's Dominion and the Market for Legal Elites in Japan," *Law and Policy in International Business* 34 (2003): 451.

17. On the ties between bureaucratic outcomes and bureaucratic jurisdictional competition, see Yoshirō Miwa and J. Mark Ramseyer, "Kyōsō seisaku no nozomashii sugata to yakuwari: Shiteki dokusen, keiji batsu, kōsei torihiki iinkai" [The Form and Function of Good Competition Policy: Monopolization, Criminal Sanctions, and the Fair Trade Commission], *Jurisuto*, no. 1261 (2004): 144, *Jurisuto*, no. 1262 (2004): 78; and Miwa and Ramseyer, "Toward a Theory of Jurisdictional Competition: The Case of the Japanese FTC," *Journal of Competition Law and Economics* 1 (2005): 247–77.

18. Joseph Sanders, "Courts and Law in Japan," in Herbert Jacob et al., eds., *Courts, Law, and Politics in Comparative Perspective* (New Haven, CT: Yale University Press, 1996), 315, 367. See also, e.g., Ulrike Schaede, "The 'Old Boy' Network and Government-Business Relationships in Japan," *Journal of Japanese Studies* 21 (1995): 293, 301 ("Effectively, there is no legal recourse to regulation in the form of administrative guidance, because compliance is 'voluntary' ").

19. Karel van Wolferen, *The Enigma of Japanese Power: People and Politics in a Stateless Nation* (New York: Vantage Books, 1989), 215.

20. Ulrike Schaede, "Understanding Corporate Governance in Japan: Do Classical Concepts Apply?" *Industrial and Corporate Change* 3 (1994): 285, 289.

21. Frank K. Upham, *Law and Social Change in Postwar Japan* (Cambridge, MA: Harvard University Press, 1987), 176.

22. Schaede, "Understanding Corporate Governance in Japan," 290.

23. Henry Rosovsky, "What Are the Lessons of Japanese Economic History?" in A. J. Youngson, ed., *Economic Development in the Long-Run* (London: Allen and Unwin, 1972), 229, 244.

24. James Fallows, *Looking at the Sun: The Rise of the New East Asian Economic and Political System* (New York: Pantheon, 1994), 218 (italics in original).

25. Wolfgang Pape, "Gyosei shido and the Antimonopoly Act," *Law in Japan: An Annual* 15 (1982): 12, 12, 13, 14–15.

26. Dore, *Stock Market Capitalism*, 156.

27. Fallows, *Looking at the Sun*, 58.

28. Ibid., 207 (approvingly quoting Eisuke Sakakibara).

29. Dore, *Stock Market Capitalism*, 17, 219–20.

30. On actual economic planning under Stalin, see Paul Gregory and Mark Harrison, "Allocation under Dictatorship: Research in Stalin's Archives," *Journal of Economic Literature* 43 (2005): 721–61.

31. Rosovsky, "What Are the Lessons of Japanese Economic History," 244.

32. Paul Krugman, *The Age of Diminished Expectations: U.S. Economic Policy in the 1990s* (Cambridge, MA: MIT Press, 1990), 142.

33. Tetsuji Okazaki and Masahiro Okuno-Fujiwara, "Japan's Present-Day Economic System and Its Historical Origins," in Tetsuji Okazaki and Masahiro Okuno-Fujiwara, eds., *The Japanese Economic System and Its Historical Origins*, trans. Susan Herbert (Oxford: Oxford University Press, 1999), 1, 11–12.

34. See Mathew D. McCubbins and Gregory W. Noble, "The Appearance of Power: Legislators, Bureaucrats, and the Budget Process in the United States and Japan," in Peter F. Cowhey and Mathew D. McCubbins, eds., *Structure and Policy in Japan and the United States* (Cambridge: Cambridge University Press, 1995), 56.

35. Randall L. Calvert, Mark J. Moran, and Barry R. Weingast, "Congressional Influence over Policy Making: The Case of the FTC," in Mathew D. McCubbins and Terry Sullivan, eds., *Congress: Structure and Policy* (Cambridge: Cambridge University Press, 1987), 493, 501 (original was italicized).

36. The classic references are William M. Landes, "An Economic Analysis of the Courts," *Journal of Law and Economics* 14 (1971): 61; and Richard A. Posner, "An Economic Approach to Legal Procedure and Judicial Administration," *Journal of Legal Studies* 2 (1973): 399.

37. See generally Stigler, "The Theory of Economic Regulation," 3; and Peltzman, "Toward a More General Theory of Regulation," 211.

38. Fred S. McChesney, *Money for Nothing: Politicians, Rent Extraction, and Political Extortion* (Cambridge, MA: Harvard University Press, 1997), 11.

39. Ibid., 14.

40. On the ineffectiveness of postwar regulation, see Miwa and Ramseyer, "The Multiple Roles of Banks"; and Miwa and Ramseyer, "Asking the Wrong Question." On the ineffectiveness of wartime and early postwar regulation, see Miwa, *State Competence and Economic Growth in Japan*; and Yoshirō Miwa and J. Mark Ramseyer, "Keizai kisei no yūkōsei: Keisha seisan seisaku no shinwa"

[On the Effectiveness of Economic Regulation: The Myth of "Priority Production" Policy], *Keizai gaku ronshū* 70(2) (2004): 2–54, *Keizai gaku ronshū* 70(3) (2004): 60–119.

41. See generally Ramseyer and Rosenbluth, *Japan's Political Marketplace*, chaps. 6–7; Ramseyer and Rasmusen, *Measuring Judicial Independence*; McCubbins and Noble, "The Appearance of Power"; and Mathew D. McCubbins and Michael F. Thies, "As a Matter of Factions: The Budgetary Implications of Shifting Factional Control in Japan's LDP," *Legislative Studies Quarterly* 22 (1997): 293.

42. See Miwa and Ramseyer, *Sangyō seisaku ron no gokai*; Miwa and Ramseyer, "Capitalist Politicians, Socialist Bureaucrats"; J. Mark Ramseyer, "Rethinking Administrative Guidance," in Masahiko Aoki and Gary R. Saxonhouse, eds., *Finance, Governance, and Competitiveness in Japan* (Oxford: Oxford University Press, 2000), 199; Miwa and Ramseyer, "The Multiple Roles of Banks"; and Miwa and Ramseyer, "Asking the Wrong Question."

43. See Miwa, *State Competence and Economic Growth in Japan*.

44. Yoshirō Miwa, "'Kin'yū seido kaikaku' to shintaku ginkō" ["Financial System Reform" and the Trust Banks], in Keimei Kaizuka and Kazuo Ueda, eds., *Henkaku ki no kin'yū shisutemu* [The Financial System in a Time of Change] (Tokyo: Tokyo University Press, 1994), 173; "Ōkura shō wa ikisugi" [Ministry of Finance Going Too Far], Nihon keizai shimbun, February 23, 1965; Miwa and Ramseyer, "The Multiple Roles of Banks."

45. Yoshirō Miwa and J. Mark Ramseyer, *The Fable of the Keiretsu: Urban Legends of the Japanese Economy* (Chicago: University of Chicago Press, 2006), chap. 6; Miwa and Ramseyer, *Sangyō seisaku ron no gokai*; Miwa and Ramseyer, "Capitalist Politicians, Socialist Bureaucrats"; Miwa and Ramseyer, "The Multiple Roles of Banks"; Miwa and Ramseyer, "Asking the Wrong Question."

46. For other evidence that the Japanese government did not mastermind growth, see Yoshiro Miwa, *Firms and Industrial Organization in Japan* (Houndsmill, Hampshire: Macmillan, 1996), pt. 3; Yoshirō Miwa, *Seifu no nōryoku* [The Competence of the State] (Tokyo: Yūhikaku, 1998); Miwa and Ramseyer, *Sangyō seisaku ron no gokai*; Miwa and Ramseyer, "Directed Credit"; Yoshirō Miwa and J. Mark Ramseyer, "Seisaku kin'yū to keizai hatten: Senzenki Nihon kōgyō ginkō no kēsu" [Policy Finance and Economic Growth: The Case of the Prewar Industrial Bank of Japan], *Keizaigaku ronshū* 66(3) (2000): 2.

47. For the relation between a bureaucracy's jurisdiction and its policy outcomes, see Miwa and Ramseyer, "Kyōsō seisaku no nozomashii sugata to yakuwari"; and Miwa and Ramseyer, "Toward a Theory of Jurisdictional Competition."

48. David G. Litt, Jonathan R. Macey, Geoffrey P. Miller, and Edward L. Rubin, "Politics, Bureaucracies, and Financial Markets: Bank Entry into Commercial

Paper Underwriting in the United States and Japan," *University of Pennsylvania Law Review* 139 (1990): 369, 375.

49. Shōken torihiki hō [Securities Exchange Act], Act No. 25 of 1948, § 65 (as in effect). The U.S. Supreme Court found commercial paper to be a security in Securities Industry Association v. Board of Governors, 468 U.S. 137 (1984).

As if to confuse matters, foreign commercial paper (the market for which was liberalized earlier than for domestic commercial paper) was treated as a security for purposes of the Foreign Exchange and Foreign Trade Control Act, but not for purposes of the Securities Exchange Act. See Takeo Kosugi and Steven M. Dickinson, "The Creation of a Domestic Commercial Paper Market in Japan," *Columbia Journal of Transnational Law* 27 (1988): 91, 100–105. According to a joint statement by two staff members of the Ministry of Finance's banking and securities bureaus, it would have been "inappropriate" to treat commercial paper the same as securities, given its short-term character and the fact that it is placed with professional investors. Moreover, they claimed, this was consistent with the practice in other countries. See Motoyasu Yoshikawa and Hiroshi Harada, "Kokunai CP shijō sōsetsu no keii to sono gaiyō" [A Summary and the Particulars of the Establishment of a Domestic Commercial Paper Market], *Kin'yū hōmu jijō* 1172 (1987): 7, 10 n. 4.

50. Yūka shōken torihiki zei hō [Securities Transaction Tax Act], Act No. 102 of 1953, §§ 2, 10.

51. A note of 1 million yen, for example, incurred a tax of 200 yen (0.02 percent); a note of 10 million incurred a 2,000-yen tax; and a note of 100 million yen incurred a 20,000-yen tax. See Inshi zei hō [Stamp Tax Act], Act No. 23 of 1967, table 1(c). The stamp tax applied to bonds as well.

52. Shōken torihiki hō, § 28 (requiring a Ministry of Finance permit to carry on securities business); Ginkō hō [Banking Act], Act No. 59 of 1981, § 4 (same for banking business; current as of 1994).

53. Hiroshi Kaneko, *Sozei hō* [Tax Act], 5th ed. (Tokyo: Kōbundō, 1995), 102.

54. Yoshikawa and Harada, "Kokunai CP shijō sōsetsu no keii to sono gaiyō," 8; Shūichi Sonoda, "Shōken gaisha ni yoru kokunai CP no toriatsukai ni tsuite" [Regarding the Handling of Domestic Commercial Paper by Securities Firms], *Kin'yū hōmu jijō* 1172 (1987): 11, 12 (1987). By the early 1990s, the rule was embodied in "Komāsharu pēpā tō no toriatsukai ni tsuite" [Regarding the Handling of Commercial Paper, Etc.], Ministry of Finance Banking Bureau Communication 610 of 1993, § I.1.(5) (as in effect; hereinafter Circular 610).

After the repeal of Circular 610 and Shusshi no ukeire, azukarikin oyobi kinri tō no torishimari tō ni kansuru hōritsu [An Act regarding the Regulation of the Receipt of Investment Capital, Deposits, and Interest Rates], Act No. 195 of 1954,

§ 2(c), along with the amendment of the relevant tax provisions, the dealer-paper requirement effectively disappeared. By March 2000, the ORIX group (including ORIX Securities) was issuing a majority of its commercial paper (over 1 trillion yen total) as direct paper. Private correspondence with the firm.

55. Sozei tokubetsu sochi hō [Special Tax Measures Act], Act No. 26 of 1957, § 91-2(a) (as in effect at the time). By the terms of the section, the lower tax rate did not apply to direct paper. Market volume figures are based on Bank of Japan data. Gordon de Brouwer, "Deregulation and the Structure of the Money Market," in Paul Sheard, ed., *Japanese Firms, Finance and Markets* (Melbourne: Addison-Wesley, 1996), 274; Litt et al., "Politics, Bureaucracies, and Financial Markets," 427 n.196.

56. On the commercial paper issues by securities firms, see *Shōken kyoku nempō* [Securities Bureau Annual] 59 (1990); and Yoshirō Miwa, *Kin'yū gyōsei kaikaku: "Yakusho banare" no susume* [Financial Industry Regulatory Reform: Toward Independence from the Bureaucracy] (Tokyo: Nihon keizai shimbun, 1993).

57. Shusshi no ukeire, azukarikin oyobi kinri tō no torishimari tō ni kansuru hōritsu.

58. Kin'yū gyō sha no kashitsuke gyōmu no tame no shasai hakkō tō ni kansuru hōritsu [An Act regarding the Issuance of Bonds, Etc., by Members of the Financial Industry for the Lending Business], Act No. 107 of 1998. It also repealed the dealer paper requirement for the lower tax rate. See Sozei tokubetsu sochi hō, § 91-2.

59. Shusshi no ukeire, azukarikin oyobi kinri tō no torishimari tō ni kansuru hōritsu, § 3, as revised. Data obtained through inquiry by the authors.

60. Litt et al., "Politics, Bureaucracies, and Financial Markets." For a detailed chronology of the liberalization from a more bureaucracy-centric perspective, see Ulrike Schaede, "The Introduction of Commercial Paper—a Case Study in the Liberalization of the Japanese Financial Markets," *Japan Forum* 2 (1990): 5.

61. Litt et al., "Politics, Bureaucracies, and Financial Markets," 371.

62. Tracking the distinction between "ex ante monitoring" and "ex post monitoring" in Hideki Kanda, "Politics, Formalism, and the Elusive Goal of Investor Protection: Regulation of Structured Investment Funds in Japan," *University of Pennsylvania Journal of International Business Law* 12 (1991): 569.

63. Litt et al., "Politics, Bureaucracies, and Financial Markets," 435, 440.

64. Ibid., 447.

65. On the use of commercial paper by nonbanks in the United States, see ibid., 425.

66. If pushed, perhaps Litt et al. would have argued that the Ministry of Finance would have surreptitiously punished a bank or securities firm that

ignored its preferences. The argument is common enough among observers who claim Japanese bureaucratic omnipotence. Ulrike Schaede, for example, claims that "[c]orporations know that by following 'advice' they may reap rewards later. On the other hand, if the ministries find a noncompliance with administrative guidance, they have numerous options to obstruct future business of the party concerned." Schaede, "The 'Old Boy' Network and Government-Business Relationships in Japan," 301. The myth is untrue, as we explain in Miwa and Ramseyer, *The Fable of the Keiretsu*, chap. 6; Miwa and Ramseyer, *Sangyō seisaku ron no gokai*; Miwa and Ramseyer, "Capitalist Politicians, Socialist Bureaucrats"; and Miwa and Ramseyer, "The Multiple Roles of Banks."

67. The committee had begun deliberations in December of 1994 and met for three years. The committee was established by the Gyōsei kaikaku iinkai setchi hō [Act to Establish the Administrative Reform Committee], Act No. 96 of 1994; see §§ 1–3.

68. Data provided by private correspondence and included here for reference. The discussion at the committee hearing itself did not disclose the actual amounts outstanding at ORIX.

69. See generally Minoru Tsuda, "Shusshi no ukeire, azukarikin oyobi kinri tō no torishimari tō ni kansuru hōritsu" [An Act regarding the Regulation of the Receipt of Investment Capital, Deposits, and Interest Rates], *Hōsō jihō* 7 (1954): 767, 767–68; Hideo Kanbayashi, "Kashikingyō tō no torishimari ni kansuru hōritsu kaisetsu" [Commentary on the Act to Regulate the Money-Lending Industry, Etc.], *Zaisei keizai kōhō*, June 10, 1949, 1; and Shigeo Tamiya, "Rishoku kikan no torishimari hō" [The Statute on the Control of Profit-Making Institutions], *Kin'yū hōmu jijō*, March 25, 1954, 4.

70. Tamiya, "Rishoku kikan no torishimari hō," 8–9.

71. Ibid., 9.

72. Comments of Michikazu Kōno, *Dai 19-kai Kokkai shūgiin ōkura iinkai giroku* 51 (May 7, 1954).

73. Kashikin gyō no kisei ni kansuru hōritsu [Act regarding the Regulation of the Money-Lending Industry], Act No. 32 of 1983.

74. Risoku seigen hō [Interest Limitation Act], Act No. 100 of 1954, § 1; Rinji kinri chōsei hō [Temporary Act for the Adjustment of Interest Rates], Act No. 181 of 1947, and accompanying regulations. See generally Miwa and Ramseyer, "Directed Credit"; Toshio Tsubaki and Shin'ichi Nishio, *Kin'yū torihiki no hōritsu sōdan* [Legal Consultation on Financial Transactions] (Tokyo: Yūhikaku, 1987), 54–55.

75. Shusshi no ukeire, azukarikin oyobi kinri tō no torishimari tō ni kansuru hōritsu, § 5.

76. E.g., [No names given] (Kyoto D. Ct., Sept. 20, 1993), *Hanrei taimuzu* 832 (1993): 227; Iwano v. Gotō (Sendai High Ct., May 27, 1987), *Hanrei taimuzu* 657 (1987): 141.

77. Circular 610, as amended June 30, 1993; Ōkurashō ginkō kyoku, Jimu renraku [Administrative Communication], June 30, 1993. Note, however, that in 1993, the ministry did promulgate an order, Ōkura shō rei 14 of March 3, 1993, § 1, that placed commercial paper within the ambit of the catchall definition given in § 2(a)(viii) of the Shōken torihiki hō.

78. Nakagawa v. Nagasaki zeimushochō (Sup. Ct. Dec. 24, 1963), *Sōmu geppō* 10 (1963): 381; see Kaneko, *Sozei hō*, 105; Jirō Tanaka, *Gyōsei hō, jō* [Administrative Law: I], new ed. (Tokyo: Kōbundō, 1984), 164.

79. Ichirō Kawamoto and Yasunami Ōtake, *Shōken torihiki hō* [Securities Exchange Act] (Tokyo: Nihon keizai shimbun, 1987), 113.

80. Akio Takeuchi, "Shasai hakkō shijō no arikata" [The Proper Bond Issue Market], *Shōji hōmu* 1100 (1987): 4, 11.

81. Note, however, that Japanese courts have not been inclined to re-characterize leases as loans. E.g., Jinshi marin K. K. v. Nishi (Tokyo High Ct., Apr. 27, 1982), *Hanrei jihō* 1048 (1982): 107; Fuyō sōgō rīsu K. K. v. Iryō hōjin shadan Tōkyō shakai byōin (Tokyo High Ct., Jan. 29, 1986), *Hanrei jihō* 1185 (1986): 104.

82. Private correspondence with the firm.

83. Alternatives we discuss in Miwa and Ramseyer, "The Myth of the Main Bank"; and Miwa and Ramseyer, "Directed Credit."

84. These dynamics are explored in Miwa, *Kin'yū gyōsei kaikaku*, 71–74; Yoshirō Miwa, "Kin'yū seido kaikaku no seiji keizai gaku" [The Political Economy of Financial Institution Reform], in Keimei Kaizuka and Kazuhito Ikeo, eds., *Kin'yū riron to seido kaikaku* [Finance Theory and Institutional Reform] (Tokyo: Yūhikaku, 1992), 307, 324–27; J. Mark Ramseyer, "Explicit Reasons for Implicit Contracts: The Legal Logic to the Japanese Main Bank System," in Masahiko Aoki and Hugh Patrick, eds., *The Japanese Main Bank System: Its Relevance for Developing and Transforming Economies* (Oxford: Oxford University Press, 1994), 230, 237–39.

85. Nihon ginkō, *Waga kuni no kin'yū seido* [Our Country's Financial System] (Tokyo: Nihon ginkō, 1986), 195.

86. The restrictions are detailed in, e.g., Shin Nihon shōken chōsa sentā, ed., *Shōken hando bukku* [Securities Handbook], 3rd ed. (Tokyo: Tōyō keizai shimpō sha, 1989), pt. 3.

87. On foreign exchange liberalization, see Yukio Yanagida et al., eds., *Law and Investment in Japan*, 2nd ed. (Cambridge, MA: East Asian Legal Studies, Harvard Law School, 2000), chap. 6.

88. Ramseyer, "Explicit Reasons for Implicit Contracts," 240, table 7.2. ORIX

had already started issuing bonds on the foreign market in 1973, with a $10 million straight bond issue.

89. For these and other details of the scope of the domestic bond issues, see Miwa, "Kin'yū seido kaikaku no seiji keizai gaku," 312–13, table 12-1.

90. E.g., Seiichirō Saitō, *Zeminãru gendai kin'yū nyūmon* [Seminar: Introductory Modern Finance], 3rd ed. (Tokyo: Nihon keizai shimbun sha, 1995), 282–83.

91. Litt et al., "Politics, Bureaucracies, and Financial Markets," 411–12.

92. See Takeo Hoshi and Anil Kashyap, *Corporate Financing and Governance in Japan: The Road to the Future* (Cambridge, MA: MIT Press, 2001), 230.

93. As of March 1993, there were eleven "city" (money-center) banks, sixty-four regional banks, sixty-six "type-2" regional banks, three long-term credit banks, and seven trust banks. There were no legal distinctions among the first three of these categories. In addition, there were a wide variety of other financial institutions. See generally Hiroshi Kusumoto, ed., *Nihon no kin'yū gyōsei, kanchō, kin'yū kikan* [Japanese Financial Administration, Bureaucracy, and Institutions] (Tokyo: Toyo keizai shimpo sha, 1994).

94. Miwa and Ramseyer, "Directed Credit."

95. See Nihon ginkō, *Waga kuni no kin'yū seido* [Our Country's Financial System] (Tokyo: Nihon ginkō, 1986), 336–42; and Miwa and Ramseyer, "Directed Credit."

96. E.g., Sanwa sōgō kenkyū sho, ed., *Nihon no kin'yū* [Japanese Finance] (Tokyo: Daiwa shuppan, 1999), 98–100.

97. Meir Kohn, *Money, Banking, and Financial Markets* (Chicago: Dryden Press, 1991), 213.

98. "Nonbanku kenkyūkai hōkokusho" [Report of the Nonbank Research Group] (April 18, 1991), reprinted in *Kin'yū*, May 1991, 31.

99. *Kin'yū zaisei jijō*, March 11, 1991, 30.

100. E.g., Act No. 74 of 1991, amending the Kashikin gyō no kisei tō ni kansuru hōritsu, Act No. 32 of 1983.

101. "Nonbanku kenkyūkai hōkokusho," 39.

102. Nonbanku mondai kondankai, "Nonbanku no yūshi gyōmu no arikata ni tsuite" [Regarding the Proper Credit Business of Nonbanks] (June 15, 1992), partially reprinted in *Kin'yū*, July 1992, 85, 86.

103. Ibid.

104. Ronald Coase, "Discussion," *American Economic Review* 54 (1964): 194, 194.

8 Legal Education

KAHEI ROKUMOTO

In his chapter "Education of the Legal Profession in Japan" in the 1963 volume, Judge Hakaru Abe comprehensively and critically outlined the Japanese legal education system and discussed some of the major issues for reform.[1] Deplorably, for the subsequent four decades very little changed for the better, while the overall situation even worsened; the urgent needs for change in legal education as well as in the legal profession that he suggested remain. Only in very recent times, a series of rather fundamental changes has been set in motion, but the reforms are not yet completed at the time of this writing. As a consequence, in my own attempt to renew Judge Abe's chapter, I find myself constantly referring back to what he wrote over forty years ago. I am able to add only a limited amount of data on the present situation and to describe some recent developments that have occurred in this area.

Legal education may be defined here as the institutional system of education for those seeking to become lawyers. Continuing education is excluded from the scope of this chapter, for that seems more pertinent to the separate subject of the legal profession. The current process of the Japanese legal education has three main stages: education in university law faculties and departments, the national Legal Examination (*Shihō shiken*), and the course of professional training at the Legal Training and Research Institute (LTRI; *Shihō-kenshū-sho*). In the following, I will first sketch the institutional mechanisms of legal education in each of the three stages mentioned, with some evaluative discussions, and then describe the changes and reforms that have taken place since the 1960s. I will finally briefly discuss the proposal for the introduction of a system of "law schools" (or graduate schools of law, *hōka-daigakuin*) that is now being undertaken as part of a series of comprehensive reforms of the justice system.[2]

I. MAIN FRAMEWORK OF LEGAL EDUCATION

A. UNDERGRADUATE LEGAL EDUCATION

1. *Generalist Orientation of Legal Education*

In Japan basic legal education is provided in universities at the undergraduate level. The four-year course leading to a "diploma in law" (*hō-gakushi*) consists of both general education courses and specialized education courses in law and other fields. Law constitutes a major field of specialized education, housed typically in a faculty of law, but at times also in a smaller unit called a "law department." While this scheme of legal education is not aimed at professional training, as will be discussed further below, it has a number of other features, likewise historically rooted, that are worth noting.

First, under the original postwar higher education system, the first two years of a university degree course were devoted to studies in general education (in essence, liberal arts education), while the last two years were for education in a specialized field. This meant that legal studies, constituting a specialized field, were confined to a mere two years, compared to the prewar university system, which allocated three years to each of the specialized studies courses including law. Some observers regarded this postwar feature as problematic, especially in view of the fact that, when the postwar system was designed, the faculty of medicine secured a three-year program following two years of general education. In fact it soon became apparent that two years were not long enough for the legal program that law faculties were prepared to offer. In order to fill the gap, arrangements were built up, in one guise or another, to introduce into the second year of general education, or even into the first year, some courses that originally belonged to specialized studies in law, such as Introduction to Law, Constitutional Law, and the first parts of Civil Law and other core law courses. This practice was expanded gradually, so that in all practical terms, one could say that university legal education came to consist of a two-and-a-half or three-year program.

In 1991, in view of this and many other gaps between the nominal form and the actual practice, the legal regulations of university organization (Standards for Establishment of University) were finally amended to abolish the distinction between the "general education" stage and "specialized education" stage and to leave the organization of the educational program to each university's discretion. However, the substance of "general education" itself is still regarded as an indispensable component of university education (as specified in Article 19[2] of the current Standards for Establishment of University), so that courses in general education may be provided in any number of units and at any stage of the four-year course of a particular faculty or department. As a result, at present, it is safe to say that the specialized education program for law is given within the four-year period of undergraduate education side by side with some courses of general education, including those in the fields of social science and the humanities, such as history, economics, political science, sociology, and so on.

Second, quite independently from the coexistence of specialized legal education and general education courses just mentioned, an undergraduate law degree is invariably combined with education in political science. This feature dates back to the formative era of the modern university system: from the beginning the law faculty was viewed as comprising a department of political science and providing some courses in economics, as well as courses in the main field of law. Economics later spun off from the law faculty to form a separate faculty, but some principal subjects of economics have been retained in the educational programs of law faculties. On the other hand, political science has always remained within the law faculty, so that the Japanese law faculties comprised not only professors of law but also professors of political science.[3] Accordingly law faculties allow their students, within their program for specialized studies, to choose to major either in "law" or in "political science," although nowadays the latter option usually is chosen by only a small minority of students.[4] Consequently, the curricula of the specialized studies in law normally also contain courses in political science and economics (the latter being taught by economics faculty members). This tradition, combined with the ongoing postwar emphasis on general education, makes the Japanese university legal education more widely based than narrowly focused on law.

Third, it is also to be noted that university legal education in itself is not aimed at professional training of lawyers; at least it is not designed to serve that purpose exclusively. To look back on history, Japan's first law faculty, the Law Faculty of the University of Tokyo, founded in 1877, and then restructured into the (sole) Imperial University in 1886,[5] was created with the objective of producing state officials trained in Western statecraft based on Western legal knowledge. This was obviously what was needed for the nation, which was newly born and hastily building itself. This subsequently became the model for the other state universities, which were gradually instituted later. Since those times, a majority of the graduates of law faculties of the state university law faculties have found jobs in government or private companies; only a handful of their graduates have become qualified lawyers, that is, judges, prosecutors, or attorneys.

A number of private university law faculties started to operate at about the time when the University of Tokyo Law Faculty was first created. These were oriented to producing private attorneys, and in fact more of their graduates became attorneys rather than judges and state officials. However, these law faculties soon came under control of the Ministry of Education, and even though they espoused mottos stressing liberty and independence from the state, they could not arrive at a separate model of legal education other than that followed by the state law faculties, but tended to be assimilated in the common pattern of legal education.[6]

Consequently, undergraduate legal education was firmly established that was oriented to training students as "generalists," who possess general abilities useful for administering organizations of various types in various fields, rather than training them in the specific professional skills required by lawyers. In fact, some of the leading law faculties, public or private, have ever since been functioning as providers of the leading national elites in civil service, business, and politics. Some of the law graduates also have become employees of local government or legal scriveners (*shihō-shoshi*, who belong to the so-called quasi lawyer category).

Fourth, a related feature of university legal education in Japan is the large number of law students (i.e., those who are registered at a law faculty or a law department), and an enormous gap between that number and the number of those who end up actually entering the legal profession. A further feature is that a majority of those who do become qualified lawyers originate from only a relatively small number of law faculties. At present, there are altogether ninety-three law faculties, of which fifteen are housed in state universities, three in municipal universities, and seventy-five in private universities. In addition, there are three faculties combining law and economics and four more combining law and humanities. The total number of student seats per year in all those 100 faculties or departments is estimated to be over forty-five thousand. Some private university law faculties have over one thousand students per year, while the larger state law faculties have a few hundred. Given the two features mentioned above, however, at all but a handful of these universities, few graduates, if any, actually enter the legal profession.

2. *Lecture-Based Law Teaching and Its Normative Character*

With respect to teaching methods, Japanese legal education has traditionally relied on the lecture method, not the case method or the Socratic method practiced in the United States. The lecture method has also been practiced in the other countries of the Continental legal system, such as France and Germany, the method being compatible with instruction for large classes, another common feature of those countries of the Continental legal system.

In a typical law curriculum in Japan—apart from the political science and economics courses mentioned earlier—the main courses are customarily called "positive law" courses. At its core are six fields of law: Constitutional Law, Civil Law, Commercial Law, Law of Civil Procedure, Criminal Law, and Law of Criminal Procedure. These six fields are referred to as the *Roppō*, or Six Codes. These six fields are flanked by the other major fields such as Administrative Law, Labor Law, Economic or Antimonopoly Law, Public International Law, and so forth. In addition, many law curricula include foreign (or comparative) laws, and the basic studies of law (legal history, legal philosophy, and legal sociology), and also some other courses in more specialized or newly developing fields of positive law. The principal subjects of the curriculum are taught as lecture courses by the holder of the chair in charge of each of those subjects. Usually, seminar courses are offered in addition in those same subjects, but a seminar course does not necessarily accompany a lecture course and in any event can accommodate only a small minority of the students who take the lecture course in the subject concerned. Each lecture course is supposed to cover systematically the whole field included in the course title, composed of the basic statutory texts, such as the Civil Code, and any relevant supplementary statutes.

As Judge Abe noted, the lectures of law professors are characterized by their theoretical and systematic nature.[7] Normally, instruction is conducted on the basis of a systematic treatise designated as the textbook for each course. Such treatises generally start by defining the particular field of law concerned, explain the structure of the main code, and gradually cover the entire field in question, discussing in accordance with an overall theoretical scheme the articles contained in the main code and the related statutes. The principal legal concepts and provisions are explained in terms of their analytical meaning, legislative circumstances and purposes, social justifications and so on, so as to guide their interpretation. Some historical and comparative discussions of those provisions may also be offered.

The main purpose of the instruction is to impart to the students not only the knowledge of the legal norms and institutions that are currently in force but also the skills of interpreting and applying those statutory norms and concepts to actual cases. However, normally in the lecture method, the "actual cases" are represented not by real cases decided by courts, or by the "raw" facts that have actually occurred in society or in a particular court case, but rather by abstract fact situations or scenarios that are composed on the basis of court cases or even purely theoretically. The general tendency in today's legal education is to emphasize the existence of "hard cases," where value or policy choice is inevitable in the legal interpretation, as well as the weighing of social interests to be protected by the law. To illustrate some difficult cases of statutory interpretation, or the way in which gaps in statutory provisions are filled by court decisions, scholarly opinions ("doctrines," *gakusetsu*) and decisions of courts are frequently mentioned and commented on. Such court decisions (referred to as "precedents" or "case law," *hanrei*) constitute indispensable elements in today's law teaching, although the cases are not reproduced verbatim in lengthy, original texts or through excerpts of the actual court decisions or opinions, but in the abstract form of a typified fact situation, which is then juxtaposed with the prevalent court decisions on it and inserted at the point where the relevant article of the statute is discussed.

As discussed above, Japanese university legal education purports to aim at generalist education in a specialized field broadly called "law" and not at practical training of students who will actually become members of the legal profession. This is reflected in the fact that analysis of particular judicial decisions does not form a central element of the teaching program, nor are the problems of fact-finding or fact-collecting dealt with, nor those of searching for and marshalling of legal materials, or client handling or drafting contracts and other documents. Such instruction would be generally incompatible with reliance on the lecture method. But Japan is by no means unique in this regard; the above features are more or less common to all the legal systems of the Continental type. Therefore, it is necessary further to examine the nature of Japanese law teaching in order to see why it has been the target of persistent criticism and controversy for the past fifty years.

To say that undergraduate law teaching is not aimed at the training of future lawyers does not mean that it is purely academic in nature. On the contrary, it is fundamentally practical and normative in nature. Even though, as mentioned above, the lectures usually incorporate analyses and comments on the law in the external perspective, such as legislative facts and historical backgrounds, undergraduate legal education is largely conducted in what H. L. A. Hart termed the "internal perspective"[8] on the existing legal system, referred to characteristically as "positive law." In other words, the instructor acts, so to speak, as a representative of the legal system and inducts the students into the legal world, directing them toward acquisition, not only of the necessary legal knowledge, but also of the point of view of someone who makes, administers, and safeguards the existing law.[9] In this broader sense, Japanese university legal education may be characterized as being of a fundamentally "practical" nature, even though its target is broader than that of professional training focused on the future members of the legal profession strictly defined, and its targets include future civil servants, company managers, "quasi lawyers," and even publicly minded citizens at large.[10]

Turning to the physical conditions of lecture-based teaching, the tendency toward "mass education" is a perennial problem of Japanese university law teaching. Lectures are usually given before a large class of students, sometimes as many as five hundred students or more. Students listen to the professor and take notes for the duration of the class session (typically 100 minutes in length). Although students are urged to prepare in advance of class by reading the textbook or other materials, and are told that they may ask questions at any time, they rarely raise their hands during the lecture. In short, these lectures are the model case of one-way instruction with a totally passive audience; those who have serious questions usually wait till the lecture is over to come to the podium to talk with the instructor individually. Both the instructor and the students are aware that the subject matter of the course must be covered within the semester. Evaluation of the students' course work is made solely on the basis of a written examination given at the end of the semester. Attendance at lectures is not controlled nor even monitored, and many students of law take the year-end examinations despite having attended the lectures only irregularly or even not at all and still pass.

Generally speaking, the norm prevails that the lectures offered in the law faculty should be carefully prepared to reflect the high academic quality of the instructor's own research in some specialized topics within his or her field, as well as to incorporate thorough and up-to-date knowledge of the law in the particular subject concerned. On the other hand, traditionally, professors were not expected to give much thought to the educational effect or efficacy of their instruction. It is only in recent times that professors began to provide students with a syllabus for their lectures, to prepare and distribute supplementary materials, and to organize the lecture carefully, so that the students could comprehend its contents.

As mentioned above, side by side with the main lecture courses, seminars are offered, albeit usually only as elective courses. Seminars provide a setting for enthusiastic students to find an opportunity to engage in self-motivated research work and actively to participate in multisided discussion in the class. However, seminar courses are small in number and can accommodate only a limited portion of the total student body.

3. *Merits and Demerits of Lecture-Based Law Teaching*

Lecture-based law teaching obviously has the great merit of giving students systematic and inclusive knowledge of the current state of law in a given field. Also, this kind of teaching gears academic legal scholars toward collective efforts, in writing and revising general treatises to be used in the classroom as well as in journal articles, and to follow the cases and statutory developments and to keep the state of art constantly updated and systematized, so that not only students but also members of the world of practice, including the legal profession, bureaucrats, and politicians, may always have at hand a reliable overview of the law in force. The scholarly treatises are not exactly regarded as "sources of law" but are viewed as most authoritative guides and also as a theoretical arsenal to be relied on in advocacy, judicial application, and administrative implementation of law, as well as in new legislation.

At the same time, the lecture method serves not only to give systematic and comprehensive knowledge of the law in the field concerned, but, above all, it serves to cultivate in the student the habit of thinking that is characterized by its systematic and comprehensive manner, and an emphasis on balancing of interests in policy making. It also cultivates the legal thinking characterized by analytical and argumentative skills of a deductive nature based on the existing statutory provisions—in other words, thinking top down from the abstract words and concepts of law, rather than bottom up from the empirical social facts. Thus, compared with the case-method teaching practiced in American law schools, the lecture method practiced in Japan tends to emphasize the systemic integrity of the law as well as its given or "established" nature.[11] It seems to me that this method also tends to encourage the view that law is accessible only to those who have mastered its esoteric language. Even though the social meaning and function of law is frequently stressed, the basic stance of law teaching tends to be that of the lawgiver rather than that of the law receiver or law user (or litigating parties) and leans toward a more or less conservative (status quo–respecting) view relying on the existing law, rather than an innovative attitude pressing for dynamic legal change in response to various social needs.

Another aspect of this teaching style must be addressed, especially in connection with the recent efforts to reform Japanese legal education. As indicated earlier, the university curricula normally offer to the students who are (broadly and in many cases vaguely) interested in law not only the main courses in the positive law subjects but also various courses in the basic science of law, political science, and economics—in addition to the various nonlegal courses in general education. On the basis of this institutional arrangement it is hoped that the future lawyers will proceed to the practical legal education in the LTRI equipped with good background knowledge of the problems and mechanisms of the society in which law operates. However, it is precisely for failure in this objective that undergraduate legal education has been persistently criticized for decades. Blame for this failure is often attributed to the stringent Legal Examination (to be discussed in a moment), which forces the students to focus narrowly on the strictly legal subjects (only those directly relevant to the Legal Examination) and to leave their wider interests aside.[12] This is certainly a valid and important criticism. However, this is not the whole story. For one thing, the problem did not start with the intensification of the competition for the Legal Examination. So we need to look at the effect of law teaching in this context as well.

In my view, it is important to ask whether the type of law teaching that is, as discussed above, practically and normatively oriented and combined with emphasis on deductive thinking premised on an existing, comprehensive system of legal norms has not certain features incongruent with the stated goal of "generalist" education common to all future professional lawyers and nonlawyers. Looking back on my own student times as well as my subsequent long years of experience in teaching first- and second-year students, I must recognize that law professors' lectures are generally received by the young students with a certain air of detachment or even disenchantment, especially by those who are just starting their university studies, almost totally lacking in a realistic sense of the world outside schools, to say nothing about the legal world. I suspect that many of these students sense something repulsive in the atmosphere of law teaching, the normatively imposing character of the whole enterprise. Instead of being intellectually stimulated, students are often put off by law lectures and become alienated, although many of them nonetheless acquiesce and follow through their studies admirably. For some of those students, legal education is just another postponement of immediate gratification in exchange for future goals. Such a situation may well generate a cynical attitude among the students—an attitude that looks at law as merely a set of technical skills to be mastered and at law teaching as an effort to mold the students' minds in terms of a closed circuit of positive law, rather than encouraging them to engage in an open-ended pursuit of their developing interests in social affairs.

In any event, it seems safe to say that there is some fundamental difference between the learning attitude required of a student taking a law course and that required of students sitting in classes in other fields, such as those in social science. In designing an undergraduate program of legal studies that combines, in some way or another, positive law teaching and studies in social and other fields, one must take into consideration the existence of a fundamental dilemma stemming from the incompatibility of the internal perspective of the positive law teaching with the other fields of study, which view the law from an "external" or social scientific perspective.

B. MECHANISM OF THE LEGAL EXAMINATION

As indicated earlier, it is not legally required of a candidate for the legal profession to have a university degree in law, or even a university diploma at all. The first step toward receiving qualification as a lawyer is to pass the Legal Examination (LE), a single national examination conducted by the Ministry of Justice once a year (in the autumn). The legal prerequisite for being able to sit for the LE is that one possesses knowledge and learning ability equivalent to the general education to be acquired at the university (Legal Examination Act, Article 3). This requirement is automatically fulfilled by students of four-year universities who have completed the first two years of coursework. Those who have not gone to a university can take a separate qualifying examination (which is officially called the "First Examination"). However, most of those who sit for the LE have obtained or are expected to obtain a university diploma, either in law or in some other field of study.

The Legal Examination itself (officially speaking, the "Second Examination") is conducted in three stages: the multiple-choice, essay, and oral examinations. The first stage tests the students' knowledge in the three core subjects of Constitutional Law, Civil Law, and Criminal Law through sixty multiple-choice questions, very elaborately prepared and to be answered in three hours and a half.[13] The second-stage examination (of the official Second Examination) consists of answering essay questions in each of the three core subjects mentioned above, plus the additional three fields of Commercial Law, Civil

Procedure Law, and Criminal Procedure Law. The candidates are asked to write answers to two legal problems in two hours for each of those subjects. (Until 1999, the candidates could choose one from the two procedure law subjects and, for another elective subject, one from among Administrative Law, Bankruptcy Law, Labor Law, Public International Law, Private International Law, and the remaining procedural subject.) At the third stage, the oral examination, the candidates are subjected to three short sessions of unstructured questions and answers about all the subjects chosen for the essay exam.

The Legal Examination is administered by the Legal Examination Control Board (LECB; *Shihōshiken-kanri-iinkai*), a body of three persons appointed by the minister of justice, consisting of the undersecretary of the Ministry of Justice, the secretary general of the Supreme Court, and a practicing attorney recommended by the Japan Federation of Bar Associations (JFBA). The examiners who conduct the actual tests are appointed by the justice minister on the recommendation of the LECB for each of the subjects tested. The result of the examination is determined by joint deliberations of the examiners (Legal Examination Act, Article 8[1]).

As indicated earlier, not all the students who graduate from law faculties and departments, but only a small proportion of them, take the Legal Examination. Many students who graduate from other faculties or departments than law also take the LE, and many also take the LE some years after graduation and after some work experience. There is no restriction as to the age of the candidates, nor as to the number of times they may sit for the LE. In any event, it has been an established pattern for some decades that only an extremely small minority (less than 3 percent) of those who take the LE pass it each year, and those who pass are relatively advanced in age (twenty-seven to twenty-eight years old on average) and have spent many years (five years on average) after graduating from the university.

C. LEGAL TRAINING AND RESEARCH INSTITUTE

1. *Legal Apprenticeship*

Those who have passed the Legal Examination are admitted to the Legal Training and Research Institute (LTRI). This institution belongs to the Supreme Court. Established in 1947, the LTRI is charged with the practical training of those who wish to become members of the legal profession as well as with providing continuing education and research for judges. Those who have passed the LE usually enter the institute immediately after passing that exam (i.e., in the following April), although they may elect to start the apprenticeship in any year thereafter. Admission to the institute amounts to appointment as a legal apprentice (*shihō-shūshū-sei*) with the Supreme Court. Apprentices acquire the status of quasi public servants and receive full salaries and benefits corresponding to that status. The training period was originally two years but was shortened to one year and a half from 1999 (as discussed further below). At the end of the training period, apprentices sit for a final examination administered by the Examination Committee of the Supreme Court. Passing this examination is the last step toward full qualification as a lawyer. By the time they take the finals, the apprentices have made up their minds on which branch of the legal profession they wish to enter. The institute is now located in the suburbs of Tokyo, and those apprentices who come from outside of the large Tokyo area may use accommodations in the institute's dormitory, located on the same premises.

2. *Teaching Program of the LTRI*

The training program for legal apprentices comprises two parts. The first part, called "classroom instruction," is conducted at the institute and takes place during the first three months of the apprenticeship and also during the last three months; the second part, called "practical training," consists of four internships of three months each—one with a civil division of a district court, one with a criminal division of a district court, one with a district prosecutorial office, and one with a law office of an attorney. (Before 1999, each of those periods was about a month longer.) During the total of twelve months of field training, apprentices are stationed in one of the prefectures (including Tokyo and Osaka) where the practical training is undertaken. The programs for the field training are undertaken and organized by the district court, the district prosecutorial office, and the bar association in each prefecture.

Classroom instruction at the institute is given by active members of the profession, who are appointed to the position of institute instructor (*Kenshū-sho-kyōkan*) by the Supreme Court for a term of three or four years.[14] The judge instructors as well as the prosecutor instructors occupy full-time positions at the institute, whereas the attorney instructors are employed on a part-time basis. The apprentices of each year are divided into classes of about seventy students. Five instructors are assigned to each class corresponding to the five subjects to be covered: civil matter judging, civil matter lawyering, criminal matter judging, prosecution, and criminal defense. The institute has no formal curriculum setting out courses and units, but conducts its instructions according to a summary set of guidelines (*Shihō shūshū-sei shidō yōkō*). Each year the instructors of each subject jointly plan the courses, prepare teaching materials, and coordinate their teaching.

After some introductory lectures on the structures and processes of civil and criminal court proceedings and on legal ethics, apprentices receive practical instruction of a seminar type in smaller groups based on case materials for each subject. The case materials, distributed to the apprentices, come in the form of a number of thick books, containing collections of comprehensive records of civil and criminal cases, carefully selected from among cases actually litigated in courts around the country.

Drafting exercises constitute the core of education at the institute. In each of the five subjects mentioned above, apprentices are asked to take the role of a judge, a prosecutor, or a counsel according to the subject at hand; to read and analyze the entire record of a particular case; and to draft their own documents appropriate for their given role on the basis of the materials provided. For example, the student may be asked to write as a judge a section of the hypothetical court decision for a civil lawsuit as well as to summarize the claims made and the facts of the case pleaded by each of the litigating parties; to draft as the counsel in civil litigation a complaint, a brief, and an answer or a settlement proposal; to write as a judge in a criminal case a court opinion and sentence together with justification; or to prepare as a prosecutor a note in support of indictment or non-indictment and a summary of the prosecutor's argument, and so on.

In the courses on civil judging, particular emphasis is placed on mastering the rules of "requisite facts" (*yōken jijitsu*). This term refers to the facts (or the type of facts) that, in accordance with the substantive rules of law, each party is deemed required to assert and to prove, as well as to the rules of proper allocation of burdens between the parties for pleading in the proper form: "claim of right," "defense," or "answer," depending on the circumstances.[15] The assignment sometimes is given as a day's homework, but mostly is given as classroom work to be completed within a few hours. Apprentices may cooperate among themselves but have to produce their own results individually. The draft work submitted is corrected, commented on, and marked by the instructor in charge and returned to the apprentices. The instructor will then conduct a session dedicated to overall review and discussion in the class.

In addition, during the last period of classroom instruction, videotapes of mock court proceedings, prepared by the instructors, are shown, and a mock trial is acted out by apprentices themselves. The training program also includes special lectures on some specialized fields of law or legal practice, such as real estate registration, corporation matters, bankruptcy matters, intellectual property, and so on, given by outside practitioners or professors. There are also some courses intended to enhance the general cultural awareness of the apprentices in the form of lectures on various topics other than law and on site visits, such as to the Kabuki theater, for example.

During their period of practical training, where the apprentices are located in various prefectures, they receive personal guidance from mentors assigned to each of them and come into contact with real situations in which actual legal cases are handled by judges, prosecutors, and attorneys. The apprentices' experience varies depending on the particular court, prosecutorial office, or attorney's office where they are stationed. The apprentices may be allowed to try their own hand in a real case by, for example, interviewing a client, preparing a letter of advice addressed to the client for their attorney teachers, questioning suspects and drafting the protocol of the interrogation in the name of their instructing prosecutors, or drafting a decision and participating in the deliberations in their guiding judges' court. However, the main part of their assignment concerns observing what their instructors do in their daily professional work. In addition, the training program includes lectures given by practitioners on various phases of the legal process and site visits to prisons, police stations, factories, airports, and so on. The apprentices may also have a chance, for example, to accompany police officers in patrolling by car or in a raid, or to view compulsory execution of a civil judgment, or to observe an autopsy session at a medical faculty.

3. Merits and Demerits of LTRI Education

As Judge Abe noted in his 1963 chapter, the practical training at the LTRI is intended to bridge the gap between the skills obtained through university legal education and the skills and abilities required of a professional lawyer.[16] Whereas law professors are persons of the academic world, normally without any experience in, or qualification for, legal practice, the instructors at the institute are all practicing lawyers in the judiciary, in the prosecution service, or at the bar. They teach the apprentices, in small classes and using actual case materials, the skills and techniques needed by qualified lawyers of all the three branches in handling actual legal matters in various aspects and phases. The teaching methods used at the institute differ markedly from typical university teaching methods that rely on unilateral lectures. The institute teaching also differs in its emphasis on the practical, rather than academic, aspect of the law. Apprentices are exposed to actual legal professional work on site, and they are given the opportunity to see behind the scenes of the legal business and to hear personal comments and advice from practitioners.

Even though, once again as Judge Abe pointed out, there are still many problems with this stage of legal education, and it is still subject to criticisms, its development since 1949 constituted a major step forward in the quality of legal education from the situation prior to World War II. The LTRI may be regarded as a unique institution that was designed on the basis of some experiences accumulated since the beginning of modern legal education in Japan. In France, one of the original mother countries for Japan's legal system, centralized professional training is afforded only to prospective judges and prosecutors, and in Germany, another model Continental law country, professional training for paid apprentices is given only in the form of field traineeship in the three branches of the legal profession. The course content and the teaching methods of the LTRI are also well grounded in the actual circumstances of the Japanese legal profession, being based on the experience and efforts for improvement accumulated by generations of dedicated instructors over the fifty years of its existence.

Another important point, which is also stressed by Judge Abe, is that the training at LTRI is recognized as representing a modified version of the "unified legal profession."[17] It has been providing an equally high level of professional training to future attorneys, judges, and prosecutors alike, as well as providing them the opportunity to foster a sense of camaraderie during the communal life spent together as apprentices. The cumulative effect of its continual operation for the past half century must be substantial in enhancing not only the capabilities, but also the status in society, of attorneys relative to judges and prosecutors, and the shared training should allow a smooth transition from the bar to the bench for experienced attorneys who might be given the opportunity to take up jobs as judges.

On the other hand, we should not overlook the fact that there are some serious limitations inherent in this institution, most of which have already been pointed out by many observers, including Judge Abe. For example, a downside of the fact that the instructors are all current legal practitioners is that they are "amateur educators."[18] This feature also means that the institute depends on the willingness of those nonprofessional teachers to expend for the public good enormous amounts of time and labor on preparation for teaching.[19] Nonetheless, we hear constant complaints that the institute suffers from lack of time.

A feature of the LTRI that deserves special attention relates to the position of the instructors. The instructors are appointed, at the discretion of the Supreme Court, only for a short period of time and as a side step from their main career paths.[20] The nature of appointment of the instructors contrasts sharply to the situation of tenured professors at universities, which ideally provides an institutional atmosphere animated by the spirit of intellectual freedom and an environment for developing an educational program, based on academic research, that is conducive to critical exercise by their students of their youthful intellect against the prevalent state of law and its administration. The current system cannot but impose certain fundamental limitations to the capacity of the institute to act as an institution charged with the task of educating the entire future body of the legal profession, including not only future judges and prosecutors but also future members of the bar. This criticism seems to be valid, even if we take into consideration the fact that the basic mission of the LTRI is to provide all new entrants to the profession with common awareness of the current state of the professional art.

A closely related criticism is that in practice, at least until recently, the LTRI served as a recruiting ground for judges and prosecutors. It is easy to see how this would happen, because for attorneys recruitment is the business of each law firm or law office, whereas instructor judges and prosecutors have their own organizations to care about and naturally wish to encourage those young lawyers who are better qualified, in their eyes, to apply for the position of assistant judge or prosecutor. It is alleged that, against this general background, some apprentices suspect discriminatory treatment depending on the future orientation of a particular apprentice. It is said that some apprentices who have already decided to become attorneys become disinterested in the coursework. This might also partly be explained by the fact that practically no one fails in the final examination. It is hard to know from the outside to what extent these allegations may reflect the reality of life for apprentices at the institute, but if true the allegations would seem to suggest a strain in the organizational structure of the institute as an educational institution.

Another frequently expressed concern is that classroom instruction at the LTRI tends to emphasize training in judging and court work at the expense of other areas of legal practice, notably in neglect of the problems actually faced by attorneys in making proof, for example. However, given that instruction must be completed within a limited time and must be given equally and in common to all apprentices in the classrooms, it seems inevitable that assignments based on the records of court proceedings are the most effective and efficient method of teaching the core elements of the professional work of all branches of the legal profession.

II. PROLONGED CRISIS OF LEGAL EDUCATION

As suggested in the above discussion, the present institutional framework of the Japanese legal education has many inadequacies and problems necessitating fundamental change. The need for restructuring the entire system of legal education was already an underlying theme of Judge Abe's 1963 chapter, which concluded with some farsighted suggestions for the direction of reform, pointing out the issues of the nature of university legal education, the role the university must play in the training of future lawyers, and the proper division of labor between the university and the LTRI.[21] For the subsequent three decades this need for fundamental change in legal education has been constantly felt by leading legal academics and practitioners, and on many occasions efforts were made to correct shortcomings in various aspects of the system. Those efforts did not bear much fruit, however. In a sense, the Japanese system, based on a delicate balance among various interests and forces, was not capable of solving its own systemic problems through its normal processes. The crisis was prolonged and problems piled up, until finally the Justice System Reform Council (JSRC) was set up and given the role of omnipotent problem solver and, in that role, pronounced a proposal for a system of Japanese-style "law schools."

Before going into the content of this proposal, however, let us review developments surrounding legal education and some of the reform efforts that were made with respect to university legal education, the Legal Examination, and the Legal Training and Research Institute, which together make up a stream forming the general background for the law school proposal.

A. EXPANDING HIGHER EDUCATION AND THE EDUCATION CRISIS

From 1945 till the 1970s the recovery and the high-rate growth of the Japanese economy continually created a strong demand for a new graduate workforce. The percentage of eighteen-year-olds aspiring to higher education grew from 26 percent in 1960 to a peak of 48 percent in 1976, and the rate of those attaining it grew from 10 percent to 39 percent in the same period.[22] In response to this overwhelming demand, the number of universities and their student enrollments grew rapidly. Law was one of the fields that expanded most rapidly. Judge Abe stated that in 1959 thirty-six universities gave instruction in law and graduated 13,165 students. The corresponding figures for 2001 were 100 universities (35 public and 65 private) with over 45,000 students enrolled.

Against this background of an expanding market for university graduates, the entrance examination for universities became extremely competitive, and passing the examination became the most important focus of learning efforts of the students. In turn, that situation gave rise to a large industry of preparatory (cram) schools for entrance examinations, not only those for universities but even right down to entrance exams for entering primary school. With this commercialization of university entrance examinations developed the notion of ranking universities according to the relative difficulty level of their respective examinations. Ironically, in parallel to the increase in competition surrounding entrance, the reputation of the education acquired at the university, as well as the students' intellectual quality and motivation once enrolled, declined. As is well known, the university came to be criticized as functioning as a mere institution to classify young people through the admissions process and to bestow a diploma with a brand attached to it, that brand reflecting the university's entrance examination rank order.

Education in the field of law was no exception. In addition, reflecting the needs of a society becoming ever more complex and constantly changing, numerous new subjects in law and political science were added to the curriculum. As the students grew in number and sank in intellectual level, the system for producing future members of a high-minded, generalist elite strained to resist the tendency toward "mass production" and its deficiencies. It was in this climate that in 1967 the Faculty of Law of the University of Tokyo came to the conclusion that its teaching program should be extended by one year, thus making it obligatory for all law students to spend an exceptional five years to obtain an undergraduate degree. The principal reason for this reform plan was that students must be given "more time to digest the knowledge made available and to cultivate further the attitude of studying and thinking by themselves."[23]

B. LOST RELEVANCE OF UNIVERSITY LEGAL EDUCATION

This bold attempt made by a leading state university law faculty was unfortunately aborted, but it brought to light the serious situation that legal education was facing, while leaving that situation unresolved; and the situation even deteriorated further as years went by. For example, in a comprehensive survey of the enrolled students conducted in 1990 by the Law Faculty of the University of Tokyo (to which fourteen hundred students, or 81 percent of the entire student body, responded), 44 percent of the respondents answered that they were not digesting the content of the lectures they take. When asked about the reasons for mal-digestion (up to two answers out of eight alternatives), students returned the responses set forth below.[24] This shows that, while the students were ready to admit their own inadequacies ([1] and [2] combined representing 75 percent), a large number of them felt they were overwhelmed by the learning materials imposed on them ([5],[6], and [7]): 85 percent).

(1)	Lack of learning ability of students	15 percent
(2)	Problems with the learning attitudes of students	60 percent
(3)	Insufficient skill or effort in the teaching methods	25 percent
(4)	Problems with the contents of teaching	8 percent
(5)	Too much material included in the lecture	12 percent
(6)	Growth and complexity of the substance to be learned	28 percent
(7)	Overcrowded curriculum leaving little time for self-study	45 percent
(8)	Don't know	3 percent
	Total	196 percent

To make matters even worse, during the 1980s a new element was added. Commercial preparatory schools (*juken juku*), specialized in preparing students for the Legal Examination, grew in influence, and soon came to operate on a large scale, not only in Tokyo but also in other large cities. Most of the students who sit for the LE, even those who are still enrolled in universities, began to attend the training courses offered by such cram schools. At the same time, law students intending to take the LE tended to begin to concentrate on preparation for it earlier than before. For example, in the survey just quoted, 43 percent of responding students (and 63 percent of those who had already taken the LE at least once) said that they had attended preparatory schools; 38 percent of those who went to a preparatory school began to do so while they were still in the first or second year of university, that is, even before they arrived in the Faculty of Law where the main part of their legal education would start.[25] Cram school courses are of course single-mindedly focused on acquisition of the narrowly technical skills for passing the LE, and the fact most LE applicants have come to be trained in this fashion began to leave visible traces on the characteristics of successful candidates, as can be inferred from the comments of exasperated examiners and LTRI instructors. Thus, the academic studies on the university campus have become increasingly irrelevant for those who intend to enter the legal profession, and louder and louder complaints have been voiced about the "double school phenomenon" and the "hollowing out of university legal education."

This large discrepancy between university legal education and the legal

TABLE 8.1. Number of Graduates Who Passed the LE, Based on University Attended

	Number of graduates passing LE		*Number of student seats in law*	
University attended	2001	2002	1990	2003
Tokyo University*	206	246	655	590
Waseda University	187	185	1,200	1,186
Keio University	100	110	1,200	1,200
Kyoto University*	90	110	400	360
Chuo University	76	104	1,710	1,414
Hitotsubashi University*	36	45	245	235
Osaka University*	34	29	210	180
Meiji University	27	26	1,180	1,150
Sophia University	19	28	300	295
Doshisha University	17	26	920	985
Tohoku University*	13	15	250	170
Kobe University*	13	20	290	260
Kansai University	13	19	790	814
Kyushu University*	12	15	280	260
Ritsumeikan University	12	17	900	810
Nagoya University*	11	15	190	175
Hokkaido University*	11	23	231	220
Nihon University	11	15	2,000	2,000
Hosei University	7	9	1,040	896
Osaka Municipal University	7	3	230	224
Rikkyo University	4	11	500	500
Aoyama Gakuin University	4	7	460	433
Kwansei Gakuin University	4	12	550	550
Tokyo Municipal University	4	9	130	175
Subtotal	918	1,099	15,561	15,082
Other passers (mostly university graduates)	72	84		
Total number of passers	990	1,183		
Total women among passers	223	227		

SOURCES: The statistics included in this table were derived from the home page of the Ministry of Justice (http: / /www.moj.go.jp); "Hōsō yōseiseido kaikaku—Kihon shiryō shū" [Reform of System for Training of Legal Profession—Collection of Basic Materials], *Jurisuto Zōkan*, 1991: 120; and *Daigaku bunkei no gakka annai* [Guide to University Departments in the Social Sciences and Humanities] (Tokyo: Gakushū kenkyūsha, 2002).
* Denotes state university.

profession can be seen in a statistical overview of the performance of Japanese law faculties and departments in the production of qualified lawyers. In 2002, for example, 990 candidates passed the Legal Examination, of whom half (493) were graduates of only three universities, while another quarter were graduates of five additional universities.

In order to have a somewhat more detailed picture, let us look at table 8.1, which shows the distribution of all those who passed the LE in 2001 and 2002, respectively, according to the universities they attended. (Note that the year 2002 marked the highest number of passers to that date.) The table identifies only those universities that produced ten or more passers in the two years combined, together with the annual number of announced seats for law students in those universities in the given years. It is to be noted, however, that, strictly speaking, the size of the enrollment in each faculty does not directly correspond to the number of those who sit for the LE each year. Not all university law students sit for the LE; those who passed the LE in a particular year may have been enrolled in their universities some years or even a decade previously, and they may not even have been enrolled in law, but in some other faculty or department.

This table includes twenty-four universities with a law faculty, which shows that out of the hundred law faculties or departments that exist, only a handful produce a sizable number of passers. This means that lawyer production is relatively concentrated in a small group of universities.[26] (It should be mentioned, though, that thirty or forty other universities, public or private, regularly produce a few—between one and five or so—lawyer graduates each year.) These figures also confirm the wide gap between the size of the law student body and the number of graduates who eventually pass the LE, even in those universities appearing in the table. Note that this gap is smaller in the state universities, whereas it is much wider in the private universities. One may also notice that, across the board, the size of enrollment in law shrunk somewhat from 1990 to 2003.

C. CHANGING SITUATIONS AND REFORM EFFORTS PRIOR TO THE LAW SCHOOL PROJECT

Since its introduction, the mechanisms of the Legal Examination have gone through a number of changes. For example, the multiple-choice exam was added in 1956 in order to cope with the rapidly growing number of applications, which threatened to make the rating of the main essay exam impracticable. This new feature was the target of criticism for some time, but it gradually came to be accepted. At the same time, great concern also was raised over the increasing difficulty for students to pass the LE while still enrolled in university or within a short period after graduation; one specific concern raised in that connection was the impact of the multiple-choice exam. Serious attempts were made to try to ensure that preparation for the multiple-choice test would not prove an unnecessary barrier for young, talented applicants, but none of those efforts had a significant impact.

In 1962, around the time Judge Abe drafted his original chapter, the Ad Hoc Committee for Investigation into the Justice System (*Rinji shihōseido chōsakai*, or *Rinshi*) was set up. The main objective of this committee was to investigate the issues of the so-called unitary system of the legal profession, but it also inquired into the method of recruitment of lawyers and recommended some reforms in the administration of the LE. That committee pointed out that the pass rate for students currently enrolled in university was sharply declining, that the average age of passers was approaching twenty-nine, and that the successful candidates were mostly mediocre in terms of their university academic records. Based on these observations, the Ad Hoc Committee stressed the importance of securing bright, talented young people with future potential for the legal profession and recommended to reform the multiple-choice test so as to focus on a general cultural foundation and basic legal knowledge.[27] However, this proposal was thwarted by concerted resistance put up by private universities and the JFBA.

Even so, various improvements were made in the examination subjects as well as the types of questions to be asked. It was not until the mid-1980s, however, that a substantial dent began to be made in the firmly established operative patterns of the LE; if anything, the situation for young applicants became even more dire. To deal with this concern, in 1991 the Legal Examination Act was amended to give the LE Control Board power to adopt a quota system to favor those taking the LE for the third time or less (Legal Examination Act, Article 8[2]). This amendment was pushed through the Diet in spite of strong resistance from the JFBA, on the justification that this was a necessary measure to enable potentially successful candidates to qualify as lawyers at a younger age. Actual implementation of this measure began in 1995, when two-ninths of the total slots available were allocated for those taking the bar exam for the third time or less; in 2002 this rate was lowered to two-elevenths.

But the greatest problem of the LE lay in the extremely small number of candidates who passed it yearly. According to the law, the purpose of the LE is to judge whether or not an applicant is qualified to become a member of the legal profession (Legal Examination Act, Article 1). This provision pre scribes the basic character of the LE as a "qualifying examination" rather than a "competitive examination" limited to a definite number of seats (as is the case for the Examination for National Civil Servants), and, as noted earlier, the final results of the LE are determined by the total score resulting from independent ratings made by examiners of different subjects. However, for three decades starting in the early 1960s, the number of passers on the Second Examination was kept constantly at the level of five hundred, which, as observers had noted for some time, not so coincidentally corresponded exactly to the capacity of the LTRI. This de facto ceiling of five hundred was finally removed in the reform of 1991, based on an agreement reached by representatives of the three branches of the legal profession (judges, prosecutors, and practicing attorneys); in accordance with the schedule agreed on, the number of passers reached about one thousand in 1999. In that year, about thirty-four hundred persons applied and about thirty thousand actually took the Legal (Second) Examination, of whom about fifty-seven hundred passed the first stage (multiple-choice) tests (of the Second Examination).

Table 8.2 and the accompanying figure 8.1 present the numbers of applicants and passers, as well as the pass rates for each year since 1949, when the current LE commenced. The column graph reflects the ceiling of five hundred that persisted for three decades and also shows a sharp stepwise increase in the number of passers since 1990. However, the angle of the rise does not look impressive at all when put in the long-term perspective, especially in view of the recent radical increase in the number of cases that are brought before courts in many different forms. The pass rate,[28] however, rose considerably in tandem with the increase in the overall number of passers in the early 1990s, but then soon began to sink back to the starting level. The reason for this can be found in the other curve, representing the number of applicants. The peak of the pass rate coincides with the lowest point in the applicant curve. The latter's long-term movement over the entire postwar period clearly shows that an increase in the number of ultimate passers is followed by an increase in the number of applicants, whereas stagnation in the number of passers brings about a decrease in applicant numbers. Once again, this seems to suggest, first, that, there has been a large deficit in the supply of lawyers. Second, there is a possibility that the increase in applicants is accounted for to some extent by the increase of repeaters as well as by those who decide to change careers after having experienced some other work.

Another observation relates to the behavior of female passers. The number of female passers exhibited a great leap of about 150 percent in 1992, a year later than a similar leap with respect to the total number of passers includ-

TABLE 8.2. Number of Applicants, Passers, and Pass Rates 1949–2002

Year	*Applicants*	*All passers*	*Pass rate (percent)*	*Passers (Male)*	*Passers (Female)*	*Percent of Passers (Female)*
1949	2,570	265	10.31	262	3	1.13
1950	2,806	269	9.59	266	3	1.12
1951	3,668	272	7.42	270	2	0.74
1952	4,761	253	5.31	246	7	2.77
1953	5,136	224	4.36	221	3	1.34
1954	5,250	250	4.76	240	10	4.00
1955	6,347	264	4.16	254	10	3.79
1956	6,737	297	4.41	283	14	4.71
1957	6,920	286	4.13	280	6	2.10
1958	7,109	346	4.87	335	11	3.18
1959	7,858	319	4.06	311	8	2.51
1960	8,363	345	4.13	330	15	4.35
1961	10,909	380	3.48	363	17	4.47
1962	10,762	459	4.27	433	26	5.66
1963	11,686	496	4.24	468	28	5.65
1964	12,698	508	4.00	483	25	4.92
1965	13,644	526	3.86	501	25	4.75
1966	14,867	554	3.73	536	18	3.25
1967	16,460	537	3.26	513	24	4.47
1968	17,727	525	2.96	490	35	6.67
1969	18,453	501	2.72	464	37	7.39
1970	20,160	507	2.51	473	34	6.71
1971	22,336	533	2.39	505	28	5.25
1972	23,425	537	2.29	511	26	4.84
1973	25,339	537	2.12	513	24	4.47
1974	26,708	491	1.84	468	23	4.68
1975	27,791	472	1.70	436	36	7.63
1976	29,088	465	1.60	426	39	8.39
1977	29,214	465	1.59	432	33	7.10
1978	29,390	485	1.65	453	32	6.60
1979	28,622	503	1.76	463	40	7.95
1980	28,656	486	1.70	437	49	10.08
1981	27,816	446	1.60	413	33	7.40
1982	26,317	457	1.74	409	48	10.50
1983	25,138	448	1.78	404	44	9.82

TABLE 8.2. *continued*

Year	Applicants	All passers	Pass rate (percent)	Passers (Male)	Passers (Female)	Percent of Passers (Female)
1984	23,956	453	1.89	401	52	11.48
1985	23,855	486	2.04	441	45	9.26
1986	23,904	486	2.03	427	59	12.14
1987	24,690	489	1.98	429	60	12.27
1988	23,352	512	2.19	451	61	11.91
1989	23,202	506	2.18	435	71	14.03
1990	22,900	499	2.18	425	74	14.83
1991	22,596	605	2.68	522	83	13.72
1992	23,435	630	2.69	505	125	19.84
1993	20,848	712	3.42	568	144	20.22
1994	22,554	740	3.28	583	157	21.22
1995	24,488	738	3.01	592	146	19.78
1996	25,454	734	2.88	562	172	23.43
1997	27,112	746	2.75	539	207	27.75
1998	30,568	812	2.66	609	203	25.00
1999	33,983	1,000	2.94	713	287	28.70
2000	36,203	994	2.75	724	270	27.16
2001	38,930	990	2.54	767	223	22.53
2002	45,622	1,183	2.59	906	277	23.42

ing males. This can be read as an indication that the widening of the gate encourages new groups of applicants, insofar as those groups perceive ample room left for new entrants into the lawyer market.[29]

Let us next turn to a profile of those who pass the LE in terms of their age and occupational status. Table 8.3 compiles the available statistics for the year 1986. This table shows that the bulk of those who passed the LE were in their late twenties and early thirties, that most passed sometime between their third and ninth attempt, and that a rather large majority devoted themselves to pursuing the examination without assuming any regular occupation even after graduating from the university.[30]

The LTRI has also been subjected to many reform proposals and controversies during the half century of its existence. For example, in 1970 the justice minister announced the intention to reexamine the LTRI system with

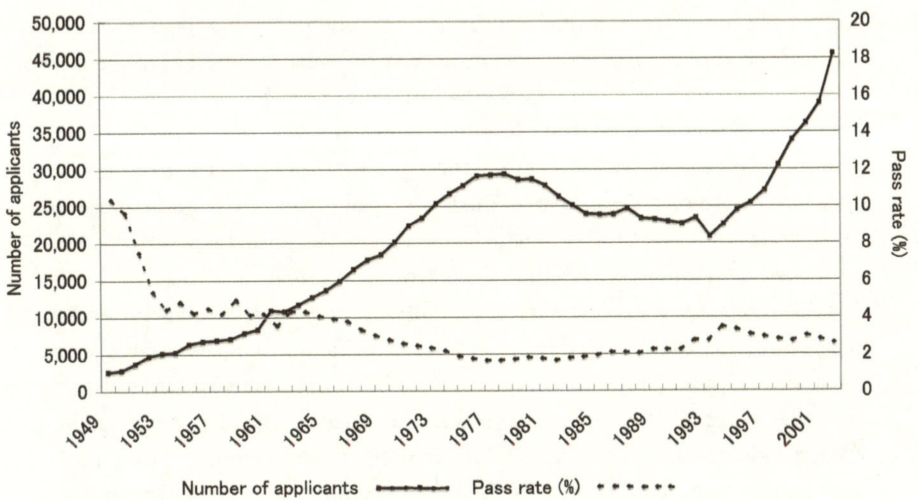

FIGURE 8.1. Number of Applicants and Their Pass Rates

a view to introducing a training program for future practicing attorneys separate from that for judges and prosecutors. This was apparently prompted by the fact that by far the greatest proportion of the beneficiaries of this state-sponsored training system are future attorneys; however, in the face of fierce opposition from the bar, this attempt did not materialize.[31]

Apart from the various improvements that have been made in the LTRI curricula and its instructional methods over the years, there has been another major institutional change. By this, I refer to the increase of the number of new entrants starting in 1991, as reflected in the columns for LE passers in table 8.2 above. In order to accommodate the growing class size, the LTRI moved in 1994 to a new site, with larger buildings, constructed in the suburbs of Tokyo. Based on the two tripartite package agreements made in 1991 and 1997 that brought about gradual relaxation of the examination results, an amendment was made in the Courts Act (Article 67[2]) in 1998, shortening the total period of LTRI training from two years to one year and a half (effective from 1999).

III. JAPANESE-STYLE LAW SCHOOL SYSTEM

A. A RADICAL REFORM PLAN

1. *Justice System Reform Council Established*

To sum up the preceding discussion, the Japanese legal education system experienced a long period of stagnation during which it was suffering from a seemingly incurable disease. Some light of hope finally began to appear when, as mentioned above, a series of piecemeal reforms were attained after the late 1980s. Those were in themselves epoch-making changes, but nevertheless represented only modest and piecemeal measures that were a far cry from real cures. However, within a decade these piecemeal reforms were absorbed by a large wave of radical change: the law school system to be put in place in April 2004. This is part of an inclusive reform scheme of the justice system proposed by the Justice System Reform Council (JSRC), aimed at overhauling the entire process of training and qualifying lawyers, including university legal education and the Legal Examination, as well as at strengthening the legal profession qualitatively and quantitatively. This is to be achieved by adding a new tier, a (principally) three-year graduate-level legal education, between the undergraduate education and the LTRI training, under the motto "From selection based on the single point (of the LE) to training based on a process."

Let us first have a look at the complicated processes by which this innovation was introduced. The JSRC was established in the Cabinet in July 1999, endowed with the mission "to clarify the role to be played by justice in Japanese society in the 21st century and to examine and deliberate fundamental measures necessary to reform the justice system and its infrastructure arrangements, such as the realization of a justice system that is easy for the people to utilize, participation by the people in the justice system, achievement of a legal profession as it should be and strengthening the functions thereof" (Act concerning Establishment of the Justice System Reform Council, Article 2[1]). The minister of justice added a comment that in the twenty-first century, Japanese society will become more complex, varied, and international; deregulation and other reforms will transform Japanese society from an "advance-control type" into a "post-check type"; and these changes will make the role of administration of justice more crucial than ever.

Placed directly under the prime minister with a special secretarial staff, the JSRC was given exceptionally high status and authority. The thirteen members of the JSRC included five academics, representing two state universities and three private universities. Presided over by a well-known constitutional law professor, Kōji Satō, the JSRC had only three members from the legal profession, the remaining five members representing associations of business, labor, and housewives. In June 2001 the council concluded its energetic two years of work and presented its bulky opinion to the prime minister, an opinion that contains a comprehensive set of recommendations amounting to a total reform of the justice system of Japan, including the establishment of a law school system.[32]

TABLE 8.3. Composition of Those Who Passed the LE in 1986

*Age**	*Number*	*Number of LE attempts*†	*Number*	*Occupational status*‡	*Number*
Under 21	0	1	1	Civil service	17
21	4	2	37	Private employee	21
22	21	3	65	Law office	9
23	42	4	71	Others	18
24	47	5	57	University	91
25	57	6	70	None	330
26	40	7	57		
27	45	8	46	Total	486
28	42	9	29		
29	42	10	14		
30	34	11	11		
31	24	12	9		
32	24	13	7		
33	17	14	4		
34	14	15	1		
35	10				
36	5	Total	479		
37	7				
38	3				
39	4				
40	3				
41	0				
42	0				
43	1				
Over 43	0				
Total	486				

*Hōmu daijin kanbō jinjika [Personnel Section of Secretariat of Justice Minister], ed., *Shihō shiken kaikaku o kangaeru: kihon shiryō shū* [Reflections on the Reform of the Legal Examination: Book of Basic Facts], *Jurisuto zōkan* [Jurisuto special issue] (1987), 39.

† Ibid., 44 (based on number who entered LTRI in 1987).

‡ Ibid., 46.

2. *Law School Vision Proposed*

This reform package purported to solve the deep-rooted and multifaceted problems of the system of recruiting, qualifying, and educating lawyers. As a plan for adding a graduate program dedicated to professional education to the existing system of legal education,[33] it inherited the legacy of the University of Tokyo's aborted 1967 attempt at extending undergraduate education to five years. At the same time, the reform plan represented one step in a broader scheme of transforming Japanese higher education as a whole, with stronger emphasis on graduate studies. The prescribed timing (the year 2004) of the introduction of law schools also coincided with the restructuring of all the state universities into so many independent corporations.

Thus, the reform plan based on a law school system in its final form was well founded in the general consensus of the community of legal academics and professionals and supported by concerted actions of governmental organs and was accepted as a plan that purported to solve long-pending problems and at the same time was compatible with the basic organizational needs of all parties involved. It would be a fascinating question to ask why such a far-reaching reform, which shakes the established structures of so many institutions fortified by an intricate network of vested interests, was initiated and could be securely put in place at this time, but it is yet premature to attempt to answer this question fully.[34] However, it is not difficult to see that it was essentially a product of larger political circumstances of the time. The JSRC itself was created in the surge of structural reforms of the Japanese system of governance that were started with a great sense of urgency around the year 1990, prompted by the end of the cold war coupled with economic globalization and the onset of a long stagnation of the Japanese economy.[35] Justice system reform was one of the major items on the reform agenda of the leading political parties, which also included the reforms of party politics and public administration as well as expanding the autonomy of local governments, and which was explained as an indispensable cornerstone of the deregulated society that was emerging.

Mention of "law schools" was first made in a policy-forming organ of the Liberal Democratic Party in 1998. This was followed by publication of some discussions of more concrete law school models by practitioners and academics, which soon produced a stream of opinion favoring the idea of law schools of Japanese style.[36] Then the University of Tokyo's Faculty of Law took initiative to announce its own version of a law school plan in a public forum, and other public and private universities followed the example one by one, thus eventually completing the lineup of prospective law schools prepared to apply for recognition by the Ministry of Education.[37]

The section of the JSRC opinion proposing the introduction of a law school system was put in place with careful preparations. Since that plan encompassed the jurisdiction of the Ministry of Education in addition to that of the Ministry of Justice, which was already involved in the council work, a separate advisory committee on the matter was established within the Ministry of Education on the request of the JSRC. This was the Conference for Consideration of the Vision for Graduate Schools of Law, composed of law professors, legal practitioners, and bureaucrats as well as some members of the JSRC itself. That body had been preceded by the Conference of Cooperators for Investigation and Study concerning Legal Education, which convened law professors of various universities under the auspices of the Ministry of Education from March 1999 to March 2000. Thus, the law school plan adopted by the JSRC was based on a consensus reached by representatives of the main institutions and groups concerned with the new venture.

Upon receiving the opinion of the JSRC, the Diet swiftly passed the Law for Promotion of Justice System Reform (December 2001). The government followed suit by setting up the Headquarters for Promotion of Justice System Reform in the Cabinet, with the prime minister as its chair, and in March 2002 the Cabinet adopted the Plan for the Promotion of Justice System Reform, officially confirming the recommendations of the JSRC. Both the Supreme Court and the Japanese Federation of Bar Associations (JFBA) followed suit by publishing outlines of their respective reform plans. Then, in connection with the reform plan, new legislation, the Linkage between Graduate Law School Education and the Legal Examination (the so-called Law School Act), was introduced by the end of 2002 to lay the legal foundation for the introduction of a law school system. Corresponding amendments were made in the Legal Examination Act and the Courts Act, as well as in the School Education Act.

B. GENERAL PRINCIPLES AND FRAMEWORK OF THE LAW SCHOOL SYSTEM

The law school vision is a reform scheme for restructuring the entire system of recruiting, qualifying, and educating the future members of the legal profession. The principal components of this project may be summarized as follows.

First, the revised School Education Act provides for graduate school for professionals (Article 65[2]). The new graduate school of law (*hōka daigakuin*, or "law school") is defined by the new Law School Act (Article 2[1]) and the Establishment Standards (Article 18[1]) as a kind of graduate school for professionals, dedicated to advanced education for professionals in law toward a professional graduate degree[38] with a standard program of three years of professional studies. Pursuant to these statutes a law school may be established subject to initial acknowledgment ("chartering") by the Ministry of Education and to subsequent continual accreditation by a third-party body (specifics of which are yet to be determined). The Law School Act prescribes that the law school is to become "the core educational institution" (Article 2[1]) for the recruitment, education, and training of the legal profession (*hōsō yōsei*). A law school may be established not only within an existing university but also by an organization without affiliation with a university, such as a local government or a bar association.

Second, according to the opinion of the JSRC, the law school is to serve as a "bridge between academic legal studies and the practical work of the legal profession" and is to provide mainly theoretical education combined with some introductory parts of practical training, such as the basics of "requisite facts" (discussed earlier) and fact-finding. Accordingly, introductory courses in the practical problems of law will constitute one of the four main areas of law school education, the other three being core legal subjects, "basic" and "neighboring" studies of law (embracing such fields as jurisprudence, legal history, comparative law, and sociology of law), and cutting-edge legal fields (Ministry of Education Notice, Article 1[1]). This practical education is a feature lacking in the existing university legal education. In order to cover the practical parts of the law school's curriculum, its regular teaching staff is required to include about 20 percent (Ministry of Education Notice 53) drawn from among professional lawyers such as judges, prosecutors, attorneys, and so on. Some special statutory measures were introduced by the Civil Servants Dispatch Act to facilitate the temporary employment of incumbent judges and prosecutors in law schools (some to be seconded on a full-time basis, others to teach on a part-time basis while maintaining their existing positions).

All this presupposes that both undergraduate legal education in law faculties and the practical training at the LTRI will continue to exist and play their roles. Indeed, although both institutions are expected to adjust the contents of their education so as to be organically integrated with the law school education, the continued existence of these two institutions represents the most distinctive feature of the "Japanese-style law schools." To accommodate these existing elements of legal education, on the one hand, the Ministry of Education Standards for Establishment, which set out the minimum standards required for the establishment of a law school, allow for a two-year course, in the place of the normal three-year course, for students who enter law school with proof of mastery of a certain degree of legal knowledge (which, in most cases, presumably would be attained through undergraduate legal education). On the other hand, the LTRI's mission is to be more sharply focused on practical training, while the length of its training may eventually be further shortened to one year.

Third, the principles of equality, openness, and diversity are declared to govern the designing of law school education.[39] The instruction will not be given in the ex cathedra style of one-way lectures delivered in large classes, but mainly in small classes (of about fifty students), using teaching methods, such as the "Socratic method," based on interactive communications between the instructor and the students, with the latter's active participation in open discussion in class. To ensure the realization of this reform of law teaching, the maximum student-faculty ratio is set at fifteen to one. It is also mandated that the student body of law schools be composed of persons of diverse backgrounds. In that regard, Ministry of Education Notice 53 (Article 3[1]) prescribes that law schools strive to ensure that those who have studied a non-law subject or have practical work experience account for 30 percent or more of the students admitted. As for the entrance examinations for law schools, a form of "law school aptitude test" has been introduced, in accordance with the prescription of the Standards for Establishment that law schools should select students for admission on the basis of accurate and objective evaluation of the students' aptitude (Article 20).

Not only are diversity and openness sought in the content of education and the students admitted, but law schools as a whole are expected to exhibit diversity and openness. Within the limits of the defined standards for acknowledgment and accreditation, the design of each law school is left up to the autonomous choice and inventiveness of each law school, with the goal that the law school system as a whole will exhibit diversity and accessibility to all those who aspire to become lawyers, offering a competitive variety of organizational forms, curricula and teaching methods, staff compositions, and so on. The JSRC also urged the achievement of a fair geographical distribution of law schools throughout Japan.

Fourth, as regards the Legal Examination, the amended Legal Examination Act provides for a New Legal Examination (NLE), which will correspond to the new system of law schools. The NLE will be administered by a new organ called the Examination Committee, made up of seven members representing the three branches of the legal profession as well as law schools. According to the law, the NLE "shall be conducted in a manner organically linked to the education in law school and to the practical training at the LTRI" (Article 2[3]). The law also prescribes that the NLE shall not overly emphasize the applicants' legal knowledge, but shall be conducted so as to ascertain "their theoretical and practical comprehension of law and ability to think and to make judgments about law" (Article 3[4]). The NLE will start in 2006 when the first classes of law schools will graduate.

The law foresees a transitional period of five years, till 2010, during which the existing LE will continue to be offered in parallel to the NLE. This is to make sure that those who have already commenced legal studies but have not graduated from law school may not lose an opportunity to become lawyers. Even after the LE is terminated in 2010, the NLE will not be limited exclusively to law school graduates, but will also be open to those who have passed a new Preliminary Legal Examination (PLE), which will start in 2011. An additional important feature is that the amended Legal Examination Act imposed a limitation on the number of times candidates may take the NLE: three times within five years of either graduation from law school or the passing of the PLE.

Fifth, under the new system, the total number of passers of the legal examination (the LE and NLE combined) is to be augmented to reach three thousand by the year 2010, which number projects to a lawyer population of fifty thousand by about the year 2018, or 2.5 times the present figure, representing a fairly substantial expansion. As to the pass rate, the JSRC pronounced that law school education must be good enough to ensure that 70–80 percent of law school graduates will pass the NLE and gain admission to the LTRI, but in view of the numbers of law schools presently proposed and their prospective number of students, many observers are already predicting that the pass rate will drop to 50 percent or below.

C. FUTURE PROSPECTS AND PROBLEMS OF THE LAW SCHOOL SYSTEM

In the summer of 2003, a total of seventy-two proposed law schools across the nation, of which twenty-two were state or municipal and fifty were private, applied to the Ministry of Education for recognition. All but two of the proposed law schools were anchored in existing law faculties; one of those two is established in cooperation with one of the three Tokyo local bar associations, with no affiliation to any existing university. While purporting to fulfill the statutory minimum requirements imposed by the government, as described above, all the law schools proposed educational programs of their own, highlighting their own sales points, such as clinical studies, business law, cooperation with the local bar, ties with the local community, and so on. After an extensive review process (including review of facilities, proposed programs, and many other aspects of the proposed law schools), four of the applications were denied; two were denied provisionally, but allowed to revise and resubmit, and were later approved; and the remaining sixty-six were approved (but, even for those schools, in nearly all cases at least some revisions were required). As a result, sixty-eight law schools were approved and were to commence operations in April 2004. Those schools range in size from 30 students per year, at the low end, to 300 per year at the largest ones; the total stated capacity for the sixty-eight schools taken together was 5,590 (table 8.4). In addition, a number of other universities, including some that feared they were not yet adequately prepared to be accepted the first year, planned to submit applications in subsequent years.

The law school project is one of the most important items of justice system reform proposed by the JSRC, with major implications for both the system of higher education and the legal profession; and there is no doubt the law school system will change the landscape of Japanese legal education. As law schools gradually take root and mature, it is expected that many of the long-pending, critical problems finally will be solved. Above all, the lost relevance of university legal education to the legal profession will be restored, in the sense that law school education will be well meshed with the reality of the practical world of law, notably by the participation of practitioner instructors in law school education, and the legal examination will be reorganized to be closely linked to law school education. As a result, the substance of legal education will be much improved so as to produce, as the JSRC pronounced, future lawyers equipped with good technical legal knowledge as well as creative thinking ability to critically review and develop the law, grounded in a broad interest in social issues and a moral sense of responsibility for the good of society and the people.[40]

Great hopes are mixed with some concerns. After all, this is the first large-scale reform that has ever been attempted by the Japanese legal system in the absence of an overwhelming external force, such as the revolutionary upheavals of 1868 or the catastrophic defeat in war of 1945. Even though these reforms were effected with a pathbreaking political approach, the reform plans were arrived at and are being carried out through deliberation and consultation of all the parties directly involved within the existing institutional settings. Thus, the new law school system has been constructed through a delicate balancing act, preserving all the components of the existing system, allowing each to participate with enthusiasm in the new scheme with its roles and missions duly redefined. Therefore, much of the ultimate success of the reform depends on how the new system is built and actually operates and on self-motivated evolution and transformation of each of the participating institutions.

An early manifestation of this dilemma was whether or to what extent law schools are allowed to monopolize the field of legal examination. As noted above, although law school graduation remains the principal prerequisite for sitting for the New Legal Examination, a bypass route was introduced in the form of the Preliminary Legal Examination. This has its own justification in that it is necessary and fair not to allow law school to become a barrier for those with insufficient resources to afford law school. However, it is still uncertain how different this examination, based on written tests, would be from the existing ones and also in what proportion the takers of the PLE will be admitted in the final NLE. This is one of the reasons it remains to be seen to what extent the motto "From selection based on the single point (of the LE) to training based on a process" will be realized.

Another issue that remains wide open is, what will be the future of undergraduate legal education? A majority of universities with existing law faculties are establishing law schools, and the core of the teaching staff at those universities, particularly those in positive law fields, will participate in the law schools, together with the newly hired practitioner instructors. At the same time, most of the existing teaching staff will retain their rights and obligations for undergraduate teaching. Those faculty members are expected to concentrate their efforts and energies on developing new law school curricula and teaching methods with a professional sense of mission for the training of future lawyers, which inevitably will lead to a reduction in the efforts and energies they will be able to spare for their teaching in the undergraduate division. On the other hand, the other law faculties and departments that are not setting up their own law schools will continue to operate, but they fear that their status or even their existence will be threatened.

In addition, there is as yet no clear image of what undergraduate legal education will look like under the new regime, either in universities with an attached law school or in those without. Will the undergraduate law faculties and departments serve as another preparatory ground for the legal exam-

TABLE 8.4. Distribution of Proposed Law Schools (2004)

Region	30–50 students	51–100 students	101–300 students	Total	Inhabitants (A)	Attorneys (B)	Students (C)	C/A*	C/B†
Hokkaido	0	0	1	1	5,643	413	100	1.8	24.2
Tohoku	1	0	1	2	9,817	501	150	1.5	29.9
Kanto	12	14	6	32	40,434	11,041	3,175	7.9	28.8
Chubu	7	3	0	10	21,628	1,682	515	2.4	30.6
Kansai	2	8	5	15	22,733	3,777	1,460	6.4	38.7
Chugoku	2	2	0	4	7,733	573	200	2.6	34.9
Shikoku	1	0	0	1	4,154	277	30	0.7	10.8
Kyushu	6	1	0	7	14,764	1,240	330	2.2	26.6
Total	31	28	13	72	126,906	19,504	5,960	4.7	30.6

* Number of law school students per 100,000 persons in population.

† Number of law school students per 100 attorneys.

inations (note that the LE and NLE will be conducted as parallel alternatives for some years) or for the entrance examination to law school, or will they become liberated from the mission of imparting systematic and comprehensive knowledge of current law and its techniques and become strongholds for the spirit of general education in the field of law? Will social science and humanities approaches to law be enhanced? What will be the guiding objective of undergraduate legal studies? Will a proper balance be struck in the undergraduate education between the normative, internal perspective of law and an analytical, observatory way of looking at law in societal context, so that it will contribute positively to the formation of lawyers with "grounding in general culture and in other social sciences," as urged by Judge Abe? And will the number of students wishing to enter law faculties and departments diminish or increase?

An important contingent factor affecting all of these issues is potential future change in the manner in which civil servants are recruited, which might be forthcoming. The increasing importance of graduate education in society at large will affect the Civil Service Examination and concomitantly undergraduate legal education as well, which long has been aiming at aspirants to the governing elite, the bureaucrats, as well as at prospective members of the legal profession. In this connection, it bears note that both the University of Tokyo and Kyoto University are establishing new graduate schools in public policy from April 2004, at the same time as the new law schools, with the expectation some law faculty graduates aiming at the civil service will enter these new public policy schools.

Similarly, there is uncertainty about the future of another component of the system, the LTRI. Introduction to the fundamentals of practical legal work is entrusted to law schools, which have become independent, decentralized providers of initial professional training and are bearing the cost of employing a fairly large number of practitioner instructors. As a consequence, the LTRI must face the task of redefining its roles. The solution may be that the LTRI's program will concentrate more on "practical training" and less on "classroom instruction," thus approaching the German model of trainee program. However, there is strong opinion pressing for eventual abolition of the LTRI among the practicing attorneys, joined by some influential academics, even though the LTRI has hitherto constituted a major, if only partial, realization of the ideal of the "unified legal profession," a catchword cherished by the bar. Issues are raised as to whether it is desirable, or even economically and physically feasible in the face of growing numbers of apprentices, to keep the centralized mechanism of educating future lawyers under the administrative control of the Supreme Court. On the other hand, as the number of attorneys who are appointed to judgeships increases as expected under the new system, it will remain important for all the members of the legal profession to have received common basic training emphasizing the skills and arts of acting as judges; it will also remain important for all members of the legal profession to have experienced a period of camaraderie at the starting point of their professional careers.

Crucial significance of the law school scheme to the structure of the legal profession lies in its coupling with the plan for expansion of the size of the legal profession itself. Inserting law schools into the legal training system has proved to be an ingenious means for revivifying and achieving wide acceptance for the long-forgotten fundamental idea that the Legal Examination is essentially a qualifying examination, not something similar to the admission test for entering a company. It seems undeniable that even if the passage rate for law school graduates drops from 70 to 50 percent or lower, law schools will serve as a powerful channel through which the societal demand for legal services is constantly fed directly into the lawyer-producing system. Also, without the prospect of the emergence of a law school system, it would have been hard to imagine that the JFBA could reach the historic decision[41] to support the JSRC 's reform package, which included a dramatic increase in the number of passers on the LE.

Nevertheless, even though the goal of three thousand passers, to be attained around 2010, is regarded by many observers not as an ultimate terminal point but only as an operative goal for the present time, it is not guaranteed that even that goal will be realized without any resistance. But another, final point bears note. In relation to the issue of expanding the provision of legal services for citizens, it is also essential to spread attorneys more evenly around the country. Accordingly, it has been stressed repeatedly that law schools also should be distributed as evenly as possible, in order to secure equal opportunity for students living in various parts of the country to acquire law school education. Table 4 above summarizes the geographical distribution of the initial sixty-eight law schools and the stated capacity of students according to region. As reflected by the columns showing the rates of aggregate number of students to the numbers of inhabitants and attorneys in each region, it is clear that law schools are being offered in a distribution pattern closely reflecting the present state of attorney distribution, whereas, as is well known, the latter has exhibited a wide discrepancy with the regional distribution of the general population. In other words, in terms of rate to population size, the initial law schools are heavily concentrated in the Kanto and

Kansai areas, while Shikoku, Tohoku, and Hokkaido are relatively neglected. This in turn implies that the law school project is so far failing to serve as a lever to attain a fairer distribution of legal services and more equal protection of law for the Japanese people.

NOTES

1. See Hakaru Abe, "Education of the Legal Profession in Japan," in Arthur Taylor von Mehren, ed., *Law in Japan: The Legal Order in a Changing Society* (Cambridge, MA: Harvard University Press, 1963), 153.

2. For lack of space for a sketch of the historical background of Japanese legal education, I must refer readers to the original chapter of Judge Abe; see ibid., 153, 153–55.

3. These circumstances may be counted as a factor to explain the fact that the true faculty-student ratio is even lower than that set forth in the law faculty guidebooks, when one focuses on the ratio of those who teach the courses in "law" to the number of students who take those courses.

4. Incidentally, under the exceptional circumstances during World War II, political science students comprised a great majority in, for example, the University of Tokyo Faculty of Law.

5. It became the present University of Tokyo Faculty of Law after World War II.

6. A comprehensive history of legal education at private universities in Japan has not yet been written, and, in my personal opinion, undertaking such a study should constitute an important task for future researchers.

7. See Abe, "Education of the Legal Profession in Japan," 160.

8. H. L. A. Hart, *The Concept of Law*, 2nd ed. (New York: Oxford University Press, 1994), 89.

9. The derogatory epithet "doctrinaire," sometimes attached to the lecture-based teaching style, may be regarded as pointing to its propensity to degenerate into preaching of law ex cathedra.

10. See Atsushi Ōmura, "Gendai Nihon no hōgaku kyōiku" [Legal Education in Current Japan], in Atsushi Ōmura, *Hōten, kyōiku, minpōgaku* [Codes, Education, and the Study of Civil Law] (Tokyo: Yūhikaku, 1999), 121–57.

11. The term *jittei-hō* (positive law), usually applied to the subjects of positive law, conveys the connotation that these subjects deal with real laws actually in force and highlights the positivistic nature of the teaching.

12. Over forty years ago, Judge Abe observed that "the fundamental function of university education is distorted by this sort of study for the examination: stu-

dents are deprived of a grounding in general culture and in other social sciences." Abe, "Education of the Legal Profession in Japan," 163.

13. The subjects to be tested have undergone many changes since the introduction of the Legal Examination.

14. Since the detailed contents of the teaching program are not officially made public, one must rely on information provided by those who have actually participated in it either as apprentices or as instructors. The following sketch of the legal education at the institute relies mainly on the precious and intriguing series of public discussions conducted by some judges and attorneys who have served as eminent instructors, as well as academics, set forth in Nichibenren hōmukenkyū zaidan [Japan Law Foundation], *Jisedai hōsō kyōiku* [Education for the Legal Profession of the Next Generation] (Tokyo: Shōji hōmu kenkyūkai, 2000). I also learned a great deal from the more personal account of Hiroaki Yanagawa, *Shihō shūshū Uwocchingu* [Watching Legal Apprenticeship] (Tokyo: Hōgaku shoin, 1993).

15. See generally Shigeo Itō, *Yōken jijitsu no kiso* [Fundamentals of Requisite Facts] (Tokyo: Yūhikaku, 2000).

16. Abe, "Education of the Legal Profession in Japan," 164.

17. Ibid., 168.

18. See ibid., 186.

19. It is noteworthy, for example, that the teaching materials have to be renewed every year so that the "answers" are not revealed to the following year's apprentices by their predecessors. It has been jokingly said that for an attorney instructor, appointment to the institute is "a three-year imprisonment plus a fine of 30 million yen." Nichibenren hōmukenkyū zaidan, *Jisedai hōsō kyōiku*, 241.

20. See Hideo Tanaka, ed., assisted by Malcolm D. H. Smith, *The Japanese Legal System* (Tokyo: University of Tokyo Press, 1976), 587.

21. Abe also pointed out the basic issue of the direct connection between the operation of the legal education system and the size of the legal profession or the bar, which has been tied to the capacity of the LTRI.

22. See Kazuyuki Kitamura, *Daigaku tōta no jidai* [The Age in Which Universities Are Eliminated] (Tokyo: Chūkō shinshō, 1990), 174–75.

23. Hideo Tanaka, "Tōkyō daigaku hōgakubu no kyōikukeikaku saikentō ni tsuite" [On the Reexamination of the Educational Program of the Faculty of Law, the University of Tokyo]," in Hideo Tanaka, *Eibei no shihō* [The Judicial Systems of England and the United States] (Tokyo: University of Tokyo Press, 1973), 572, 584.

24. Tōkyō daigaku hōgakubu [University of Tokyo Faculty of Law], *Hōgakubu kyōiku ni kansuru jittaichōsa hōkokusho* [Report on the Survey Research concerning Education at the Faculty of Law] (1990), 23–24.

25. Ibid., 33–35.

26. Note that our criterion of at least ten passers in the most recent two years as of this writing is an arbitrary one, and the universities included in the list and their rank order will vary somewhat from year to year.

27. *Rinji shihō seido chōsakai ikensho* [The Opinion of the Ad Hoc Committee for Investigation into the Justice System] (1964), 100–114.

28. There is a gap between the number of applicants and the number who actually take the examination. Each year, a few thousand applicants default. As a result, the pass rate calculated on the basis of the actual applicants is somewhat higher than that presented in table 8.2. However, I have elected to use the applicant-based rate, because this is the rate that has long been used in past discussions of this subject. In any event, the difference between the two has consistently remained below 1 percent in recent years.

29. These changes must also be closely related in various ways to the shifting economic situation of the time, but lack of data precludes further analysis of those points. For one thing, the suppliers of the statistics and analyses so far have concentrated their attention on those who are ultimately selected in neglect of those who constitute the pool for selection. Analysis of the behavior of applicants will also be indispensable in explaining why the average age of those who are ultimately selected has not radically decreased as the result of the recent reforms.

30. It would be interesting to explore the effect of the recent increase in the number of passers on the composition of applicants, but unfortunately, and curiously, there are no data available.

31. See Morio Takeshita, *Saibanhō* [Laws concerning the Administration of Justice], 4th ed. (Tokyo: Yūhikaku, 1999), 413. This attitude of the bar is predictable in view of its traditional posture of stressing equal treatment of the three branches of the legal profession in the process of the recruitment and training of its members. However, the same problem is bound to arise sooner or later in Japan, as it recently has in Germany, where the number of attorneys has been growing explosively under a similar type of state-provided training system.

32. Shihō seido kaikaku shingikai [Justice System Reform Council], *Shihō seido kaikaku shingikai ikensho—21 seiki no Nihon o sasaeru shihō seido* [Recommendations of the Justice System Reform Council—for a Justice System to Support Japan in the Twenty-first Century] (June 12, 2001), available in English at (http://www.kantei.go.jp/foreign/judiciary/2001/0612report.html).

33. From the early 1990s, some leading national universities had instituted a special graduate program (*senshū kōsu*) in law and political science, offering a mas-

ter's degree aimed at students who intended to use the learning attained for their later occupations, as well as those who were already engaged in careers. That graduate program did not aim at the training of future members of the legal profession per se, however.

34. For my own views on the reform plan at an earlier stage of development, see Kahei Rokumoto, "Law and Culture in Transition," *American Journal of Comparative Law* 49 (2001): 545.

35. The fact the JSRC was established directly under the prime minister signified at least a formal rejection of the traditional method of securing informal three-party (the Ministry of Justice, the Supreme Court, and the JFBA) agreement prior to formal legislative procedures, an established practice in the lawmaking process in matters concerning the justice system (see ibid., 553).

36. See Yukio Yanagida, "Nihon no atarashii hōsō yōseiseido—Hābādo rōsukūru no hōgaku kyōiku o nentō ni oite" [A New System for Training the Japanese Legal Profession—with Reference to Legal Education at Harvard Law School], *Jurisuto*, nos. 1127, 1128 (1998); Shigeaki Tanaka, "Hōsō yōseiseido kaikaku to hōgakukyōiku" [The Reform of Training for the Legal Profession and University Legal Education], in *Kyōto daigaku hōgakubu hyakushūnen kinen ronbunshū* [Collected Papers Commemorating the One-Hundredth-Year Anniversary of the Faculty of Law, Kyoto University] (Tokyo: Yūhikaku, 1999), 1:53.

37. As a consequence of the administrative reorganization in 2001, the Ministry of Education became the Ministry of Education, Culture, Sports, Science and Technology. For the sake of convenience, the title "Ministry of Education" is used throughout this chapter.

38. The degree to be awarded by the law schools is formally designated as *Hōmu Hakase* (literally, "doctor of legal affairs"), evidently based on the U.S. designation Juris Doctor.

39. Shihō seido kaikaku shingikai, *Shihō seido kaikaku shingikai ikensho.*

40. See ibid.

41. On November 1, 2000, the JFBA held an extraordinary general meeting to pass a resolution supporting the scheme calling for the establishment of law schools. This was a bold leap from the federation's own previous resolution of just three years previously to accept an increase in passers to one thousand. The draft resolution prepared by the executive committee also included, among other points, a demand that the assistant judgeship system should be abolished, that judges should be appointed principally from among the ranks of practicing attorneys and other lawyers, and that the promotion and related processes of personnel administration of judges should be made more transparent and objective. The draft resolution also included a demand to introduce the jury system, particu-

larly for serious criminal offenses. Attorneys who opposed the resolution formed groups and mounted campaigns, and a rumor went around that the resolution might be defeated. However, after a long and turbulent session, the resolution was adopted by an overwhelming majority of seventy-four hundred to thirty-four hundred votes. A summary is available at (http://www.nichibenren.or.jp/jp/katsudo/syuppan/shinbun/2000/322_1.html).

PART II

The Individual, The State, and the Law

IN THE FIRST OF THE NINE CHAPTERS in part II, "Ongoing Changes in the Infrastructure of a Constitutional System: From 'Bureaucracy' to Democracy," Kazuyuki Takahashi explores the very foundations of Japan's constitutional system. Based on an examination of the reforms of the political system, the administrative system, and the justice system, he argues that the goals of these various reforms are converging toward one ultimate objective: overcoming the traditional "rule by bureaucrats" and establishing strong and effective political leadership based on popular support.

In the second chapter, "The Constitution of Japan: 'Pacifism' and Mass Media Freedom," Lawrence W. Beer addresses other fundamental issues regarding Japan's Constitution. As the title suggests, the chapter focuses primarily on Japan's unique quasi pacifism—the constitutional issue that has generated by far the most debate within Japan over the past half century—and mass media freedom. Beer concludes his chapter by discussing constitutional amendment, or, rather, the absence of any constitutional amendment in the nearly sixty years since Japan's Constitution was adopted.

The next two chapters focus on administrative law. In "Development of the Concepts of Transparency and Accountability in Japanese Administrative Law," Katsuya Uga provides a thorough explanation of the two most important new laws in the administrative law field: the Administrative Procedure Act of 1993 and the Information Disclosure Act of 1999. In analyzing the forces that led to the enactment of these two laws and the impact of the laws, Uga focuses on two fundamental concepts: "transparency" and "accountability."

The following chapter, Tom Ginsburg's "The Politics of Transparency in Japanese Administrative Law," is framed primarily as a comment on the Uga chapter. In his chapter, Ginsburg elaborates on the political dynamics behind the Administrative Procedure Act, the Information Disclosure Act, and a Cabinet resolution requiring public notice of administrative rule making. In addition, Ginsburg focuses on one particular procedural requirement—the requirement that administrators give reasons to regulated parties—and the likely impact of that requirement. He concludes by considering the likely impact of the reforms on public demands for transparency.

In "The Development of Criminal Law in Japan since 1961," Kōya Matsuo begins by providing a decade-by-decade review of the most important pieces of legislation in the field of substantive criminal law, focusing on key trends in each era. After focusing in the first part of his chapter on legislation, or "law in books," Matsuo turns to "law in action," discussing the activities of courts and prosecutors. As he observes, while the number of new laws over the past four decades may appear at first glance to be rather impressive, during most of that period the legislature was not particularly active in the field of criminal law. To the contrary, Matsuo concludes, "[l]egislative activity was stagnant as far as the revision of the Penal Code was concerned," and as a consequence in some cases the courts had to take the lead in expanding the scope of laws through interpretation. Matsuo closes with a discussion of prospects for the future, focusing on such issues as the death penalty and corporate crimes.

The next chapter, Joseph L. Hoffmann's "Globalization and Japanese Criminal Law," is framed as a comment on Matsuo's chapter. As the title indicates, Hoffmann focuses on the impact of globalization on Japanese criminal law. His conception of globalization is broad; he argues that three different types of globalization—economic globalization, social and cultural globalization, and the globalization of law itself—have significantly affected, and in some instances have been affected by, recent developments in Japanese criminal law.

In "Criminal Justice in Japan," David T. Johnson undertakes a broad examination of Japanese criminal justice. He begins by looking back at major patterns in postwar criminal justice. As distinguishing characteristics of Japan's criminal justice system, Johnson discusses such features as commitment to truth, correction, consistency, and convictions, along with a confession-centered approach. Turning to the future, Johnson identifies and discusses a wide range of social changes and new challenges for the criminal justice system.

He argues that Japan is in the throes of major social change that could transform the ways in which criminal justice is administered.

The last two chapters in this part address subjects that lay beyond the scope of the 1961 Law in Japan conference: environmental law and health law. Although the Minamata tragedy was not mentioned at the 1961 conference, by that time, as Kōichirō Fujikura discusses in his chapter, "Litigation, Administrative Relief, and Political Settlement for Pollution Victim Compensation: Minamata Mercury Poisoning after Fifty Years," Minamata already had attracted public attention. Indeed, a Supreme Court decision issued in 2004 held that the central government and prefectural government possessed sufficient information that they could and should have taken steps to minimize the tragedy no later than the start of 1960. They failed to do so, and, as Fujikura explains, the legal saga surrounding Minamata has continued for nearly fifty years since. Fujikura explores the ramifications of Minamata and lessons to be learned from the tragedy.

In the final chapter in this part, "Medical Error, Deception, Self-Critical Analysis, and Law's Impact: A Comparative Examination," Robert B Leflar explores Japanese and U.S. approaches to medical error. As he observes, both nations have engaged in debates over the proper design of systems of liability, information management, and institutional incentive structures to best deal with the problem of medical error. Both nations face similar tensions with regard to these various measures. Yet the nature of the debates differs, Leflar explains, because of differences in the allocation of accountability in the two nations: the United States relies on civil malpractice lawsuits as the primary accountability mechanism, whereas Japan relies primarily on the criminal justice system and the media. This chapter provides a fascinating study revealing the impact of legal standards on the behavioral patterns of individuals and institutions.

9 Ongoing Changes in the Infrastructure of a Constitutional System

From "Bureaucracy" to Democracy

KAZUYUKI TAKAHASHI

The Constitution of Japan remains unchanged since its enactment in 1946; and we celebrated its fiftieth anniversary just a few years ago. Recent years, however, have witnessed unprecedentedly rapid changes in the environment in which the Constitution functions. Some efforts to adjust to those changes have taken place not on the constitutional level but rather on the level of laws. These efforts nonetheless have generated profound constitutional transformations by restructuring what can best be described as the "infrastructure" that determines to a large extent the way in which the Constitution functions. What I have in mind here are those various reforms that have been triggered first in the political field by the Hosokawa government, leading to a chain reaction of successive reform plans in the administrative and judicial fields. Although each reform plan resulted from its own causes, we now begin to realize that the goals of these various reforms are converging toward one important idea: to overcome the traditional "rule by bureaucrats" and establish strong and effective political leadership based on popular support. In this chapter, I will briefly sketch the main motives underlying the political, administrative, and judicial reforms and show that those reforms are converging, hopefully, toward that goal.

I. POLITICAL REFORMS

A. ELECTORAL SYSTEM

From the time the current Constitution came into effect in 1947 until the political system reforms of 1994, Japan adhered to an election system for the members of the House of Representatives that we refer to as a "multi-seat constituency system" or "system of medium-sized electoral districts." Under this system, each constituency elected three to five members, depending on the size of population, with each voter entering on his or her ballot only one name chosen from among the officially declared candidates. After forty years of experience, we came to understand that this system was not only totally inappropriate for the establishment of policy-centered politics but also might be one of the major causes of corruption. Under this system, it was not uncommon for two or more candidates of the same party (usually the Liberal Democratic Party [LDP]) to compete against each other rather than against the candidates of other parties. Unable to distinguish themselves from each other in terms of the policies advocated by the party, the candidates tended to emphasize, not their party's policies, but their own capability, demonstrated by past achievements, to channel central government money to their constituency through governmental aid and public works investments. Business circles in the constituency profited from government money and returned votes and donations to the politicians they supported, thus fostering cozy relations and causing corruption scandals from time to time.

The solution advanced for this problem was to introduce a new election system that would put the focus on policy differences and promote competition among, not within, political parties. There are two election system models that promote policy- and party-centered politics: single-seat constituency and proportional representation systems. The former was favored by the LDP and the latter by smaller parties. A compromise resulted in a combined single-seat constituency and proportional representation system, with voters casting two ballots, one for each system. The total number of lower house members was set at 500 (reduced to 480 by amendment in 2000), 300 of whom were to be elected by single-seat constituency and the rest (180) by proportional representation. For the latter system, the nation was divided into eleven blocs, each receiving an allocation of seats in accordance with the size of the population; the "qualified parties"[1] can present their fixed lists of candidates; voters vote according to the list, and the number of seats each list obtains is calculated using the d'Hondt formula for each bloc; and successful candidates are to be decided for each list according to the order fixed in advance.[2]

Several constitutional questions have been raised with respect to this system. First, malapportionment resulted with regard to the single-seat constituency system. The law that set up the panel to draft the drawing of lines for the election districts specified that the maximum disparity among constituencies must be less than a one-to-two ratio. At the same time, that law directed the panel to respect the existing prefectural and municipal boundaries in order to avoid gerrymandering. The law further stipulated, as the apportionment procedure to be followed by the panel, that every prefecture first be given one seat (47 in total) before the remaining seats (253) could be distributed to prefectures in proportion to population and that each prefecture be divided into as many districts as it was thus entitled to. Achieving all of the above stipulations did not prove possible. Utilization of the specified formula forced the panel to abandon the efforts to stay within the one-to-two ratio and instead to propose a plan containing the maximum disparity of 1-to-2.3, and the Diet passed that plan into law. Despite the disparity, the Supreme Court, over dissents from five justices, ruled it constitutional in the Grand Bench decision of November 10, 1999,[3] concluding that the formula constituted a permissible exercise of legislative discretion.

A second constitutional objection raised against the new system was that it favored candidates from the "qualified parties" in election campaigns over candidates not belonging to such parties, by allowing the "qualified parties" to conduct election campaigns of their own, which would surely benefit their candidates. Most importantly, TV broadcast of policy stances is only afforded to the "qualified parties." The Supreme Court also rejected challenges on this ground. The Court held that the goal of achieving party-centered politics is reasonable and acceptable under the Constitution and that the advantages the candidates of the "qualified parties" enjoy as a result of those parties' independent campaign activities have not yet exceeded the permissible degree of inequality.[4] Here again, five justices dissented with regard to the evaluation of the impacts resulting from the unequal treatment.

The new system is expected gradually to generate a two-party system or at least a polarization of parties into two blocs. As of this writing, we have had general elections twice, in 1996 and 2000, under the new system. Contrary to the above expectation, no clear sign has yet been seen that a new framework is emerging. The trend observed is rather toward a moderated multiparty system, partly due to the effect of the proportional representation element built into the new system. To be sure, the monopolization of power by the

LDP has long since ended, and coalition governments have become the norm. But it remains to be seen whether a stable two-bloc system will emerge.

B. POLITICAL FUNDS CONTROL

In light of the fact that donations by business firms to individual politicians were often implicated in corruption scandals, the eighth Election System Research Council recommended in its reports of 1992 that private corporations be banned from making donations. The Political Funds Control Act, revised in 1994, provided in Article 9 of its appendix that within five years from the enactment of the law steps be taken to ban donations by private corporations (companies, trade unions, and all other organizations except political organizations) to individual politicians. This was effectively accomplished in 1999, with the changes taking effect in January 2000. Article 10 of the appendix also provided for a review of donations from private corporations to political parties within five years, but a ban on such donations was not effectuated in the 1999 revision because of strong objections from the LDP, which argued that the donations to political parties would not conflict with the goal of party-centered politics. The political parties, in the context of Political Funds Control, are defined as those political organizations that either have five or more Diet members or obtained 2 percent or more of valid votes in the most recent Diet member elections. It turned out, as many political observers predicted, that the donations to political parties function as a conduit for corporate money to reach individual politicians through local chapters of political parties, which are given legal status as separate political parties with regard to receiving donations. The number of party chapters is not legally limited and the LDP Diet members, who usually dominate local chapters by serving as their heads, rushed to set up local chapters by transforming their support groups into chapters in name only. Chapters and support groups of individual politicians are not clearly separated, and it is often said that those politicians have two political purses at their disposal, their own purses and those of the chapters.[5]

There are four main sources of political money under the current system: first, donations from individuals, who can donate up to either 10 million yen or 20 million yen in total per year, depending on to whom the donations are made, with the lower limit for donations to individual politicians (or their designated political funds management organizations) or political organizations other than political parties, and the higher limit for donations to political parties (or their designated political funds organizations), and the maximum amount each politician or political organization can receive from one and the same individual is 1.5 million yen, except in the case of political parties, which are subject to no ceiling; second, donations from private corporations, which can donate to political parties (or their designated political funds organizations) up to the maximum of 100 million yen in proportion to the size of capital, in the case of companies, and to the size of membership, in the case of trade unions, with corporations other than companies and trade unions being subject to a lower ceiling; third, revenues from fund-raising parties, the maximum price of party tickets one person or corporation can purchase being set by the act at 1.5 million yen; and fourth, state subsidies to political parties (to be explained in the next section).

In order to assure the transparency of money flow, the accountants of political organizations are required to submit to the minister of general affairs or local election administration commissions financial reports that declare the names of donors of fifty thousand yen or more, as well as the names of those to whom payments of fifty thousand yen or more are made. Those reports are made available to the public.

Some commentators have pointed out several constitutional problems attributed to this system, two of which seem to me to be most serious. First, all the political organizations, defined in the act as organizations that have as their primary objective to promote, support, or oppose political causes or policies, or to recommend, support, or oppose particular candidates for public offices, as well as organizations that constantly and methodically perform the abovementioned activities as their main activities, are required to register with the general affairs minister or with the election administration commissions of the respective prefectures before they start receiving donations or making expenditures for the purpose of conducting political activities. This regulation might be overbroad in that even organizations that have no intention of participating in election processes and that confine themselves to exercising freedom of speech are subject to a prior-registration requirement. Second, if companies enjoy freedom of political activities, including freedom to make donations, as the Supreme Court has ruled,[6] is it possible to totally ban private corporations including companies from giving money to individual politicians? Companies may be able to achieve the same goal by donating to political parties instead of to individual politicians, but there might be some political or nonpolitical organizations that may want to associate with particular politicians through donations with the aim of promoting certain causes. Political organizations can do this if they register in advance, but nonpolitical organizations are prohibited from doing the same.

C. STATE SUBSIDIES TO POLITICAL PARTIES

The political reform package of 1994 contained a plan to provide state subsidies to political parties in order to make up for the envisaged restriction on corporate donations.[7] It was decided for that purpose to make an appropriation of the sum of 250 yen per capita multiplied by the size of the population,[8] amounting in total to more than 30 billion yen. Half of the total amount is to be distributed to the eligible parties in proportion to the number of their Diet members and the other half in proportion to the number of votes they have collected in the most recent nationwide elections.[9] The eligible parties are defined as those that either have five or more Diet members, or have at least one Diet member and obtained 2 percent or more of total valid votes nationwide in the most recent national election.[10] The eligible parties that intend to receive the subsidy are required to register with the general affairs minister.[11]

It was expected that these subsidies would constitute, hopefully, a third of the total revenue for each party, but parties recently have been becoming more and more dependent on the state subsidies. In 2000, the LDP relied on subsidies for 59.8 percent of its income, and the Democratic Party of Japan for more than 60 percent.[12]

This system is not immune to constitutional defects either. For instance, it disproportionately favors the existing major parties over future parties because the act does not limit the purposes for which the subsidies may be used,[13] on the pretext of respecting freedom of political activities. The only burden imposed on recipient parties is the duty to submit financial reports on how they expended the money, with receipts attached for each expense exceeding fifty thousand yen. Parties were expected to use the money for such activities as policy studies, but in most of the cases to date, the money has been divided and distributed to individual Diet members to be used for election campaigns or for maintenance of their offices, producing unjustifiable advantages for the incumbents.

II. ADMINISTRATIVE REFORMS

Administrative reforms surfaced as a top-priority item on the political agenda of Prime Minister Ryūtarō Hashimoto, who pledged to stake his political career on the issue. The Administrative Reform Council, headed by the prime minister, energetically worked on drawing the outline of reforms and issued its final report in December 1997. In accordance with that report, many laws related to the administrative reforms were enacted and the new scheme took effect in January 2001.

The main purpose of the reform was to reorganize and revive administration so as to respond effectively and promptly to the needs of the time. The final report called for streamlining the bloated and sclerotic administration through decentralization, privatization, and deregulation. The underlying philosophy was to reduce central government functions to a minimum, making the best use of local autonomy and market mechanisms. Alleviation of the central administration's duties was to go hand in hand with the reinforcement of political functions as compared with the administrative functions of the central government. For that purpose, the separation of policy making and policy implementation was set forth as a guiding principle for the reorganization, the former being assumed by the central government, the latter to be outsourced to the private sector or to independent administrative agencies, patterned after a British model.

Among many aspects of the reform efforts undertaken to achieve these goals, two issues warrant comment here: (1) the strengthening of the prime minister's power and (2) decentralization. Each has potential for reversing Japan's longstanding practice of acceding to bureaucrats' rule.

A. LEADERSHIP OF THE PRIME MINISTER

According to the Constitution, executive power is vested in the Cabinet (Article 65), which consists of the prime minister and other ministers of state (Article 66). As the Constitution talks about "various administrative branches" (Article 72) and "competent Minister of State" (Article 74), we can interpret it as assuming the existence, under the Cabinet, of an administrative organization consisting of several branches (ministries and agencies), each headed by a minister of state. The Cabinet is a collective organ, collectively responsible to the Diet (Article 66), but the prime minister is not "primus inter pares," as was the case under the Meiji Constitution. Rather, the prime minister is the head of the Cabinet (Article 66), the status of which is materialized by the power of appointing and removing ministers of state as he or she chooses. So, in theory, the prime minister is now in the position to lead the Cabinet and control the entire administration. But the reality had been completely different.

Traditionally, politics in Japan has been characterized by the preeminence of the bureaucracy. Ever since the Meiji Restoration, Japan's political center has been occupied by bureaucrats not elected directly or indirectly by the people, but appointed by the emperor. Under the Meiji Constitution, most of the ministers of state, including the prime ministers as primus inter pares, were recruited from outside the Diet, except during a short period commonly called the period of Taisho Democracy. All the important policies were drafted by bureaucrats who monopolized the expertise in policy making, the role of the Imperial Diet being confined to restraining excessive use of power by bureaucrats.

This practice was carried over into practice under the new Constitution, partly because the administration of the "ancien regime," together with its personnel, survived the General Headquarters (GHQ)–ordered purge. When the postwar turmoil settled down, it was again the bureaucracy that assumed a central role in politics. The Diet members, who were expected to lead policy making but lacked experience and know-how, tended to define their own role as transmitting aspirations of their constituencies to bureaucrats and began to act more like lobbyists than legislators. The Constitution introduced a British-style parliamentary system, but, influenced by an American vision of strict separation of powers, the ruling party and the Cabinet distanced themselves from each other. Being unable to ensure strong support from the ruling party, and, to make matters worse, facing, from time to time, an allied resistance of party members and bureaucrats, the prime minister and his or her Cabinet failed to demonstrate strong leadership in policy making.[14] The fact that the Cabinet, supported by the LDP, which maintained uninterrupted power for thirty-eight years from 1955 to 1993, heavily relied on a delicate factional balance, further weakened the prime minister's position. Notwithstanding the Constitution's vesting in the prime minister of the power to appoint and remove ministers of state, in reality the prime minister could not appoint the right persons to the right posts, but instead was obliged to accept the persons recommended by faction leaders to the posts demanded by them as a reward for contributing to his or her election or as a gift to appease a grudge relating to a severe contest. It is quite natural, then, that the ministers of state do not represent the prime minister's policy but the interests of their own factions. Furthermore, faction leaders recommend their candidates for ministers of state in order of seniority rule within their factions, not based on talent or expertise. Serving only for a very short period because of the frequent reshuffling of the Cabinet, most of the ministers of state leave the posts before obtaining a thorough knowledge of the relevant ministry's affairs, thus allowing bureaucrats to control policy making in a "bottom-up" style. Accordingly, ministers of state tend to act as representatives of bureaucrat-made policy rather than as the prime minister's agents directing and supervising bureaucrats to draft policies in line with the prime minister's policies.

It is said that this system with the bureaucracy as its center worked well until toward the end of the 1980s. Japan's prime goal after World War II was to recover from war damage and catch up with Western countries in terms of economic growth. Once that national goal was set, there was no better-suited organ than the bureaucracy, the best think tank in Japan, to work out ways and means to achieve the goal. Bureaucrats worked hard with a noble sense of mission. Businesspeople trusted them and accepted, sometimes demanded, a wide range of business regulations in exchange for protection from "excessive competition." Firmly united under the direction of the bureaucracy, Japan succeeded in achieving rapid growth and catching up with developed nations.

But, at the same time, this style of politics fostered collusive relations among bureaucrats, politicians, and businesses, causing occasional bribery scandals. When the sense of mission gradually eroded following the attainment of the national goal and the morality of the people involved began to deteriorate, the negative aspects of this cozy relationship loomed intolerably large in the public mind. Especially after the bubble economy burst and the distribution of economic fruits began to present a zero-sum game feature in the 1990s, the absence of politics, understood in the sense of efforts to choose among competing values, came to be regretted.

Bureaucrats who are not elected and lack democratic legitimacy cannot perform this role of choosing among competing values. Without letting people participate in decision making, value-choice cannot be achieved. Furthermore, achieving value-choice requires strong initiative in proposing new goals and policies on the part of politicians. And it is the prime minister and his or her Cabinet who are best situated to assume this role. This is why the Administrative Reform Council called for enhancing the Cabinet functions and the prime minister's role in its final report.[15] Details of the council's proposals worth mentioning here include revision of the Cabinet Act to the effect of allowing the prime minister to take initiative at Cabinet meetings, reinforcement of the Cabinet secretariat, and establishment of the Cabinet office.

Article 72 of the Constitution stipulates that the prime minister, representing the Cabinet, exercises control and supervision over the various administrative branches, and Article 6 of the Cabinet Act stipulates that the prime minister exercises control and supervision on the basis of the principles adopted at the Cabinet meetings. In the current practice, the agenda of the

Cabinet meeting is set by the de facto meeting of the administrative vice ministers held prior to the Cabinet meeting. Only the items having reached consensus among ministries concerned are put on the agenda of the Cabinet meeting. Given the vertically divided structure of administrative organization, the rigid ministry boundaries, and tough turf wars between ministries, consensus building is not always easy and the prime minister's leadership in coordinating policy directions and ensuring consensus between ministries has long been hoped for. Although the Cabinet Act stipulates that a minister of state has the right to bring up any item to the meetings and to ask for a decision by the Cabinet, it was not clear whether the prime minister had the same right, and this made it difficult for the prime minister to secure the basis on which to intervene in disputes with an aim of bringing entire ministries in line with his or her policies. This is the reason the final report called for the revision of the Cabinet Act, and as a result Article 4, paragraph 2, of the revised act now stipulates that the prime minister can introduce, on the agendas of Cabinet meetings over which he or she presides, any item concerning fundamental principles regarding the Cabinet's important policies as well as other items. With this clarification, the prime minister is now equipped with legal power to exercise strong leadership in conducting the nation's policies in line with the policies he or she promised before assuming the post.[16]

Legal empowerment alone is not enough for the prime minister to exercise leadership effectively. He or she needs substantial staff assistance. For this purpose, the Cabinet secretariat was strengthened and the new Cabinet office was created. The Cabinet Act added a provision[17] empowering the Cabinet secretariat to take charge of the task of drafting fundamental principles concerning important policies of the Cabinet and of general planning and coordination, which corresponds to the abovementioned new power of the prime minister. The number of staff members was increased; of especial note is the fact that the maximum number of the prime minister's aides was raised from three to five. The newly created Cabinet office assumes the task of helping the Cabinet with regard to key policies,[18] and in pursuit of this task it helps and cooperates with the Cabinet secretariat.[19] To achieve its task, it takes charge of the policy planning and general coordination that will be required in order to ensure policy consistency among various ministries, without sharing, nevertheless, the abovementioned task of the Cabinet secretariat. I would say that the core task of the Cabinet secretariat is to draft key policies of the Cabinet, whereas the core task of the Cabinet office is inter-ministerial coordination in line with the key policies.[20] In view of its nature, the Cabinet office is not governed by the National Administrative Operation Act, which governs all the ministries, but is created by a special law titled the Cabinet Office Establishment Act and is deemed in its legal status as superior to ministries and agencies. The Cabinet office has under it several advisory councils assigned to contribute to the tasks of the Cabinet office, headed by the prime minister or chief Cabinet secretary, and consisting of concerned ministers of state and experts. The most important of these councils is the Economic and Financial Advisory Council, which is expected to take over budgetary drafting that used to be assumed by the Ministry of Finance.

The reform was put into effect in January 2001. The Koizumi government that was formed right after the new scheme started seemed to demonstrate strong initiative based on overwhelming popular support against bureaucracy as well as coalition parties, but it later encountered difficulties from the joint resistance from *zoku giin* (Diet members who are closely identified with certain interests and, in turn, have close relations with the ministries representing those interests) and bureaucrats. It will take more time to see whether Japanese constitutional politics finally produces a break from the traditional evils or a return to them after a desperate struggle.

B. DECENTRALIZATION

The Constitution of Japan guarantees local autonomy, with relevant rules set forth in Chapter 8, Articles 92–95. As its basic provision, Article 92 stipulates that regulations concerning organizations and operations of local public entities shall be fixed by law in accordance with the principle of local autonomy, but the Constitution contains no definition of the principle of local autonomy. It is left to interpretation and common understanding that that principle contains two prongs: one being the autonomy of local entities, meaning their independence from central or intermediate-level governments in dealing with their own functions, and the other being the autonomy of local residents, meaning their participation in dealing with local affairs. But the problem is to decide what constitute local functions or affairs. There are some functions for which a central government is best suited, such as defense, foreign affairs, maintenance of domestic market order, and so on. If certain other functions concern only local entities, the concerned entities should have the right to handle them autonomously. But most governmental functions are neither exclusively central nor local in nature, but rather show characteristics of both; that is, they can be handled either singly or jointly. If the central government assumes authority, uniformity in dealing with the functions will be accentuated, whereas if those matters are left to local governments, local differences will be respected at the sacrifice of uniformity. The distribution between central and local governments is regarded as being mainly a question of policy choices. To be sure, how to distribute authority depends on the size and structure of local entities.[21] Large entities can assume more functions and attain strengthened local autonomy, but participatory autonomy by residents would become difficult.

In order to harmonize the two prongs of local autonomy, the Local Autonomy Act adopted a two-tiered structure, with municipalities (cities, towns, and villages) as lower, basic entities expected to promote effective participation, and prefectures (*to*, *dō*, *fu*, and *ken*) as upper, wide-area entities expected to block interference from central government. However, this system did not live up to expectations. In traditional practice, the central government tended to absorb as many functions as possible and used local government organs (chief executive officers) as instruments for carrying those functions out in conformity to the uniform rules it dictated. Central bureaucrats made minute rules to handle the so-called state-mandated functions and strictly subjected chief executive officers to those rules by tolerating neither their own interpretation of the rules nor intervention of local assemblies for the purpose of adapting the rules to various local situations. This practice went so far that critics tabbed local autonomy as "30 percent" autonomy, meaning that state-mandated functions occupied 70 percent of the total functions conducted by local governments. The traditional practice was tolerable in the phase of economic growth, during which the central government took leadership in devising and carrying out nationwide plans to promote development in the most effective and efficient manner. But when a national minimum level of decent life was achieved and people began to seek a better environment in which to live, this practice could not continue. It was quite natural that proponents of local autonomy viewed this practice as the origin of all evil, and a government panel to promote decentralization came up with the idea of abolishing state-mandated functions and reclassifying them into the three categories of (1) state functions to be conducted by the central government itself, (2) functions legally entrusted to municipalities, and (3) functions of municipalities.[22] The main point of the new scheme consists of the creation of the second category; its purpose is not only to reduce the volume of functions to be regulated by central government but to strengthen the "rule of law." That is, when the central government entrusts local entities to conduct functions that involve a normal role of the state, specific measures needed to ensure appropriate management must be decided not by bureaucratic direction or *gyōsei shidō* (administrative guidance) but by law and regulations.

Local entities have the power to interpret the law and regulations on equal footing with the central government, and when local entities do not agree with the central government's legal interpretation, they can seek an advisory opinion of the Commission for Resolving Disputes between Central and Local Governments, to be newly created for that purpose. In case the local entities are not satisfied with the commission's opinion, they can bring the dispute with the central government to the courts of appeal. This mechanism was set up to ensure the equality of the central and local governments, but given the traditional hesitance on the part of local entities to argue against central government, it remains to be seen whether this procedure will produce the desired results.

Autonomy requires not only power but also money. The Committee for the Promotion of Decentralization released its final report on the reform of fiscal relations between the central and local governments in June 2001, calling for strengthening the fiscal autonomy of local governments. The current main revenue sources of local entities are local taxes, tax grants, subsidies, and local bonds. It is often pointed out that revenue from local taxes provides only 40 percent of total tax revenue, whereas expenditures made by local governments amount to 60 percent of total expenditures. The difference is made up for by the transfer of money from the central government to local governments through tax grants and subsidies. Generally speaking, the conventional reallocation of tax revenues has worked to benefit rural communities where the LDP had strongholds. Tax grants are the transfer of tax revenues from central government for the purpose of narrowing gaps in fiscal capabilities among local governments and ensuring the equal quality of administrative services nationwide. The amount of grants to each local government is calculated by a fixed formula, avoiding the discretion of central bureaucrats, and put into its general budget allowing free use by the recipient local government. In contrast, central government subsidies are extended to help finance specified policy goals approved by the central government. It is said that because of a permanent shortage of money, local bureaucrats concentrate their energies on drafting applications for the subsidies instead of drafting their own plans for what their entities really need. Central bureaucrats wield power to allocate the subsidies, and Diet members act as lobbyists around the central bureaucrats in a bid to pressure them to approve the applications for the benefit of local governments and business firms within their constituencies. Understandably, the government panel called for the reduction of subsidies to a minimum. As for the local government bonds, their issuance had to be approved by the central government, but this control is to be relaxed a bit, and now local governments are required only to consult with the central government.[23]

True reform calls for transferring national tax resources to local entities and ensuring the financial basis of local autonomy together with the transfer of government tasks. That is what the government panel recommended, but the central government is very slow to put that recommendation into practice.

III. JUSTICE SYSTEM REFORM

The final report of the Justice System Reform Council[24] advanced quite radical reform proposals, and implementation of some of those proposals is now under way. Those proposals are not immune from constitutional issues and deserve thorough analysis before they are cleared of constitutional defects. But here I confine myself to making a brief comment on the characteristic way of thinking, the philosophy or the spirit that underlies those proposals, and leave specific topics to other chapters.

What attracted my attention the most in the report is its first chapter, titled "Fundamental Philosophy and Directions for Reform of the Justice System." There it starts by declaring that "the fundamental task for reform of the justice system is to define clearly what we must do to transform both the spirit of the law and the rule of law into the flesh and blood of this country, so that they become 'the shape of our country.'" In the next paragraph, the phrase "to transform the spirit of the law and the rule of law into the 'flesh and blood' of Japan" is paraphrased as "to make the law . . . broadly penetrate the entire state and all of society and become alive in the people's daily life." The report seems to interpret the rule of law in terms of people's daily life being ruled by law.

The report next relates the justice system reform to the political and administrative reforms discussed above: "These reforms have sought to transform the excessive advance-control/adjustment type society to an after-the-fact review/remedy type society." In the traditional "advance-control/adjustment type society," said the council's report, people are used to conceiving themselves as "governed objects" instead of "governing subjects," which prevented the emergence of autonomous and active citizens indispensable for a well-functioning democracy based on the fundamental value of the "respect for individuals" (Article 13 of the Constitution). Now that political and administrative reforms are paving the way to a new type of society, "people will break out of viewing the government as the ruler (the authority) and instead will take heavy responsibility for governance themselves."

The report then asks: What is the proper role for the justice system in such a new society? Here the report compares the judicial branch with the political branches (the Diet and the Cabinet) and states that whereas the latter "seek[s] to create order by mapping out policies against the backdrop of majority rule and by fixing and conclusively executing norms in the form of law for the future," the former is expected to "maintain and to develop the law." The metaphor of the human body paraphrases this observation:

> [W]hen likened to the human body, if the political branches constitute the heart and arteries, the judicial branch shall be said to be the veins. The series of reforms mentioned above, such as political reform and administrative reform, are, so to speak, an effort to restore and strengthen the functions to make blood flow swiftly by removing extraneous crudescence in the heart and arteries. According to this metaphor, justice reform shall be considered to be aiming at harmonizing the body and improving its health by expanding and strengthening the scale and function of the justice system as part of what the "shape of our country" should be in the 21st century, with fundamental reflection on whether or not the existing veins were excessively small.

We may recall that the administrative reforms aimed at streamlining the bloated government by privatization, deregulation, and decentralization are expected to generate "an after-the-fact review/remedy type of society" by eliminating the excessive, in-advance intervention by government. If, as a result of these reforms, people can no longer expect an interventionist government to exercise this harmonizing function and instead anticipate a massive increase in legal disputes, "expanding and strengthening the scale and function of the justice system" becomes unavoidable. That line of thinking is very clear. What is at issue here is to realign a judicial role in accordance with the change in the roles of the political branches, especially the administrative branch.

Recall that the leading philosophy of administrative reforms was to establish the political leadership of the prime minister and his or her Cabinet on the one hand and to vitalize civil society by restricting state intervention on the other. Depending on which aspect we emphasize, the conception of the judicial role can be different. If the emphasis is on the former, the judicial role will tend to be viewed in terms of a check on abuse by the majority. If the emphasis is on the latter, the judicial role will be viewed in terms of adjudication of disputes among autonomous citizens. To my dismay, the report does not clearly distinguish these two roles of the judiciary. But it would not be unfair to say that, with respect to the image projected by the report, the latter is disproportionately favored over the former.

The report states that "the concept of the rule of law, stating that all people are equal under the law, most clearly appears in the fundamental nature of the justice system, that being that all people are treated equally and an impartial third party makes a decision based on fair and clear legal rules and principles through fair procedure." If the aim of the judicial system reform is to transform the rule of law into "flesh and blood" and the rule of law requires judges to serve as an impartial third party, the most urgent task should have been to work out reform plans to establish the impartial third-party status of judges with respect to disputes between political branches and citizens, because that is precisely where the maintenance of that status has faced and still faces all kinds of difficulties, whereas it is not so difficult for judges to act as an impartial third party with respect to disputes among citizens.

Generally speaking, it is very important, when we consider the proper role for the judiciary, to distinguish two fields in which the judiciary plays a role. In one field, the judicial branch assumes the function of administering legal order in tandem with the political branches. This image is supported by the separation of state and civil society; and the judicial branch plays, as a coworker with the political branches, a different role in performing the same state function of administering civil society, with the political branches assuming a role of legal order formulation and the judicial branch a role of maintaining legal order. In the other field, the judicial branch stands in opposition to the political branches and supervises their compliance with law. When we talk about the rule of law, it is usually this side of the issue that we have in mind.

Maintaining legal order in civil society is, to be sure, a very important task, but it does not seem to raise much difficulty in terms of the rule of law. I agree that the concerns pointed out in the report, such as excessive delay of trials, judgments not reflecting the general sentiment of ordinary people, and lack of easy access to legal professionals are big problems in Japan. Ameliorating those problems certainly will promote the rule of law, but that deals with the issue of state function, not the core issue of rule of law in Japan. It seems to me that by misapplying the concept of rule of law the report lost sight of the real issue of the rule of law. That is why, it seems to me, the report fails to come up with concrete recommendations on the reform of administrative and constitutional litigation systems, despite the quite radical, even revolutionary, reform designs it proposes concerning administration of justice in civil society.

IV. IN LIEU OF CONCLUSION

The establishment of more active leadership by the prime minister and his or her Cabinet has been one of the central issues of constitutional politics in Japan in the past decade. But faced with this issue raised not by constitutional scholars but by political studies experts, a majority of constitutional scholars have been rather hesitant to join the movement, pointing out the danger of dictatorship. All of us concur in the analysis of our system's problems: the most serious evils amalgamate in the "bureaucracy," that is, usurpation of policy making by bureaucrats. But we are deeply divided over the course the reform should take: should we strengthen the prime minister and the Cabinet or the Diet? A majority of constitutional scholars advocate the latter. They argue that democracy requires the Diet members directly elected by the people to make political decisions, the Cabinet being an instrument to loyally execute the Diet's decisions with the help of the bureaucracy, and that the Constitution assumes the Diet to be the center of political decision making by stipulating in Article 41 that the Diet shall be the highest organ of state power.

The problem with this stance is that the Diet, with more than seven hundred members, is not in a position to deal with the tasks society today constantly calls for. The Diet may be able to regain the policy-planning power (if it ever had it before) from the bureaucracy by setting up many specialized small committees within the Diet and providing them with sufficient staff consisting of experts in their respective fields. Still, the Diet needs someone to achieve coordination and adjustment among those committees in order to ensure coherence and consistency among policies. In the current increasingly complex world, this role cannot be performed without strong leadership, and who can provide it in our constitutional scheme better than a prime minister who exercises strong leadership? A strong prime minister and a strong Diet are not incompatible. The point is to assign the proper role to each and to strengthen them in their respective roles. The prime minister and his or her Cabinet govern and the Diet controls. The former should be provided with the means by which to govern, the latter with the power to control.[25]

The best way to strengthen the leadership of the prime minister is to create a tie between his or her will and that of the people. The question is how to achieve this within the framework of the parliamentary system where the prime minister is elected not by the people but by the Diet. The British model offers one answer, and the political and administrative reforms no doubt sought to move toward that direction without yet producing a definite result. Although strengthening the de facto tie between the prime minister and the people carries with it a danger of dictatorship, the risk can be contained by strengthening political control by the Diet as well as legal control by the courts.[26] I interpret the total design of recent reform efforts as aiming to establish the political structure in which the prime minister and his or her Cabinet, supported by the people and aided by bureaucrats, take active initiative in drafting policy plans, seek approval by the Diet through legislation and control, and have bureaucrats implement the approved policies, under the legal control of the judiciary. The reforms are now under way and their success depends largely on how we conceive and actualize the goal.

NOTES

1. The qualified parties are defined in art. 83-2, clause 1, of the Kōshoku senkyo hō [Public Office Election Act], Act No. 100 of 1950, as those falling into one of the following three categories: (1) holding five or more Diet members, (2) having obtained 2 percent or more of effective votes in the most recent general elections of the Diet members, or (3) putting on the party list as many or more candidates as two-tenths of the total number of seats in the relevant bloc.

2. See "Tokushū: Seiji kaikaku rippō" [Special Issue: Electoral Reform Legislation], *Jurisuto*, no. 1045 (1994).

3. Suits from dozens of districts were decided on the same day, of which the most important decisions are the following two: Ōkura et al v. Central Election Commission (Sup. Ct., Grand Bench, Nov. 10, 1999), *Minshū* 53 (1999): 1577, and Koshiyama v. Tokyo Election Commission (Sup. Ct., Grand Bench, Nov. 10, 1999), *Minshū* 53 (1999): 1704.

4. Koshiyama v. Tokyo Election Commission, 1704.

5. See "Tokushū, Seiji kaikaku rippō."

6. Yahata Steel Company case (Sup. Ct., Grand Bench, June 24, 1970), *Minshū* 24 (1970): 625.

7. See "Tokushū, Seiji kaikaku rippō." As discussed in section I.B. above, the envisaged ban on corporate donations to political parties was not realized in the 1999 revision.

8. Seitō josei hō [Subsidies to Political Parties Act], Act No. 5 of 1994, art. 7.

9. Ibid., art. 7. The details of the distribution formula are stipulated in art. 8. Originally, the total amount each recipient party could receive was restricted to no more than two-thirds of its revenue in the previous year, but this ceiling was abolished by the 1999 revision.

10. Ibid., art. 2.

11. Ibid., art. 5. The Communist Party of Japan declined to register. The current number of registered eligible parties is nine.

12. *Asahi shinbun*, September 14, 2001, morning edition.

13. Seitō josei hō, art. 4.

14. The ruling party (the LDP), which constitutes a political power independent of the government, and the bureaucracy, which concentrates in its hands expertise in legislation, have been two main obstacles to the establishment of strong leadership by the prime minister. The prime minister cannot draft bills implementing his or her policies without the help of bureaucrats, and he or she cannot send bills to the Diet without obtaining prior approval by the LDP's General Affairs Committee. The alliance of bureaucrats and LDP members concerned with a given issue often blocked the prime minister's policy preferences. Concerning these problems, see Atarashii Nihon o tsukuru kokumin kaigi (21 seiki rinchō) [People's Council for Creating a New Japan (Twenty-first-Century Provisional Council)], ed., *Seiji no kōzō kaikaku—Seiji shudō kakuritsu taikō* [Structural Reform of Politics—Fundamental Principles for Achievement of Political Initiative] (Tokyo: Tōshindō, 2002).

15. Gyōsei kaikaku kaigi [Administrative Reform Council]. For analyses of the interim and final report of the Administrative Reform Council, see "Tokushū: Kokka no yakuwari to tōchi kōzō kaikaku" [Special Issue: The Role of the State and Reform of the Structure of Control], *Jurisuto*, no. 1133 (1998); "Tokushū: Gyōsei kaikaku no rinen, genjō, tenbō" [Special Issue: The Ideals, Actual Situation, and Prospects for Administrative Reform], *Jurisuto*, no. 1161 (1999).

16. The subcommittee of the Administrative Reform Council further discussed the ideas of empowering the prime minister to give direct orders to ministry officials without prior consultation with the minister concerned, as well as to command in emergencies without prior approval of the Cabinet, but failed to reach an agreement. The introduction of majority rule in decision making at Cabinet meetings also was envisaged but was dropped from the revision draft.

17. Naikaku hō [Cabinet Act], Act No. 5 of 1947, art. 12, clause 2, item 2.

18. Naikakufu setchi hō [Cabinet Office Establishment Act], Act No. 89 of 1999, art. 3, clause 1.

19. Ibid., art. 3, clause 3.

20. A figurative explanation advanced by a member of the council is that the Cabinet office is expected to function as the brains of the prime minister while the Cabinet secretariat functions as his or her hands and feet.

21. Businesses to be assumed by local entities and the size of local entities are interdependent matters, and which of them should be taken as the starting point

in designing the organization and structure of local autonomy raises an important question. It is not practical to start from scratch. The more practical approach is to start from the existing system and amend defects in businesses as well as in size. Our government finds many of the current municipalities too small to shoulder the businesses to be transferred from the state and prefectures and is encouraging them to merge by promising to give favorable financial treatment to those that decide to merge before 2005. Some critics warn, however, that enlarging the size by merger might result in erosion of participation by residents.

22. "Tokushū: Chihō bunken dai 4ji hōkoku to sono kadai" [Special Issue: Fourth Report on Local Autonomy and Related Issues], *Jurisuto*, no. 1127 (1998); "Tokushū: Chihō bunken suishin iinkai dai 1ji hōkoku" [Special Issue: First Report of the Committee to Promote Local Autonomy], *Jurisuto*, no. 1110 (1997).

23. Chihō zaisei hō [Local Finance Act], Act No.109 of 1948, art. 5-3.

24. See "Recommendations of the Justice System Reform Council—for a Justice System to Support Japan in the Twenty-first Century" (June 12, 2001), reprinted in "Tokushū: Shihō seido kaikaku shingikai ikensho o megutte" [Special Issue: Reflections on the Recommendations of the Justice System Reform Council], *Jurisuto*, no. 1208 (2001). See also "Tokushū: Shihō seido kaikaku no tenbō" [Special Issue: Prospects for Justice System Reform], *Jurisuto*, no. 1170 (2000). The English version of the final report is accessible at (http://www.kantei.go.jp/judiciary/2001/0612report.html) (accessed June 14, 2006).

25. See Kazuyuki Takahashi, "Tōchi kikō no shiza tenkan" [A Shift in Vantage Point regarding the Machinery of Government], *Jurisuto*, no. 1222 (2002): 108.

26. See Kazuyuki Takahashi, "'Kokumin naikaku sei' sairon" [Revisiting the Debate over the "People's Cabinet System"], *Jurisuto*, no. 1136 (1998): 65, no. 1137 (1998): 92.

10 The Constitution of Japan

"Pacifism" and Mass Media Freedom

LAWRENCE W. BEER

For over fifty years, commitments to international peace, human rights, and popular sovereignty have been central to Japan's constitutionalism. Article 9's rejection of war and force to settle international disputes continues in effect. Over time, social, economic, and political rights of the individual have enjoyed increased protection and promotion under law.

This chapter summarizes the current state of Japan's unique quasi pacifism and mass media "rights and freedoms of the spirit" (*seishinteki jiyūken*) and concludes with a word on constitutional amendment.[1]

I. ARTICLE 9 PACIFISM

Since World War II, more has been written in Japan about Article 9 pacifism than about any other topic of Japanese legal discourse. Article 9 is rooted in the preamble to the Constitution:[2]

> We, the Japanese people, desire peace for all time . . . and we have determined to preserve our security and our existence, trusting in the justice and faith of the peace-loving peoples of the world. We desire to occupy an honored place in an international society striving for the preservation of peace. . . . We recognize that all the peoples of the world have the right to live in peace, free from fear and want.

Article 9 reads:

> Aspiring sincerely to an international peace based on justice and order, the Japanese people forever renounce war as a sovereign right of the nation and the threat or use of force as a means of settling international disputes . . .
>
> 2. In order to accomplish the aim of the preceding paragraph, land, sea, and air forces, as well as other war potential, will never be maintained. The rights of belligerency of the state will not be recognized.

Theoretically consistent philosophical or religious pacifism rules out violent response to individual or collective violence.[3] Pure pacifism requires, in all circumstances, that a person or community turn the other cheek and refrain from hostile reaction, based on faith in human goodness and disciplined conviction in the face of provocation, or on a belief that, on balance, violent response is counterproductive according to some other cost-benefit calculus. Only peaceful resistance to evil violence is permissible. That does not describe the official or popular pacifism of Japan, although some Japanese believe that Japan should not respond militarily even to an invasion, so horrible is war.

For decades after World War II there was strong popular rejection of militarism and war in response to national suffering, defeat, and ideological disillusionment. A psychological pacifism permeated public debate, the mass media, and both popular culture and high culture.[4] The passion of that era has softened, but its influence continues.

At the turn of the century, Japan's Article 9 was supported at home and was drawing increased respectful attention abroad,[5] rather than cynical dismissal as absurdly idealistic or dangerous to a nation's security. Political parties and opinion leaders seemed close to a consensus in favor of paragraph 1 of Article 9, but not on the proper interpretation of paragraph 2.[6]

Like all governments, Japan's recognized in practice a natural-law right of self-defense and the legitimacy of police violence in response to some crimes; so Japan's is a qualified, "quasi pacifism." On the other hand, Japan denied the legitimacy of taking violent initiatives to settle international disputes (e.g., to contest territorial claims).[7] It would not be more "natural" or politically wise, as some have suggested, for Japan to engage in a maximal military buildup.

Like most peoples of the world, a large majority of Japanese strongly opposed the U.S.'s unnecessary and preemptive invasion of Iraq in 2003. Prime Minister Jun'ichirō Koizumi supported the U.S. action, but would have preferred acting consensually under the United Nations umbrella. In the first deployment of ground troops to a war zone since World War II, Japanese contingents of the Ground Self-Defense Forces (SDF) were sent to Samawa in southern Iraq early in 2004. The Air SDF and Maritime SDF also contributed to Iraq's peace and reconstruction (e.g., building roads and airfields, purifying water, and hauling and protecting fuel, vehicles, and relief supplies).

The government has taken "war potential" in paragraph 2 to mean any military capacity beyond the minimum "land, sea, and air forces" needed for self-defense. In the new century, debate has often centered on whether a particular deployment policy, weapons system, or logistical support system (e.g., long-distance tanker aircraft) was essential for defense and in compliance with Article 9.[8] Although the military budget usually has been less than 1 percent of gross domestic product since 1976, Japan's economy is the second largest, so the military budget is one of the largest. According to James Auer, however, the SDF would be insufficient for defense (e.g., against North Korea) without the U.S. supplement in heavily militarized Northeast Asia.[9] In spite of its blustering, North Korea seems unlikely to use nuclear weapons, because it would trigger near genocide in response.

A substantial majority of Japanese constitutional lawyers criticize some government policies for violating the letter and/or spirit of Article 9.[10] They contend the SDF are unconstitutional, not because of a mindless idealism in most cases, but because the text of the 1947 Constitution does not lend itself to a less rigorous interpretation. Many support Japan's mode of constitutional pacifism.

Opposition political parties have modified long-held positions. For example, in the 1990s under Prime Minister Tomiichi Murayama the Social Democratic Party first recognized the constitutionality of the SDF.[11] In 2000 the Japan Communist Party changed a policy established in 1958 and approved use of the de facto military, the SDF, in "emergencies" while continuing to claim the SDF are unconstitutional.[12] The largest parliamentary opposition party, the Democratic Party of Japan, reversed its policy of supporting a ban on using the SDF in U.N. peacekeeping operations.[13]

Japan has long been the leading provider of nonmilitary Official Development Assistance (ODA) under the policies of the Organization for Economic Cooperation and Development (OECD) and a generous supporter of the United Nations. Since the hotly contested passage of the 1992 U.N. Peace-Keeping Operations Cooperation Act ("PKO Act"), Japan has expanded considerably its overseas monitoring and logistical support, but without participating in hostilities (e.g., in Cambodia, East Timor, Afghanistan, African countries, and the Indian Ocean).[14] In October 2001 (in part because of the

September 11 tragedy in the United States), under new law Japan first allowed SDF personnel to use arms abroad not only to defend themselves but to protect those "under their care," such as refugees and wounded foreign troops.[15]

The general public has long considered the SDF constitutionally acceptable only as long as the SDF did not fight abroad and were of relatively modest capability.[16] When asked in 2000 to name up to two primary functions of the SDF in the twenty-first century, about 70 percent felt the primary function was disaster relief, while about 41 percent cited military deterrence and 36 percent cited international peacekeeping and emergency aid abroad to be most important. Only 10.7 percent supported an increase in the size of the SDF, while 13.9 percent called for cutbacks and 61.7 percent thought current levels appropriate.[17] How the public would respond if Japan suffered combat casualties in Iraq remained unclear in 2006 because the SDF had not become militarily engaged.

Japan's implementation of Article 9 and the preamble of the Constitution in international relations was long premised on a realistic popular and governmental perception that Japan was not likely to be militarily threatened by a foreign state, a perception that continued all through the cold war. Other countries, by no means most, realistically see no credible threat on their borders.[18] Japan may see itself as too useful to other nations' economies and technologies to make attack a rational option. Many in the militarized political cultures of the United States and other nations that see themselves as persistently, even permanently, threatened have found Japan's approach hard to understand. History suggests that its opposite, a rush to military solutions, results more often than not in unnecessary barbarism and a crushing drain on resources. Under its comprehensive security policy, balancing economic, cultural, and political concerns, and its Security Treaty with the United States, Japan has felt no need for military power commensurate with its economic strength and has been leery of military influence on domestic politics, which led to the disaster of World War II.[19]

To illustrate a practical consequence, the recent development of Japan's NEC Earth Simulator, which works at a speed of 35,000 gigaflops (a gigaflop equals a billion mathematical operations per second), was driven by a desire to understand climate change, global warming, and earthquake patterns.[20] In contrast, the policy priority served by U.S. supercomputers, which in combination have only a fraction of the capacity of the NEC Earth Simulator, is simulation of weaponry. Like Japan's dual-use technology (e.g., in optics), the simulator may benefit the U.S. military. The Japan–United States Treaty of Mutual Cooperation and Security (1960)[21] has served Japan's legitimate geopolitical needs. And Japan's operative priorities have been served well by Article 9 pacifism.

The Supreme Court has never directly decided whether the Self-Defense Forces founded in 1954 are unconstitutional. The Supreme Court's 1959 Sunagawa Decision refrained from finding the Japan–United States Security Treaty unconstitutional, in an Article 9 case contesting extension of a runway at the Tachikawa Air Base of the United States.[22]

In the famous Naganuma Nike Missile Site Case, the Sapporo District Court (1973)[23] found the SDF unconstitutional, but the High Court (1976) and the Supreme Court (1982) reversed on technical grounds, avoiding the constitutional issue. Farmers in Naganuma in northern Japan had challenged a government decision to establish a Nike antiaircraft missile site in a forest reserve, alleging that the base illegally interfered with their water supply and flood control system and also violated their Article 9 "right to peace." The appellate courts decided that the farmers had lost their standing to sue when the government eliminated their water problems.

A 1987 Tokyo High Court decision,[24] let stand by the government, denied that in time of peace Defense Agency activities involve a higher public interest than those of civilian airports or other government agencies. In the spirit of Article 9, noise pollution was seen as a legitimate public concern and noise from military aircraft as a violation of the personal rights of citizens. In other cases the courts have ordered the government to compensate local residents for noise from U.S. and SDF aircraft.

On March 6, 2002, the Kanazawa District Court[25] ordered the government to pay 810 million yen to compensate 1,729 (of 1,776) plaintiffs for SDF aircraft noise around the Komatsu Air SDF Base exceeding the tolerable level under the international environmental standard, at a weighted equivalent continuous perceived noise level (WECPNL) of 75. For the first time in such noise-pollution cases, the plaintiffs claimed the SDF are unconstitutional. The court declined to judge the issue of constitutionality or to require the SDF to limit its flights and make future compensation payments.

What Japan has not done under Article 9 is as instructive as what it has done. Japan's government maintains that Article 9 does not permit Japan to come to the assistance of another state (principally, the United States) under a collective self-defense arrangement.[26] Japan has no independent military command structure.[27] Japan is sworn not to develop, possess, introduce, or use nuclear weapons. Unlike some European democracies, Japan has no national security law under which freedom of expression might be restricted during times of emergency. The Constitution has not—nor have other laws until 2003—had provisions related to acts of war, such as declaring war or concluding peace treaties. No article refers to martial law or military courts. Until a controversial amendment of November 2001, the SDF Act mandated no "defense secrets" (except under the Japan–United States Security Treaty).

In June 2003, however, for the first time since 1945, Japan adopted laws that ease efficient governmental and SDF response to "military attack situations," while reaffirming its rigorously defense-oriented foreign policy under Article 9 and "utmost" protection of fundamental human rights. A supplementary Diet resolution required other laws within one year to assure the safety and rights of citizens during emergencies, and those laws were passed in 2004.[28] Military emergencies remained unlikely to occur. The new laws enable SDF forces establishing frontline battlefield positions, for example, to use or expropriate privately owned land, houses, and trees. The SDF also became exempt in wartime from a number of peacetime legal procedures affecting, for example, road traffic, hospital activities, building standards, medical use of narcotics, and protection of national parks.

Under 1954 law, the primary duty of the SDF is the defense of Japan. If Japan is attacked or in imminent danger of attack, under 2003 law the government is to draft a plan of action that must be approved by the Cabinet and the Diet. If the situation is extremely urgent, the government may mobilize the SDF without a plan of action; however, the Diet has authority to halt by resolution measures taken by the government in response to military attack.

Among the "auxiliary duties" of the SDF are U.N.-sponsored peacekeeping activities, civil engineering projects (e.g., the 690 SDF personnel in East Timor in 2003), transport of state guests, and response to natural disasters and acts of terrorism. The new laws and attendant policy changes look toward a regime with an emergency management agency that deals with both military and other emergencies, an expanded Security Council under the prime minister, prime ministerial power to issue orders to local government officials in time of war, and enhanced status for international peacekeeping activities. Peacekeeping activities have become a "primary duty" of the SDF, leading to new SDF equipment and organizational needs. In place of past ad hoc response to emergency situations, for example, the SDF will have specialized standby units for quick dispatch at home and abroad.

All efforts to establish a state secrets law have been effectively opposed and government information disclosure has been strengthened.[29] However, civil servants in general are forbidden by law from revealing secrets learned in the course of their work.[30] Conscription is considered unconstitutional under Article 18, which bans "bondage of any kind" and "involuntary servitude" except as punishment for crime.

It is not clear whether Article 9 should be or will be amended, to clarify Japan's right of self-defense.[31] As many as 74 percent of Japanese have opposed amending Article 9.[32] Should there come a time for amendment, Japan might seriously consider adding a third paragraph to Article 9, forever renouncing the development, manufacture, possession, introduction, or use of nuclear, chemical, biological, or other (e.g., electronic) weapons of mass destruction. Might not Japan then credibly urge others to do likewise? Any progress in that direction would be a victory for humankind.

II. MASS MEDIA FREEDOM

The individual Japanese enjoys a wide spectrum of rights and freedoms under Chapter 3, Articles 11–40 and Article 97 of the Constitution of Japan. "All of the people shall be respected as individuals," and generally these rights and freedoms are to be "the supreme consideration in legislation and in other governmental affairs" (Article 13).

Here the focus is on mass media freedom under Article 21, which is categorized in Japan as one of the "rights and freedoms of the spirit." That article provides, in part: "Freedom of assembly and association as well as speech, press and all other forms of expression are guaranteed. 2. No censorship shall be maintained." Other such rights include the right to petition the state (Article 16), freedoms of thought and conscience (Article 19), religious freedom (Article 20), and academic freedom under Article 23, the first such provision in the world.[33]

Japan's mass media system is one of the largest, most free, and technologically most advanced in the world.[34] With a newspaper diffusion rate of 576 per thousand population, Japan leads other nations by a wide margin.[35] Japan has 108 daily newspapers, including five national dailies.[36] In 2000, Japan published almost three thousand magazines and fifty-six thousand book titles (counting only first editions), and produced 270 films (298 were imported).[37]

"The Canons of Journalism" (last revised in June 2001) of the private Japan Newspaper Publishers and Editors Association (Nihon shinbun kyōkai, or NSK) guide the self-regulation of the newspaper and broadcasting industries. They begin: "The people's right to know is a universal principle that sustains a democratic society. That right cannot be ensured without the existence of media, operating with the guarantee of freedom of speech and expression, while being totally committed to a high moral standard and fully independent of all powers."[38]

The text then expounds on the importance of freedom and responsibility, accuracy and fairness, independence and tolerance, respect for human dignity and human rights, and decency and moderation. The long-term challenge for media professionals is to sort out and assess the impact of new technologies on society in light of free speech legal principles and respect for the development rights of children.

The educated public tends to trust the fairness and competence of newspaper and TV news coverage more than political parties and politicians.[39] Self-regulation under the NSK code and counterparts in other mass media and individual companies generally has been more important to the protection, promotion, and limitation of freedom than state law.[40]

Over a twenty-year period, the freedom of information movement achieved passage of information disclosure ordinances in all prefectures and major cities.[41] This progressive wave led finally to Diet passage of the Information Disclosure Act, in effect since April 1, 2001.[42] Any individual Japanese or foreigner may submit a request for information at a service window, and so may organizations. The law requires all local governments to establish information disclosure ordinances. A critically important feature of all ordinances and the law is provision for an independent review system for appeals against refusal of disclosure of part or all information requested at an agency.

The "citizen ombudsman movement" has also led to greater government openness since 1994.[43] Activists use local disclosure ordinances to audit local government finances, to uncover possibly fraudulent expense vouchers and excessive entertainment of national officials to gain support for local projects. The movement annually publicizes a ranking of local governments in terms of cooperative transparency. The media lavish attention on local and national scandals as lovingly as their colleagues in other democracies.

Media excesses have led to Diet debates, judicial decisions, and nongovernmental efforts on privacy and defamation issues. In 2001 a nonpartisan Human Rights Protection Deliberation Council of the Justice Ministry recommended creation of a new independent government agency to strengthen the justice system's protection of human rights.[44] Among the old and new problems coming under its purview will be abusive treatment of women and the elderly, ethnic minorities, HIV victims, and resident foreigners and stalking, and privacy violations and defamation by the mass media.

In response to such human rights violations by television and radio broadcasters, in 1997 specialists and industry began to develop Japan's first third-party entity to deal with viewer and listener complaints and to protect freedom of expression.[45] The result was the Broadcasting Ethics and Program Improvement Organization (BPO; *Hōsō rinri-bangumi kōjō kikō*), in effect since July 1, 2003. The BPO is an independent, autonomous umbrella system sponsored and paid for by the public Japan Broadcasting Corporation (*Nihon hōsō kyōkai;* NHK) and the 190-member National Association of Commercial Broadcasters (NAB; *Nihon minkan hōsō renmei*) to protect freedom of expression and other rights in broadcasting with respect for the perspectives of viewers and listeners. The BPO's structure includes a board of directors, a secretariat, and an advisory council that selects the members of three committees: the Broadcast Program Committee (*Hōsō bangumi iinkai*), to assess and recommend improvements in programming; the Committee on Broadcasting and the Young (*Hōsō to seinen iinkai*); and the centrally important Committee on Human Rights and Other Related Rights (known as the BRC; *Hōsō to jinken tō kenri ni kansuru iinkai*). The council (headed in 2004 by Masami Ito, distinguished civil liberties scholar and former Supreme Court justice) consists of five prominent men and women, none of whom may have a connection with the broadcasting industry. The president of the BPO and head of the board (in 2004 Hideo Shimizu, eminent media law specialist) must also be from outside the industry.

The BRC was founded in 1997 to represent the public and stand between the government and industry. The council appoints up to eight highly credible members for three-year terms, none with a relationship with government or the mass media industry. Recent members have included a former Supreme Court justice, a past president of the Japan Federation of Bar Associations (*Nichibenren*), a person of great international experience (required representation), human rights attorneys, a specialist in broadcasting law, a novelist, and a film director.

The BRC acts on its own initiative when a serious infringement of rights comes to its attention, but more commonly is activated by an individual's complaint. The BRC will consider a claim of rights violation only when it focuses on a specific broadcast program, when the complainant and the broadcaster are unlikely to reach agreement by discussion, when the case is brought to a broadcaster within three months of the date of the program and to BRC within twelve months of that date, and when the case is not on trial in court and does not ask an award of damages. The BPO is accessible twenty-four hours a day and receives most of its complaints and inquiries, thousands each year, by telephone. The BRC services are offered at no cost. The secretariat requires the complainant to fill out and return a Rights Infringe ment Complaint Form (*mōshitatesho*) and puts together a complete file for the BRC to consider and act on. The BRC's decisions (*kettei*) are communicated to the parties and to the public, with "views, opinions, and recommendations" (*teigen*), and a broadcaster may be required to broadcast a holding. Broadcasters agree to comply with the BRC's decisions as an exercise in social responsibility. In this manner, a considerable number of grievances have been settled without formal legal action.

In addition, hundreds of media defamation suits have been filed in recent years, with mixed results. For example, on January 29, 2002, the Supreme Court delivered a landmark decision,[46] siding with Kazuyoshi Miura and holding newspapers responsible for their use of biased reports written by wire services such as Kyodo News. Miura was charged with arranging his wife's murder in Los Angeles (the L.A. Affair Defamation Case) in 1981 in order to collect insurance benefits. Some newspapers convicted Miura even before his trial was concluded, some relying on reports produced by Kyodo News. In point of fact, however, he was acquitted by the Tokyo High Court in July 1998. (That acquittal was appealed to the Supreme Court.)

The media's argument, following the earlier view of some Japanese and U.S. courts, was that newspapers should not be held responsible for publishing defamatory reports if they have come from credible wire service sources. Some critics of the 2002 decision felt that to protect freedom of information, only the wire service, if anyone, should be held responsible for defamation, not the newspapers. Local newspapers particularly, with their limited resources for corroboration, could be negatively affected by the Supreme Court decision and freedom of information diminished.

"Reporters clubs" (*kisha kurabu*) have had a near monopoly on gathering domestic news.[47] Each of these many groups includes representatives of major news organizations and has special access to news while on assignment to cover a ministry, the Diet, a political party, a union federation, economic organizations, a court, the prime minister's office, or other entity to which it is attached. Reporters from different media companies may form a consensus on what should be reported, rather than compete with each other. Deviation from the shared view may bring ostracism, even reassignment as a result of pressure on a reporter's company. Nonmembers, foreign and domestic, have been excluded in many cases from the main news-gathering process.[48] Such in-group dependence could discourage independent investigative journalism. In general, however, these "clubs" do an excellent and efficient job, contending, like U.S. journalists, with the spins of interest groups and reliable anonymous sources.

The mass media have been attacked most persistently, not by the government, law, victims of personal rights violation, or ordinary pressure groups, but by small organizations of right-wing nationalists who, unlike Emperor Akihito, are hypersensitive to "anti-Japanese" discussions in the press and in history textbooks of the imperial institution and the brutal behavior of the military during World War II.[49]

Although Japan was ethnically homogeneous until the late twentieth-century immigration of diverse hundreds of thousands, the spectrum of institutionalized, social, political, and humanist thought in Japan has been very wide. Tolerance for the existence of such variety is the social foundation of media freedom. Unlike the United States, but like most of the democratic world, Japan has no taboo regarding socialism, in public discourse or in party politics. The "conservatism" of the Liberal Democratic Party is that of a democratic socialist state mixed with a distinctive capitalism. In contrast to the behavior patterns of other actors, the modus operandi of the extreme right has been characterized by violence, threats, and small but noisy demonstrations.

On Constitution Day, May 3, 1987, Tomohiro Kojiri (age twenty-nine), a reporter for the *Asahi shinbun* newspaper, was shot dead at his office with a shotgun.[50] His colleague Hyoe Inukai was seriously injured. The case has not been solved. A rightist group, Sekihōtei, claimed responsibility, but corroborating evidence has not been found. The fifteen-year statute of limitations ran out on May 3, 2002. On that day the president of *Asahi shinbun*, police officials, journalists, detectives, and other concerned citizens offered prayers and flowers before a photograph altar in the office where Kojiri was gunned down. The investigation continues, to honor the community commitment to press freedom.

Legal scholars, newsmen, and others have on occasion received threatening calls.[51] Even conservative prime ministers Yasuhiro Nakasone and Noboru Takeshita have received death threats for being insufficiently nationalistic.[52] Over the postwar decades such crimes have been few and the mainstream mass media have not often been intimidated, but rightists must be kept in mind when assessing mass media freedom in Japan.

III. AMENDMENT

Under Article 96 of the Constitution, amendment requires approval by a two-thirds majority of all members of each house of the Diet, followed by approval by a majority of those voting in a special or regular election.[53] For half a century, the possibility of amendment has been much discussed, but no amendment has been passed. In 1999 the Diet approved the establishment of two Committees to Investigate the Constitution (*Kempō chōsakai*). The House of Representatives committee has fifty members, and the House of Councilors committee forty-five. Their mission is to conduct a "broad and comprehensive" study and to submit separate reports with recommendations to the speaker of each house. Each speaker will then submit the report to the full house for debate and possible action.[54] What the results of this multiyear study will be is not clear. The lengthy research of the earlier Commission on the Constitution (1958–64) unearthed no flaws, omissions, or needed corrections regarding the basic principles of the document. In 2006, at the time of writing, some have called for revision. Others would confine change to clarifications of the peace provision (Article 9) and the rights to privacy and a clean environment. Although imperfect of execution, like all democratic constitutions, it seems poignant that Japan's, one of the longest established, most enlightened, most successfully implemented and unamended constitutions should also be the world's most exhaustively studied by its government on a questioned assumption that change is needed.

IV. CONCLUSION

All but a few of the over 190 nation-states in the United Nations in 2006 have a single-document national constitution, over 135 ratified since 1970. The exceptions are the United Kingdom, New Zealand, Israel, and three who use the Koran as their basic document, Saudi Arabia, Libya, and Oman. The 1947 Constitution of Japan is one of the world's oldest and most effectively implemented basic laws, but like all constitutional systems Japan's functions imperfectly, as political culture generates aberrations from constitutional democracy.[55]

Since 1948 Japan has enjoyed an unbroken succession of national and local elections under democratic law. All men and women over twenty have had the right to vote. Since the early 1990s, an ongoing legal reform process has attacked stubborn problems of malapportionment and excesses in political fund-raising, which have eased occasional corruption. Much creative improvement has been achieved; problems remain.

In addition, far-reaching administrative reforms have looked to strengthening the prime minister, the Cabinet, and the Diet in their relations with the formally subordinate but powerful bureaucracy and to enhancing the position of local government units vis-à-vis the central government. The goal is a more democratic leadership structure. Noteworthy judicial reforms are also afoot early in the twenty-first century to better integrate reform policies with the daily lives of the self-governing people. A new system of "citizen judges" (*saiban'in*) sharing decision-making power with judges in serious criminal cases was approved by the ruling coalition in 2004. The courts continue to enforce and develop the law while monitoring compliance.

In law related to foreign relations, the constitutional debate will continue to revolve around the limits Article 9 places on Japan's military capacities and SDF activities other than disaster relief, such as participation in U.N. peace-related projects. Continuing differences between Japanese and U.S. perceptions and national security policies may become more apparent in the decade ahead. In any case, debates, whether about Article 9, electoral reform, prime ministerial power or administrative restructuring, the global environment, or the world economy, will take place in an atmosphere of public and private freedom of expression lending authenticity and legitimacy to the results.

NOTES

1. Elsewhere the other constitutional and human rights are discussed—rights in criminal justice, social and economic rights, and equality rights.

2. Nihonkoku kempō [Constitution of Japan], art. 9. For extensive recent commentary on art. 9, see "Tokushū: Kempō 9 jō o kangaeru" [Special Issue: Thinking about Article 9 of the Constitution], *Jurisuto*, no. 1260 (2004).

3. Toshihiro Yamauchi, "Nihon no 'bōeiseisaku'—Tenkan e no shiten" [Japan's "Defense Policy"—a View of the Change], *Jurisuto*, no. 1192 (2001): 44; Tadakazu Fukase, *Sensō hōki to heiwateki seizonken* [Renunciation of War and the Right to Live in Peace] (Tokyo: Iwanami shoten, 1987); Nobuya Bamba and John F. Howes, eds., *Pacifism in Japan: The Christian and Socialist Tradition* (Kyoto: Minerva Press, 1978); Toshihiro Yamauchi, "Constitutional Pacifism: Principle, Reality, and Perspective," in Yoichi Higuchi, ed., *Five Decades of Constitutionalism in Japanese Society* (Tokyo: Tokyo University Press, 2001), 27; and James E. Auer, "Article Nine: Renunciation of War," in Percy R. Luney Jr. and Kazuyuki Takahashi, eds., *Japanese Constitutional Law* (Tokyo: Tokyo University Press, 1993), 74.

4. Kendall A. Whitney, "Pacifism and Japanese Politics" (master's thesis, University of Colorado, Boulder, 1969); Thomas U. Berger, *Cultures of Antimilitarism: National Security in Germany and Japan* (Baltimore: Johns Hopkins University Press, 1998).

5. Proceedings of the World Congress, International Association of Constitutional Law (Tokyo, 1996); Lawrence W. Beer, "National Security and Freedom of Expression in Japan," in Sandra Coliver et al., eds., *Secrecy and Liberty: National Security, Freedom of Expression and Access to Information* (Boston: M. Nijhoff Publishers, 1999), 349; Beer, "Peace in Theory and Practice under Article 9 of Japan's Constitution," *Marquette Law Review* 81 (1998): 815. In 2003, after the fall of the Saddam Hussein regime, some Iraqi constitutionalists were hoping for a constitutional provision like Japan's art. 9.

6. See Yamauchi, "Constitutional Pacifism"; and Auer, "Article Nine."

7. See Yamauchi, "Constitutional Pacifism"; and Auer, "Article Nine."

8. Considerable opposition was expressed to equipping SDF ships with the sophisticated Aegis detection and defense systems as possibly unconstitutional. Interpretations of existing law have also been modified occasionally. For example, in April 2002, the legal basis for SDF investigation of unidentified ships changed from "research purposes," under art. 5 of the SDF Establishment Act, to "sea patrols" approved by the prime minister, under art. 82 of the law.

9. See Auer, "Article Nine."

10. See ibid.; Yamauchi, "Nihon no 'bōeiseisaku"; and Toshihiro Yamauchi, "'Bōei' hōsei" [The Defense Legal System], *Jurisuto*, no. 1073 (1995): 18.

11. See, e.g., *Asahi shinbun*, July 20–24, 1994.

12. See, e.g., *Asahi shinbun*, November 24–25, 2000; *Japan Times*, November 25, 2000.

13. See, e.g., *Japan Times*, December 12, 2000.

14. See, e.g., *Asahi.com*, October 23, 30, 2001; November 9, 21, 26, 2001; December 3, 2001; January 12, 2002; February 5, 2002. See also *Japan Times*, October 30, 2001; November 14, 2001; December 8, 2001.

15. See Lawrence W. Beer and John M. Maki, *From Imperial Myth to Democracy: Japan's Two Constitutions, 1889–2002* (Boulder: University Press of Colorado, 2002), 96.

16. Foreign Press Center, ed., *Facts and Figures of Japan* (Tokyo: Foreign Press Center, 2002), 26–29. On the controversial 1997 "Guidelines for Japan-U.S. Security Cooperation," see *Asahi shinbun*, September 24, 1997; January 6 and April 2, 1998.

17. U.S. Information Agency, Office of Research, "'Global Partnership': Views of the Japanese Public" (2002).

18. Militarism is not inevitable. A good number of nations, large and small, are secure in their borders without substantial military capacity, while the palpable security threats in some countries are internal. See Beer, "National Security and Freedom of Expression in Japan," 350.

19. See Reinhard Drifte, *Japan's Foreign Policy for the 21st Century: From Economic Superpower to What Power?* (New York: St. Martin's Press, 1998).

20. See John Markoff, "Japanese Computer Is World's Fastest, as US Falls Back," *New York Times*, April 20, 2002.

21. Treaty of Mutual Cooperation and Security between the United States and Japan, Treaty No. 6 of June 23, 1960, reprinted in Hiroshi Itoh and Lawrence W. Beer, *The Constitutional Case Law of Japan: Selected Supreme Court Decisions, 1961–70* (Seattle: University of Washington Press, 1978), 104.

22. Japan v. Sakata et al. (Sup. Ct., Grand Bench, Dec. 16, 1959), *Keishū* 13 (1959): 3225. J. Mark Ramseyer and Eric Rasmusen found twenty-five district court decisions that dealt with art. 9, "three of which held either the SDF or the bases unconstitutional." J. Mark Ramseyer and Eric B. Rasmusen, "Why Are Japanese Judges So Conservative in Politically Charged Cases?" *American Political Science Review* 95 (2001): 335.

23. Itō et al. v. Minister of Agriculture and Forestry (Sapporo Dist. Ct., Sept. 7, 1973), *Hanrei jihō* 712 (1973): 24 (1973); Minister of Agriculture and Forestry v. Itō et al. (Sapporo High Ct., Aug. 5, 1976), *Gyōsai reishū* 27(8) (1976): 1175; Uno et al. v. Minister of Agriculture and Forestry (Sup. Ct., lst Petty Bench, Sept. 9, 1982), *Minshū* 36(9) (1982): 1679. All three are available in translation in Lawrence W. Beer and Hiroshi Itoh, *The Constitutional Case Law of Japan: 1970 through 1990* (Seattle: University of Washington Press, 1996), 103. The other Supreme Court decision is in translation at 130. That case, the Hyakuri Air SDF case, questioned unsuccessfully the constitutionality of sales contracts for the construction of an air SDF base. Also much discussed was the Eniwa Case (Japan v. Nozaki [Sapporo Dist. Ct., March 29, 1967], *Kakyū keishū* 9[3] [1967]: 359), in which two farmers were acquitted of destroying "defense equipment and facilities" under the SDF Act; they had cut telephone lines in an SDF base area.

24. Tokyo High Ct., July 15, 1987, decision reported in *Asahi shinbun*, July 15, 1987, evening edition.

25. Kanazawa Dist. Ct., March 6, 2002.

26. *Asahi.com*, April 27, 1999. On opposition to expanded cooperation with the U.S. military, see also *Christian Science Monitor*, April 28, 1999.

27. Osamu Nishi, *The Constitution and the National Defense Law System in Japan* (Tokyo: Seibundo Publishing, 1987), 123.

28. Special Criminal Act to Implement the Agreement under Article 6 of the Treaty of Mutual Cooperation and Security between Japan and the United States of America regarding Facilities and Areas and the Status of United States Forces in Japan, Act No. 138 of 1952, as amended; Japan Newspaper Publishers and Editors Association [Nihon shinbun kyōkai (NSK)], *Prcss Laws in Japan* (Tokyo: Nihon

shinbun kyōkai, 1993), 10–11. See *Asahi shinbun*, March 9, 2004, evening edition, and *Asahi shinbun*, March 10, 2004, for reports of laws regarding government response to "military attack situations."

29. Since 2001, significant efforts have been made to restrict leakage of military secrets. See, e.g., *Asahi.com*, October 18, 2001. Useful guidelines are provided by the Johannesburg Principles on National Security, Freedom of Expression and Access to Information after the Cold War. For the agreement of the mass media and the government on the ground rules for covering Iraq, see *Asahi shinbun*, February 29 and March 12, 2004.

30. Kokka kōmuinhō [National Public Employees Act], Act No. 120 of 1947, art. 100, para. 1. No employee in the national public service is to divulge any secrets that may have come to his or her knowledge in the performance of his or her duties. This duty also applies after the public employee has retired from office. Under arts. 109 and 111, any person "who has divulged a secret in violation of art. 100" is subject to imprisonment for not more than one year or a fine of not more than thirty thousand yen, and any person who induces or assists in such acts is subject to the same penalty.

31. The SDF attracted an increasing number of recruits as unemployment rose late in the twentieth century. For decades, though, the SDF did not meet its recruitment goals. See *Japan Times*, February 7, 2004.

32. See *Asahi shinbun*, May 2, 2001.

33. Masami Ito, "The Rule of Law: Constitutional Development," in Arthur Taylor von Mehren, ed., *Law in Japan: The Legal Order in a Changing Society* (Cambridge, MA: Harvard University Press, 1963), 205; Lawrence W. Beer, *Freedom of Expression in Japan: A Study in Comparative Law, Politics, and Society* (New York: Kodansha International, 1984), 248.

34. See, e.g., Japan Newspaper Publishers and Editors Association [Nihon shinbun kyōkai], *The Japanese Press, 2001* (Tokyo: Nihon shinbun kyōkai, 2001); Beer and Maki, *From Imperial Myth to Democracy*, chap. 7; Ellis S. Krauss, *Broadcasting Politics in Japan: NHK and Television News* (Ithaca, NY: Cornell University Press, 2000); and Susan J. Pharr and Ellis S. Krauss, eds., *Media and Politics in Japan* (Honolulu: University of Hawai'i Press, 1996).

35. Foreign Press Center, *Facts and Figures of Japan*, 101; Keizai Koho Center, *Japan 2001: An International Comparison* (Tokyo: Keizai Koho Center, 2000), 115.

36. Keizai Koho Center, *Japan 2001*, 115; Foreign Press Center, *Facts and Figures of Japan*, 105–7; Japan Newspaper Publishers and Editors Association, *The Japanese Press, 2001*.

37. *Eirin*, the Motion Picture Ethics Commission, is the independent industry self-regulatory organ. The customs office regulates the import of foreign films

under a system of doubted constitutionality. See Beer, *Freedom of Expression in Japan*, 337.

38. Japan Newspaper Publishers and Editors Association [Nihon shinbun kyōkai], "The Canons of Journalism" (June 21, 2000).

39. James Marshall, *Japan's Successor Generation: Their Values and Attitudes* (Washington, DC: U.S. Information Agency, 1985).

40. The Newspaper Advertising Code of Ethics is contained in the NSK annual, Japan Newspaper Publishers and Editors Association, *The Japanese Press, 2001*. Examples of individual newspaper advertising codes are discussed in Japan Communist Party v. Sankei Newspaper Co. (Tokyo Dist. Ct., July 13, 1977), *Hanrei jihō* 857 (1977): 30 (1977), in translation in Beer and Itoh, *The Constitutional Case Law of Japan: 1970 through 1990*, 575.

41. See Lawrence Repeta, *Local Information Disclosure Systems in Japan* (Seattle: National Bureau of Asian Research, 1999); and Repeta, "The Birth of the Freedom of Information Act in Japan: Kanagawa 1982," MIT Japan Program, Working Paper 03-01 (2003), available at (http://www.freedominfo.org/reports/japan.htm).

42. Act No. 4 of May 14, 1991, an act concerning the disclosure of information held by administrative agencies. Yoshirō Kitagawa and Hiroshi Miyake, *Jōhō kōkai hō kaisetsu* [Commentaries on the Information Disclosure Act], 2nd ed. (Tokyo: Sanseido, 2003); Masahiro Uzaki et al., eds., *Jōhō kōkai hō: Rippō no ronten to shiru kenri* [The Information Disclosure Act: Legislative Arguments and the Right to Know] (Tokyo: Sanseido, November 30, 1997). See Beer and Maki, *From Imperial Myth to Democracy*, 115.

43. See Repeta, "Local Information Disclosure Systems in Japan."

44. See *Asahi.com*, May 26, 2001. Passage of implementing legislation was expected in 2002. The admirable grassroots human rights commissioners (*jinken yōgoiin*) and administrative counselors (*gyōsei sōdan iin*) have needed a new agency to strengthen human rights enforcement. See Lawrence W. Beer, *Human Rights Commissioners (Jinken Yōgo Iin) and Lay Protection of Human Rights in Japan*, Occasional Paper no. 31, International Ombudsman Institute (October 1985); and Joel Rosch, "Institutionalizing Mediation: The Evolution of the Civil Liberties Bureau in Japan," *Law and Society Review* 21 (1987): 243.

45. See, e.g., Hōsō to jinken tō kenri ni kansuru iinkai [Committee on Human Rights and Other Related Rights (BRC)], "BRC nenji hōkokusho: 2002 nendo" [BRC Annual Report: 2002] (2003); and Hōsō rinri-bangumi kōjō kikō [Broadcasting Ethics and Program Improvement Organization (BPO)], "BPO hōkoku" [BPO Report] (periodic reports on activities).

46. See *Asahi shinbun*, January 29, 2002, evening edition; and *Asahi shinbun*, January 30, 2002.

47. See Beer and Maki, *From Imperial Myth to Democracy*, 114; Laurie Anne Freeman, *Closing the Shop: Information Cartels and Japan's Mass Media* (Princeton, NJ: Princeton University Press, 2000); and "Gaikoku medeia e no kaiken kaihō" [Opening of Press Conferences to Foreign Media], *Asahi shinbun*, February 19, 2004.

48. For a liberating decision on courtroom note taking, see Repeta v. Japan (Sup. Ct., Grand Bench, March 8, 1989), *Minshū* 43 (1989): 89, translated in Beer and Itoh, *The Constitutional Case Law of Japan: 1970 through 1990*, 627. An authoritative compilation of analyses of 122 major judicial decisions affecting the media is *Medeia hanrei hyakusen* [One Hundred Selected Precedents on the Mass Media], *Jurisuto*, no. 179 (2005).

49. Japan's Constitution reduces the emperor from a sacred god to a human symbol of the unity of the Japanese people without any governmental powers (chap. I, arts. 1–8). Some Japanese identify the imperial family with certain traditional values and customs. As a member of a model nuclear family, the "people's emperor" is of modest interest to most Japanese. Premodern Japan had an occasional empress, but the Meiji Constitution and the Imperial House Act (Koshitsu tenpan) limited the throne to men. Princess Aiko's birth in 2001 raises the possibility of the first empress in modern Japan. Eighty-three percent of voters favor allowing a woman to become empress; 64 percent (73 percent of women) view the imperial family in a positive light, while 28 percent see it negatively. *Asahi.com*, December 24, 2001. The gender discrimination in the Imperial House Act provision appears unconstitutional. See generally Kenneth James Ruoff, *The People's Emperor: Democracy and the Japanese Monarchy, 1945–1995* (Cambridge, MA: Harvard University Asia Center, 2001).

50. On the Kojiri Case, see *Asahi.com*, May 3 and 4, 2002. Ten major rightist attacks on the mass media since 1960 are described at *Asahi.com*, December 1, 2001.

51. See *Asahi.com*, December 1, 2001.

52. See ibid.

53. Art. 96 provides: "Amendments to the Constitution shall be initiated by the Diet, through a concurring vote of two-thirds or more of all members of each House and shall thereupon be submitted to the people for ratification, which shall require the affirmative vote of a majority of all votes cast thereon, at a special referendum or at such election as the Diet shall specify. 2. Amendments when so ratified shall immediately be promulgated by the Emperor in the name of the people, as an integral part of this Constitution."

54. These Diet committees differ from the Commission on the Constitution (*Kenpō chōsakai*) of 1957–64, in that they are two entities, unconnected with the

Cabinet, and without members who are independent "persons of learning and experience." See Beer and Maki, *From Imperial Myth to Democracy*, 158; and John M. Maki, *Japan's Commission on the Constitution: The Final Report* (Seattle: University of Washington Press, 1980).

55. The Asian context of Japan's constitutionalism is elucidated in Lawrence W. Beer, ed., *Constitutional Systems in Late Twentieth Century Asia* (Seattle: University of Washington Press, 1992).

11 Development of the Concepts of Transparency and Accountability in Japanese Administrative Law

KATSUYA UGA

I. INTRODUCTION

More than forty years have passed since the historic conference on Japanese law was held at Harvard Law School in 1961. It is easy to recognize remarkable progress in some areas of Japanese administrative law, such as administrative procedure and freedom of information, during those forty years. If you simply compare the textbooks of Japanese administrative law written forty years ago with the current ones, the difference is clear. Forty years ago, very few, if any, pages were devoted to administrative procedures in Japanese administrative law textbooks. Today, all of them include, as an essential element, a chapter on administrative procedures, with a particular focus on the Administrative Procedure Act (APA).[1] Forty years ago, no textbooks on Japanese administrative law even mentioned freedom of information. Today, a textbook would be considered defective if it did not contain a chapter on that topic.

On the other hand, there are some areas where progress has been very slow during the past forty years. Examples include the Administrative Case Litigation Act (ACLA) and the Administrative Complaints Investigation Act (ACIA).[2] The ACLA, enacted in 1962, is a law of general applicability concerning administrative case litigation brought before courts of law. The ACIA, enacted in 1962, is a law of general applicability concerning appeals against dispositions by administrative agencies, but it concerns appeals to administrative agencies, not to courts.[3] These laws have undergone no substantive amendment. Although case law has developed in the meantime, it cannot be said that there has been any dramatic change. (It bears note, however, that, based on a recommendation of the Justice System Reform Council, an investigative committee on administrative litigation was set up by the government. In January 2004, that committee published its final report, which included recommendations for reform of these laws; it is expected that these laws will be amended in the near future.)

In this chapter, I will focus on the development of the concepts of "transparency" and "accountability" in Japanese administrative law. Forty years ago, there were no statutes in Japan that used the words *transparency* or *accountability*. Even public law scholars seldom used those words. Today, those words have become very popular not only among public law scholars but also among politicians, bureaucrats, journalists, and even the general public. And it is not surprising any more to find those words in statutes or local ordinances. This chapter analyzes the cause of this change and its impact.

II. ENACTMENT OF THE ADMINISTRATIVE PROCEDURE ACT

On November 5, 1993, an administrative procedure bill was passed into law by the Japanese Diet's House of Councilors, and that bill was promulgated seven days later. Looking through the introduction to the midterm report of the Management and Coordination Agency (Second) Research Group on Administrative Procedures (RGAP2), prepared by its chairperson, we notice his painstaking efforts to keep "the beacon to the passage of an administrative procedure code" ablaze. Borrowing this phrase to describe the postwar history of administrative procedures in Japan, we can say that up until the APA's recent passage a total of three such beacons were lit along the way.

Before going into the content of the act itself, let us take a look at the process by which it was passed into law. As early as 1948, the Provisional Deliberative Council on Administrative Structure Reform recognized the necessity of making preparations for the passage of an administrative operations act. Then, in October 1950, the Deliberative Council on Legal Institutions set up a section on administrative procedures under a directive from the Allied Forces General Headquarters (GHQ). This is not to say that the GHQ was particularly enthusiastic about passing an administrative procedures law, and given the very poor understanding among lawmakers in Japan concerning the significance of such a law, the subcommittee on administrative procedures was unable to produce any practical results on the subject.

In May 1952, a draft bill on national administrative operations was introduced in the House of Representatives during the thirteenth session of the Diet. Yet that bill was permanently shelved upon dissolution of the Diet during its fourteenth session. As its name implies, that bill was aimed at improvement in administrative operations and therefore was mostly admonitory in its tone and content; however, within the fourteen articles that made up the bill, there were several administrative procedures stipulations that have remained important up to the present day. If this bill had been passed in the early 1950s, administrative procedures might have been improved at a very early point in Japan's postwar history.

Again in 1953, the Operations Section of the Deliberative Council on Administrative Affairs published proposed guidelines for a twenty-one-article administrative operations bill, and during the following year the Japan Public Law Society (JPLS) adopted as the theme for its annual conference the topic of an administrative operations bill and administrative procedures. Concerning the above twenty-one-article guideline proposal, a joint debate was held between the JPLS and the Japan Public Administration Society. The twenty-one-article guideline proposal combined both admonitory provisions for administrative operations and stipulations for administrative procedures. However, there were criticisms that the former were hardly worth putting into legislation and that the latter had not been satisfactorily prepared. The guideline proposal did not find its way into the law books.

Still later in 1953, on December 21, the plenary assembly of the Deliberative Council on Administrative Affairs proposed that agencies conduct hearings in a fair and democratic manner and amend and unify stipulations contained in the statute books pertaining to procedures for hearings. Of course, these actions on the part of the council by no means constituted a clear commitment to passage of an administrative procedures law, nor were they included in the Cabinet decisions on improving administrative operations, issued on December 12, 1954. It is difficult to say, therefore, that the council's decisions on administrative procedures were given very high priority. Nonetheless, these various proposals show that the first beacon in leading the way to an administrative procedures law was illuminated in the 1950s, only to be extinguished.

Gradually, however, spurred in part by the progress made in research on the subject by public law scholars, the importance of legal stipulations for administrative procedures came to be widely recognized within the public law community. In 1960 the JPLS devoted its twenty-fifth annual conference to the theme of administrative procedures, and in February 1962, the Provisional Commission for Administrative Reform (PCAR) was formed, with a subcommittee section on administrative procedures. This subcommittee published a detailed 168-article draft of an administrative procedure act in February 1964, and the PCAR as a whole issued its recommendations on improving administrative procedures based on this draft in September of that year.

It was this series of events that set the spark to light the second beacon leading to an administrative procedures law for Japan. Japanese lawmakers, however, were not ready to follow the path so illuminated. Let us take a look at what happened. The Administrative Management Agency at that time proceeded to make a budget proposal in 1965 for the establishment of a provisional investigative committee on administrative procedures. The proposal was turned down, however, and that spelled the end for a draft for an administrative procedures bill that can be rated excellent even by today's standards. Even so, that draft played a valuable role, for it exerted significant influence on the research that has since accumulated within Japan on administrative procedures.

One more event that proved influential in increasing interest in administrative procedure legislation in Japan was the passage of a similar law in West Germany during 1976, since the German administrative law community has profoundly influenced its Japanese counterpart from the very outset.

The next phase began with the uncovering of the Douglas-Grumman airplane bribery scandal in the mid-1970s and the resulting establishment of a council to come up with measures for preventing such backroom dealings in the future. The council issued its proposals in September 1979, stating in part that in order to prevent such affairs in the future, it was necessary to consider the long-term issue of preparing legislation for general administrative procedures. As a result, the (First) Research Group on Administrative Procedures (RGAP1) was set up as a private advisory committee to the chief of the Administrative Management Agency's Administrative Management Bureau. Once again a beacon was lit to guide Japan toward administrative procedure legislation. In November 1983, RGAP1 published its proposals in the form of guidelines for the draft of a seventy-one-article administrative procedure bill. During the following year, the JPLS reviewed these guidelines.

Other significant developments occurred in that same period. During March 1983 the (Second) Provisional Commission on Administrative Reform (PCAR2) included in its report a recommendation to set up a provisional investigative body of experts to prepare for the passage of an administrative procedures law. This direction was affirmed in Cabinet decisions in May 1983 and January 1984; in June 1985, RGAP2 was set up as a private advisory committee to the chief of the Administrative Management Bureau of the Management and Coordination Agency.

The RGAP2 report was presented before a subcommittee on deregulation of the Provisional Council for Promotion of Administrative Reform (CPAR2) in October 1988. This report included guidelines for a forty-five-article draft of an administrative procedure law. In turn, CPAR2 published its report in April 1990. That report contained a recommendation to consider and implement as quickly as possible the setting up of an investigative body of experts with the purpose of unifying administrative procedures. Based on that recommendation, the Third Provisional Council for Promotion of Administrative Reform (CPAR3) was organized in October of that year, and in January of the following year it set up a subcommittee on advancing fair and transparent administrative procedures.

Thereafter, events moved rather steadily toward the enactment of the APA. In July 1991, the RGAP1 guidelines for an administrative procedure law were made public, and in November of that year the subcommittee on fair and transparent administrative procedures presented its final report to CPAR3. CPAR3 in turn issued its recommendations in December 1991, and, on the basis of those recommendations, later that same month the Cabinet decided to introduce an administrative procedure bill to the Diet. From that time on the draft was zealously perfected in the APA enactment preparation section set up in the Management and Coordination Agency.

The Cabinet decided in May 1993 to introduce the bill during the 126th session of the Diet; however, it was shelved when the Diet was dissolved. The bill was then reintroduced to the 128th session the following September in identical form. The bill was discussed at the JPLS conference in October 1993; it was passed by the Diet in November 1993 and came into effect in October 1994.

III. CONTENTS OF THE ADMINISTRATIVE PROCEDURE ACT

The APA is made up of six chapters and thirty-eight articles. This section will be devoted to summarizing and commenting on the major features of the law.

A. GENERAL PROVISIONS

According to its purposes clause, the APA exists for the purpose of advancing the guarantee of fairness and transparency in the administrative process and thus promoting the protection of the rights and interests of Japan's citizens (Article 1[1]). This is the first time the term *transparency* has been used in an enacted piece of legislation, and its use signifies that the content and process of administrative determinations shall be made as clear as possible to the citizenry.[4] Including increased transparency with respect to administrative operations as a definite goal of the APA must be given due praise, not only for the influence it will have on the actual implementation process of the APA, but also for its effects on other aspects of public administration.

A second significant general provision specifies that the APA, as a general piece of legislation, does not take precedence over special provisions for administrative procedures contained in other laws (Article 1[2]). Therefore, in order to know whether any particular procedure is covered by the APA, it is not sufficient to rely on the provisions of the APA alone; it is necessary to check whether special provisions are made in other laws.

B. DISPOSITIONS RELATING TO APPLICATIONS

Chapter 2 of the APA governs dispositions[5] relating to applications, while chapter 3 covers adverse dispositions. Adverse dispositions do not include dispositions that deny permissions, licenses and the like sought by application (Article 2[4]b). Rather, the term *adverse disposition* refers to a disposition that takes away an *already existing* permission, license, or other benefit.

In the abstract, if we compare dispositions relating to applications with adverse dispositions, the latter are indeed very important. However, when taking into consideration actual administrative practices in Japan, procedural provisions covering applications are at least as important as the latter, and possibly more important. This is because in Japan, adverse dispositions do not have very many uses, since it is often possible to achieve the same result through administrative guidance (discussed in more detail below). In contrast, the number of applications made on a daily basis is enormous, and Japanese in general were not necessarily satisfied with the situation regarding the manner in which they were treated. There were many cases in which, for example, application review standards were not made available to the public; administrative offices, against the will of the applicants, refused to "receive" applications (and instead kept the applications effectively in limbo); applicants were kept uninformed as to the status of their applications for long periods of time after receipt; and the reasons for denying applications were not made available. These problems were the focus of particular attention during deliberations of CPAR3, and chapter 2 of the APA is designed to correct the situation, thus giving it a very important place in the act.

Under the APA, administrative agencies are obligated to (1) enact standards necessary for judging, according to law, whether an application will be granted or not (i.e., determinate review standards); (2) make those determinate standards as concrete as possible in light of the nature of the permission, and so forth, in question; and (3) make the review standards available to the public (except in the case where making such standards available would cause extraordinary administrative inconvenience) by means of posting them at the administrative office legally in charge of receiving each application, or by other methods (Article 5). Up until the enactment of the APA, it is believed that many administrative agencies established review standards internally, but few were made available to the public. The third requirement described above was designed to rectify that situation.

In terms of judicial precedents prior to the enactment of the APA, the Supreme Court, in a case concerning the issuance of taxi operator permits to individuals, ruled that the administrative agency in question, as an office responsible for granting permits to a small group out of a large number of competing applicants on the basis of items of concrete information, was prohibited from using procedures that lead to the appearance of arbitrariness in the actual permit issuance process. Moreover, because the basic statute in question (Road Transport Act, Article 6) had provided only very abstract taxi-permit standards, these standards (whether internal or not) should be converted, said the Court, into a set of concrete review standards to be applied in a fair and rational manner. When such standards require subtle, highly technical review processes, applicants must be given the opportunity to argue and present evidence that they meet the necessary requirements. However, it seems that the Court, in insisting that review standards be established, had in mind only situations with competitive applications and even then did not require that the standards be made available to the public. In addition, although the above decision did touch on the question of freedom of occupational choice, it did not undertake a constitutional interpretation of the due process requirement, thus limiting itself to an interpretation of the Road Transport Act. Therefore, the decision is definitely limited in the breadth over which it can be applied.

Article 5 of the APA covers applications in general and makes it obligatory that administrative agencies enact review standards and make them available to the public. This point signifies a great leap forward. Because of this provision, it is now easier for anyone who files an application to assess prospects beforehand. Together with Article 9(2), which requires administrative agencies to provide applicants and prospective applicants with information relevant to their applications, upon request, Article 5 now makes it possible for anyone to know for certain what preparations must be made in order to file an application. These provisions also make it possible to judge whether an application will be accepted or not, thus enabling potentially unsuccessful applicants to stop the process at an early stage and save them and the agency involved from wasting time and effort. The obligation on the part of administrative agencies to make their review standards available to the public also puts pressure on agencies to establish their standards rationally and with care. Review standards do not constitute legislative rules that bind courts. However, any diversion from them that is not supported by a rational reason might be interpreted by a court as grounds for finding an illegal action.

The APA also makes it obligatory for administrative agencies to establish standards for the amount of time typically needed in the application review process and requires that these standard time periods, when determined, be made available to the public (Article 6). The provision requires only that the agencies make an effort to establish these time frames, implying an understanding that, because of the varying nature of application processes, it may sometimes be difficult to set deadlines. Nonetheless, it is expected that this article will motivate administrative agencies to handle applications without undue delay.

Of course, even if standard time periods are established and made available to the public, there is a definite possibility that agencies might undertake deliberate practices of not "receiving" applications when filed. Indeed, provisions concerning standard time periods could ironically result in furthering this practice to avoid running over deadlines in processing applications. Here the APA requires that administrative offices begin review procedures without delay as soon as an application is filed, and demands that, in the event an application has deficiencies of the merely formal type, administrative agencies must seek corrections to the application within a specified period of time or reject it (Article 7). In the past, the practice of not "receiving" an application when filed—in effect, treating the application as though it had never arrived—was one tool used in the administrative guidance process. In outlawing this practice, Article 7 does not seek to outlaw administrative guidance itself. Essentially, the APA is not intended to suppress administrative guidance; however, administrative guidance practices that demand withdrawal of applications or changes in content against the wishes of the applicant are banned by the act as obstructing the applicant's exercise of rights (Article 33). Therefore, it is clear that if an applicant who does not desire administrative guidance files an application, the receiving agency must begin reviewing it immediately.

Even though some legislative provisions existed concerning the notification of reasons for rejecting applications, up until the passage of the APA, there was not one judicial decision finding that such notification is required under the Constitution. Article 8 of the APA rectified this situation by making the declaration of reasons for rejection obligatory in general.

When an application (or a number of related applications from one applicant) requires processing by more than one administrative agency, it is not at all rare in Japan for delay to occur. Concerning such cases, the APA urges that when necessary, each of the agencies involved maintain contact with one another and receive explanations from the applicant in joint session (Article 11[2]). It was hoped that this essentially admonitory provision would form the basis for creating guidelines and concrete measures to build a system of interagency exchange on application matters. Under the electronic government policy, promotion of "one-stop service" has made this hope a reality.

C. ADVERSE DISPOSITIONS

Chapter 3 of the APA contains provisions regarding dispositions rendered by administrative agencies that are of a disadvantageous or adverse nature. Article 12 states that agencies should make an effort to enact and make available to the public standards for these dispositions. In contrast to the handling of application review standards, the APA here does not go beyond an admonitory stance; however, compared to applications, adverse dispositions are rare in Japan, and creating standards for such action beforehand could sometimes be rife with difficulties. We should also consider the possibility that publication of such standards might hinder legal efficacy. For example, the publication of standards for dispositions that demand a verbal warning for the first offense, a formal written warning for the second offense, and the shutdown of operations for the third offense would inform pernicious operators beforehand that the first two offenses would not cause any actual detriment to their operations. Therefore, it is probably necessary that the provision regarding standards for adverse dispositions be merely admonitory in nature. However, in cases where standards for adverse dispositions are actually enacted and made available to the public, this article, along with Article 14 requiring a declaration of reasons for adverse dispositions, will help ensure care and rationality in deciding on such action.

The APA has divided the adverse disposition procedure into two parts.

The first concerns the hearing, and the second concerns providing opportunities for explanation and rebuttal. While the former procedure is carried out orally, the latter is in principle carried out through written documents. This dual procedure follows the draft of the APA that had been recommended as early as the First Provisional Committee for Research on Administration. How many stages are appropriate in the procedures for adverse dispositions is an important question. It can be said that simple, unitary, as well as complicated, multiphase procedures both tend to defeat the purpose of establishing fully integrated administrative procedures. The APA's choice of a two-stage procedure allows formal adjudicative procedures, which use quasi-judicial, trial-type hearings, to be invoked on the basis of special provisions made in other laws. In other words, concerning the three possible levels of adverse disposition procedure of formal adjudication, hearing, and explanation/rebuttal, the first has been relegated to determination by specific laws, while the other two have been determined generally by the APA as to content and utilization standards.

In the opinion of this author, the APA is probably correct in adopting the dual-stage procedural method from the viewpoint of reaching a balance between the need for uniformity and concern for flexibility in responding to a variety of possible actions. Of course, we can imagine cases in which the dual-stage method would not be appropriate. Such cases, however, can be covered by provisions for exceptions made in specific laws; filling the APA with too many kinds of procedure might cause difficulties as to which procedure to choose for any given case. The APA, while making clear legal determinations of standards for choosing to grant hearings and opportunities for explanation/rebuttal, has also left room for hearings to be decided via administrative discretion (Article 13[1]), resulting in a wise piece of legislation that avoids confusion as to which route to choose, while at the same time providing the possibility of flexible responses.

While limited to the hearing procedures, the APA guarantees to the parties in an adverse disposition, and to other persons disadvantaged by such action, the right to request access to the documents filed in the case and other materials that were used as a basis for the adverse disposition (Article 18). Even though Article 33(2) of the ACIA already guarantees this right to the claimant and any other participants in the case, the APA provision goes beyond this article. The APA is not only limited to materials "issued from the agency in question," and when viewed from the standpoint of bolstering the right to hearings, the access to materials recognized by the APA can be said to be epoch making. Also, the existence of this provision will have the desired effect of improving the way in which administrative agencies structure, manage, and control their documents.

Another facet of the APA that deserves note vis-à-vis adverse dispositions is the provisions concerning who presides over the hearing. In Japan, despite the fact that Article 16 of the National Administrative Operations Act Guidelines already required that the agency employee presiding over a hearing must not have been involved in the action that gave rise to the hearing, consideration had seldom been given to the impartiality of the hearing's presiding officer, except in the case of formal adjudication. Article 19 of the APA goes beyond the guidelines established by CPAR3 in setting forth the grounds for disqualification of a hearing officer in the act itself. While this problem may seem somewhat mundane in character, this approach should be praised as a step in the right direction. The presiding officer draws up a report containing his or her opinion as to whether the party in the case has just cause (Article 24). When an administrative agency decides to render an adverse disposition, it is obligated to study in detail the records of the hearing and the report containing the opinion of the presiding officer (Article 26). No matter how they choose to hold their hearings, if administrative agencies render decisions for adverse dispositions completely independent of the opinions given by presiding officers, the role of hearings will decline in significance in the administrative process. Article 26 of the APA is an attempt to avoid such a situation and thus has a particularly important meaning for hearing procedures.

D. ADMINISTRATIVE GUIDANCE

The APA is the first law of this kind in the world to contain regulations, both procedural and substantive, pertaining to administrative guidance.[6] Chapter 4, Articles 32–34 contain the substantive regulations. These provisions set forth the general principles that administrative guidance is voluntary in nature; a recipient of administrative guidance may not be forced to follow the guidance nor subjected to adverse treatment for refusal to follow it. These points may seem obvious from the principle of administration according to law. But when we consider actual administrative practices, which do not always completely reflect that principle, it is far from superfluous to state clearly the limits to which administrative guidance can be applied.

Articles 35 and 36 contain the procedural regulations. Article 35 is especially noteworthy. Clause 1 of that article makes it obligatory for those imposing administrative guidance to state clearly to the receiving party the subject, content, and agent responsible for administrative guidance. Clause 2, in turn, provides that in the case of oral guidance, the receiving party may request written clarification of the items covered in the previous clause and that the agent responsible must comply with that request unless an extraordinary administrative inconvenience exists. In the Japan–United States Structural Impediments Initiative, Japan promised to conduct as much administrative guidance as possible in writing. The APA does not go so far as to require that all administrative guidance be conducted in writing. With the requirement that oral administrative guidance be put in writing upon request, though, Article 36, clause 2, embraces the objective of memorialization of administrative guidance; this provision was expected to restrict arbitrary and uncalled-for use of administrative guidance.

E. NOTIFICATIONS

Chapter 5 of the APA states that as soon as a notification from a subject party reaches the relevant agency, so long as it is in accordance with formal requirements, all of the procedural requirements shall be considered fulfilled (Article 37). This provision seems quite obvious in principle, but similar to the case of applications mentioned above, in actuality there had been instances in which receipt of a notification had been refused against the wishes of the subject party. Article 37 was intended to correct this situation. (Incidentally, the term *procedural requirements* refers to required deadlines and items to be included in the notification. Thus, Article 37 by no means prevents the imposition of penalties for the filing of fraudulent information, even if the notification meets all of the procedural requirements of the filing process.)

F. APPLYING THE APA TO LOCAL PUBLIC ENTITIES

The scope of applicability of the APA is an important issue, and one topic that has received great attention is the extent of applicability to actions of local public entities. Article 2(5)(b) of the APA places under its jurisdiction all administrative agencies, including local public entities (excluding legislative assemblies). Article 3(2), however, states that the provisions contained in chapters 2–5 are not applicable to dispositions and notifications (only when enabling provisions are contained in ordinances and regulations) or administrative guidance carried out by local public entities.

Together, these two provisions mean that even if an adverse disposition is taken by an agency of a local public entity, the APA is applicable to actions taken according to a statute. This holds true no matter what kind of work the local public entity is involved in.

As for administrative guidance, however, even when interpreted as related to dispositions based on statutes, chapter 4 is not applicable as long as the guidance is carried out by an agency of a local public entity. Basically, this non-applicability reflects deference to local governmental autonomy. In the case of administrative guidance, initially CPAR3 was of the opinion that administrative guidance related to dispositions taken based on statutes should come under the APA, but in its final recommendations, it chose to exempt all administrative guidance by agencies of local public entities, partly because in practice it would be extremely difficult to judge whether actual cases of administrative guidance are in fact related to a disposition based on the statute.

Nonetheless, local public entities had no call to be content with such exclusion from APA provisions, for Article 38 clearly urged that necessary steps be taken, in the spirit of the APA, in order to achieve fairness and increase transparency in local public entities. In this manner, local public entities were being requested to make concerted efforts to review their existing administrative procedures and to undertake necessary reforms through the enactment of ordinances, regulations, guidelines, or other methods. And, in fact, local public entities responded to this prompting: all forty-seven prefectures and about 99 percent of municipalities have already enacted administrative procedure ordinances that are basically the same as the APA.[7]

IV. EVALUATION OF THE OPERATION OF THE ADMINISTRATIVE PROCEDURE ACT

The APA went into effect on October 1, 1994. From the beginning, it was not expected that this law would cause a dramatic change in the relationship between the government and citizens. Rather, it was expected that it would bring about a gradual change in the bureaucrats' perception of the government-citizen relationship. As predicted, the act has not caused a fundamental shift of power between the government and its citizens during the roughly eight years of its operation. On the other hand, in cases in which companies and citizens challenged government actions with resolve, the APA turned out to be a valuable weapon.

A well-known example is the Amakusa Gas case. A gas supplier, Amakusa Gas had been trying to expand its service area but had been blocked by local Ministry of International Trade and Industry (MITI) officials' administrative guidance. The content of the administrative guidance rendered to Amakusa

Gas was that it should consult in advance with propane gas companies that would be affected by the expansion. Local MITI officials refused to accept Amakusa Gas's application unless a report was attached documenting negotiations with the local propane gas companies. The administrative guidance did not go so far as to demand approval by the local propane gas companies, but, in effect, Amakusa Gas was expected to obtain the consent of those companies. It used to be the custom to pay money to competitors to obtain such consent. Amakusa Gas found the custom irrational and refused to follow the practice, and as a result it faced difficulty in having its application processed.

On the day the APA went into effect, Amakusa Gas resubmitted its application, but it was not accepted and the company received the same guidance. Amakusa Gas then requested local MITI officials to put this administrative guidance in writing based on Article 35, clause 2, of the APA, but this request was turned down. The company next used Keidanren's Administrative Guidance Hotline. Keidanren investigated the case and found that the local MITI bureau's practice was a clear violation of the APA. Keidanren notified MITI of its intent to make the matter public. The MITI had to admit that this administrative guidance was not appropriate; at that point Amakusa Gas's application was handled and approved. In an editorial, *Nikkei shimbun* commented that in this incident David used the APA as a weapon and beat a giant Goliath. This incident received wide media coverage, and other gas suppliers subsequently had their applications to expand their service areas approved by the local MITI bureaus.

In another case, an affiliate of Amakusa Gas submitted an application to sell high-pressure gas to hospitals. As in the Amakusa Gas case, it received administrative guidance to attach a letter of approval from its competitors. The company refused to follow the guidance and asked the administrative agency to handle the application according to the APA, following which the application was approved.

Another example concerning administrative guidance is the "Internet" case. Internet is the name of a company that imports foreign cars. The company used to be able to clear customs without entrusting the customs entry to clearance traders, but it received administrative guidance to consign the procedures to clearance traders. The commission that would be charged by those traders, however, would have been so expensive that it would be difficult for Internet to make a profit. Accordingly, Internet refused to follow the administrative guidance. Internet called the Keidanren hotline and also requested the customs official to put the administrative guidance in writing. Without waiting for Keidanren's intervention, the customs official withdrew the guidance.[8]

If we turn our eyes to court decisions, we can find some examples in which the APA has made a major difference. Let me cite two examples. The first case is related to the "declaration of reasons" requirement of Article 8 of the APA. In the past, whenever statutes had required the "declaration of reasons," Japanese courts had reversed those dispositions that were not supported by sufficient reasons. However, the number of statutes requiring declarations of reasons had been small. As discussed above, the APA vastly broadened the "declaration of reasons" requirement, by establishing a general principle that the reasons must be given when applications are rejected (Article 8) or adverse dispositions are rendered (Article 14).

When one plaintiff's application for registration as a horse owner was turned down, he filed a suit to revoke the decision for lack of sufficient reason as required by Article 8 of the APA. In that case, the Tokyo District Court reversed the agency's decision, holding that the reason attached to the disposition was not sufficiently concrete.[9] As this example shows, Japanese courts do not demand that plaintiffs explain whether agencies' decisions are wrong in substantive terms. Thus, attacking on the ground of insufficient reasons is a good strategy for plaintiffs.

The second example is related to review standards. Article 5, paragraph 3, of the APA makes it mandatory for administrative agencies to make review standards available to the public except in cases of extraordinary administrative inconvenience. When a Chinese student was disqualified from taking a national medical examination and challenged that determination, the Tokyo High Court cited Article 5, paragraph 3, to reverse the decision of the minister of health and welfare denying the application, because the minister did not make the review standard available to the applicant. It is worth mentioning that the Tokyo High Court also cited Article 8 as a ground for reversal. In doing so, the court required the reasons given by the administrative body to contain a reference not only to the legal authority for the decision but also to the review standard on which the decision was based. Before the APA went into effect, agencies were not expected to refer to review standards in their reasons. However, since the APA made it mandatory, in principle, to establish review standards and make them available to the public, it is very natural, as the Tokyo High Court determined, to require administrative agencies to explain the reasons for decisions by reference to the applicable review standards.

A further interesting aspect of this case is that neither the plaintiff nor his lawyers seemed to notice that the APA could be a useful weapon for them in the first instance; they only asserted a violation of the APA for the first time in the second instance. Even more interesting is that the Tokyo District

Court, which handled the first instance of this case, also seemed oblivious to the fact that the APA could be an important issue in this case. Thus, one lesson that can be drawn from the cases mentioned above is that the APA is still not necessarily widely recognized even among lawyers. One of the reasons for this is that few lawyers, including judges, have studied administrative law.

On the other hand, in cases where citizens actively use the APA, the act can make an important difference. It should be noted, moreover, that the APA's use of the word *transparency* in its purposes provision had an important symbolic impact. Though the pace of progress still cannot be said to be fast, the notion that public administration should be transparent has started to permeate throughout the government, and the APA's recognition of the fundamental principle of transparency has played a valuable role in that process. As mentioned above, all forty-seven prefectures and more than 99 percent of municipalities already have administrative procedure ordinances. As with the APA itself, nearly all of those ordinances also recognize the basic principles of procedural fairness and transparency. As this reflects, procedural fairness and transparency have become important principles of Japanese administrative law, and it is expected that courts will use the APA and the ordinances more often in judicial review of administrative actions in the future.

V. PUBLIC COMMENT

Although the Japanese APA does not contain provisions on rule making, such provisions have been discussed in academia for many years. Recently, business organizations and foreign countries also have pressured the Japanese government to introduce rule-making procedures. Against this background, the Administrative Reform Council proposed the introduction of "public comment" procedures in its final report issued in December 1997. Based on this report, in March 1998, the Cabinet pledged to investigate this procedure in regulatory areas in its "3 year plan for the promotion of deregulation." And Article 50, paragraph 2, of the Basic Act for the Reform of the Central Ministries obliged the government to introduce and use public comment procedures in order to listen to public opinions and insure fairness and transparency.

On March 23, 1999, the Cabinet issued a resolution on public comment procedures in connection with regulation; this resolution went into effect on April 1, 1999. It is worth noting that the draft of this resolution was itself made public and amended, taking into account the comments that were received. This was not the first time such public comment procedures had been used by the government. For example, in March 1998, MITI employed a public comment procedure with regard to important matters that were being discussed at an advisory panel. However, it is significant that this procedure was introduced throughout the central government.

Several points should be mentioned with respect to this public comment procedure. First, it is based on a Cabinet resolution, not a statute, which means agency actions under it are not appealable to the courts. For this reason, it is hoped that legislative codification of this Cabinet resolution will be undertaken in the near future. (In this connection, it should be mentioned that the Japanese government has a plan to amend the APA and incorporate the "public comment" procedures into the statute. If that plan is followed, an avenue for judicial review should become available.)

Second, the coverage of this resolution is broad in some respects yet narrow in others. It is broad in the sense that it covers not only legislative rules, such as Cabinet orders and ministerial ordinances, but also non-legislative rules, such as review standards and disposition standards under the APA. Since notice and comment procedures under the U.S. Administrative Procedure Act do not extend to those rules that are not legally binding, the fact that the Cabinet resolution included non-legislative rules deserves note. On the other hand, it is narrow in the sense that it covers only regulatory rules. This shows clearly that increasing transparency in government regulation, which was a source of concern to both Japanese business circles and U.S. and European Union trade negotiators, was the main objective of this policy. From the citizens' viewpoint, however, there is no reason to limit this public comment procedure to regulatory rules.

Third, under this Cabinet resolution, administrative agencies are supposed to explain the reasons why some comments were not adopted. In this connection, the reasons must be made public together with the comments received. This represents a major step forward in the evolution of transparency and accountability in Japanese administrative law. In contrast, before the Cabinet resolution went into effect, even in those cases where public comments had been solicited, there was no need to reply to any comments that were received. It must be pointed out, however, that controlling the quality of the reasons given remains a formidable task, particularly given the absence of a right to judicial review.

Fourth, ex parte contacts between the agencies and the commenting parties are not prohibited and need not be documented. For obvious reasons, this may serve as a loophole in the objective of improving transparency.[10]

It is too early to tell how effective this public comment procedure has been.

According to a survey conducted by the Management and Coordination Agency's Administrative Management Bureau, in fiscal year 1999, the original drafts were revised in 15.2 percent of the cases where public comments were received. How to evaluate this number is a difficult question, but at least it can be said that the Cabinet resolution has had some positive impact on certain areas of the rule-making process. On the whole, it is fair to say that this Cabinet resolution is a major step in the development of Japanese administrative law, but it is not yet fully developed and further efforts are needed to improve it.

As for local public entities, some administrative procedure ordinances, such as that of Tottori prefecture, include provisions on public comment procedure. It is also worth mentioning that the first public comment ordinance was enacted in 2001, in Yokosuka City. By embodying the public comment requirement in ordinance, the potential for judicial review has been assured. As of this writing, however, it is too early to say how effective the ordinance will be.

VI. ENACTMENT OF INFORMATION DISCLOSURE LAWS

As early as the 1970s, some academics, lawyers, and citizen groups began to discuss the possibility of enacting information disclosure laws. In 1982, the first information disclosure ordinance was enacted in Kanayama Town of Yamagata Prefecture. That same year, Kanagawa became the first prefecture to adopt an information disclosure ordinance. Since then, the number of local governments enacting information disclosure ordinances has increased steadily. Today, all forty-seven prefectures and more than 80 percent of municipal governments have information disclosure ordinances.[11]

At the national level, it was the Lockheed Payoff Scandal that stirred public opinion that an information disclosure law should be enacted. In 1980, a nongovernmental organization (NGO) called Citizens Movement for an Information Disclosure Act was established. In 1981, that NGO promulgated a "Declaration of Rights to Information Disclosure," together with eight basic principles on freedom of information. That same year, the Japan Civil Liberties Union published a model disclosure ordinance. The opposition parties started to submit information disclosure bills in the Diet. All such bills died, however, because they were not supported by the ruling party, the Liberal Democratic Party (LDP). The LDP had been indifferent to information disclosure because it had continued to enjoy the privilege of being the ruling party since 1955. Under the circumstances in which the ruling party and opposition parties were fixed and unlikely to change positions, bureaucrats gave favorable treatment to the LDP by providing it with information that was not accessible to the opposition parties. In other words, the LDP received much more information and more valuable information from the bureaucrats. Enactment of an information disclosure law would deprive the LDP of this privilege, because it would enable opposition parties to obtain access to the documents that used to be inaccessible to them.

The myth that the LDP would always remain the ruling party proved wrong, however. In 1993 the LDP finally lost its majority in the lower house and for the first time since 1955 became an opposition party. The new coalition of ruling parties made the enactment of an information disclosure law a high priority in their political agenda. This new coalition was short-lived, however, and the LDP along with the Social Democratic Party and New Party Sakigake regained the status of ruling party. As one condition to forming this coalition, though, the LDP had to pledge to the other two parties that it would cooperate to enact an information disclosure law. It should be mentioned that the LDP itself also overcame its strong allergy to information disclosure once it had experienced a period as an opposition party. Through that experience, the LDP discovered that information disclosure would strengthen its position vis-à-vis bureaucrats, whether it was a ruling party or an opposition party.

At the national level, the Information Disclosure Act (IDA) was enacted in 1999 and went into effect on April 1, 2001. Citizens have learned how to use local information disclosure ordinances for the past twenty years, so from the beginning, national government agencies received a massive number of requests to disclose documents; it was expected that this law would cause a dramatic change in the way the national government is run.

VII. CONTENTS OF THE INFORMATION DISCLOSURE ACT

A. PURPOSE

In accordance with the principle that sovereignty resides in the people, and by providing for the right to request the disclosure of administrative documents, the purpose of the IDA, as set forth in its purposes provision, is to strive for greater disclosure of information held by administrative organs, thereby ensuring that the government is accountable to the people for its various operations. Along the lines of this provision, many local information disclosure ordinances have been revised to clearly include government accountability in their purpose provisions.

B. COVERED ORGANS

The IDA covers virtually all administrative organs. It includes organs established by law within the Cabinet (the Cabinet Secretariat, etc.), organs under the jurisdiction of the Cabinet (such as the National Personnel Authority), organs established as national administrative organs (ministries, commissions, and agencies), as well as the Board of Audit. However, the Diet and the courts are not covered. Although the Supreme Court has established an internal rule on information disclosure, the legislative codification of that rule remains an important task.

C. THE SCOPE OF ADMINISTRATIVE DOCUMENTS COVERED

The IDA is applicable to documents, drawings, and electromagnetic records that, having been prepared or obtained by an employee of an administrative organ in the course of his or her duties, are held by the administrative organ concerned for organizational use by its employees. It is wider in scope in two respects as compared with previous local information disclosure ordinances. First, it includes all types of electromagnetic records. Second, all organizational records are included in its coverage. This also had a significant impact on local information disclosure ordinances, as many of them were revised to widen the scope of the documents covered by their provisions.

D. DISCLOSURE OF ADMINISTRATIVE DOCUMENTS

Any person may request disclosure of administrative documents. Except for administrative documents in which one or more of the following types of information are recorded, heads of administrative organs are required to disclose the documents requested. The scope of non-disclosable information is as follows:

a. Information concerning an individual from which a particular individual can be identified, etc. However, this exception excludes information required to be made public by law or custom, and information concerned with the offices of public officials, and so forth.
b. Information concerning a corporation where there is a risk that, if made

public, the corporation's legitimate interests would be harmed, where the information was voluntarily provided on the condition that it not be disclosed and it normally would not be made public, and so forth.

c. Information as to which the head of the administrative organ deems, with adequate reason, that disclosure would pose a risk of harm to the security of the state or a risk of damage to trustful relations with another country, and so forth.

d. Information as to which the head of the administrative organ deems, with adequate reason, that the disclosure would pose a risk of hindering the maintenance of public order and safety through crime prevention and criminal investigations, and so forth.

e. Information concerning deliberations or examinations, and so forth, internal to or between either organs of the state or local public entities, and so forth, that if made public would risk unjustly harming the frank exchange of opinions, and so forth.

f. Information that concerns the affairs or business conducted by organs of the state or local public entities, and so forth, which, if made public, would risk causing hindrance to the proper performance of such affairs or business.

It should be noted that even when information not ordinarily subject to disclosure (hereinafter referred to as "non-disclosure information") is recorded, it may be disclosed if there is deemed to be a particular public interest necessitating disclosure. When non-disclosure information would be disclosed merely by answering whether or not administrative documents exist, the disclosure request may be refused without making clear the existence or nonexistence of the documents. This is what is called a Glomar denial (taking its name from a U.S. Freedom of Information Act case involving the Central Intelligence Agency and the *Glomar Explorer*, a ship).

E. PROCEDURE FOR THE DISPOSITION OF DISCLOSURE REQUESTS

Under the IDA, disclosure decisions are to be made within thirty days of the date of the disclosure request. When information relating to a third party is recorded in an administrative document, the third party may be given the opportunity to submit a written opinion. That opportunity is to be afforded when disclosure is to be made because of public interest reasons. Disclosure of documents and the like is to be made either by providing for inspection or by providing copies, and electromagnetic recordings are to be disclosed by a method to be determined by Cabinet order. The fees for disclosure requests and the implementation of disclosure are to be within the scope of actual expenses, to be determined by Cabinet order. Consideration is to be given to ensure that the fee is as affordable as possible.

F. APPEALS, AND SO FORTH

An Information Disclosure Review Board was established within the Cabinet office in order to examine and deliberate appeals, in response to cases referred from the heads of administrative organs concerning appeals of disclosure decisions, and so forth. The Review Board consists of nine members appointed by the prime minister and approved by both houses of the Diet. The Review Board may request that the reference agency (1) present the administrative documents concerned with the appeal or (2) produce and submit materials classifying or arranging in a manner specified by the Review Board the information recorded in the administrative documents concerned with the appeal. The Review Board may have a designated member hear statements of opinion by the appellant, and so forth.

G. JURISDICTION OVER LAWSUITS

Lawsuits may be brought demanding the revocation of a disclosure decision or the revocation of a ruling or decision regarding the appeal of a disclosure decision. In addition to the court provided for by Article 12 of the ACLA, such cases may also be brought before the district court that has jurisdiction over the seat of the high court that has jurisdiction over the seat of the plaintiff's general forum.

H. MANAGEMENT OF ADMINISTRATIVE DOCUMENTS

To contribute to the proper and smooth application of the law, the IDA provides, the heads of administrative organs are to properly manage administrative documents. In that connection, the heads of administrative organs are responsible both to establish rules regarding the management of administrative documents, as provided for by Cabinet order, and to make those rules available for inspection by the public. The Cabinet order determines standards for the classification, preparation, maintenance, and disposal of administrative documents, along with other items necessary for the management of administrative documents. Administrative organs have observed these requirements: they have established rules for the proper management of administrative documents in accordance with the relevant Cabinet order, and they have made those rules available for public inspection.

I. INFORMATION DISCLOSURE BY LOCAL PUBLIC ENTITIES

The IDA does not apply to local public entities. However, in keeping with the spirit of this law, local public entities are obliged to strive to formulate and implement measures necessary for the disclosure of the information that they hold. Quite a few local public entities have already amended their information disclosure ordinances. Moreover, the number of local public entities with information disclosure ordinances has increased dramatically.

J. INFORMATION DISCLOSURE BY PUBLIC CORPORATIONS

The IDA does not apply to public corporations. However, the IDA made it obligatory for the government to promote the disclosure and provision of information held by public corporations, in accordance with their character and type of business, and to take necessary measures such as legislation relating to the disclosure of information held by those corporations. In keeping with that call, the Information Disclosure Act for Public Corporations was enacted in 2001; 135 public corporations are covered by that law.[12]

VIII. EVALUATION OF THE OPERATION OF THE INFORMATION DISCLOSURE ACT

For many years, information disclosure ordinances have been actively used by citizens at the local and prefectural levels, and those ordinances have proven to be effective tools for scrutinizing government activities. In many cases, the requests have resulted in disclosure of information without the need for further action. And, in cases in which the requests were initially rejected, both information disclosure committees and courts have played important roles in providing effective relief to the requesters.

Information disclosure committees are neutral, third-party organs composed of academics, private attorneys, and others. They have authority to conduct in camera inspections, a very powerful tool to check whether decisions to withhold documents were wrong. According to a survey conducted by an NGO, the Citizens Movement for Freedom of Information, at the prefectural level, information disclosure committees recommended disclosure beyond that of the original decisions by administrative organs in more than 50 percent of the cases brought before them.

As for litigation, it is now well known that it is difficult for plaintiffs to prevail in administrative litigation in Japan, but information disclosure suits are exceptional. Data compiled by Professor Masahiro Uzaki of Dokkyo University show that plaintiffs have prevailed, at least partially, in nearly two-thirds of the cases they have brought. There are several reasons for this. First, unlike other administrative litigation, threshold requirements are almost nonexistent in information disclosure suits. Since requesters are allowed to request documents without explaining the reasons for their request, standing does not become an issue. Second, the burden of proof rests with the heads of the administrative organs; that is, it is necessary for agencies to prove that the withheld documents are exempted from disclosure by the information disclosure ordinances. Third, it is rare in information disclosure suits that courts have to defer to administrative discretion.

At the national level, the government has compiled statistics on the first and second years of operation of the IDA. There were 48,650 requests in total in the first year and 59,580 requests in the second year. In the first year 45,071 initial decisions were made by the heads of administrative organs and in the second 58,598 initial decisions were made. Both years, the administrative documents were totally or partly disclosed in about 90 percent of the cases. In the first year, the initial decisions were rendered within the thirty-day deadline in more than 80 percent of the cases; in the second year, the percentage of decisions issued within thirty days increased even further, to over 90 percent.

Turning to the appeals situation, in the first year, 1,354 administrative appeals were filed, of which 384 cases were referred to the Information Disclosure Review Board of the Cabinet office; in the second year, there were 910 administrative appeals, of which 703 cases were referred to the board. As these figures reflect, in the first year there was a wide disparity between the number of administrative appeals filed and the number of cases referred to the board. Since heads of administrative organs are, in principle, obliged to seek opinions of the board, most of this gap presumably was caused by delay in referrals (and the figures for the second year seem to bear out this conclusion). Whether this delay was inevitable or not is a matter to be investigated.

Among the 384 cases referred to the board in the first year, the board issued recommendations in 178 cases that year. With three subcommittees in the board, this means that, on average, each subcommittee issued recommendations in about sixty cases that year. This number increased sharply in the second year, when the board issued 546 recommendations. One reason for the relatively low number in the first year is that the board had to wait for the first couple of months before the first wave of cases was referred to it. A second major factor accounting for the sharp increase in the second year is that the commissioners accumulated experience. In particular, once precedents were established, cases falling within those precedents could be handled quickly. Although it was feared the board would be overwhelmed by an influx of referred cases and would take a very long time before issuing recommendations, so far, backlogs have not been such a serious problem. Based on the first two years of experience with the Information Disclosure Review Board, it would probably be fair to say that the board has proven to provide effective remedies at a reasonable cost.

Turning to the situation in the courts, fifteen lawsuits were filed in the first year and twenty-five lawsuits in the second year; several court decisions have already been handed down. Since the number of court decisions remains low, however, it is premature to tell how effective judicial review has been in implementing the IDA.

Perhaps the most interesting question is what impact the IDA has had on the bureaucrats' culture of secrecy. It is unlikely that the enforcement of the IDA has changed this culture overnight. On the other hand, it would be wrong to suggest that the professed goal of the IDA, to ensure government accountability to the people through information disclosure, had no influence on bureaucrats' way of thinking. The fact that the word *accountability* was used in the purpose provisions of the IDA, in my view, has been affecting Kasumigaseki culture to a certain extent. Today it is not rare to hear bureaucrats saying things such as, "In order to make the government accountable to the citizens for what it is doing, we will publish the minutes of the meetings on the Internet," or "In view of accountability, we have decided to publish our interim reports and seek public comment," even when such actions are not required by law. In fact, *accountability* has become such a popular word among bureaucrats that we very often see the word in government reports.

IX. CONCLUSION

In closing, let me address the question of what ramifications the APA, public comment procedures, and IDA will have on the doctrines of administrative law. Under the traditional administrative law theory, citizens were just the recipients of administrative actions. From that standpoint, the main focus of administrative law doctrine was on how to afford redress for aggrieved citizens by providing for such remedies as administrative suits against administrative organs and governmental tort actions.

From around the 1960s, public participation in government decision making has been stressed by public law scholars. The APA did not tackle this problem frontally. Rather, in keeping with traditional administrative law theory, its main focus was on how to protect direct recipients of administrative actions. The Cabinet resolution on public comments ameliorated this situation to a certain degree. Recently, in city planning and other planning processes involving matters such as road construction, public involvement in the planning processes has been stressed by bureaucrats themselves. "Public administration in partnership with citizens" has become a very popular slogan in those fields. However, public involvement of citizens in the decision-making processes of the government can be accomplished only when government information is made available to citizens in a timely manner. Preferably, the government should make this information available to the public voluntarily and proactively. This does not always happen, however, and the IDA serves as a safety net when the government does not do so.

The Cabinet resolution on public comments and the IDA have accelerated the trend of recent administrative law doctrine, which positions citizens not only as recipients of administrative actions but also as active participants in government decision-making processes. For example, a characteristic of some of the recently published textbooks on administrative law is their emphasis on interactive communication between the government and citizens.[13] Japan still has far to go to achieve this ideal, but the trend toward public participation has been steady and increasing in force, and that trend seems certain to strengthen even further in the years to come.

NOTES

1. Gyōsei tetsuzuki hō [Administrative Procedure Act], Act No. 88 of 1993. For an overview of the development of the theories on administrative procedures in postwar Japan, see Katsuya Uga, *Gyōsei tetuzuki jōhō kōkai* [Administrative Procedure and Information Disclosure] (Tokyo: Kōbundō, 1999), 2.

2. For overviews of the ACLA and ACIA in English, see Katsuya Uga, "Procedure in Administrative Law in Japan," *Journal of the Japan-Netherlands Institute* 7 (2001): 184, 194; Shokitsu Tanakadate, "A Summary of the Limitation on Administrative Adjudication under the Japanese Constitution," *Law in Japan: An Annual*

18 (1986): 108 (1986); and Ichiro Ogawa, "Outline of the System of Administrative and Judicial Remedies against Administrative Actions," in Kiyoaki Tsuji, ed., *Public Administration in Japan* (Tokyo: University of Tokyo Press, 1984) 237.

3. Accordingly, both the APA and the ACIA deal with procedures within the administrative process. It can be said that the former concerns pre-disposition procedures, while the latter concerns post-disposition procedures.

4. For further details on the provisions concerning transparency in the APA, see Katsuya Uga, *Gyōsei tetuzuki hō no riron* [Theory of Administrative Procedure Law] (Tokyo: Tokyo University Press, 1995), 17.

5. *Disposition* is a technical term unfamiliar to many American lawyers because it is derived from a German concept. For details, see Robert W. Dziubla, "The Impotent Sword of Japanese Justice: The Doctrine of Shobunsei as a Barrier to Administrative Litigation," *Cornell International Law Journal*, 1985, 37, 52.

6. Books and articles explaining Japanese "administrative guidance" in English are rather numerous. See, e.g., Michael K. Young, "Judicial Review of Administrative Guidance," *Columbia Law Review* 84 (1984): 923; Frank K. Upham, *Law and Social Change in Postwar Japan* (Cambridge, MA: Harvard University Press, 1987), 166–227; J. Mark Ramseyer and Minoru Nakazato, *Japanese Law: An Economic Approach* (Chicago: University of Chicago Press, 1999), 205; Hiroshi Shiono, "Administrative Guidance," in Tsuji, *Public Administration in Japan*, 221–35; Russell A. Yeomans, "Administrative Guidance: A Peregrine View," *Law in Japan: An Annual* 19 (1986): 125; Malcolm D. H. Smith, "Prices and Petroleum in Japan: 1973–1974—a Study of Administrative Guidance," *Law in Japan: An Annual* 10 (1977): 81; Wolfgang Pape, "Gyosei Shido and the Antimonopoly Law," *Law in Japan: An Annual* 15 (1982): 12; Yoriaki Narita, "Administrative Guidance," *Law in Japan: An Annual* 2 (1968): 45; Paul A. Davis, "Administrative Guidance in Japan—Legal Considerations," *Sophia University Socio-economic Institute Bulletin* 41 (1972): 1; Takashi Wakiyama, "The Nature and Tools of Japan's Industrial Policy," *Harvard International Law Journal* 27 (1986): 467. For further readings, see also the publications listed in Yukio Yanagida, Daniel H. Foote, Edward Stokes Johnson Jr., J. Mark Ramseyer, and Hugh T. Scogin Jr., eds., *Law and Investment in Japan—Cases and Materials* (Cambridge, MA: East Asian Legal Studies, Harvard Law School, 1994), 125.

7. For further details on the contents of the APA, see Katsuya Uga, Gyōsei tetuzuki hō no kaisetu [Commentary on the Administrative Procedure Act], 5th ed. (Tokyo: Gakuyō shobō, 2003). A number of articles on the APA have appeared in English. See, e.g., Tom Ginsburg, "System Change? A New Perspective on Japan's Administrative Procedure Law," in Tom Ginsburg et al., eds., *The Multiple Worlds of Japanese Law: Disjunctions and Conjunctions* (Victoria, BC: Centre

for Asia-Pacific Initiatives, University of Victoria, 2001), 107; Ginsburg, "Dismantling the "Developmental State"?—Administrative Procedure Reform in Japan and Korea," *American Journal of Comparative Law* 49 (2001): 585; Mark Levin, "Bureaucratic Sumo Wrestling," *Asian Law Journal* 4 (1995): 16; Ken Duck, "Now That the Fog Has Lifted: The Impact of Japan's Administrative Procedures Law on the Regulation of Industry and Market Governance," *Fordham International Law Journal* 19 (1996): 1686; and Lorenz Ködderitzch, "Japan's New Administrative Procedure Act: Reasons for Its Enactment and Likely Implications," *Law in Japan: An Annual* 24 (1991): 105.

8. For further details on these cases, see Uga, *Gyōsei tetuzuki*, 40. For other examples, see Ginsburg, "System Change," 124; Duck, "Now That the Fog Has Lifted," 1747.

9. X v. Japan Racing Association (Tokyo Dist. Ct., Feb. 27, 1998), *Hanrei jihō* 1660 (1998): 44.

10. See Michael J. Markus, "Regulatory Transparency in Japan: Half Full or Half Empty?" *Asia Perspectives* 3 (2001): 20, 21.

11. For details on local information disclosure ordinances, see Lawrence Repeta, "Local Government Disclosure Systems in Japan," *NBR Executive Insight* (Seattle: National Bureau of Asian Research, 1999), available at (http://www.nbr.org/publications/executive_insight/); David M. Schultz, "Japan's Information Disclosure Law: Why Law of Loopholes Is Better than No Law at All" (master's thesis, University of Washington School of Law, 2000), 17–34 (on file with the author); and David Boling, "Access to Government-Held Information in Japan: Citizens' 'Right to Know' Bows to the Bureaucracy," *Stanford Journal of International Law* 34 (1998): 1.

12. For further details on the contents of the IDA, see Katsuya Uga, *Shin jōhō kōkai hō no chikujō kaisetsu* [New Commentary on Information Disclosure Laws] (Tokyo: Yūhikaku, 2002). As for English materials, see Schultz, "Japan's Information Disclosure Law," 39–83; Lawrence Repeta and David Schultz, "Japanese Government Information: New Rules for Access" (2002), available at: (http://www.freedominfo.org/analysis/japan1/index.htm); and Narufumi Kadomatsu, "The New Administrative Information Disclosure Law in Japan," *Zeitschrift für Japanisches Recht* 8 (1999): 34.

13. See, e.g., Yōichi Ōhashi, *Gyōsei hō* [Administrative Law and Process] (Tokyo: Yūhikaku, 2001).

12 The Politics of Transparency in Japanese Administrative Law

TOM GINSBURG

The 1990s will likely be seen as a major turning point in Japanese administrative law. During the decade, Japan adopted three major legal reforms that substantially impact the Japanese administrative system: the Administrative Procedure Act (APA), the Information Disclosure Act (IDA), and the Cabinet resolution requiring public notice of administrative rule making.[1] The first two of these reforms are statutory in character and have received some attention abroad. The Cabinet resolution has received less attention but may prove to be equally significant, especially if it is expanded and strengthened to include provision for judicial review. Together, these three reforms bring Japan into alignment with many other countries of the Organization for Economic Cooperation and Development (OECD) in terms of basic structure of regulation of administrative action and administrative policy making.

This comment seeks to elaborate on some of the political dynamics behind the reforms and to speculate on possible implications. First, I consider the broader political environment. Second, I focus on one mode of procedural requirement that appears in the new legal reforms, namely, the requirement that administrators give reasons to regulated parties under particular circumstances. Third, I consider the impact of the reforms on public demand for administrative transparency.

I. THE BROADER POLITICAL CONTEXT OF ADMINISTRATIVE REFORM

My first theme is that it is important to explain why reforms made sense from the point of view of those political forces that had dominated the postwar system. It is sometimes argued that *demand* from the public is the key factor in legislative change. But academics and others in Japan had argued for greater transparency for many years, to little avail. In fact, legal change did not occur until the Liberal Democratic Party (LDP) fell out of power briefly in 1993. This turned out to be a crucial if short interlude for administrative reform.

While it would be tempting to claim that the Hosokawa government passed the APA to constrain the bureaucracy, it made no substantive changes to a bill that had been sitting on the shelf as drafted by the bureaucracy under LDP scrutiny. The particular provisions of the APA, then, must have been more or less acceptable to the LDP, and they became desirable to the LDP once it fell out of the governing coalition. A party that realizes it cannot govern forever needs transparency during periods when it is out of power. The timing of the adoption of long-standing proposals suggests that underlying the shift toward transparency was a changing relationship between the LDP and the bureaucracy that culminated in the brief fall of the LDP. Whether the reforms will themselves contribute to further deterioration in this relationship remains to be seen.

Another factor underlying the shift toward greater transparency is the changing role of the business community. Keidanren pressure for more transparent administration was very important in catalyzing reforms, a point that is illustrated by the central role played by the Keidanren "hotline" in implementation of the APA.[2] Here it is arguable that the prolonged recession, combined with numerous bureaucratic failures and scandals, actually strengthened the power of business within Japanese domestic politics. The clear need for reform to restructure the economy has strengthened the hand of those arguing for transparency and government accountability. In the high-growth and bubble eras, there was little need to rock the boat when things were going well. But the economic troubles of the 1990s have contributed to pressure for change.

A final noteworthy point on the political context is that many of the reforms have been organized around the Cabinet office (formerly the prime minister's office). The prime minister has historically been a weak figure in Japan's party-centered political system. But it might make sense for a prime minister who is unable to control independent ministries to expand public account ability as a way of reducing the ability of the ministries to hide information. In this regard, it is important that the Management and Coordination Agency,[3] one of fourteen external bureaus in the prime minister's office, played an important role in shepherding both the APA and IDA through the legislative process and monitored the line ministries' performance of APA requirements.[4] The Cabinet office also hosts the IDA Review Board and implemented the recommendation to allow public comments on delegated legislation. Perhaps we are witnessing internal political dynamics *within* the government, whereby the center seeks to exert greater control over the line ministries.

Probably no single one of these explanations is sufficient to explain the developments in administrative law, and elements of all three are at play in the shift toward transparency. The main point is that administrative law reforms reflect underlying political dynamics, in Japan and elsewhere. Although transparency and accountability are slogans that focus on the relationship between government and the public, these reforms would be unthinkable unless they also served the interests of powerful forces in the Japanese governance system. The incentives of the LDP, business, and the Cabinet office all converged on moving toward greater transparency.

II. CONSTRAINING ADMINISTRATIVE POLICY MAKING THROUGH "GIVING REASONS" REQUIREMENTS

Administrative law reforms not only *reflect* political factors, they can shape politics as well, sometimes in unanticipated ways. The Japanese state has historically operated on the basis of broadly worded statutes with large delegations to the administration. While a large amount of administrative policy making is inevitable in any modern state, since bureaucrats fill in the details of statutes, it has been especially apparent in Japan because of broad delegations. Less precise legislation requires more making of new rules by ministries.

In addition, the Japanese state has operated primarily through case-by-case ad hoc determinations, made on the basis of flexible "guidance" rather than preannounced rules. In such a circumstance, without legislative clarity or clear rules, private actors have no choice but to cultivate relationships with the bureaucrats who will in fact be making distributive decisions on a discretionary basis. The extent to which this discretion was exercised in the shadow of LDP power need not concern us here. For now, it is sufficient to say that the entire structure of Japanese postwar political economy was reflected in and sustained by the structure of Japanese public law.

The seemingly minor procedural step of requiring bureaucrats to give reasons for decisions, found in both the APA and the Cabinet order (and which also governs the IDA), may in fact become profoundly important in constraining the discretion of bureaucrats. There are at least two reasons for this. First of all, an administrator who must give reasons for his or her actions will be more careful to make more rational, or at least more justifiable, decisions than will a bureaucrat who can exercise purely by fiat. This was the result that was likely contemplated by the drafters of these "giving reasons" requirements: making the bureaucracy more accountable and transparent to the public will tend to improve bureaucratic performance and responsiveness.

Second, comparative experience in both the United States and the European Union indicates that "giving reasons" requirements can become a major beachhead of judicial review.[5] This is because bureaucrats who must give reasons automatically create a record that can serve as the basis for judicial inquiry. A bureaucrat who makes a phone call "suggesting" an outcome to a private party is much more impervious to review, since there is no record of his or her decision. But once reasons are given, the reasons are open to scrutiny by judges as to whether or not they are adequate. Although the requirement to give reasons appears to be procedural in character, it can easily and naturally lead to substantive evaluation by judges of the reasons proffered by bureaucrats.

This second point is relevant at least as far as the APA and IDA are concerned (the giving reasons requirement in the Cabinet order is not reviewable by courts). And it appears that some version of this dynamic is already occurring in Japan, as evidenced by the fact that two early cases that rely on the APA (both discussed in the chapter by Professor Uga in this volume) drew on the giving reasons requirement of Article 8. Professor Uga notes the significance of Japanese judges choosing to refer to the ministries' review standards in evaluating the reasons offered by bureaucrats. Once a court can independently evaluate the reasons given in light of the review standards, the notion that giving reasons is merely a procedural requirement becomes a fiction. The examination of reasons is no longer procedural but substantive as well, in the sense that judges will now be able to assert that the reasons did not meet the ministries' internal standard of review. To make such an assertion the judge will have to examine the facts of the application in light of the standard, a substantive evaluation if ever there was one.

One might welcome this kind of scrutiny by judges. Certainly it means that arbitrariness is constrained at its outer limits: a bureaucrat cannot offer as a reason "because I felt like it" or "because an LDP Diet member told me so." But comparative experience also suggests that judges involved in reviewing administrative action themselves become deeply involved in policy making. The court that scrutinizes reasons quickly becomes involved in substantive questions of administration. And this leads to the proverbial problem of "who guards the guardians" as bureaucratic discretion is traded for judicial discretion.[6] In this way, greater transparency involves a shift in policy-making authority within the government, from ministries to courts, and is not merely limited to providing reasons for citizens for greater accountability.

Of course, bureaucrats have many tools at their disposal for resisting judicial control. Once reasons are required, bureaucrats learn what reasons are acceptable to judges. Reasons themselves tend to coalesce around certain formulas that have been found to pass judicial scrutiny. Administrative practice becomes tailored to the requirements of judicially created administrative law. All this reflects a perhaps inevitable process of judicialization once reasons are required, but it is by no means clear that discretion can actually be eliminated.

Another related question is how tight a link judges will require between reasons given for administrative action and statutory language. A requirement of close connection between reasons given and explicitly delegated powers might lead bureaucrats not only to search for justifications in statutory language but ultimately to draft more detailed statutes so as to be able to protect themselves from judicial scrutiny. In such a circumstance, bureaucrats can say to judges "we had no discretion here and were just following the statutory commands." But in fact, those commands may have been planted in the law by the bureaucrats themselves. This further illustrates the difficulty of truly constraining bureaucratic discretion.

Giving reasons can also shape the process of public comments on regulatory rules. The story of how judges turned the "informal rule-making" provisions of the U.S. Administrative Procedures Act into an extensive and formal record-gathering process has been told elsewhere.[7] One aspect of this involved turning the notice and comment requirement into an enforced exchange, with reasons to be given by the bureaucracy for rejected comments. The Japanese Cabinet order requires such reasons, but without judicial reviewability, there is little potential for judicial scrutiny in this regard.

In conclusion, the fact that Japanese judicial scrutiny has focused on the "giving reasons" requirement at this early stage is not surprising. We do not know, of course, whether the two cases related to the APA described by Professor Uga will be a harbinger of things to come. But the potential bears watching, and, as I have suggested, some of the downstream effects may not have been contemplated by the drafters of these legal reforms. In particular, these cases might be a sign of a nascent judicialization of Japanese administration.

III. CHANGING DEMAND FROM THE PUBLIC?

Whether these new legal tools will be widely utilized by the public remains to be seen. Professor Uga is no doubt correct when he suggests that the bureaucrats' "culture of secrecy" will not be transformed overnight. But the very passage of these laws may change behavior, even if formal constraints on the bureaucracy are still limited. We must remember that laws can be expressive, meaning that they can be effective independent of the formal sanctions attached to their provisions.[8] From this perspective, the mere passage of a law signals a change in expectation to both regulators and regulated parties and can change behavior significantly. Professor Uga's emphasis on the symbolic value of including transparency in the purpose provisions of the APA seems to contemplate this kind of mechanism.

Another example is the APA's approach toward administrative guidance. With the exceptions of some slight formalization (e.g., the requirement that guidance be given in writing if requested), the APA mainly restated existing law. Existing law allowed firms to refuse to follow guidance, but few did so. If more firms begin to refuse to follow guidance, as did the "Internet" firm described in Professor Uga's chapter, the passage of the law may be effective in changing the power relations between government and governed simply by informing parties of their legal rights.

We have an indication of changing demand from the public in the number of requests for information disclosure in the first two years of the IDA's operation. These numbers are surprisingly high, though we do not yet know if they reflect many years of pent-up demand or will remain at a high level. By one estimate, roughly 80 percent of requests for information disclosure under the IDA have come from reporters. Some of the more prominent documents obtained under the IDA include minutes from the meeting of the Financial Rehabilitation Committee, details on *amakudari* appointments disclosed by the Cabinet office in 2001, and documents on the San Francisco Peace Treaty. Reporters were behind some of these prominent disclosure requests.

Of course, the lack of standing limitations in the IDA makes it a more likely tool of ensuring transparency than the APA, which is still subject to the limited framework of the still-unreformed Administrative Case Litigation Act. The early cases handed down on the IDA so far support this preliminary assessment that it will be a more effective mechanism for the public.

In December 2001, the Nagoya District Court rejected the Ministry of Economy, Trade and Industry's (METI) assertion that information on the planning for the 2005 World Expo fell within the "business information" exception under the IDA.[9] While this case is still on appeal, it shows that courts may be willing to closely scrutinize ministry claims of non-disclosability.

One other initiative mentioned in passing by Professor Uga, but which may also become important, is the E-Government initiative. In 2001, the Japanese government adopted an "E-Japan strategy" that aims to make all government-related transactions, such as registration, application, and procurement procedures, electronically available over the Internet. As a separate matter, some *shingikai* are now making available their meeting agendas and minutes over the Internet. Thus, information from the Japanese government is clearly becoming more accessible to the public, and there are signs that transparency is becoming not merely a slogan but a reality in Japan, at least for routine government matters. This can also contribute to changing expectations on behalf of the public, leading to demand for more effective and accountable government.

IV. CONCLUSION

The major shifts of the 1990s in Japanese administrative law will have important and perhaps unanticipated effects on Japanese governance for many years. Although the APA has been criticized by many (including this author) for not going far enough, creative judges may have a window for greater scrutiny of administration through the giving reasons requirement of Article 8.[10] Subsequent reforms, especially the IDA and the Cabinet order, have had more obvious and immediate impact, and revision of the Administrative Case Litigation Act will also be an important step, should it occur. All of these reforms will change the dynamics of relationships among the business community, the bureaucracy, the LDP, and the public and will create new pressures for reform or retrenchment of Japanese governance in the years ahead.

NOTES

1. These are described in Katsuya Uga, "Development of the Concepts of Transparency and Accountability in Japanese Administrative Law" (this volume).

2. On the other hand, in the case of the IDA, early data indicate that requests for information are not primarily drawn from businesses. This contrasts with the

U.S. Freedom of Information Act (FOIA), which has become primarily a tool for business.

3. The Management and Coordination Agency has subsequently been restructured into the Ministry of Public Management, Home Affairs and Posts and Telecommunications.

4. See APA Databook (2000).

5. See Martin Shapiro, "The Giving Reasons Requirement," *University of Chicago Legal Forum* 1992 (1992): 179, 179–220.

6. See Martin Shapiro, *Who Guards the Guardians? Judicial Control of Administration* (Athens: University of Georgia Press, 1988).

7. See generally Peter Schuck, ed., *Foundations of Administrative Law* (New York: Oxford University Press, 1994); and Christopher Edley, *Administrative Law: Rethinking Judicial Control of Bureaucracy* (New Haven, CT: Yale University Press, 1990).

8. Richard McAdams, "A Focal Point Theory of Expressive Law," *Virginia Law Review*, 86 (2000): 1649.

9. Nagoya Citizen Ombudsman v. METI (Nagoya Dist. Ct., Dec. 13, 2001), *Hanrei taimuzu* 1083 (2001): 310.

10. See also Tom Ginsburg, "Dismantling the 'Developmental State?' " *American Journal of Comparative Law* 49 (2001): 585, 602.

13 The Development of Criminal Law in Japan since 1961

KŌYA MATSUO

Japan is a nation of 380,000 square kilometers, with a population of 126 million. The criminal law endeavors to keep the society safer, cleaner, and more efficient. It touches many aspects of people's lives deeply. My task here is to describe the development of criminal law in Japan from 1961 until the present and, hopefully, try to foresee somewhat the future progress in the twenty-first century.

I. LEGISLATION

A. FAILURE OF THE FULL-SCALE REVISION OF THE PENAL CODE OF 1907

In the year 1961, the original Law in Japan conference coincided with the publication of the Preliminary Draft Revised Penal Code (*Kaisei keihō junbisōan*) by the government of Japan. It is firmly recognized in Japan that the criminal law must find its source in legislation.[1] Although an immense number of statutes establish crimes, the most basic among those statutes is the Penal Code.[2] Consequently, that code is always the center of attention for criminal lawyers.

As early as the 1920s, the government of Japan took the position that the Penal Code of 1907 was unsatisfactory and created a special commission to review that code. The commission worked for five years, from 1921 to 1926, and adopted a platform for revision of the Penal Code consisting of forty items. If we look back now, that proposal reflected a combination of ultraconservatism and modern penal philosophy. In 1927, a second commission undertook the task of drafting a penal code that would embody the principles set forth in that platform. After a number of years, that commission tentatively finished its work in 1940 when it produced the Provisional Draft of a Revised Penal Code (*Kaisei keihō karian*). But at that time the government was not able to afford the time and resources that would have been needed to continue the project.

Following the end of World War II in 1945, the drastic postwar law reform effort commenced. The new Constitution was promulgated in 1946. The new Code of Criminal Procedure and the new Juvenile Act were enacted in 1948. A number of criminal statutes were repealed. Yet, apart from a partial revision in 1947,[3] the Penal Code of 1907 remained the same as before.

In 1956, the government resumed preparing an overall revision of the Penal Code. The committee established for that purpose was composed of fifteen members, headed by eminent criminal law scholar Dr. Seiichirō Ono.[4] After five years of intensive efforts, the committee issued the aforementioned Preliminary Draft Revised Penal Code.[5] As the next step in the revision process, the minister of justice referred the matter officially to the Legislative Council (a more formal organ than the said committee). The Criminal Law Section of the council had approximately fifty senior members and as many junior members. The chairperson of that section was again Dr. Ono. Subcommittees were formed and those subcommittees met often to prepare the first draft.

It is to be noted that there were two trends in the council. One was inclined to stress the moralistic character of criminal law as well as the security of society. That view attached some importance to the achievements of the prewar commission for the revision of the Penal Code. The other was conscious of the significance of the new Constitution and tried to pay more attention to the liberty of the individual. According to the views of the latter group, the work done by the prewar commission should have been ignored.

The Legislative Council completed its work in 1974, when the Draft Revised Penal Code (*Kaisei keihō sōan*) was published. Generally speaking, that draft was unpopular. Dean Shigemitsu Dandō states that the draft was subjected to sharp criticism within scholarly circles and bar associations because of its conservative tendencies.[6] Although the proposals contained in the draft were not so dramatic, the draft was denounced as a code of more crimes and more penalties.[7] In the 1970s, the infiltration of the concept of decriminalization among Japanese criminal law scholars was conspicuous, and many of the scholars were skeptical about establishing new crimes. To make matters worse, there was another stumbling block, namely, the introduction of authorization for a commitment order for mentally disturbed criminals. The psychiatrists group strongly opposed this measure and the Japan Federation of Bar Associations supported the opposition movement. The Ministry of Justice and the Japan Federation of Bar Associations held a number of meetings to seek to reconcile their views, but the efforts were in vain. The bill based on the draft has never been introduced to the Diet.

B. PARTIAL REVISION OF THE PENAL CODE AND ADOPTION OF VARIOUS CRIMINAL STATUTES, 1960–89

1. *Developments, 1960–69*

Japan's rapid economic growth started in the 1960s. This growth made the whole nation wealthier, but at the same time it caused many problems to which criminal law is relevant. First, the rise of the price of land and houses invited wrongdoers to take possession of immovable property illegally. Commentators were divided over whether such wrongdoers could be prosecuted and punished for larceny under Article 235 of the Penal Code. To avoid any doubt in this regard, in 1960 Article 235-2 was added; that article provides that a person who wrongfully takes possession of immovable property of another shall be punished with *chōeki* (imprisonment with prescribed work) for up to ten years. A somewhat related provision, Article 262-2 (Destruction of Boundary), was added at the same time.

Kidnapping for ransom is rather rare in Japan, but it does occur. In 1964 it was felt that the existing provision on abduction was insufficient, and Article 225-2 on abduction for ransom was added. That article states that a person who kidnaps or abducts someone for the purpose of making a near relative or any other person concerned about the safety of the kidnapped or abducted person surrender any property shall be punished with *choēki* for life or for not less than three years.

In the 1960s, the motorization of Japan expanded rapidly. An inevitable result was a remarkable increase in traffic accidents. The number of traffic-related casualties stood at 82,880 in 1955, but rose more than twelvefold in just a decade, to nearly one million in 1965. The death toll rose from 6,379 to 16,765 in the same period. The government undertook strenuous efforts to improve the situation. Among the measures adopted was more severe punishment for traffic offenders. A person who failed to use such care as was required and thereby killed or injured another became subject to punishment with imprisonment for up to three years or a fine. In 1968, the maximum penalty was raised to five years' *chōeki*.

Various kinds of pollution also proved to be a serious problem for Japanese society. Among the many pollution cases, the worst case of water pollution occurred in Minamata, a city in Kumamoto Prefecture.[8] The first cases of Minamata disease, a disease that attacks the central nervous system, began to appear in the 1950s. But for many years there was a dispute over what caused the illness. In 1968, the government expressed the official view that wastewater from factories was responsible. This represented the first step to the solution of the tremendous difficulties in Minamata. As to air pollution, the Yokkaichi asthma case is representative. Yokkaichi City in Mie Prefecture was well known for its petrochemical complex. A number of people suffered from asthma; a group of plaintiffs filed suit in 1967, and in 1972 the district court affirmed the causal relationship between operations of the complex and the outbreak of asthma. Here again the government had to do its best to control the state of affairs. Among the many pieces of legislation dealing with pollution, one was related to criminal law. That is the statute of 1970 titled the Act of Environmental Pollution Offense concerning Human Health. That law establishes criminal penalties, with punishment for both intentional and negligent offenders.

2. *Developments, 1970–79*

In March of 1970, Japan was struck by hijackers for the first time in its history. Offenders who claimed to be members of the Red Army hijacked a Japan Airlines plane flying from Tokyo to Fukuoka and demanded the pilots go to North Korea. Eventually they succeeded to arrive at Pyongyang. (Recently it has been reported that most of the hijackers still live there.) After the incident the Diet quickly approved the Aircraft Protection Act and that act became effective in June 1970. In December of the same year, the Hague Treaty against illegal capture of aircraft was agreed on, and Japan signed and ratified that treaty in 1971. Through this experience, Japan became aware of the significance of international agreements in the field of criminal law as well as in connection with prevention of terrorist activity.

In 1976, the Lockheed scandal shocked Japan, especially because former prime minister Kakuei Tanaka was involved. He was indicted on the charge of having received 500 million yen in bribes from the Lockheed Aircraft Corporation in order to influence an airline in Japan to buy Lockheed jets. After a long seven-year trial, the Tokyo District Court found Tanaka guilty in 1983.[9]

In the meantime public opinion in Japan had become furious regarding corrupt behavior by public figures. The government had to take some action, and one of the measures taken soon after Tanaka's indictment was introduction of a bill to stiffen punishment for corruption. The maximum penalty for bribery provided by the Penal Code had been three years' *chōeki*, which could be raised to five years if aggravating circumstances existed. The bill proposed to alter these penalties to five years and seven years, respectively. The Diet was not so quick to act on the bill, but it ultimately was enacted in 1980. Five articles in the Penal Code related to bribery were amended to include the harsher penalty. The revision also had the effect of changing the statute of limitations. Considering that detection of bribery takes time and the prosecution is often barred by the statute of limitations, the prolongation of the period of time was important.

3. *Developments, 1980–89*

During the 1980–89 period, economic crimes emerged as a major problem.[10] To deal with one prominent type of economic crime, in 1981 a new provision was added to the Company Act to punish fixers of stockholders' meetings (*sōkaiya*). A director of a company who gives benefits to a fixer is also subject to punishment under the revised law. Although the prescribed maximum penalty was only six months' *chōeki*, the new law proved to be useful because a number of companies, including large corporations, were investigated and their directors were found guilty.

The need for consumer protection was also recognized as a serious matter.[11] Dishonest businesses were multiplying and an increasing number of unwitting persons were being exploited. The background for these developments was a rapid expansion of credit sales. It has been reported that the amount of credit sales more than tripled in just a decade, rising from 4,362 billion yen in 1973 to 13,587 billion yen in 1982. Troubles between credit companies and their customers occurred frequently. The Sales on the Installment Plan Act of 1961 was amended in 1984 in an effort to protect consumers more effectively. Criminal sanctions against crooked dealers were stiffened slightly, but the effect of this change was limited. Direct sales were also a cause of critical damage to helpless consumers. The Door-to-Door Sales Act of 1976 was also amended in 1984, mainly by way of extending the cooling-off period to seven days.

Reflecting the spread of technology, in 1987, new provisions on computer crimes were added to the Penal Code. This was accomplished by modifying the chapters on forgery of documents, obstruction of business, and fraud. A proposal to establish new crimes specifically related to computers, such as illegal access, was shelved. But the revision of the Penal Code without referring to the Draft Revised Penal Code was a significant step because it implied that the existence of the draft would not impede the reform of the Penal Code any longer.

In 1988, the Securities Exchange Act was revised and insider trading became punishable for the first time in Japan. At the time, the lack of awareness of illegality concerning such conduct was severely pointed out. The criminalizing of insider trading had a clear symbolic effect.

C. THE PENAL CODE OF 1907—OBSOLETE?

1. *The Problem of the Amount of Fines—Revision of 1991*

In 1989, the era of Japan changed from Shōwa to Heisei. It is only a coincidence, but almost at the same time the public attitude changed toward acceptance of revision of the Penal Code. The view that the Penal Code of 1907 was too old on several points to meet the present social conditions began to be voiced in discussions.

An initial obvious problem was that the amounts of fines prescribed by the Penal Code were absurd because those amounts were based on the economic situation at the start of the twentieth century. Negligent homicide, for example, carried a fine of up to one thousand yen under the Penal Code of 1907. The monetary value had fluctuated since then, and, particularly after 1945, sharp inflation had attacked Japan. As a reflection of the dramatic changes, in the 1930s 1 dollar was equivalent to 2 yen, but by the 1960s 1 dollar was equivalent to 360 yen. Since 1907, Laws for Temporary Measures concerning Fines had been enacted twice, and, as a result, the amount of fines was raised to two hundred times the face value set force in the Penal Code. These were stopgap measures, however. In 1991 at last, the Diet passed a law to revise the Penal Code completely as far as the amount of fines is concerned. The fine for negligent homicide, for example, is now set at up to five hundred thousand yen.

Other old criminal statutes, some as old as the Penal Code itself, involve the same problem concerning the amount of fines. As with the Penal Code prior to the 1991 amendment, the above-mentioned Laws for Temporary Measures have taken care of the problem to some extent. But it has been realized that modern statutes face another fundamental shortcoming, particularly when applied to corporations. If an employee of a corporation commits an offense in connection with the business of the corporation, the corporation itself is subject to punishment, as well as is the employee. In the event of a serious offense, the employee-defendant is likely to receive the penalty of *chōeki*, but for the corporation, the only form of punishment available is a fine. Yet the amount of fines for the corporation has been fixed at the same level as for the individual employee, and, especially in the case of a major corporation, the amount of fines was often ridiculously small.

Both the Ministry of Justice and the Fair Trade Commission undertook research on the level of fines, and in 1992 the Antimonopoly Act introduced a new provision to impose a maximum fine of 100 million yen in the case of a juristic person, in contrast to a maximum of 5 million yen in the case of an individual. Since that time, several other statutes have been amended in the same fashion. At present the Securities Exchange Act sets the amount of fines for juristic persons at 500 million yen, the Unfair Competition Act at 300 million yen, the Patent Act at 150 million yen, and so on. There has also been a trend toward increasing the amount of fines imposed on individual actors in the fields of financial crimes, drug crimes, and environmental crimes.

2. The Problem of Language—Revision of 1995

Japanese language changes rather quickly. The wording and style of statutes are no exception to this linguistic evolution. Before 1945, people wrote in literary style, utilizing classical wording, complicated characters and *katakana* (angular Japanese phonetic syllabary) for legal documents.[12] The Penal Code of 1907 was of course written in that manner. After 1945, however, the practice changed remarkably. New statutes and legal documents are now written in a modern style, using simple characters and *hiragana* (rounded Japanese phonetic syllabary). Since young people are completely accustomed to this modern style, they have much difficulty in reading old statutes. In addition to the problems of style and wording, the Penal Code contained more than fifty complicated characters now deemed obsolete.

All concerned felt that the situation had reached the limits of patience. A project to reform the language of the Penal Code commenced in 1990, and the resulting Act to Simplify the Penal Code was adopted in 1995. The basic principle of this reform was that the code was to be simplified only in terms of language without altering content. Five articles falling into two categories, however, were repealed. First, Article 40, which provided that "an act of a deaf-mute is not punishable or punishment therefore shall be reduced," was abolished. This article was clearly intended to benefit the deaf and mute. But the educational system for disabled persons has much improved since 1907, and the disabled themselves were calling for equal treatment in the application of penal sanctions. Second, controversial articles on extraordinary protection for ascendants were repealed. The representative provision was Article 200 on patricide. That article provided that a person who kills one of his or her own or his or her spouse's ascendants is to be punished with death or *chōeki* for life. In 1973, the Supreme Court, in *Aizawa v. Japan*,[13] declared this article unconstitutional because it violated the equal protection clause of the Constitution. Whereas punishments under Article 200 were limited to death or *chōeki* for life, the range of punishments available under Article 199, which is applicable to other cases of intentional killing, includes *chōeki* for not less than three years. Public opinion largely supported the decision of the Supreme Court, but the reasoning rendered by justices was not uniform. Some justices held that the basic principle of higher penalties for crimes against ascendants was valid but the disparity in minimum penalty between Article 200 and Article 199 was impermissible. Other justices concluded that the victim's status as a father or a mother should not be an aggravating factor at all. The Diet hesitated to delete Article 200 and it remained in the code, although it was never again used after the Supreme Court decision. In 1995, all four provisions of that sort were omitted.

Looking back on these two revisions, I believe that the Penal Code of 1907 was practically saved, after 1995, from the charge of being obsolete. Moreover, through the reforms of 1991 and 1995, a consensus was reached that the improvement of the Penal Code should be achieved by piecemeal reforms, instead of a single comprehensive revision.

D. LEGISLATION SINCE 1990—ANIMATING FORCES

1. *International Cooperation*

These days, criminal law cannot be isolated from international trends. The United Nations adopted the Convention against Illicit Traffic in Narcotic Drugs and Psychotropic Substances in 1988. Japan ratified that convention in 1992 and thereby committed itself to enacting a statute implementing the relevant standards. The new law punishes the crime of money laundering in connection with drug offenses, and permits controlled delivery for investigation of drug criminals. Both measures were alien to the traditional Japanese legal system; their adoption reflects the direct influence of international trends.

Soon the concerns of international society expanded to organized crime in general. The so-called Group of Seven (G7) summit conferences expressed worries about the growing threat posed by international organized crime. The government of Japan took the position that a new law was needed, and in 1999 the Diet passed the Act for Punishment of Organized Crime, Control of Crime Proceeds, and Other Matters. Among other matters, that act provides for enhanced punishment for offenses committed by organized crime and confiscation of proceeds.

On the same occasion, the Act concerning Interception of Communications for the Purpose of Criminal Investigation was adopted after a heated debate both in the Legislative Council and in the Diet. The new law permits wiretapping for investigation of drug offenses, firearm offenses, and organized homicide. Although there were already a few precedents in which courts had authorized wiretapping via judicial warrant, it was not easy for police officers to obtain such a warrant. As a matter of law, the situation has changed. But police forces are still circumspect in using the measure of wiretapping, even under the new law.[14]

Protection of children from sexual abuse is another matter of international concern. The Act on Child Prostitution and Child Pornography of 1999 punishes, with *chōeki* for up to three years or a fine, offenders who have sexually abused a child under eighteen for payment and those who have distributed or sold child pornography. These provisions also apply to Japanese nationals who commit such crimes outside the territory of Japan.

2. *The Threat of Terrorism*

On March 20, 1995, several persons belonging to the cult named Aum Shinrikyo carried out an attack on the Tokyo subways, using the nerve gas sarin, a deadly poison. Twelve people died and more than three thousand were injured; Japan had experienced massacre-type domestic terrorism for the first time. The government and the Diet took quick action. Just over a month later, a new statute, on the Control of Sarin, was promulgated on April 21. Another statute prohibiting the production and use of chemical weapons was also enacted, in accordance with the International Treaty on Chemical Weapons of 1993, which Japan subsequently ratified in 1997.

3. *Impact of Victims' Predicament*

There is a worldwide trend to pay more attention to victims of crime, and Japan is part of the same trend. In 2000, the Code of Criminal Procedure was revised in order to deal with injured persons and their relatives in a more appropriate manner. Major points of the legislation were protecting victims as vulnerable witnesses[15] and also offering them the chance to state their opinions in court. When a victim dies, his or her relatives are afforded the same opportunity to state their opinions in court. The view that the family of the deceased victim must be taken care of also had an impact on the reform of the Juvenile Act in 2000; pursuant to that reform, a juvenile offender older than sixteen years of age is now more likely to be sent to a criminal court if he or she intentionally killed another.

Based on the same principle of recognition of victims' rights, a new crime of causing death or injury as a result of extremely dangerous driving was established. Under the prior law, if an automobile driver killed or seriously injured another person owing to his or her driving under the strong influence of alcohol, the offender was subject to punishment with *chōeki* of up to five years. But bereaved families who had lost their beloved husband, wife, or children were not at all satisfied with that sentence. Families of traffic accident victims began to protest, and their voice became louder and louder. Spurred by this outcry, the government reexamined the situation and concluded that extremely dangerous driving is tantamount to using violence against another. As a consequence, a new provision added to the Penal Code in 2001 punishes extremely dangerous driving with *chōeki* for up to ten years in the event of injury and for not less than one year nor more than fifteen years in the event of the death of a victim.

4. *Diffusion of Computers*

Society has become highly information oriented and computers are used everywhere. That has led to a need for information to be protected more carefully. The above-mentioned revision of the Penal Code in 1987 was insufficient. In 1999, the Act on the Prohibition of Illegal Access was adopted. Under this act, a person who commits the offense of illegal access is to be punished with *chōeki* for up to one year or a fine of up to five hundred thousand yen.

II. COURTS' AND PROSECUTORS' DECISIONS

Section I examined the development of criminal legislation: in other words, law in books. Law in action, to which I now turn, is largely dependent on judgments rendered by courts and decisions made by prosecutors.

1. *Nulla poena sine lege*

I am afraid section I, by concentrating on a description of criminal legislation, may have given the impression that the legislative organs always have been active in enacting and reforming penal statutes. That is not the truth by any means. Legislative activity was stagnant as far as the revision of the Penal Code was concerned, especially during the period from 1961 through 1986. New types of misconduct occasionally appeared but discussions on criminalizing such misconduct and amending the Penal Code were shelved. When a prosecutor dared to indict in such a case, judges had to endeavor to find the appropriate boundary line within which to permit flexible or extensive construction of law, bearing in mind that the principle of legality (*nulla poena sine lege*) forbids the application of penal provisions by analogy.

A typical example is the forgery of documents by means of photocopier. The leading case in this connection is a Supreme Court decision rendered in 1976.[16] The defendant sought to make a forged copy of a receipt for deposit money. He attached a form with a false statement to a part of an authenticated form and then photocopied it. He uttered this paper and was indicted for forgery of an official document as well as for uttering a forged document. The trial court and the appeals court held that the defendant produced only a copy, not an original document, and refused to convict the defendant. But the Supreme Court declared that a photocopy is a duplicate with complete accuracy and is usually trusted to the same extent as the original document. The defendant was eventually convicted. Opinions of commentators on this precedent were divided, and subsequent Supreme Court decisions involving similar cases were often accompanied by dissenting opinions.[17]

2. *Constitutional Limitations*

Article 81 of the Constitution states that the Supreme Court is the court of last resort with power to determine the constitutionality of any law, order, regulation, or official act. In keeping with this recognition of the important power of the Supreme Court, the Code of Criminal Procedure provides that an appeal to the Supreme Court is to be accepted for review when an appellant alleges violation of the Constitution. In practice, many appellants allege constitutional violations, but their challenges are seldom successful. In the field of criminal law, *Japan v. Aizawa*, discussed in section I.C.2. above, is the only case where a provision in the Penal Code had been squarely declared unconstitutional.

It can be pointed out that government bills are always examined carefully with respect to their constitutional validity before being submitted to the Diet. For that reason, constitutional disputes of importance rarely occur concerning laws. The situation is slightly different with regard to local ordinances, which sometimes implicate constitutional issues. In *Shigeto v. Japan*,[18] for example, the defendant was indicted under the Fukuoka Ordinance for the Protection of Juveniles, which prohibits acts of debauchery and obscenity. The male defendant had sexual intercourse with a girl under eighteen years of age. The Kokura Summary Court convicted him and imposed a fine of fifty thousand yen, and the Fukuoka High Court affirmed. The defendant appealed to the Supreme Court, asserting that the concept of debauchery is too broad to be constitutionally valid. Twelve justices of the Supreme Court rejected the assertion, with two concurring opinions, but three justices filed dissenting opinions. The majority restricted the act of debauchery to conduct in which the offender abuses a juvenile victim and, as so interpreted, held the ordinance constitutional.

B. PROSECUTORS' DECISIONS

1. *Discretionary Prosecution*

Public prosecutors are granted wide discretion with regard to the bringing of formal charges. The Code of Criminal Procedure expressly states that prosecution may be suspended if it is deemed unnecessary after considering the character, age, and situation of the offender; the gravity of the offense; the circumstances under which the offense was committed; and the conditions subsequent to the commission of the offense (Article 248). In the year 2000, whereas public prosecutors indicted 122,805 persons for trial and requested conviction of 912,377 persons by summary order (to be explained below), they gave 842,106 persons the benefit of the suspension of prosecution. Consequently, the ratio of suspension was 44.9 percent.

It must be noted that individual prosecutors usually follow implicit standards gradually formulated by decisions of their senior colleagues. For difficult cases a prosecutor would consult with his or her superior and try to obtain approval for any disposition. As a result, the unwritten guidelines work well and disparity of decisions is almost completely avoided.

Exceptionally it occurs that a guideline is clearly changed. A rather astonishing example was the alteration of the standard for handling traffic accidents that result in minor injury. Before 1986, a person who negligently injured another while driving a car used to be formally charged. The ratio of suspension of prosecution in such cases was as low as 23 percent. But after 1987 the figure rose markedly, and in 2000 the ratio of suspension reached 88 percent. The public prosecutors' office explained the grounds for this radical change as follows:[19] (1) In this era of automobiles it is not appropriate to punish so many people for minor injury cases; (2) the insurance system has spread and damage is usually well covered; (3) prevention of traffic accidents should depend not solely on criminal sanctions but also on administrative measures; and (4) for minor injury cases the sentence usually has been a small fine, which has very little practical impact in any event. Fifteen years later, this policy statement was formalized by legislation. The 2001 revision of the Penal Code provided that, if the injury caused by a negligent driver is slight, the punishment may be remitted in the light of the circumstances (Article 211, paragraph 2). This is effectively a sort of decriminalization, and public prosecutors suspending prosecution of such offenders now have legal justification for doing so.

In addition to the power of deciding whether or not to prosecute, public prosecutors enjoy another form of discretion when the offense to be charged is punishable with a fine not exceeding fifty thousand yen. In such cases, summary procedure is available provided that the defendant has no objection. In this simple procedure a summary order is issued designating the amount of fine not exceeding half a million yen. If the defendant obeys the order, the whole procedure quickly comes to an end. Each year, the number of defendants who receive summary orders is nearly ten times the number of defendants who are indicted for trial and processed according to ordinary procedures.

2. *Quasi Desuetude and Infrequently Used Statutes*

Public prosecutors use some criminal statutes infrequently and some practically never. Various examples of the latter may be found in the Penal Code. Chapter 14 establishes crimes relating to smoking opium. Those provisions played an important role in the old days. However, many other drug laws are now in operation and Chapter 14 is obsolete. The Draft Revised Code of 1974 proposed to abolish this chapter but it still remains in the present Penal Code. Similarly, Chapter 29 is devoted to crimes of abortion. They were also deemed essential provisions for many years. But the Eugenic Protection Act of 1948, which legalized abortion to a considerable extent, has changed the situation dramatically. Since 1975 there have been very few reports of prosecution for the crime of abortion.

Among the many infrequently used criminal statutes, the Antimonopoly Act is especially worthy of note. That act was enacted in 1947 under the influence of the U.S. Antitrust Act. Illegal monopoly and unfair competition are subject to penal sanctions. But these crimes are to be prosecuted only on complaint by the Fair Trade Commission (FTC) of Japan. The commission was very circumspect about filing complaints, and almost no complaints were made before 1990. In 1990, however, the FTC officially announced a change in policy concerning complaints. Between 1991 and 2000, complaints were filed in ten cases. It is hoped that the commission will become even more active in the future and will cooperate with public prosecutors with respect to antimonopoly violations.

3. *Quantum of Proof for Prosecution and the Conviction Rate*

Public prosecutors in Japan are expected to file formal charges only if they are convinced of the guilt of the defendant. Needless to say, their belief of guilt must be supported by evidence. Therefore prosecutors endeavor to collect evidence strong enough to guarantee proof beyond a reasonable doubt. As a result, it is rare for a defendant to obtain an acquittal. Each year the conviction rate is higher than 99 percent. In 2000, only 71 defendants out of 77,933 were found not guilty, totally or partially, by district courts and summary courts.

This practice is perhaps unique to Japan. At the original Law in Japan conference this practice was discussed earnestly with evaluations split pro and con. Since then we have had some debate within Japan on this issue. Although a few commentators criticize the present practice and argue that prosecutors should undertake prosecutions more actively, bringing indictments in more borderline cases, many lawyers, including most defense attorneys, support the circumspect attitude of public prosecutors. The latter school of thought stresses that being indicted itself often causes serious damage to an accused.

Article 40 of the Constitution of Japan seems to support the current practice indirectly. It states that any person who is acquitted after being arrested or detained may sue the state for redress as provided by law. Its implied message is that state officials engaged in criminal investigation and prosecution should avoid indicting innocent persons. Incidentally, a defendant who is acquitted can claim 12,500 yen per day as redress for his or her detention.

C. COURTS' DECISIONS ON SENTENCING

Judges have considerable discretion in sentencing. The Penal Code of Japan prescribes a wide range of penalties for many crimes. For example, intentional homicide of all types is to be punished with death, or *chōeki* for life, or *chōeki* for not less than three years, and larceny is to be punished with *chōeki* for not less than one month and not more than ten years. It is the judges' responsibility to fix the proper sentence, avoiding the evil of disparity, and without the benefit of a presentence report.

At the original Law in Japan conference, the lenient attitude of Japanese judges was emphasized.[20] Within the range of prescribed penalties, Japanese courts tend to impose rather short sentences. Moreover, execution of the sentence is often suspended. The ratio of suspended sentences was 52.4 percent in 1963. That trend continued and the ratio stood at 64.8 percent in 2000. The number of prisoners actually sent to correctional institutions was 37,285 in 1961. Notwithstanding a population increase of over 30 percent, that number dropped to 24,496 (including 4,349 foreigners) as of 1999.

Of late, however, the situation has been slightly changing. Some defendants are sentenced to heavier terms than before and stay in prison longer. In 1961, only 2.7 percent of new prisoners were under a sentence of longer than five years' imprisonment, but in 1999 that proportion had risen to 4.6 percent. It is not easy to explain what caused this change, but the growing concern for the suffering of victims is certainly a relevant factor. The new law on dangerous driving, discussed in section I.D.3. above, accelerated the change. At the original Law in Japan conference a case was described in which the defendant, heavily intoxicated, drove a car at tremendous speed at night and killed one person and seriously injured two others. He was sentenced to imprisonment for eight months. The reporter stated that the defendant would have incurred a far heavier penalty if the case had been tried in the United States.[21] In Japan today the sentence for such a case is likely to be the same as in the United States.

III. PROSPECTS FOR THE FUTURE

A. CRIMES

Since crimes and criminal sanctions are regulated absolutely by statutes, I examined the development of legislation in section I. At the end of that section, I observed that recent criminal legislation is promoted by needs for international cooperation, growing threats of terrorism, strong concern for victims, and the rapid diffusion of computers. If a single key word for recent trends is to be sought, that word would be *globalization*. Terrorism inevitably demands international cooperation, and concern for victims and diffusion of computers are recognized everywhere in the world. Formerly criminal law was deemed fairly local by nature, compared to other laws, particularly commercial law. Now the character has changed to some extent. The tendency to establish new criminal laws focusing on the trend of globalization will continue in the twenty-first century.

It is evident that the United States is the leading figure in globalization. Each country, however, has its own culture built up through history. If I were to offer an example from the field of criminal procedure, use—or nonuse—of wiretapping may be a remarkable instance to show differences between the United States and Japan. As mentioned earlier (section I.D.1.), the Act concerning Interception of Communications for the Purpose of Criminal Investigation was adopted in Japan in 1999. In the legislative debate, many materials on wiretapping practice in the United States and Europe were introduced and the understanding was shared that, good or bad, every developed country is dependent on wiretapping as an investigative measure. Based in part on that understanding, the new law was enacted and came into force in August 2000. As of the end of 2002, however, only two cases had been reported in which wiretapping was actually conducted.[22]

Another example is the penetration—or slow penetration—of the *Miranda* rules. Article 38 of the Constitution of Japan provides that no person shall be compelled to testify against himself. The Code of Criminal Procedure states that a suspect is to be notified before interrogation of the right to silence and that the accused can retain counsel at any time. But the accused cannot request a lawyer to be appointed by the state on the ground of poverty (at the suspect stage) before being charged formally (the defendant stage). There have been heated discussions on introducing the public defense system for suspects. In its recommendations, issued in June 2001, the Justice System Reform Council called for establishment of such a system; it is likely that in a few years' time indigent suspects will be entitled to appointed counsel, as the U.S. Supreme Court called for in its *Miranda* decision. I should add that the right to be accompanied by a lawyer during interrogation, which is another principle set forth in *Miranda*, is another matter. Police officers and public prosecutors usually attach great importance to the person-to-person talk with a suspect, and they are hesitant to allow counsel to attend interrogations.

B. PENALTIES

In contrast to "crimes," there has been little reform of "penalties" since 1961 except for those relating to financial punishment. As discussed earlier, the amount of fines for some offenses was raised and confiscation of crime proceeds was expanded. But the major provisions of the Penal Code concerning penalties have been unchanged since 1907. The code simply states that the principal penalties are death, *chōeki*, *kinko* (imprisonment without prescribed work), fine, penal detention, and minor fine, confiscation being an additional penalty. A thorough reexamination of penalties is overdue; a great deal of research must be done with respect to penalties in the near future. Some of the important issues are discussed below.

1. *Death Penalty*

The biggest issue with regard to punishment is whether to retain or to abolish capital punishment. According to public opinion polls, a majority of the Japanese people seems to be in favor of retaining the death penalty as far as the most vicious crimes are concerned. The government reflects this attitude and is reluctant to abolish it immediately. Japan has been a member state of the International Covenant on Civil and Political Rights since 1979, but it has not signed the Second Optional Protocol to the International Covenant on Civil and Political Rights, Aimed at the Abolition of the Death Penalty (CCPR-OP2-DP).

A trend toward abolition of the death penalty, however, is discernible. The most important move in this regard was the formation in 1994 by some Diet members of the League to Promote Abolition of Capital Punishment, a nonpartisan group including influential politicians. Then, in 2000, the three parties in the ruling coalition started a project team on life confinement without parole, a system that is indirectly related to abolition of the death penalty. Among criminal law scholars, Dean Shigemitsu Dandō is the most influential advocate of abolition.[23] Although Dean Dandō has buttressed his views in part by reference to his own experiences as justice of the Japanese Supreme Court, the response of the judicial branch has been modest so far. The Supreme Court upheld the constitutionality of capital punishment in 1993, citing its own decision of forty-five years earlier, and, while lower court judges are always prudent in the assessment of capital punishment, they continue to sentence convicted defendants to death in exceptional cases.

2. Imprisonment

The most vexing subject in the area of punishment is the revision of the Prison Act of 1908. That act is largely obsolete, and prison practice has been improved greatly pursuant to administrative ordinances. The government proposed a full-scale reform of the Prison Act and produced a bill for a new Criminal Institution Act in 1982. But the Diet did not pass the bill, mainly owing to a vigorous dispute over police detention of suspects. This was rather a collateral issue but the opposition was too severe for the Diet to ratify the bill. It is hoped that the ongoing gap between the law and practice in this area can be bridged as soon as possible.

The punishment of incarceration consists of three forms: *chōeki*, *kinko*, and *kōryū*. *Chōeki* signifies confinement in prison with prescribed work; *kinko* signifies confinement in prison without prescribed work; and *kōryū* signifies confinement in a house of detention for less than thirty days. *Kōryū* is used very infrequently and has small importance. *Kinko* is imposed on offenders who have committed crimes of negligence or crimes with political motives. Such offenders were deemed to deserve treatment in prison different from that of other infamous criminals. Most of the convicts sentenced to *kinko*, however, petition to engage in the prescribed work, and practically there is little difference between *chōeki* and *kinko*. In the 1970s integration of these two forms of confinement was advocated. But traffic accidents increased rapidly at that time, and the significance of retaining *kinko*, as a special form of incarceration for negligent offenders, was recognized and the argument for "integration" faded away.

Short-term confinement is often criticized on the ground that several months in prison is too short to rectify a person but long enough to deprave him or her. But in Japan that sort of evil is not readily apparent. In 2000, 9,261 defendants were sentenced to *chōeki* or *kinko* of less than six months, but execution of the sentence was suspended for 80 percent of them. Safety and order in prisons, generally speaking, are well maintained. There has been no escape since 1997. Prison work is conducted regularly and effectively. Some prisoners enjoy the opportunity for vocational training or community service.

3. Financial Penalties

The Penal Code recognizes two forms of financial penalties—fines and minor fines. The minor fine, which is set at less than ten thousand yen, is rather useless as punishment and the number of convicts who receive a minor fine is very small. By contrast, fines are very widely utilized, mainly in the summary procedure. In 2000, 911,760 defendants were sentenced to fines. Of these, only 1,053 came through ordinary criminal trial and all others through summary procedure. The amount of fines is rather moderate; in 2000, only 225 defendants were sentenced to fines of more than 1 million yen.

It has been realized that the present system of financial penalties needs reexamination. As early as 1993, the subcommittee of the Legislative Council sent the minister of justice a report titled "Essential Problems of Financial Penalties." That report discussed a number of items, such as introducing daily fines, prescribing financial penalties for crimes against public officials on duty, establishing new types of sanctions such as community service, and so on. Opinions of subcommittee members were divided, and the Legislative Council will take over the task of reexamining financial penalties in the near future.

4. *Miscellaneous*

Japanese criminal law has paid a limited amount of attention to corporate crimes. Corporations are punished only when the statute expands the criminal sanction to a juridical person in connection with the criminal act of its employee. The form of sanction for corporations is exclusively fines and nothing else. Probably Japan has to learn much from the United States in this regard.

Another feature of the Japanese legal system is a rigid distinction between criminal cases and civil cases. Owing to this distinction, the Japanese legal system is inhospitable to such ideas as punitive damages rendered in civil court.[24] But the growing concern for victims may change the situation because the effective combination of criminal sanctions and civil remedies is deemed desirable to some extent.

Apart from punishment, medical care should be provided for mentally disabled persons who commit serious crimes. As mentioned earlier, the proposal of adding a commitment measure to the Penal Code was not accepted in the 1970s. At the time of writing, a bill on compulsory hospitalization by court order was under consideration by the Diet. The court for such cases was to be composed of a judge and a psychiatrist.

IV. CONCLUDING REMARKS

In closing, I would like to add a few words concerning the similarities and differences between Japan and the United States in the field of criminal law.

Fifty years ago, soon after the new Code of Criminal Procedure was adopted in Japan, some lawyers asserted that it introduced a discrepancy between penal law and criminal procedure because the former, received from the European Continent, remained unchanged while the latter was revised in an Anglo-American style. They also predicted that the conviction rate would drop significantly under the new procedure.

In the intervening years, the worry over discrepancy disappeared, and, far from falling, the conviction rate rose to over 99.9 percent. The administration of criminal procedure, which heavily relies on close investigation conducted by both police officials and public prosecutors, has attained this result. I have coined the term *minute justice* to express the trait of the present Japanese criminal procedure. It is effective, truth oriented, but costly and sometimes coercive. In any event, it is rather different from criminal procedure in the United States.[25]

In contrast, the substantive criminal laws in the two nations are largely similar. Particularly since the Model Penal Code was promulgated in the United States in 1962, we can compare the penal codes of both countries without much difficulty, and we can find many aspects that are substantially in common[26] (although technicalities in codification differ[27]). The lingering question is whether the differences in criminal procedure will diminish or not. My prediction is that Japan will gradually approach the United States on many points, but the basic differences will remain.[28]

NOTES

1. See Shigemitsu Dandō, *The Criminal Law of Japan: The General Part*, trans. B. J. George (Littleton, CO: F. B. Rothman, 1997), 33.

2. Keihō [Penal Code], Act No. 45 of 1907. Keihō is also often translated as Criminal Code. See Hiroshi Oda, *Japanese Law*, 2nd ed. (New York: Oxford University Press, 1999), 413.

3. The 1947 revision reflected the mandates of the new Constitution.

4. Dr. Ono (1891–1986) was a professor of criminal law and procedure at the University of Tokyo and for many years remained a key person in the efforts for revision of the Penal Code.

5. The Preliminary Draft and commentary were published in English. See B. J. George, ed., *A Preparatory Draft for the Revised Penal Code of Japan, 1961* (South Hackensack, NJ: F. B. Rothman, 1964).

6. See Dandō, *The Criminal Law of Japan*, xiv.

7. In contrast to the Penal Code of 1907, which ended with Article 264, the

draft contained 369 articles. The special part was responsible for about half the increase in the number of articles.

8. See Kōichirō Fujikura, "Litigation, Administrative Relief, and Political Settlement for Pollution Victim Compensation: Minamata Mercury Poisoning after Fifty Years" (this volume); David T. Johnson, *The Japanese Way of Justice: Prosecuting Crime in Japan* (New York: Oxford University Press, 2002), 63.

9. Japan v. Tanaka et al. (Tokyo Dist. Ct., Oct. 12, 1983), *Hanrei jihō* 1103 (1984):15. Many issues were contested in the trial, particularly the scope of the authority of the prime minister and the legitimacy of granting immunity to witnesses.

10. Economic offenses continue to be a matter of vital importance to this day. Reflecting the continued importance, the White Paper on Crime 2000 included a featured segment titled "Economic Offenses: Current Conditions and Countermeasures."

11. During this same period, it was pointed out in England that criminal legislation was effective for consumer protection. See Sir Gordon Borrie, *The Development of Consumer Law and Policy: Bold Spirits and Timorous Souls* (London: Stevens and Sons, 1984), 45.

12. For a brief introduction to the Japanese language, with reference to the legal system, see Hideo Tanaka, ed., *The Japanese Legal System: Introductory Cases and Materials* (Tokyo: University of Tokyo Press, 1976), 25.

13. Aizawa v. Japan (Sup. Ct., Grand Bench, Apr. 4, 1973), *Keishū* 27 (1973): 265. This case involved an egregious pattern of child abuse, in which a father repeatedly raped his own daughter over a period of years. The daughter eventually killed him. Despite the extenuating circumstances, under Article 200 the daughter would have faced a sentence of either death or *chōeki* for life.

14. The situation with regard to wiretapping is discussed further in section III.A. below.

15. Under the law, such witnesses may testify behind a curtain or via two-way closed circuit television.

16. Japan v. Watanabe (Sup. Ct., Apr. 30, 1976), *Keishū* 30 (1976): 453.

17. For example, Justice Shimatani filed a dissenting opinion in Sasahara v. Japan (Sup. Ct., June 27, 1986), *Keishū* 40 (1986): 340.

18. Shigeto v. Japan (Sup. Ct., Grand Bench, Oct. 23, 1985), *Keishū* 39 (1985): 413.

19. Government of Japan, *Summary of the White Paper on Crime 1993* (Tokyo: Research and Training Institute of the Ministry of Justice, 1993), 26.

20. See Haruo Abe, "The Accused and Society: Therapeutic and Preventive Aspects of Criminal Justice in Japan," in Arthur Taylor von Mehren, ed., *Law in Japan: The Legal Order in a Changing Society* (Cambridge, MA: Harvard University Press, 1963), 324.

21. See ibid., 331 n. 24.

22. In May 2002, the Tokyo Metropolitan Police Department announced that it intercepted one or more telephone conversations concerning a drug offense in January of that year and arrested three suspects. It was later reported that in another case in late 2002, one or more telephone conversations concerning a drug offense were intercepted and four suspects were arrested.

23. See, e.g., Shigemitsu Dandō, "Toward the Abolition of the Death Penalty," *Indiana Law Journal* 72 (1996): 7.

24. See, e.g., Dan Fenno Henderson, "Comparative Law in the Japanese Courts: Punitive Damages," *Law in Japan: An Annual* 24 (1991): 98. On an appeal of the case analyzed in Professor Henderson's article, the Supreme Court of Japan rendered a decision in 1997 rejecting the enforcement of punitive damages approved by the court of appeals in California.

25. See Daniel H. Foote, "The Benevolent Paternalism of Japanese Criminal Justice," *California Law Review* 80 (1992): 317.

26. On the significance of the promulgation of the Model Penal Code, see Sanford H. Kadish, "Fifty Years of Criminal Law: An Opinionated View," *California Law Review* 87 (1999): 943.

27. See Paul H. Robinson, Michael T. Cahill, and Usman Mohammad, "The Five Worst (and Five Best) American Criminal Codes," *Northwestern University Law Review* 95 (2000): 1. If Professor Robinson and his coauthors were to evaluate the Penal Code of Japan, they would not give it a high score because of such problems as the lack of comprehensiveness and the use of legal terms without providing definitions.

28. See Daniel H. Foote, "Confessions and the Right to Silence in Japan," *Georgia Journal of International and Comparative Law* 21 (1991): 415; Kōya Matsuo, *Keijisoshōhō* [Treatise on Japanese Criminal Procedure], new ed. (Tokyo: Kōbundō, 1999), 1:136.

14 Globalization and Japanese Criminal Law

JOSEPH L. HOFFMANN

I. INTRODUCTION

More than four decades after the conference that led to the publication of *Law in Japan: The Legal Order in a Changing Society,* it is certainly a most opportune time to examine the recent evolution of Japanese criminal law and also to speculate about the future. I am deeply honored to have the opportunity, in this chapter, to do a little bit of both.

Professor Kōya Matsuo's wonderful chapter in this book, "The Development of Criminal Law in Japan since 1961," has already outlined the key changes in Japanese criminal law over the past four decades, and he has also presented a thoughtful and insightful analysis of those changes. I propose to focus my attention and comments on a few of the specific aspects of those changes and to discuss those particular aspects within the larger context of globalization.

First, however, I would like to define the term *globalization*, which is used so often nowadays but not always in the same way. In this chapter, I will use the term *globalization* to describe the processes by which global forces affect, and are in turn affected by, events and changes that occur at the national, subnational, and local levels.

I would like especially to distinguish the term *global* from the related term *international*. As I will use it, the term *global* is broader than the term *international*. In the context of law, for example, the phrase *international law* usually refers to legal doctrines arising out of treaties or other similar bilateral or multilateral agreements between nation-states; customary law arising out of the consistent behavior of those nation-states over time; and supranational institutions, such as the United Nations, that have been created in large part to further the development and enforcement of such "international law."

The term *global*, as I will use it, certainly includes "international." But it also includes much more. Again, to use the example of the context of law, the term *global* might refer to changes in a particular nation-state's domestic laws that are produced by global economic, social, cultural, or legal forces. Or the term *global* might refer to the consequences of events occurring in one particular nation-state on the domestic laws of other nation-states, or on the traditional doctrines of "international law." And the term *global* would also include the legal implications of the rise of such "global" nongovernmental organizations (NGOs) and institutions as multinational corporations, international NGOs, and even worldwide criminal organizations.

Used in this broad sense, the most significant development in Japanese society over the past four decades undoubtedly has been the dramatic and ongoing impact of globalization. During this period, Japan has transformed itself from a recovering nation, still emerging from the ravages of war, into a true global power. In the process, Japan has substantially opened itself up to the larger world—at least by comparison to most of earlier Japanese history—and, at the same time, has left its own indelible marks on that larger world.

Globalization has played a key role in the evolution of Japanese criminal law and seems likely to continue to do so in the future. Three different kinds of globalization have significantly affected, and in some instances have been affected by, recent developments in Japanese criminal law. These three kinds of globalization are (1) economic globalization, (2) social and cultural globalization, and (3) the globalization of law itself. I will now discuss each of these three kinds of globalization in turn.

II. ECONOMIC GLOBALIZATION

One area in which Japanese criminal law has changed significantly as a result of globalization is the area of economic crime. Within the past ten years alone, Japan has enacted new and tougher criminal laws to address organized crime, money laundering, international drug trafficking, and computer crime. Each of these domestic legal changes was related, at least in some way, to the fact that the global economy has made it much easier for criminals to engage in illegal activity without regard to national borders and boundaries.

Today, money, drugs, guns, valuable information, and even people can be moved from place to place around the world with lightning speed. This has required all nation-states not only to improve dramatically their own domestic criminal laws and law-enforcement methods but also to work together to investigate and prosecute such crimes around the world. Japan has been at the forefront of this kind of international cooperation.

For example, in 1992, Japan ratified the U.N. Convention against Illicit Traffic in Narcotic Drugs and Psychotropic Substances, which led directly to the enactment of new Japanese criminal laws prohibiting certain drug crimes as well as money laundering. Similarly, in March of 1996, the first Asia/Pacific Operational Drug Enforcement Conference, attended by representatives of nineteen countries as well as the U.N. Drug Control Program, was sponsored in Tokyo by the National Police Agency. These examples show how the continuing globalization of crime, which is simply one form of economic globalization, has caused Japan to make major changes in its domestic criminal laws and also to work more closely with other nation-states to combat such global crimes.

But globalization can be a double-edged sword. For instance, in the area of organized crime, recent changes in Japanese criminal law may have had the unintended effect of actually speeding up the globalization of crime. For many years, Japanese society seemed to be relatively tolerant with respect to certain kinds of crimes traditionally committed by domestic organized criminals, or *bōryokudan*. In fact, Professors Curtis Milhaupt and Mark West have argued that such criminals in Japan prospered because they performed many useful services that were otherwise difficult to obtain through legitimate means, such as settling civil disputes, collecting debts, facilitating land transactions, and obtaining negative information from and about large corporations.

In 1991, Japan cracked down on domestic criminal organizations by enacting the Bōryokudan Countermeasures Act. This law allowed the government to identify certain organizations as "designated *bōryokudan*," which in turn allowed police and prosecutors to intervene much more aggressively to prevent many kinds of traditional fund-raising activities by such organizations. The primary motivation for this change in Japanese criminal law undoubtedly was the desire to combat the corrupting influence of organized crime on various aspects of Japanese society, as well as the fact that, during a period of severe economic recession, organized crime could no longer be so easily tolerated as it had been before.

In the years immediately after the Bōryokudan Countermeasures Act became effective, however, there were disturbing reports that Japanese organized crime groups were forming closer relationships with similar criminal organizations in other countries. Moreover, an increasing number of violent crimes in Japan, including murders, suddenly were being committed by mentally unstable persons who had obtained guns, allegedly by buying them from *bōryokudan* in at least some instances.

The problem, it seems, is that because *bōryokudan* no longer could obtain funds through their traditional illegitimate means, they were forced to begin to look elsewhere—including to the established international business of trafficking in drugs and guns. The domestic crackdown on Japanese organized crime groups, in other words, may have effectively compelled such groups to become assimilated more fully into the global criminal economy. At the same time, organized crime groups from outside Japan, including from South Korea, Nigeria, Hong Kong, and elsewhere, continued to increase their activities within Japan, with or without the cooperation of domestic organized crime groups. These developments led the Diet to enact, in 1999, the new Act for Punishment of Organized Crimes, Control of Crime Proceeds, and Other Matters, which substantially toughened the punishment for various organized crimes.

In the future, it seems inevitable that economic globalization will continue to break down the traditional geographical barriers that have protected individual nation-states from the harm caused by criminals in other countries. No nation-state can afford to opt out entirely from the process of economic globalization; economic isolationism would mean missing out on the many benefits of worldwide free trade, thus leading quickly to relative national impoverishment. But whenever a nation-state makes itself more available for free trade, it simultaneously makes itself more vulnerable to global economic crimes.

The long-term solution to this dilemma may lie in the direction of even more significant forms of international cooperation than we have seen in the recent past. For example, just as most nation-states (but not the United States) have recently joined together in the formation of the new International War Crimes Tribunal, it is foreseeable that we may someday witness the creation of an International Court for Economic Crimes, which would serve to adjudicate alleged violations of international norms of behavior in the economic realm. The same thing might happen for drug crimes, gun smuggling, and computer crimes. Perhaps even more controversial, but also foreseeable, would be the development of full-fledged international police forces, with authorization to operate without regard to national borders, and charged with the mission to investigate global crimes and to apprehend those persons responsible for committing them.

III. SOCIAL AND CULTURAL GLOBALIZATION

Turning to the realm of social and cultural globalization, we find additional strong evidence of the effects of globalization on Japanese criminal law. Over the past four decades, Japan has made the transition from an almost completely homogeneous society to one that now includes numerous persons of foreign descent. This is an important aspect of globalization. The massive migration of persons around the globe—often motivated primarily by the sincere desire of migrants to work and thereby achieve a higher standard of living, a desire generally supported by multinational corporations that benefit from a free (and thus relatively cheap) labor market—has begun to transform the very nature of many traditional societies. Japan is especially sensitive to this kind of transformation, precisely because it was one of the most isolated countries in the world for an extended period of several hundred years.

The slowly but steadily increasing diversity of Japanese society has engendered societal concern, which is perhaps overstated but nevertheless real, about crimes committed in Japan by foreigners. To be sure, there is some data to support this concern. From 1986 to 1995, for example, the number of crimes cleared by the police and found to have been committed by foreigners in Japan increased from 2,537 to 17,213, although the total number of foreign visitors in Japan during the same period did not even double. And violent crimes by foreigners increased from 94 cases in 1986 to 247 cases in 1995.

At the same time, it must be noted that even in 1995, the number of foreign visitors arrested for crimes in Japan represented only a tiny fraction—only 2.2 percent—of the total number of persons arrested for crimes in Japan. In other words, despite the substantial increases in crimes committed by foreigners in Japan during the late 1980s and early 1990s, it remains the case that crimes in Japan overwhelmingly are committed by Japanese, not by foreigners.

Nevertheless, it seems likely that the aforementioned societal concern about crimes by foreigners, whether well founded or not, has had—and will continue to have—a significant effect on Japanese criminal law and especially penal policy. The Japanese criminal justice system traditionally has emphasized the rehabilitation and reintegration into society of the offender as its primary goals. But these laudable goals may not seem so appropriate to the situation of a foreign visitor who commits a crime in Japan and who may not care to be "rehabilitated" or "reintegrated" into Japanese society. In such cases, the logical societal response may be either to impose a more severe punishment, in the form of lengthier imprisonment, or simply to expel the foreign visitor from Japan altogether. This may explain the fact, already noted by Professor Matsuo, that prison sentences for certain crimes seem to have increased recently in Japan. It may also help to explain why, in 1999, more than 17 percent of those persons sent to prison for crimes in Japan were foreigners, a percentage much higher than the proportion of foreigners within the overall population of persons committing crimes in Japan.

If my speculation is correct in this regard, then as the population of Japan continues to diversify, we should expect to see a continuing increase in the overall punitiveness of Japanese society, based on increasing concerns about crimes committed in Japan by foreigners. This is also likely to be a reflection of the well-known fact that, in all societies, criminal punishment is not merely a matter of practicality, but it also serves an important symbolic function. Whenever the members of a particular society feel that they are losing control, or that the society is becoming generally more unruly and dangerous, then the criminal laws are likely to be changed—and toughened—in an effort to respond to such public concerns and thereby restore public confidence. In the United States, for example, public support for the death penalty tends to peak during periods of social unrest—even if such unrest does not involve any crimes that would be eligible for the death penalty. In such situations, the death penalty often serves mostly as a symbol, and a rallying point, for those who advocate greater law and order. In Japan, lengthier terms of imprisonment may be serving a similar symbolic societal function.

This leads naturally to a discussion of the one area that has witnessed perhaps the most significant recent changes in Japanese criminal law, namely, juvenile crime. Japan continues to experience a perceived crisis of juvenile crime. Crime rates among juveniles have increased, especially for violent crimes, and several notorious cases of shockingly brutal, high-profile murders committed by juveniles have focused the attention of the Japanese public squarely on this problem.

After a period of study lasting several years, Japan's Diet recently enacted very substantial reforms of the Juvenile Act. These reforms have made more juveniles subject to criminal punishment as if they were adults, and they have also changed the procedures used in family court to make those procedures more closely resemble the ones used in adult criminal courts, in at least some cases. To be more specific, the new Juvenile Act, passed in November of 2000, implements the following changes: (1) the fact-finding procedures in family court have been changed to allow the participation of prosecutors in cases where the juvenile denies guilt; (2) public defenders are also allowed to participate in such cases; (3) the minimum age at which a juvenile can be transferred to the adult criminal court, and face regular criminal prosecution, has been lowered from sixteen to fourteen; (4) the traditional presumption against transfer of a juvenile to the adult criminal court has been eliminated in cases involving serious crimes, especially those resulting in the death of the victim; and (5) victims of crimes allegedly committed by juveniles have been given the opportunity to receive notice about the proceedings in family court, as well as to participate in such proceedings by expressing their opinions about the case.

While these reforms of the Juvenile Act are interesting and significant in and of themselves, I think they are even more interesting and significant as a manifestation of growing concerns in Japan about the social and cultural effects of globalization. It is clear that a kind of "generation gap" has emerged recently in Japan. Within the older generation, there seems to be a widespread belief that many younger Japanese today are quite different from their counterparts in earlier times. Some of these perceived differences might appear trivial (e.g., fashions in clothing and hairstyles). Others, however, seem to be legitimate matters for societal concern. Among these is the perception that many younger Japanese today are relatively less concerned about the collective welfare of Japan as a nation-state and relatively more concerned about their own personal and financial futures, than were earlier generations.

For better or for worse, of course, Japan *is* changing as a result of globalization. And, for better or for worse, Japanese young people today *are* different from those in earlier generations. This is quite inevitable. But it is also inevitable that older generations are likely to react to such changes in a negative way. In Japan, this negative reaction seems to have crystallized, at least for the moment, around the specific issue of juvenile crime. The closest analogy here may be to the United States of the mid-to-late 1950s—another historical period during which an older generation became very concerned about the direction in which the country, and particularly its young people, was starting to move. Then, in the United States, as now, in Japan, the older generation often expressed such concerns in the form of widespread fear and outrage over the specific issue of juvenile crime.

I do not intend to minimize, of course, the seriousness of juvenile crime, either in Japan today or in the United States during the 1950s. This is especially true with respect to the kinds of extremely violent juvenile crimes that have occurred recently in Japan and that are clearly a matter of legitimate societal concern. But it is important to keep in mind that the recent increases in the overall crime rate for juveniles in Japan are somewhat similar to increases that previously occurred in 1951, 1964, and 1983. Indeed, the increase in the overall crime rate for juveniles around 1983 was especially severe. Yet the Juvenile Act was not substantially changed at that time, nor was it substantially changed during the two earlier periods of increases in juvenile crime. This suggests that the recent changes in the Juvenile Act may have been motivated not only by well-founded societal concerns about juvenile crime but also by broader concerns about fundamental changes in the nature of Japanese society—changes that may reflect the impacts of social and cultural globalization. The existence of such broader concerns also may partially explain the recent conservative shift in Japanese politics.

IV. THE GLOBALIZATION OF LAW

The third and final kind of globalization that I would like to discuss is the globalization of law itself. Over the past four decades, the comparative study of law has contributed to a growing number of situations in which the domestic laws of one nation-state have been changed on the basis of lessons learned from the experiences of another nation-state. Examples of this globalization of law can be found everywhere, including in many of the areas of law discussed in this volume.

In criminal law, Japan today seems to be moving very slowly in the direction of a more "American-style" approach. What I mean by this is that the Japanese criminal justice system, once described by Professor Daniel Foote as being based on a concept of "benevolent paternalism," recently seems to have taken on some of the more retributive and punitive aspects of the American criminal justice system. For example, Japan—like the United States—continues to adhere to the use of the death penalty, even though many other nation-states around the world have abolished capital punishment and even though influential Japanese scholars such as Justice Shigemitsu Dandō argue strenuously that Japan should do so as well. In addition, as noted by Professor Matsuo, imprisonment in Japan recently seems to be on the increase, even if only modestly. More significantly, and as described above, juveniles in Japan are now subjected more frequently to adult criminal punishment and at a younger age. The procedures in family court have also been formalized, with more rigorous fact-finding and the increased participation of both prosecutors and defense lawyers, developments that are quite similar to those that occurred within the American juvenile justice system during the 1960s and 1970s. Finally, another recent change in the law of Japan has granted the victims of crimes the opportunity to express their views and opinions about those crimes in court, an opportunity that seems inconsistent with the prior emphasis on rehabilitation and much more consistent with a retributive approach to criminal justice.

Why have these changes taken place? There are undoubtedly many reasons, but one of them may be the increasing exposure of Japanese lawyers, especially younger ones, to the legal rules that prevail in other countries—and especially in the United States. As Japanese lawyers learn more about the so-called due process, adversarial model of American criminal justice, they seem to be somewhat more supportive of adopting at least some aspects of that approach in Japan. Such an approach, however, cannot easily be reconciled with the traditional rehabilitative focus of Japanese criminal justice.

But, once again, globalization is a double-edged sword. The great irony here is that, at the same time that Japan seems to be moving gradually in the direction of the more retributive and punitive American criminal justice system, we in America are just now beginning to learn the lessons of Japan's great success in this area of the law. Professor John Haley has been particularly diligent in informing Americans that Japan's low crime rate is not simply the product of inherent cultural differences, but it also reflects a set of very deliberate choices about how to structure the Japanese criminal justice system in order to encourage the rehabilitation and reintegration of offenders into mainstream Japanese society. Professor Haley's writings on restorative justice have struck a resonant chord with many Americans, and even though restorative justice does not yet represent the dominant theme of American criminal justice today, there are some signs of movement in that direction. This movement can be seen most clearly in "progressive" reforms like peer tribunals for juvenile offenders and victim-offender reconciliation programs, which have been adopted in locations across the United States during recent years.

Will Japanese criminal law in the twenty-first century turn increasingly punitive, thus coming to resemble the American criminal law of the twentieth century? Or will American criminal law in the twenty-first century return to a primary focus on rehabilitation, thus emulating the approach that served Japan so well during the twentieth century? Most likely, any near-term changes in the criminal laws of both Japan and the United States will occur incrementally, and thus both countries will long retain their distinctive approaches to criminal justice. But the forces of globalization, in the end, are likely to prove inexorable. The end result of economic, social, cultural, and legal globalization is likely to be a world in which virtually every nation-state has gradually evolved toward some kind of legal "middle ground" and in which the differences between legal systems are far less significant than their similarities.

15 Criminal Justice in Japan

DAVID T. JOHNSON

Civilization is a movement and not a condition,
a voyage and not a harbor.—ARNOLD TOYNBEE

Change is not progress.—H. L. MENCKEN

I. INTRODUCTION

In some respects, criminal justice in Japan has served the nation well for the past forty years. There are several notable achievements. At the front end of the system, police clearance rates were (until recently) higher than in other industrialized democracies, and once a suspect has been identified, prosecutors routinely "construct the truth" so thoroughly that the criminal process has come to be called a system of "precise justice."[1] Prosecutors and judges take into account the needs and circumstances of suspects in order to individualize justice and thereby foster rehabilitation and reintegration, while at the same time attempting to dispense consistent justice through their organized efforts to treat "like cases alike." At the system's back end, conviction rates are high (and rising), yet imprisonment rates remain low. Japan's per capita incarceration rate has increased 50 percent since 1992, but the country still imprisons just one person for every twenty-five prisoners in the United States. Of course, Japan has had the lowest crime rates of any industrialized democracy for most of the postwar period, but at least some of that crime control success can be credited to its institutions of criminal justice. These patterns—efficiency, truth, correction, consistency, and parsimony of punishment—reflect the realization of values that are pursued by most democratic systems. They therefore merit praise.[2]

One must ask, however, at what cost these achievements have come, for in criminal justice as in economics there are few free lunches. Research shows that investigations in Japan are often intrusive and occasionally coercive.[3] Facts are sometimes fabricated, stretched, and concealed.[4] Mistakes are made.[5] Innocent people have been wrongfully arrested, convicted, and imprisoned.[6] Police and prosecutors are unaccountable and defense lawyers all but impotent.[7] Victims are sacrificed at the conviction-rate altar.[8] White-collar offenders are above the law.[9] Prosecutors target progressive defense attorneys and whistle-blowing colleagues.[10] And most fundamental, the guardians of the system are so averse to outside scrutiny that it is often impossible to see or say what the problems are.[11]

This chapter explores the achievements and costs of doing criminal justice in the Japanese way. It unfolds in two installments. First, it summarizes some of the major themes that have characterized criminal justice in Japan for the past four decades. It shows that although some things have changed, Atsushi Nagashima's[12] depiction of Japanese criminal justice, which appeared in 1963 in the original *Law in Japan: The Legal Order in a Changing Society,* is, in important respects, as apt today as it was when he wrote it. Next, this chapter explores some of the social changes and challenges that Japan will confront as it administers criminal justice in the twenty-first century. There is likely to be more change over the next forty years than there has been in the preceding forty, because the environments of Japanese criminal justice—the social, economic, and political contexts that shape the administration of criminal sanctions—are evolving in ways that seem to be evoking significant adjustments in the Japanese way of justice.

II. LOOKING BACK: PATTERNS IN POSTWAR CRIMINAL JUSTICE

Many of the patterns Nagashima[13] observed have persisted. Most notably, prosecutors are still granted such wide discretionary power that Japanese criminal justice is in large part determined by the ways they investigate, charge, and try cases.[14] Similarly, criminal trials continue to be primarily paper affairs (*chōsho saiban*) in which dossiers (not oral testimony in open court) play the pivotal evidentiary role.[15] Rehabilitation remains a cardinal objective for prosecutors and judges,[16] and one of the main mechanisms of correction is still the strategic use of leniency through suspended charges and sentences.

However, at least three features of Nagashima's analysis do require revision. First, Nagashima argued that "the administration of criminal justice in Japan has been changing clearly and steadily from an inquisitorial to an accusatorial process."[17] If the seeds of adversarialism were ever evident in Japan's criminal process, they have not blossomed.[18] Confession remains the "king of evidence," and police and prosecutors still seek admissions of guilt single-mindedly. In so doing, they remain largely unchecked by judges or defense attorneys during the critical pre-charge period. The second revision is related, for the role of defense lawyers in Japanese criminal justice has expanded less than Nagashima anticipated.[19] Indeed, in ordinary cases such as larceny, robbery, and assault, Japan's Code of Criminal Procedure so advantages the prosecution that even the most determined defense lawyer can have little effect during the crucial investigatory stages.[20] Despite a few modest changes, "the invisibility of Japanese defense lawyers continues."[21] For this reason, Japan's criminal process has been called "an unbalanced adversary system,"[22] a "cooperative adversary system,"[23] and a "pseudo-adversary system."[24] Finally, Nagashima omitted two key actors from his analysis: police and victims of crimes. Japanese police have vast discretion to decide matters that matter. As "street-corner politicians," they influence "who gets what" in the currencies that count: life, liberty, property, and reputation. Since police possess immense power over people, outcomes, and information, they provide an especially revealing window onto criminal justice in Japan.[25] Some views through that window are discomforting.[26] Victims are also absent in Nagashima's account of the accused and society. Because their role has expanded considerably,[27] they, too, are featured in this chapter.

A. TRUTH, CORRECTIONS, CONSISTENCY, AND CONVICTIONS

In criminal justice as in scholarship, truth is fundamental to everything else.[28] In fact, truth—or a reasonable approximation to it—is nearly a necessary condition for making just decisions. Without it, justice is an accident. Although the concept of "truth" is difficult to define, in broad terms there is substantial agreement about what constitutes its core: accurate accounts by competent people of what they genuinely believe from sensory experience, and the honest production of papers and objects relevant to legal questions.[29]

The first distinguishing characteristic of Japanese criminal justice is its commitment to uncovering, clarifying, and constructing the *truth*.[30] Although analogous commitments characterize most criminal justice systems, different systems attach different weights to this task,[31] and Japan's system—and the prosecutor especially—seems to invest it with special significance.[32] Many of the country's criminal justice achievements are premised on a faith that facts can be explicated and evidence organized so as to say with precision who did what to whom.

The "truth" of a case is primarily determined by police and prosecutors, through investigations and interrogations during which dossiers are composed to summarize their findings. At trial, judges make the final, authoritative findings of fact, but most courts validate the prosecutor's version of events, and many cases never even go to trial because prosecutors believe the truth that they discern does not merit indictment. Commitment to truth is one of the hallmarks of an effective system of criminal justice.[33] Though this value must be balanced with other principles such as fairness, openness, and respect for the dignity of victims and suspects, truth should also be recognized as a precondition for making sound discretionary decisions—decisions that in the aggregate constitute a country's criminal justice policy.[34]

A commitment to *correction*—to rectify offenders—is the second theme in Japanese criminal justice. The strength of this commitment has been debated,[35] but the available evidence suggests that the Japanese system pursues rehabilitation in ways and to degrees that are seldom seen in American or British criminal justice.[36] The threshold decision concerns which offenders are correctable—a judgment that is more than merely a choice between two binary options, correctable and not. Rather, investigators locate offenders along a continuum ranging from "not at all correctable" on one end to "highly correctable" on the other. Compared to their counterparts in the U.K. or U.S.A., prosecutors in Japan construct a distribution of offenders that is centered markedly more on the correctable part of the continuum. Once an offender is deemed deserving of correctional efforts, officials employ two main mechanisms to encourage reform: instruction and leniency.[37] Through *instruction* (especially during interrogation), officials make moral appeal to norms, both as external realities in the accused's social world ("we believe theft is wrong") and as internal realities in the accused's conscience ("you know theft is wrong"). Through *leniency*, officials aim to accord offenders the time and opportunity to change without stigmatizing them unduly or pushing them into subcultures that reinforce criminal tendencies. Indictments and sentences are frequently suspended for these reasons.

Correction without consistency would be a chimerical achievement, but Japanese criminal justice manages the tension between these two imperatives of justice that Western jurists regard as often incompatible and always in tension—the need to individualize case dispositions so as to promote rehabilitation, and the need to treat like cases alike so as to achieve *consistency*.[38] Many prosecutors in Japan reject the tenet that there is a necessary trade-off between individualized decision making in the service of correction and ordered decision making in the service of consistency. In fact, where prosecutors have sufficient time, resources, power, and information, they are able to apply a regularized set of standards to a case and still take into account a broad range of factors related to the individual's circumstances. Since these "conditions" have often prevailed in postwar Japan, the country has achieved an impressive level of consistency in criminal justice decision making.[39]

Criminal justice in Japan may be best known for its *high conviction rates*. Almost every person who is tried is convicted, and even among defendants who contest the state's case, conviction rates range between 95 and 97 percent—substantially higher than comparable rates in other democratic countries.[40] The interesting question is not whether Japanese rates are high—on this matter disagreement exists only over how big the gap is between Japan and other nations—but rather what explains the disparity. The causal candidates are many: a compliant judiciary,[41] hamstrung defense lawyers,[42] the absence of juries,[43] and so on. The primary proximate cause, however, is prosecutor prudence about whether and when to indict.[44] Prosecutors screen cases so carefully that suspects with a chance of being acquitted rarely receive a trial. Their prudence is both individual and institutional. Prosecutors who charge or try cases that end in acquittal are called to account for the outcome, and if the acquittal is considered the result of a "mistake," the responsible person is rebuked by superiors and the job and case assignments received thereafter may reflect the error. At the same time, the procuracy's practice of *kessai*, or collective deliberation over case dispositions, targets and eliminates acquittal-risky cases.[45]

Japan's high conviction rate has mixed consequences. Although some analysts argue that the system must be "tilted" toward the state since so few people get acquitted,[46] this view ignores the fact that many suspects who would be tried in other systems never get indicted in Japan. In this sense, the high conviction rate reflects prosecutors' preference for the risk that an uncharged offender will re-offend over the converse risk that a charged suspect will be acquitted.[47] Although this approach "favors" correction in that it exposes suspects to less stigma and punishment, it generates unwelcome consequences as well. Some victims who desire vindication never get a chance to exercise their voice in open court. The supply of vigorous defense lawyering gets suppressed (who wants to do defense work when there is little chance of success?). The public loses the extra deterrence that a more aggressive charging policy would generate. And judges sometimes slide into two troublesome tendencies: a penchant for thinking (or feeling) that if a defendant has been charged then he is probably guilty, and an inclination to expand the meaning of "reasonable doubt" so as to counteract the risk of a pro-prosecution lean. As judges increase the quantum of evidence required to reach conviction, prosecutors respond accordingly—by increasing the quantum of evidence required to indict. Fewer "gray" cases get charged, the conviction rate climbs higher, acquittals become even more newsworthy, prosecutors grow more prudent, and the causal circle accelerates. Some prosecutors regard this circle as "vicious" because it crowds out their capacity to ensure that the guilty do not escape justice, and many consider it one of the system's most pressing problems. One elite prosecutor declared that it is "a disgrace" for prosecutors to charge only clear winners:

> You asked me why we prosecutors do not take adventures. In one sense the answer is easy. *We require proof beyond an unreasonable doubt*. The fewer acquittals there are, the more attention and criticism each one gets, and the more careful we become to avoid acquittals in the future. It's a vicious circle; don't you see? In this way it is natural that the acquittal rate is declining over time. But it is not a good thing.[48]

B. CONFESSIONS AND COBWEBS

It has often been said that *confessions* lie at the heart of Japanese criminal justice.[49] Though the syntactic difference is slight, it may be more revealing to say that confessions *are* the heart—the pump that keeps cases circulating in the system and that helps generate the achievements described above. Most police and prosecutors believe confessions reveal aspects of the truth that cannot be illuminated any other way.[50] If so, then confession helps create the factual foundation for the pursuit of consistency. Similarly, confession with contrition facilitates correction, and admissions of guilt make indictment feasible and conviction all but certain. Since confession is the precondition for many of the achievements in Japanese criminal justice, the people who pursue them—police and prosecutors especially—are reluctant to embrace reforms that might make suspects less likely to sing. Ironically, confessions are becoming more important even as they become more difficult to obtain. The public's rights consciousness has strengthened.[51] Defense lawyers have become more likely to counsel their clients to remain silent.[52] Foreign suspects, many of whom are less likely to confess than Japanese are, not only constitute a growing proportion of the criminal caseload,[53] they also may "infect" Japanese suspects with alien, unrepentant attitudes.[54] Since suspects increasingly recognize that prosecutors seldom charge without a confession, the view that silence is golden seems to be spreading.[55]

Thus, if confession is the heart of Japanese criminal justice, its pulse has started to slow. Whatever the causes, the increased difficulty of eliciting admissions of guilt concerns many officials. Some believe the proper response is to redouble efforts to obtain confessions so as to preserve the consequent achievements.[56] On this view, the problem is not excessive reliance on confession but rather excessive deference to alien notions of fairness. In contrast, other analysts argue that the system must ease its reliance on confessions by instituting reforms to permit plea bargaining and immunity, practices long considered anathema by many Japanese.[57] As one prosecutor sees it:

> The distinguishing characteristic of our country's criminal justice system is the demand for detailed proof. Until now, the method for satisfying this demand has been obtaining confessions and statements through interrogation. However, getting these statements has become very difficult in recent years. . . . If there is not some kind of alternative to interrogation as a method for obtaining such statements, it is greatly feared that our country's criminal justice system may very well collapse.[58]

By this perspective, if Japan's confession-centric system does not ease up it will break down. Moreover, until alternatives to interrogation are introduced, many offenders who should be charged and convicted will not be, especially in cases—corporate crimes, crimes of corruption, and organized crimes by the *yakuza*—that are difficult to investigate in the traditional way.[59]

The British satirist Jonathan Swift once said that "laws are like cobwebs, which may catch small flies but let wasps and hornets break through." Viewed from an Anglo-American perspective, Swift's aphorism captures the "schizophrenia" that helps define criminal justice in Japan.[60] Compared to most of their Western counterparts, Japanese police and prosecutors work in a deeply *dualistic* legal environment. On the one hand, in "ordinary" cases of street crime, Japan's rules of criminal procedure confer powers on investigators that enable them to control the criminal process and "make" cases more easily than investigators can in the U.K., U.S.A., Canada, and elsewhere.[61] On the other hand, Japanese investigators lack many of the procedural powers—such as the authority to plea-bargain, offer immunity, or conduct undercover stings—that are routinely used in other countries to "make" cases against politicians and other white-collar offenders. This dualism renders Japan's criminal process a cobweb, highly enabling of efforts to indict and convict run-of-the-mill offenders—Swift's "small flies"—yet disabling of efforts to bring "wasps and hornets" to justice.

One of the best-known propositions in the sociology of law is that "downward law is greater than upward law," a theorem that says more law gets directed at low-ranking persons than at high-ranking ones.[62] If this proposition applies to all societies and at all times, as its proponents claim and as appears to be true, then some may suppose that Japan is nothing special: all societies are marked by legal dualism. Such a conclusion would be misplaced. The fact of legal dualism is not peculiar to Japan, but what is notable is just *how much* downward law exceeds upward law in its force and effects.

This contrast between the enabling power of downward law and the disabling features of its upward counterpart raises an important question: What are the consequences of Japan's legal cobweb? Forbidding particular investigative techniques "may be tantamount to sanctioning high levels of the types of crime associated with those investigative sanctions."[63] Japanese politics are widely perceived to be structurally (and extravagantly) corrupt.[64] Indeed, it is now clear that corruption exacerbated the economic troubles—trillions of yen in bad loans, record bankruptcies, and three recessions—which Japan experienced during the "lost decade" of the 1990s. If upward law had been more vigorous, would these problems have been less severe? A more fundamental question of fairness is this: Is it *just* to have a criminal process that enables investigators to make cases out of crimes committed mainly by the poor and powerless but simultaneously disables them from making cases against the criminal "haves"? If the answer is no, then Japan may need to mend its cobweb. However, doing so without empowering defense lawyers risks exacerbating the existing imbalance of power in Japanese criminal procedure. As the next section shows, "solutions" often breed their own new needs and problems.

III. LOOKING AHEAD: SOCIAL CHANGES AND CRIMINAL JUSTICE CHALLENGES

During the past forty years there has been more continuity than change in the administration of Japanese criminal justice. As one scholar has observed, if officials from the 1930s could be transported "to today's prosecution scene, [they] would recognize quickly that, despite extensive legal reforms, the essence of the old system remains intact."[65]

Change may be in the offing. In the years to come, Japanese criminal justice will face major challenges in addition to the problems of confessions and cobwebs. Most importantly, the future of criminal justice in Japan depends at least as much on what happens outside the system as inside it, for legal systems everywhere are embedded in and shaped by social, political, economic, and cultural forces.[66] More normatively, criminal justice should be *responsive* to the influences of some of these environments.[67] The patterns described above—corrections, consistency, convictions, and so on—have specific preconditions. Throughout the postwar era, Japanese criminal justice has benefited from several salutary contexts, including low crime rates, light caseloads, insulation from public and political pressure, the absence of juries, and (in ordinary street crime cases) enabling laws of criminal procedure.[68] These contexts and conditions are changing.[69] As they do, criminal justice in Japan may be compelled to pursue a different mix of values than the one it has pursued heretofore.

A. THE CHANGING CONTEXTS OF CRIMINAL JUSTICE

Consider a few of the most consequential changes. In 2001, a million more crimes were committed in Japan than just a decade earlier. Thefts rose 1.5-fold, rapes doubled, and muggings and purse snatchings jumped 400 percent.[70] One factor in these rises has been an increase in the number of crimes committed by minors. In Osaka, for example, more than 80 percent of muggings are committed by juveniles, and 80 percent of those robberies are committed in groups of three or more.[71] As many police officials see it, "juvenile delinquents have made Japanese streets dangerous."[72] Since fear sells, the Japanese media frequently depict children as "predators." In the wake of a high-profile stabbing, for example, one of the country's most widely read columnists asked whether Japan is creating "a whole new breed of outsider,"[73] and other commentators have called juveniles "shameless" and "self-intoxicated."[74]

Though it is true that children have committed a number of seemingly "senseless" crimes in recent years,[75] the most important criminological pattern may not be kids as "predators" but rather kids as "prey." Reports of child abuse and neglect have soared in recent years, as have deaths and injuries.[76] If Japan's young victims are as likely to enter a "cycle of violence" as are their American counterparts (the causal mechanisms linking victimization to victimizing would seem to be the same), then the crime problems generated by child abuse could be formidable.[77] Youngsters are also staying home from school in record numbers. In 1998, 139,000 elementary and junior-high school students refused to attend classes for at least thirty straight days—a 100 percent increase since 1991. Many of these truant children reject school because they have been hurt by bullying classmates and abusive teachers.[78]

But youth are not Japan's only law-and-order problem. "Crimes by foreigners" (*rainichi gaikokujin hanzai*) quintupled in the ten years from 1992 through 2001,[79] and more than 40 percent of arrested foreigners are now from China.[80] During the same interval, robberies rose almost threefold, sex crimes increased by two-thirds, extortion went up by half, and methamphetamine arrests and crimes involving knives or guns each rose by 15 percent. In Tokyo, rape cases have increased more than 40 percent since 1999.[81] In Kabuki-cho, Tokyo's largest entertainment district, drug and arms deals are said to be "rampant,"[82] and police have installed dozens of surveillance cameras on poles, roofs, and walls in order to maintain order in the area.[83] Gun crimes reached a ten-year high in 2001.[84] On some street corners (as in Osaka's Nishinari-ku), drug dealers peddle their wares with unprecedented brazenness, and on the streets in Tokyo's Shin-Okubo district, prostitutes are equally intrepid. Corporate crimes and government corruption, though difficult to count, seem as conspicuous as ever. And so on. In the first decade of the twenty-first century, many Japanese believe crime control problems are more serious than they have been for fifty years.

Only about ten years ago the *New York Times* published a front-page story praising Japan as "a safer society."[85] Although Japan remains a safer place than the United States and most other democracies,[86] it appears the crime gap may be closing from both directions.[87] Of course, media images of crime shape public opinion and crime policy as much as actual crime rates.[88] Since crime is easily packaged as entertainment, the Japanese media (like their American counterparts) often focus on the social facts of crime, fear, and insecurity,[89] and one regularly hears lamentations that "law and order in Japan, once considered as stable and secure as the water supply, is now on the brink of collapse."[90]

Though such sentiments are hyperbolic they are also widely shared. Indeed, residents of Japan feel more insecure than at any time since World War II.[91] In a nationwide poll conducted in January 2002, for example, 60 percent of Japanese adults expressed some or a lot of "anxiety" (*fuankan*) about the present, and almost nine in ten respondents said they felt uneasy about "crime and traffic accidents," making them the biggest source of concern among the ten types of anxiety listed.[92] In the same poll, the vast majority of respondents said they expected their own "safety" (*anzen*) to be no better in ten years than it is now. A similar poll in December 2001 revealed that 90 percent of respondents believed "order" (*chian*) in Japan had "gotten worse over the last few years," while 86 percent felt sentences are "often" or "sometimes" too lenient.[93]

Public concern about crime has turned "law and order" into an increasingly salient political issue. Politicians now adopt "get tough" positions on crime policy, and their rhetoric helps push law in an increasingly punitive direction. One result is that prisons in Japan are over capacity for the first time since the early 1950s. In many cases, cells built for six inmates now hold eight or more, and the Justice Ministry predicts that the combination of more crime and more punishment will drive the inmate population above eighty thousand by 2004—a near-doubling of prisoners in only twelve years.[94] As of 2002, sixty-two of seventy-four prison and detention facilities were overcrowded, and some twenty municipalities in sparsely populated areas of the country were vying to construct prisons in their communities.[95] For the first time since the end of World War II, the government is planning to expand its prison complex.

Criminal law and its enforcement have also become more severe against a variety of offenses, from domestic violence and sexual molestation to child prostitution, stalking, drunk driving, and reckless driving that results in death or injury.[96] The Juvenile Law has been revised to allow children as young as fourteen to be tried as adults, thereby tempering Japan's historic commitment to rehabilitate youth with retributive and deterrent considerations.[97] Beginning with the Bōryokudan Countermeasures Act (*Bōtaihō*) in 1991, the Diet has passed numerous laws that target organized crime, including a narrowly circumscribed wiretapping law.[98] The Mental Health Welfare Act is being reformed in order to shift responsibility for determining whether a suspect is mentally ill away from professional psychiatrists (who tend to focus on questions of treatment and rehabilitation) and toward a mixed panel of psychiatrists and legal professionals. The impetus for this movement appears to be the perception that too few mentally ill suspects are charged and convicted. The most fundamental "get tough" shift is occurring among prosecutors and judges, who are imposing more punishment on more people than they have heretofore. In the year 2000, for example, the average prison term was 26.4 months, four months longer than in 1991.[99]

Broad shifts in Japan's economy and society may portend more crime problems to come. Economic inequality and concentrated disadvantage foster much serious crime.[100] Japan's economy was moribund throughout the 1990s, and the nation has weathered several recessions in just the past decade. Many experts believe that without major structural reforms in Japan's economy and polity, more trouble is on the way.[101] As of 2002, economic growth is stagnant, prices are declining, permanent employment is crumbling, unemployment is at record levels, and the jobless rate for young men (the most crime-inclined group in any society) is almost double the rate for the rest of society (10.7 percent vs. 5.5 percent). The most troubling sign may be the fact that inequality in Japan is serious and growing.[102] In fact, average household income before taxes and transfers is more unequal in Japan than in the United States, and Japan has more unequally distributed assets, larger wage differentials, and higher rates of poverty than Australia, New Zealand, and much of Europe.[103] Moreover, income disparities in Japan grew by 50 percent between 1995 and 2000.[104] In an effort to stimulate growth, corporations and policy makers are embracing greater inequality by setting pay through performance instead of seniority, by instituting tax reforms that benefit the wealthy while pushing less affluent citizens to pay more, and by cutting welfare payments to single mothers.[105]

The most important victims of these economic problems are young people entering a job market that differs radically from the one earlier cohorts encountered.[106] Not long ago, high school graduates in Japan were cherished as "golden eggs" full of potential. In retrospect, that era could turn out to be an abnormal period in Japanese history.[107] As of 2002, about half of work-bound high school graduates drift into part-time, temporary positions as *freeters* (or "free workers"), who receive low pay, few benefits, and no job security. Although some stories glamorize their flexible lifestyles and iconoclastic attitudes, in most cases these outcomes are more a product of hopelessness than of the conscious pursuit of some preferred path.[108] Graduates who become trapped in this kind of work risk entering a new kind of lower class—with the criminal risks attendant thereto. Because their future as *freeters* seems dim, some students who do remain in school see little reason to conform and perform in ways that previously were taken for granted.[109]

In addition to the growing class differences in Japanese society, major changes are occurring in other criminal justice contexts. One of the most fundamental is a shift in ideology and socioeconomic organization, toward a greater emphasis on personal freedom and individual initiative. This change seems to be driven from the political Right by the perceived needs of business to compete in the globalized economy.[110] At the same time, the number of foreigners residing in Japan has risen every year for the past three decades, and the growing ethnic diversity has been accompanied by a parallel diversification of values.[111] The spread of the automobile, the expansion of train networks, and the emergence of new dwelling patterns—especially suburban housing—are significant because they alter how daily life is lived. These ecological developments help explain a number of noteworthy features in postmodern Japan: lengthy commutes to work and school, the increased mobility of the labor force, the suburbanization of employment, the declining importance of local loyalties, and the privatization of individual and family life.[112] Although strong informal controls may be the key to explaining Japan's historically low crime rates,[113] those constraints on conduct may be weakening, driven in part by the developments described above. At the same time, scandals in government have so undermined confidence in officialdom that the country's once vaunted bureaucracy now enjoys the trust of just 8 percent of Japanese adults. By comparison, more than two-thirds of American adults say they trust their federal bureaucracy.[114] Since scandal involves real or alleged transgressions that become known to others, the media constitute a crucial link in the causal chain whose last link is public disaffection with government.[115] The media's propensity to show "how it really is" by exposing backstage behavior also undermines traditional notions of authority, privacy, and intimacy. Of course, the media also help "democratize" culture, but democratization brings its own criminogenic consequences, including a more pronounced moral individualism that may further fuel the decline of informal social control.[116]

The most fundamental changes in Japanese society are demographic, for population patterns shape and determine many social facts.[117] Japan is undergoing a "demographic shock."[118] Birthrates are at record lows, largely because women postpone marriage and childbearing longer than ever before.[119] In 2000, the number of lifetime births per Japanese woman was 1.35, nearly three times fewer than in 1950. The fertility rate was still lower in trend-setting Tokyo—just 1.06.[120] On the other end of the demographic curve, Japan's life expectancy rates are the longest in the world: seventy-seven years for men and eighty-four for women. Because demographic projections are more accurate than weather or economic forecasts, population realities can be predicted with more than the usual confidence. By 2050, average life expectancy in Japan will reach eighty-eight, and 42 percent of Japanese will be over the age of sixty.[121] The country's population will peak in 2007 and (if present trends continue) could fall continuously for 100 years thereafter. To keep its population stable, Japan will need to admit 17 million immigrants by 2050, which would make foreigners almost 20 percent of the population (compared with just 1 percent today). Family and household patterns are also shaped by divorce rates, which have doubled to 2.0 per thousand people in twenty-five years.[122] Although just 1 percent of Japanese children are born "out of wedlock,"[123] women's labor force participation rates have risen steadily for the past twenty years,[124] leaving more children "home alone" and subject to less social control than previous cohorts of children have experienced.[125]

Japan's demographic changes will aggravate the country's fiscal crunch. The soaring ratio of retirees to workers will require raising the retirement age, scaling back retirement benefits, and redefining the seniority-based wage system. Nonetheless, even the most optimistic forecasts predict that taxes will have to be raised in order to pay for pensions, health care, and other costs of caring for the elderly. The American Center for Strategic and International Studies forecasts that Japan's demographic changes will keep the country mired in recession for much of the period between 2025 and 2050, not least because a smaller workforce paying higher taxes will further depress consumption and growth.

In these demographic circumstances there are few attractive alternatives. "Reneging on pension commitments could undermine public confidence, but running up the red ink makes Japan more vulnerable to rising interest rates."[126] One result of the demographic shock could be a significant increase in political tension between the generations—a possibility premised on the notion that inequality will increase between older people who have reaped the benefits of Japan's previous prosperity and younger people who are not fairing as well. If, as many criminologists believe, inequality breeds crime and fosters punitive attitudes, then Japanese criminal justice will be shaped by these demographic trends, too. On the other hand, the nation's fiscal crisis could make it difficult to invest in the police, prisons, and other institutions of governmental control that more crime and punishment would seem to require.

Although there are a lot of "ifs" and "coulds" in this section, one scenario seems especially striking: Japan may confront the same kind of "criminological predicament" that the U.K. and U.S.A. have faced since the 1970s—"a new and problematic set of structural constraints that form the policy horizon within which all [criminal justice] decisions must be made."[127] The British and American predicaments are rooted in two large social facts: the normality of high crime rates and the acknowledged limitations of the criminal justice state.

What is clear is that Japan is in the throes of major social change that could transform the ways in which criminal justice is administered. Economic dynamics are the most basic transformative force, but other currents contribute to change as well, including the welcome spread of egalitarian sentiments in Japanese society.[128] When the United States and Britain underwent similar changes, their approaches to crime control responded in remarkably parallel ways.[129] Chief among those changes were the following twelve developments:

1. The decline of the rehabilitative ideal
2. The reemergence of punitive sanctions and expressive justice

3. An increase in the emotional tone of crime policy
4. The felt need, above all, to "protect the public"
5. The victim's move to center stage of the criminal process
6. The politicization of crime issues and the increased importance of populist sentiments
7. The reinvention of the prison as a place of control, not correction
8. The academic embrace of control theories and "criminologies of everyday life"
9. An expanded infrastructure of crime prevention and community safety
10. The commercialization of crime control
11. New management styles and ideologies in criminal justice organizations
12. A perpetual sense of law-and-order "crisis"

The social forces that forged these crime control arrangements in the United States and Britain—especially the distinctive social organization of "late modernity" and the emergence of free market, socially conservative politics—could stimulate parallel responses in Japan's crime control field. Convergence is not inevitable,[130] but my reading of the Japanese landscape is that there are signs of movement in all twelve directions. How long they will continue and how deeply they will run are difficult to predict, but whether criminal justice in Japan converges toward an Anglo-American "culture of control" or not, it is certain to face challenges to its standard operating procedures.

B. CHALLENGES

A *challenge* is "a call to respond" or "a difficult and demanding task." Criminal justice in Japan will face at least three challenges in the decade to come: how to preserve the system's commitment to correction, how to cultivate perceptions of fairness so as to bolster the system's legitimacy, and how to devolve responsibility for crime control away from the state and toward organizations and communities in civil society. This section explores some of the forces generating these challenges and some of the ways that officials might respond.

1. *Conserving Corrections*

Japan's commitment to correction is being challenged on several fronts. In the first place, the correctional impulse is premised on the possibility of efficiently identifying offenders. Change the premise and you risk undermining the deterrent effect of the criminal sanction. Research shows that deterrence is a function of two main variables—the severity of punishment and its certainty. In general, deterrence depends less on sanction severity than on the probability of apprehension (or the perception of that probability). For most of the past forty years the likelihood of being punished in Japan (even if only by arrest or interrogation) was substantially higher than in other democratic countries. Criminal justice officials could therefore pursue parsimony in punishment without sacrificing much of the law's deterrent potential. In recent years, however, Japan's clearance rates have plummeted, from 40 percent in 1997 to less than 20 percent in 2002—a 50 percent decline.[131] As the certainty of punishment declines, prosecutors and courts may feel the need to recover some of the "lost deterrence" by seeking and imposing more severe sentences. The collapsing clearance rate also subverts corrections less directly, by increasing the public's sense of insecurity and by decreasing their confidence in the system. In Japan as elsewhere, when these sentiments strengthen, they stimulate calls for stronger punishment. As Japan's largest newspaper sees it, it is "time to get tough on crime."[132]

Correction in Japanese criminal justice has been more strongly supported by professionals working within the system—prosecutors, judges, and attorneys—than by the public at large. In the original volume of *Law in Japan*, for example, Haruo Abe described and lamented the "gap" between Japan's too-lenient judiciary and the public's more punitive preferences.[133] Subsequent studies have confirmed that a gap still exists, and experimental research shows that when judging serious crimes such as robbery, Japanese citizens are at least as harsh as their American counterparts and at least as willing to support retributive, incapacitative, and deterrent rationales for punishment.[134] When it comes to correction, therefore, the crucial difference between Japan and the United States is not public attitudes about crime but rather the insulation that Japanese officials have enjoyed from the fear, fury, and wishful thinking that drives crime policy in the United States.[135]

That insulation is eroding. Criminal justice officials in Japan have become less capable of resisting the impact of public opinion, partly because the character of policy making has become more politicized, but also because those officials have lost status and credibility.[136] The clearance rate, for example, has fallen for a variety of reasons, but two of the most important reflect (and reinforce) the declining influence of official expertise: a scandal wave that has induced lower levels of public confidence in and cooperation with the police, and heightened public scrutiny of police record keeping, which makes it more difficult to fudge the facts about cleared cases.[137] As the expertise and autonomy of criminal justice officials decline, so, too, does their capacity to pursue rehabilitative ends that diverge from the public's more punitive preferences.[138] Although this could make Japanese criminal justice more responsive to public opinion, it is worth reflecting on a more fundamental question: Will it make it more just?

The challenge of preserving the correctional impulse in Japanese criminal justice is further complicated by the increasingly politicized nature of criminal justice policy making. In particular, the bureaucrats who once defined the direction and content of criminal justice must now consider the interests of victims more fully than they have before.[139] Where once the victim's role was routinely reduced to that of complainant and witness, now the victim is becoming a favored constituency whose interests must be served by all criminal justice agencies. Victims are to be kept informed about their cases, treated with sensitivity, offered access to support, given compensation for their injuries, and accorded rights and a voice that they have not previously possessed. As victims move closer to center stage of the criminal process, the system's various agencies come to see themselves more as service providers for individual victims than as agents of the public interest. When decision making is transformed in this way, the process of "individualization" increasingly centers on victims instead of offenders. Dispositions that once were selected to suit the needs of offenders become shaped instead by the need to reflect victims' sentiments.[140] In the process, the interests of victims and offenders come to be seen as diametrically opposed. On this "zero-sum" view, what is good for the offender must be bad for the victim, and so it becomes imperative to marginalize the needs of "the criminal."

The needs of foreign offenders are especially likely to be discounted and ignored. In fact, there are signs that political leaders want to cut back on the commitment to corrections for foreign suspects, defendants, and convicts. Writing in one of Japan's leading monthly magazines, Atsuyuki Sassa, chairman of the Cabinet Safety Security Office, and Tomoko Sasaki, an upper house member of Parliament, argued that Chinese residents of Japan commit a disturbingly large number of "heinous crimes" (*kyōaku hanzai*). More importantly, Sasaki says, when she was a prosecutor,

> if someone said "Chinese Crime" the image was strong that the offender and the victim were both Chinese. Now, however, their target has shifted to the Japanese. . . . Recently, the recognition has spread among Chinese offenders that "the Japanese are easier to target than the Chinese are." In 1991, 53.6 percent of robbery victims were Japanese; in 2001, 80.9 percent were. Since the

people being targeted are us Japanese, we absolutely must not neglect this issue.[141]

Neglect seems unlikely. According to Sassa and Sasaki, Chinese residents of Japan commit six times more crime than they did ten years ago, so that they now account for fully half of all crimes committed by foreigners in Japan. Moreover, when Chinese offenders are caught, they "never talk" to police because they "are more afraid of revenge from their comrades than they are of the police." Their refusal to confess and cooperate drives the clearance rate down, not only because Chinese crimes are harder to solve, Sassa and Sasaki say, but also because they require police resources that cannot be used in other cases. The concern for protecting foreigners' rights has gone so far that it has become an "obstacle" to more urgent crime control needs. In Sassa's view, the most troubling fact of all is that Chinese offenders find Japanese prisons to be such "a pleasant environment" that when he led a Chinese judge on a tour of Fuchu prison in Tokyo, the jurist reportedly confessed that "if it is this nice a prison, all Chinese people will want to come here."[142] Because "the cost performance" of Japanese criminal justice is favorable for Chinese offenders, the price of crime must be raised (by increasing punishments) and commitments to rights and rehabilitation must be cut back accordingly. Otherwise Japan will remain a "thieves' paradise."[143] Sassa and Sasaki conclude by urging the Japanese Diet to "wrestle with this problem" as soon as possible. If it does not, they say, many more Japanese will become "pitiful victims" of predatory Chinese.[144]

The final source of the challenge to correction comes from the changing composition of criminal caseloads in Japan. Two such changes are notable: the rise in the number of foreign suspects and offenders, and the erosion in the percentage of suspects who confess to crimes. Daniel Foote has observed that the influx of foreigners poses one of the greatest external challenges to the individualizing "benevolence" of Japanese criminal justice.[145] In his view, since foreign suspects subscribe to different values and speak different languages than the police and prosecutors who handle their cases, the latter are less likely to devote resources to rehabilitation or reintegration. Instead of reform through individualized decision making, these officials concentrate on "processing cases efficiently." At the same time, foreign suspects seem less inclined to make the kind of penitent confession that prosecutors consider the primary sign of remorse and the first necessary step on the road to correction. The leniency that officials offer remorseful suspects is an opportunity for reform that cannot be extended to suspects whose absence of remorse is deemed a form of rebellion against the system that officials represent.[146] The approach to unrepentant foreign suspects is paralleled by a similar style of handling Japanese suspects who do not confess. Rigorous longitudinal analysis has not been done, but most informed observers agree that the propensity to confess has declined among Japanese suspects as well. If confessions are the heart of Japanese criminal justice—the pump that keeps cases circulating in the system and the primary prerequisite for the pursuit of correction—then tracing the trajectory of Japan's rehabilitative ideal will require attending to changes in the state's capacity to obtain remorseful admissions of guilt. The next section suggests that pursuing penitent confessions may conflict with the need to bolster the legitimacy of Japanese criminal justice.

2. *Enhancing Legitimacy*

The second challenge confronting Japanese criminal justice is the need to cultivate belief in the propriety of the process through which criminal dispositions are reached. The issue is legitimacy, which at root involves *public perceptions* of official behavior. Crime policy in Japan has ceased to be a matter that can be entrusted to professional experts. "Ordinary people"—especially victims and an increasingly insecure public—now have voices that must be heard and heeded. One question concerns how to balance their demand that authorities "clarify case facts" with the countervailing requirement to treat the accused fairly. This, of course, is neither a new issue for Japan nor a distinctively Japanese concern. Article 1 of Japan's Code of Criminal Procedure articulates both objectives—truth and fairness—and even hints at the strain between them, while crime control–due process tensions characterize many systems of criminal justice, not just Japan's.[147] Still, this issue seems urgent in Japan for a variety of reasons. As crime rates rise, criminal justice becomes politicized, law and order occupy more of the media's attention, and institutions of criminal justice come to be considered inadequate organs of crime control, what the system *says* about crime and justice may become at least as important as what it *does*.[148] For criminal justice in Japan to retain the legitimacy it has enjoyed for much of the postwar period, its managers will have to attend more keenly and respond more consistently to public perceptions. Two issues are primary: the legitimacy of the investigative process by which confessions are obtained and the truth is constructed, and the legitimacy of a trial process that in its present form (as of 2002) leaves little room for civilian participation.

The need to "uncover and clarify the truth" has been the cardinal objective in Japanese criminal justice since at least the end of World War II.[149] Other objectives—such as rehabilitating offenders and treating like cases alike—are important, but their achievement depends on the system's capacity to construe and construct the truth.[150] For the most part, it is prosecutors who clarify and construct the truth during pretrial investigations. They do so mainly by preparing written documents, or dossiers, that record the content of conversations they have had with various witnesses. In the vast majority of cases, the most important of these dossiers is the suspect's confession, which is treated as crucial at all subsequent stages. In fact, confession plays such a critical role in Japan's criminal process that it can be called the animating reality of Japanese criminal justice. This is the system's primary postulate: no confession, no truth, no correction, no consistency, no conviction, no justice.[151]

We have seen that confessions are becoming more difficult to obtain. At the same time, the process of interrogation by which confessions are elicited is being criticized on several fronts.[152] Internationally, United Nations committees on human rights have repeatedly rebuked the Japanese state for violating protocols about the length, location, and methods of interrogation; for excessive reliance on confessions as evidence; and for inadequate disclosure of evidence to the defense.[153] These admonitions have had little discernible effect so far, but many Japanese, including Ryūichi Hirano, the dean of Japanese criminal justice studies, believe that in this globalized era, Japan "cannot go on forever ignoring the UN's counsel."[154] The system's heavy reliance on confessions, the increased difficulty of obtaining them, and the sustained criticism of the process by which admissions of guilt are elicited have combined to create a question in the minds of many in Japan's officialdom: Can reliance on interrogation and confession continue in its present form?

There are two main responses to this issue. Some officials reject critiques of present practice as misleadingly "Anglo-centric" and aim to reinforce the system's commitment to find the truth through obtaining confessions.[155] What this response overlooks, of course, is that many of the system's most trenchant critics have decidedly non-Anglo origins.[156] In contrast, other officials insist that the system must ease its reliance on confessions by instituting reforms that make it legally possible to "make" cases through methods, such as plea bargaining and immunity, that currently are forbidden in Japan.[157]

Here lies the first problem of legitimacy in Japan's present system. Will it react by redoubling the commitment to interrogate suspects, or will it search for alternatives to the "truth through confession" axiom that has long been the system's bedrock belief?[158] The response to this challenge is as likely to be determined by developments outside the system as by what insiders desire. Criminal justice officials in Japan are becoming less capable of directing their own fate and shaping their own policies.[159] As their control wanes, politicians become more directive, and public opinion and media perceptions become increasingly key reference points for evaluating options. In this changed and charged environment, image is not everything but it does matter immensely. Prosecutors, for example, no longer can subscribe to the dictum that they do not and should not explain their behavior.[160] Instead, they have entered "the PR era" by establishing "public information officers" in some prefectural offices.[161]

Two related issues of image concern the criminal justice system's limited transparency. Ironically, police, prosecutors, and prisons in Japan are more closed to outside scrutiny than their American counterparts even though, on the whole, those in Japan seem to have less that "needs hiding."[162] The obstacles to research and investigative reporting are so formidable that it is difficult to document in detail even the most basic patterns of behavior.[163] All too often, citizens have to rely on the good faith of officials to tell it like it is. In this sense, the "truth" that preponderates in the media is like the "truth" that prevails in criminal investigations: both are constructed by officials in backstage settings. In either case, claims about the status of "truth" depend on perceptions of the legitimacy of the process—and the officials who control the process—for construing and constructing it.[164] If information is the currency of democracy, then in criminal justice as in other areas of government activity, the Japanese public lacks the key to the treasury.

The most glaring absence of openness occurs when the death penalty is administered in complete secrecy.[165] Hangings in Japan are only announced after the fact, to the public and to the condemned's family. Inmates on death row do not even know whether or when they will be hanged until a guard arrives at their cell on the morning of the execution day to announce that "your time has come." As a result, many inmates "spend years or even decades not knowing if they are living their last day."[166] The Ministry of Justice maintains that a policy of prior notification would inflict "major pain" on inmates and could even encourage suicide or escape, but Sakae Menda, who spent thirty-four years on death row before being exonerated in 1983, says that the current practice produces "absolutely unbearable anxiety" and is really designed to make death row inmates as docile as possible. "The reality," he says, "is that [the secrecy policy] is done for the convenience of the authorities."[167]

At present, the United States is the only other rich democracy that still practices capital punishment (albeit more openly than Japan). In the long run, both countries will probably be compelled to abolish the practice.[168] Democratic governments must attend to public perceptions, and when it comes to capital punishment the public that most matters may be as much international as domestic.[169] In the international court of public opinion, the death penalty is widely perceived to be uncivilized.[170]

There is a parallel problem of legitimacy in Japanese criminal trials, where judges currently decide guilt and impose punishment without input from lay judges or jurors. Many believe this trial system is deeply "undemocratic."[171] In one recent poll, almost 70 percent of Japanese adults said they are "dissatisfied" with judicial opinions,[172] and another survey revealed some of the reasons for discontent: 92 percent said the legal system takes so much time and money that it "is hard to use," and 89 percent called it "difficult and authoritarian."[173] It is therefore unsurprising that 81 percent of Japanese adults said the legal system must be reformed, compared with just 10 percent who said reform is unnecessary. Surveys also show that most Japanese favor using citizens as lay assessors for serious criminal trials (by a 2-to-1 ratio), but that most people do not want to serve themselves.[174]

As a result of these perceptions and other pressures for change, Japan's trial system will integrate laypeople into the adjudication process in 2009.[175] In criminal cases where the sentence could be death or life in prison and in criminal cases where a victim has died, the current panel of three professional judges will share its authority with six lay assessors. At present, these kinds of cases constitute about 4 percent of Japan's criminal caseload. The decision rule in mixed court trials will be majority rule with one amendment: at least one judge and one lay assessor must vote with the majority.

Japan's new lay assessor system could have several consequences. First, prosecutors will not be able to predict the result of charge decisions as reliably as they have in the past (lay assessors do not have "track records"), which may make their charging policies less cautious and thereby push conviction rates down. In addition, since lawyers will need to convince laypeople of the merits of their positions, trials could evolve from the deliberate, paper-processing sessions they are today into more vigorously adversarial forums of contestation and debate. At the same time, trial sessions will need to be held more continuously so as not to interfere too much with lay assessors' other obligations. Finally, if the new style of criminal trial becomes substantially more costly and time-consuming than what participants have grown used to, they could adapt by devising informal methods of adjudication (such as plea bargaining) in order to save time and money and avoid uncertainty. In these ways, efforts to increase the legitimacy of trials by promoting citizen participation could create new perceptions of illegitimacy elsewhere in the system.[176]

3. *Devolving Responsibility*

The need to share authority for doing justice and maintaining order extends beyond criminal trials. Indeed, Japanese criminal justice officials are being pressured to support, cooperate with, and devolve authority to victims, private organizations, and civil society much more than they have in the past.

In Japan as in most countries, the state has long been "the chief custodian of criminal justice."[177] Recently, however, state-based criminal justice is being challenged on two fronts. First, the provenance of security is being "multilateralized" through privatization and volunteerism. Security is increasingly provided by business firms and residential communities, and volunteers have come to share responsibility for safety with the public police (as in citizen patrol programs of the kind one can see in many Japanese cities). In 1996, for example, 377,140 private security guards were employed in Japan, compared with just 224,985 public police officers.[178] In the same year, Japan had only one thousand professional probation officers, most of whom were confined to their desks. Casework was delegated to fifty thousand voluntary probation officers who performed the frontline duties of controlling and caring for the probationers and parolees in their communities.[179] In addition, the character of criminal justice is being challenged in some nations by a "restorative justice" movement that aims to "heal the harms caused by crime" instead of merely "assigning blame and delivering pain" as states customarily have done. Both of these trends—multilateralization and restorative justice—involve relocating authority to nonstate actors or to lower levels of government,[180] and in both developments criminal justice is being decentralized for a variety of reasons: so that it can better respond to local needs, reflect local morality, and take advantage of local knowledge, but also because of deepening distrust in government, fiscal constraints on the state, increases in "mass private property" (such as shopping centers), and the "marketing of insecurity" by businesses that see the potential for profit in providing products and services for insecure citizens.[181]

In the world of "late modernity" that Japan now inhabits, government may need to devolve power and share the work of social control with local organizations and communities in order to remain effective and legitimate.[182]

The limited capacity of the sovereign state to control crime and do justice is the most fundamental lesson to be learned from studies of crime and social order in the United States and Britain. Fortunately, since Japan has not moved as far as the U.K. or U.S.A. toward a punitive "culture of control," it does not face the risk of being locked into an "iron cage" of punishment that is financially and socially costly and that could continue unabated long after its originating conditions have ceased to exist.[183] But as we have seen, if the intensity of change in Japanese criminal justice is not as great as in the U.K. or U.S.A., the direction does look familiar. The challenge for criminal justice officials is to respond intelligently to the forces described in this chapter rather than stand by and watch those pressures push policy and practice in unwelcome directions. As the contexts of Japanese criminal justice continue to change—as crime becomes a bigger and more politicized problem, victims more central actors, and security a more salient concern—the challenge of responding in ways that attend to new needs without undermining the achievements of the current system will probably grow more formidable.

Although pressure to devolve authority and share the work of social control can be seen in a number of fields, it seems most significant in two areas: the development of commercial methods for controlling crime and managing risk, and the victims' rights movement. In Japan as in other late modern societies, crime control and criminal justice are no longer solely the province of government. Private police, segregated spaces, security audits, surveillance cameras, and managerial approaches to crime and security stress the strategies of crime prevention and reduction over the traditional techniques of prosecution and punishment. Japan's burgeoning commercial crime control industry will not displace the formal agencies of criminal justice, but it will affect how criminal justice professionals define, identify, and respond to security concerns. In particular, the value of cost-effectiveness that constrains choice in the commercial sector is likely to become a more important concern to official agencies as well, especially if Japan continues to run large budget deficits. At the same time, the commercial orientation to serve specific "customers" could pull criminal justice officials away from their traditional obligation to "serve the public interest" and toward a greater interest in being responsive to the preferences of specific "constituencies" such as specific communities, businesses, or victims.

Security-conscious Japanese are buying up commercial crime-control devices at an increasingly rapid rate. Precise statistics are unavailable, but many analysts believe the amount spent on security products and services is "growing by leaps and bounds."[184] Secom, Japan's largest security company, says its home-protection business is expanding 20 percent annually. Demand for Miwa Lock Company's high-end products has tripled in two years, and demand for Kagino Kyukyusha's pick-proof locks has risen rapidly as well. Asahi Glass reports strong interest in its tempered windows. Secom and toy maker Tomy coproduce a global positioning system that enables parents to track their children over the Internet for four dollars a month, and if a child goes missing, the companies will send out a search team for eighty dollars an hour. Security cameras are widely used on roads and streetlights and in banks, shopping centers, and schools.[185] Mace is selling well, especially among young women. Misawa Homes sells "panic rooms" so that residents under attack can retreat to a sealed-off chamber with protected phone lines. Exsight Corporation reports strong interest in a variety of crime-control gizmos, from gas masks and bulletproof helmets to stun guns, pepper sprays, and briefcases that emit smoke. In short, many Japanese seem to feel like Nobuko Koshitaka, who travels with a loud buzzer in her purse. "I don't trust the police," the thirty-one-year-old says. "I feel like I have to watch out for myself."[186] For a fee, scores of commercial security providers are willing to help do the watching.

The victims' rights movement will confront Japanese officials with another strong demand to share responsibility for doing justice. That, at least, is what has happened in the United States, Britain, Australia, France, and elsewhere.[187] This movement presents Japanese officials with a difficult choice. On the one hand, they could respond to victims' needs as their counterparts have in other nations: by choosing dispositions and changing policy so as to satisfy demands for harsher punishment.[188] If crime rates continue to rise in Japan, and if (as seems likely) more citizens come to believe that it is beyond the state's capacity to secure a tolerable level of security, then attending more to the *consequences* of crime—by satisfying victims and managing fears—will become an increasingly attractive option to politicians and criminal justice officials alike. If so, concern about the *causes* of crime and the *reform* of offenders will become less central.

There may be a better way. "Restorative justice" has many incarnations, but most proceed from premises that are consistent with the need for states to share responsibility for providing security and doing justice. To start with, restorative justice regards crime as more than merely an offense against the state, for crime also injures victims, communities, and even the offenders themselves. Restorative justice further insists that the criminal process should help repair the harms caused by crime while resisting the tendency for governments to monopolize control over responses to it.[189] In these ways, restorative justice offers a vision for administering criminal justice in a manner that takes seriously the interests of victims without sacrificing the needs of offenders.[190] Becoming more restorative is one way that Japanese officials could share responsibility for criminal justice without shedding their commitment to care for, not merely control, offenders.[191]

IV. CONCLUSION

Civilization is a movement and not a condition, a voyage and not a harbor. At the same time, change does not necessarily mean progress. Over the past three decades, dramatic developments have occurred in American criminal justice that can hardly be called "progressive." As of 2002, 2 million U.S. citizens are incarcerated on any given day—about six times the number for 1973—and the various U.S. governments put one or more offenders to death every week. What is more, about 40 percent of young black men in the United States are under control of the criminal justice system—either in prison or jail or on probation or parole. This chapter has argued that social changes like the ones that transformed U.S. crime control arrangements are now shaping the administration of Japanese criminal justice—in ways that are both difficult to discern and, in direction if not intensity, surprisingly familiar. If a third edition of *Law in Japan* is published in 2045, the chapter on administering criminal justice is unlikely to exhibit as much consistency with this chapter as this one has with its predecessor. The future is uncertain, of course, not least because history is born of general causes but completed by "accidents" such as the Aum Shinrikyo attacks and September 11. What is clear is that the many values criminal justice could serve are not mutually compatible. As Isaiah Berlin put it, "Some among the Great Goods cannot live together."[192]

Citizens and officials in Japan will have to choose from among a number of competing values. Every choice (to serve victims) could entail a loss (of the rehabilitative ideal?), and every solution (to devolve responsibility) could create a new situation (public-private security partnerships?) that breeds its own needs and problems. Since one cannot have everything, priorities must be established, trade-offs must be made, and values and principles must be allowed to yield to each other in varying degrees—depending on the specific circumstances. In my view, the priorities for administering criminal justice during the first decades of the twenty-first century should include preserving the country's commitment to correction, bolstering the legitimacy of the criminal process, and spreading responsibility for the coproduction of law and order to actors and institutions in civil society. The voyage continues.

NOTES

1. Kōya Matsuo, "Keiji soshōhō no Nihonteki tokushoku: Iwayuru moderu ron to mo kanren shite" [Special Characteristics of the Japanese Code of Criminal Procedure: In Relation to the So-Called Model Theory], *Hōsō jihō* 46 (1994): 1249.

2. David T. Johnson, *The Japanese Way of Justice: Prosecuting Crime in Japan* (New York: Oxford University Press, 2002).

3. Sumio Hamada, *Jihaku no kenkyū* [Research on Confessions] (Tokyo: 31 Shōbo, 1992); Daniel H. Foote, "The Benevolent Paternalism of Japanese Criminal Justice," *California Law Review* 80 (1992): 317–90; Futaba Igarashi, "Crime, Confession, and Control in Contemporary Japan," trans. by Gavan McCormack, *Law in Context* 2 (1984): 1–30.

4. Tomomi Hirata, *Zen'in muzai: 122nin senkyo ihan jiken o ou* [Everyone Innocent: The Election Violation Case Involving 122 Acquittals] (Tokyo: Gyōsei, 1992); Masafumi Miyamoto and Tokushubu Sankei Shimbun, *Kensatsu no hirō* [Prosecutor Fatigue] (Tokyo: Kadokawa shōten, 2000), 233; Elmer H. Johnson, "Punitivity in Japanese Prisons? Testing the Policy of Tolerance" (paper delivered at the annual meeting of the American Society of Criminology, Chicago, November 13, 2002), 248.

5. Setsuo Miyazawa, "Introduction: An Unbalanced Adversary System—Issues, Polices, and Practices in Japan, in Context and in Comparative Perspective," in Malcolm Feeley and Setsuo Miyazawa, eds., *The Japanese Adversary System in Context: Controversies and Comparisons* (Hampshire, UK: Palgrave Macmillan, 2002), 1; Chalmers Johnson, *Conspiracy at Matsukawa* (Berkeley: University of California Press, 1972).

6. Daniel H. Foote, "From Japan's Death Row to Freedom," *Pacific Rim Law and Policy Journal* 1 (1992): 11–103; Nihon Hyōronsha, "Nihon no enzai" [Miscarriages of Justice in Japan], special edition, *Hōgaku seminā* 27 (July 1983).

7. Hiromitsu Ochiai, "Corruption: Who Polices the Police?" *Japan Quarterly*, April–June (2000): 50–57; Daniel H. Foote, "Nichibei hikaku keiji shihō no kōgi o furikaette" [Looking Back at Lectures on Comparative Criminal Justice in Japan and the United States], *Jurisuto*, no. 1148 (1999): 165–73; Masayuki Murayama, "The Role of the Defense Lawyer in the Japanese Criminal Process," in Feeley and Miyazawa, *The Japanese Adversary System in Context*, 42.

8. Eri Atarashi, *Hanzai higaisha shien* [Helping Victims of Crime] (Tokyo: Komichi shobo, 2000); D. Johnson, *The Japanese Way of Justice*, 201.

9. Tetsurō Murobushi, "Kensatsu to seiji: Kenryoku chūkaku to no kōbō" [Prosecutors and Politics: Struggles with the Nucleus of Power], *Hōgaku seminā*

zōkan 16 (1981): 265–72; Susumu Mukaidani, *Chiken tokusōbu* [The Special Investigation Division of the Tokyo Prosecutors Office] (Tokyo: Kōdansha, 1993); Eiichi Murakushi, *Kensatsu hiroku* [The Prosecutors' Secret Records] (Tokyo: Kōbunsha, 2002).

10. Akira Uozumi, *Tokusō kensatsu no yami* [The Dark Side of Special Prosecutors] (Tokyo: Bungei shunjū, 2002); Takashi Tachibana, "Kono taiho wa zettai ni okashii!!" [This Arrest Is Absolutely Improper], *Shūkan asahi*, May 17, 2002.

11. David H. Bayley, *Forces of Order: Policing Modern Japan* (Berkeley: University of California Press, 1991); Michio Kobayashi, *Nihon keisatsu: Fuhai no kōzō* [Japan's Police: The Structure of Corruption] (Tokyo: Chikuma shobo, 2000).

12. Atsushi Nagashima, "The Accused and Society: The Administration of Criminal Justice in Japan," in Arthur Taylor von Mehren, *Law in Japan: The Legal Order in a Changing Society* (Cambridge, MA: Harvard University Press, 1963), 297–323.

13. Ibid.

14. D. Johnson, *The Japanese Way of Justice*, 201.

15. Takeo Ishimatsu, "Are Criminal Defendants in Japan Truly Receiving Trials by Judges?" trans. Daniel H. Foote, *Law in Japan: An Annual* 22 (1989): 143–53; Satoru Shinomiya, "Adversarial Procedure without a Jury: Is Japan's System Adversarial, Inquisitorial, or Something else?" in Feeley and Miyazawa, *The Japanese Adversary System in Context*, 114.

16. Foote, "The Benevolent Paternalism of Japanese Criminal Justice."

17. Nagashima, "The Accused and Society," 321.

18. Feeley and Miyazawa, *The Japanese Adversary System in Context*.

19. Takashi Takano, "Miranda Experience in Japan," in Feeley and Miyazawa, *The Japanese Adversary System in Context*, 29.

20. Setsuo Miyazawa, *Policing in Japan: A Study on Making Crime* (Albany: State University of New York, 1992).

21. Murayama, "The Role of the Defense Lawyer in the Japanese Criminal Process," 43.

22. Miyazawa, "Introduction: An Unbalanced Adversary System."

23. Daniel H. Foote, "Reflections on Japan's Cooperative Adversary Process," in Feeley and Miyazawa, *The Japanese Adversary System in Context*.

24. Kōya Matsuo, "Tōjishashugi to bengo" [The Adversary System and Criminal Defense], in *Keiji saiban no riron: Kamo Yoshisuke sensei koki shukuga ronshū* [Theories of the Criminal Trial: Essays in Honor of Professor Yoshisuke Kamo] (Tokyo: Nihon hyōronsha, 1979).

25. Masayuki Murayama, *Keira keisatsu no kenkyū* [Research on Police Patrol] (Tokyo: Seibundō, 1990).

26. Kobayashi, *Nihon keisatsu*; Ochiai, "Corruption"; Akihiro Ōtani, *Nihon keisatsu no shōtai: Jiken no inpei, sōsa misu, fushōji wa naze okoru?* [The True Colors of Japan's Police: Why Do Cover-ups, Investigative Mistakes, and Scandals Occur?] (Tokyo: Nihon bungeisha, 2000).

27. Atarashi, *Hanzai higaisha shien*; Norio Takahashi, *Shūfukuteki shihō no tankyū* [The Quest for Restorative Justice] (Tokyo: Seibundō, 2003).

28. Felipe Fernandez-Armesto, *Truth: A History and a Guide for the Perplexed* (New York: St. Martin's Press, 1997), 3.

29. Marvin E. Frankel, *Partisan Justice: Too Much Fight? Too Little Truth? Equal Justice?* (New York: Hill and Wang, 1978).

30. D. Johnson, *The Japanese Way of Justice.*

31. William T. Pizzi, *Trials without Truth: Why Our System of Criminal Trials Has Become an Expensive Failure and What We Can Do to Rebuild It* (New York: New York University Press, 1999).

32. Tomoko Sasaki, *Nihon no shihō bunka* [Japan's Judicial Culture] (Tokyo: Bungei shunjū, 2000).

33. Joseph D. Grano, *Confessions, Truth, and the Law* (Ann Arbor: University of Michigan Press, 1993).

34. D. Johnson, *The Japanese Way of Justice,* 99.

35. Antonie Peters, "Some Comparative Observations on the Criminal Justice Process in Holland and Japan," *Journal of the Japan-Netherlands Institute* 4 (1992): 247–94; Igarashi, "Crime, Confession, and Control in Contemporary Japan."

36. Foote, "The Benevolent Paternalism of Japanese Criminal Justice"; David Garland, ed., "Mass Imprisonment in the USA," special issue, *Punishment and Society* 3 (2001): 1–199.

37. D. Johnson, *The Japanese Way of Justice,* 185.

38. David T. Johnson, "The Organization of Prosecution and the Possibility of Order," *Law and Society Review* 32 (1998): 247–308; Lief H. Carter, *The Limits of Order* (Lexington, MA: Lexington Books, 1974); Lloyd E. Ohlin and Frank J. Remington, eds., *Discretion in Criminal Justice: The Tension between Individualization and Uniformity* (Albany: State University of New York Press, 1993).

39. D. Johnson, "The Organization of Prosecution and the Possibility of Order."

40. D. Johnson, *The Japanese Way of Justice,* 217.

41. J. Mark Ramseyer and Eric B. Rasmusen, "Why Is the Japanese Conviction Rate So High?" *Journal of Legal Studies* 30 (2001): 53.

42. Hiroshi Yamaguchi, *Shihō fuhai* [The Deterioration of the Judiciary] (Tokyo: PHP Kenkyūjo, 1999).

43. Masahiro Hayashi, "Sendai no baishin saiban ni tsuite" [On Jury Trials in Sendai]. *Hanrei taimuzu*, 630 (1987): 17–24.

44. D. Johnson, *The Japanese Way of Justice*, 219.

45. Ibid., 129.

46. Karel van Wolferen, *The Enigma of Japanese Power: People and Politics in a Stateless Nation* (New York: Alfred A. Knopf, 1989), 221.

47. D. Johnson, *The Japanese Way of Justice*, 106.

48. Quoted in ibid., 242.

49. Daniel H. Foote, "Confessions and the Right to Silence in Japan," *Georgia Journal of International and Comparative Law* 21 (1991): 415–88.

50. Akio Harada, "Higisha no torishirabe: Kensatsu no tachiba kara" [Interrogating Suspects: A Prosecutor's Point of View], in Makoto Mitsui, Yoshifusa Nakayama, Kazuo Kawakami, and Masayoshi Tamura, eds., *Keiji tetsuzuki* [Criminal Procedure] (Tokyo: Chikuma shobō, 1988), 1:177–86.

51. Eric Feldman, *The Ritual of Rights in Japan: Law, Society, and Health Policy* (Cambridge: Cambridge University Press, 2000).

52. Miranda no Kai, *"Miranda no Kai" to bengo katsudo* [The Miranda Association and Defense Lawyer Activities] (Tokyo: Daigaku tosho, 1997).

53. As of March 2000, 10 percent of criminal trials in Japan had foreign defendants. Ten years earlier the analogous figure was 1 percent. See Jeff Horwich and Taro Karasaki, "Cultural Conflicts Intensify in Prison System," *Asahi Evening News*, June 20, 2000.

54. Wolfgang Herbert, *Foreign Workers and Law Enforcement in Japan* (New York: Kegan Paul International, 1997); Kei Chō, *Rainichi gaikokujin hanzai: Bunka shōtotsu kara mita rainichi chūgokujin hanzai* [Crimes by Foreigners in Japan: Culture Conflict and Crimes by Chinese Residents of Japan] (Tokyo: Akashi shōten, 2003).

55. D. Johnson, *The Japanese Way of Justice*, 269.

56. Shigeru Ōta, "Kensatsu jitsumu no kadai" [Practical Problems for Prosecutors], *Jurisuto*, no. 1148 (1999): 276–81.

57. Kinko Satō, *Torihiki no shakai: Amerika no keiji shihō* [The Bargaining Society: Criminal Justice in America] (Tokyo: Chūō kōronsha, 1974); Fumio Aoyagi, *Nihonjin no hanzai ishiki* [The Japanese Crime Consciousness] (Tokyo: Chūō kōronsha, 1986).

58. Haruhiko Ukawa, "Shihō torihiki o kangaeru" [Thinking about Plea Bargaining], *Hanrei jihō* 1583 (1997): 31–47, quoted in D. Johnson, *The Japanese Way of Justice*, 270.

59. Miyamoto and Tokushūbu, *Kensatsu no hirō*.

60. David T. Johnson, "Kumo no su ni shōchō sareru Nihonhō no tokushoku" [Japan's Legal Cobweb], *Jurisuto*, no. 1148 (1999): 185–89.

61. Miyazawa, *Policing in Japan*.

62. Donald Black, *The Behavior of Law* (New York: Academic Press, 1976).

63. Phillip B. Heymann, "Understanding Criminal Investigation." *Harvard Journal on Legislation* 22 (1985): 314.

64. Jacob Schlesinger, *Shadow Shoguns: The Rise and Fall of Japan's Postwar Political Machine* (Stanford, CA: Stanford University Press, 1996); Richard H. Mitchell, *Political Bribery in Japan* (Honolulu: University of Hawai'i Press, 1996).

65. Richard H. Mitchell, *Justice in Japan: The Notorious Teijin Scandal* (Honolulu: University of Hawai'i Press, 2002), 5.

66. Garland, "Mass Imprisonment in the USA"; Bayley, *Forces of Order*.

67. Philippe Nonet and Philip Selznick, *Law and Society in Transition: Toward Responsive Law* (New York: Harper Colophon, 1978).

68. D. Johnson, *The Japanese Way of Justice*, 21.

69. Kōya Matsuo and Masahito Inouye, "Hashigaki" [Foreword], *Jurisuto*, March 18 (2002), 2–3.

70. *Hanzai hakusho: Keizai hanzai no genjō to taisaku, heisei 12 nenpan* [The White Paper on Crime: The Current State of Economic Crime and Countermeasures against Them] (Tokyo: Hōmushō hōmu sōgō kenkyūsho, 2001). The overall crime rate is driven mainly by the category of theft (*settō*), which comprises about two-thirds of all crimes (ibid.).

71. "Most Minors Held for Theft Repeaters," *Daily Yomiuri*, August 17, 2002.

72. "Crime Hits Record High on Japan's Mean Streets," *Japan Times*, August 10, 2002

73. "Creating a New Breed of Outsiders?" *Asahi shinbun*, September 20, 1999.

74. Michael Hoffman, "The Kids Are Not All Right," *Japan Times*, October 20, 2002.

75. In 2001, ten children under age fourteen were arrested for murder or attempted murder. See "Crime Hits All-Time High [in 2001]," *Mainichi Daily News*, December 21, 2001. By comparison, in 1999, approximately seventy-five Americans under age fourteen committed murder or nonnegligent manslaughter. See Bureau of Justice Statistics, *Sourcebook of Criminal Justice Statistics—2000* (Washington, DC: U.S. Department of Justice, 2001), 315.

76. According to a study by the Ministry of Health, Labor and Welfare, five main factors increase the risk of child abuse: poverty, social isolation, postnatal depression, young parents, and rapid remarriage by parents who had children with a previous partner (*Daily Yomiuri*, June 22, 2002).

77. Cathy Spatz-Widom, "The Cycle of Violence" (Washington, DC: National Institute of Justice, 1999).

78. Yohji Morita, Haruo Soeda, Kumiko Soeda, and Mitsuru Taki, "Japan,"

in P. K. Smith, Y. Morita, J. Junger-Tas, D. Olweus, R. Catalano, and P. Slee, eds., *The Nature of School Bullying: A Cross-National Perspective* (London: Routledge, 1999), 309–23.

79. *Hanzai hakusho.*

80. Chō, *Rainichi gaikokujin Hanzai.*

81. "New Law Sees Rise in Child Abuse Deaths," *Mainichi Daily News*, December 13, 2001.

82. "Foreigners' Crimes Up," *Asahi.com*, October 2, 2001.

83. Matthew Green, "Cleaning up the Capital," *Kansai Time Out*, July (2002): 44.

84. "Gun-Related Crimes Mark 10-Year High," *Daily Yomiuri*, August 2, 2001.

85. Nicholas D. Kristof, "A Safer Society: A Special Report; Japanese Say No to Crime; Tough Methods, at a Price," *New York Times*, May 14, 1995.

86. Although crime has increased in Japan, overall offense rates remain about three times lower than in the United States, four times lower than in France, five times lower than in Germany, and six times lower than in England. See *Hanzai hakusho.*

87. Alfred Blumstein and Joel Wallman, *The Crime Drop in America* (Cambridge: Cambridge University Press, 2000).

88. Research on the effects of television viewing reveals that the more one watches TV, the more one thinks the real world is like the TV world. Since the TV world is saturated with violence, heavy watchers have especially unrealistic views about the scope and seriousness of crime in society. See Sissela Bok, *Mayhem: Violence as Public Entertainment* (New York: Perseus, 1999).

89. "Terebi Tōkyō settōdan hōdō" [Tokyo Television's Reporting on the Theft Gang], *Asahi shinbun*, July 4, 2002. For example, on the day I edited this paragraph (October 22, 2002), the Web site for the *Mainichi Daily News* (the English version of one of Japan's four major dailies) listed twelve "top news" stories; nine dealt with crime. They included "Gang Kidnaps, Robs, and Beats Total Stranger;" "Armed Robbers Net 70 Million Yen from Aomori Cash Car;" and "Businessman Bandit Stalks Tokyo Convenience Stores." Other recent headlines from Japanese newspapers include "Cops Call Tokyo a Rapist Haven, Warn Women to Be Wary"; "Crime Hits Record High on Japan's Mean Streets"; "Crime's Brutal Upswing"; "Deteriorating Public Safety"; "Time to Get Tough on Crime"; "Prisons Bursting at the Seams"; and "Crime Wave Now Becoming a Political Issue."

90. Shigeo Masui, "Back to Basics to Beat Crime," *Daily Yomiuri*, January 17, 2002.

91. Mikio Kawai, *Anzen shinwa hōkai no paradokkusu: Chian no hōshakaigaku* [The Paradox of the Shattered Safety Myth: A Socio-legal Study of Order] (Tokyo: Iwanami shoten, 2004).

92. "Asahi shinbunsha teiki kokumin ishiki chōsa" [The Asahi Newspaper Company's Regular Citizen Consciousness Survey], *Asahi shinbun*, January 8, 2002.

93. "Yomiuri shimbunsha seron chosa" [The Yomiuri Newspaper Company Public Opinion Poll], *Yomiuri shinbun*, December 14, 2001. (Similar surveys published on November 30, 2001; January 18, 2001; December 19, 1999; December 20, 1998; March 17, 1997; June 22, 1995; and November 7, 1993).

94. Shigeo Masui, "Japan's Prisons Overflowing," *Daily Yomiuri*, April 28, 2002.

95. Akihiro Ishihara, "Overcrowded Jails May Be Dangerous," *Daily Yomiuri*, August 19, 2002; "Prisons Bursting at the Seams," *Mainichi Daily News*, September 26, 2002.

96. Matsuo and Inouye, "Hashigaki."

97. Toshiko Takemura, "Youth Crime Debate Continues," *Daily Yomiuri*, June 25, 2002.

98. Peter B. E. Hill, *Botaiho: Japanese Organized Crime under the Boryokudan Countermeasures Law* (Stirling: Scottish Centre for Japanese Studies, University of Stirling, 2000); Hill, *The Japanese Mafia: Yakuza, Law, and the State* (New York: Oxford University Press, 2003).

99. Mari Yamaguchi, "Packed Prisons Worry Japanese Officials," *Honolulu Advertiser*, November 11, 2001. The increase in punishment may be partly a function of a rise in the average level of crime seriousness, but prosecutors and judges insist it is not just that. Independent of crime seriousness, there is also a shift toward heavier sanctions.

100. Elliott Currie, *Crime and Punishment in America* (New York: Metropolitan Books, 1998).

101. Richard Katz, *Japan, the System That Soured: The Rise and Fall of the Japanese Economic Miracle* (New York: M. E. Sharpe, 1998); Leonard Schoppa, "Japan: The Reluctant Reformer," *Foreign Affairs* September–October (2001): 76–90.

102. Olivier Zunz, Leonard Schoppa, and Nobuhiro Hiwatari, *Social Contracts under Stress: The Middle Classes of America, Europe, and Japan at the Turn of the Century* (New York: Russell Sage, 2002); Toshiki Satō, *Fuheitō shakai Nippon* [Japan the Unfair Society] (Tokyo: Chūko shinsho, 2000); Hiroshi Ishida, *Social Mobility in Contemporary Japan: Educational Credentials, Class and the Labor Market in Cross-National Perspective* (Palo Alto, CA: Stanford University Press, 1995).

103. Toshiaki Tachibanaki, *Nihon no keizai kakusa: Shotoku to shisan kara kangaeru* [Economic Inequality in Japan: An Analysis in Terms of Income and Assets] (Tokyo: Iwanami shoten, 1998). Measuring inequality is complicated, and there is no consensus about the seriousness of the problem in Japan. See Junsuke Hara and Kazuo Seiyama, *Shakai kaisō: Yutakasa no naka no fubyōdō* [Social Stratification: Inequality in an Affluent Society] (Tokyo: University of Tokyo Press, 1999)

Some analysts believe that the rise in income and consumption inequality since the mid-1980s is largely explained by the aging of the population, not (as in the United Kingdom and the United States) by increases in inequality between and within different age-groups. See Fumio Ohtake, "Aging Society and Inequality," *Japan Labor Bulletin* 38(7) (July 1, 1999): 1–9. There is, however, substantial agreement about certain features of the big picture, including the fact that recent increases in crime "reflect the social costs brought about by the worsening of unemployment and inequality" in Japan. See Fumio Ōtake and Kazuaki Okamura, "Shōnen hanzai to rōdō shijō: Jikeiretsu oyobi todōfuken betsu paneru bunseki" [Juvenile Crime and the Labor Market: A Panel Analysis by Time and Place], *Nihon keizai kenkyū* 40 (March 2000): 40–65.

104. Doug Struck and Kathryn Tolbert, "Japan Faces Growing Class Differences," *Honolulu Advertiser*, January 6, 2002.

105. Stephanie Strom, "Japan Slowly Embraces Greater Income Inequality over Social Harmony," *New York Times*, January 4, 2000; "Govt to Tighten Purse Strings on Single Mothers," *Daily Yomiuri*, June 8, 2002.

106. James Brooke, "Young People Feel a Chill in Japan's Hiring Season," *New York Times*, April 1, 2002.

107. Strom, "Japan Slowly Embraces Greater Income Inequality Over Social Harmony"; Deborah J. Milly, *Poverty, Equality and Growth: The Politics of Economic Need in Postwar Japan*, Harvard East Asian Monographs (Cambridge, MA: Harvard University Press, 1999).

108. Yumiko Ono, "Outlook Grim for Japanese Graduates: Economic Slump Means Fewer Jobs for Young Adults," *Honolulu Advertiser*, December 26, 2001.

109. Struck and Tolbert, "Japan Faces Growing Class Differences."

110. Ronald Dore, "Japan's Reform Debate: Patriotic Concern or Class Interest? Or Both?" *Journal of Japanese Studies* 25(1) (1999): 65–90.

111. David Matsumoto, *The New Japan: Debunking Seven Cultural Stereotypes* (Yarmouth, ME: Intercultural Press, 2002). A survey of registered voters by the *Yomiuri shinbun* (June 14, 2002) found that 90 percent of respondents felt the manners and behavior of Japanese people have "worsened."

112. David Garland, *The Culture of Control: Crime and Social Order in Contemporary Society* (Chicago: University of Chicago Press, 2001), 84.

113 Nobuo Komiya, "A Cultural Study of the Low Crime Rate in Japan," *British Journal of Criminology* 39 (Summer 1999): 369–90; Bayley, *Forces of Order*; T. R. Reid, *Confucius Lives Next Door: What Living in the East Teaches about Living in the West* (New York: Random House, 1999).

114. *Yomiuri shinbun*, November 30, 2001.

115. John B. Thompson, *Political Scandal: Power and Visibility in the Media Age*

(Cambridge, UK: Polity Press, 2000); Susan J. Pharr, "Public Trust and Corruption in Japan," in Arnold J. Heidenheimer and Michael Johnston, eds., *Political Corruption: Concepts and Contexts* (New Brunswick, NJ: Transaction Publishers, 2002).

116. Garland, *The Culture of Control*, 88.

117. Jacob S. Siegel, *Applied Demography: Applications to Business, Government, Law, and Public Policy* (New York: Academic Press, 2001).

118. Sonni Efron, "Japan's Demography Shock," *Los Angeles Times*, June 24–26, 2001.

119. Japanese women postpone marriage and childbirth for two main reasons: because it is expensive to raise and educate children, and because to become a wife and mother is to say *sayonara* to freedoms that many single women enjoy. The costs of motherhood—what demographers call "the mommy tax"—are "far more punishing for Japanese women" than for their American and European counterparts. See ibid.

120. Some European nations are experiencing similar demographic trends. Unlike Italy, however, Japan is loath to allow immigrants to solve labor shortages, and unlike Sweden, which makes it financially attractive for single mothers to bear and raise children, social norms in Japan discourage out-of-wedlock births. See ibid.

121. Japan's annual longevity statistics are released on September 15, Respect for the Aging Day. In recent years "the tenor of media coverage has changed from celebratory to 'Oh no, [the average life span] has increased again.'" Ibid.

122. The comparable rate for the United States is 4.2 divorces per 1,000 population. See ibid.

123. In the United States, 32.8 percent of births are registered as "nonmarital." See ibid.

124. Between 1987 and 1995, the number of Japanese who believed that women should "stay at home and look after their families" declined by almost 40 percent. Ibid.

125. This section stresses pressures that could push Japanese criminal justice toward "convergence" with countries like the United Kingdom and the United States. However, since crime is committed disproportionately by young males, Japan's low birthrates may also be a countervailing pressure against that high-crime, high-punishment pattern.

126. Efron, "Japan's Demography Shock."

127. Garland, *The Culture of Control*, 105.

128. Matsumoto, *The New Japan*.

129. Garland, *The Culture of Control*, 163.

130. Michael Tonry, "Symbol, Substance, and Severity in Western Penal Policies," *Punishment and Society* 3 (2001): 517–36; Nils Christie, *Crime Control as Industry*, 3rd ed. (London: Routledge, 2000).

131. Kaoru Nakada, Shin'ya Horita, and Chiharu Nagasawa, "Hanzai kenkyoritsu 24.2% ga imi suru mono" [The Meaning of the 24.2 Percent Clearance Rate], *Spa*, January 31 (2001): 20–23.

132. "Time to Get Tough on Crime," *Daily Yomiuri*, August 11, 2002.

133. Haruo Abe, "The Accused and Society: Therapeutic and Preventive Aspects of Criminal Justice in Japan," in von Mehren, *Law in Japan*, 331.

134. V. Lee Hamilton and Joseph Sanders, *Everyday Justice: Responsibility and the Individual in Japan and the United States* (New Haven, CT: Yale University Press, 1992), 157. A poll in 2001 revealed that 86 percent of Japanese adults believe criminal sentences are "often" or "sometimes" too lenient (*Yomiuri shinbun*, December 14, 2001). Compared to California, the mean length of sentence in Japan is especially short for sex crimes, kidnapping, assault, and murder, while mean sentence length is more similar for robbery, theft, and drug and gun offenses. See E. Johnson, "Punitivity in Japanese Prisons"; see also D. Johnson, *The Japanese Way of Justice*, 190–201.

135. Franklin E. Zimring, Gordon Hawkins, and Sam Kamin, *Punishment and Democracy: Three Strikes and You're Out in California* (New York: Oxford University Press, 2001).

136. In national polls conducted in January 2001, just 28.7 percent of Japanese adults said they trust (*shinrai*) the courts, and only 19.0 percent said they trust police and prosecutors. The comparable figures for American adults were 60.7 percent and 64.5 percent, respectively. Across all of the fourteen institutions surveyed (from legislatures to labor unions), the average Japanese trust level was almost three and one-half times lower than the American average. *Yomiuri shinbun*, January 18, 2001.

137. David T. Johnson, "Nihon ni okeru shihō seido kaikaku: Keisatsu no shozai to sono jūyōsei" [Justice System Reform in Japan: Where Are the Police and Why It Matters], *Hōritsu jihō*, no. 2 (February 2004): 8–15. In July 2002, police in Ibaraki Prefecture became the first to acknowledge cooking the clearance-rate books. "Juribo ni keibi na nusumi shirusazu: Kenkyo appu no ura waza?" [Minor Thefts Not Recorded in [Ibaraki] Police Books: A Backstage Trick to Raise Clearance Rates?], *Yomiuri shinbun*, July 8, 2002. At least ten incumbent and former officers admitted that police hid crime data for more than twenty years. The lying, they claim, ended around 1996, but that is not the case (D. Johnson, "Nihon ni okeru shihō seido kaikaku"). One incumbent officer has said that "the prefectural police headquarters instructed us to raise the rate. We had no choice but to do so."

138. Mitsuaki Sasaki, Yasuyuki Sakai, and Akira Morio, "Keiji rippō katei" [The Criminal Legislation Process] (panel held at the annual meeting of the Keihō Gakkai, Nanzan University in Nagoya, Japan, May 18, 2002); Zimring, Hawkins, and Kamin, *Punishment and Democracy*.

139. Atarashi, *Hanzai higaisha shien*; "Hotto mōningu: Hanzai higaisha chiiki de dō uketomeru ka" [How Are Victims of Crime Dealing with It?], *NHK News*, July 9, 2002 (Tokyo channel 1).

140. Garland, *The Culture of Control*.

141. Atsuyuki Sassa and Tomoko Sasaki, "Zainichi chūgokujin kyōaku hanzai jijō" [The Circumstances of Heinous Crimes Committed by Chinese Residents of Japan], *Bungei shunjū*, August (2002): 270.

142. Amnesty International disagrees with the judge, as do other critics of prison conditions in Japan. Amnesty International, *Japan: Abusive Punishments in Japanese Prisons*, Report ASA 22/04/98 (New York: Amnesty International, 1998); Vivien Stern, *A Sin against the Future: Imprisonment in the World* (Boston: Northeastern University Press, 1998); Horwich and Karasaki, "Cultural Conflicts Intensify in Prison System"; "Aichi Prison Guards Accused of Assaulting Inmates," *Mainichi Daily News*, November 8, 2002. In 1998, the U.N. Human Rights Commission published a report condemning Japan for violating the "cruel and inhumane treatment" clause of the International Convention on Human Rights. "Editorial: Crimes in Nagoya Prison," *Asahi.com*, November 12, 2002. Among other recommendations, the commission urged Japan to institute credible procedures for investigating prisoners' complaints. Inmates in Japan long have complained that prison guards retaliate against them when they attempt to bring grievances about prison conditions to lawyers or other outside bodies. Takuya Asakura, "Prison Abuses in Spotlight Following Guard Arrests," *Japan Times*, November 13, 2002.

143. Mark Schreiber, "Chinese, Japanese Clash in 'Mafia Town,'" *Japan Times*, October 20, 2002.

144. Chō, *Rainichi Gaikokujin Hanzai*.

145. Foote, "The Benevolent Paternalism of Japanese Criminal Justice," 374.

146. D. Johnson, *The Japanese Way of Justice*, 189.

147. H. Richard Uviller, *The Tilted Playing Field: Is Criminal Justice Unfair?* (New Haven, CT: Yale University Press, 1999).

148. Tom Tyler, *Why People Obey the Law* (New Haven, CT: Yale University Press, 1990).

149. Makoto Mitsui, Yoshinobu Baba, Hiroshi Satō, and Ritsurō Uemura, eds., *Keiji tetsuzuki*, 3 vols. (Tokyo: Yūyūsha, 2002).

150. D. Johnson, *The Japanese Way of Justice*, 99.

151. Ibid., 268.

152. Harada, "Higisha no torishirabe," 1:185.

153. Defendants in Japan possess very limited discovery rights. Prosecutors have worked hard to delimit those rights, and their arguments have been successful but self-serving. For an organization that trumpets truth telling so much, it is ironic that the procuracy opposes disclosing to the defense more of the building blocks—the draft dossier especially—that investigators use to construct the truth. Discovery rights are much broader in the United States, Germany, Holland, and elsewhere, and they were substantially broader in prewar Japan. See Thomas Weigend, "Nihon no keiji bengo ni tai suru Doitsuhō no kanten kara no komento" [Comment on Japanese Criminal Defense from the Standpoint of German Law], *Jurisuto*, no. 1148 (1999): 193–97; D. Johnson, *The Japanese Way of Justice*, 41, 75, 272. When defense lawyers are disabled in this way, they too often provide "a supplementary service to the prosecution" instead of playing the advocacy role that is prescribed by the adversary system. See Murayama, "The Role of the Defense Lawyer in the Japanese Criminal Process," 54.

154. Ryūichi Hirano, "Sanshinsei no saiyō ni yoru 'kakushin shihō' o: Keiji shihō kaikaku no ugoki to hōkō" [For a "Reformed Justice" through the Adoption of a Lay Participation System: Movements and Direction of Criminal Justice Reform], *Jurisuto*, no. 1148 (1999): 4. Concern about how to balance facts and fairness was not born recently. Indeed, Atsushi Nagashima's essay ends by calling for a shift in Japanese criminal justice "from an inquisitorial to an accusatorial process." See Nagashima, "The Accused and Society," 321. Calls for that change continue, from a variety of quarters. Feeley and Miyazawa, *The Japanese Adversary System in Context*.

155. Ōta, "Kensatsu jitsumu no kadai"; Sasaki, *Nihon no shihō bunka*.

156. Hirano, "Sanshinsei no saiyō ni yoru 'kakushin shihō' o; Ryūichi Hirano, "Diagnosis of the Current Code of Criminal Procedure," trans. by Daniel H. Foote, *Law in Japan: An Annual* 22 (1989): 129–42; Hamada, *Jihaku no kenkyū*; Ishimatsu, "Are Criminal Defendants in Japan Truly Receiving Trials by Judges"; Yamaguchi, *Shihō fuhai*; Miyazawa, *Policing in Japan*; Masayuki Murayama, "Postwar Trends in the Administration of Japanese Criminal Justice: Lenient But Intolerant or Something Else?" *Journal of the Japan-Netherlands Institute*, 4 (1992): 221–246; Takano, "Miranda Experience in Japan." For example, Hirano argues that "the real substance" and "the truly distinctive character" of Japan's criminal process lie in an inquisitorial investigative process that is dominated by police and prosecutors. Hirano, "Diagnosis of the Current Code of Criminal Procedure." Hirano regards trials in Japan as mere "ceremonies" for "ratifying" prosecutors' decisions, and he concludes that Japanese criminal justice is "abnormal," "diseased," and "really quite hopeless."

157. Ukawa, "Shihō torihiki o kangaeru"; Satō, *Torihiki no shakai*; Aoyagi, *Nihonjin no hanzai ishiki*.

158. Shingo Yoshimura, "Wakayama Case May Be Model for Trials in Future," *Daily Yomiuri*, May 14, 1999.

159. Matsuo and Inouye, "Hashigaki."

160. The traditional formula is "*Wareware wa benkai shinai*," which means, roughly, "We [prosecutors] do not explain, justify, or defend our actions."

161. "Kensatsu mo PR no jidai: Tōkyō nado 4 chiken ni 'kōhōkan' o shinsetsu" [It's the PR Era for Prosecutors Too: Four District Prosecutors Offices, including Tokyo, Establish the Position of 'Public Information Officer'], *Asahi shinbun*, January 25, 2002.

162. Bayley, *Forces of Order*, 78; D. Johnson, *The Japanese Way of Justice*, 11.

163. Jurg Gerber and Susan L. Weeks, "Some Reflections on Doing Cross-Cultural Research: Interviewing Japanese Prison Inmates," *Criminologist*, November–December (1992): 7–13.

164. Christopher Bracey, "Truth and Legitimacy in the American Criminal Process," *Journal of Criminal Law and Criminology* 90 (Winter 2000): 691–728.

165. Petra Schmidt, *Capital Punishment in Japan* (Leiden: Brill, 2002).

166. Doug Struck, "On Japan's Death Row, Uncertainty by Design: Condemned Never Know When Executioner Will Call," *Washington Post*, May 2, 2001.

167. Howard W. French, "Secrecy of Japan's Executions Is Criticized as Unduly Cruel," *New York Times*, June 30, 2002.

168. Franklin E. Zimring, *Wrestling with Destiny: The Contradictions of American Capital Punishment* (New York: Oxford University Press, 2003).

169. In a poll by the prime minister's office, 76 percent of Japanese adults said the death penalty should be retained, 9 percent said it should be abolished, and 15 percent were undecided. Schmidt, *Capital Punishment in Japan*, 166.

170. Shigemitsu Dandō, *Shikei haishiron* [For Abolition of Capital Punishment] (Tokyo: Yūhikaku, 1997); Peter Hodgkinson and William A. Schabas, *Capital Punishment: Strategies for Abolition* (Cambridge: Cambridge University Press, 2004). A study of capital punishment in global perspective found that as of January 2001 there were "76 totally abolitionist countries, 11 abolitionist for ordinary crimes, 36 abolitionist de facto, and 71 still retentionist." Roger Hood, "Capital Punishment: A Global Perspective," *Punishment and Society* 3 (2001): 334. Besides Japan and the United States, the only other democracies that regularly execute offenders are India and Taiwan.

171. Shinomiya, "Adversarial Procedure without Jury."

172. *Yomiuri shinbun*, November 30, 2000.

173. Kyodo News Service, December 1, 2001.

174. *NHK News*, May 4, 2001; Kyodo News Service, December 1, 2001.

175. Shihō seido kaikaku shingikai [Justice System Reform Council], *Ikensho* [Recommendations], June 12, 2001; Kent Anderson and Mark Nolan, "Lay Participation in the Japanese Justice System" (unpublished paper, February 4, 2004), 1–55. Atsushi Nagashima predicted that "the road will be opened, eventually, to the introduction of the jury trial" in Japan. Nagashima, "The Accused and Society," 321. The emerging lay assessor system partly vindicates his prediction. Anderson and Nolan, "Lay Participation in the Japanese Justice System."

176. In June 2001, Japan's Justice System Reform Council published other recommendations in addition to the ones aimed at enhancing public participation in criminal proceedings. Some pertain directly to prosecutors and, if adopted, seem likely to push them in a more punitive direction. In particular, the council recommended "greatly increasing" the number of prosecutors, perhaps by as much as one thousand (Japan presently has about two thousand prosecutors). It suggested that decisions made by prosecution review commissions—citizen councils that review non-charge decisions—be made binding on prosecutors (at present they are merely advisory). And it argued that prosecutors must hear and heed the voices of three constituencies not known for their leniency: victims, police, and the general public. Shihō seido kaikaku shingikai, *Ikensho*.

177. David H. Bayley, "Security and Justice for All," in Heather Strang and John Braithwaite, eds., *Restorative Justice and Civil Society* (Cambridge: Cambridge University Press, 2001), 211.

178. Naoko Yoshida, "The Taming of the Japanese Private Security Industry," *Policing and Society* 9 (1999): 246.

179. E. Johnson, *Japanese Corrections: Managing Convicted Offenders in an Orderly Society* (Carbondale: Southern Illinois Press, 1996).

180. Setsuo Miyazawa, "The Private Sector and Law Enforcement in Japan," in William T. Gormley Jr., ed., *Privatization and Its Alternatives* (Madison: University of Wisconsin Press, 1991).

181. Bayley, "Security and Justice for All," 212; David H. Bayley and Clifford D. Shearing, "The Future of Policing," *Law and Society Review* 30(3) (1996): 585–606.

182. Garland, *The Culture of Control*, 205.

183. Ibid., 203.

184. Mark Magnier, "Rising Crime Drives Japanese to Fight Back with Gizmos," *Los Angeles Times*, September 9, 2002.

185. "Monitoring the Monitors," *Mainichi Daily News*, October 31, 2002.

186. Magnier, "Rising Crime Drives Japanese to Fight Back with Gizmos."

187. Garland, *The Culture of Control*.

188. "Hotto mōningu: Hanzai higaisha chiiki de dō uketomeru ka."

189. Daniel Van Ness and Karen Heetderks Strong, *Restoring Justice* (Cincinnati: Anderson, 2002).

190. John Braithwaite, *Restorative Justice and Responsive Regulation* (New York: Oxford University Press, 2002).

191. Strang and Braithwaite, *Restorative Justice and Civil Society.*

192. Isaiah Berlin, *The Proper Study of Mankind: An Anthology of Essays,* ed. Henry Hardy and Roger Hausheer (New York: Farrar, Straus and Giroux, 1997).

16 Litigation, Administrative Relief, and Political Settlement for Pollution Victim Compensation

Minamata Mercury Poisoning after Fifty Years

KŌICHIRŌ FUJIKURA

I. INTRODUCTION

The process of industrializing modern Japan since the Meiji Restoration (1868) involves a long history of environmental disruptions and disputes.[1] After World War II, Japan's national goals became economic recovery and rebuilding of the basic industries, which had been totally destroyed by the war; those goals were pursued at almost any cost. As was soon discovered, the cost was enormous in terms of environmental destruction and loss of lives and health; for its industrial development, Japan paid a dear price in human suffering. Japanese environmental law and policy were formed in response to the pressing need to compensate victims of industrial pollution. Thus, Japanese environmental law and policy may be termed a victim-compensation approach.

Among Japan's many environmental disasters, Minamata stands out. Minamata disease, a disease caused by mercury poisoning brought on by the intensive industrial activities of a chemical company and its disregard of the surrounding environment and communities, represents a tragic by-product of Japan's push for industrial development. The events in Minamata have deeply affected the course of development for Japanese environmental law and policy ever since.

II. THE MINAMATA STORY

The first incident of mercury poisoning in Japan appeared in the mid-1950s during a period of growing economic prosperity. In 1954, several people were hospitalized with similar symptoms. They all were suffering from violent shaking, a narrowing field of vision, and loss of control and coordination over their body movements. The number of victims increased rapidly. All were living in fishing villages in the vicinity of Minamata Bay, in Kumamoto Prefecture, which is located in Kyushu, the southernmost of Japan's four main islands. In the initial period after the outbreak, it was feared that Minamata disease, as it came to be known, was contagious; the victims and their families suffered the further indignity of discrimination by the rest of the community.

It took more then ten years before teams of scientists determined the cause of disease to be methylated mercury. The Ministry of Public Health officially recognized that as the cause and made a public announcement to that effect in 1968. Methylated mercury was a by-product of the Japan Chisso (Nitrogen Manufacturing) Company. For years the Chisso plant, located in Minamata, had discharged methylated mercury in its effluent directly into Minamata Bay.[2] Gradually the chemical had become concentrated in the tissues of fish, other marine organisms, and ultimately in the inhabitants of the Minamata fishing community. Mercury affected the central nervous system after it entered the human body through the food chain.

In 1965 a similar outbreak of Minamata disease was reported in Niigata City, on the Japan Sea side of the main island of Honshu. There, the Showa Denko Corporation operated a plant employing the same production process and method as Chisso.

Although the cause of disease was not determined until the 1960s, fishermen and village people instinctively knew from the beginning that the effluent with a sickening color discharged from the Chisso plant was killing fish and also birds and cats that fed on fish. The villagers repeatedly sought to negotiate with Chisso to have it stop the discharge, but Chisso was never responsive. The local residents then resorted to such traditional means of dispute settlement as conciliation, mediation, and arbitration. They asked the governor of the prefecture to intervene and appealed to the central government for help. They protested, demonstrated, picketed, staged sit-ins, and even attempted to break into the plant forcefully. All their efforts, however, produced little result. Chisso, denying any wrongdoing, continued its operations.

III. STAGE ONE: MINAMATA VICTIMS SUE FOR DAMAGES

The victims finally decided to take the polluters to court. The Niigata group (of 77) sued Showa Denko in 1967, and the Minamata group (of 139) sued Chisso in 1969. The only cause of civil action available was one for damages based on a theory of negligence under Article 709 of the Civil Code, which provides: "A person who violates intentionally or negligently the rights of another is bound to make compensation for damages arising therefrom." In a negligence action, the plaintiff must prove the critical elements of liability, namely, breach of duty of care, foreseeability of harm, and causation.

In both cases, the courts found the polluters negligent and awarded the plaintiffs substantial damages.[3] In applying the traditional negligence principle to the modern pollution context, the courts utilized an innovative approach in determining the defendants' liability. First, the courts imposed an extensive and high degree of care on the defendants' chemical plants. Second, the courts found that the defendants could have foreseen injuries from their discharges to people living in the surrounding areas. Third, the courts created a presumption of causation in favor of the plaintiffs.

As to each of the above issues, the courts set forth the following reasoning:

(1) Degree of care. The defendants owed a high degree of care since the production process of the chemical industry generally utilized large quantities of dangerous substances such as raw materials and catalysts. There was an extremely high probability that unpredictably harmful substances would be contained in the factory's wastewater. When dangerous materials were discharged into the rivers and seas, harm to plants, animals, or people could easily be anticipated. Therefore, when a chemical plant discharged wastewater, it must always use "the best knowledge and technology" to determine whether harmful substances were present and what effect there might be on plants, animals, and humans. In addition to assuring the safety of its wastewater, if by any chance harm became apparent or there arose doubt about its safety, the factory should immediately suspend operations and adopt the necessary maximum preventive measures. Especially with regard to the life and health of area residents, the factory must exercise a high degree of care to prevent harm before it occurs.

(2) Foreseeability. The defendants contended that foreseeability was limited to the foreseeability of the production of the specific causal agent, and that they did not violate any duty since they could not possibly have foreseen this specific outcome. However, the courts found that if one were to accept the defendants' contention, the degree of danger could be proven only after

the environment was polluted and destroyed and lives and health of people harmed. Until that point, the discharge of dangerous wastewater would have to be tolerated. The inevitable consequence would be that the encroachment on the lives and health of residents would be tantamount to allowing the residents to serve as human subjects for experimentation. The courts found this clearly unjust.

(3) Causation. The courts analyzed causation in three parts: (a) the characteristic symptoms of the disorder and its causal (etiological) agent, (b) the pathway of pollution, and (c) the discharge of the causal agent by the wrongdoer. With regard to (a) and (b), the courts held that causation might be proved by an accumulation of circumstantial evidence if the plaintiffs' explanation was consistent with the relevant scientific findings (of clinicians, pathologists, epidemiologists, and other medical specialists). When the above level of proof was obtained, and the search for the source of pollution led to the very doorstep of the factory, it should be factually presumed that the factory was the source, and legal causation should be fully established.

In these cases of mercury poisoning, the courts in essence imposed strict liability on the polluters, while still using the terminology of negligence under Article 709: such terms as *breach of care, probability* and *foreseeability of harm.* The courts also created a presumption of causation in favor of the plaintiffs. Once the plaintiffs demonstrated the causal agent and the pathway implicating defendants, the burden of proof then shifted to the defendants to prove that the causal agent could not be discharged from its plant.

Other victims of air and water pollution in other parts of Japan also sued. In all of the major litigation efforts, the victims won.[4] These decisions played an important role in structuring the overall approach to relief for pollution victims. The courts' holdings on the above issues were adopted into and formed the foundation of a national administrative compensation system established in 1973.

The courts played another important role, as well. The courts provided the victims with a public forum where they could confront and expose the polluters' wrongdoing. The victims were morally outraged, and their assertion of civil rights in a very basic sense was finally vindicated by the courts.

IV. STAGE TWO: ADMINISTRATIVE COMPENSATION SYSTEM ESTABLISHED

The Diet in 1970 enacted a dozen environmental protection measures. Then, in 1973, the Act for the Compensation of Pollution-Related Health Injury was enacted, thereby establishing a national administrative compensation system. The law was supported by all major actors, namely, pollution victims, business and industry, politicians, and bureaucrats. Organizations of pollution victims supported the law because the administrative compensation system could offer victims much-needed monetary relief promptly and fairly. Business and industry supported it because the system could provide some predictability and control as to the costs of compensation. (In contrast, business and industry could not predict nor control the magnitude and extent of tort liability that the courts might impose in potential lawsuits against them.) Politicians and bureaucrats supported the law because, through it, they could take credit for doing something for the victims and at the same time retain control over the national pollution crises.

The law established an administrative system to provide scheduled compensation payments for certified victims of air and water pollution. Polluted areas were designated around major industrial cities and sites. In the case of air pollution, forty-one areas eventually were designated by using the level of sulfur oxide (SOx) concentration as an index. Seven areas of water and soil pollution caused by mercury, cadmium, and arsenic were also designated. In these areas, usually a specific source of toxic pollution had been identified. People living in designated areas who developed certain prescribed symptoms were certified by doctors, and a special Health Damages Certification Council (composed of medical, legal, and other experts) was set up for the purpose of reviewing certification. Upon certification, victims became eligible to receive compensation for medical expenses, lost earnings, and other incidentals.

The costs of compensation were imposed on polluters. In the case of air pollution, a graduated emission charge was levied on stationary sources (factories with smoke stacks) and a tonnage tax on automobiles, with those two categories of polluters respectively contributing 80 percent and 20 percent of the amount paid into the central fund each year. The emission charge was collected at the national level. Thereafter, the fund was distributed to provincial governments for payment to the victims. In the case of water-related pollution traceable to a specific substance and source, identified polluters (such as Chisso in Minamata) were required to pay directly to certified victims at the local level.

The administrative system provided relief to large numbers of victims. In 1988, for example, when the system had been in operation for fifteen years, 108,489 certified victims of air pollution and 1,898 certified victims of toxic pollution were receiving compensation under it.

The administrative system was designed primarily for two purposes: (1)

providing compensation for pollution-related health damages and (2) making polluters pay for the costs. However, the system may also serve the following functions: (3) identifying harm caused by pollution, (4) legitimating compensation to victims, (5) providing polluters an incentive to reduce emissions, (6) providing an accounting of the costs of pollution, and (7) generating information vital for environmental policy making. Functions (3)–(7) may not have been intended, but it is worthwhile to explore them.

(3) Identifying harm caused by pollution. The system identifies and defines the extent and nature of the harm of pollution. It makes people in designated areas aware of a possible link between pollution and their illness by prescribing typical symptoms caused by harmful substances. It also provides an incentive for victims to come forward to be identified.

(4) Legitimating victim compensation. The system legitimates payments to victims by admitting officially that pollution exists and by recognizing that victims are entitled to receive compensation. In the past, pollution victims often suffered discrimination and were accused of using their personal misfortune to obtain public assistance. The system publicly recognizes that pollution-related health damage does exist in many parts of Japan and that victims are indeed entitled to receive compensation for their suffering. Once certified, victims as a group become a symbolic existence whose force cannot be ignored politically.

(5) Providing an incentive to reduce emissions. The system provides polluters with an incentive not to pollute or to reduce the amount of pollutants. In the case of air pollution, the system charges the emission sources according to the amount of SOx discharged. In addition to direct regulation through the setting of certain emission standards, the administrative compensation system provides an economic incentive for polluters to pollute less by adopting antipollution measures, if those measures would cost less than the emission charges imposed. The air quality in designated areas improved sufficiently that the law was amended in 1987 and all area designations as to air pollution were removed. The marked reduction in SOx was largely brought about by the industrial policy of importing low sulfur oil. However, the emission charges under the system may, theoretically at least, have had some effect.

(6) Accounting for the costs of pollution. The system provides an accounting of the costs of pollution in terms of health damages every year. The system reports on the number of applications for certification, by area; on the number of certified victims; on the amount of compensation paid to them; and on the amount of charges imposed on polluters. These numbers otherwise would not be accounted for and would not be produced for the public to see.

(7) Generating vital information. Finally, the system generates general information relating to pollution and public health. This information is vital for making the public aware of pollution as well as for establishing long-range and medium-range environmental policy. In the absence of the administrative system, this information likely would not be available. A large-scale public health survey might produce similar data, but it would be costly to undertake such a survey and it would be difficult to obtain funds to conduct such a survey every year in a systematic way.

The above administrative system worked well for providing compensation for victims of air pollution. The typical symptoms of those victims were clearly defined, and the funds necessary to pay the victims were generated by imposing charges on numerous emission sources.

However, the system experienced many difficulties with respect to compensating Minamata victims. First, the number of applications for certification greatly increased once Chisso's liability was clearly established by the court decisions. Soon, toward the end of the 1970s, the backlog of applications to be processed reached several thousand. Second, the medical standards for certification became progressively uncertain as many applications involved not acute mercury poisoning, but milder, cumulative effects of poisoning indistinguishable from ordinary ailments. The doctors on the certification board could not agree on what the typical symptoms were. The courts, reviewing several cases of appeals from persons whose applications for certification had been denied, held the board's standards too strict. The Environment Agency also proposed more flexible guidelines for certification. However, these judicial and administrative attempts could not resolve the certification problem. Third, Chisso, the sole party responsible for continuously paying compensation to the certified victims, reached the brink of bankruptcy many times. Each time, the prefectural government rescued Chisso by issuing public bonds, a large portion of which the central government purchased, and by making the capital generated therefrom available in the form of low interest loans to Chisso. Nobody could afford to see Chisso go bankrupt.

As of 1995, there were 2,950 certified victims of mercury poisoning (2,260 Chisso-related and 690 Showa Denko–related). Upon certification, a victim received on average a lump sum payment of US$180,000 (¥100 = US$1) and annual payments of $20,000. Chisso paid $27,500 per certified victim, a total of $31 million. Showa Denko paid $16,500 per certified victim, a total of $7 million. From 1973 to 1994, the two companies together paid a total of $1,288 million to certified victims.

Meanwhile, litigation involving other issues, civil as well as criminal, continued after the initial damages action against Chisso.[5] A criminal charge was brought against a plant manager of Chisso for criminal negligence in discharging the water, and he was convicted. The victims sued the certification board to contest its determination denying them certification. The courts found the board's certification standards too strict and inflexible and ordered some of the plaintiffs to be certified.

The victims also sued the governments (national and local) for their failure to take necessary and prompt action. Major issues involved in this set of litigation were (a) whether the government should have banned fishing and sale of fish caught in Minamata Bay under the food safety act (the central government said no in response to the inquiry from the local government because there was no clear evidence that all fish and shellfish in the bay were contaminated), and (b) whether the governments should have ordered Chisso to stop its operations because it was in violation of the water quality preservation act (the governments contended that there was no violation because the area was not designated for preservation under the act). The decisions of six district courts in rulings on these issues were evenly divided, three holding the government liable and three not liable. Both parties appealed to appellate courts. Toward the end of the 1980s, a total of 2,300 plaintiffs were involved in those suits, with actions pending before a total of eleven district and appellate courts.

Meanwhile, in 1992, the central government, in cooperation with the local governments, initiated a health care plan for uncertified victims. By the end of 1995, about 4,600 people were receiving on average $2,900 for medical care annually.

By the mid-1990s it became apparent that the certification process for Minamata victims had broken down. Chisso had been in a chronically precarious financial situation. Litigation was at an impasse. The only option remaining seemed to be a political resolution of the problem.

V. STAGE THREE: POLITICAL SETTLEMENT

In April 1994, the ruling political party, a coalition of Liberal Democrats, Socialists, and one other faction, decided to make a national political settlement with the Minamata victims. The major political issue was the treatment of and remedies to be accorded to those who were claiming some effects of mercury poisoning, but who were still uncertified and uncared for. The government proposal contained the following features: (1) the polluters shall make a lump sum payment to those who meet certain requirements; (2) the national government and the Kumamoto prefecture government shall make a statement expressing sincere regret for their handling of the Minamata problem; (3) the parties who sign this agreement shall terminate all pending lawsuits; and (4) the central and prefectural governments shall continue the comprehensive health care plan, shall provide financial measures to assist Chisso and to develop the affected areas, and shall reopen the application process for health care payments.

In May of that year, accepting and acting on the government proposal, the National Coordinating Conference of the Minamata Victims-Plaintiffs and the Plaintiffs' Lawyers (the National Conference), and Chisso Corporation (Chisso) entered an agreement for the purpose of achieving the "final and comprehensive solution of all problems" concerning the Minamata disease. The following text of the agreement captured in its preamble the events leading to the final settlement:

> (1) On March 20, 1973, the Kumamoto District Court rendered judgment for the plaintiffs, holding Chisso liable for damages. Following the court decision, a compensation agreement was signed by patients. Since the conclusion of the compensation agreement, however, the number of applications for certification has markedly increased, and so correspondingly has the number of rejected applications. Several rejected patients-applicants filed suits, contesting the determination of the certification board as well as its procedure and standards.
>
> (2) The Fukuoka Appellate Court, on August 16, 1985, held that four of five plaintiffs deserved to be certified. The court found that, although the loss of feeling in the skin and loss of sensation in the hands and feet might be caused by deformation of the neck bone, these were quite distinctive symptoms of mercury poisoning. It was reasonable to presume, the court held, that the symptom was in fact that of the Minamata disease, unless it should be proved otherwise, and that even a diagnosis of such symptom alone, when accompanied with those epidemiological conditions and cumulative symptoms observable among the family members of a particular patient, should warrant the finding of Minamata disease with high probability.
>
> (3) Since 1980, a series of suits was brought against the central government and Kumamoto prefectural government under the government torts claims act. The plaintiffs alleged that the governments were liable for the occurrence and the spread of Minamata disease. During September to October of 1990, several courts where those suits were pending recommended the parties to settle. The plaintiffs, the Kumamoto prefectural government, and Chisso par-

ticipated in settlement negotiations, but the central government refused to join in. On January 7, 1993, the Fukuoka Appellate Court drafted and proposed the terms of settlement. However, the settlement was not finally reached since Chisso did not accept the proposal. Meanwhile, several district courts found for uncertified patients, ordering Chisso to compensate them.

(4) The central government initiated a comprehensive medical care measure which provided 4,600 persons with medical care. In June 1994, a new cabinet was formed under Prime Minister Tomiichi Murayama, the head of the Socialist Party, and finding a solution for Minamata disease was placed on a high priority list of his government's political agenda. The government agreed on a framework for a political solution of the Minamata disease problems. Murayama, speaking for the government, issued the following official statement on December 15, 1995: "I express deeply felt condolences for those who died in the midst of sufferings and frustration and when I consider those who have been put under indescribable sufferings for many years and must have felt irreparably hurt, I am filled with the sincere feeling of regret."[6]

In the above context, the National Conference and Chisso, "taking into consideration, to the utmost degree, the urgent necessity for early resolution," entered an agreement to settle the Minamata disease problems. The agreement sets forth the following terms of settlement:

(1) Chisso gravely accepts the following: that Chisso's legal responsibility for causing Minamata disease by its own discharge of methyl mercury was adjudged by the court on March 20, 1973; that Chisso's legal responsibility for four uncertified plaintiffs was affirmed by the appellate court judgment on August 16, 1985; and that a series of other district court decisions, while appealed, held Chisso liable for uncertified-patient plaintiffs. Chisso shall make apology to the plaintiffs, the residents of the affected areas and to society in general for the fact that, since the beginning of the Minamata problem, it has taken such a long time to reach the resolution today.

(2) Among those who were possibly exposed to an above-natural level of methyl mercury in the past and were suffering from the loss of sensation in their hands and feet, the administrative compensation act has set those certified apart from the others whose certification was denied. The diagnosis of Minamata disease has been made on the basis of exposure to methyl mercury and of a combination of symptoms of mercury poisoning. This agreement intends to provide some relief for those whose certification was denied. However, since the medical determination of the Minamata disease is depend-

ent on a matter of degree of probability, the fact that their applications were denied does not mean that they are entirely without the effects of methyl mercury. Therefore, the agreement provides relief for those who are suffering from the loss of sensation in their hands and feet, and who consent to the termination of their litigation.

(3) The National Conference and Chisso actively shall work with the residents of the area for reviving and redeveloping the community, by participating and coordinating in the efforts of repairing and reconstructing the community's bonds.[7]

Under the agreement, Chisso is required to make lump sum payments to (1) those who are currently registered and receiving health care under the comprehensive health care measure and (2) those who are determined to be eligible in the reopened application process for the comprehensive health care measure by the prefecture governor in consultation with the review board. The amount of lump sum payment to each eligible person is $26,000 plus a $3,000 medical care payment per year for those who applied between January and August 1996.

The number of renewed applications was over 9,300, of which 5,885 were determined eligible (roughly 60 percent). In March 1997, when the review of all applications was completed, the final number of persons eligible for receiving lump sum payments and continuing medical payments reached 10,350 (including about 4,400 who were determined to be eligible before the reopening of the application process). It is estimated that those who have been determined eligible would continue to receive medical care payments, on average, for ten to fourteen years. Assuming these estimates are accurate, the total amount of medical care payments per person would amount to around $29,000–$40,000. Together with the lump sum payment, the total amount one person would receive would be comparable to the average damage award ($58,000) granted by the courts in six cases where the plaintiffs sued the governments as well as the polluting companies.[8]

Aside from the individual lump sum payments, a total of $50 million was allocated to six victims organizations involved in the litigation. If an eligible person was a member of one of those organizations, he or she might receive an additional amount determined by each organization, in addition to his or her lump sum payment. This portion of payments came from Chisso. The medical care costs were to be borne by the central and local governments as a part of the costs of the public health insurance system.

The National Conference and its members agreed, upon receiving the lump sum payments, to settle all disputes and pending litigation, and to refrain in the future from litigation for damages, attempting negotiations, and activities for demanding official certification under the administrative compensation system.

The group of people in Niigata who sued Showa Denko also reached a settlement with terms similar to that for the groups in Minamata. Showa Denko agreed to contribute $2.5 million for the reconstruction of community ties, in addition to lump sum payments to eligible persons.

VI. KANSAI REGION LITIGATION: THE FINAL CHAPTER?

About ten thousand people accepted the 1995 settlement. All lawsuits and claim applications then pending before courts and administrative boards were withdrawn. However, one group of Minamata disease victims refused to join in the government-proposed political settlement and continued litigation. This group consisted of people who lived in fishing villages on the coastal area near Minamata Bay but left the area in the 1950s and 1960s and moved to the Kansai region to find new jobs. They organized and filed a suit in 1982 against Chisso, the central government, and the Kumamoto prefectural government. The plaintiffs (fifty-eight persons) claimed that (1) the governments were responsible for causing and spreading Minamata disease by failing to take proper measures, (2) plaintiffs should be recognized as suffering from Minamata disease, and (3) plaintiffs should duly be compensated.

In 1994, the Osaka District Court rendered a decision that held Chisso, but not the governments, liable for damages. The plaintiffs appealed. In 2001, the Osaka High Court held that Chisso and the central and prefectural governments were liable for compensating the victims. Three issues were contested in the appeal. First, were the medical standards applied to determine those suffering from Minamata disease correct? Second, were the central government and prefectural government liable under the Government Torts Liability Act? Third, at what point did the statute of limitations (twenty years) start in the instant case?

As to the medical standards for determining the disease, the high court found that methyl-mercury poisoning affected the cerebral cortex and resulted in sensory impairments of the distal parts of victims. A doctor could objectively confirm, the court opinion stated, the existence of sensory impairments by examining victims. Those who were determined to have compounding sensory impairments alone could duly be recognized as suffering from methyl-mercury poisoning.

On the issue of government liability, the high court held that the central and prefectural governments failed to take effective regulatory measures under the Water Quality Conservation Act and other regulations at critical stages in which they could have contained and terminated the discharges of wastewater from the Chisso plant. The neglect and delays in taking necessary actions around the end of 1959 on the part of the governments were judged to constitute illegal inaction.

As to the statute of limitations, the high court held that plaintiffs' cause of action was preserved since they did apply for official certification. Otherwise, the high court stated, the statute of limitations would have run four years after plaintiffs left the Minamata Bay area.

The high court substantially reduced the amount of damages claimed by plaintiffs, however. The plaintiffs claimed $330,000 on average per person. The high court awarded amounts ranging from $45,000 to $85,000 per person. It is interesting to note that the Osaka District Court had awarded damages slightly less than these on a novel theory of "probable causation." The district court assigned each plaintiff who was exposed to methyl-mercury pollution a probability for suffering from Minamata disease, ranging from 15 to 40 percent. It is, to say the least, a questionable and dubious theory. The district court's reasoning certainly made no sense to plaintiffs. In contrast with the district court's findings of probable causation, the high court clearly found that plaintiffs were suffering from Minamata disease, but nonetheless reduced the amount of damage awards.

Chisso, which the Osaka High Court held liable for 75 percent of the harm and resulting damages, accepted the judgment and did not appeal. Both the central government and Kumamoto Prefecture, though, appealed to the Supreme Court. On October 15, 2004, the Supreme Court rendered a decision that upheld the Osaka High Court judgment in nearly all respects.

As to the central government, the Supreme Court held that, under the Water Quality Conservation Act and the Factory Water Discharge Regulation Act, the central government had the authority to order improvements in water treatment processes, temporary shutdowns, or other measures to ensure the protection of water quality. The Court continued, "Safeguarding the lives and health of residents of surrounding communities from deterioration in water quality being a primary objective of the above authority, that authority is to be exercised in a timely and appropriate fashion."[9] By the end of November 1959, the Court found, (1) severe damage to lives and health had been continuing for some three and a half years since the first official discovery of Minamata disease, and the central government was aware that many people had become ill and a substantial number had died; (2) the central government could have known, with a high degree of probability, that the cause of disease was some type of organic mercury compound and that the Chisso factory was the source of discharge; and (3) it would have been possible for the central government to test the discharge water and determine that it contained mercury. Even allowing time for the necessary procedural steps, the Court ruled, by no later than the end of December 1959, the central government could and should have ordered steps to ensure improvement in water quality. "It is clear that, if [the central government's] regulatory authority had been exercised at that time, the subsequent spread of Minamata disease could have been prevented, but, because the authority was not actually exercised, the damage grew." The Court continued, "[J]udging from the nature and purposes of the two Acts relating to water quality, from January 1960 on, [the central government's] failure to exercise its authority . . . was markedly lacking in rationality (*ichijirushiku gōrisei o kaku*), and is illegal under the Government Torts Liability Act."[10]

In the case of the prefecture, the authority to act rested, not on the water quality legislation, but rather on authority to regulate fisheries within the prefecture. In other respects, though, the Court found that the prefectural government stood in essentially the same position as the central government; the Supreme Court upheld the Osaka High Court's judgment that the prefecture also bore liability under the Government Torts Liability Act.

As to the statute of limitations, the Supreme Court adopted a somewhat different approach from that of the high court. "In cases in which damage to health arises from the accumulation of substances within the human body, and in which there is a latency period before symptoms appear," the Court concluded, "the statute of limitations should begin to run from the point at which all or a portion of the injury has manifested itself." To hold otherwise, and to allow the statute of limitations to begin to run before the injury has manifested itself, the Court stated, would be "extremely harsh" to victims.[11] Furthermore, said the Court, this interpretation of the statute of limitations was appropriate to put tortfeasors on notice that, when damage from their acts is likely to manifest itself only after a substantial period of time has past, they still are subject to liability for claims by victims.

The Supreme Court upheld, without discussion, the Osaka High Court's reasoning regarding application of the medical standards for certification of victims. The Supreme Court did narrow the range of the high court's judgment in one respect, however. As mentioned above, the Supreme Court found that the central government and prefecture were liable for their inaction from

January 1960. Eight of the plaintiffs had already moved away from the Minamata region before that date, and the Supreme Court held that they were not eligible for compensation from the governments.

This judgment, which came a half century after the outbreak of Minamata disease, represents the Supreme Court's first decision on government liability for the disease. At one and the same time, it in theory should represent the final legal word on Minamata disease. As mentioned above, the 1995 settlement in principle brought to a close all lawsuits and claims except those of the Kansai group; the Supreme Court judgment signals the end of the Kansai litigation. Whether the Supreme Court judgment will in fact represent the final chapter in the legal saga is doubtful, however. As soon as the judgment was announced, two major victims organizations that had participated in the 1995 settlement announced plans to seek a reexamination of the terms of the settlement, including an expansion of the class of certified victims. And another group announced plans to file new litigation on behalf of 110 additional plaintiffs who had moved to another region in Kyushu.

VII. SOME LESSONS

Whether or not the legal saga is at an end, the suffering is not. Some people fear that the political settlement, and now the Supreme Court judgment, might create a false impression on the part of the general public that the Minamata story is over. The steel net that sealed the mouth of the bay to prevent fish from going out was finally removed in 1997. Fish caught in the bay were tested for mercury and declared safe. Commercial fishing is now possible in and around the bay, but few fishermen remain in the area. A large portion of the bay (about 138 acres) was landfilled, and a layer of concrete was poured to cover the heavily contaminated sediments at the bottom of the bay. A memorial museum was built on the site. Other use of the acquired space remains undecided. The Chisso plant is still there and still operating; the sole purpose of its existence seems to be continuing to pay compensation to the certified victims of mercury poisoning.

These appearances should not mislead us into thinking that Minamata is a thing of the past. Reading through a score of court decisions involving victims, Chisso, and regulatory agencies, and following the social and political events surrounding the Minamata disease, one cannot help but state that it has been and still is a continuing tragedy. The magnitude and full extent of harm caused by mercury pollution in Minamata have yet to be determined. It has been reported that about twenty thousand people living along the nearby coast have been affected. About seventeen thousand applied for official certification, and of those about four thousand were certified. About twelve hundred have died from mercury poisoning. The compounding effects of forty years of litigation, the administrative compensation system, and the final political settlement have been very divisive within the community. People are divided between those who sued and those who did not, those who applied for certification and those who did not, and those certified and those not certified. Indeed, at one time, the victims were fragmented into twenty different factions.

The tragedy was caused by Chisso in its reckless pursuit of profits through mass production, promoted by the industrial policy on the part of national and local governments. The government agencies' unofficial interventions and informal directions were prevalent. Their inaction for containing and preventing pollution and negation of their duties for environmental safety at critical junctures were apparent. From the beginning of the Minamata disease, almost ten years were spent in officially determining the cause of the disease while the discharge of wastewater from the plant continued. Chisso was not cooperative at all and apparently misled the Minamata residents and regulatory officials, as later proved in the trial of the plant manager found guilty of criminal negligence. Chisso and regulatory agencies made full use of scientific uncertainty as to the cause of disease as their excuses for their inaction.

As recounted above, three different institutional approaches have been used over the past forty years: judicial, administrative, and political.

The courts served as a vital first step. Victims resorted to the courts for the vindication of their rights after all traditional means of dispute settlement had failed. The courts provided the victims with a forum to confront the polluters and gain public attention. Through litigation, a local incident of mercury poisoning far away from Tokyo finally drew the attention of politicians and bureaucrats in the central government. The victim-centered litigation provided a much-needed focus and forum to draw public attention to what was happening in Minamata. At the early stage of litigation, courts faced social issues squarely and decided for victim-plaintiffs by innovatively interpreting and applying traditional tort provisions of the Civil Code. Plaintiffs' claims were vindicated. The courts created a presumption of causation in favor of the plaintiffs and imposed a very high degree of care on the polluting companies. The courts awarded damages to the plaintiffs in all major pollution cases in the early part of the 1970s and in the process laid the foundation for the administrative compensation system.

In the case of air pollution, the administrative compensation system served its function sufficiently in terms of providing compensation to victims. In that context, scientific and medical standards for designating heavily polluted areas and certifying victims were relatively clear and never in dispute. Moreover, a sufficient fund was created at the national level by imposing charges on numerous emission sources. The amount needed to pay certified victims each year was assessed and charged to those sources. The collection of charges was effectively made through relevant industrial associations, and the fund remained solvent all through the years of its operation.

In contrast, the administrative compensation system did not function well in the case of mercury poisoning. The victim certification process was initially flooded with a large volume of applications; it quickly became apparent that the medical standards for certifying Minamata victims did not work. A main reason for this failure was that certification standards were not medically sound. This in turn resulted in large part from the fact that, from the beginning, certification standards were closely tied to Chisso's financial ability to pay required compensation to certified victims. The certification process was manipulated to control and to confine the number of certified victims so as to keep Chisso financially afloat. Even since the courts found it liable for damages, Chisso has been on the verge of bankruptcy several times and has been kept afloat by infusions of public money in the form of low interest loans. If Chisso were to go under, about two thousand certified victims currently receiving compensation directly from the company would be left uncompensated. Under these circumstances, medical opinions were sharply divided and medical standards for certification were constantly disputed. The certification process resulted in a large number of victims going uncertified even though they were as deserving as others who were certified. This in turn led to a strong sense among people who applied for certification but were denied that the process was unfair and unjust.

The political settlement came only after forty years had passed. It was offered by the national government as a comprehensive and ultimate solution to the Minamata problem. It certainly extended remedies to a large number of uncertified victims. It offered a lump sum payment to people who had been exposed to mercury pollution and claimed to be suffering from symptoms of methyl-mercury poisoning, even though they were not officially certified. If medical standards for certification were sound, these recipients could not be suffering from Minamata disease. The political settlement thus created a gray zone where people could receive a one-time payment, despite not being recognized as official Minamata victims. The political settlement also incorporated a comprehensive health care plan designed to improve public health care in the affected community. The measure has provided such treatments as acupuncture and hot spring bathing to those who were not eligible for medical care payments. Furthermore, the political settlement emphasized the need to heal the divided community and made some attempts to promote cooperation among the once-adverse parties.

In mass tort cases around the world, litigation often leads to political settlements. In some of those cases, judges are actively involved in formulating the terms of the settlement. Possible advantages and disadvantages of setting up administrative compensation systems also have been widely debated. Unless a society decides to adopt a comprehensive national health and welfare system, it takes all three of the above approaches—judicial, administrative, and political—to resolve a mass tragedy such as Minamata.

Given the many benefits of the 1995 settlement package, almost all the victims and their organizations accepted the offered settlement in exchange for giving up all pending litigation and claims. Yet the settlement had one major weakness: it left government responsibility for the tragedy ambiguous. Although the prime minister expressed pro forma regret at the time of political settlement, the responsibilities of governments for their actions and inactions over the years in dealing with Minamata disease seemed to have been buried forever.

In this respect, the Kansai region victim-plaintiffs deserve gratitude. They are the one group who persisted and appealed their case to the Supreme Court, placing the issue of government responsibility squarely before it. And by doing so, they have secured a judgment recognizing the responsibility of the central and prefectural government to take action to avoid the Minamata tragedy and sharply rebuking both governments for their failure to do so. The effort of this group of victim-plaintiffs in achieving this historic Supreme Court judgment deserves to be recorded in the annals of Japanese environmental law.

The Supreme Court judgment has conclusively established government responsibility. Yet, in hindsight, several questions still remain to be answered. Why was Chisso not ordered to stop the discharge when mercury was found in the wastewater? Why was commercial fishing in Minamata Bay not prohibited? Why did Chisso continue its operations even after an internal experiment on cats established its wastewater caused the disease? Why were only damages and not injunctions sought in all those suits? Why did regulatory agencies remain unconcerned and not initiate actions in the critical stages? What is the most effective and efficient combination and sequence of litigation, regulatory relief and political intervention? Why did it take forty years to reach the settlement? To find answers to these questions would certainly be a step toward preventing such tragedies from happening again.[12] The Minamata story urges all of us to do so.

NOTES

1. For a brief history of Japanese environmental disruptions and disputes, see Julian Gresser, Koichiro Fujikura, and Akio Morishima, *Environmental Law in Japan* (Cambridge, MA: MIT Press, 1981), 3–27. See also Jun Ui, ed., *Industrial Pollution in Japan* (Tokyo: United Nations University Press, 1992).

2. Chisso had operated its plant on the site since 1938. Why did Minamata disease suddenly appear in 1953 and why did it appear only in Minamata, not in the vicinities of other chemical plants producing the same products? These two unanswered questions concerning causation were finally analyzed and solved by two chemical engineers in a book published in 2001 by Hajime Nishimura and Tatsuaki Okamoto, *Minamata byō no kagaku* [The Science of Minamata Disease] (Tokyo: Nihon hyōronsha, 2001). The authors identify the cause of the sudden outbreak of the disease in 1953 as a change of the sub-catalytic agent in Chisso's acetaldehyde production process and find the disease appeared only in Minamata because of the physical setting of the bay and surrounding area.

3. Translations of the Niigata and Kumamoto court opinions are available in Gresser, Fujikura, and Morishima, *Environmental Law in Japan*, 66, 86. See also Ui, *Industrial Pollution in Japan*, chap. 4 (Minamata Disease), 103; the Social Scientific Study Group on Minamata Disease, National Institute for Minamata Disease, *In the Hope of Avoiding Repetition of a Tragedy of Minamata Disease: What We Have Learned from the Experience* (Minamata, Japan: National Institute for Minamata Disease, 2001); W. Eugene Smith and Aileen M. Smith, *Minamata: Words and Photographs* (New York: Holt, Rinehart and Winston, 1975).

4. There were four major pollution decisions around 1970. These are discussed in Gresser, Fujikura, and Morishima, *Environmental Law in Japan*, 55–132. See also Frank K. Upham, "After Minamata: Current Prospects and Problems in Japanese Environmental Litigation," *Ecology Law Quarterly* 8 (1979): 213.

5. A score of court cases involving Minamata disease have been brought and decisions have been rendered. They are (1) victims suits against Chisso for damages under the Civil Code, (2) suits against the national and local governments under the State Compensation Act, (3) a criminal charge against the plant manager, and (4) victims suits contesting determination of the certification board and asking damages for long delays in processing their applications. For a list of court decisions, see Sadao Togashi, *Minamata byō jiken to hō* [Minamata Disease Incidents and the Law] (Fukuoka, Japan: Sekifūsha, 1995), 468–73.

6. Shushō Danwa [Prime Minister's Statement], *Asahi shinbun*, December 15, 1995, evening edition, 1.

7. "Kyōteisho" [The Agreement (May, 19, 1996)], in Minamatabyō kenkyūkai [Minamatabyō Study Group], ed., *Minamatabyō kenkyū* [The Annals of Minamata Disease] (Fukuoka: Asi Book Publishing, 1999), 124.

8. See Takeshi Kojima, "Minamata byō mondai no seijiteki kaiketsu" [Political Solution to the Minamata Disease Problem], *Jurisuto*, no. 1088 (1996): 5.

9. Araki v. State (Sup. Ct., Oct. 15, 2004), *Minshū* 58 (2004): 1802, 1814.

10. Ibid., 1815.

11. Ibid., 1816.

12. See Social Scientific Study Group on Minamata Disease, *In the Hope of Avoiding Repetition of a Tragedy of Minamata Disease*. In spite of a promising and ambitious title, this report is disappointing. One of the reasons for disappointment is that the group confined its study to the period from May 1956, when Minamata disease was officially discovered, to September 1968, when the government made a public statement concerning the cause of the disease.

17 Medical Error, Deception, Self-Critical Analysis, and Law's Impact

A Comparative Examination

ROBERT B LEFLAR

I. INTRODUCTION

The problem of medical error has become a focus of major public concern in both Japan and the United States, as it has around the world.[1] Proposals for legislative and institutional reform of liability and health care delivery systems to address the patient safety issue have emanated not merely from affected interest groups and academic commentators on both sides of the Pacific but from the highest levels of national politics.[2] Headlines about appalling mistakes and gruesome statistics on hospital casualties have impelled even the most sluggish of health care and regulatory institutions to attempt to change traditional methods and procedures, or at least to appear to be doing so.

At the core of the debates in each nation about the proper design of systems of liability, information management, and institutional incentive structures is a tension between two worthy principles: public accountability for medical harm and the promotion of patient safety. This tension arises in the following way. Quality improvement requires accurate information. For a hospital to reduce the frequency and severity of preventable medical harm, the key health care personnel—administrators, doctors, and nurses—must know what risks are present and how to eliminate or minimize them. This knowledge can be developed from self-critical analyses of accidents and near misses, the lessons ideally to be disseminated to other health care institutions. But, for fear of public accountability, health care personnel in both Japan and the United States have a history of covering up information about accidents, impeding hospitals from conducting self-critical analyses and preventing safety measures from being devised and implemented.

Responding to this concern, administrative policies and legislative measures have been advanced in each country aimed at promoting patient safety by shielding providers from the legal consequences of public information disclosure about adverse events. But such measures are likely to come at a potential cost to public accountability.

The stakes over this issue are somewhat different in the two countries, however, because of differences in the loci of accountability. In the United States, the civil malpractice action is a major public accountability mechanism. In Japan, by contrast, the chief accountability mechanisms are the media and the criminal justice system. It is not so much the plaintiff's attorney as the whistleblower, the reporter, and the police that Japanese hospitals fear.

II. SOURCES OF *SATORI*: HOW THE UNITED STATES AND JAPAN AWOKE TO THE MEDICAL ERROR EPIDEMIC

In the United States, the escalation of public concern about medical error was fueled by science politics: the employment of the discipline of epidemiology by physicians, public health specialists, and lawyers with a view to building a factual foundation for public advocacy.[3] Publication of the Harvard Medical Practice Study on iatrogenic injuries in New York State in 1991,[4] and of a follow-up study in Colorado and Utah,[5] led the Institute of Medicine of the National Academy of Sciences to the conclusion that U.S. medicine is afflicted with alarmingly high error rates, a public health problem of enormous significance. The institute's report, *To Err Is Human*,[6] put the issue on the national political agenda.

That report estimated that between forty-four thousand and ninety-eight thousand hospital patients die from medical mismanagement each year in the United States.[7] This estimate excludes deaths from medical error outside the hospital, for example in nursing homes. With regard to the incidence of preventable deaths and nontrivial injuries combined, the best estimate is that 3–4 percent of hospitalized patients suffer those levels of harm[8] (a far greater number than the volume of malpractice cases filed).

To Err Is Human generated wide publicity and led President Clinton to form a presidential commission recommending national legislation to improve patient safety. A Quality Interagency Coordination Task Force began the process of implementing the Institute of Medicine's recommendations in federal agencies dealing with health care.[9] A quasi-public National Quality Forum was created to collect detailed information about specific safety problems and ways of addressing them and to disseminate the findings throughout the nation's health care systems.[10] The federal government is investing hundreds of millions of dollars in researching patient safety issues and attempting to disseminate conclusions and implement improved safety systems.[11] Some state governments are engaging in significant safety initiatives.[12] Most importantly, it has become de rigueur among hospitals in today's competitive environment to take a hard look at existing practices and to attempt to remedy the problems identified.

In Japan, what put the medical error problem on the map was not scientific studies, as in the United States;[13] it was the mass media,[14] giving front-page coverage to a series of medical mishaps stunning in their quotidian banality, most of them followed by a cover-up and deception of patients and families suffering harm.[15] Among the many recent cases, four have attained representative significance: the Yokohama Municipal University Hospital patient mix-up in 1999,[16] the Hiroo Metropolitan Hospital fatal injection in 2000,[17] the Tokyo Women's Medical University heart-lung machine blunder in 2001,[18] and the Aoto Hospital greenhorn "keyhole surgery" foul-up in 2002.[19] Patient safety activities by professional groups and the health ministry would not likely have been undertaken but for the spur of public outrage at cases such as these.

III. PATIENT SAFETY, THE CIVIL JUSTICE SYSTEM, AND DISCLOSURE OF ACCIDENTS

A. THE UNITED STATES

An essential part of the project of creating a "culture of safety" in a hospital is self-critical analysis: the gathering and analysis of reliable information on preventable mistakes within the hospital and the implementation of corrective measures. In the United States, hospitals are pushed to perform self-critical analyses by developing professional standards, by the hospital accreditation process, and by a new requirement for participation in the major government health insurance programs of Medicare and Medicaid. But some fear that the quality of those self-critical analyses may be undermined by the operation of the U.S. civil justice system.

The Institute of Medicine's pathbreaking report, *To Err Is Human*, stressed the importance of self-critical analyses as one means of avoiding medical mistakes.[20] Similar recommendations abound in the medical literature,[21] to the point that the institution of in-hospital systems for producing self-critical analyses of accidents and near misses may be considered to have become an established standard for health care institutions. Since 2001, the Joint Commission for Accreditation of Healthcare Organizations (JCAHO) has made the conduct of "thorough and credible root cause analyses" of all "sentinel events," or serious preventable events adversely affecting patient safety, a subject for hospitals' triennial inspections.[22] Since 2003, the Department of Health and Human Services has required all hospitals participating in the Medicare and Medicaid programs—the vast majority of U.S. hospitals—to develop and maintain a quality assessment and performance improvement program, incorporating self-critical analyses as part of the process.[23]

Many physicians and hospital administrators, cautioned by defense counsel, fear that these self-critical analyses, in the hands of plaintiffs' attorneys, will serve as weapons for infliction of legal liability and professional embarrassment. Some contend that this fear may deter honest, thorough reviews of adverse events, hindering quality improvement efforts. As Troyen Brennan, a lead author of the Harvard Medical Practice Study, observed: "Any effort to prevent injury due to medical care is complicated by the dead weight of a litigation system that induces secrecy and silence. No matter how much we might insist that physicians have an ethical duty to report injuries resulting from medical care or to work on their prevention, fear of malpractice litigation drags us back to the status quo."[24]

These concerns may be somewhat overblown. Hospital self-critical analyses are generally protected by state-law peer review privileges. (The great majority of U.S. medical malpractice litigation takes place in state courts.) These privileges protect the deliberations of hospital committees reviewing the course of individual patients' care and the performance of medical personnel. Evidence of what happens in peer review and quality assurance committees typically is neither subject to discovery nor admissible as evidence in civil trials.[25] But there are some variations from one state to another as to the scope of the peer review privilege.[26] Additionally, there is sometimes a gray area between original medical records and factual "incident reports," both of which are typically discoverable and admissible in evidence,[27] and evaluative or deliberative documents protected by the peer review privilege, which are non-discoverable and inadmissible. The existence of this gray area creates a potential for some documents with evaluative content to fall into plaintiffs' attorneys' hands.[28] Moreover, some courts have refused to recognize the peer review privilege in federal cases.[29] So caution on the part of some U.S. physicians about the legal consequences of conducting self-critical analyses is not without reason.

This caution is reinforced by the general concern in the health care industry about rising liability insurance premiums, attributed by many to excessive medical negligence judgments and settlements. Medical societies, business groups, and the liability insurance industry, trumpeting these concerns, have persuaded most states in the past few years to enact "tort reform" legislation protective of health care and other defendants.

To alleviate physicians' concerns about adverse legal ramifications of conducting self-critical analyses, Congress enacted the Patient Safety and Quality Improvement Act of 2005.[30] This new law creates a voluntary system allowing medical providers to report medical errors in confidential fashion to independent entities called Patient Safety Organizations. The reports will be protected from use in civil and criminal proceedings.

Whether or not hospitals' self-critical analyses are ever made available to plaintiffs' attorneys as a matter of civil law, a consensus has formed that the fact that an error was made harming the patient must be disclosed to the patient and family as a matter of medical ethics. Medical mistakes must not be covered up. This ethical duty of truth telling about error may not be universally observed—in fact, in actual practice it may be disregarded as often as not[31]—but the duty is made clear in the American Medical Association's Code of Medical Ethics,[32] and the JCAHO hospital accreditation process now reinforces that ethical principle as an accreditation requirement.[33]

Health care, even in private for-profit hospitals, is a public or at least a quasi-public enterprise affecting the public's health and safety, largely paid for by public programs (such as Medicare and Medicaid in the United States and the national health insurance scheme in Japan). Accordingly, information about errors is not limited to disclosure to individual patients and family members. Statistical information about the general quality of performance of providers of medical care is gradually becoming available to government regulators, health care providers, purchasers of health care such as employers and employer groups, and the general public. Beginning with the publication of reports on risk-adjusted mortality data for heart bypass surgery by New York State hospitals and individual cardiac surgeons in 1991,[34] hospital safety statistics have proliferated, although their significance to the public is subject to debate.[35] Hospitals nationwide are publicly rated, for example, on how well they perform on ten evidence-based measures of good medical treatment for acute heart attack, congestive heart failure, and pneumonia.[36] The trend toward transparency in matters of U.S. hospital performance seems unstoppable.

B. COMPARISON WITH JAPAN

Unlike U.S. hospitals, Japanese hospitals are required to perform self-critical analyses neither by hospital accreditation authority[37] nor by government reimbursement policy. Nevertheless, many Japanese hospitals are beginning to do self-critical analyses, spurred in part by recommendations from the university hospital presidents[38] and guidance from the Ministry of Health, Labor and Welfare (MHLW).[39] Japanese medical leaders have raised concerns, similar to those voiced in the United States, about the possibility that such analyses could be used to medical defendants' detriment in civil malpractice actions.[40]

Japanese physicians have far less to fear from the civil justice system than U.S. physicians do, as an objective matter. This fact is statistically demonstrable, as seen in tables 17.1–17.3. Medical malpractice statistics are available for claims *closed* in the United States as a whole[41] and for claims *filed* in Japanese courts[42] and with the Japan Medical Association and its Osaka chapter.[43] Precise comparisons from these differing statistical compilations are difficult, but it is nevertheless clear that claims rates are much lower in Japan than in the United States. For example, in 1996 there were 123,410 claims closed in the United States[44] as compared with 1,157 claims filed in Japanese courts and with the Japan and Osaka Medical Associations[45] (compare tables 17.1 and 17.2 with table 17.3[46]). Likewise, medical malpractice premiums in Japan, which could be considered a very rough proxy for payouts, are but a small fraction of those charged in the United States.[47]

Overall levels of claims and payouts tell only part of the story, however. Trends, and perceptions of trends, are also important. The quantity of civil medical malpractice cases in Japan is *accelerating* at a rate that outstrips increases in most other categories of litigation,[48] and payout amounts are likewise accelerating. The plaintiffs' malpractice bar is expanding in number and sophistication,[49] a fact well known to physicians. Of greatest significance is the media attention devoted to medical cases. Even though the number of litigated cases and therefore the likelihood of being sued are small in Japan compared to the United States, media coverage of Japanese cases magnifies their impact on the consciousness of individual physicians and hospitals. The adverse reputational consequences of publicized litigation are significant.[50] If the performance of self-critical analyses adds to the risk of such adverse consequences, many physicians will hesitate to conduct them.

Three separate legal grounds are of concern to Japanese physicians on this point: (1) national and local freedom of information rules applicable to

TABLE 17.1. Medical Malpractice Actions Filed in Court, Japan, 1975–2001

Year	*Actions Filed*	*% Compensated**
1975	140	N/A
1976	234	N/A
1977	257	37.0
1978	238	34.7
1979	252	39.3
1980	310	30.3
1981	195	39.0
1982	270	32.6
1983	271	35.3
1984	255	26.6
1985	272	31.7
1986	335	30.0
1987	335	17.6
1988	352	21.3
1989	369	27.6
1990	364	30.3
1991	357	27.0
1992	378	37.3
1993	444	29.2
1994	504	38.8
1995	434	38.9
1996	581	41.3
1997	593	37.3
1998	622	44.0
1999	663	30.3
2000	775	46.7
2001	805	38.4

SOURCE: Administrative Office of the Supreme Court of Japan.
*Not including cases settled or withdrawn.

public hospitals and (2) the liberalized discovery rules under Article 220 of the civil procedure law, discussed in this section, and (3) the reporting requirements under Article 21 of the Physicians' Act, discussed in the next section on the role of criminal law.[51]

Under the national information disclosure law, records kept by public hos-

TABLE 17.2. Medical Malpractice Claims Filed with Medical Associations, Japan, 1975–2001

Year	*Japan Medical Association*	*Local medical association*
1975	233	96
1976	N/A	N/A
1977	N/A	N/A
1978	N/A	N/A
1979	N/A	N/A
1980	276	123
1981	N/A	N/A
1982	N/A	N/A
1983	N/A	N/A
1984	N/A	N/A
1985	258	143
1986	N/A	N/A
1987	267	149
1988	N/A	N/A
1989	N/A	N/A
1990	297	168
1991	N/A	N/A
1992	256	170
1993	N/A	N/A
1994	281	166
1995	N/A	N/A
1996	351	225
1997	321	171
1998	361	N/A
1999	349	N/A
2000	N/A	N/A
2001	N/A	N/A

SOURCE: Kazue Nakajima et al., "Medical Malpractice and Legal Resolution Systems in Japan," *Journal of the American Medical Association,* 285 (2001): 1632, 1633, 1638.

pitals are potentially subject to disclosure unless an exception to disclosure applies, for example, to protect individual patients' privacy.[52] However, the names of individual physicians are not necessarily protected by this exception. For example, in response to an *Asahi shinbun* request for information on an accident at a public hospital, the Cabinet's Information Disclosure Review

TABLE 17.3. Medical Malpractice Closed Claims, U.S., 1991–2000

	*Occurrence policies**		*Claims-made policies*			
Year	*With payment*	*Without payment*	*With payment*	*Without payment*	*Total*	*% Compensated*
1991	8,515	22,049	22,326	53,299	106,189	29.0
1992	8,299	22,834	22,780	59,903	113,816	27.3
1993	8,103	23,026	24,718	64,702	120,549	27.2
1994	8,720	23,583	22,427	69,205	123,935	25.1
1995	8,664	20,800	22,573	73,380	125,417	24.9
1996	7,667	17,129	22,855	75,759	123,410	24.7
1997	5,984	14,896	18,342	64,282	103,504	23.5
1998	3,962	10,696	13,873	56,398	84,929	21.0
1999	2,293	6,496	8,126	43,867	60,782	17.1
2000	557	1,494	2,478	20,786	25,315	12.0

SOURCE: *Best's Aggregates and Averages, Property-Casualty*, 2001 ed. (Oldwick, NJ: A.M. Best Co., 2001), 238 (first four data columns).

* "Occurrence policies" cover events occurring during the period of coverage, for which claims may later be filed; "claims-made" policies cover claims filed during the period of coverage. The last two columns are the author's sums of these two incommensurate categories, purely for the purpose of constructing a rough comparison of the relative magnitudes of the number of claims filed and compensated in the United States and Japan.

The number of closed claims diminishes markedly from 1996 to 2000 because the later the claims were filed, the lower the likelihood of their having been closed by 2001, when these statistics were collected.

Board called for disclosure of the names of attending physicians, the minutes of internal hospital committees investigating the accident, and the contents of apology letters to patients and families.[53] Although such disclosures are apparently uncommon,[54] they contain the potential for considerable embarrassment to medical personnel.[55]

Liberalization of the discovery rules of the civil procedure law[56] has opened up the possibility that hospital incident reports and internal analyses of adverse events might become available to plaintiffs' attorneys. Article 220 of the civil procedure law recognizes a general principle of discoverability of specifically identified documents, but contains several exceptions. The Supreme Court in 1999 recognized that documents produced solely for internal use (*naibu bunsho*) are exempt from discovery under one such exception.[57] Hospitals' internal reports arguably fall within this *naibu bunsho* exemption.

The Tokyo High Court ruled in 2003 that a hospital's internal report concerning a patient's death was disclosable, in part, to attorneys for the patient's family.[58] The high court drew a distinction between the part of the report containing fact-gathering interviews with hospital personnel, on the one hand, and the part containing "objective" conclusions about the patient's course, causes of his or her death, proposed corrective measures, and accident prevention strategies, on the other. The court held the fact-gathering section of the report non-disclosable on the ground that disclosure would interfere with a protectable interest that the court characterized as "free formation of ideas" (*jiyū na ishi keisei*) on the part of the medical personnel, and that the fact gathering was solely for internal use. However, the court ruled that the part of the report containing factual conclusions and quality improvement strategies was disclosable. Although this part of the report was in part for internal use, it was also the basis for the hospital's report on the case to prefectural health authorities, and it contained an apology to the family and a prayer for the eternal happiness of the departed patient—factors that took this part of the report out of the *naibu bunsho* exception.

This appears to be a disclosure principle somewhat broader than that generally applied under the American peer review privilege statutes, which typically call for disclosure of incident reports but protect from discovery all documents with evaluative content.

A major issue facing MHLW in structuring its patient safety programs has been what type of system to implement regarding the analysis and reporting of medical errors. The ministry has wobbled somewhat on this issue. The ministry initially required *tokutei kinō byōin* (an administrative category of advanced-level hospitals) to establish safety management systems incorporating systems for *internal* reporting to hospital patient safety committees of accidents involving injury.[59] Fearing physician resistance, MHLW originally required neither *tokutei kinō byōin* nor general hospitals to submit any *external* reports, either of accidents involving injury or of "near misses" in which an error did not result in harm. All hospitals, however, were encouraged to send in reports of near misses on a voluntary basis.

The ministry's original reporting program was not a success. The near miss reports, which the MHLW had hoped would contain virtually as much information useful in identifying specific problems and risks as reports of actual accidents might contain, were entered into a rigid, unhelpful coding system that made root cause analysis difficult. There were vast variations in the thoroughness with which *tokutei kinō byōin* conducted their internal reporting systems for accidents involving harm.[60] The ministry had no reliable information on the actual extent of medically caused injury.[61]

In 2003, acting on an advisory committee report,[62] MHLW changed course and determined that accidents causing harm to patients, rather than near miss events, would be the focus of the redesigned reporting system. Since April 2004 reporting has become mandatory rather than voluntary. Reports are made not to any governmental entity with enforcement powers, such as MHLW, but rather to an independent entity whose purpose is the collection and analysis of medical accident data and the formulation and dissemination of corrective measures[63]—a structure somewhat analogous to the air safety reporting system in the United States. Although reporting is required, no penalty is associated with failure to report—a compromise policy aimed at simultaneously mollifying media and patients groups' criticisms of the previous voluntary reporting system and appeasing Japan Medical Association opposition to strictly enforced mandatory accident reporting.

Legal compulsion, however, is not the only means by which hospital accident reports may be disclosed to affected patients, families, and the public. Some hospitals have adopted policies of rather thoroughgoing voluntary disclosure. For example, after its nationally publicized heart and lung surgery patient mix-up and other misadventures, Yokohama Metropolitan University implemented a policy of public disclosure of all cases of malpractice resulting in death, serious injury, or lesser injury where hospital safety practices are called into question.[64]

Consumer demand for information about hospital quality is high, and the media are attempting to respond. Various publications have issued reports purporting to rank hospitals in various fields of medicine, by reputation, by volume of procedures performed, and so on.[65] The objectivity of these rankings may be questionable, but sales of these publications can leave no doubt of the public's interest in availability of health care quality information.

However, public access to reports of patient safety hazards through the civil justice system, administrative mechanisms, and private sector initiatives is not the only means by which the principle of public accountability for medical error can be vindicated. In Japan, far more than in the United States, a significant locus for the accountability function is the criminal justice system, amplified by the power of the media.

IV. PATIENT SAFETY AND THE CRIMINAL JUSTICE SYSTEM

Criminal prosecutions of medical personnel for medical acts[66] resulting in harm to patients are rare in both Japan and the United States. Barriers to successful criminal prosecution are high, and properly so. Nevertheless, the criminal law is available in both nations as a restraint on patient-endangering acts of uncommon turpitude.

A. THE UNITED STATES

In the United States, it has been estimated that the past two decades have seen perhaps twenty-five to thirty cases of criminal prosecutions for medical negligence.[67] These cases were typically brought, and convictions sometimes obtained, on the basis of the defendants' reckless disregard for patients' safety—a standard considerably stricter than the negligence standard applied in civil cases.[68] The rarity of these prosecutions is at least partly explained by the factual complexity typical of medical cases and the need for expertise regarding matters such as causation and professional standards of care, the discretion afforded physicians in matters of medical judgment, the high burden of proof beyond a reasonable doubt, and the fact that responsibility for prosecution decisions typically falls on busy local prosecutors' offices lacking ready access to medical expertise. These factors together make the prosecution of medical personnel a costly and difficult endeavor.

Accordingly, in comparison with the relative frequency of civil medical malpractice actions, the threat of criminal prosecution does not loom large as a concern of U.S. physicians and hospitals. Injured patients and their families seldom seek to have a harm-causing physician indicted; the private law remedy is vastly preferred.

B. COMPARISON WITH JAPAN

1. *Social Significance of Criminal Prosecutions*

In contrast to the United States, a major source of concern to Japanese hospitals and physicians is the prospect of a police investigation and criminal prosecution. Even before the recent surge of public attention to the problem of medical error, an average of two to three prosecutions per year were brought in medical cases in Japan[69]—a per capita frequency somewhat higher than that reported in the U.S. literature.[70] In the past four years, the annual rate of prosecutions in Japan has increased.

More important than the absolute number of prosecutions is the level of media coverage. The front-page publicity accorded to prosecutions for recent medical disasters has set the medical profession on edge and has helped create a public expectation of sorts that police and prosecutors have a routine role to play in sorting out medical mishaps. This expectation is evident in the actions of medical malpractice victims. Attorneys experienced in representing Japanese medical malpractice plaintiffs report that patients and families sufficiently indignant about medical injuries to consult an attorney frequently also seek police investigations and want to see medical wrongdoers prosecuted. This sense of indignity is due in part, but only in part, to anger over the not uncommon practice of deceit about harm suffered in the hospital and to falsification of patients' medical records.

2. *Legal Grounds for Criminal Prosecutions*

Japanese prosecutors employ several legal weapons in medical cases that are not part of U.S. prosecutors' standard arsenal. Most importantly, the standard charge brought against medical personnel under the Japanese Criminal Code is "professional negligence causing death or injury"[71]—a crime not found in U.S. statute books. (As noted above, the few convictions in recent years in U.S. medical cases almost always involve charges of recklessness or intent—a higher level of mens rea than negligence.) Additional sanctions are available in the Criminal Code for attempts to cover up medical wrongdoing by altering patients' charts[72] and under the Physicians' Act for failing to report "unnatural deaths" to police.[73] Japanese prosecutors may be reluctant to bring medical crime cases for various reasons including the factual difficulties, but as these provisions demonstrate, their statutory obligation to protect the public certainly extends into medical facilities.

The crime under Article 21 of the Physicians' Act of failing to report an "unnatural death," though infrequently prosecuted,[74] is causing considerable controversy within Japanese medical circles. Disagreement exists about whether this ambiguous provision of the Physicians' Act requires only the reporting of deaths in which ordinary nonmedical criminal activities might be suspected—the traditional interpretation—or whether the provision extends to cover deaths in which professional negligence might be involved.[75] If the latter, more expansive interpretation is correct, some have charged that the reporting requirement, if applied to a physician whose acts may have contributed to a patient's death, might violate the constitutional protection against self-incrimination.[76] However, the Supreme Court rejected this constitutional argument in 2004.[77]

The issue exemplifies the tension between the principles of public accountability and patient safety. Accountability considerations demand that circumstances raising suspicions of medical error be communicated to some competent, neutral entity outside the hospital, rather than be kept under wraps in the traditional fashion. At present, there are few external entities capable of effective response to such communications, except the media (to whom whistleblowers within the hospitals have increasingly turned) and the police. So despite the limitations of police in terms of medical expertise, it is understandable that some people might favor a structure encouraging reporting to the police as a public accountability mechanism.[78] However, the corresponding possibilities of criminal sanctions and adverse reputational consequences could create, in the minds of medical personnel, the opposite incentive to cover up medical mishaps, thereby losing opportunities for analysis and correction of errors.

As indicated above, MHLW recently adopted a mandatory reporting system for adverse events, with reports to be submitted to an independent entity without enforcement powers. As this new system gains traction, the accountability-based pressure for reporting to police will diminish. Whether the lodging of a part of the public accountability function in the new reporting system will affect the interpretation of the ambiguity in the Physicians' Act remains to be seen.

3. *Prosecutorial Considerations*

According to Tokyo prosecutors experienced in medical cases, several factors are most important in decisions about whether to prosecute. These factors are (1) the bringing of a complaint by the patient or family, (2) the seriousness of the harm, (3) the egregiousness of the medical personnel's acts or omissions, (4) the clarity of proof of negligence, and (5) whether the medical personnel provided compensation and apologies to the injured.[79] Other relevant considerations include the extent of media coverage, the current weakness of professional disciplinary sanctions within medicine, and perhaps the deterrent effect of prosecution on other harm-causing behavior.[80] Few cases meet these criteria, but those that do, when they become public, have enormous impact.

4. *Criminal Law's Role in Medical Error Cases in Japan and the United States*

Criminal law plays a far greater role in the public regulation of medical error in Japan than in the United States. Japanese aggrieved by perceived medical error have a greater tendency to call for police and prosecutorial involvement than Americans. The lack of other accountability mechanisms in medicine—for example, the weakness of peer review and professional discipline structures,[81] the absence of objective hospital-by-hospital statistics on outcomes of medical treatment, and the relative infrequency of civil malpractice litigation—enhances the social importance of the criminal law as a way of increasing transparency in the medical world.

Various theories have been offered for the tendency of Japanese to rely on police and prosecutors in cases of medical harm. One explanation draws on a traditional predilection among Japanese to look to public authorities, *ōyake*, to resolve private disputes that Americans would resolve privately.[82] Another explanation emphasizes the practical difficulties and delays in obtaining civil law remedies through malpractice actions, impelling victims to turn to public officials who are more accessible and who may be more likely to act.

One other possible explanation, drawing on the work of David Johnson,[83] focuses on a comparison between the goals of victims of medical error and the goals of prosecutors. Recent scholarship on medical error victims' experiences and goals,[84] and victims' own accounts,[85] indicates that their objectives include compensation, a sincere apology, knowledge of the truth about what happened, sometimes revenge, and the institution of measures to avoid similar injuries in the future.

Prosecutorial objectives are rather well aligned with those of medical error victims. Japanese prosecutorial culture emphasizes establishing the exact facts of each case and pursuing defendants' rehabilitation by encouraging remorse. As noted above, considerations in the charging decision include whether the victim has received compensation and apology. It is reasonable to assume these prosecutorial priorities are known to the public, at least in a general way. Although law enforcement officials have recently been criticized for inattention to victims' needs,[86] prosecutors claim to be responding to these criticisms. It is not surprising, then, that Japanese medical error victims should turn to prosecutors for assistance. By contrast, U.S. prosecutors, lacking the same regard for the importance of remorse and apology and less exacting about determining the precise facts, are less appealing allies to injured patients and families.

V. CONCLUSION

Both Japan and the United States are coming to realize that the reduction of the human toll from medical error is a social objective of the first importance.

Leaders in both nations recognize that accurate information on the nature, frequency, and causes of medical errors is essential to any successful quality improvement program. Both nations are grappling with the fact that obtaining accurate information through programs of self-critical analysis in medical facilities creates serious tension between the principles of patient safety and public accountability.

Differences in the two societies' legal structures, however, have forced efforts to resolve this tension into somewhat different trajectories. In the United States, where civil malpractice litigation and the hospital accreditation process play critical roles in medical quality control and peer review is relatively well developed, the debate has largely centered on protecting from plaintiffs' attorneys internal hospital information developed for purposes of quality improvement and accreditation requirements. In Japan, where the pressure on hospitals from civil litigation and hospital accreditors is much less stringent and peer review and professional discipline are weak, the debate is focusing more on the proper role of the criminal justice system as regulator of medical quality.

It may well be that police and prosecutors are not ideally suited for the medical quality control role that has been thrust on them. But democratic societies demand public accountability, and the relative weakness of other social structures regulating medicine has made the criminal justice system (together with the media) into an accountability mechanism of last resort. Unfortunately, the threat of criminal prosecution and accompanying adverse publicity may undercut sorely needed initiatives within hospitals to perform self-critical analyses.

With regard to one important point, however, the involvement of the criminal justice system in the medical error arena has offered Japan an unqualified benefit. The traditional practice of systematic deception of patients about medical harm cannot long endure. Whistleblowers within hospitals have uncovered these deceptions, prosecutors are not inclined to tolerate them, and the media are unforgiving. Thanks in part to the criminal justice system, the practice of medical dishonesty, by doctors seeking to cover up their mistakes, is likely in decline.

NOTES

The author thanks Takanori Abe, Norio Higuchi, Futoshi Iwata, Tatsuo Kuroyanagi, and Michiyuki Nagasawa for their kind assistance. This research project was supported by an Abe Fellowship granted by the Japan Foundation Center for Global Partnership and the Social Science Research Council, and by the University of Arkansas School of Law.

Earlier versions of this essay have appeared in Japanese in Robert B Leflar, "Iryō misu, anzen, kōteki sekinin—Nichibei ni okeru iryō misu jōhō shūshū shisutemu no kōchiku" [Error, Safety, and Accountability: Crafting Information Systems on Medical Mistakes in America and Japan], trans. Tomoko Mise, *Amerika-hō* 2003 (2003): 1–24, and Robert B Leflar, "Iryō jiko ni taisuru Nichibei no taiō—Kanja no anzen to kōteki sekinin no sōkoku" [Two Societies' Responses to the Problem of Medical Error: The Tension between Patient Safety and Public Accountability], trans. Tomoko Mise, *Hanrei taimuzu* 1133 (2003): 20–27.

Professor Futoshi Iwata and I have addressed this topic in Robert B Leflar and Futoshi Iwata, "Medical Error as Reportable Event, as Tort, as Crime: A Transpacific Comparison," *Widener Law Review* 12 (2005): 189–225.

1. See, e.g., Alice L. Bhasale et al., "Analyzing Potential Harm in Australian General Practice: An Incident-Monitoring Study," *Medical Journal of Australia* 169 (1998): 73 (the "Quality in Australian Health Care Study"); Charles Vincent et al., "Adverse Events in British Hospitals: Preliminary Retrospective Record Review," *British Medical Journal* 322 (2001): 517; Department of Health [United Kingdom], *An Organisation with a Memory* (London: The Stationery Office, 2000); "Gesundheitsministerkonferenz, Ziele für eine einheitlichen Qualitätsstrategie im Gesundheitswesen" [Health Minister's Conference, Goal for a Unified Quality Strategy in the Health Care System] (http://www.gesetzeskunde.de/Rechtsalmanach/Gesundheitswesen/gesundheitsministerkonferenz.htm) (1999) (Germany) (accessed March 23, 2005); Emmy M. Sluijs and Cordula Wagner, *Kwaliteitssystemen in zorginstellingen: De stand van zaken in 2000* [Quality Systems in Health Care Institutions: The State of Affairs in 2000] (Utrecht: Nivel, 2000) (Netherlands); Synnöve Ödegård, "Säkerheten i vården bör fokusera på prevention: Låar av flyget, kärkraftsverken och offshoreindustrin" [Prevention Should Be the Focus of Measures in Health Care: Lessons to Be Learned from the Aviation, Nuclear Energy, and Offshore Oil Industries], *Läkartidningen* (1999): 3068 (Sweden).

2. President Bush has spotlighted the nation's medical malpractice system as a cause of hospitals' failure to improve care, to patients' detriment, and his supporters in Congress have introduced legislation attempting to remedy some of the perceived deficiencies. See "President Discusses Medical Liability Reform," White House press release, January 5, 2005 (http://www.whitehouse.gov/news/releases/2005/01/20050105_4.html) (visited March 23, 2005); Help Efficient, Accessible, Low-Cost, Timely Healthcare (HEALTH) Act of 2005, H.R. 534, 109th Cong. (2005). Prime Minister Koizumi's Council for Regulatory Reform has pro-

posed a major restructuring of hospital care, one primary aim of which is the improvement of patient safety. See Sōgō kisei kaikaku kaigi [Council on Regulatory Reform], "Kisei kaikaku no suishin ni kansuru daiichiji tōshin" [First Report Regarding Promotion of Regulatory Reform] (December 11, 2001), chap. 1.1 ("Medical Care"), (http://www8.cao.go.jp/kisei/en/011211report/1.html) (English translation) (visited February 9, 2004). Of course, in both cases the executive is attempting to enlist the public's concern over patient safety for partisan advantage.

3. To be sure, media exposés, in particular the *Boston Globe*'s 1995 account of the death of one of its columnists at the Dana Farber Cancer Institute as a result of medication mistakes, drew attention to the scientific evidence of the widespread incidence of medical error and helped spark the national debate over the issue. See Michael L. Millenson, "Moral Hazard vs. Real Hazard: Quality of Care Post-Arrow," *Journal of Health Policy and Law* 26 (2001): 1069, 1074. For a useful summary of the upsurgence of patient safety initiatives in the United States, see Stephen D. Small and Paul Barach, "Patient Safety and Health Policy: A History and Review," *Hematology/Oncology Clinics of North America* 16 (2001): 1463.

4. Troyen A. Brennan et al., "Incidence of Adverse Events and Negligence in Hospitalized Patients: Results of the Harvard Medical Practice Study I," *New England Journal of Medicine* 324 (1991): 370; Lucian L. Leape et al., "The Nature of Adverse Events in Hospitalized Patients: Results of the Harvard Medical Practice Study II," *New England Journal of Medicine* 324 (1991): 377; Russell Localio et al., "Relation between Malpractice Claims and Adverse Events due to Negligence: Results of the Harvard Medical Practice Study III," *New England Journal of Medicine* 325 (1991): 245.

5. Eric J. Thomas et al., "Incidence and Types of Adverse Events and Negligent Care in Utah and Colorado," *Medical Care* 38 (2000): 261.

6. Linda T. Kohn et al., eds., *To Err Is Human: Building a Safer Health System* (Washington, DC: National Academy Press, 2000).

7. Ibid., 1, 26, 31. The report relied for these estimates on the Harvard Medical Practice Study and the Colorado-Utah study, discussed above.

8. Troyen A. Brennan, "Reporting of Errors: How Much Should the Public Know?" *Effective Clinical Practice* 3 (2000): 298.

9. Quality Interagency Coordination Task Force [United States], *Doing What Counts for Patient Safety: Federal Actions to Reduce Medical Errors and Their Impact; Report of the Quality Interagency Coordination Task Force to the President* (Rockville, MD: Quality Interagency Coordination Task Force, 2000).

10. See, e.g., National Quality Forum, *Serious Reportable Events in Healthcare: A Consensus Report* (Washington, DC: National Quality Forum, 2002).

11. Among other federal initiatives are a $250 million five-year research program undertaken by the Agency for Healthcare Research and Quality and a $478 million three-year program budgeted by the Department of Veterans Affairs. Small and Barach, "Patient Safety and Health Policy," 1468, 1470–71.

12. See, e.g., Jill Rosenthal et al., *Medical Errors and Adverse Events: A Report of a 50-State Survey* (Portland, ME: National Academy for State Health Policy, 2000); Kohn et al., *To Err Is Human*, 254–65.

13. An official at the Ministry of Health, Labor and Welfare explained, perhaps somewhat disingenuously, why no quantitative studies of the extent of medical error had been carried out in Japan: "It's impossible. Our medical records are too bad." Interview with Tetsuya Fujimori, MD (deputy director; Ministry of Health, Labor and Welfare; General Affairs Division; Health Policy Bureau; Tokyo), April 12, 2001.

14. On the role of the Japanese media in creating the climate of public opinion as well as reporting on it, see Ofer Feldman, *Politics and the News Media in Japan* (Ann Arbor: University of Michigan Press, 1993), 17, 22–25; and John C. Campbell, "The Media and Policy Change in Japan," in Susan J. Pharr and Ellis S. Krauss, eds., *Media and Politics in Japan* (Honolulu: University of Hawai'i Press, 1996).

15. This phenomenon has received sporadic international attention. See, e.g., Yumiko Ono, "In Japan, a Doctor Shakes up Medicine in Malpractice Case," *Wall Street Journal*, June 10, 2002, A1 (physician's negligence action against hospital in which her daughter died).

16. A heart patient had part of his lung removed, and a lung patient with a similar name had part of his heart valve excised. The mistake was not discovered until the evening after the operations. Three doctors and two nurses were found criminally liable for professional negligence. "Court Fines Medical Staff for Heart, Lung Mix-up," *Japan Times*, September 21, 2001.

17. A patient died after a nurse injected her with what the nurse believed to be a heparin solution. In fact the syringe contained a disinfectant, and had been left on the cart by another nurse. The two nurses were convicted of the crime of professional negligence causing death or injury, and the hospital director was convicted of forging a death certificate containing a false cause of death and of failing to report the case to police. "Nurses Get Suspended Sentences in Hiroo Malpractice Case," *Japan Times*, December 28, 2000; "Cover-up of Patient's Death Gets Director Suspended Term," *Japan Times*, August 31, 2001.

18. Improper operation of a heart-lung machine by one doctor during heart surgery led to a decreased blood flow to the brain of the twelve-year-old patient, who later died. Another doctor, in charge of the surgery, falsified data on the

patient's chart in a cover-up attempt. "Two Doctors Arrested in Malpractice Death," *International Herald Tribune / Asahi shinbun*, June 29, 2002, 1. The first doctor was arrested and indicted for professional negligence causing death, the second for falsifying an official document. "2 Doctors Indicted for Girl's Death," *International Herald Tribune / Asahi shinbun*, July 20–21, 2002, 22. The hospital was stripped of its prestigious and remunerative status as a special function hospital.

19. Three neophyte surgeons performed a "keyhole" laparoscopy on a prostate cancer patient using sophisticated equipment with which they were unfamiliar. Having also failed to procure an adequate supply of blood of the correct type in case of need, they were unable to cope with the patient's excessive blood loss during surgery. Following the patient's death, they were arrested for professional negligence, along with the senior surgeon who had authorized the operation despite the physicians' inadequate experience and the anesthesiologist on duty who had failed to put a stop to the procedure at the critical juncture. See "Three Urologists Held over Patient's Death; Inexperienced Doctors Read from Manual While Performing Surgery," *Japan Times*, September 26, 2003; "Jikei Medical School Fires Three Doctors Standing Trial for Malpractice Death," *Japan Times*, December 27, 2003.

20. See Kohn et al., *To Err Is Human*, 86–108.

21. See, e.g., Lucian L. Leape et al., "Promoting Patient Safety by Preventing Medical Error," *Journal of the American Medical Association* 280 (1998): 1444; David Blumenthal, "Making Medical Errors into 'Medical Treasures,'" *Journal of the American Medical Association* 272 (1994): 1867.

22. Joint Commission on Accreditation of Healthcare Organizations, *Hospital Accreditation Standards* (Oak Brook, IL: Joint Commission Resources, 2002), 200, Standard LD.5.2; JCAHO Sentinel Event Policy and Procedures (January 2002), available at (http://www.jcaho.org/accredited+organizations/hospitals/sentinel+event/index.htm) (visited February 16, 2004). See also Harold Bressler, "The Sentinel Event Policy: A Response by the Joint Commission," *Journal of Health Law* 33 (2000): 519, 531 and n.38 (2000) (views of JCAHO general counsel).

23. "Medicare and Medicaid Programs; Hospital Conditions of Participation: Quality Assessment and Performance Improvement," *Federal Register* 68 (2003): 3435 (codified at 42 C.F.R. § 482.21).

24. Troyen A. Brennan, "The Institute of Medicine Report on Medical Errors—Could It Do Harm?" *New England Journal of Medicine* 342 (2000): 1123, 1125. See also, e.g., Bryan A. Liang, "Risks of Reporting Sentinel Events," *Health Affairs* 19(5) (September–October 2000): 112.

25. Representative peer review statutes include, e.g., Ala. Code Ann. § 22-21-8 (2001); Ark. Code Ann. § 16 46 105 (Michie 2001); Minn. Stat. Ann. §§ 145.61 and

145.64 (West Supp. 2002). The first case recognizing and explaining the self-critical analysis privilege in a medical context was Bredice v. Doctors Hospital, Inc., 50 F.R.D. 249, 250–51 (D.D.C. 1970), aff'd, 479 F.2d 920 (D.C. Cir. 1973). See generally Donald P. Vandegrift, Jr., "The Privilege of Self-Critical Analysis: A Survey of the Law," *Albany Law Review* 60 (1996): 171; Daniel Mulholland, "Unanticipated Consequences of Unanticipated Outcomes Disclosures," *Journal of Health Law* 35 (2002): 211, 214–19 (surveying statutes and case law as applied to hospital reports to JCAHO).

26. Kohn et al., *To Err Is Human*, 120–21; Susan O. Scheutzow, "State Medical Peer Review: High Cost but No Benefit—Is It Time for a Change?" *American Journal of Law and Medicine* 25 (1999): 7, 28; Melissa Chiang, "Promoting Patient Safety: Creating a Workable Reporting System," *Yale Journal on Regulation* 18 (2001): 383, 400–401.

27. See John C. Lincoln Hosp. v. Superior Court, 768 P.2d 188 (Ariz. Ct. App. 1989); Chicago Trust Co. v. Cook County Hosp., 698 N.E.2d 641 (Ill. App. Ct. 1998); Columbia / HCA Healthcare Corp. v. Eighth Judicial Dist. Court, 936 P.2d 844 (Nev. 1997). Cases on both sides of this issue are collected in William D. Bremer, "Scope and Extent of Protection from Disclosure of Medical Peer Review Proceedings relating to Claim in Medical Malpractice Action," American Law Reports, *ALR 5th, Annotations and Cases*, 69 (Rochester, NY: Lawyers Cooperative Publishing, 2000), 559.

28. In jurisdictions in which "incident reports" are discoverable, hospital attorneys will often counsel devising "incident report" forms calling for only minimal information, so that other internal communications containing even a hint of evaluation or potentially damaging factual information can be otherwise characterized and thereby be sheltered by the peer review privilege. Other tactics of experienced hospital counsel are explained in Bressler, "The Sentinel Event Policy," 532–33.

29. E.g., Syposs v. United States, 63 F. Supp. 2d 301 (W.D.N.Y. 1999). Contra, Weekoty v. United States, 30 F. Supp. 2d 1343 (D.N.M. 1998). In Veterans Administration hospitals, a specific federal statute exempts peer review and quality assurance documents from discovery. Kohn et al., *To Err Is Human*, 123.

30. Patient Safety and Quality Improvement Act of 2005, Pub. L. No. 109-41, 119 Stat. 424.

31. Rae M. Lamb et al., "Hospital Disclosure Practices: Results of a National Survey," *Health Affairs* 22(2) (March–April 2003): 73.

32. American Medical Association, Current Opinions of the Council on Ethical and Judicial Affairs E-8.12, "Patient Information" (updated 1994). See also National Patient Safety Foundation, "Talking to Patients about Health Care Injury:

Statement of Principle," at (http://www.npsf.org/html/statement.html) (2000) (visited February 16, 2004); Stephen Jencks, "Public Reporting of Serious Medical Errors," *Effective Clinical Practice* 3 (2000): 299, 301 ("Almost all ethicists agree that the patient has an absolute right to know what has happened and whether what has happened is the result of an error").

33. Joint Commission on Accreditation of Healthcare Organizations, *Hospital Accreditation Standards*, 73, Standard RI.1.2.2. See generally Nancy LeGros and Jason D. Pinkall, "The New JCAHO Patient Safety Standards and the Disclosure of Unanticipated Outcomes," *Journal of Health Law* 35 (2002): 189.

34. See, e.g., Aaron D. Twerski and Neil B. Cohen, "Comparing Medical Providers: A First Look at the New Era of Medical Statistics," *Brooklyn Law Review* 58 (1992): 5; Robert B Leflar, "Infōmudo konsento o koete—Iryō jōhō no kōkai to chiryō kekka ni motozuku iryō teikyōsha hyōka no reimei" [Beyond Informed Consent: Public Access to Medical Information and the Dawn of Physicians' Accountability for the Results of Medical Treatment], trans. Hiroo Sono, *Hokkaido Law Review* 44 (1994): 1039; Mark R. Chassin et al., "Benefits and Hazards of Reporting Medical Outcomes Publicly," *New England Journal of Medicine* 334 (1996): 394.

35. One recent study found that making quality information public tends to stimulate hospitals to improve areas in which their performance was low. Judith Hibbard et al., "Does Publicizing Hospital Performance Stimulate Quality Improvement Efforts?" *Health Affairs* 22(2) (March–April 2003): 84. Another study concluded, however, that the existence of "report cards" for cardiac surgery actually led to worse health outcomes for sicker patients, because hospitals sometimes declined to treat them. David Dranove et al., "Is More Information Better? The Effects of 'Report Cards' on Health Care Providers," *Journal of Political Economy* 111 (2003): 555.

36. See, e.g., David Brown, "Hospitals Will Be Rated on Their Performance," *Washington Post*, December 13, 2002, A1.

37. The Japan Council for Quality in Health Care (JCQHC) (Nihon iryō kinō hyōka kikō), conducts hospital accreditation surveys on a voluntary basis, but does not check as part of the survey whether hospitals carry out self-critical analyses of adverse events. Interview with Hisashi Ōmichi (JCQHC director), July 31, 2003.

38. Kokuritsu daigaku igakubu fuzoku byōinchō kaigi jōchi iinkai [National University Hospital Presidents' Conference], *Iryō jiko bōshi no tame no anzen kanri taisei no kakuritsu ni tsuite—Nakama hōkoku* [Interim Report: Establishing Safety Systems for the Prevention of Medical Accidents] (Tokyo: MHLW, 2000).

39. E.g., Ministry of Health, Labor and Welfare, "Risuku manējimento manyuaru sakusei shishin" [Guidelines for the Creation of Risk Management Manuals] (2000).

40. See, e.g., Takashi Yokota et al., "Will Accident Reports Filed in Hospitals in Japan Be Used in the Future as Evidence in Malpractice Lawsuits?" *American Journal of Emergency Medicine* 19 (2001): 597.

41. See *Best's Aggregates and Averages, Property-Casualty*, 2001 ed. (Oldwick, NJ: A. M. Best Co., 2001), 238. These figures include all insurance payouts, whether the claims were filed in the judicial system or not.

42. Data on claims filed within the judicial system are available annually from the Administrative Office of the Supreme Court (table 17.1).

43. See Kazue Nakajima et al., "Medical Malpractice and Legal Resolution Systems in Japan," *Journal of the American Medical Association* 285 (2001): 1632, 1633, 1638. These statistics (table 17.2) represent claims filed with the nationwide non-judicial dispute resolution system under the auspices of the Japan Medical Association (JMA) liability insurance program, which covers 43 percent of Japanese physicians, and with a local chapter unnamed in the article. Claims filed with the JMA encompassed the larger claims (¥1 million or more), while those filed with the local chapter—the second largest in Japan, presumably Osaka, where Nakajima is based—represent the smaller claims (1634, 1637–38).

44. See *Best's Aggregates and Averages, Property-Casualty*, 238; see also table 17.3.

45. See Nakajima et al., "Medical Malpractice and Legal Resolution Systems in Japan," 1632; see also tables 17.1 and 17.2.

46. It would be inaccurate simply to take the number of lawsuits (table 17.1) plus the number of JMA and local Osaka claims filed (table 17.2) as even a rough estimate of the number of medical malpractice claims in Japan as a whole. About 8 percent of the claims filed in the JMA system are also filed in court, see Nakajima et al., "Medical Malpractice and Legal Resolution Systems in Japan," 1635; the Osaka claims represent only a fraction, albeit a substantial one, of all the small claims filed with local medical associations. Moreover, some other medical injury claims are filed only with the special compensation system for drug adverse events. Still, comparing the figures in table 17.1 and table 17.2 with those in table 17.3 demonstrates convincingly the magnitude of the difference between the propensity to file medical claims in the United States and Japan.

47. The premium paid by a physician member of the Japan Medical Association liability insurance program in 2000 was ¥55,000 (US$500). (Unlike in the United States, premiums in Japan do not vary by specialty or location.) General hospitals insured by Yasuda Fire & Marine Co. paid ¥16,130 (US$150) annually per bed. Nakajima et al., "Medical Malpractice and Legal Resolution Systems in Japan," 1633 (table 1). By contrast, U.S. internists pay more than ten times as much; physicians in high-risk specialties in high-verdict locales may pay three hundred times as much; and hospital premiums are far higher as well. See U.S. Depart-

ment of Health and Human Services, *Confronting the New Health Care Crisis: Improving Health Care Quality and Lowering Costs by Fixing Our Medical Liability System* (Washington, DC: Office of the Assistant Secretary for Planning and Evaluation, Department of Health and Human Services, 2002), 16 (table 6), available at (http://aspe.hhs.gov/daltcp/reports/litrefm.pdf) (visited February 16, 2004).

48. See Tatsuo Kuroyanagi, "Iryō jiko soshō no shori ni tsuite" [The Management of Medical Accident Litigation], *Hō no shihai* 130 (2003): 5, 12 (fig. 1).

49. Informal plaintiff-side medical malpractice groups (*iryō bengodan*) in most major metropolitan areas are backed by specialized resource centers such as Iryō jiko chōsadan [Medical Accident Research Group] and Iryō jiko jōhō sentā [Medical Accident Information Center]. They have collected and published expert opinion testimony in a wide variety of cases, together with lists of medical experts willing to testify for plaintiffs, and made these available to attorneys nationwide. E.g., Iryō jiko jōhō sentā, *Iryō kago soshō kanteishoshū dai-13-shū* [Collection of Expert Witness Reports in Medical Malpractice Litigation No. 13] (Nagoya: Iryō jiko jōhō sentā, 2002). A measure of the expansion of the plaintiffs' malpractice bar is the number of full members of Iryō Jiko Jōhō Sentā, all of whom are attorneys devoting at least a significant part of their practice to medical cases. The number has increased from 111 in 1990 to 451 as of May 2000 (Iryō jiko jōhō sentā, *Iryō higaisha no kyūsai o mezashite* [Striving for Compensation for Medical Victims] [Nagoya: Iryō jiko jōhō sentā, 2002], 7 [table 4]), and to 522 as of August 2002 (personal communication from attorney Yoshio Katō, August 12, 2002). (This number is still orders of magnitude smaller than the number of plaintiff-side malpractice specialists in the United States.)

50. For an American perspective on this point, see William M. Sage, "Reputation, Malpractice Liability, and Medical Error," in Virginia A. Sharpe, ed., *Promoting Patient Safety: An Ethical Basis for Policy Reform* (Washington, DC: Georgetown University Press, 2004), 159–83.

51. A fourth source of legal obligation to disclose information about hospital accidents, an obligation implied from the contract between the patient and the medical provider, has been recognized in two recent district court decisions. (Kyoto Dist. Ct., July 12, 2005), *Hanrei jihō* 1907 (2005): 112, 124–25; (Tokyo Dist. Ct., Jan. 30, 2004), *Hanrei taimuzu* 1194 (2006): 243 (Hiroo Hospital civil case). These cases are discussed in Leflar and Iwata, "Medical Error as Reportable Event, as Tort, as Crime," 212–13.

52. Gyōsei kikan no hoyū suru jōhō no kōkai ni kansuru hōritsu [Act concerning Access to Information Held by Administrative Organs], art. 5(1).

53. Jōhō kōkai shingikai [Information Disclosure Review Board], Opinion of January 9, 2002, 13–14. See "Kokuritsu byōin no iryō jiko, 'Tantōi nado kaiji o':

Jōhō kōkai-shin ga shokijun" ["Disclose Physicians' Names" in National Hospital Medical Accident: Information Board Sets Standards], *Asahi shinbun*, January 9, 2002, evening edition, 1.

54. Interview with Professor Katsuya Uga (University of Tokyo Faculty of Law), August 7, 2003.

55. The MHLW official in charge of patient safety efforts stated in mid-2003, however, that he believed the possibility of disclosure of hospital documents under information disclosure rules had not decreased the number of incident reports submitted to MHLW by public hospitals. Interview with Kazuhiro Araki, July 29, 2003.

56. Analyses of the new discovery provisions useful to English-language readers include Shozo Ota, "Reform of Civil Procedure in Japan," *American Journal of Comparative Law* 49 (2001): 561; and Toshiro M. Mochizuki, "Baby Step or Giant Leap? Parties' Expanded Access to Documentary Evidence under the New Japanese Code of Civil Procedure," *Harvard Journal of International Law* 40 (1999): 285, 299–309.

57. (Sup. Ct., Nov. 12, 1999), *Minshū* 53 (8) (1999): 1787 (holding that bank *ringisho* are for internal use and not subject to discovery) (Fuji Bank Case).

58. (Tokyo High Court, July 15, 2003), *Hanrei jihō* 57 (2003): 1842; *Hanrei taimuzu* 298 (2003): 1145 (Saitama Medical University case).

59. MHLW later established similar internal reporting systems for general hospitals as well. Ministry of Health, Labor and Welfare, *Shōrei* 111 (August 30, 2002), available at (http://www.mhlw.go.jp/topics/bukyoku/isei/i-anzen/2/kaisei/index.html) (visited February 16, 2004).

60. For example, Kitasato University Hospital conscientiously reported about three thousand incidents—a fifth of the total reported nationwide. By contrast, neither Asahikawa Medical College Hospital nor Hamamatsu University Hospital reported a single incident. "Medical Accident Tally at 15,000," *International Herald Tribune / Asahi shinbun*, April 24, 2002.

61. Interview with Kazuhiro Araki, July 29, 2003.

62. Ministry of Health, Labor, and Welfare, "Iryō ni kakaru jiko jirei jōhō no toriatsukai ni kansuru kentō-bukai hōkokusho" [Report of the Subcommittee for the Study of the Handling of Information on Medical Accident Events] (2003).

63. This function is performed by the Japan Council for Quality Health Care (Nihon iryō kinō hyōka kikō).

64. Yokohama shiritsu daigaku byōin kaikaku iinkai [Yokohama Metropolitan University Hospital Reform Committee], Iryō jiko no kōhyō kijun [Standards for Public Disclosure of Medical Accidents] (February 16, 2001) (on file with the author). The policy requires patients' or families' consent before public disclo-

sure, to protect their privacy. Incidents not involving harm to patients, in principle, are not to be disclosed.

Some private hospitals not subject to information disclosure ordinances have adopted similar policies, even despite the extensive media coverage about medical error. Interview with Dr. Isao Mori (president, Ishinkai Yao General Hospital), July 8, 2001 (describing hospital policies).

65. E.g., "'Erabareru byōin' no jidai" [The Era of Hospital Choice], *Aera*, November 4, 2002, 34–39; "Daichōgan shuyō 103 byōin, 'shujutsu jisseki' wa konna ni chigau" [Vast Differences in Colon Cancer Surgery Results at 103 Leading Hospitals], *Sunday Mainichi*, July 28, 2002, 44–49; "Kanja ya chiiki ni hirakareta byōin, jōhō kōkai de shinrai kankei jōsei e" [Accountable Hospitals: Building Trust with Patients and Community through Information Disclosure], *Nikkei Business*, August 20, 2001, 118–19.

66. I exclude from consideration criminal acts committed by medical personnel outside the course of usual medical care, such as billing fraud, assaults on patients, violations of controlled drug laws, euthanasia, and physician-assisted suicide.

67. James A. Filkins, "'With No Evil Intent': The Criminal Prosecution of Physicians for Medical Negligence," *Journal of Legal Medicine* 22 (2001): 467, 471–72 and nn. 51, 53 (describing nine appellate cases, and estimating from "fifteen or so" to "perhaps two dozen" more non-appellate cases over the twenty-year period 1981–2001, based on a Westlaw database search and a canvass of other studies). The actual number of prosecutions may be somewhat higher than Filkins's estimate, because the cases are not recorded in any systematic way and the Westlaw database Filkins searched is incomplete. See also George J. Annas, "Medicine, Death, and the Criminal Law," *New England Journal of Medicine* 333 (1995): 527 (criminal prosecution of physicians for patients' deaths "extraordinarily rare").

68. Filkins's review of modern appellate cases, Filkins, "With No Evil Intent," reports convictions upheld for reckless or intentional acts in Pennsylvania v. Youngkin, 427 A.2d 1356 (Pa. Super. Ct. 1981) (involuntary manslaughter); People v. Einaugler, 618 N.Y.S.2d 414 (N.Y. App. Div. 1994) (reckless endangerment); Wisconsin v. Chem-Bio Corp. (reckless homicide) (discussed at 477–78 of the Filkins article); and People v. Klvana, 15 Cal. Rptr. 2d 512 (Cal. App. 1992) (second-degree murder). In all these cases recklessness or conscious disregard for a known risk to life was proven.

Physicians have occasionally been prosecuted for crimes with mens rea less than recklessness, for example, negligent homicide (under a concept of negligence stricter than that applied in civil cases). E.g., Utah v. Warden, 813 P.2d 1146 (Utah 1991). But in the modern cases except for *Warden*, either they were found not guilty or their convictions were overturned. See United States v. Billig, 26 M.J. 744 (1988) (military case); Colorado v. Verbrugge, No. 98CA0262, 1999 WL 417965 (Colo. App. June 24, 1999). In an earlier era, negligent homicide cases against physicians were sometimes successful. Donald C. Barrett, "Annotation, Homicide Predicated on Improper Treatment," American Law Reports, *ALR 3rd, Annotations and Cases*, 45 (Rochester, NY: Lawyers Cooperative Publishing, 1972), 114, 142–49. However, the modern cases typically require intent or recklessness. See Kara M. McCarthy, "Note, Doing Time for Clinical Crime: The Prosecution of Incompetent Physicians as an Additional Mechanism to Assure Quality Health Care," *Seton Hall Law Review* 28 (1997): 569, 607–13.

69. According to one recent report, 73 prosecutions were brought in medical cases over the period 1974–99—a rate of 2–3 per year. "'Shohoteki misu': Iryō kago yūhatsu keiji saiban 73-ken: Kyūdai joshu bunseki" ["Elementary Mistakes": 73 Criminal Cases Triggered by Medical Malpractice, Kyushu University Researcher Finds], *Nishi Nippon shinbun*, August 25, 2003, available at (http://www.nishinippon.co.jp/media/news/news-today/20030825/morning_news001.html) (last visited August 26, 2003) (reporting study by Dr. Shōichi Maeda). This study found 21 prosecutions during the 1970s, 22 during the 1980s, and 27 during the 1990s. This rate appears not to have varied much in the fifty years following the end of World War II. See Hideo Iida and Issei Yamaguchi, *Keiji iryō kago* [Criminal Medical Malpractice] (Tokyo: Hanrei taimuzu-sha, 2001), 1 (reporting 137 prosecutions brought in the fifty years following the end of World War II).

70. Filkins's estimate, based on incomplete data though it is, puts the U.S. prosecution rate at slightly more than one per year—less than half the Japanese rate, though the U.S. population is more than double Japan's. See Filkins, "With No Evil Intent."

71. Keihō [Criminal Code], Law No. 45 of 1907, art. 211, providing a prison sentence of up to five years and a fine of up to ¥500,000. This crime is most commonly charged in connection with traffic offenses. Arts. 209 and 210 also criminalize negligence causing injury and negligence causing death, respectively, but they are seldom used in medical prosecutions.

72. Keihō, art. 156. This provision formed the basis for the indictment of one of the physicians in the recent Tokyo Women's Medical University case, discussed in section II of this chapter.

73. Ishihō [Physicians' Act], Law No. 201 of 1948, as amended by Law No. 1 of 2002, art. 21.

74. The charge was brought against the administrator of Hiroo Metropolitan Hospital in Tokyo for failing to report a patient's accidental death. The admin-

istrator was convicted, as discussed in section II of this chapter. The author is aware of only four other prosecutions under this provision.

75. This expansive interpretation was originally offered in a 1994 position paper of Nihon hōi gakkai, an association of forensic medicine specialists. Nihon hōi gakkai, "'Ijōshi' gaidorainu" [Guidelines on 'Unnatural Death'] (1994), reprinted in Toshiharu Furukawa, "Shinryō kōi ni kanren shita kanja no shibō, shōgai no hōkoku ni tsuite" [Reporting to Police of Patients' Deaths and Injuries Connected with Medical Acts], *Nihon geka gakkai zasshi* 104 (2003): 9, 13–14.

76. See, e.g., Hitoshi Saeki, "Ijō shitai no todokede gimu to mokuhiken" [The Duty to Report Unnatural Deaths and the Right to Remain Silent], *Jurisuto*, no. 1249 (2003): 77; and Yasushi Kodama, "Ishihō 21-jō o meguru konmei" [The Confusion Surrounding Article 21 of the Physicians' Act], *Jurisuto*, no. 1249 (2003): 72.

77. (Sup. Ct., Apr. 13, 2004), *Keishū* 58(4) (2004): 247 (Tokyo Hiroo Hospital case).

78. In fact, the Japan Surgical Society [Nihon geka gakkai] issued a position paper contesting the idea that art. 21 of the Physicians' Act requires the reporting to police of deaths potentially connected to medical error, but nevertheless calling on its members to voluntarily report to police both deaths and serious injuries resulting from clear breaches of the standard of medical care, as a matter of medical ethics. Nihon geka gakkai, "Shinryō kōi ni kanren shita kanja no shibō, shōgai no hōkoku ni tsuite" [Reporting to Police of Patients' Deaths and Injuries Connected with Medical Acts], reprinted in Hiroyuki Katō, "Iryō jiko jōhō no hōkoku no mondaiten" [Issues in Reporting Medical Accidents to Police], *Jurisuto*, no. 1249 (2003): 69, 70–71; and Furukawa, "Shinryō kōi ni kanren shita kanja no shibō, shōgai no hōkoku ni tsuite." This position, like the position paper of the National University Hospitals Presidents' Conference that preceded it, discussed in section III.B of this chapter, in effect acknowledges the importance of reporting to a public entity as an accountability mechanism in a time of shaken public confidence in physicians' skill and candor. Interview with Dr. Toshiharu Furukawa, Tokyo, July 16, 2003.

79. Interview with Shūji Iwamura, Takayuki Aonuma, and Atsushi Satō, Tokyo district prosecutor's office, July 25, 2001. The author is grateful to Professor Futoshi Iwata of Sophia University, who helped design the interview questionnaire and accompanied the author at the interview, and to Mr. Akio Harada, through whose kind offices the interview was arranged.

80. Futoshi Iwata, "Kashitsu ni yoru iryō kago ni taisuru keijiteki kisei: Nichibei hikaku-kō" [Regulation of Medical Malpractice through Criminal Negligence Actions: Japan-U.S. Comparative Research], in Yasushi Kodama, ed., *Iryō*

anzen suishin ni kansuru hōteki mondai ni kansuru kinkyū: Heisei 14-nendo kinkyū seika hōkokusho [Research Report on Legal Problems in the Promotion of Medical Safety] (2003), 6 (on file with author).

81. See Robert B Leflar, "Informed Consent and Patients' Rights in Japan," *Houston Law Review* 33 (1996): 1, 9 and nn. 22–23.

82. For a classic exposition of this view, accompanied by a certain skepticism about its continued explanatory power, see Hideo Tanaka and Akio Takeuchi, "The Role of Private Persons in the Enforcement of Law: A Comparative Study of Japanese and American Law," *Law in Japan: An Annual* 7 (1974): 34.

83. See David T. Johnson, *The Japanese Way of Justice: Prosecuting Crimes in Japan* (New York: Oxford University Press, 2002).

84. For a fascinating study of the importance to patients of candor, apology, and willingness to undertake safety corrections, see Steven S. Kraman and Ginny Hamm, "Risk Management: Extreme Honesty May Be the Best Policy," *Annals of Internal Medicine* 131 (1999): 963 (describing Lexington, Kentucky, Veterans Administration Hospital's successful policy of openness toward patients and apology in cases of error); see also Jonathan R. Cohen, "Apology and Organizations: Exploring an Example from Medical Practice," *Fordham Urban Law Journal* 27 (2000): 1447 (same; legal analysis).

85. For an English-language treatment of a Japanese parent/physician's journey through a medical malpractice dispute over her daughter's death, illustrating most of the motivations noted herein, see Tsuneko Kunou, *A Promise to Akiko: A Mother's Notes* (Berkeley, CA: Creative Arts Book Co., 1998). Experiences of families of U.S. patients who died from malpractice are well portrayed in, e.g., Sandra M. Gilbert, *Wrongful Death: A Memoir* (New York: W.W. Norton, 1995); and "Blunt Instruments: Medicine, Law and the Death of Nancy Lim," at (http://www.nancylim.org) (visited February 16, 2004). Japanese-language victims' accounts range from, e.g., Kuniko Nagao, *Musume kara no shukudai* [Homework from My Daughter] (Tokyo: Soushisha, 1988), to Fumie Sugino, *"Waribashi ga nō ni sasatta wagako" to "daibyōin no taido"* [The Chopstick Stuck into Our Child's Brain, and the Giant Hospital's Attitude] (Tokyo: Shōgakukan, 2000).

86. See, e.g., "Higaisha no tachiba ni tatta shihō: Hikinige jiko de musuko o nakushite" [Toward a Justice System That Stands on the Victims' Side: Son Lost in Hit-and-Run], *Gekkan shihō kaikaku* 2 (1999): 15–17 (1999), available at (http://www2.tky.3web.ne.jp/~norin/katayama.html) (visited February 16, 2004). Police and prosecutors have also been criticized for failing to act on citizen complaints of sexual harassment.

PART III

The Law and the Economy

IN THE FIRST CHAPTER in this part, "Reexamining Legal Transplants: The Director's Fiduciary Duty in Japanese Corporate Law," Hideki Kanda and Curtis J. Milhaupt introduce the intriguing saga of Article 254-3 of the Commercial Code, which sets forth the fiduciary duty of corporate directors. Introduced in 1950 as a direct import from the United States, for nearly forty years thereafter that provision was never independently applied by the courts and played little role in corporate governance. Then, beginning with a landmark 1989 decision, Article 254-3 took on a life of its own and began to play an increasingly important role in Japanese corporate law. Kanda and Milhaupt utilize this case study to address two of the major themes raised by the 1961 Law in Japan conference: the role of law in corporate governance and the impact of foreign influences on Japanese corporate law. As their primary focus, though, they explore a much broader topic: the theory of legal transplants.

Takashi Uchida and Veronica L. Taylor argue in their chapter that Japanese contracting in the late 1990s and early 2000s exhibits a marked shift from the regulatory framework and norms of the 1960s. They find contract in the twenty-first century in Japan to be a contested domain, with visible turning points in the mindset of policy elites. They characterize the current period of debate and transition as a return to classical contract theory grounded in economic analysis—what they call Japan's "era of contract." In addition, they explore the ways in which new policy preferences are infusing the regulation of contracts in Japan and look at the courts, the use of contracts by commercial actors, and the intermediation of the legal profession in which the design, interpretation, and enforcement of contracts in Japan are changing. The treatment of contracts by each of these institutions evidences significant deviation from the received images of Japanese contract law and practice that were current in the 1970s and 1980s.

In the next chapter, "From Security to Mobility? Changing Aspects of Japanese Dismissal Law," Ryūichi Yamakawa addresses one of the most significant features of Japanese labor law, regulation of dismissals. As he explains, despite the absence of a specific statutory mandate, courts have established comprehensive limitations on an employer's right to dismiss workers. After discussing the historical development of the dismissal doctrine, Yamakawa explores the relationship between law and employment practices. He then discusses new aspects of dismissal law that have arisen as a result of recent socioeconomic changes and looks forward to likely trends in coming years.

Harry First and Tadashi Shiraishi begin their chapter, "Concentrated Power: The Paradox of Antitrust in Japan," with a quote from Yoshio Kanazawa's essay on antitrust in the 1963 edition of *Law in Japan*. In discussing Japan's Antimonopoly Act, Kanazawa observed that enforcement "is anemic today," and "there is . . . no immediate prospect" of the act being resuscitated. In their chapter, First and Shiraishi discuss the development of antitrust over the intervening four decades. During that time, they observe, much has changed. Among other developments, the act has been strengthened and antitrust principles have come to be embraced by government policy makers. Despite these changes, they conclude, antitrust enforcement, while "not quite anemic," has not been robust. After examining Japan's antitrust enforcement system, First and Shiraishi introduce comparisons to the U.S. system, contrasting the deconcentrated, networked approach in the United States to Japan's hierarchical system. Drawing on lessons from the United States, they then offer suggestions for opening up antitrust enforcement in Japan.

In recent years, the field of intellectual property has assumed great prominence. Influenced by U.S. law and policy, Japanese approaches to intellectual property have undergone major changes over the past decade, with an increasingly pro-patent tilt. In their chapter, "The Changing Roles of the Patent Office and the Courts after *Fujitsu/TI*," Naoki Koizumi and Toshiko Takenaka explore one of the most important sets of developments relating to the patent enforcement process. After comparing the U.S. and Japanese patent enforcement traditions, Koizumi and Takenaka discuss the landmark Supreme Court decision of 2000 in the *Fujitsu/TI* case. As they explain, that decision greatly expanded the authority of the courts to determine the validity of patents. In doing so, it shifted the balance between the Patent Office and the courts and at the same time signaled movement from the traditional German approach to patent validity toward the U.S. approach. As Koizumi and Takenaka discuss, however, the decision has given rise to a new set of serious problems.

The next two chapters address the field of taxation. In "The Reform of the Japanese Tax System in the Latter Half of the Twentieth Century and into the Twenty-first Century," Hiroshi Kaneko traces the development of the Japanese tax system and important problems facing that system. He begins the chapter by reviewing the postwar reforms to Japan's tax system and reaffirming the continued importance of those reforms in setting the basic philosophy of that system. After discussing some of the modifications adopted from the 1950s through the 1970s (modifications that, Kaneko suggests, represented a retreat, or "deterioration," from the ideals of the postwar system), the chapter focuses on the tax reforms from 1986 through 1988, "the major turning point" for Japan's postwar tax system. After discussing the significance of the 1986–88 reforms and subsequent modifications to those reforms, Kaneko closes by examining major current issues and offering a forecast of future developments.

Christopher H. Hanna's chapter, "Some Observations on the Japanese Tax System at the Beginning of the Twenty-first Century," is framed as a comment on the Kaneko chapter. Of the many major issues raised by Kaneko, Hanna focuses on a few high-profile tax issues that have arisen in recent years, including issues related to consolidated tax returns, partnerships, and the new United States–Japan Income Tax Treaty, which entered into force in 2004.

The final chapter in this part, Kent Anderson and Makoto Itō's "Insolvency Law for a New Century: Japan's Revised Framework for Economic Failures," addresses another topic that was not included in the 1963 *Law in Japan* volume. Times have changed. As Anderson and Itō note, insolvency filings increased by over 1000 percent in the ten years between 1992 and 2001, and the bankruptcies have included some of Japan's largest companies, which once were thought too big to fail. As Anderson and Itō explain, the huge swell in filings brought attention to limitations in and problems with the insolvency system, which in turn has led to intensive review and extensive revision of the system. In their chapter, Anderson and Itō provide a general overview of the revised formal insolvency regime and explore how that system operates. In doing so, they highlight major issues relating to each of the main components of the system and the policy determinations Japan has made regarding those issues. They conclude by arguing that the revisions to Japan's insolvency system do indeed constitute a "turning point" in how Japan manages economic failure.

18 Reexamining Legal Transplants

The Director's Fiduciary Duty in Japanese Corporate Law

HIDEKI KANDA & CURTIS J. MILHAUPT

I. INTRODUCTION

The transplantation of legal rules from one country to another is commonly observed around the world. Legal transplants[1] can range from the wholesale adoption of entire systems of law to the copying of a single rule. Japanese law, particularly the legal rules governing economic organization, is a prime example of the transplant phenomenon, both in its systemic and single-rule variations. Japan imported its original Commercial Code (including legal rules on business corporations) from Germany in 1898 as part of a fundamental reform of its legal system and made large-scale amendments to the corporate law in the immediate postwar period by importing many specific legal rules from the United States.

Despite the importance of legal transplants to legal development around the world, scholarly understanding of this ubiquitous form of legal development is still fairly rudimentary. As Alan Watson, the most prominent contributor to the transplants literature, has noted, while "[t]he act of borrowing is usually simple, . . . build[ing] up a theory of borrowing on the other hand, seems to be an extremely complex matter."[2] For example, there is little agreement among scholars on transplant feasibility and the conditions for successful transplants, or even how to define "success." Moreover, there is little analysis of how the success or failure of legal transplants relates to the achievement of larger goals, such as economic development.

This chapter attempts to shed light on the role of legal transplants in corporate law by examining Japan's transplantation of a single corporate rule:

the director's duty of loyalty.[3] In 1950, Japan added to its Commercial Code a new statutory provision, Article 254-3, as a direct import from the United States.[4] Article 254-3 provides: "directors owe to the company the duty to perform their functions faithfully, in compliance with laws, the company's charter provisions, and resolutions of shareholders' meetings." The importation of this provision in an attempt to improve Japanese corporate law is not surprising: the duty of loyalty is central to U.S. corporate law, playing a major role in addressing agency costs associated with the corporate form. As we will see below, however, for almost forty years after it was transplanted, the duty of loyalty was never separately applied by the Japanese courts, and played little role in Japanese corporate law and governance. It finally began to be used in the late 1980s, long after Japan had achieved high economic growth. This suggests that transplanting this core U.S. corporate law rule did not contribute to Japan's postwar economic success, although it apparently did not detract from that success either.

This topic seems particularly appropriate for a volume designed to parallel and update the classic volume *Law in Japan: Legal Order in a Changing Society*. Two essays in that volume anticipate the major debates in comparative corporate law scholarship today as well as the main themes of this chapter—the role of law in corporate governance and the impact of foreign influences on the quality of corporate law.[5]

More broadly, understanding whether and how this specific transplant worked has significance beyond Japanese corporate law. Today, there is growing discussion of the possibility that greater attention to fiduciary duties could enhance corporate governance in many countries, with attendant analysis of the feasibility of transplanting fiduciary principles.[6] More broadly, Japan is widely viewed as a rare example of a "successful legal transplant," yet there is very little analysis of what this means, beyond the fact that subsequent to Japan's enactment of a European code system, it developed into a highly prosperous and politically stable nation. Deeper analysis of Japan's experience with the transplantation of the duty of loyalty standard may advance both debates.

First, we review existing literature and provide a simple analytical framework for determining the success or failure of a legal transplant. We then turn to our specific example. We begin with a brief examination of the central role of duty of loyalty doctrine in U.S. corporate law. We contrast the situation under Japanese corporate law, tracing the duty of loyalty from its transplantation to its eventual application by the Japanese courts. Next, we evaluate the transplantation of the duty of loyalty in Japan in light of our theoretical discussion and end with a brief conclusion.

II. SOME ELEMENTS OF A THEORY OF LEGAL TRANSPLANTS

Alan Watson is right—building a theory of legal transplants is hard. Although the discussion in this section represents only a first step toward a systematic mode of analysis, we believe it provides a useful way to begin thinking about the transplant phenomenon. We begin by asking why transplants are a major form of legal development. Next we briefly discuss existing explanations for the phenomenon, noting some shortcomings in these approaches. Finally, we provide a simple conceptual framework for determining the success or failure of a specific legal transplant.

Why are legal transplants ubiquitous? Several interrelated answers are possible. First and most obviously, they are a cheap, quick, and potentially fruitful source of new law (particularly given the possible learning effects associated with the foreign rule) and may be the only feasible means of law reform in some instances (the "practical utility" motivation). Second, this form of legal change often follows colonization or military occupation (the "political" motivation). Third, law reform is typically the province of the legal profession (broadly defined to include lawyers, judges, and ministry of justice officials), and this has implications for legal borrowing. As one commentator puts it, "all law making, apart from legislating, desperately needs authority,"[7] and law borrowed from an esteemed foreign source often fills that need among the legal profession (the "symbolic" motivation). Finally, some rules are transplanted in haste and without adequate preparation or familiarity with the operation of the rule in the home country ("blind copying"). As we will discuss below, the motive for a transplant, as well as the motives of the legal professionals charged with its subsequent application and enforcement, have implications for its success or failure.

Indeed, the literature reveals fundamental disagreement on transplant feasibility. Commentators are split between those who proclaim the feasibility of transplantation as a device of legal change and those who claim that they are impossible. In large measure, this debate reflects disagreement about the relationship of law to the society in which it exists. At one extreme is the optimism of Alan Watson, who views law as existing apart from political and social institutions and primarily significant for its authoritative qualities. For Watson, "the transplanting of legal rules [by which he means both individual rules and large parts of a legal system] is socially easy."[8] At the other extreme are skeptics who take the position that "rules cannot travel [because their meaning is culture-specific]. Accordingly, 'legal transplants' are impossible."[9]

Between these two extremes, several intermediate positions are also present in the literature. Otto Kahn-Freund argues that distinctive "environmental" conditions in each country—particularly the political environment in the form of constitutional structure and interest group coalitions—make successful transplants rare.[10] Finally, the economically oriented commentator Ugo Mattei has suggested that legal borrowing can best be explained as a movement toward efficiency. That is, competition in a "market for legal culture" determines which rules are transplanted from abroad; the most efficient legal doctrine survives around the world.[11]

While these perspectives are valuable, neither optimists nor skeptics have drawn on rigorous theory in support of their positions. Watson's optimism rests on several questionable assumptions, including (a) that what matters most is the *idea* behind the law being transplanted, rather than the law itself,[12] and (b) that "many legal rules make little impact on individuals."[13] At the same time, the view that legal transplants are impossible is contradicted by a variety of empirical evidence. And while it may be true that efficient legal rules survive and proliferate around the world, this fact (even if true) does not address the *conditions* under which a particular legal rule is efficient in a given country.

So we turn to the main question: what are the conditions of successful legal transplants? Obviously, "success" depends on the baseline one uses for measurement, and this too is controversial.[14] Here, we take success to mean simply use of the imported legal rule in the same way that it is used in the home country, subject to adaptations to local conditions. Conversely, failure occurs when the imported rule is ignored by relevant actors in the host country, or the application and enforcement of the rule lead to unintended consequences. This definition is broad enough to countenance "success" where law contributes to the development of social norms but is otherwise unenforced. We stress that by defining the terms *success* and *failure* in this way, they carry no normative implications. Our aim here is simply to explain why transplants are used or ignored, not to evaluate the economic consequences of their use or nonuse. Indeed, as we will discuss in our transplant case study below, it is not obvious that heavy reliance on the duty of loyalty is optimal in the corporate law of the host country (United States). Thus, it is difficult to draw normative conclusions about the initial nonuse and subsequent use of the duty of loyalty transplant in the host country (Japan).

We believe that "fit" between the imported rule and the host environment is crucial to the success of a transplant. A rich and dynamic analytical conception of "fit" might provide traction on the question why some transplants are used and others are ignored. "Fit" might be thought of as having two components—micro and macro. *Micro-fit* is how well the imported rule complements the preexisting legal infrastructure in the host country. *Macro-fit* is how well the imported rule complements the preexisting institutions of the political economy in the host country.

Central to analysis of both micro-fit and macro-fit is the *availability of substitutes*. The fewer the available substitutes for the transplanted rule, either within the legal system (in the form of other laws and legal procedures) or outside the legal system (in the form of norms, informal state interventions, or market constraints), the more likely it is that the transplanted legal rule or institution will be adapted to local conditions and thus used by relevant actors in the host country.

Motivation is also highly relevant to the analysis. Motivation must be analyzed both from the perspective of the law reformers initially responsible for the transplant and from the legal actors (courts, attorneys, government officials) with the potential to make use of it. From the former perspective, the more predominant practical utility is in the mix of motives for the transplant, the more likely it is that the transplant will be successful from the outset, if only because motivation is likely to affect law reformers' attention to micro-fit. Other motives, such as politics or symbolism, are far less conducive to success. Yet the initial motivation for the transplant (whether conducive to success or not) can be overcome by those with the authority to apply or enforce the law subsequent to its codification in the local regime. Thus, motivation is an ongoing issue.

Having sketched a few theoretical ideas on transplantation as a device of legal change, we now turn to an important example, the transplantation of the duty of loyalty from U.S. to Japanese corporate law.

III. THE DUTY OF LOYALTY: FROM U.S. TO JAPANESE CORPORATE LAW

A. THE UNITED STATES

As Robert Clark notes, "Directors, officers, and, in some situations, controlling shareholders owe their corporations, and sometimes other shareholders and investors, a fiduciary duty of loyalty. This duty prohibits the fiduciaries from taking advantage of their beneficiaries by means of fraudulent or unfair transactions."[15]

This duty plays a large role in U.S. corporate law. It is the key doctrinal desideratum of some of the most venerable (or at least well-known) cases of the Delaware courts.[16] It ranges over vast areas of the standard U.S. law school course, from the treatment of self-interested transactions and corporate opportunities, through executive compensation and controlling shareholder problems, to the sale of control and corporate combinations.[17]

Not only is the duty of loyalty appropriately deemed central to *existing* U.S. corporate law; it is viewed as a key facilitator of the ongoing *development* of U.S. corporate law. To quote Clark again: "Most importantly, this general fiduciary duty of loyalty is a residual concept that can include factual situations that no one has foreseen and categorized. The general duty permits, and in fact has led to, a continuous evolution in corporate law."[18]

In the process of occupying large tracts of U.S. corporate law, duty of loyalty jurisprudence—particularly as developed by the Delaware courts—has also greatly influenced the structure of corporate governance and transactional mechanics in the United States. The cases provide numerous legal incentives for directors facing conflicts of interest to structure the deal substantively and procedurally to approximate an arm's-length transaction.[19] It is widely accepted, for example, that Delaware's approach to the duty of loyalty has influenced the use of independent committees of directors and the retention of independent legal and financial advisors in corporate transactions.

The influence of the duty of loyalty on U.S. corporate law and governance is all the more striking given that there is widespread dissatisfaction with the actual state of the law. In the words of one commentator, "Perhaps no area of corporate law is as beset with conflicting judicial opinions, variations among statutes, and confusion and uncertainty concerning the likely outcome of litigation as is the duty of loyalty."[20]

This last point raises a puzzle within U.S. corporate law—precisely how and why does the duty of loyalty work? Two points should be made. First, not all scholars agree that it does in fact work well as an organizing legal principle of corporate governance.[21] Second, even in the United States, the duty of loyalty has undergone a substantial transformation over the past century, from an outright prohibition against transactions that pose a conflict of interest to a flexible standard applied ex post by the courts. Interestingly, the duty of loyalty is itself a legal transplant in U.S. corporate law—not a cross-border transplant of the type we are discussing in this article, but a cross-doctrinal transplant from the law of trusts.[22]

B. JAPAN

As noted above, Article 254-3 of the Commercial Code was imported from the United States in 1950. The exact process by which this provision was transplanted is not entirely clear from the historical record, but the U.S. Occupation authorities in charge of corporate law reform sought inclusion of this provision as part of a package of reforms designed to improve minority shareholders' rights under the Japanese Commercial Code.[23] The Occupation authorities were apparently not satisfied that the preexisting provisions on the duties of directors were adequate, and perhaps since the duty of loyalty was considered to be one of the most important provisions in U.S. corporate law, a decision was made to codify it in the Japanese code.[24] There is no evidence that this provision was controversial or even widely debated at the time of the transplant.[25]

Several interesting developments subsequent to the introduction of Article 254-3 into the code should be noted. First, the provision generated a large amount of doctrinal discussion among commentators concerning whether a director's duty of loyalty (*chūjitsu gimu*) in Article 254-3 is different from the preexisting duty of care (*zen kan chūi gimu*) under Article 254(3) (which incorporates Civil Code Article 644). The details of this debate are beyond the scope of this chapter. But a famous Supreme Court decision of June 24, 1970, adopted the view that Article 254-3 clarifies and restates the duty of care—it does not constitute a separate or higher duty for corporate directors.[26] Equally importantly, as discussed below, until a new trend emerged, the Japanese courts never separately applied the duty of loyalty in Article 254-3. In each case where it was cited, the court simultaneously cited the duty of care provision, so the meaning of Article 254-3 was not clear and its application had no practical significance.[27]

Second, even prior to the 1950 amendments, the Commercial Code contained important rules governing director conduct. These include Articles 264 (regulation of competition), 265 (regulation of self-dealing), and 269 (regulation of compensation). After Article 254-3 was introduced, commentators viewed these specific provisions as special applications of the general duty of loyalty principle under Article 254-3, and the courts often applied these specific provisions. This leads to the fundamental question: why did Japanese corporate law need Article 254-3?

Third, as a matter of legal change, the statutory language of Articles 264 and 265 was altered several times subsequent to the 1950 amendments, while Article 254-3 has never been altered. It must be noted that most statutory changes in Japanese corporate law are motivated by domestic forces and reasons rather than pressure or other forces from outside Japan; the original Commercial Code and the 1950 amendments are exceptions.

Fourth, Articles 264 and 265 provide procedural ex ante rules. Under Article 264, when a director engages in an activity in the same line of business as that of the company, he must disclose the facts and obtain ex ante approval of the board of directors.[28] Similarly, when a director attempts to engage in a self-dealing transaction—for example, the purchase of land from the company—he must disclose the facts and obtain ex ante approval of the board of directors. In most cases applying the relevant provisions of the code, the courts struggled with such issues as the activities covered by Articles 264 or 265, and the effect of a transaction where the director had not complied with the procedural requirements of Article 265.

In contrast, Article 254-3 is a standard—a legal provision that is given content only ex post, by an adjudicator who determines both the bounds of permissible conduct and factual issues related to the dispute.[29] In the United States, the duty of loyalty is judicially enforced ex post, and courts have wide discretion to fashion appropriate procedural requirements and remedies in the absence of specific statutory guidance. By contrast, courts in civil law jurisdictions, including Japan, tend to grant only those remedies explicitly recognized in the statutes. While this difference in judicial mind-set can be exaggerated, it is fair to say that, at least historically, common law judges have been more comfortable than their civil law counterparts in working with open-ended standards. In order for a standard to take hold in a civil law system, it must overcome the predisposition of judges working in such systems to apply specific provisions of the code in favor of more general provisions.

Yet any simple explanation of why the transplant of Article 254-3 was initially unsuccessful—for example, that Articles 264 and 265 served as adequate substitutes, or a standard like Article 254-3 has a high enforcement cost because Japan lacks an active judiciary—must contend with the confounding reality of more recent developments. In a well-known case in 1989, the Tokyo High Court gave separate application to Article 254-3 (i.e., without coupling it with any other provision) and awarded damages to the aggrieved company.[30] In this case, a director of a computer support company resigned to set up his own firm. He successfully persuaded several key employees of his former firm to move to his start-up. The court ruled that poaching key employees was a violation of the director's duty of loyalty to his former company as provided in Article 254-3 and held him liable to the company for damages.

Doctrinally, the court appeared to assume that Article 264—which regulates "competition" with the firm in the same line of business—does not reach the distinct activity of luring employees away from the firm. Thus, there was room for the application of Article 254-3, despite the existence of a more specific provision in the code. In the United States, this sort of case would probably be handled by the doctrine of corporate opportunity. In Japan, however, as shown by this case, the scope of Article 264 is too narrow to cover all corporate opportunity cases. So Articles 254-3 and 264 are not perfect substitutes even for the subgroup of self-dealing cases known as corporate opportunity.[31]

Transplantation of the general duty of loyalty provision was not accompanied by the remedial rules recognized in the United States. One common remedy when the duty is breached in the United States is disgorgement of the director's profits rather than damages to the firm. In Japan, however, the violation of Article 254-3 implicates Article 266(1)(v)—providing only for the payment of damages. This reduced the practical significance of applying Article 254-3 (duty of loyalty) apart from Article 254(3) (duty of care).

Nevertheless, after the above-mentioned landmark case, in some factually similar cases, the courts have applied Article 254-3 independently and awarded damages for breach of the duty of loyalty.[32] In a different context, one court held that a director of an insurance company violated the duty of loyalty by revealing nonpublic corporate information to the media, and awarded damages to the company.[33] Thus, it is fair to say that Article 254-3 now plays an important role in Japanese corporate law, though the scope of application of the duty of loyalty is still more limited than in the United States.

The extent to which a director's activity in relation to corporate opportunities should be regulated is a difficult question, and U.S. case law is complex (some would say confused) in this respect. Our point here is simply that courts must exercise wide discretionary power in resolving corporate opportunity and other self-dealing cases, and the relevant law in the United States relies heavily on "standards" for this purpose. The Tokyo High Court case is a watershed in the history of Japanese corporate law in that the court exercised ex post judicial intervention, U.S. style, to control director conflicts of interest. In subsequent cases, Japanese courts have followed its lead, finding directors liable for breach of the general duty of loyalty standard in Article 254-3.[34]

IV. EVALUATION

The discussion above raises a puzzle. Why was Article 254-3 dormant in Japan for almost forty years after it was transplanted? And why was it suddenly awakened from its long slumber in the late 1980s? There is no evidence that the Japanese judiciary abruptly became more activist in the 1980s.[35] It is also highly unlikely that directors suddenly became "more greedy" at this time.

Our theoretical discussion of legal transplants allows us to shed at least some light on this puzzle. We hypothesize that at the time the duty of loyalty was transplanted and throughout the period of high economic growth, conditions were not ripe for success (as we have defined the term). However, by the late 1980s, a variety of legal, economic, and institutional changes began to improve the micro-fit between the duty of loyalty standard and the legal infrastructure, and the macro-fit between the duty of loyalty standard and the institutions of the political economy.

At the time of the transplant in 1950, the micro-fit between Article 254-3 and the existing legal infrastructure was not close.[36] As noted above, the duty of loyalty provision is a standard. The application of a standard, particularly one as open-ended and vague as the duty of loyalty (which in essence simply prohibits "selfish" behavior on the part of directors), places high demands on the legal infrastructure. At a minimum, that infrastructure must include a viable derivative suit procedure and attorney incentives to bring such suits, judges and attorneys familiar with the use of broad legal standards as opposed to narrowly tailored rules, and courts capable of detecting and fashioning remedies for self-dealing in the absence of explicit statutory guidance. This infrastructure was not highly developed at the time of the transplant. The law reformers appear to have been motivated primarily by politics (Article 254-3 was introduced under military occupation) and symbolism (as noted above, it was generally thought that the duty of loyalty was an important rule in the United States). Notably lacking was a practical motivation for the transplant. There is no historical evidence that curbing managerial expropriation of shareholders was a chief concern of the Occupation's corporate law reformers, who seemed principally concerned about advancing "shareholder democracy" in Japan. The Japanese legal community itself did not seem concerned by this problem. The lack of a clear practical motive for the transplant may have lessened the reformers' attention to micro-fit and dampened the incentives of the local legal community to make the duty of loyalty standard an integral part of the legal system.[37]

At a macro-level, the duty of loyalty was orphaned by the distinctive institutions characterizing Japan's high economic growth period, which helped prevent the taking of corporate opportunities and other self-dealing by directors. High growth may itself have discouraged the taking of corporate opportunities, because the rewards of remaining with a company were high.

Conversely, the lifetime employment system, in which rewards were directly tied to seniority and lateral career opportunities were limited, made it costly to leave the firm and establish a competing company.[38] Moreover, managers operating on thin margins in highly competitive, export-oriented markets, or operating under extensive governmental oversight, may have been unable to extract rents for personal consumption. While takeovers provide managers with opportunities to reap significant gains from one-time disloyal conduct, such transactions were rare in postwar Japan because of cross-shareholding arrangements, virtually eliminating opportunities for this form of managerial rent extraction.[39] Thus, it is not evident that there were significant corporate fiduciary lapses to be addressed by the legal system in the high-growth period.

Both micro-fit and macro-fit were also affected by the existence of partial substitutes for the duty of loyalty standard. For example, as noted above, the Commercial Code contained specific provisions covering at least a subset of the conduct addressed by Article 254-3. Note, for example, that if the concept of "competition" in Article 264 were broader, the Tokyo High Court may have resolved the erstwhile seminal case on poaching employees to form a new venture without resort to Article 254-3, postponing this important doctrinal development. Efficient private substitutes for some corporate law rules may also have existed outside the legal system, weakening macro-fit. One of us has argued that a series of nonlegal rules ("norms") governing the conduct of Japanese firms in the high-growth period was a reflection of the "transplant effect," in which unfamiliar legal rules are bypassed by the legal community and private sector.[40] These norms—including the main bank system of contingent corporate monitoring (at least in crisis situations), the lifetime employment system, and social constraints on takeovers—dampened the demand for corporate law and legal professionals. In so doing, they relieved pressure for the creation of a closer micro-fit between the provisions of the Commercial Code—including the duty of loyalty—and the surrounding legal infrastructure.[41]

However, over time the micro- and macro-fit between the duty of loyalty and other Japanese institutions became closer, substitutes became less viable, and motivations were altered. At a micro-level, the legal community gained experience and became more comfortable with the use of a standard such as Article 254-3. The derivative suit mechanism was reformed.[42] The existence of a growing body of precedent highlighted the distinctness of the duty of loyalty from the duty of care, motivating legal professionals to use the transplanted provision more extensively and in new situations. At a macro-level, high growth was followed by prolonged recession and the extralegal structure for Japanese corporate governance weakened, changing the incentives of managers and increasing the demand for corporate law.

Our analysis suggests that the importance of the duty of loyalty in Japanese corporate law doctrine will continue to grow outside the realm of corporate opportunity, although it is difficult to predict the pace of this development. For example, as shareholder activism and takeovers increase (further tightening macro-fit between the legal standard and the political economy of Japan), the duty of loyalty is likely to become a more central and actively utilized corporate governance principle in Japan.

While we are obviously working from a very limited empirical base in a single case study, this account of Japan's transplantation of an important corporate law from the United States casts doubt on the accuracy (or at least universality) of existing attempts to explain the transplantation phenomenon. Contrary to Alan Watson's view, it was not the *idea* that was important in this transplant—the duty of loyalty concept already existed in several specific provisions of the Japanese Commercial Code. And Watson's claim that law generally does not matter beyond its symbolic importance is refuted by our example and numerous other empirical studies. Thus, the basis for his contention that transplanting law is "socially easy" is open to question. Contrary to Otto Kahn-Freund's analysis, politics (defined on his terms as the constitutional structure of government and interest group dynamics) played virtually no role in the initial nonuse and eventual utilization of this transplant. Moreover, Ugo Mattei's efficiency perspective does not contribute significantly to the analysis of this transplant episode. While efficient rules may indeed tend to survive and proliferate outside their home jurisdictions, this bare fact has little explanatory power in the absence of a fine-grained examination of how a specific rule fits into the existing legal infrastructure and political economy of a given system, and the alternatives available to relevant actors.

Rather, at least in this limited example, the success or failure of the legal transplant varied over time and was determined largely by the degree to which the transplant fit the prevailing legal and nonlegal infrastructure of which it was a part. This observation, while not entirely surprising, has several important implications that run counter to the existing literature.

First, measuring the success or failure of a legal transplant may take decades of observation. Japan's experience with the duty of loyalty shows that even a poorly motivated and ill-fitting legal transplant may become a core rule in the host country over time, as the legal infrastructure and political economy change. This occurs as legal and nonlegal developments alter the mix of substitutes available and affect the motivation of the legal professionals who interpret and enforce the transplant.

For other countries experimenting with the codification of the duty of loyalty as a means of improving corporate governance, this lesson could be either reassuring or discomforting. For Korea and Taiwan, which recently imported the duty of loyalty by copying Article 254-3, the Japanese experience may suggest that the duty of loyalty is poised to play a role in corporate governance. The legal and political-economic environments of these countries bear many similarities to those of Japan, suggesting that micro- and macro-fit are conducive to success of the transplant. For countries less far along the path of judicial development and with classes of investors and lawyers less motivated to use this tool of corporate governance, Japan's long, dormant post-transplant period may be more representative of the role the duty of loyalty will play in their corporate law systems in the coming decades. Of course, it is possible that other institutions in these systems might already exist or develop to provide adequate substitutes for judicial enforcement of this legal standard.

Second, the analysis here suggests that, contrary to the approach of most scholars to date, it is virtually impossible to discuss the "success" or "failure" of wholesale transplants of entire bodies of law (such as Japan's transplantation of codes in the European civil law tradition in the late nineteenth century) or to extrapolate meaningfully from a single rule to the feasibility of legal transplants in general. Each legal rule or institution must be examined individually, and assessment of the overall feasibility of legal transplants as a form of legal change requires a more rigorous theoretical base than existing literature has provided. We hope this essay constitutes at least a step toward the formation of such a base.

V. CONCLUSION

In this chapter, we have reexamined the legal transplant phenomenon by analyzing the movement of a single legal rule from U.S. to Japanese corporate law. We have developed a simple analytical framework using the concept of "fit" to evaluate the conditions for the success or failure of a legal transplant and employed the framework to explain why the duty of loyalty transplant failed for four decades to take hold in Japanese corporate law but suddenly emerged as an important rule.

As analyzed here, the development of the duty of loyalty in Japanese corporate law parallels trends noted by other contributors to this volume, particularly the "judicification" of Japanese law. The increasing use by the legal community of broad legal standards such as that provided in Article 254-3 of the Commercial Code is one indication of the transformation under way in the Japanese legal system and political economy.

We hope this reexamination of the duty of loyalty deepens understanding of the influence of foreign law on the Japanese legal system and spurs further theoretical and empirical work on the role of transplants in legal adaptation.

NOTES

Milhaupt gratefully acknowledges the support of the Abe Fellowship program administered by the Social Science Research Council, with funds provided by the Center for Global Partnership. We benefited from the comments of Kon Sik Kim, Mark West, attendees at the "Law in Japan: A Turning Point" conference at the University of Washington, and participants at a workshop in Kanagawa, Japan, sponsored by the Research Institute of Economy, Trade and Industry. This essay was originally published in the *American Journal of Comparative Law* 51 (2003): 887–901. It is reproduced here with minor modifications with permission.

1. We define a legal transplant as a body of law or individual legal rule that was copied from a law or rule already in force in another country, rather than developed by the local legal community. For a host of reasons (including most basically a lack of familiarity among the local legal community charged with interpreting and enforcing it), a legal transplant might "behave" differently than a locally developed body of law or rule.

2. Alan Watson, "Aspects of Reception of Law," *American Journal of Comparative Law* 44 (1996): 335, 335.

3. In this chapter, we focus on the transplantation of a specific rule as opposed to systemic transplants of entire bodies of law. As discussed below, we believe it is difficult to analyze meaningfully the success or failure of systemic transplants.

4. As originally enacted, this provision was art. 254-2 of the Commercial Code. It was renumbered art. 254-3 by amendments to the code in 1981. For convenience, we use the latter code provision throughout this article.

5. See Makoto Yazawa, "The Legal Structure for Corporate Enterprise: Shareholder-Management Relations under Japanese Law," in Arthur Taylor von Mehren, ed., *Law in Japan: The Legal Order in a Changing Society* (Cambridge, MA: Harvard University Press, 1963), 547; and Shinichiro Michida, "The Legal Structure for Economic Enterprise: Some Aspects of Japanese Commercial Law," in von Mehren, *Law in Japan*, 507.

6. For example, both Korea and Taiwan transplanted the duty of loyalty into their commercial codes in the wake of the Asian financial crisis by copying the Japanese art. 254-3. For scholarly discussions of fiduciary duty transplants, see, e.g., Lynn Stout, "On the Export of U.S.-Style Corporate Fiduciary Duties to Other Cultures: Can a Transplant Take?" in Curtis J. Milhaupt, *Global Markets, Domestic Institutions: Corporate Law and Governance in a New Era of Cross-Border Deals* (New York: Columbia University Press, 2003), 46–76; and Katharina Pistor and Chang-gang Xu, "Transplanting the Concept of 'Fiduciary Duty': Evidence from Transition Economies," in Milhaupt, *Global Markets, Domestic Institutions*, 77–106.

7. Watson, "Aspects of Reception of Law," 346.

8. Alan Watson, *Legal Transplants: An Approach to Comparative Law*, 2nd ed. (Athens: University of Georgia Press, 1993), 95.

9. Pierre Legrand, "What 'Legal Transplants'?" in David Nelson and Johannes Feest, eds., *Adapting Legal Cultures* (Oxford: Hart Publishing, 2001), 55, 57.

10. Otto Kahn-Freund, "On Uses and Misuses of Comparative Law," *Modern Law Review* 37 (1974): 1. By *politics*, Kahn-Freund means constitutional structure of government as well as interest group pressures.

11. Ugo Mattei, "Efficiency in Legal Transplants: An Essay in Comparative Law and Economics," *International Review of Law and Economics* 14 (1994): 3.

12. Alan Watson, "Comparative Law and Legal Change," *Cambridge Law Journal* 37 (1978): 313, 315.

13. Watson, *Legal Transplants*, 96.

14. See David Nelken, "Towards a Sociology of Legal Adaptation," in Nelson and Feest, *Adapting Legal Cultures*, 7, 37–39.

15. Robert C. Clark, *Corporate Law* (Boston: Little Brown, 1986), 141.

16. E.g., Guth v. Loft, 5 A.2d 503 (Del. 1939); Sinclair v. Levien, 280 A.2d 717 (1971); Weinberger v. UOP, Inc., 409 A.2d 701 (Del. 1983); Revlon v. McAndrews & Forbes, 506 A.2d 173 (Del. 1985).

17. See, e.g., Melvin A. Eisenberg, *Corporations and Other Business Organizations*, 8th ed. unabridged (New York: Foundation Press, 2000).

18. Clark, *Corporate Law*, 141.

19. See E. Norman Veasey, "Duty of Loyalty: The Criticality of the Counselor's Role," *Business Lawyer* 45 (1990): 2065 (1990); and Edward Rock and Michael Wachter, "Islands of Conscious Power: Law, Norms, and the Self-Governing Corporation," *University of Pennsylvania Law Review* 149 (2001): 1619, 1662–63.

20. A. A. Sommer Jr., "The Duty of Loyalty in the ALI's Corporate Governance Project," *George Washington Law Review* 52 (1984): 719. Henry Hansmann and Reiner Kraakman note the "notoriously vague and open-ended U.S. case law that articulates the fiduciary dut[y] of loyalty." Henry Hansmann and Reiner

Kraakman, "The End of History for Corporate Law," *Georgetown Law Journal* 89 (2001): 439, 459.

21. E.g., Roberta Romano, "The Shareholder Suit: Litigation without Foundation?" *Journal of Law, Economics and Organization* 7 (1991): 55.

22. Edward Rock and Michael Wachter, "Dangerous Liaisons: Corporate Law, Trust Law, and Interdoctrinal Legal Transplants," *Northwestern University Law Review* 96 (2001): 651.

23. See generally Masafumi Nakahigashi, *Shōhō kaisei shōwa 25 /shōwa 26* [The 1950–51 Amendments to the Commercial Code] (Tokyo: Shinzansha, 2003).

24. See Michiyo Hamada, in 6 *Shinpan chūshaku kaishahō* [Annotated Company Law, new edition, vol. 6] (Tokyo: Yūhikaku, 1987), 27–28.

25. See Nakahigashi, *Shōhō kaisei shōwa 25 /shōwa 26*. It is possible that art. 254-3 was not controversial because the U.S. and Japanese negotiators attributed different meanings to this provision. The Americans may have believed they were introducing a new duty into the corporate law, while the Japanese may have viewed the provision as an amplification of specific, preexisting legal duties. There is no specific evidence of such a failure in "meeting of the minds," although this interpretation is consistent with the subsequent events detailed in the text.

26. Arita v. Kojima (Sup. Ct., June 24, 1970) (Yahata Seitetsu case), *Minshū* 24 (1970): 625. (In a shareholder derivative suit challenging a steel company's political donation to the ruling Liberal Democratic Party, the Court held that the donation was not a violation of the directors' duty of care or loyalty.)

27. To be precise, there was one case prior to the trend discussed in text below in which a court stated in passing that the director had violated the duty of loyalty, without reference to the duty of care. However, the court was not precise in its analysis and held the director liable to his company for the commission of a tort. Sanrei Yamako Kabushiki Kaisha v. Korumu Bōeki Kabushiki Kaisha (Osaka High Ct., Mar. 3, 1983), *Hanrei jihō* 1084 (1983): 122.

28. Shareholders' approval was required until an amendment in 1981.

29. See Louis Kaplow, "Rules versus Standards: An Economic Analysis," *Duke Law Journal* 42 (1992): 557.

30. Nihon Setsubi Kabushiki Kaisha v. Takada (Tokyo High Ct., Oct. 26, 1989), 835 *Kin'yū shōji hanrei* 835 (1989): 23.

31. Note that there is a case where the court applied both art. 254-3 and art. 264. See Kabushiki Kaisha Miyako Seisō Keibi Ryokka Kōgyō v. Inoue (Maebashi Dist. Ct., Mar. 14, 1995), *Hanrei jiho* 1532 (1995): 135.

32. See, e.g., Zenken Top Kabushiki Kaisha v. Unnamed (Tokyo Dist. Ct., Feb. 22, 1999), *Hanrei jihō* 1685 (1999): 121.

33. Chiyoda Hoken Sōgō Kaisha v. Unnamed (Tokyo Dist. Ct., Feb. 15, 1999), *Hanrei jihō* 1675 (1999): 107.

34. A computer search revealed five reported cases finding directors liable for breach of the duty of loyalty following the seminal Tokyo High Court decision. In numerous other cases, plaintiffs alleged violation of art. 254-3, but the court held for the defendant directors.

35. One commentator suggested that the development of the capital markets in the 1980s in Japan might have affected judicial "mind-set," leading to the more expansive view of the duty of loyalty. While this is plausible, it is virtually impossible to verify.

36. Japanese corporate law commentators recognized this point long ago. See Yazawa, "The Legal Structure for Corporate Enterprise," 557 (speculating that the nonuse and underdevelopment in Japan of judicially applied standards to regulate directors' fiduciary obligations is the result of the legal education system, judicial training, and the administration of justice).

37. For example, although a derivative suit mechanism was transplanted in the 1950 amendments to the Commercial Code, plaintiffs were required to pay a high filing fee to initiate such suits. This dampened incentives to bring this type of litigation until the fee was lowered in the early 1990s.

38. See Ronald J. Gilson and Mark J. Roe, "Lifetime Employment: Labor Peace and the Evolution of Japanese Corporate Governance," *Columbia Law Review* 99 (1999): 508 (a labor market closed to lateral movement complements the lifetime employment system).

39. See J. Mark Ramseyer, "Takeovers in Japan: Opportunism, Ideology, and Corporate Control," *UCLA Law Review* 35 (1987): 1.

40. Curtis J. Milhaupt, "Creative Norm Destruction: The Evolution of Nonlegal Rules in Japanese Corporate Governance," *University of Pennsylvania Law Review* 149 (2001): 2083.

41. To cite just one example, duty of loyalty jurisprudence in the United States advanced significantly during the takeover boom of the 1980s. In a system where hostile takeovers are virtually unknown because of cross-shareholding practices or social norms, courts will face fewer opportunities to give content to the abstract command of the duty of loyalty.

42. Note that the derivative suit mechanism was altered to lower enforcement costs in 1993, but this development occurred *after* the seminal case and its early progeny, so lower enforcement costs alone do not explain why the duty of loyalty was activated in Japanese corporate law.

19 Japan's "Era of Contract"

TAKASHI UCHIDA & VERONICA L. TAYLOR

I. INTRODUCTION: JAPANESE CONTRACT LAW THEN AND NOW

The classic work *Law in Japan: The Legal Order in a Changing Society*, edited by Arthur Taylor von Mehren, treats Japanese contract as a fairly uncontroversial field of positive law.[1] In that volume, Professor Takeyoshi Kawashima's chapter on dispute resolution was destined to become widely read outside Japan, but Charles Stevens's later translation of another of Kawashima's essays was the real catalyst for the concept of a Japanese "contract consciousness" receiving wide recognition outside Japan.[2] Kawashima's characterization of Japanese contracting as informal and infused with social norms was a useful counterpoint to doctrinal accounts of the Civil Code principles governing contract in Japan. More often, however, Kawashima's assessment was read as a claim that Japanese contract consciousness was unique—leading to enduring but ultimately unhelpful debates.[3]

In this chapter we argue that Japanese contracting in the 1990s and early 2000s exhibited a marked shift from the regulatory framework of the 1960s. Here we contest the idea of homogenous contracting norms in Japan and the implicit claim that there is widespread consensus about the content and direction of contract law. Instead, we find contract in the twenty-first century in Japan—as elsewhere—to be a contested domain, with visible turning points in the mind-set of policy elites. Takashi Uchida characterizes the current period of debate and transition as a return to classical contract theory grounded in economic analysis—what he calls Japan's "era of contract."

We can analogize this to Hugh Collins's "contractualization,"[4] but in the context of Japanese society, it is more accurately labeled as an "era" because of the way in which the phenomenon marks a break with the past.[5]

In the sections that follow we explore the ways in which new policy preferences are infusing the regulation of contracts in Japan. We then look at some other regulatory forums in which the design, interpretation, and enforcement of contracts in Japan are changing: the courts, the use of contracts by commercial actors, and the intermediation of the legal profession. The treatment of contracts by each of these institutions evidences significant deviation from the received images of Japanese contract law and practice that were current in the 1970s and 1980s, both within and outside Japan.

II. THE "ERA OF CONTRACT" APPEARS

A. ORIGINS

Kawashima's account of Japanese-style contract consciousness depicted Japan in the immediate post–World War II period as a place in which, on the one hand, the binding power of mere agreement was relatively weak, while on the other hand, oral agreements underpinned by social trust predominated. He argued that explicit, tightly drafted agreements ran contrary to Japanese "cultural values." His critics countered that this was, in fact, not a distinct phenomenon, but something universal in nature. Both sides of the debate, however, shared a common presumption—the idea that the classical view of contract within law, and the market model of contract employed within economics, played a more limited role in Japanese society than it did in the West.[6] Whether this was the case is debatable.[7] What is clear today, however, is that the dominant analytic framework for thinking about contracts in Japan is changing markedly.

After the dramatic economic growth following the end of World War II, Japanese society experienced what we might call a tragic reckoning: the "bubble economy" of the late 1980s. The 1990s saw a massive restructuring of economic and legal institutions, symbolized by a new role for contracts within Japanese society. Contract forms and practices grounded in the classical view of contract are beginning to sweep across Japanese society.

In what sense is the role of contract in Japan broadening? In this chapter we focus on the role of contract within Japanese society since the 1980s. It was in the 1980s, of course, that Reaganomics appeared in the United States, Thatcherism appeared in Europe, and the Chicago School of Economics claimed the spotlight. During this period, policy makers belonging to these schools of thought exercised enormous influence in fields beyond economics. Within Japan too, the then prime minister, Yasuhiro Nakasone, sought to stay in step with President Reagan and moved to implement deregulation (*kisei kanwa*).[8] We can see the emergence of the era of contract as a product of that kind of deregulation. In this sense, we may consider the emergence of the era of contract in Japan to be simply manifesting a phenomenon common to the world's industrialized countries. The question of whether the emergence of the era of contract in Japan and the United States (or other Western countries) is in fact the same or not is an interesting one. Here we see, perhaps, not the differences between East and West per se, but rather the differences between countries that legitimize the creation of the state through the mechanism of contract and those that do not. In the discussion that follows we seek to follow the ripples of the era of contract in Japan and thereby trace some distinct characteristics of Japanese society in the 1990s and beyond.

B. ATTRIBUTES

Japan's era of contract manifests itself in many different ways. Below, we try to sketch a typology of situations in which contract exerts a new influence or prominence in Japan.

1. *The Shift toward Personal Responsibility*

In the period between 1960 and 1990, the legislative regulation of contract was confined to the provisions on the classical type contracts of the Civil Code, supplemented by some special laws that were designed to combat the most egregious problems of consumer contracting, such as those arising from door-to-door sales or installment sales.[9] Industries that created "problem" transactions such as home tutoring, aesthetic salon services,[10] and loan-sharking were regulated through a combination of administrative guidance, specific regulation, and the formation of industry-wide standard form contracts.[11] These techniques were intended to be preemptive. What they had in common was the bureaucratic focus on the industry, rather than the end user.[12]

As the momentum for deregulation increased throughout the 1990s, however, the policy emphasis in contracts shifted from industry regulation to risk assumption in contracting by the end user. The policy shift is epitomized by the following key passage in the 1997 *Final Report of the Administrative Reform*

Council established by the Hashimoto Cabinet. In conjunction with strengthening the function of the Cabinet, it states: "In relation to justice, in order to fully develop the 'rule of law' it is necessary to establish some proactive measures. Indeed, 'rule of law' is the essential basis for pursuing [public] welfare and securing the trust of international society through pursuit of domestic deregulation, and through the transformation of society from one predicated upon opaque, preemptive administrative regulation to one based upon ex post facto oversight and remedies."[13] From this point onward the transformation of Japanese society from a preemptive regulatory model to an ex post facto remedial model based on personal responsibility has been attempted through the adoption of numerous subsequent policies. The 2001 recommendations of the Justice System Reform Council established under the Koizumi Cabinet[14] also adopted the same line and proposed wide-ranging reforms to the justice system including the introduction of graduate-level legal education.[15]

The manifestation of these policies in relation to legislative regulation of the market is found in the passage and implementation of new regulatory legislation such as the amended House Lease Act, the Financial Products Act, the Consumer Contracts Act, and the Product Liability Act.[16] These enactments give emphasis to individual choices grounded in personal responsibility and attempt to limit the role of legal intervention to simply supporting these choices. The legal mechanism that communicates choice in the market is "contract," and so here we can also discern an important transition within the legal system to the era of contract. This new consumer legislation brings into being the "consumer" as a class of actor with legal rights and remedies that exists independently of the particular contract or any relationship with a commercial party. This legal "empowerment" of "consumers" in Japan is both a central plank of the Justice System Reform Council agenda since 2001 and the focus of great enthusiasm among legal professionals and consumer advocates.[17]

a. The Product Liability Act

The enactment of the Product Liability Act in 1994 was the first symbolic representation of the emergence of the era of contract. The law draws its impetus and norms from the European Community directive on product liability[18] and appears to be a rather restrained piece of legislation in comparison with what we might call the radical jurisprudence of product liability developed within American case law. However, for Japanese society, this legislation marks a complete change of direction in consumer protection policy. Japanese administrative agencies had frequently tried to effect consumer protection by utilizing administrative guidance, requiring the creation of voluntary industry organizations in industries where problems occurred, and encouraging self-regulation. Law in the form of preemptive regulation, including unnecessary industry protections and standards, was also common. The Product Liability Act represents a change of direction away from consumer protection as legal and practical preemptive regulation to consumer protection that gives rise to incentives for industry to improve products through the ex post facto consumer reliance on legal remedies.[19]

This legislation did not create the explosive increase in product liability litigation that industry had initially feared[20] but, rather, spurred a huge increase in premiums collected by insurance companies and a visible increase in the volume of "warning" notices. In other words, companies that, when selling a product, had previously used a single page describing its dangerous characteristics, now began to attach ten pages of warnings. Between contracting parties, these frequently functioned as standard form exclusions of liability.

Of course the drafters had anticipated that a product liability law based on the principle of strict liability would result in warnings and the abuse of exclusion clauses. However, the policy choice was that, rather than pursue preemptive administrative regulation, it was preferable to have a situation in which consumers are given information about potential dangers at the point of contracting and then exercise their own judgment about whether to purchase or not. That same policy stance informs the legislation relating to consumer contracts that was enacted after the Product Liability Act.

b. Consumer Contracts

The year 2000 was an important one for consumer law. First, the Consumer Contracts Act that had been subject to long years of drafting was finally established.[21] The law, created after many twist and turns, gives consumers the right to rescind a contract in a situation where their misunderstanding has been caused by the practice of providing inappropriate information (Article 4). However, it stops short of intervening in the content of the contract and allows invalidation of contract provisions where there is a clear, unjust exclusion of liability or limitation of liability, or where there is an excessively harsh liquidated damages or penalty clause (Articles 8, 9). Further, it provides that "[t]he consumer, when concluding a consumer contract, shall make use of information provided by the business/retailer and make efforts to comprehend the rights and obligations of the consumer and other matters contained in the consumer contract" (Article 3[2]). The insertion of this provision, which in legal terms is virtually meaningless, suggests harsh confrontation in the process of drafting between consumer protection policy and trenchant opposition from industry to the enactment of this law.

If we compare this Consumer Contracts Act with the European Union (EU) regulations on unfair terms in consumer contracts, it is relatively easy to point out the difference in stance on the question of emphasis given to market mechanisms.[22] Considering the wealth of research conducted on the EU by legal scholars and policy makers in Japan prior to the Consumer Contracts Act drafting, it is clear that, when the law was enacted, Japan consciously chose a policy position that sought consumer protection only to the extent that the function of the market mechanism was supported. At the time, this choice was labeled the product of intense compromise in order to prevent the defeat of legislation on consumer contracts. In the result, we can see it as legislation colored by the desire of business to usher in an "era of contract."

The same trend is even more clearly apparent in the Act concerning the Sale of Financial Products, enacted in the same year.[23] This law, introduced as a measure to protect the users of financial services, applies broadly to financial services transactions including savings deposits. It charges the business (*jigyōsha*) with the obligation to explain important terms of a contract, centering on the risk of loss of capital (*ganpon kesson*) (Article 3), and creates liability for damages where there is a breach of the duty to explain (Article 4). It then includes an article that links the amount of damages to the amount of lost principal (Article 5). The stance here is clear: consumer protection is limited to provision of information, falls short of intervention in the content of the contract, and makes it easier to seek a remedy through ex post facto litigation.

c. The Rhetoric of "Personal Responsibility"

The shared characteristic of these consumer protection laws is that, rather than preemptive prevention of injury to consumers, the focus is on preventing future injury by the ex post facto attribution of liability. This kind of approach is a familiar one within American law. However, whether in fact it has the effect of preventing future injury, and to what extent, depends on the commencement of ex post facto litigation seeking damages. Moreover, when we consider the scale of the cost of bringing ex post facto litigation, whether the anticipated deterrent effect will then be invoked in Japan is unclear. These are all issues for which there is, as yet, little empirical evidence.[24]

Nevertheless the reason this kind of legislation was supported was a preference for a scheme in which consumers are provided with adequate information and are able to choose on the basis of a wide range of options. As a result, even where consumers suffer injury, it is judged to be "one's own responsibility" to seek legal remedy. As the Justice System Reform Council report puts it: "[Citizens are expected to] break out of the consciousness of being a governed object and . . . become a governing subject, with autonomy and bearing social responsibility, and . . . take heavy responsibility for governance themselves."[25] Here contract is used as a means of manifesting one's will, or taking "personal responsibility." But a scheme that charges consumers with personal responsibility has not traditionally been supported in Japanese society and in our view does not yet attract widespread support. This kind of consumer "empowerment" also comes at a price. Infrastructure, such as consumer complaint centers, is expensive and may prove vulnerable over time; remedies delivered through the courts are contingent on access (now made easier through the introduction of a small-claims procedure) and on legal assistance. Justice system reform plans to increase the number of attorneys in Japan might swell the ranks of those able and willing to provide pro bono or consumer-oriented service, but it is unclear whether the current extreme maldistribution of legal services in Japan will be corrected in a way that makes this uniformly achievable across the country. What we see, however, is the concept of personal responsibility being invoked as part of the rhetoric well suited to justifying the slimming down of a bloated government through deregulation.

2. *The Shift toward Efficiency Maximization*

a. Labor Law

In earlier periods, Japanese labor law was classified as a field of "social law," that is, part of the range of regulations in a welfare state designed to protect workers disadvantaged by inequality of bargaining power. Today, the wave of deregulation is bringing about significant changes in this area. Symbolic of that change is the debate surrounding termination of employment and recent changes to labor law.

In contrast to the United States, courts in Japan prior to the 1990s actively intervened in the termination of labor contracts and had developed case law principles that severely restricted termination at will. A termination at will (or layoff) was not valid unless four elements could be fulfilled: (1) the necessity of reducing the workforce, (2) fulfilling the obligation to make efforts to avoid retrenchment, (3) a justifiable reason for selecting those to be terminated, and (4) a justifiable process for explanation and consultation. These kinds of case law principles differ from those in the United States, where adjustment of the workforce through termination (or layoff) is common, but they closely resemble labor law requirements in European countries such as Germany and France. Rather, we can say that, among industrialized countries, those having a termination system such as that of the United States are the exception. Japan's case law principles were developed in the period following World War II, when Japan experienced strong economic growth and while the economic pie was growing. It was said that the stabilization of employment and the creation of the Japanese paradigm of lifetime employment were supported through these case law principles.

However, as economic growth stalled, a move to change the case law through legislation emerged. Business and industry organizations, as proponents of this movement, asserted that the restructuring of employment through termination should be made easier by introducing complete freedom of contract. The goal of the policy that was invoked in order to justify the proposed reform was "labor mobility." The argument runs that, as the structure of industry changes dramatically, in order to realize an efficient transfer of labor from declining industries to new industries, it is desirable that termination can be undertaken freely.

We cannot say that this argument has a particularly strong empirical basis. Japan's labor market is still experiencing some of the highest levels of unemployment in the postwar period, so that much of the additional labor sought by new industries is already in the market. Consequently, it is difficult to see that making termination easier to accomplish will have the effect of helping employment flow into new industries. Rather, making it easier for declining industries to effect termination of those with nowhere to go will simply result in an increase in the number of unemployed.

On the other hand, prominent business executives are consistently repeating the message that it is critical to maintain a posture of valuing employment during a time of recession. In short, what is at issue is not lack of labor mobility but management philosophy on employment. Managers who aim at efficient management and ideologues both proclaim the necessity of a return to freedom of contract during the current period, in which forms of employment are becoming diverse.

b. House Lease Act

A further domain in which a large-scale debate about the return to freedom of contract occurred is the House Lease Act. In Japan, since the 1941 revision of the House Lease Act, it has been difficult for the owner to demand that the tenant vacate even when the contract period has expired.[26] A refusal to renew the lease has required a "justifiable reason." This system has been supported for sixty years as a legislative policy that ensured the stable provision of housing for tenants. However, the system has now come to be cited as a prize example of an unjust regulation. To be sure, the House Lease Act provisions also apply to contracts where a large corporation leases office space. Where a corporation concludes a lease contract for a designated number of years and has more than adequate negotiation power, a regulation requiring the landlord to renew the contract period is unnecessary. However, the group of scholars who commenced a campaign to abolish this provision did not assert that protection of large corporations was unnecessary. Rather, they maintained that the requirement of a "justifiable reason" was an unjust regulation because it prevented the provision of good-quality rental housing to the ordinary person.[27] They claimed, because of this regulation, building owners feared that once a building is leased as housing they would be unable to evict the tenants and would be prevented from making optimum use of their real estate. This attitude of building owners would restrict the supply of rental housing. The scholars who supported deregulation enthusiastically asserted that if the justifiable reason regulation were abolished, good-quality rental housing would become available and those workers who own homes outside of the metropolitan area and commute long distances would be able to rent much more spacious housing within the city for the same cost.

As a consequence, new revisions to the Land Lease and House Lease Act[28] were enacted in 1999 and it became possible to conclude lease contracts to which the "justifiable reason" standard did not apply and so at the expiration of the contract term it would be possible to evict the tenants. Nevertheless, in practice, the new type of lease contract, termed the fixed-period lease contract (*teiki shakuya keiyaku*), has not been taken up to the extent expected following the coming into force of the amended Land Lease and House Lease Act. At present the fixed-term lease contract seems to be used for the lease of office buildings by corporations, rather than for residential leases. In the case of residential housing, the tenant often does not know at the outset how long he or she intends to live in that property and so it is an excessive demand for the tenant to behave like a Homo economicus with complete information and conclude a contract for a fixed term. On the other hand, the house owner cannot gain rental income without tenants and so, provided that he or she does not plan to demolish the building within a certain number of years, there is little incentive to conclude a fixed-term contract that randomly stipulates a period.

In the result, to date evidence of the rose-colored, simple market model envisioned by those championing deregulation—increased supply of high-quality low-cost housing—has not materialized. Nevertheless, those who argue in support of a fixed-term lease right continue to assert the need to abolish completely the existing land lease law. This speaks to the issue that deregulation is not simply an academic debate about the best means to reach a certain policy goal, but is an ideology.

c. A Return to the Principle of Freedom of Contract

What we see above is an era of contract taking place in which corporations are restructuring their contracts based on the belief that economic efficiency can be achieved solely on the basis of discrete contracts grounded in the principle of freedom of contract.[29] At the same time, state regulation such as labor law and tenancy law is employing "freedom of contract" as a device for achieving a policy objective such as labor mobility or the provision of good-quality housing. However, in either case, it is open to question whether a return to the principle of freedom of contract is an effective device for achieving those policy objectives. The principle of freedom of contract appears to be grounded in, and legitimated by, an empirical economic model—but in fact is not.

Another significant change is the extent to which lateral regulation has begun to impact contracts in Japan. Perhaps the leading example of this is the Antimonopoly Act,[30] although, to be sure, we still see enforcement concentrated on horizontal rather than vertically restrictive contracts. Amendments in the past decade permit actions to be commenced by individuals, so that parties claiming loss resulting from anticompetitive behavior cataloged in the law are not limited by the Fair Trade Commission's willingness to commence an action. Add to this the potential personal liability of company directors for breaches of the Antimonopoly Act and you have a regulatory landscape that is significantly different from what prevailed even ten years ago.[31]

3. Escaping State Intervention

a. Electronic Commerce

As the twentieth century neared its close, a hitherto unknown form of contract began to be employed. One model is the creation of contracts establishing the systemic infrastructure for electronic commerce. For transactions to be concluded using a computer network, a certain amount of systemic infrastructure is necessary. However, electronic transactions using the Internet take place on a global scale, and in this case different regulatory regimes envisioned as jurisdictions bounded by geographical borders are nothing more than barriers to commerce. For this reason, the development of systemic infrastructure, based on contract that is not affected by any particular jurisdiction, is progressing. First, a system of electronic authentication, establishing individual identity, has been established through a network of contracts. To this has been added—in the case of business-to-business transactions—multiple parties linked by electronic data interchange (EDI) networks and consent to netting that allows mutual settlement and the incorporation of settlement by financial institutions. In the case of consumer transactions, credit cards are used for settlement and conclusion of the transaction within the network. Further, in the case of disputes, alternative dispute resolution (ADR) services are now in the process of being provided through such networks.

The function of contract in this setting is not simply one of acting as a means for expressing a choice made of one's own volition. By conjoining contracts composed of complex provisions, it becomes possible to construct autonomously an infrastructure for commercial transactions that in the past was provided by the state through the legal system. Thus, to the extent that "principle of freedom of contract" is accepted, the infrastructure operates effectively, regardless of the law that governs in the final analysis.

Of course, in order for electronic commerce to be carried out in a stable way, a legal system that supports it is necessary to some extent. The 1996 UNCITRAL Model Law on Electronic Commerce (revised in 1998) and the 2001 UNCITRAL Model Law on Electronic Signatures were both international attempts to unify the laws of individual countries.[32] In Japan, too, in the area of electronic verification (electronic signatures), the 2000 Law concerning Electronic Signatures and Verification was enacted in order to create a legal framework for electronic commerce.[33] However, the national law necessary for advancing the systemic infrastructure for electronic commerce created through contracting is—with the exception of enforcement of valid contracts—extremely limited. In other words, what is required is recognition of the principle of freedom of contract, the principle of equal treatment (nondiscrimination against foreign law), and the principle of technological neutrality (nondiscrimination against any given technology). In this sense, although electronic commerce is not completely severed from the state because it relies on state enforcement of the contract as the final stage, it shows that it is possible to construct a complex system in which multiple parties bind themselves consensually and in which state intervention is kept to a minimum.

To date there have been theories that explain the legal system or institutions by employing contractual concepts. We could say that the typical example of this is the economic theory that explains corporations as a nexus of contracts. However, these theories, along with the social contract theories that use contract to explain the emergence of the state, are complete fictions. That is, by explaining social institutions in contractual terms, they highlight previously invisible aspects of these institutions and legitimate decisions that would have been previously inconceivable, such as the overthrow of governments.[34]

By contrast, electronic commerce is, in reality, a scheme for constructing complex institutional infrastructure for commercial transactions through contract. If this is possible, it would not be surprising if the other systems, too, prove to be not fictions for the sake of explanation but rather attempts at actual construction through contract.

b. The Family as Contract

As we saw previously with electronic commerce, there are systems and institutions that can be substituted for by contract and are in fact in the process of being replaced by contract. In an ever-widening world governed only by consent of parties, it would seem to many Japanese that the last residual area to escape from the conquest of contract as the embodiment of market mechanism is the family. However, we now see the beginning of an assertion that the legal system of family be replaced by contract.[35]

Of course, those making the arguments are still few in number. But the impact of the contractual approach to the family lies in its persuasiveness, compelling serious deliberation. Logical rebuttal demands considerable reflection. Commentators employing the contractual approach criticize the way in which the state legally defines the shape of the family and discriminates against forms of the family that fall outside of these parameters. For example, the law stipulates that a child born to unmarried parents is an illegitimate child whose share in succession will be half of that of a legitimate child, that is, one whose parents registered their marriage by recording it in their family register (*koseki*). The Supreme Court has held that this discrimination, when viewed from the vantage point of protection of legal marriage, does not contravene the "equality under the law" provided for in Article 14(1) of the Constitution.[36] Many scholars, while supporting the protection of legal marriage, are critical of this decision because of the way in which it works an injustice on a child, who bears no responsibility for his or her illegitimate status.[37]

Such scholarly criticism is well founded. However, if we consider that, within the Civil Code, one of the important functions of legal marriage is to confer legitimacy at birth, the abolition of a distinction between legitimate and illegitimate birth may have the effect of relaxing the character or classification (*Merkmal*) of legal marriage. It follows that, hypothetically, if we remove the legal discrimination between legally married couples and those couples who are not, then the necessity of creating a provision or having a provision within the law specifically to designate the form of marriage becomes unnecessary. Rather, the form of family would be a choice that would be delegated to the free consent of individuals (whether or not linked as a same-sex couple). Commentators favoring the contractual approach make this argument. They also assert that, within the provisions of laws relating to families, what cannot be delegated to the free consent of the parties is the relationship between parents and children. Therefore, it is sufficient to retain minimum provisions for that purpose. In consequence, they argue, the law should retreat from most of the provisions relating to spouses, because it is possible to create these relationships completely through contract.

On the other hand, there are a number of lawyers who, although vocal in their criticism of a system that legally mandates the form of the family and extends protection to that form, do not concur with the radical claim that family law should be abolished and replaced by contract. This kind of ambivalence is visible in most industrialized societies today including France, Germany, and Australia and may not seem to be indigenous to Japan. The result is typically hybrid—some contract-based family forms supported by administrative law or decriminalization, and the preservation of the classical form of marriage as the de facto model.

In reality, the debate on legal marriage set out above is not simply a defense of discrimination against illegitimate children or the validity of same-sex marriage. What is being contested is whether the form of the family is a matter that can be decided consensually among individuals, or whether it is a public matter, decided communally through public discourse and debate. The fact that the legislative proposal presented to the Legislative Reform Council in 1996 recognizing separate family names for spouses, to date, has been repeatedly debated but not enacted demonstrates that in Japan the form of spousal (or family) relations is quintessentially a question for public decision. During this period, a strategy adopted by business and government has been to permit the use of separate family names as a matter of custom, in the spirit of the 1999 Basic Law for a Gender-Equal Society.[38] This notwithstanding, in response to calls for separate family names for spouses as a legal framework for marriage, opposition remains deep-rooted, and majority support for the idea appears not to have emerged. It may be that we can discern here a manifestation of a Japanese qualification to the extent of private domain governed by contract.

C. CONTRACT AS IDEOLOGY / "CONTRACT AS LEGAL TECHNIQUE" / "CONTRACT AS PHILOSOPHY"

The focus on contract that seeks to expand personal responsibility and efficiency originally appeared as part of the trend toward deregulation. For that reason, the standard pattern in the argument is to remove the regulations attaching to contract and to return to classical freedom of contract. It goes without saying that the relaxation of unnecessary regulation is desirable, but within the legal norms that are labeled "regulation" are those that respond to the particular characteristics of certain contractual relationships and have their own rationality, and so careful and detailed debate is necessary to establish whether a return to freedom of contract constitutes an appropriate means to achieving the ultimate policy goal.

In the case of the enactment of the Product Liability Act, Uchida has argued that in a country such as Japan, where administrative regulation is relatively effective, rather than hope for a deterrence of future harm through placing the burden of litigation on victims of defective products, it would be cheaper and more effective to refine the system of preemptive regulation of product safety.[39] In relation to the introduction of the fixed-term house lease right, we suggest that the legal principle that requires a "justifiable reason" for refusing renewal of the lease was not a regulation that worked for the protection of "the weaker party"; rather, it was a contractual legal principle that suited the long-term contractual relationship of residential property and abolishing it would not return us to a position of no regulation but would instead forcibly impose a contract model unsuited to this kind of contractual relationship.[40] Our criticism of the debate concerning labor contracts is similar, in that we support the legal principle limiting termination of employment as a legal scheme that is suited to a continuing contractual relationship such as a labor contract.

In these debates, the issue is whether it is appropriate to employ contract in order to fulfill a particular policy objective, and what type of contract it may be appropriate to employ. In this sense, contract as a legal system is a means for achieving a particular purpose. However, in reality, contract is not simply a means. As far as labor contracts are concerned—as between a legal system that allows termination at will, in the way that U.S. law does, and a legal system that treats termination as the last resort for cost reduction after management has made strenuous efforts—the choice is not confined to which is the more effective means for achieving efficiency, but rather the question is, within an employment system in which efficiency can be achieved, what kind of employment system is "preferred." In other words the inquiry is really about a desired vision of society and the extent to which people find meaning in communal values, a question that economics is not equipped to answer.[41]

In this sense, the "contract" of the era of contract is not simply a legal technique that is legitimated through consequentialism. It is a type of philosophy. We can say the same about the move to create social systems through contract outside state law. Social contract theory used this kind of contract to explain the state. However, that was posited on the natural assumption that this explanation was a fiction. Now we have social contracts that are not a fiction and which are emerging as real plans for social systems.

III. CONTRACTS AND COURTS IN JAPAN

A. THE ROLE OF COURTS

One of the often-cited features of Japanese corporate organization prior to the 1990s has been the prevalence of continuing relational contract ties between companies. One typical example is the manufacturer-supplier contracting in Japan's auto industry, where—in contrast to the vertical integration achieved in the United States through merger and acquisition—quality control, reliability, and interdependency were managed in Japan through the vehicle of explicit or implicit contracts. Another often-cited example is the existence of supportive transactions within *keiretsu*, integrated vertical or horizontal corporate groupings, however defined.[42] This led some American scholars to assert that one of the drivers in organizational choice in Japan—that is, a preference for transacting within a corporate grouping—has been the lack of contract enforceability that would allow more "market-based" transactions at arm's length.[43] A counterargument is that the *keiretsu* (and thus, presumably, their preference for internal contracting) are fictional.[44] Both these views, however, are predicated on a fairly static and formalist view of corporate governance and contracting norms.[45]

The implicit argument in some views of commercial contracting in Japan up to the 1990s is that the Kawashima-style preference for relational contracting is structurally induced because of deficiencies in the formal legal institutions. The problem with this view is that the empirical evidence runs the other way. Commercial actors in Japan, as elsewhere, certainly do not favor litigation as a primary means of resolving transactional problems. However, even if we leave aside cases commenced but settled and cases unreported, the reported case law of the past fifteen years or so shows ample use of the courts by Japanese litigants across a wide range of contractual disputes, notwithstanding structural barriers to litigation such as cost and a relatively small commercial bar.[46] The result has been a highly developed Japanese contract jurisprudence, albeit one that differs from Anglo-American approaches to contract law in some respects. What is striking about the Japanese contract jurisprudence from the 1970s to the present is the way in which case law has been used to expand significantly the scope of Civil Code doctrine, and the deeply divided opinions, both among judges and scholars, about what the values animating contract decisions should be—that is, whether courts should support a communitarian vision of commerce in which smaller or weaker transaction parties are protected through operation of law, or whether "the market" should dictate transaction outcomes, with minimal interference from the courts. Professor Noboru Kashiwagi, for example, is highly critical of current distribution contract jurisprudence and expresses a strong preference for a more "market-based" conception of contracts over what seem to him excessive social welfare concerns by Japanese courts.[47]

Uchida's own work on the development of Japanese contract law jurisprudence in the postwar period illustrates how the courts have gradually fleshed out the general provisions of the Civil Code (e.g., the abuse of rights doctrine and the good faith doctrine) in a way that provides fairly clear case law guidelines about what constitutes good faith pre-contractual negotiation, post-formation performance of contract, protection of reasonable expectation for renewing contracts, and good faith negotiation of contracts that prove difficult to perform according to their original terms.[48]

Uchida's taxonomy of good faith is borne out in case law, particularly as it relates to continuing contracts. Contract law scholars, judges, and attorneys have had no difficulty identifying continuing contracts in Japan as a category of transaction occurring across consumer transactions, employment contracts, subcontracting situations, distribution, franchising, and supply of goods settings that warrants an analysis different from that of the discrete contract contemplated by classical contract theory. In many cases, the courts also take note of the particular identity of the parties, the circumstances in which the contract was formed, and the practices that obtain elsewhere in the industry, in an analysis that resonates with the application of equitable principles in the common law world. This has led Uchida and other theorists to explore theoretical justifications for the courts' inquiry into, and application of, social norms or evidence of norms developed by the parties themselves, whether or not these are immediately apparent from contract-related documentation (where this exists).

This process has been particularly evident in areas where new forms of transactions have emerged in the absence of detailed regulation, franchising contracts being but one example.[49] In Japan, as elsewhere, the example of the franchise transaction is the franchisor as business developer who seeks to expand the system by soliciting capital contributions in the form of franchise fees. The franchisee typically contributes start-up capital, labor, and energy in return for the right to operate a tested (and thus less risky) business system for a limited time. In theory small franchisees in Japan are supported by the bureaucratic oversight of small and medium-sized enterprises that is provided by the Ministry of Economy, Trade and Industry (METI).[50] In practice, the insulation from exploitation by a more powerful transaction partner (such as requirements that franchisors make adequate disclosure of their business operations to prospective franchisees) has come from case law, based on the general provisions of the Civil Code, rather than from legislation.[51]

In other types of transactions, the courts have been invoked as a way of protesting social or financial dislocation stemming from contracts affected by the dramatically changed economy of the 1990s. Clusters of cases involving lease agreements between property owners and real estate developers and litigation against insurance companies over financial products providing "guaranteed" annual returns are examples. The so-called cosmetics cases are another cluster of well-known cases. Here, contract breaches and terminations of long-term continuing distribution contracts between leading cosmetics manufacturers and some of their distributors/retailers became a proxy for challenging tightly drafted contracts aimed at preventing discounting of luxury products, at a time when the introduction of information technology and the globalization of economies was exerting competitive pressures on the distribution sector to become more efficient. During this period, so-called price destruction (*kakakuhakai*), or heavy discounting, emerged as a trend in the distribution and retailing sectors.[52] A key feature of the cosmetics cases, in particular the Shiseido litigation, was the way in which the Antimonopoly Act was invoked as a way of challenging the continuing contracts between the parties by characterizing their restrictive provisions as devices for resale price maintenance.[53] Although Professor Hiroo Sono points out that these cases should really be read as contract rather than as competition cases,[54] the mobilization of the Antimonopoly Act in this way and the courts' willingness to engage in a (limited) competition law analysis after decades of "anemic" Antimonopoly Act inaction are legally and politically significant. Scholarship that uses this case study to explore the links between contract and competition law in Japan[55] clearly resonates with our observations about the ways in which contract has been harnessed in the service of "deregulation" in Japan.

B. EMPIRICAL STUDIES

The desire to inscribe contract practices with cultural value (and virtue) runs deep, and so we see in the 1990s in Japan a range of empirical projects focused on whether and how Japanese business norms are changing and what impact this may be having on contract practice.

The multi-country survey by Professors Masanobu Katō and Michael Young and their collaborators represented a reexploration of Japanese contract consciousness through a 1980s-era problem involving renegotiation of a Japan-Australia long-term supply contract.[56] A core issue in this study was the nature of the long-term agreement, in contrast to a discrete contract. It probes the expectations of businesspeople and lawyers (in this study through university students as proxies) in regard to ongoing business relationships and the extent to which different national groups invoke doctrinal law in the service of resolving problems that emerge in the course of the transaction.

A different cluster of studies explores a more fundamental issue at the domestic level: the incidents of contractual norms and communicative strategies in contract formation, particularly in the provision of goods and services to consumers.[57] At one level research of this kind functions as a critique of positivist assumptions about contract that are grounded in classical contract doctrine. At another level, this research is significant in relation to the emergence of "consumers" as a distinct focus for legislative regulation, as we identify in this chapter.[58]

A third cluster of mid-1990s interviews compared commercial contracting practices by Japanese and U.S. corporations across a range of transaction types and industries.[59] To some extent this project was predicated on the fairly widespread use of continuing contracts in different industries, but part of its significance lies in the way that it catalogs both similarities between U.S. and Japanese corporations and wide variations in both countries across transaction type and industry at that time. What the interview responses showed was that it was possible to trace the origins and use of "indigenous" contract practices and patterns of contracting that appear deeply embedded in their social context and that these practices become institutionalized over time. Those institutionalized practices, however, are also the product of other institutional factors, such as economic organization, the use of technology, and the legal and regulatory framework.[60] As each or any of these factors changes, they induce change in related contractual transactions. In this sense, "Japanese" contracting can be observed in a given setting at a given time and may be different from, similar to, or indistinguishable from its non-Japanese counterpart; however, to seek "Japanese contracts" as an aggregated entity, abstracted from their particular context, is to seek a chimera.

C. THE ROLE OF INTERMEDIATE ACTORS

One systemic change that has allowed this sea change in contract to occur in Japan has been the rise of professional intermediaries. An axiomatic feature of "Japanese contracts" prior to the 1990s was the brevity and perfunctory language of contract documentation. The evidence of the past decade is that this is less and less the case. As we point out in relation to product liability, some of the wordy documentation now in evidence has the explicit function of excluding strict liability and shifting risk. More broadly, however, our preliminary interview data suggested that attitudes toward risk management, legal compliance, and documentation by intermediate professionals, including attorneys, in-house counsel, and business managers, are changing.

In our interviews in the mid-1990s and in annual surveys of in-house legal staff in Japan, respondents almost uniformly report that their working lives are busier and more complex because of an increase in legal regulation impacting on their organization.[61] In the case of large corporate mergers and reorganizations this has been manifested, for example, as a need to articulate and document intercorporate relationships between a newly established holding company and its related entities, or to document the outsourcing of functions previously performed in-house by permanent full-time employees. In other cases the 1990s emergence of "corporate governance" (*kōporēto gabanansu*) in Japan has spurred the emergence of "compliance departments" in many large corporations. Much of the initial work of the compliance departments seems to have been documenting or re-documenting transactions now explicitly constructed as "contractual." Written contract is the device for constructing the relationship, for apportioning risk, and also for articulating new concerns such as the ownership of, and liability for, intellectual property rights.

Attorneys and paralegals are also actively re-managing the scope of their work in the wake of justice system reforms that expand both their scope of practice and their personnel numbers.[62] These changes have interacted in ways that have made current contractual relationships progressively more formalistic and have contributed to the appearance that classical contract models are being overlaid on, or perhaps are coming to dominate, social relations.

IV. CONCLUSION: THE FUTURE OF JAPANESE SOCIETY

Kawashima presented an outline in which Japanese contract consciousness, in comparison with that of the West, was not modern and lagged behind the West. Quite apart from the issue that the theory was predicated on the presumption that views of contract proceed lineally from premodern to modern, his approach embodies a critical flaw: the reference point for evaluating Japanese contract consciousness was not the contract consciousness of actual "Westerners" existing within "Western" society, but a synthetic construct of modern contract consciousness.

Following Ian Macneil, we can separate the modern law (or the modern civil code) concept of contract—or in common law parlance, classical contract theory and concepts of contracts in action—into discrete contract and relational contract and in this way immediately create a richer analytic framework than the one provided by Kawashima.[63] When we evaluate the contract consciousness subsisting in Japanese society, too, we should be able to provide a more granular analysis than simply deeming a modern (or classical) view of contract to be "lagging." For example, where contract consciousness cannot be explained by reference to modern concepts of contract, it may be that this is strengthened by the structure of power relations within a particular industry, or that it is efficient and economically rational because it is the product of particular conditions within a given industry or social sector. On the other hand, values other than economic efficiency may also be embraced by the parties.

Adopting this framework of analysis, how would we evaluate the ninety-some years preceding Japan's era of contract? We should certainly note that the sharp division between law and society postulated by Kawashima in the past does not exist. In the examples we have given in this chapter, changes in the positive law and changes in Japanese contract behavior at the level of social strategy have been clearly induced by policy objectives. This is demonstrated clearly in the policy forms and processes taking place in the era of contract that we see from the Administrative Reform Council through to the Justice System Reform Council. In other words, this is the transformation of a "preemptive regulatory society" into an "ex post facto check and remedy society." Here, law relating to contract is a direct means of achieving social transformation, and contract strategies employed at the social level are induced by positive law, rather than independently (pre)existing.

From the outside, the new laws that embody conceptions of contract appear similar to the concepts of contract in modern law (or classical contract law), but the philosophy underlying them is different. In the past, when a modern contract concept (or classical contract concept) was created, the liberalism that was the underlying philosophy was significant because it confirmed the individual freedom that was opposed to feudal power that had overborne freedom. By contrast, the philosophy ushering in today's era of contract rejects the welfare state that had attempted to safeguard individual freedom in practice. Instead, it is a philosophy that perceives the realization of substantive contractual justice by the state as an excessive intrusion into society.

Today, if it is meaningful to debate Japanese views of contract and contact consciousness, it is not to engage in a naïve search for some kind of static goal such as differences between Japan and "the West"—although the approach in this chapter may be suggestive of fruitful comparisons with countries beyond Japan. Rather, the inquiry is important because what is being unveiled in the setting of Japanese society is an era of contract in which noncontractual social relations and social relations governed by relational contracts are being displaced by the discrete contract. To what extent is Japanese society likely to commit to this philosophy? To what extent can it commit? These are the questions we should be asking as we go forward.

NOTES

1. Takeyoshi Kawashima, "Dispute Resolution in Contemporary Japan," in Arthur Taylor von Mehren, ed., *Law in Japan: The Legal Order in a Changing Society* (Cambridge, MA: Harvard University Press, 1963), 41.

2. Takeyoshi Kawashima, "The Legal Consciousness of Contract in Japan," *Law in Japan: An Annual* 7(1) (1974). This article was still being used as an authoritative extract in Japanese law textbooks as late as 2000. See, e.g., Yukio Yanagida et al., eds., *Law and Investment in Japan: Cases and Materials*, 2nd ed. (Cambridge, MA: East Asian Legal Studies Program, Harvard University, 2000). For a critique of Kawashima's concepts and argumentation, see Takao Tanase, "The Empty Space of the Modern in Japanese Law Discourse," in Johannes Feest and David Nelken, eds., *Adapting Legal Cultures* (Oxford: Hart, 2001), 187–98.

3. For an application of the Kawashima conceptualization, see Shinichiro Michida, "Contract Societies: America and Japan Contrasted" [Keiyaku shakai: Amerika to Nihon no chigai o miru], trans. Veronica Taylor, *Pacific Rim Law and Policy Journal* 1 (1992): 199–224. For a comparison of the Kawashima contract typology with Japanese case law during the 1980s and 1990s and a rebuttal of the conceptual framework, see Veronica Taylor, "Continuing Transactions and Persistent Myths: Contracts in Contemporary Japan," *Melbourne University Law Review* 19 (1993): 352–97.

4. Hugh Collins, *Regulating Contracts* (Oxford: Oxford University Press, 1999). On the role of contract law as a pivotal element in the governance mechanisms of the post-regulatory state, see Hugh Collins, "Regulating Contract Law," in Christine Parker et al., eds., *Regulating Law* (Oxford: Oxford University Press, 2004), which argues, inter alia, that "the objective of meta-regulation should be to try to align general contract law with the state's welfare and social inclusion goals and to coordinate the imposition of restraints on the reflexivity of private law, in order to ensure that individual rights or welfare goals are secured" (29). This is a very different regulatory argument from the description of policy elites' adoption of neoclassical concepts of contract in Japan in the 1990s, described in this chapter.

5. Takashi Uchida, *Keiyaku no jidai* [The Era of Contract] (Tokyo: Iwanami shōten, 2000).

6. Here we use the binary distinction used in that literature of "Japan" contrasted with "the West," the latter often standing in for the United States. We prefer more nuanced comparisons and acknowledge the vast body of literature detailing national and regional variations in contracting norms and practice. For examples based on empirical studies of other Asian economies during the 1990s, see Jane Kaufman Winn, "Relational Practices and the Marginalization of Law: Informal Financial Practices of Small Businesses in Taiwan," *Law and Society Review* 28 (1994): 801, and John McMillan and Christopher Woodruff, "Dispute Prevention without Courts in Vietnam," *Journal of Law, Economics, and Organization* 15(3) (1999): 637.

7. For a study of premodern contract formality in Japan, see Dan Fenno Henderson, "'Contracts' in Tokugawa Villages," *Journal of Japanese Studies* 1 (1974): 51–90, arguing that village "contracts" in writing were the product of careful design, notwithstanding the deliberate obstacles to their enforcement using state apparatus. For a study of sex industry contracts in the prewar period, covering prostitution and geisha indenture, the regulatory system, and related case law, see J. Mark Ramseyer, *Odd Markets in Japanese History: Law and Economic Growth* (Cambridge: Cambridge University Press, 1996), 109–34.

8. For a concise history of deregulation debates dating from the 1920s in Japan, see Gregory W. Noble, "Reform and Continuity in Japan's *Shingikai* Deliberation Councils," in Jennifer Amyx and Pete Drysdale, eds., *Japanese Governance: Beyond Japan Inc.* (London: RoutledgeCurzon, 2003).

9. See, e.g., the Installment Sales Act [Kappu hanbai hō], Law No. 159 of 1961 (as amended), and the Specified Commercial Transactions Act [Tokuteishō-torihiki ni kansuru hōritsu] (formerly the Act concerning Door-to-Door Sales, Etc.), Law No. 57 of 1976 (as amended). The Specified Commercial Transactions Act covers, in addition to door-to-door sales, other direct-marketing methods such as mail, telephone, and e-mail sales solicitation.

10. See, e.g., Nihon bengoshi rengōkai shōhisha mondai taisaku iinkai [Japan Federation of Bar Associations Consumer Problem Strategy Committee], ed., *Keizokuteki sābisu torihiki: Shōhisha toraburu kaiketsu saku* [Continuing Contracts for Services: Remedial Strategies for Consumer Problems], Bessatsu NBL No. 32 (Tokyo: Shōjihōmu kenkyūkai, 1995); Veronica Taylor, "Consumer Contract Governance in a Deregulating Japan," *Victoria University of Wellington Law Review* 27(1) (1997): 99–120.

11. Regulations to control the imposition of high levels of interest on loans previously existed, such as the Restrictions on Interest Act [Rishi seigen hō], Law No. 100 of 1954, but following the 1970s, the emergence of so-called *sara-kin* loans (extortionate loans to wage earners) led to subsequent legislative amendments. In 1983 the Act on Lending Businesses [Kashikingyō no kisei tō ni kansuru hōritsu] was established, and the 1954 Act Governing Interest on Capital Contributions and Deposits [Shusshi no ukeire, azukarikin oyobi kinri tō no torishimari ni kansuru hōritsu]—aimed at regulating financial services providers—was amended and strengthened three times after 1983. These statutes were then revisited again in the wake of the consumer and commercial loan problems of the 1990s.

12. This is true except to the extent that problems experienced by end users and reported publicly had an impact on the viability of the industry. In many cases, when end users experienced loss or damage, those cases were reported to Diet

members via their respective electoral liaison offices and were publicized not through the courts but through questions in the Diet, to which administrative agencies would then respond. This kind of public-sector response to a social problem, taking place outside the court system, can be viewed as a function of Japanese-style dispute resolution. However, this is clearly very different from the social vision being pursued by the current government.

13. *Final Report of the Administrative Reform Council* (December 3, 1997), available at (http://www.kantei.go.jp/foreign/971228finalreport.html).

14. Justice System Reform Council, *Recommendations of the Justice System Reform Council—a Justice System to Support Japan in the Twenty-first Century* (June 12, 2001), available at (http://www.kantei.go.jp/foreign/judiciary/2001/0612report.html). The council's original mandate at the time of its establishment in 1999 is described at (http://www.kantei.go.jp/foreign/policy/sihou/singikai/991221_e.html).

15. Japan's graduate-level law schools [*hōkadaigakuin*] were created pursuant to the justice system reform agenda outlined by the Justice System Reform Council in 2001 and began operation in April 2004.

16. House Lease Act [Shakuyahō], Law No. 50 of 1921 (as amended, 1941, 1966, and abolished effective August 1, 1992), replaced by the Land Lease and House Lease Act [Shakuchishakuyahō], Law No. 90 of 1991 (amended by Law No. 110 of 1996 and Law No. 153 of 1999); Act concerning the Sale of Financial Products, Etc. [Kinyūshōhin no hanbai tō ni kansuru hōritsu], Law No. 101 of 2000; the Consumer Contracts Act [Shōhisha keiyaku hō], Law No. 51 of 1993; and the Product Liability Act [Seizōbutsu sekinin hō], Law No. 85 of 1994.

17. The recommendations of the Justice System Reform Council state:

> Japan, which is facing difficult conditions, has been working on various reforms, including political reform, administrative reform, promotion of decentralization, and reforms of the economic structure such as deregulation. What commonly underlies these reforms is the will that each and every person will break out of the consciousness of being a governed object and will become a governing subject, with autonomy and bearing social responsibility, and that the people will participate in building a free and fair society in mutual cooperation and will work to restore rich creativity and vitality to this country. This reform of the justice system aims to tie these various reforms together organically under "the rule of law" that is one of the fundamental concepts on which the Constitution is based. Justice system reform should be positioned as the "final linchpin" of a series of various reforms concerning restructuring of "the shape of our country." (Justice System Reform Council, *Recommendations of the Justice System Reform Council*)

18. Reform Council directive of July 25, 1985, on the approximation of the laws, regulations, and administrative provisions of the member states concerning liability for defective products (85/374/EEC)(OJ L 210, 7.8.1985, 29).

19. Luke Nottage, *Product Safety and Liability Law in Japan* (London: RoutledgeCurzon, 2004).

20. Luke Nottage and Yoshitaka Wada, "Japan's New Product Liability ADR Centers: Bureaucratic, Industry or Consumer Informalism?" *ZJapanR* 6 (1998): 40.

21. Consumer Contracts Act. See also the Electronic Consumer Contracts Act and Electronic Transmission of Assent Act [Denshi shōhisha keiyaku oyobi denshi shōdaku tsūshin ni kansuru minpō no tokurei ni kansuru hōritsu], Law No. 95 of 2001.

22. See Reform Council Directive 93/13/EEC on Unfair Terms in Consumer Contracts (OJ L95, 21.4.93, 29).

23. Act concerning the Sale of Financial Products, Etc., available at (http://www.fsa.go.jp/p_mof/houan/hou11c.pdg) (only in Japanese).

24. For earlier related work in the United States, see Carl Shapiro, "Symposium on the Economics of Liability" *Journal of Economic Perspectives* 5(3) (1991), available at (http://www.jstor.org). Shapiro points out that responses to accidents through ex post facto remedies represent a policy choice that is very costly. In contrast to the Japanese approach described in this chapter, in Australia the Regulatory Institutions Network at Australian National University (RegNet [http://regnet.anu.edu.au/]) has partnered with the Australian Consumer and Competition Commission in a multiyear empirical study to test different types of regulatory, compliance, and enforcement techniques. The range of approaches within the project extends beyond the simple dichotomy between prophylactic bureaucratic protection and market-led litigation following injury that seems to be contemplated in the Japanese policy settings discussed above. See the RegNet/ACCC 2003 Preliminary Report: (http://cccp.anu.edu.au/Preliminary%20Research%20Report.pdf). This project is modeled on earlier empirical research on protection of consumers in nursing home regulation. See John Braithwaite, Toni Makkai, Valerie Braithwaite, and Diane Gibson, *Raising the Standard: Resident Centred Nursing Home Regulation in Australia* (Canberra: Australian Government Publishing Service, 1993). This earlier research forms the basis of a new affiliated project, RegHealth (http://reghealth.anu.edu.au/).

25. Justice System Reform Council, *Recommendations of the Justice System Reform Council*, 10–11.

26. House Lease Act.

27. Scholars who shaped the debate included Hideo Fukui and Tatsuo Hatta. Their views are collected in Yasutaka Abe, Yoshihiro Nomura, and Hideo Fukui,

eds., *Limited Term Lease Rights* [Teikishakkaken] (Tokyo: Shinzansha, 1998). Professors Fukui and Hatta were subsequently appointed to the government's Council for Regulatory Reform established on April 1, 2001 (chair: Yoshihiko Miyauchi, Orix Corporation) (http://www8.cao.go.jp/kisei/en/).

28. Land Lease and House Lease Act.

29. It is possible, of course, to look at contract practices of the past as also being attempts to pursue efficiency. What is significant, however, is the current strengthening tendency among policy elites in Japan to conceive "efficiency" solely in terms of the simple market model imagined by classical contract law.

30. Antimonopoly Act [Shiteki dokusen no kinshi oyobi kōsei torihiki no kakuho ni kansuru hōritsu], Law No. 54 of 1947 (as amended).

31. Veronica Taylor, "Re-regulating Japanese Transactions: The Competition Law Dimension," in Amyx and Drysdale, *Japanese Governance*, 134.

32. Available at (http://www.uncitral.org/uncitral/en/uncitral_texts.html).

33. Act concerning Electronic Signatures and Verification [Denshi shōmei oyobi ninshō gyōmu ni kansuru hōritsu], Law No. 102 of 2000.

34. Robert Nozick's renowned work *Anarchy, State, and Utopia* (Oxford: Blackwell, 1974) explored the extent to which the state can be constructed through contract, providing an example of one such stimulating intellectual experiment.

35. Ayako Nozaki, *Seigiron ni okeru kazoku no ichi—Riberaru feminizumu no saiteii ni mukete* [The Position of the Family in Moral Theory—toward a Liberal Feminist Repositioning] (Tokyo: Keisoshobō, 2003); Junji Annen, "Kazokukeisei to jikokettei" [The Form of the Family and Individual Choice/Self-Determination], *Iwanamikōza gendaihō 14 Jikoketteiken to hō* [Iwanami Seminars on Contemporary Law, No. 14, Self-Determination and Law] (Tokyo: Iwanami shōten, 1998), 129–45; Annen, "'Ningen no songen' to kazoku no arikata: 'Kaiyakutekikazokukan' sairo'" ["Human Dignity" and the State of the Family: Redebating the "Contractual Approach to Family"] *Jurisuto*, no. 1222 (2002): 21–29.

36. Supreme Court Grand Bench, July 5, 1995.

37. A representative of the contractual approach argues that, as far as the discrimination against illegitimate children and their legal share in succession is concerned, the problem can be overcome through stipulation in the will left by the person conferring property and this does not interfere with the exercise of individual choice/self-determination. On this point the argument differs from that of many academic theories but in effect supports the Supreme Court finding of constitutionality.

38. Also translated as the Basic Law on Equality in Social Participation, Law No. 78 of 1999 (http://www.gender.go.jp/english/basic_law/). For a critical analysis of the legislation and its underlying policy objectives, see Mari Osawa, "Koi-

zumi's 'Robust Policy': Governance, the Japanese Welfare Employment Regime and Comparative Gender Studies," in Glenn D. Hook, ed., *Contested Governance in Japan* (London: RoutledgeCurzon, 2005), 111.

39. Takashi Uchida, "Kanken seizōbutsu sekinin" [Product Liability], *NBL*, nos. 494–97 (1992).

40. Uchida, *Keiyaku no jidai*, particularly chap. 6.

41. Takashi Uchida, "Kaiko o meguru hō to seisaku—Kaikohōsei no seitōsei" [Law and Policy concerning Termination of Employment: The Legality of the Law Governing Termination], in Fumio Ōtake, Shinya Ōuchi, and Ryuichi Yamakawa, eds., *Kaikohōsei o kangaeru* [Thinking about the Law Governing Termination of Employment] (Tokyo: Keisoshobō, 2004).

42. We accept that *keiretsu* is not a particularly well-defined concept and that—however defined—has less applicability than is often claimed, particularly in competitive industries such as auto manufacturing.

43. E.g., Ronald J. Gilson and Mark J. Roe, "Understanding the Japanese Keiretsu: Overlaps between Corporate Governance and Industrial Organization," *Yale Law Journal* 102 (1993): 871. Significantly, however, none of the corporations that we spoke with in a series of interviews in Japan in the mid-1990s cited legal unenforceability of contracts as a problem, despite the fact that, like commercial contracts everywhere, some of those described to us would have real validity problems if litigated (from interview notes on file with the authors). This is consistent with the extensive literature on self-enforcement of contracts through legal substitutes such as reputation, information, technology, and financing strategies.

44. E.g., Yoshirō Miwa and J. Mark Ramseyer, "Banks and Economic Growth: Implications from Japanese History," *Journal of Law and Economics* 45 (2002): 127 (arguing that prewar Japanese corporate finance did not rely on relationship banking, but that firms raised capital through competitive capital markets).

45. For a more recent examination of this problem, see Ichirō Kobayashi, "Practitioner Note: The Interaction between Japanese Corporate Governance and Relational Contract Practice," *New York University Journal of Law and Business* 2 (2005): 269 (arguing that "insufficient infrastructure of business contract practice was one of the primary factors leading Japanese corporate governance to pave its own way. An evolutional view of the interaction of corporate governance and contract practice . . . reveals that Japanese corporate governance has functioned primarily as a signal of reputation. Only a firm that adopts a particular corporate structure is able to establish a good reputation, which in Japan, is the most important self-enforcement device in relational contract practice" [273]).

46. See, e.g., Tom Ginsburg and Glenn Hoetker, "The Unreluctant Litigant?

An Empirical Analysis of Japan's Turn to Litigation," Illinois Law and Economics Working Paper No. LE 04-009, College of Law, University of Illinois at Urbana-Champaign, 2004, available at (http://ssrn.com/abstract=608582).

47. Noboru Kashiwagi, "I Can't Turn You Loose: The Termination of Distributors in Japan" (paper presented at the conference "Change, Continuity and Context: Japanese Law in the Twenty-first Century," University of Michigan, Ann Arbor, April 2001).

48. Takashi Uchida, "Gendai keiyakuhō no aratana tenkai to ippanjōkō" [New Developments in Contemporary Contract Law and General Clauses], *NBL*, nos. 514–17 (1994).

49. For a scholarly treatment of how Japanese civil law has adapted to the needs of continuing contracts, of which franchises can be a subset, see Hiroyasu Nakata, *Keizokutekitorihiki no kenkyū* [Les affaires successives: Étude juridique (A Study on Successive Transactions)] (Tokyo: Yūhikaku, 2000).

50. See, e.g., the limited scope of "protection" provided in art. 11 of the Small and Medium-Size Retail Enterprise Promotion Act [Chūshokourishōgyō shinkōhō], Law No. 101 of 1973 (as amended), which requires parties concluding contracts that bring a new entity into a chain-store system or retail system linked through use of a common trademark or trade dress to disclose to the prospective entrant specified documents that include the financial statements of the system, the duration of the contract, and restraints on the use of trademark and trade dress. The law has been revised multiple times since its enactment; art. 11 was revised by Law No. 160 of 1999. For a summary in Japanese of responses to the public comment on the proposed revision of art. 11, see (http://www.meti.go.jp/feedback/downloadfiles/i20328bj.pdf).

51. Kenji Kawagoe's compendium of franchise case law is representative of an extensive literature on how to interpret Japanese jurisprudence in the field of franchise contracts. See Kenji Kawagoe, *Furanchaizu shisutemu no hanrei bunseki* [Analysis of Reported Cases on Franchise Systems], Bessatsu NBL No. 56, shinpan [rev. ed.] (Tokyo: Shōjihōmu kenkyūkai, 2000).

52. We should note, however, that the shift toward discounting in the cosmetics market in Japan—of which so-called price destruction [*kakakuhakai*] and the "revolution in distribution" [*ryūtsūkakumei*] are aspects—began in the late 1980s. These phenomena have different roots from those of the collapse of the bubble economy epitomized by real estate and share price drops. Although it overlaps in time with the collapse of the bubble economy, what drove price destruction were changes to information technology that allowed new efficiencies in distribution and, within the globalized economy, consumer dissatisfaction with the differential between domestic and overseas prices.

53. See Antimonopoly Act, including regulations on prohibition on resale price maintenance (art. 12). For a commentary in English, see Masahiro Murakami, *The Japanese Antimonopoly Act* [Nihon no dokkinhō] (Tokyo: Shōjihōmu, 2003); and Mitsuo Matsushita, *International Trade and Competition Law in Japan* (Oxford: Oxford University Press, 1993). A list of the related guidelines and advice documents published by the Japan Fair Trade Commission can be found at (http://www.jftc.go.jp/dokusen/3/index.htm).

54. Hiroo Sono, "'Dokkinhō ihan kōi no shihōjō no kōryokuron': Oboegaki: keshōhin hanbai tokuyakuten keiyaku no kaiyaku jirei o sozai ni" ["A Memorandum on the Validity of Contacts in Violation of Antimonopoly Law": With Reference to Cosmetic Distributorship Cancellation Cases], *Kanazawa hōgaku* 38 (1996): 263.

55. Willem M. Visser 't Hooft, "Termination Disputes within the Japanese Distribution System for Luxury Cosmetics: A Case Study," in Willem M. Visser't Hooft, *Japanese Contract and Anti-trust Law: A Sociological and Comparative Study* (London: RoutledgeCurzon, 2002), 81–129.

56. Reviewed in Veronica Taylor, "Ōsutoraria kara mita Nihon keiyakutorihiki" [Japanese Commercial Contracts from an Australian Perspective], *Jurisuto*, no. 1096 (1996): 71–73.

57. Takao Tanase, ed., *Keiyakuhōri to keiyakukankō* [Legal Principles of Contract and Customary Contractual Practices] (Tokyo: Kōbundō, 1999).

58. Taylor, "Consumer Contract Governance in a Deregulating Japan," 99.

59. Unpublished research; interview notes on file with the authors.

60. For a more recent application of this idea to bank lending to Japanese corporations, see Kobayashi, "Practitioner Note," 269.

61. See generally *Dai8ji hōmubumon jittaichōsa hōkokusho* [Report on the 8th Annual Survey of Corporate Counsel], Bessatsu NBL No. 63 (Tokyo: Shōjihōmu kenkyūkai, 2001), available in outline at (http://www.keieihoyukai.jp/examine/hyoshi.html).

62. See, e.g., Kyoko Ishida, "The Legal Profession of Japan," in Veronica Taylor, ed., *Japan Business Law Guide* (loose-leaf) (Singapore: CCH, 1998), 7–101.

63. For a summary of and response to Macneil's scholarship on relational contract, see "Relational Contract Theory: Unanswered Questions; A Symposium in Honor of Ian R. Macneil," *Northwestern University Law Review* 94 (2000): 847.

20 From Security to Mobility?

Changing Aspects of Japanese Dismissal Law

RYŪICHI YAMAKAWA

I. INTRODUCTION

One of the most significant features of Japanese labor law lies in regulation of dismissals. With no specific statutory mandate, courts have established restrictions on the employer's right to dismiss workers.[1] This case law is consistent with the long-term employment—sometimes referred to as "lifetime employment"—that is one of the most distinctive aspects of traditional Japanese employment practices. As James Abegglen noted in 1958, Japanese employers emphasize maintaining their workers' employment even in economic crisis, while at the same time the workers commit themselves to their companies.[2] Thus, security in employment has been a key concept both in Japanese employment practices and in Japanese labor law.

For many years it has been debated whether Japanese employment practices would be faced by fundamental change. Although Japanese-style management became the object of praise in the 1970s and 1980s, the debate over whether employment practices would face fundamental change has been resurrected since the collapse of the "bubble" economy in the early 1990s. This time, predictions of the demise of the traditional Japanese practices have been far more widespread and intense. Indeed, journalistic publications cry out that Japanese employment practices are already a thing of the past.[3] In addition to the questions of whether and to what extent this is the correct description of the current situation, the question of whether the law of dismissals is also changing naturally arises.

Against this background, this chapter analyzes current trends in Japanese dismissal law. Section II describes the historical development of the case law regarding dismissals over the past half century and lays out the key features of Japanese law from a comparative viewpoint. Section III examines the relationship between legal standards—the law regulating dismissals—and Japanese employment practices, in view of the background of such practices including the control structure in Japanese corporations. Section III also briefly describes recent changes in these practices and the underlying assumptions. Section IV then introduces several new aspects in Japanese dismissal law that have developed in recent years as a result of recent socioeconomic changes. These new aspects include both developments in case law and in legislative/administrative measures, such as the recent amendment to the Labor Standards Act that codified case law regarding abusive dismissal. This chapter concludes by noting that Japanese labor law regarding dismissal is beginning to change, gradually recognizing the importance of the promotion of workers' employment opportunities in the external labor market in addition to security in employment in the internal labor market.

II. HISTORY OF JAPANESE DISMISSAL LAW

A. DISMISSAL UNDER THE CIVIL CODE

The Civil Code of Japan, enacted in 1896, contains several provisions relating to employment contracts. One of those provisions, Article 627, paragraph 1, states, "Each party to an employment contract without a fixed term may give notice of termination of the contract at any time. In such case, the contract shall be terminated two weeks after the notice is given." According to one drafter of the Civil Code, parties to an employment contract, in most cases, do not expect the employment relationship to continue permanently.[4] Thus, the drafters believed that although the parties should be provided with freedom to terminate the contract, the two weeks' notice requirement was necessary to avoid disadvantaging the other party in the case of sudden termination.[5]

Accordingly, under Article 627 of the Civil Code, an employment contract is supposed to be at will, since there are no restrictions on the reason for termination of the contract. Indeed, in 1924, one of the leading commentators on the Civil Code stated that this article provided the parties with the right to terminate the employment contract in order to prevent the parties from being unduly bound, even when no specific reason for termination exists.[6] This is true regardless of whether the employer or the employee is the party who terminates the contract. Therefore, under this provision and its prewar interpretation,[7] the employer had an almost unrestricted right to dismiss the employee.[8]

B. SEMINAL LIMITATIONS ON DISMISSAL: POSTWAR CASE LAW AND LEGISLATION

Shortly after World War II, however, statutory limitations on the employer's right of dismissal were enacted. First, Article 11 of the Trade Union Act of 1945 prohibited disadvantageous treatment, including dismissals, based on union membership or protected acts by trade unions.[9] Second, the Labor Standards Act, enacted in 1947, prohibited dismissals during the periods of leave given for pregnancy or for injuries that occurred in the course of employment and during the thirty-day period after such leave (Article 19). The Labor Standards Act also prohibited employers from discriminating with respect to working conditions, including dismissals, because of nationality, creed, or social status (Article 3). Furthermore, the latter law required employers to give thirty days' advance notice, as opposed to the fourteen days' notice required under the Civil Code, when discharging employees (Article 20). Still, these regulations were limited to dismissals based on specific reasons or were mere procedural requirements.

Nevertheless, in the early 1950s, when many employers discharged employees during the drive for business reorganization based on the policy called the "Dodge Line"[10] and during the recession that followed the end of the Korean War, courts began to tackle the issue of whether dismissals should be based on just cause. During this period, courts' views were split.

At first, a number of decisions maintained the position embodied in Article 627 of the Civil Code and held that employers could discharge workers without just cause.[11] Scholars noted that this was the prevailing view,[12] although some of these decisions acknowledged that it was possible for an employer's exercise of this right to dismiss to be abused and, thus, be illegal.[13] On the other hand, a few decisions emerged holding that an employer may lawfully discharge workers only for just cause, such as when the worker at issue does not contribute to the productivity of the enterprise or when the worker disrupts the order of the business entity (the just cause theory).[14]

Over time, however, an increasing number of lower court decisions came to regulate dismissals by relying on Article 1-3 of the Civil Code, which generally prohibits the abuse of private rights (the abusive dismissal theory). For example, one decision stated, "In light of the current situation where workers live almost solely on the income earned from employment, a dismissal without reasonable cause shall usually be an abuse of the right to dismiss, because, while it is relatively easy for employers to hire workers, workers face difficulty in obtaining jobs once they are discharged and are vulnerable to hardships."[15]

Although decisions that relied on the abusive dismissal theory represented the prevalent view by the mid-1950s, the specific content of this doctrine was not yet established at that time. Rather, there were considerable differences in opinion with regard to when a dismissal constituted an abuse of right. A number of decisions took the position that there was no abuse of the right to dismiss where a dismissal merely lacked just cause. For example, a lower court stated in 1956, "Although it is evident that the employer's right to discharge should not be abused, the dismissal need not be based on just cause. . . . The employer may lawfully discharge its workers because its suspicions, even if the facts on which those suspicions are based have not been demonstrated by evidence, endanger the trust and confidence of the employment relationship."[16] Thus, this court held that the abuse of the right to discharge may be established through the potential loss of confidential relationship regardless of the existence of just cause.

C. ESTABLISHMENT OF THE DOCTRINE OF ABUSIVE DISMISSAL

Around 1960, many courts began to apply the abusive dismissal theory more stringently. It has been pointed out that, interpreted in that manner, this doctrine hardly differed from the just cause theory.[17] Finally, after these lower court decisions had accumulated, the Supreme Court of Japan stated in 1975, "The exercise of the employer's right to dismiss shall be null and void as an abuse of right if the dismissal is not based on reasonable cause or is viewed as improper from the general viewpoint of society."[18] In 1977, the Supreme Court also held, "The employer may not always discharge workers even when there exists a fact that constitutes a reason for dismissal stipulated under work rules. If a dismissal is excessively unreasonable and impermissible from the viewpoint of general society, such a dismissal shall be null and void as an abuse of right."[19] Thus, case law established the doctrine of abusive dismissal.

Under this doctrine, courts have held a dismissal to be permissible only when (1) a worker is incapable of providing service, (2) a worker is incompetent or lacks ability to work, (3) a worker violates his or her job duties or is engaged in misconduct, (4) there is a compelling business necessity such as financial difficulties, or (5) a union shop agreement compels the employer to discharge a worker who leaves or is dispelled from the union.[20] Also, even when a worker lacks ability or violates job duties, courts have considered mitigating factors favorable to the worker or have required employers to take other less detrimental measures, such as transfers or demotions.

When a court finds a dismissal to be an abuse of the employer's right to dismiss, it will declare the dismissal to be null and void. As a result, the severance of the contractual relationship between the employer and the worker is declared to have never happened and the employment contract between the employer and the worker is restored. The conclusion of the judgment in such cases typically reads, "The court hereby declares that plaintiff has a position where he or she has rights under the employment contract." Although such a judgment merely affords declaratory relief, the employer is expected to reinstate the plaintiff.[21] Still, it is reported that actual reinstatement is difficult in practice, and even the plaintiffs who win their cases frequently leave their company (with a special retirement allowance) shortly after their reinstatement.[22]

D. RESTRICTION ON ECONOMIC DISMISSALS

When the case law regarding abusive dismissal began to develop, courts generally refrained from overruling an employer's decision to carry out economic dismissals. For example, a 1950 decision held that economic dismissals were not unfair even though the employer took no steps to find alternatives to dismissals, such as transfers or solicitation of voluntary retirement, and that the employer did not violate the principle of good faith even though the employer did not take care of the workers who became unemployed.[23]

However, as the doctrine of abusive dismissal developed, restrictions on economic dismissals gradually strengthened. One district court stated in 1966 that it is essential to consider workers' interests when determining the validity of economic dismissals, since the reasons on which the dismissals are based are within the control of the employer.[24] Among scholarly commentaries, there was a contention that, in order to carry out economic dismissal lawfully, the employer should satisfy three prerequisites. These were (1) the necessity of cutting the workforce in order to maintain profits as a business enterprise, (2) reasonableness in the selection of workers to be discharged, and (3) good-faith procedures in relation to the trade union.[25] This framework is quite similar to the "four-requirement" doctrine that developed later and is explained below.

Nevertheless, the framework for evaluating the validity of economic dismissals was not yet established at this time, since some courts maintained a lenient attitude, deferring to the employer's judgment with regard to reductions-in-force. For example, one court stated in 1965 that the employer has the discretion to decide how many workers should be reduced, how to reduce the workforce, and how the workers to be dismissed should be selected. Furthermore, the court held that a mistake in the application of the selection standards did not automatically render the dismissal unlawful.[26]

A new development occurred after the first oil crisis hit the Japanese economy in 1973. At this time, the courts developed a framework called the "four-requirement" test for determining the validity of economic dismissals. According to this framework, the employer must satisfy four requirements in order to lawfully carry out economic dismissals. The employer needed to establish the existence of (1) a necessity for a reduction-in-force; (2) a good-faith effort to avoid dismissals through other methods, such as transfers, temporary plant closings, solicitations of voluntary retirement, and so on; (3) a reasonable standard for selecting workers to be discharged and the fair application thereof; and (4) a procedural effort to explain to and obtain the understanding of the trade union or workers regarding the necessity of and steps for economic dismissals.[27]

Although questions remained regarding the precise contents of the "four requirements,"[28] a large number of lower court decisions adopted this framework,[29] and this approach became established case law doctrine. Since its establishment, there has been a bit of fluctuation in the application of this doctrine. This is especially true with respect to the requirement of the necessity for reduction-in-force. In some cases, the courts' intervention in the employers' business judgment appears to have been unnecessary. In one case, for instance, a district court held that economic dismissals brought about by the closing of a maintenance department that continually had suffered from deficits was unlawful. The court asserted that the employer should have avoided hastily closing the department totally without attempting to transfer employees or should have proposed voluntary retirement.[30]

E. FEATURES OF JAPANESE DISMISSAL LAW

As described above, Japanese law has developed comprehensive limitations on the exercise of the employer's right to dismissal. Limitations such as these exist in most industrialized countries, with the notable exception of the United States, where the doctrine of employment at-will basically remains in force. It must be noted that, unlike European countries, Japan's limitations on dismissals were established via case law rather than by statute. In other words, as Professor Daniel Foote has pointed out, the judiciary created the Japanese dismissal law.[31]

With respect to the contents of restriction on dismissals, Japan and European countries share much common ground. For example, the circumstances that may justify dismissals are expressed through general and abstract terms, such as "reasonable cause" or "permissible from the viewpoint of general society" in Japan, "socially justified (*sozial gerechtfertigt*)" in Germany, and "real and serious reasons" (*les causes réelles et sérieuses*) in France.[32]

However, when we look closely, there are some differences in the substance of the permissible reasons for dismissals. This is especially the case with regard to the degree of judicial intervention in the employer's business judgment in the case of economic dismissals. In Germany, for example, economic dismissals are socially justified if it is impossible for the employer to retain the workers because of compelling business necessity. Although compelling business necessity is required, courts have deferred to the employer's business judgment as to whether or not to take particular organizational measures, unless the judgment is clearly unreasonable.[33] Likewise, in the United Kingdom, where redundancy is one of the reasons that may justify dismissals,[34] courts do not interfere with the employer's right to decide the size, scope, and direction of enterprises, so long as the redundancy actually exists.[35]

Unlike the situation in these countries, it is notable that, as stated above, the necessity for reduction-in-force is subject to judicial review under the "four-requirement" test in Japan. Indeed, there are cases where courts have substituted their judgment for that of the employer regarding such matters as the timing of the closing of the department.[36] Although the number of such cases may not be large, the Japanese courts show less deference to the employer's judgment than do courts in Germany and the United Kingdom.

On the other hand, procedural regulations regarding dismissals are scarce under Japanese labor law. In many other countries, employers are required to exhaust certain procedures in order to carry out dismissals. In Germany, for example, employers must generally obtain the opinion of the works council before discharging workers. In the case of economic dismissals, it is necessary to conduct consultation with the works council and to codetermine the "social plan" to provide compensation for the affected workers.[37] In France, employers are required to conduct an interview with the worker in the case of individual dismissals, while consultation with the workers' representative is necessary in the case of economic dismissal. This is also true in England, where employers have a duty to consult with the workers' representatives when they discharge twenty or more workers for economic reasons.

To be sure, procedural fairness is considered in Japan under the "four-requirement" test in the event of economic dismissal. Still, the content of the procedural requirement, which is described generally as a good-faith effort to obtain the understanding of workers, is abstract in comparison with the obligation to consult in other countries. This may be because the restriction on dismissal in Japan has developed through case law. Since each case is decided on its own facts, it may be difficult for the court to formulate generally applicable procedural steps for employers to follow.

With respect to remedies for unlawful dismissals, one of the unique features of Japanese law is that courts declare such dismissals null and void. Such declaratory judgments assume that the employment contract remains intact and that the defendant has an obligation to treat the plaintiff as an employee. Although the plaintiff is entitled to back pay as well as compensatory damages for the emotional distress in certain cases, he or she cannot choose payment of damages rather than payment of lost wages without contesting the validity of dismissal. In other countries, monetary relief is the ordinary remedy for an unlawful dismissal, regardless of the availability of reinstatement under statutory law. In actuality, however, reinstatement is rarely successful in Japan. As noted above, in practice, even workers who win their cases often leave the employer.[38]

Another problem relating to remedies for unlawful dismissal is the need for effective dispute resolution systems. The number of civil labor and employment cases filed with the district courts was 3,120 in 2002, including both ordinary cases and preliminary injunction cases.[39] Among these, 1,013 were cases contesting the validity of a termination of employment including dismissals.[40] The number of such cases almost tripled since 1990, probably due to the increase in employment disputes in the course of the recession. However, Japanese courts are not easily accessible in labor and employment cases when compared with courts in other countries. In Germany, for example, the number of cases filed with the labor courts is far larger, amounting to about 570,000 in 1999.[41]

Thus, in recent years, several proposals have been made for the improvement of the dispute resolution processes in labor and employment cases, and some of those proposals have been implemented. One of the most important changes was the enactment of the Individual Labor Dispute Resolution Act in October 2001. This law created a comprehensive administrative dispute consultation/resolution system for employment disputes. Another notable change under this act was the establishment of the Dispute Adjustment Commissions. These commissions are a neutral and independent administrative agency in charge of the resolution of employment disputes through conciliation (mediation with respect to disputes under the Equal Employment Opportunity Act).

In addition, in 2004 the Diet passed the Employment Tribunal Act, which creates a new judicial proceeding (Employment Tribunal Proceeding) for resolving employment disputes. Under this proceeding, an Employment Tribunal Commission, composed of one professional judge and two lay members with expertise and experience in labor and employment relations, is to render an award after no more than three hearing days. If either party files an objection to the award, the proceeding will automatically move to ordinary litigation.

Of course, the lack of accessibility of judicial or administrative forum is not the only reason for the small number of labor and employment claims. Where the long-term employment and seniority-based wage systems prevail, it is difficult for a worker to sue his or her employer while continuing to work, because such action will often disrupt their relationship and result in unfavorable treatment. Even in cases involving dismissals where the relationship is already terminated, some workers may find it difficult to obtain new employment opportunities because they may gain a reputation as "difficult" by suing the former employer.[42] Still, in view of the large number of cases that went to the consultation procedure under the Individual Labor Dispute Resolution Act,[43] it is likely that the number of dismissal cases will increase at least to a certain extent, if the disputes can be resolved in a quick and inexpensive manner.

III. BACKGROUND OF JAPANESE DISMISSAL LAW

Each country's labor law is closely related to the labor market and the employment practices of the country. This is especially true where, as in Japan, the regulation of dismissal has developed through case law. This section contains a brief description of Japanese employment practices as well as an analysis of their relationship with Japanese labor law, especially with respect to dismissal.

A. JAPANESE EMPLOYMENT PRACTICES

1. *Overview*

The two main features of the employment practices of Japan are long-term employment and seniority-based wages. Although the ongoing changes to these practices will be introduced and evaluated later, this section will begin by discussing those practices as they have developed so far.

In the Japanese practice of long-term employment, mandatory retirement at the age of sixty has played an important role. Mandatory retirement means that workers are assured employment until the set retirement age, although the existence of this system does not mean that employers may not discharge workers or that workers may not resign before reaching the set age. Still, at least in recent years, workers have found it difficult to remain until the retirement age in the companies that they entered after graduating from schools. Workers are often farmed out to subsidiaries or affiliated companies.[44] Thus, although they do not necessarily remain in the same company throughout their careers, long-term employment is maintained by assuring employment within the group of related companies. In this sense, it is true that employers in Japan have tried to maintain employment security and avoid dismissals, while making flexible use of the workforce through transfers, farming out, and overtime work.

The second main characteristic of Japanese employment practices, seniority-based wages, does not necessarily imply that the amount of wages is determined directly based on the age or years of service of workers. Since the 1970s, many companies, at least large- and medium-sized companies, have determined workers' base wages according to a job-related grade classification system (*shokunō shikaku seido*). Under this system, workers are classified on the basis of their ability. However, "ability" is often defined in general terms, such as "the ability to supervise and train rank-and-file workers," with little relationship to the specific duties for each job. Such classifications are useful in transferring workers among different jobs, because the transfers do not require a change in base wages, so long as the worker remains in the same grade. However, these ambiguous, nonspecific criteria make it difficult to differentiate between workers' abilities so that, in practice, the classifications tend to be based on seniority rather than job-related ability. Therefore, ultimately, even under the classification system, wages tend to rise with seniority.

It must also be noted that long-term employment and seniority-based wages apply only to regular workers who conclude employment contracts without fixed terms. Atypical workers, such as part-timers and workers with fixed-term contracts, have been excluded from these long-term employment practices. Rather, they have functioned as a "buffer" for periods when employers have needed to reduce their workforces. Employers have often terminated these workers before discharging regular workers.

2. *Background of Japanese System*

There has been a debate about the historical origins of Japanese employment practices, especially long-term employment. Some argue that these practices can be traced back to the Edo era, when head clerks of large merchant families served their masters for decades.[45] Those who share this view often emphasize the influence of Japanese culture, such as loyalty to the organization.[46]

On the other hand, the more prevalent view is that the typical Japanese employment pattern began when heavy industries in Japan started to develop in the first few decades of this century.[47] Before that, the turnover rate of Japanese workers was quite high, as compared with the postwar period.[48] Indeed, a Japanese engineer who had work experience in the United States commented in 1901 that Japanese workers with some education preferred not to remain in one company and instead moved from one job to another.[49] In response, large companies began to implement schemes to provide economic incentives designed to keep workers from leaving,[50] although long-term employment did not take root because of the recession around the 1920s.[51]

Whatever their historical origin, Japanese employment practices were "established" or came to be accepted widely during the period of economic growth after World War II.[52] The turnover rate of Japanese workers sharply declined during this period even as compared with the 1930s, when the Japanese practices were developing.[53]

Many factors contributed to the background for the establishment of modern Japanese employment practices.[54] These include stable economic growth during the postwar period, a need to train employees within the company, a population structure where young workers were abundant, bitter experiences with violent strikes in the 1950s, and other factors. However, what appears to have played an especially important role in the development of the modern employment practices is the structure of control or "corporate governance" in Japanese companies.[55]

Under the Commercial Code of Japan,[56] stockholders have the right to control their corporation, as is the case in the United States. However, at least in the case of large, publicly traded corporations, most stockholders in Japan have not been enthusiastic in exercising their right to control. One reason for such behavior lies in the structure of stockholding in Japanese companies. In Japan, it has been quite common for large companies that routinely do business with each other to own each other's stock (cross-stockholding). When such cross-stockholding evolves among the banks from which the companies obtain long-term credit, these banks become so-called main banks for the corporations. The purpose of the cross-stockholding is to build a long-term, stable relationship rather than to gain short-term profit.

This pattern of stockholding developed after World War II against the background of the dissolution of large financial combines as well as the corporations' policy of protecting themselves from hostile takeovers.[57] At the beginning of the twentieth century, in contrast, Japanese corporations were far more "capitalistic" or stockholder-oriented.[58] In 1930, a leading economist at that time complained that the "short-sighted tyranny" and "greed for fat dividends" on the part of stockholders had considerably weakened the stable development of enterprises.[59]

The structure of control in Japanese corporations during the postwar period apparently influenced the behavior of their directors. Generally speaking, directors in modern Anglo-American corporations are the "agents" of the stockholders and are supposed to prioritize the stockholders' interests over the interests of other stakeholders such as employees.[60] However, where stockholders are not interested in exercising their right to control a corporation, directors enjoy wide discretion and autonomy in administering the corporation. In this situation, directors are likely to consider their own interests and the interests of other stakeholders in the company, especially their employees. This is especially true when directors (including presidents) are promoted up from managerial employees' positions, as is often the case in Japanese corporations.

Corporations that have such a structure, as opposed to those that are actively controlled by stockholders, tend to become a sort of "employees' community," typified by a cooperative relationship between labor and management (figure 20.1).[61] This "employee community" model accounts for various aspects of Japanese corporate systems, including the practice of long-term employment. Although multiple factors may have contributed to the development of long-term employment, this practice fits the mind-set of Japanese management, since it benefits both the management and employees. As a matter of course, long-term employment assures security in employment for the employees. Long-term employment also benefits management because it (coupled with seniority-based wage systems) contributes to the stable development or the long-term profits of the corporation by providing incentives for employees to accumulate firm-specific skills that are valuable to the corporation.[62]

The seniority-based wage system is also consistent with Japanese corporate behavior, based on the structure of control in Japanese corporations. Seniority-based wage increases reflect the workers' increasing contributions

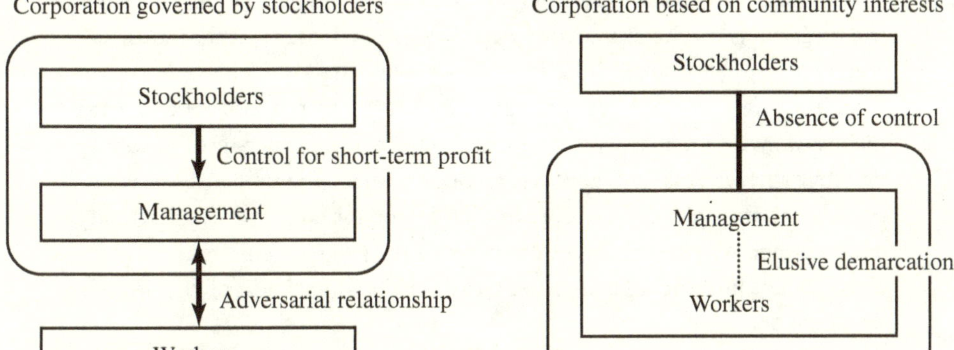

FIGURE 20.1. Two Models of Worker-Management Relations

to the corporation through the development of ability in the course of employment, and workers tend to remain in their corporations until they receive increased wages. In addition, the seniority-based wage system is also beneficial to workers because it serves the workers' financial needs in their life cycle.

B. RELATIONSHIP OF EMPLOYMENT PRACTICES TO DISMISSAL LAW

It is apparent that the employment systems adopted by Japanese corporations have had much influence on Japanese labor and employment law. One of the most significant examples is the case-law limitation on the exercise of the employer's right to dismiss.[63] It is often difficult for discharged workers to find comparable new employment opportunities. This situation becomes more serious in a labor market where the long-term employment system prevails.[64] Furthermore, even when the discharged worker can find a new position, his or her income usually decreases because of the loss of seniority, in a system in which seniority plays a major role in the determination of wages. Thus, given the Japanese employment practices, there is an increased need to restrict unjust dismissals. Since one of the important contributing factors to Japanese employment practices, including long-term employment, is the structure of corporate control in Japan, it is safe to say that such structure of control has exerted an influence on the shaping of Japanese labor law regarding dismissals.[65]

Of course, the Japanese employment practices are not the only basis for the limitations on the employer's right to dismissal. Many other industrialized countries have such limitations, and the International Labor Organization, in Convention No. 158, has called for the protection of workers from dismissals without just cause. Indeed, despite the influence of Japanese employment systems on dismissal law, courts have not required plaintiff workers who contest dismissals to prove that defendant employers had actually adopted such systems. Thus, the existence of the Japanese employment practices has not become a legal prerequisite for the application of the abusive dismissal doctrine.

Nevertheless, the fact that the restrictions on dismissals developed in the form of case law can be best explained by the influence of the Japanese employment practices. For the judiciary to develop case law regulation inconsistent with a statutory provision, the social norm or custom that serves as a basis for such regulation must be firmly established and acknowledged in the society. In the case of the doctrine of abusive dismissal, employment security had become such a strong social norm that it effectively overrode the principle of at-will employment embodied in Article 627 of the Civil Code.

This explanation is buttressed by the historical development of the abusive dismissal doctrine. Decisions relying on the prohibition of abuse of rights in order to restrict unjust dismissals appeared soon after World War II, when the condition of the labor market was quite poor because of the devastated economy and confusion after the war. At that time, however, there were also a number of decisions that maintained the principle of at-will employment. Even as the number of decisions adopting the abuse-of-rights theory increased, the contents of the restriction, that is, the criteria for determining when the exercise of the right to dismissal constitutes abuse of the employer's right, were not firmly established. It was not until well after 1950 that this doctrine was established. At that time, the condition of the labor market in Japan had improved dramatically and the unemployment rate was remarkably low.[66] As stated above, the Japanese employment systems developed mainly after 1950. It is not simply coincidental that the abuse-of-right doctrine developed during the same period.

This is also true with respect to the restriction on economic dismissals. Against the background of the long-term employment system, Japanese employers have tended to avoid dismissals by relying on other means of reducing labor costs or utilizing human resources as efficiently as possible, even when their business has suffered from financial loss. This attitude contrasts sharply with that of employers in the United States (figure 20.2). Generally

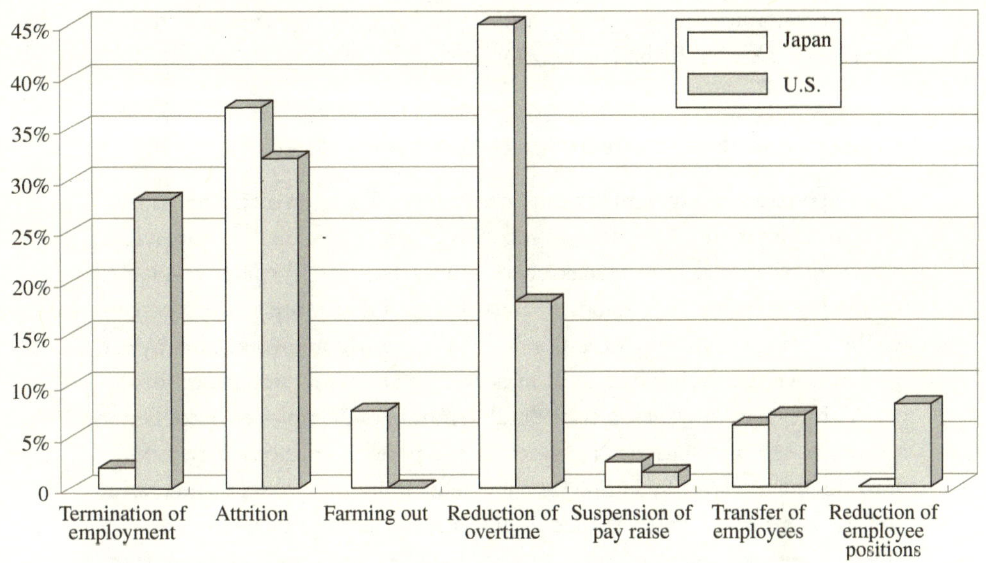

FIGURE 20.2. Most Likely Measures to Reduce Labor Costs
SOURCE: Ministry of International Trade and Industry, Nichibei no kigyō kōdō hikaku chōsa [Comparative Japan–US Survey of Corporate Behavior] (1988).

speaking, employers in the United States are more likely to carry out dismissals than Japanese employers as a means to reduce labor costs when their business is suffering.

Where, as in Japan, employers respect the security of employment, it is natural for courts to review closely the employer's judgment concerning the necessity for reduction-in-force or the effort to avoid dismissals. Indeed, it has been pointed out that the so-called four-requirement test established in case law in the late 1970s was influenced by the general pattern of measures for reducing labor costs undertaken by large Japanese companies after the first oil crisis in 1973.[67]

The policy emphasizing employment security has been reflected not only in case law but also in statutory law. Under the scheme of *koyō chōsei josei kin* (subsidies for employment adjustment) provided under the Employment Insurance Act, employers in financial crisis can receive subsidies from the Employment Insurance Fund if they intend to avoid economic dismissals through such measures as temporary closing of factories, farming out of employees, and so on, in cooperation with the workers' representative (such as the majority union).[68] This scheme, the purpose of which is the prevention of economic dismissals, was introduced in 1974, after the Japanese employment practices already had taken root.

C. CHANGES IN BACKGROUND CIRCUMSTANCES

That Japanese employment systems are changing has been oft noted. Indeed, the unemployment rate reached a record high 5.5 percent in November 2001. Many employers are actively seeking to reduce labor costs. A survey conducted by the Japan Institute of Labor in 2002 reported that more than 50 percent of the 1,683 companies who responded to the questionnaire had already carried out, were carrying out, or at least were planning reductions-in-force.[69]

With respect to wages, a considerable number of employers have begun to change seniority-based wage systems into performance-based systems by introducing the so-called annual salary determination system or increasing the importance of performance appraisals in making salary adjustments. According to a survey conducted by Shakai Keizai Seisansei Honbu (Japan Productivity Center for Socio-economic Development), 34.8 percent of the companies that employ one thousand or more workers utilized an annual salary determination system in 2001, up from 25.2 percent the previous year.[70]

Furthermore, regular-worker positions, which enjoy the security of Japanese employment practices, are decreasing and are being replaced by atypical or non-regular workers, such as part-timers and workers who conclude fixed-term employment contracts. According to the Rōdōryoku Chōsa (Labor Force Survey), atypical workers accounted for 27.2 percent of all employees in 2001.[71] While such workers have much more mobility in the labor market, most such workers lie outside the protection of long-term employment practices as well as the abusive dismissal doctrine.[72] In addition, many of these workers are women and the elderly who do not wish to obtain the position of regular worker, which is accompanied by duties to work overtime or the possibility of being transferred to distant workplaces. For such workers, promoting employment opportunities in the external labor market is especially important.

A number of factors have precipitated these changes. Among these are the decade-long recession after the collapse of the "bubble economy" and the difficulty in maintaining seniority-based wage systems when the workforce is aging. However, in light of the assumption that the absence of stockholders' control in corporate governance has played an important role for the establishment of Japanese employment practices, it is necessary to ask whether this structure is also changing.

In recent years, the ratio of cross-stockholding has been declining. In 1987, the ratio of cross-stockholding was 18.39 percent; by 2001, it had declined to 8.9 percent.[73] Although the ratio of stable stockholders such as banks or other related companies is still high, at 33 percent, this ratio too has also been declining.[74] Also, foreign stockholders are increasing remarkably. The percentage of stock held by foreign shareholders increased from 3.6 percent in 1987 to 18.3 percent in 2001.[75] Thus, it is often noted that stockholders in Japan are beginning to exercise control over their corporations. In reflection of this view, a recent survey by the Ministry of Finance reported that an increasing number of institutional investors are becoming more active in exercising their stockholder rights.[76]

At present, however, many stockholders do not yet actively exercise their right to control corporations. Although presidents and directors are beginning to recognize the importance of the "sovereignty" of stockholders, there have been no drastic changes in the practical reality of corporate governance in Japan.[77] According to a recent survey of directors of large corporations, 85.8 percent of the respondents thought that the corporation should be managed reflecting the views of various stakeholders, not limited to stockholders.[78] At present, most stockholders appear to be more interested in selling their stock in the market rather than in controlling directors in order to gain profit. Thus, the employee-centered as opposed to the stockholder-centered view of corporate governance still continues as an important background condition for employment practices.[79] Similarly, many employers, even while carrying out changes in the seniority-based wage systems, still assume that long-term employment is the norm, although they recognize the need for some modifications.[80] Such an attitude of Japanese employers is shown in their selection of measures for reductions-in-force. Although many employers have been carrying out some forms of reduction-in-force, they prefer to achieve these reductions through attrition, decreased recruiting, or solicitation of voluntary retirement, rather than through dismissals.[81]

Still, Japanese companies are struggling to restructure themselves in order to survive in competition in the global market. In order to maintain profitability, many companies are now moving their manufacturing plants to other Asian countries such as China. Also, business reorganization has become quite common, with frequent mergers and transfers of business. The division of corporation, a new measure of business reorganization, was introduced under an amendment to the Commercial Code in 2000.[82] Through these reorganization measures, employers select profitable or promising departments and concentrate their resources on them, while selling or spinning off other depart ments. Furthermore, corporations are now taking seriously the evaluation of their profitability in the capital market. This is especially true because many large Japanese corporations are now relying on stocks or bonds rather than loans from banks for financing. Thus, employers in Japan appear to attach more importance than ever to the profitability of the corporation.[83]

In response to these recent developments, Japanese labor law has undergone several important changes in recent years.[84] In 1999, the amendment of the Worker Dispatching Act relaxed the limitations on permissible jobs for worker dispatching in response to the increasing demand for atypical employment.[85] When, as stated above, the Commercial Code was amended to introduce the scheme of the division of corporation, the Labor Contract Succession Act was enacted in order to balance the need for smooth implementation of the corporate division against the protection of workers involved in such a process.[86] However, despite the significance of these reforms, the core of Japanese labor law has not yet seen any major changes.[87] With respect to dismissal law, courts have maintained the doctrine of abusive dismissal and have invalidated a number of dismissals. Still, several aspects of dismissal law indicate that gradual changes are beginning to take place. Section IV explores such changes.

IV. CHANGING ASPECTS OF JAPANESE DISMISSAL LAW

A. EMPLOYMENT CONTRACTS SPECIFYING JOB CONTENTS

Under the abusive dismissal doctrine, as stated earlier, courts review not only whether there is a reasonable ground for the dismissal but also whether it is socially appropriate to discharge the worker under the facts of each case. Even when workers are found to be incompetent in their assigned positions, their dismissal may still constitute an abuse of right if there are less drastic, alternative measures available, such as demotion or transfer.[88] In other words, as in the case of economic dismissals, the employer should make a reasonable effort to avoid dismissals.

However, several decisions have recently held that such efforts are not necessary under certain circumstances. Most notably, this is the case with workers who conclude an employment contract that limits their duties to specific jobs or positions. For example, in a case where the employer (a subsidiary of a U.S. corporation) hired a plaintiff via an executive search firm as a senior manager of the human resource management department and later discharged him because of incompetence, the Tokyo High Court upheld the dismissal.[89] The court stated that, in such a case, it suffices for the court to determine whether the plaintiff is incompetent for the specific job for which he was employed and that the employer is not required to consider transfers or a demotion to lower positions.[90] A similar result was reached in a case involving the dismissal of a professional employee.[91]

Workers who conclude an employment contract that limits their duties to specific jobs or positions need not obey the employer's order of transfer. At the same time, such workers usually receive considerably higher salaries than ordinary workers for the specific job that they are supposed to perform under the employment contract. Since they are in a different situation than ordinary workers in Japan, it is natural to apply a different standard to determine the validity of the dismissal for such workers. It must be noted, however, that in the cases described above, the employers made some efforts to avoid the dismissal by issuing warnings and giving the plaintiffs the opportunity to improve their performance. Thus, these cases imply that the employers still have a duty to make some effort to avoid dismissals even where the worker is specialized.

B. *ÄNDERUNGSKÜNDIGUNG*: CONDITIONAL DISMISSAL

Änderungskündigung is a term under German labor law that means a dismissal because of a worker's refusal to accept proposed changes in working conditions. The dismissal is conditional because the employer does not carry it out if the employee accepts the proposal. Thus, its purpose is to obtain changes in working conditions rather than the termination of the contract itself. In Japan, however, the employer may unilaterally change working conditions under certain circumstances. For example, the employer may change workers' job contents or places of work via transfer orders.[92] In addition, by unilaterally revising work rules, the employer may change collective working conditions, such as wage standards, provided that such revisions are "reasonable."[93]

Therefore, Japanese employers rarely need to discharge workers who do not accept changes in working conditions. Nevertheless, in cases, for example, where the employment contract specifies a worker's job contents or place of work, it may become necessary for the employer to make use of conditional dismissal. Conditional dismissals may also become necessary in cases where the revision of work rules does not fulfill the requirement of "reasonableness" needed for a unilateral change of work rules by the employer.

In a 1995 case,[94] workers for Scandinavian Airlines contested the validity of conditional dismissals. The employer had proposed that some of the employees change their positions from those specified in their contracts and that the term of their employment contracts be revised to a one-year fixed term. The employees refused and the employer discharged them. The Tokyo District Court upheld the dismissals and laid out the criteria for evaluating the validity of a conditional dismissal. According to the court, a conditional dismissal is lawful if (1) the change in the working conditions at issue is essential for the employer's business; (2) the necessity for the change overrides the disadvantages the workers may suffer from it, so that the dismissal of those who refused the proposal for the change is inevitable; and (3) the employer made a good-faith effort to avoid the dismissal.[95]

A key element in the background to this decision was the fact that the employment contract limited the plaintiffs' jobs to specific positions, prohibiting the employer from unilaterally ordering transfers. Also, the employer could not force employees, even through the revision of work rules, to accept a fixed-term employment contract when they had already concluded a contract without fixed term, because the fixed-term contract is not protected from termination under the abusive dismissal doctrine. Thus, the criteria of the Tokyo District Court decision may not apply to cases where a worker's position is not specified in the contract or where the employer may change working conditions unilaterally.

Furthermore, there is a criticism that conditional dismissals will effectively compel the workers to choose to accept the employer's proposal for changes in working conditions, because workers who face such a choice will not be able to take the risk of being discharged for refusing the proposal. Indeed, after the Scandinavian Airlines case, the Osaka District Court rendered a decision invalidating a conditional dismissal.[96] This court expressed concern about compelling employees to make a decision between dismissal and changed conditions and stated that the conditional dismissal should be subject to the same strict scrutiny as economic dismissal. The Scandinavian Airlines case itself was settled before the higher court could render a decision.

Nevertheless, a number of scholars maintain that conditional dismissals should be permitted in certain appropriate circumstances. Under the influence of German legislation, some propose that a worker may continue to work after the employer gives notice of the conditional dismissal through a temporary acceptance of the employer's proposal.[97] In such a case, the worker maintains the employment relationship until the courts determine the reasonableness of the proposal.

Both conditional and economic dismissals are means by which management can reduce labor costs. In Japan, both require a showing of business necessity. In a sense, the conditional dismissal is a modified form of economic dismissal in that the employer's proposal for the new working conditions can be regarded as one of the efforts to avoid dismissal. As the contents of the employment contract in Japan become more diversified because of the diversification of the labor market and the individualization of personnel management, it will become more difficult for the employer to change working conditions unilaterally. Thus, in the future, employers may need to rely on conditional dismissals more and more heavily. If the problem of the "forced choice" described above can be resolved through legislative measures or interpretation of the current law, the conditional dismissal may become an instrument that can help strike a balance between the workers' need for employment security and the employers' need to change working conditions based on fluctuating business conditions.

C. CURRENT CASE LAW ON ECONOMIC DISMISSALS

As stated earlier, case law after the first oil crisis established the framework called the "four-requirement" test with respect to economic dismissals.[98] Under this framework, economic dismissals or layoffs are permitted only after the court has established (1) the necessity of a reduction-in-force, (2) the employer's good-faith effort to avoid dismissals through other methods to reduce labor costs, (3) the reasonableness of the standard used to select workers to be discharged, and (4) the existence of adequate procedural effort to explain to and obtain the understanding of the trade union or workers regarding the necessity of the economic dismissals and the steps taken for the economic dismissals. In the past few years, however, several decisions by the Tokyo District Court challenged this framework, thereby giving rise to a heated discussion.[99]

One of the most debated decisions was rendered in the Westminster Bank case.[100] This decision expressly renounced the four-requirement test, stating that the determination of whether a dismissal amounts to an abuse of the employer's right must be based on a consideration of the totality of circumstances in each case and that the four "requirements" are merely typical factors to be considered in that determination.[101] Although not so drastic, other decisions have also indicated an understanding that the four requirements are not "requirements" in the strict sense but merely "factors."[102] If these are regarded only as factors, an economic dismissal can be lawful even when the court cannot find one of the factors, whereas under the traditional interpretation, a dismissal becomes automatically unlawful if even one of the requirements is not fulfilled.

These recent developments regarding economic dismissal are due in part to the fact that the specific contents of the traditional four-requirement test, including the precise meaning of the term *requirement*, have not been fully explored. More importantly, however, these decisions reflect changes in the situation surrounding economic dismissals. As described above, employers in Japan are presently busy restructuring their corporations in order to become more competitive. One of the most prevalent measures for such restructuring is the reorganization of corporations, including the closing of unprofitable departments and the concentration of resources into more promising departments. The Westminster Bank case was one such case. In that case, the employer, a Japanese branch of a foreign-based bank, decided to close its trade finance department because of its dim prospects and discharged the plaintiff, who specialized in trade finance and had been working in that department. The Tokyo District Court held that the employer's business judgment to close the department should be respected and that a reduction-in-force is inevitable in such a case, whether or not the corporation is suffering from financial crisis.[103] This view can also be seen in other cases involving the closing of unprofitable departments.[104]

Thus, recent court decisions have shown considerable deference to the employer's business judgment in the context of restructuring. This indicates that judges are aware of the current trends and changes in Japan's economy. If so, the difference in the framework for determining the validity of economic dismissals is not as significant as it appears to be, because, even under the traditional four-requirement test, courts may defer to the employer's business judgment, and they have sometimes done so when determining whether there is a necessity for the reduction-in-force.[105] Thus, the "four-factor" test and the "four-requirement" test may lead to similar results. Indeed, many of the decisions after the Westminster Bank case appear to have returned to the traditional framework in most respects. Although these decisions take the position that the so-called four requirements are merely factors used to determine whether an economic dismissal is an abuse of the employer's right, they focus on the four factors in the same manner as they did under the traditional framework.[106]

Theoretically, even under the traditional framework, the "requirements" should really be characterized as "factors," since under certain circumstances these requirements may become unnecessary or be replaced by other relevant factors.[107] Again, the situation in the Westminster Bank case provides an illustration. The plaintiff was an assistant manager of the defendant's trade finance department, which was to be closed down, and the Tokyo District

Court found that it would have been difficult for the defendant to transfer the plaintiff to other departments, because the comparable positions in other departments required expertise for specific job duties and the only available position was a clerical one, for which the salary was much lower than what the plaintiff was earning. Under these circumstances, the court ruled that the dismissal of plaintiff was lawful, considering, among other things, that the defendant made a good-faith effort to maintain the plaintiff's livelihood by paying a considerable premium for retirement allowance and assisting in the plaintiff's job search by providing for outplacement services with no time limit and free of charge.[108]

Thus, the court in the Westminster Bank case effectively replaced the factor of a "good-faith effort to avoid dismissal" with a "good-faith effort to maintain the worker's livelihood and to make accommodations to aid in his or her job search," in cases where transfers are not a feasible means of avoiding economic dismissals. With the increase of corporate restructuring with corporations streamlining by closing unprofitable departments, it is likely that it will become more difficult for employers to transfer redundant workers to other available positions or to find other means of avoiding dismissals.

Moreover, transfers are not always beneficial for workers. Transfers may sometimes require workers to move to other locations or to perform new duties that are different from what they have done. In these cases, it may be better for the worker to find a new employment opportunity, if the employer makes a good-faith effort to minimize the worker's loss as exemplified in the Westminster Bank case. In this sense, although the traditional four requirements are still the main factors to be considered in the case of economic dismissals, it may sometimes be appropriate and necessary to consider other factors.

D. RECENT DISCUSSIONS AND LEGISLATION ON DISMISSAL LAW

In recent years, discussion of dismissal law has been quite lively.[109] In addition to the recent developments in the case law described above, there have been several proposals for legislation regulating dismissals. However, there are two different viewpoints among the proponents of the legislation.

On the one hand, some commentators argue that legislative measures are necessary so that employers can carry out dismissals, especially economic dismissals, more easily in appropriate cases. They reason that the present, judicially established dismissal standards lack predictability about which dismissals are lawful. This inflexible law, they argue, deters companies from creating new employment opportunities, because of the difficulty in discharging workers when the need arises.[110] Meanwhile, other proponents of new legislation contend that it is necessary to have statutory provisions establishing the principle of protection from dismissals without just cause and strengthening the procedural regulation of dismissals through measures such as requiring joint consultation with trade unions.[111]

In connection with the discussion on legislation, economists and labor law scholars have begun to reexamine the necessity of regulating dismissals. Economists are discussing whether it is possible to justify the prohibition of unjust dismissals by relying on the "incomplete contract theory." Those who favor dismissal regulation contend that, under this theory, regulation is necessary to prevent opportunistic dismissals that allow the employer to escape the contractual obligation to pay workers more wages as the workers accumulate skills.[112] Opponents of this view counter that courts are incapable of enforcing such regulation because they cannot determine whether the worker has fulfilled his or her obligations.[113]

Apparently stimulated by the discussion among economists, labor law scholars too are discussing the normative basis for regulating dismissals. Some rely on the traditional view that such regulation is necessary to guarantee the workers' right to maintain minimum standards of living and right to work (set forth in Articles 25 and 27 of the Constitution), in view of the special nature of the employment contract.[114] Meanwhile, others have introduced new arguments. These include the need to protect workers' expectations for the maintenance of the continuing employment relationship,[115] as well as for preventing the loss of the workers' opportunity for self-realization through working.[116]

Even though these new views are appealing, the traditional view still appears most viable, if one considers the fact that, for the majority of workers, their bargaining power vis-à-vis the employer is relatively weak even today. This is because the nature of employment is such that the worker cannot save his or her time for working in order to sell later at higher prices, with the result that he or she often cannot help but conclude an employment contract under unfavorable conditions. Moreover, in the context of dismissal, it is often difficult for the worker, once discharged, to find comparable employment opportunities in the labor market.

Notwithstanding the debate over the necessity for dismissal regulation from the economic point of view, labor law scholars are generally in agreement about the necessity of legislative measures. However, it appears difficult to guarantee predictability regarding the validity of dismissals. As in other measures for personnel management, the validity of dismissals depends on various factors in each case. It will do more harm than good to create mechanical rules. Thus, one of the best alternatives is to enact a provision declaring the principle that unjust dismissals are prohibited and to create guidelines or a code of practice that illustrates typical fact patterns to exemplify whether a given dismissal is lawful or unlawful.[117] Although such a code of practice would not itself be binding on the judiciary, courts may in actuality rely on it unless circumstances in a given case necessitate deviation. A code of practice that is similar to this proposal is already functioning in the United Kingdom regarding the procedures for dismissals.[118]

Another proposal for new legislation addresses remedies for unjust dismissals. As stated earlier, at present, a dismissal that constitutes an abuse of the employer's right becomes null and void under the abusive dismissal doctrine. Although workers in such cases are generally entitled to back pay for the periods when they could not work, the dismissed worker is required to contest the validity of the dismissal.[119] In other words, the worker may not concede that the dismissal is valid and ask only for monetary remedies. Since reinstatement is often not a practical option, some scholars call for a legislative provision that gives workers a right to choose monetary remedies.[120] In addition to these proposals addressing clarification of dismissal law and remedies, there have been other proposals regarding dismissal procedures and the burdens of proof in court procedures.[121]

After much discussion regarding the necessity for and contents of new dismissal regulation, a bill to amend the Labor Standards Act was passed by the Diet on July 4, 2003. As regards the limitation on the employer's right to dismissal, the amendment added a new provision, Article 18-2, which states, "[A] dismissal shall be null and void as an abuse of right if the dismissal is not based on reasonable cause or is viewed as improper from the general viewpoint of society." It is clear that this provision is modeled after the 1975 Supreme Court opinion that established the abusive dismissal doctrine.[122]

Before the Ministry of Health, Labor and Welfare submitted the bill to the Diet, the Labor Policy Council proposed that the amendment should include a provision regarding monetary remedies. However, trade unions strongly opposed the proposal on the ground that employers would opt for monetary remedies in certain cases where the dismissal is invalid and the employee seeks reinstatement. Thus, this proposal was not incorporated into the bill.

Also, the original text of Article 18-2, as drafted by the Ministry of Health,

Labor and Welfare, stated that "the employer may dismiss its employees unless the right to dismissal is restricted under this Act or other laws, provided that the abuse of the right to dismissal shall be null and void as an abuse of right if the dismissal is not based on reasonable cause or is viewed as improper from the general viewpoint of society." Trade unions and the opposition parties in the Diet expressed serious concern that the statement clarifying the employer's right to dismissal would make dismissals easier, or that the burden of proof regarding the reasonable cause of the dismissal would shift to the employee in spite of the current practice to the contrary. As a result, the bill was modified by the Diet so that Article 18-2 contained only the rule regarding abusive dismissal. In addition, the Diet committees that were in charge of the amendment passed an ancillary resolution, which clarified that Article 18-2 would not change the practice regarding the burden of proof in litigation in abusive dismissal cases. Thus, it was made clear that the new provision on abusive dismissal is only a codification of the existing case law.[123]

E. RELATED LEGISLATIVE AND ADMINISTRATIVE DEVELOPMENTS

Although not directly aimed at the regulation of dismissals, a 2001 amendment to the Employment Measures Act indicates the Diet's concern about the increasing numbers of reductions-in-force. Article 24 of the Employment Measures Act, as amended, requires employers who intend to reduce their workforce at an establishment by thirty or more workers to take specific measures. These measures include drawing up and submitting to the Public Employment Security Office a "Plan for Assistance for Reemployment," after hearing the opinion of the majority union or, if no such union exists at the establishment, the person representing the majority of workers. In contrast to traditional measures, such as the Subsidy for Employment Adjustment,[124] which emphasized the prevention of dismissals, this provision is intended to facilitate the smooth movement of redundant workers to new employment opportunities.

In addition to this scheme, new measures that facilitate workers' mobility are being enacted and existing measures are being strengthened. This is a policy response to the present situation in which employers are finding it difficult to maintain redundant workers. The policy is shifting toward assisting redundant workers in finding employment opportunities in the external labor market. One example of this recent trend is found in a 1999 amendment to the Employment Security Act that relaxed stringent regulations on private employment agencies. One of the purposes of this amendment was to facilitate workers in finding employment opportunities in the external labor market by enhancing the function of private employment agencies.[125]

In addition, the Ministry of Health, Labor and Welfare is now providing several subsidies to promote the reemployment of workers. One of these subsidies is the *shinki-seichō bun'ya koyō sōshutsu tokubetsu shōrei kin* (special subsidy for creating employment opportunities in new or promising industries). This program, created under the Employment Insurance Act, is intended to provide employers in promising industries, such as telecommunications and biotechnology, with subsidies to aid in hiring or training workers who have lost their jobs. Although the Ministry still maintains most of the subsidies for preventing economic dismissals, the smooth reallocation of workforce gradually has become important as a labor policy.

V. CONCLUSION

Traditionally, Japanese labor law has emphasized employment security. The employer's right to discharge workers has been restricted, not only with respect to dismissals based on an individual worker's conduct, but also with respect to economic dismissals. These restrictions developed after World War II through the doctrine of abusive dismissal established by the courts. The establishment of this case law was influenced by the Japanese employment practices, especially long-term employment, which in turn was based on the structure of corporate control in Japan. This case law was incorporated in the Labor Standards Act in 2003.

However, several emerging trends represent substantial changes from traditional dismissal law. In the case of an employment contract that specifies the worker's position or job contents, dismissal based on incompetence has become relatively easier. Although several issues remain to be resolved, conditional dismissal provides a vehicle for changing working conditions in conjunction with the termination of employment. Regardless of the debate on the necessity of a new framework for economic dismissals, recent decisions indicate that the stance of the judiciary toward economic dismissals is wavering against the background of increased corporate restructuring. Finally, there has been considerable development in legislative and administrative measures for assisting workers to find new employment opportunities in the external labor market.

In view of such recent developments as a whole, it can be argued that Japanese labor law regarding dismissal is gradually beginning to recognize the importance of the protection or creation of employment opportunities in the external labor market, in addition to the security of employment within a corporation (including affiliated companies).[126] As in other aspects of labor law reform now taking place, such changes reflect responses to the recent socioeconomic situation in Japan, including changes in employment practices. Since the Japanese dismissal law developed against the background of the Japanese employment practices, it is only natural that the contents of the law will be modified in response to the changes in its background.

Nevertheless, it is difficult to determine the extent of changes that Japanese labor law is experiencing. Despite the tendency to emphasize the importance of mobility in the labor market, the core assumption of Japanese labor law, long-term employment, basically remains intact. With regard to dismissal law, the abusive dismissal doctrine has not undergone significant changes. Indeed, the "four-requirement (factor)" test regarding economic dismissals has basically survived the challenges of the recent lower court decisions. In the background, many employers still recognize the importance of long-term employment, and the structure of control in Japanese corporations has not changed drastically yet. When the Diet finally directly addressed the issue of dismissals in Article 18-2 under the 2003 amendment to the Labor Standards Act, it merely codified the existing case law regarding abusive dismissal without any substantive changes.[127] Therefore, it remains to be seen how far Japanese dismissal law will go in the direction of mobility and how it will strike the balance between security and mobility.

NOTES

I would like to thank Professor Daniel Foote for his insightful comments and suggestions. I am also indebted to Mr. Brian Hersey for his valuable comments and editorial assistance. This chapter is partly based on Ryūichi Yamakawa, "Nihon no kaiko hōsei" [Japanese Dismissal Law], in Fumio Ōtake et al., eds., *Kaiko hōsei o kangaeru* [Reflections on Dismissal Law], supp. ed. (Tokyo: Keisō shobō, 2004).

1. These judicially developed restrictions are discussed in section II of this chapter.

2. James C. Abegglen, *The Japanese Factory: Aspects of Its Social Organization* (Glencoe, IL: Free Press, 1958), 11–25.

3. E.g., *Nihongata jinji wa owatta* [Japanese-Style Personnel Management Is Gone) (Tokyo: Nihon keizai shinbun-sha, 1993).

4. Kenjirō Ume, *Minpō yōgi kannō san: Saiken hen* [Summarized Explanation of the Civil Code (3): Obligation Law] (Tokyo:Yūhikaku, 1912), 693.

5. Ibid., 693.

6. Hideo Hatoyama, *Zōtei Nihon saikenhō kakuron gekan* [Specific Issues on Japanese Obligation Law (2)], supp. ed. (Tokyo: Iwanami shoten, 1924), 49.

7. There appears to be no reported decision before World War II that restricted the employer's right to dismissal through the abuse-of-right doctrine as explained below or other provisions in the Civil Code.

8. When the employment contract has a fixed term, the parties' right to terminate is limited. Under art. 628 of the Civil Code, the parties may terminate the contract without advance notice only for a compelling reason. If such reason is based on the negligence of one party, he or she shall be liable to the other party for the damages resulting from such negligence.

9. Although the Trade Union Act was substantially amended in 1949, this prohibition of disadvantageous treatment was basically maintained and included in a more comprehensive provision regarding the prohibition of unfair labor practices (art. 7 of the current Trade Union Act).

10. In 1949, Joseph Dodge, a special minister from the United States, came to Japan and advocated policies to combat inflation and stabilize the Japanese economy. As the government took the fiscal policy for retrenchment, many enterprises could not help restructuring themselves.

11. E.g., Tsubakii v. Japan (Otsu Dist. Ct., Mar. 14, 1953), *Rōminshū* 4 (1953): 50 (Otsu Camp case); Itō v. Ōsaka Tōgyō K.K. (Osaka Dist. Ct., May 26, 1950), *Rōminshū* 2 (1950): 410; Tohara v. Chūgai Seiyaku K.K. (Tokyo Dist. Ct., Aug. 8, 1951), *Saibansho jihō* 88 (1951): 6.

12. E.g., Junryō Honda, "Kaiko jiyū no hōri" [Doctrine of Freedom of Dismissal], *Minshōhō zasshi* 35(5) (1957): 43.

13. Tohara v. Chūgai Seiyaku K.K., 8.

14. Iwata v. Tōkyō Seimei Hoken Sōgō Kaisha (Tokyo Dist. Ct., May 8, 1950), *Rōminshū* 1 (1950): 230.

15. Tohara v. Chūgai Seiyaku K.K., 8.

16. Okada v. Japan (Fukuoka Dist. Ct., Kokura Branch, Sept. 8, 1956), *Rōminshū* 7 (1956): 1098.

17. Munehiko Mishima, "Kaiko ken no ran'yō" [Abuse of Right to Dismiss], in Tōru Ariizumi and Teruhisa Ishii, eds., *Rōdōhō taikei 5: Rōdō keiyaku & shūgyō kisoku* [The System of Labor Law: Labor Contract and Work Rules, vol. 5] (Tokyo:Yūhikaku, 1963), 288.

18. Ichikawa v. Nihon Shokuen Seizō K.K. (Sup. Ct., Apr. 25, 1975), *Minshū* 29 (1975): 456.

19. Shiota v. Kōchi Hōsō K.K. (Sup. Ct., Jan. 31, 1977), *Rōdō hanrei* 268 (1977): 17.

20. Kazuo Sugeno, *Japanese Employment and Labor Law*, trans. Leo Kanowitz

(Durham, NC: Carolina Academic Press, 2002), 480. However, the employer may not discharge a worker when he or she joins another union or organizes a new union. Mitsui Sōko Kō'un K.K. v. Miura (Sup. Ct., Dec. 14, 1989), *Minshū* 43 (1990): 2051.

21. However, courts may not usually enforce the reinstatement itself, since an employer may not be compelled to accept the work of employees unless extraordinary circumstances apply. See Sugeno, *Japanese Employment and Labor Law*, 77.

22. Junko Yamaguchi, "Kaiko o meguru hōteki kyūsai no jikkōsei" [Effectiveness of Legal Relief relating to Dismissal], *Nihon rōdō kenkyū zasshi* 491 (2001): 62.

23. Nagayoshi v. Matsuura Tankō K.K. (Nagasaki Dist. Ct., Sasebo Branch, Nov. 20, 1950), *Rōminshū* 1 (1950): 945.

24. Shimamine v. Tsugami Seisakujo K.K. (Niigata Dist. Ct., Aug. 26, 1966), *Rōminshū* 17 (1966): 996.

25. Mishima, "Kaiko ken no ran'yō," 298.

26. Aiura v. Mitsui Kōzan K.K. (Fukuoka Dist. Ct., June 27, 1970), *Hanrei jihō* 608 (1970): 3.

27. One of the most famous cases in an early stage of this doctrine is Hamada v. Ōmura Nogami K.K. (Nagasaki Dist. Ct., Omura Branch, Dec. 24, 1975), *Rōdō hanrei* 242 (1976): 14.

28. In recent years, the precise meaning of *requirement* under this doctrine has often been discussed. This debate is explored in section IV.C.

29. Tōyō Sanso K.K. v. Shimazaki (Tokyo High Ct., Oct. 29, 1979), *Rōminshū* 30 (1979): 1002, is one of the leading cases that adopted the four-requirement test. The Supreme Court, while sometimes upholding lower court decisions that relied on this doctrine (e.g., Asahi Hoikuen v. Miyake [Sup. Ct., Oct. 27, 1983], *Rōdō hanrei* 427 [1983]: 63), has not expressly adopted it.

30. Fukutomi v. Hyōgo Ken Propane Gas Hoan Kyōkai (Kobe Dist. Ct., Apr. 28, 1998), *Rōdō hanrei* 743 (1998): 30.

31. Daniel H. Foote, "Judicial Creation of Norms in Japanese Labor Law: Activism in the Service of—Stability?" *UCLA Law Review* 43 (1996): 635.

32. Sometimes the permissible reasons for dismissals are classified into several subcategories, depending on the type of dismissals such as economic dismissals or dismissals based on the worker's conduct or ability. See § 98(2) of the Employment Rights Act of 1996 of the United Kingdom.

33. Manfred Weiss and Marlene Schmidt, *Labour Law and Industrial Relations in Germany*, 3rd rev. ed. (The Hague: Kluwer, 2000), 107. On the other hand, courts should determine whether the worker could be retained through other measures such as transfer and whether the selection of workers to be discharged is reasonable from the social viewpoint. Ibid., 107–8.

34. § 98(2)(b) of the Employment Rights Act of 1996. The dismissal because of redundancy may still be unfair for other reasons, such as unfairness of selection of workers to be discharged.

35. Simon Deakin and Gillian S. Morris, *Labour Law* (London: Butterworths Tolley, 2001), 503. The elements of redundancy are set forth in § 139(1) of the Employment Rights Act of 1996.

36. See, e.g., Fukutomi v. Hyōgo Ken Propane Gas Hoan Kyōkai, 30.

37. Weiss and Schmidt, *Labour Law and Industrial Relations in Germany*, 108, 204.

38. See Yamaguchi, "Kaiko o meguru hōteki kyūsai no jikkōsei," 62.

39. Saikō saibansho jimusōkyoku gyōseikyoku, *Heisei 14 nen rōdō kankei minji-gyōsei jiken no gaiyō* [Summary of Civil and Administrative Cases regarding Labor Relations in 2002], *Hōsō jihō* 55 (2003): 2169, 2169–70.

40. Ibid., 2170.

41. See Katsutoshi Kezuka, "Doitsu ni okeru kobetsu rōdō funsō shori shisutemu" [The Systems for Resolving Employment Disputes in Germany], in Katsutoshi Kezuka, ed., *Kobetsu rōdō funsō shori seido no kokusai hikaku* [International Comparison of Systems for Resolving Individual Labor Disputes] (Tokyo: Nihon rōdō kenkyū kikō, 2002), 146.

42. It must also be noted that, since the ordinary remedy for an abusive dismissal is a judgment declaring the dismissal null and void, meaning that the plaintiff has a position as the defendant's employee, a discharged worker who does not wish to be reinstated sometimes gives up the idea of suing the employer.

43. During the period from April 1, 2002, to March 31, 2003, the number of consultations involving civil employment disputes handled by the Ministry of Health, Labor and Welfare was 103,194. Among these civil cases, those related to dismissals were the largest component, about 28.6 percent (32,454 cases). See (http://www.mhlw.go.jp/houdou/2003/04/h0425-1.html).

44. See generally Sugeno, *Japanese Employment and Labor Law*, 447–52.

45. E.g., Haruhito Takeda, *Nihonjin no keizai kannen* [Sense of Economy of the Japanese] (Tokyo: Iwanami shoten, 1999), 195–201.

46. E.g., Kazuhiro Arai, *Bunka, soshiki, koyō seido* [Culture, Organization, and Employment System] (Tokyo:Yūhikaku, 2001), 90–91.

47. E.g., Kōnosuke Odaka, *Rōdō shijō bunseki* [Analysis of the Labor Market] (Tokyo: Iwanami shoten, 1984), 277–80.

48. See Chiaki Moriguchi, "The Evolution of Employment Systems in U.S. and Japanese Manufacturing Firms, 1900–1960: A Comparative Historical and Institutional Analysis" (2000), 9, available at (http://papers.nber.org/papers/W7939).

49. See Kōnosuke Odaka, "Sangyō no ninaite" [Those Who Bore Industry],

in Shunsaku Nishikawa and Takeshi Abe, eds., *Sangyōka no jidai* [Era of Industrialization] (Tokyo: Iwanami shoten, 1990), 314.

50. Koji Taira, *Economic Development and the Labor Market in Japan* (New York: Columbia University Press, 1970), 151–64. In recent years, a growing number of scholars have emphasized the importance of wartime regulations, such as the restriction on the exercise of shareholders' rights, in the historical development of the Japanese economy. See, e.g., Tetsuji Okazaki, "Nihon ni okeru kōporēto gabanansu no hatten" [The Development of Corporate Governance in Japan], in Masahiko Aoki and Ronald Dore, eds., *Shisutemu to shite no Nihon kigyō* [Japanese Enterprise as a System] (Tokyo: NTT shuppan, 1995), 437.

51. Andrew Gordon, *The Evolution of Labor Relations in Japan: Heavy Industry, 1853–1955* (Cambridge, MA: Council on East Asian Studies, Harvard University, 1985), 132–34.

52. See, e.g., Akira Takanashi, ed., *Kawaru Nihongata koyō* [Changing Employment Practices in Japan] (Tokyo: Nihon keizai shinbun-sha, 1994), 24 (observing that Japanese employment practices were established in the 1950s). For a brief description of the postwar history of Japanese labor and employment relations, see Yasuo Kuwahara, *Rōshi no kankei* [Labor-Management Relations] (Tokyo: Hōsō daigaku kyōiku shinkō kai, 1995), 21–35. See also Kuwahara, "Employment Relations in Japan," in Greg J. Bamber and Russell D. Lansbury, eds., *International and Comparative Employment Relations: A Study of Industrialised Market Economies* (London: Sage Publications, 1998), 249–62.

53. See Moriguchi, "The Evolution of Employment Systems in U.S. and Japanese Manufacturing Firms," fig. 1.

54. See Ronald Dore, *Stock Market Capitalism: Welfare Capitalism; Japan and Germany versus the Anglo-Saxons* (New York: Oxford University Press, 2000).

55. See Ryūichi Yamakawa, "The Silence of Stockholders: Japanese Labor Law from the Viewpoint of Corporate Governance," *Japan Labor Bulletin* 38(11) (1999): 6.

56. In 2005, the Company Act was enacted and replaced the second part of the Commercial Code that governed the organization and administration of corporations. However, the principle that stockholders have the right to control their corporation was not changed.

57. See Jun'ichi Shishido, "Reform in Japanese Corporate Law and Corporate Governance: Current Changes in Historical Perspective," *American Journal of Comparative Law* 49 (2001): 653, 662–67.

58. See Okazaki, "Nihon ni okeru kōporēto gabanansu no hatten," 439–53.

59. Kamekichi Takahashi, *Kabushiki kaisha bōkokuron* [Corporations Will Ruin the Country] (Tokyo: Banri kaku, 1930), 4.

60. As Berle and Means pointed out in 1933, the power of stockholders in the United States around that time was not strong and corporations were under the control of management. Adolf A. Berle Jr. and Gardiner C. Means, *The Modern Corporation and Private Property* (New York: Commerce Clearing House, 1933; repr., New Brunswick, NJ: Transaction Publishers, 1991), 64–65, 244–52. However, at least in comparison with the Japanese situation as explained above, stockholder control in the United States has been strengthened through the latter half of the twentieth century, mainly due to the increase in the role of institutional investors. See Margaret M. Blair, *Ownership and Control: Rethinking Corporate Governance for the Twenty-first Century* (Washington, DC: Brookings Institute, 1995), 44–48.

61. For a brief explanation of the Japanese model, see Blair, *Ownership and Control*, 267–71.

62. See Masahiko Aoki et al., "Kigyō no koyō shisutemu to senryaku teki hokansei" [Employment System of the Corporation and Strategic Complementarity], in Masahiko Aoki and Masahiro Okuno, eds., *Keizai shisutemu no hikaku seido bunseki* [Comparative Institutional Analysis of the Economic Systems] (Tokyo: Tōkyō daigaku shuppan kai, 1996), 123–52.

63. Another notable feature of Japanese labor and employment law relating to Japanese employment practices is the employer's wide discretion in personnel management. Case law has established that employers have a right to transfer their employees to new workplaces or positions unless employment contracts, work rules or collective agreements provide otherwise. In one case, for example, the Supreme Court held that an employee must accept a transfer to a distant workplace even if he had to move without his family because of his wife's work commitments (Yoshida v. Tōa Paint K.K. [Sup. Ct., July 14, 1986], *Hanrei jihō* 1198 [1986]: 149). Japanese employers also exercise great flexibility with respect to overtime work. The Supreme Court held that an employer may compel its employees to do overtime work if the employer had a collective agreement as required under the Labor Standards Act (art. 36) and work rules that provided a reasonable basis for the order to work overtime (Tanaka v. Hitachi Seisakujo K.K. [Sup. Ct., Nov. 28, 1991], *Minshū* 45 [1991]: 1270). While employers are not free to discharge employees even in the case of business slowdown, they may transfer (or farm out) redundant employees to divisions or related companies where they can be absorbed. Also, when employers have excess work, they typically order their employees to work overtime without hiring new regular workers (although it should be noted that employers sometimes hire part-time workers or dispatched workers). This means that they do not need to discharge the employees whom they would have hired when the additional workforce was necessary. In other words, transfers and overtime work are a means of workforce adjustment in place

of discharge. Management flexibility in the internal labor market is, in a sense, a price for the employment security. See Ryūichi Yamakawa, "The Role of Employment Contract in Japan," in Lammy Betten, ed., *The Employment Contract in Transforming Labour Relations* (The Hague: Kluwer, 1995), 109–13.

64. For a judicial decision that acknowledged such a relationship between Japanese employment practices and the abusive dismissal doctrine, see Volonakis v. Singer Sewing Machine Co. (Tokyo Dist. Ct., May 14, 1969), *Hanrei jihō* 568 (1969): 87.

65. As regards the influence on the features of collective labor relations law, see Yamakawa, "The Silence of Stockholders," 9–10.

66. From 1950 to 1975, the unemployment rate generally remained below 2.0 percent. See Japan Institute of Labor, ed., *The Labor Situation in Japan 2001/2002* (Tokyo: Japan Institute of Labor, 2001), 4.

67. Sugeno, *Japanese Employment and Labor Law*, 53.

68. See ibid., 60n.

69. See (http://www.jil.go.jp/statis/doko/saiko/saiko.htm) (last visited July 1, 2002).

70. See (http://www.hrd-net.com/news/020204.html)(last visited July 1, 2002).

71. See (http://www.jil.go.jp/statis/shuyo/200205/0203.htm) (last visited July 1, 2002).

72. For a contract worker who has a reasonable expectation for the renewal of the employment contract as a result of the repetitive renewal and other factors that give rise to such expectation, case law has established that the abusive dismissal doctrine can be applied by analogy. Tōkyō Shibaura Denki K.K. v. Maeda (Sup. Ct., July 22, 1974), *Minshū* 28 (1974): 927.

73. See Nissei kiso kenkyūjo, *Kabushiki sōgō mochiai chōsa 2001 nendo ban* [Survey on Cross-Stockholding 2001], available at (http://www.nli-research.co.jp/stp_repo.html) (last visited March 3, 2003). Since the method of this survey went through several changes in the past few years, the ratios of cross-stockholding in the past were also modified, and they are different from those contained in the previous reports.

74. See ibid.

75. See Tokyo Stock Exchange, *2001 Shareownership Survey 5*, available at (http://www.tse.or.jp/english/data/research/shareownership.html) (last visited March 3, 2003).

76. See (http://www.mof.go.jp/jouhou/soken/kenkyu/zk054.htm) (last visited March 3, 2003).

77. See Michio Nitta, "Nippon kigyō no kōporēto gabanansu: Genjō to tenbō" [Corporate Governance of Japanese Corporations: Status Quo and Future

Prospects], in Takeshi Inagami et al., eds., *Gendai Nippon no kōporēto gabanansu* [Corporate Governance in Current Japan] (Tokyo: Tōyō keizai shinpō-sha, 2000), 98.

78. See ibid., 95.

79. On May 22, 2002, the Diet passed an amendment to the Commercial Code that recognized a new scheme for corporate governance for large corporations, in which a board of directors, the majority of whom are selected from outside, would oversee the management in place of auditors. However, Japanese corporations have been very slow or reluctant in adopting this new system. According to a survey conducted by the Japan Auditors Association in May 2003, only 2.5 percent of the respondent corporations chose to do so. See Nihon kansayaku kyōkai [Japan Auditors Association], *Shōhō kaisei e no taiō ni kansuru ankēto shūkei kekka* [Results of the Questionnaire Survey on the Response to the Revised Commercial Code] (2003), 2.

80. See Jinji rōmu kanri kenkyūkai, *Shin seiki no keiei senryaku, kōporēto gabanansu, jinji senryaku* [Management Strategy, Corporate Governance, and Personnel Strategy in the New Century] (Tokyo: Japan Institute of Labor, 2000), 16–17.

81. According to a survey by the Japan Institute of Labor, the most favored measures that the respondent companies selected in the process of reductions-in-force were attrition (81.6 percent), decrease in recruiting (76.9 percent), and solicitation of voluntary or early retirement (34.2 percent), while only 6.9 percent carried out dismissals. See (http://www.jil.go.jp/statis/doko/saiko/saiko.htm) (last visited July 1, 2002).

82. See Ryūichi Yamakawa, "Japan," in Roger Blanplain, ed., *Corporate Restructuring and the Role of Labor Law* (The Hague: Kluwer, 2003), chap. 5.

83. See Jinji rōmu kanri kenkyūkai, *Shin seiki no keiei senryaku, kōporēto gabanansu, jinji senryaku*, 4.

84. See generally Ryūichi Yamakawa, "Labor Law Reform in Japan: A Response to Recent Socio-economic Changes," *American Journal of Comparative Law* 49 (2001): 627. The background of the recent labor law reform is not limited to the economic difficulties that Japanese employers are facing. On the supply side of the labor market, aging of the population and feminization of the workforce are continuing. The amendment to the Child Care and Family Care Leave Act reflects such changes, although it is not the subject of this essay. For a discussion of that topic, see ibid., 631.

85. See Takashi Araki, *Labor and Employment Law in Japan* (Tokyo: Japan Institute of Labor, 2001), 40–47.

86. See Yamakawa, "Japan," chap. 5, 107–8.

87. See Yamakawa, "Labor Law Reform in Japan," 648.

88. See, e.g., X v. Sega Enterprises K.K. (Tokyo Dist. Ct., Oct. 15, 1999), *Rōdō hanrei* 770 (1999): 34.

89. X v. Ford Jidōsha (Nippon) K.K. (Tokyo High Ct., Mar. 30, 1984), *Rōminshū* 35 (1984): 140.

90. Ibid., 152.

91. X v. Praudofutto Japan K.K. (Tokyo Dist. Ct., Apr. 26, 2000), *Rōdō hanrei* 789 (2000): 21 (upholding the dismissal of a consultant because of incompetence).

92. See Yoshida v. Tōa Paint K.K., 149.

93. See, e.g., Satō v. Daishi Ginkō K.K. (Sup. Ct., Feb. 28, 1997), *Rōdō hanrei* 710 (1997): 12.

94. Nagai v. Aerotoransuporuto K.K. (Tokyo Dist. Ct., Apr. 13, 1995), *Hanrei jihō* 1526 (1995): 35 (Scandinavian Airlines case).

95. Ibid.

96. Takahashi v. Ōsaka Rōdō Eisei Center (Osaka Dist. Ct., Aug. 31, 1998), *Rōdō hanrei* 751 (1998): 38.

97. E.g., Takashi Araki, *Koyō shisutemu to rōdō jōken henkō hōri* [Employment Systems and Variation of Terms and Conditions of Employment] (Tokyo: Yūhikaku, 2001), 309. But see Nippon Hiruton K.K. v. Funaki (Tokyo High Ct., Nov. 26, 2002), *Rōdō hanrei* 843 (2003): 20 (holding that the employer may refuse to recognize such temporary acceptance).

98. See section II.D. above.

99. See, e.g., the articles contained in "Reexamination of the Doctrine Regarding Economic Dismissal," special issue, *Kikan rōdōhō* 196 (2000): 12–120.

100. Yasuda v. National Westminster Bank, Ltd. (Jan. 21, 2000), *Rōdō hanrei* 782 (2000): 23 (third decision in the preliminary injunction proceeding).

101. Yasuda v. National Westminster Bank, Ltd., 32.

102. E.g., Okubo v. Singapore Development Bank Ltd. (Osaka Dist. Ct., June 23, 2000), *Rōdō hanrei* 786 (2000): 16 (ordinary procedure).

103. Yasuda v. National Westminster Bank, Ltd.

104. E.g., Okubo v. Singapore Development Bank Ltd.

105. Matsushima v. Nihon Kōkan K.K. (Yokohama Dist. Ct., Kawasaki Branch, July 19, 1982), *Rōminshū* 33 (1982): 695.

106. E.g., Tazaki v. Varig K.K. (Tokyo Dist. Ct., Dec. 19, 2001), *Rōdō hanrei* 817 (2003): 5.

107. However, since the four "requirements" are primarily representative "factors" for determining the validity of economic dismissals, it usually suffices for a court to base its decision on these four factors, unless circumstances of the case necessitate the consideration of other factors. Ryūichi Yamakawa, *Koyō kankei hō* [The Law of Employment Relations], 3rd ed. (Tokyo: Shinsei-sha, 2003), 255.

108. Yasuda v. National Westminster Bank, Ltd., 34.

109. For analysis by both economists and lawyers, see Ōtake et al., *Kaiko hōsei o kangaeru*.

110. See, e.g., Norihiro Yashiro, *Koyō kaikaku no jidai* [The Era of Employment Reform] (Tokyo: Chūo kōron-sha, 1999), 85; and Fumio Ōtake, *Koyō mondai o kangaeru* [Reflections on Employment Issues] (Osaka: Ōsaka daigaku shuppan kai, 2000).

111. Nihon rōdō bengodan, "Rōdō keiyaku hōsei rippō teigen" [Proposals for Labor Contract Legislation], *Kikan rōdōsha no kenri* 210 (1995): 59.

112. Hiroyuki Chūma, "Kaiko ken ran'yō hōri no keizaigaku" [Economics of the Abusive Dismissal Doctrine], in Yoshirō Miwa et al., ed., *Kaishahō no keizaigaku* [Economics of Corporation Law] (Tokyo: Tōkyō daigaku shuppan kai, 1998), 425.

113. Jun Tsuneki, "Fukanbi keiyaku riron to kaiko kisei hōri" [Job-Security Regulations from the Viewpoint of the Economic Theory of Incomplete Contracts], *Nihon rōdō kenkyū zasshi* 491 (2001): 18.

114. See, e.g., Hajime Wada, "Seiri kaiko hōri no minaoshi wa hitsuyō ka" [Is the Reexamination of the Law of Economic Dismissal Necessary?], *Kikan rōdōhō* 196 (2001): 12.

115. Michio Tsuchida, "Kaiko ken ran'yō hōri no hōteki seitōsei" [Normative Legitimacy of the Abusive Dismissal Doctrine], *Nihon rōdō kenkyū zasshi* 491 (2001): 4. Relying on the relational contract theory, Professor Takashi Uchida has emphasized the importance of the maintenance of the employment relationship as a basis of legal limitation on dismissals. See, e.g., Takashi Uchida, "Koyō o meguru hō to seisaku" [Law and Policy regarding Employment], in Ōtake et al., *Kaiko hōsei o kangaeru*.

116. Takashi Muranaka, "Nihonteki koyō kankō no hen'yō to kaiko seigen hōri" [The Transformation of Japanese Employment Practices and Law of Dismissal Regulation], *Minshōhō zasshi* 119 (1999): 602.

117. For an example of the guidelines, see Yōichi Shimada, "Kaiko kisei o meguru rippōron no kadai" [Legislative Issues on Dismissal Regulation], *Nihon rōdōhō gakkaishi* 99 (2002): 74.

118. Advisory, Conciliation and Arbitration Service (ACAS) Code of Practice 1: Disciplinary and Grievance Procedures, available at (http://www.acas.org.uk/publications/pdf/cop.pdf) (last visited July 1, 2002).

119. This does not necessarily mean that the plaintiff needs to seek a judgment that declares that the dismissal is null and void. As long as the plaintiff contests the validity of dismissal, he or she may ask the court only for a back-pay order.

120. See Fumito Komiya, "Koyō shūryō ni okeru rōdōsha hogo no saikentō" [Reexamination of Protection of Worker's Protection in the Termination of Employment], *Nihon rōdōhō gakkaishi* 99 (2002): 32.

121. See Shimada, "Kaiko kisei o meguru rippōron no kadai," 74.

122. The opinion of the Supreme Court in that case, Ichikawa v. Nihon Shokuen Seizō K.K., is summarized in section II.C. above.

123. With respect to the debate in the legislative process regarding art. 18-2 as well as the contents of the other provisions included in the amendment that may affect dismissals, see Ryūichi Yamakawa, "Rōki hō kaisei to kaiko rūru" [Amendment to the Labor Standards Law and the Rules on Dismissals], *Jurisuto*, no. 1255 (2003): 48.

124. See generally Sugeno, *Japanese Employment and Labor Law*, 60n.

125. See Araki, *Labor and Employment Law in Japan*, 6.

126. See ibid., 227–29.

127. Most recently, it is proposed that comprehensive legislation regarding the employment contract is necessary in order to clarify legal rules governing employment relationships. A study group established by the Ministry of Health, Labor and Welfare published a report in September 2005 containing such a legislative proposal. See (http: / /wwwmhlw.go.jp / shingi / 2005 / 09 / s0915-4.html) (last visited June 7, 2006). Although the proposal does not change the abusive dismissal doctrine codified under article 18-2 of the Labor Standards Act, it is suggested that this provision should be incorporated in the new legislation. Also, the study group proposed that the monetary remedies for abusive dismissal in lieu of declatory judgment should be introduced. As a result of discussion in the Labor Policy Council, a bill entitled "Labor Contract Act" was submitted to the Diet in March 2007. Although the bill contains a provision that codifies the abusive dismissal doctrine (which would replace article 18-2 of the Labor Standards Act, which would be deleted at the same time), the proposal for monetary remedies was not incorporated in the bill.

21 Concentrated Power

The Paradox of Antitrust in Japan

HARRY FIRST & TADASHI SHIRAISHI

I. INTRODUCTION

In his essay about the Antimonopoly Law in the 1963 edition of *Law in Japan*, Yoshio Kanazawa observed that enforcement of Japan's Antimonopoly Act[1] "is anemic today" and, although the act could be resuscitated, "there is, of course, no immediate prospect of this happening."[2] Kanazawa pointed to the "negative attitude toward the underlying philosophy" of the law exhibited by recently appointed commissioners of the Fair Trade Commission (JFTC),[3] to the many exemptions from the Antimonopoly Act that had followed its adoption in 1947,[4] and to the growth of what has come to be called administrative guidance by the ministries, particularly the Ministry of International Trade and Industry (MITI).[5] He concluded by wondering whether the Antimonopoly Act "serves a useful function in the social and economic environment of Japan." Although he hoped that the JFTC would "revitalize itself and assume a positive role in the administration of the law," he also thought that the Antimonopoly Act should be better fit to its "social environment" so that it would "permit restrictive practices when they demonstrably benefit the Japanese economy or society as a whole."[6]

Kanazawa's account of antitrust in Japan was written only sixteen years after the enactment of the Antimonopoly Act. We write some forty years after Kanazawa, fifty-five years after the statute's enactment. Much has changed in that time. There have been substantial legislative changes in the act, strengthening its provisions rather than narrowing them. There has been substantial scholarly attention paid to the act, both in Japan and elsewhere, exploring the importance and effect of antitrust enforcement in Japan. The policies behind the act have even come to be embraced by government policy makers. In the late 1980s and early 1990s increased antitrust enforcement was seen as important in Japan and elsewhere as a way of curing United States–Japan trade problems and opening Japan's markets. In the early 2000s antitrust enforcement has come to be seen in Japan as a way to improve the operation of a sluggish and overregulated economy. Even the prime minister has pronounced on the importance of strong antitrust enforcement.[7]

And yet, doubts remain about antitrust in Japan, similar to the doubts expressed by Kanazawa. These doubts are not addressed to the utility of antitrust in today's economy in Japan. They are more addressed to the perceived lack of antitrust enforcement by the JFTC. As one commissioner expressed it, the JFTC is often viewed as "a watch dog that does not bite."[8] Indeed, the very acknowledgment that the JFTC needs to be strengthened is an indication that it is perceived as too weak to be an effective enforcer of the antitrust laws.

The actual record of antitrust enforcement in Japan is, of course, more complicated than can be expressed in a political catchphrase. Unlike the record when Kanazawa wrote, enforcement has turned out to be not quite anemic, nor has the JFTC been without bite. Nevertheless, it would also be difficult to characterize the commission's enforcement record as robust.

There are many reasons for the relatively weak performance of the commission over time, including Japan's often negative view of the utility of antitrust as economic policy and the position of the JFTC in relation to other government ministries. One area that has been overlooked as an explanation for weak antitrust enforcement in Japan, however, is the very concentration of enforcement authority in the JFTC. The Antimonopoly Act follows the model of concentrating enforcement in an apparently powerful single administrative government agency and, as a result, only a small number of private litigants invoke antitrust protections. This concentration, we believe, has actually led to weaker antitrust enforcement than might otherwise have occurred in Japan. It is, we think, the paradox of antitrust in Japan.

Our chapter proceeds as follows. We begin with a description of Japan's antitrust enforcement system, with a particular focus on the current position and activities of the JFTC. We then compare that to the antitrust enforcement system that has evolved in the United States. Our review of the U.S. system is not so much to detail that system as to provide the contrast of a system where enforcement is much more deconcentrated and enforcers operate in a networked environment rather than a hierarchical one. We conclude with three suggestions for opening up antitrust enforcement in Japan: increase the networking of the JFTC and other ministries with regard to competition matters, strengthen the support structure for private litigation, and have the JFTC participate fully in the growing internationalization of antitrust enforcement.

II. CONCENTRATED ANTITRUST ENFORCEMENT: JAPAN

A. THE BASIC STRUCTURE OF JAPAN'S ANTITRUST ENFORCEMENT[9]

1. *JFTC*

a. General Organization

The Antimonopoly Act prescribes not only the substantive rules but also the organization of the JFTC. The JFTC consists of one chairperson and four commissioners (Article 29), with the General Secretariat attached to the commission (Article 35).[10] The commission is guaranteed independence (Article 28) and the prime minister has the authority to appoint its members (Article 29). Although from 2001 to 2003 the JFTC was formally placed under the jurisdiction of the Ministry of Public Management, Home Affairs, Posts and Telecommunications (MPHPT), it is now formally placed under the jurisdiction of the Cabinet Office.[11] The officials of the General Secretariat, antitrust professionals led by the secretary general, have substantial involvement in antitrust policy making, although it is the commission itself that has the legal power to authorize them to act (Articles 27 and 34).

b. JFTC Procedures

The JFTC can compulsorily investigate to determine whether the Antimonopoly Act has been violated (Article 46). When it finds a business entity to be in violation of the act, the JFTC usually recommends that the entity should cease and desist from violating the law (Article 48).[12] If the entity accepts the recommendation, the JFTC issues a "recommendation decision" to legally empower the recommendation (Article 48); most JFTC decisions take this form. If the business entity does not accept the recommendation, a hearing procedure will take place to determine whether a violation has occurred, after which an "after-hearing decision" will be issued (Article 54). During the hearing, however, the respondent entity can decline to continue, in which case the JFTC issues a "consent decision" (Article 53-3).

The JFTC has a variety of alternatives to the issuance of formal decisions. The most visible are "warnings" (*keikoku*) and "cautions" (*chūi*), which it issues when it claims not to be able to amass sufficient evidence to prove a violation, but, nevertheless, is suspicious that illegal conduct has occurred.[13] Another alternative is the conditioning of activities. The JFTC does not like to give administrative guidance, having criticized other agencies for doing so,[14] but it does permit companies to consult with it as to the legality of particular transactions. The JFTC will provide a "yes" or "no" to companies that engage in such consultations. In the case of a negative response, the commission will then wait for the offending company to "spontaneously" offer improvement measures, to which the commission will again respond.[15] This kind of conditioning can most often be observed in the context of premerger notifications.[16]

c. Penalties

When a business entity has committed an "unreasonable restraint of trade" in the meaning of Article 2(6), which roughly means an anticompetitive horizontal restraint, including price-fixing and bid rigging, the Antimonopoly Act requires the JFTC to order the entity to pay an "administrative surcharge" (fine) based on a percentage of sales of the product affected.[17] This order can be appealed to the hearing panel at the JFTC (Article 48-2).

Some categories of violations, practically limited to price-fixing and bid rigging, can be charged criminally. Individuals responsible for these violations can be prosecuted under Article 89 of the Antimonopoly Act, but these cases are rare and no individual has ever been imprisoned for a violation. Corporations can be prosecuted and fined under Article 95, up to ¥500 million (approximately $4 million) pursuant to a 2002 amendment to the Antimonopoly Act.

The public prosecutor's office can proceed under the Antimonopoly Act only when the JFTC officially files a criminal accusation with it (Article 96). The JFTC has adopted a rule that it will file an accusation in cases that have significant effects on the Japanese general public and/or concern repeat offenders.[18]

2. *Private Actions*

a. Damages

An injured person can sue under the Antimonopoly Act Article 25 to recover single damages, but only after a JFTC decision as to illegal conduct has become "final and conclusive."[19] Plaintiffs who sue under the Antimonopoly Act need not prove negligence or willfulness by the defendants and the court has to request the JFTC to provide it with an opinion on damages.[20]

Parties injured by antitrust violations can also sue under the general tort provision of Civil Code Article 709. It is well established that "unlawful conduct" under the meaning of Article 709 includes antitrust violations. This interpretation enables injured persons to take legal action in cases where the JFTC has not rendered a formal enforcement decision. Plaintiffs may also prefer Civil Code Article 709 for procedural reasons. Suits brought under the Antimonopoly Act must be brought in the Tokyo High Court before a panel of five judges, while Civil Code suits are brought in the relevant district court. Moreover, the Tokyo High Court's jurisdiction is limited to Antimonopoly Act violations that appeared in the preceding JFTC decision; a plaintiff that wishes to litigate other conduct allegedly committed by the defendant, whether related to competition policy or not, cannot join such claims before the Tokyo High Court. Thus, even in cases where the JFTC has rendered a formal decision, some plaintiffs have chosen to file in district court under Article 709 because of the procedural disadvantages of appearing before the Tokyo High Court.[21]

b. Injunctions

Any person whose interests are significantly injured, or likely to be significantly injured, by an antitrust violation can seek injunctive relief pursuant to the Antimonopoly Act Article 24, which took effect in April 2001. The amendment to permit private injunctive relief came after considerable study of the effectiveness of private antitrust litigation and is based on the view that allowing plaintiffs to obtain injunctive relief will lead to greater use of private remedies.[22] Plaintiffs can join damage claims (Civil Code Article 709 and/or others) and injunction claims (Antimonopoly Act Article 24).

c. Other remedies

Another avenue for private litigation is the use of the Antimonopoly Act as a defense in a suit for breach of contract. Civil Code Article 90 nullifies, in whole or in part, a contract incompatible with "public order." "Public order" has been held to include compliance with the Antimonopoly Act.[23]

B. THE IMPORTANCE OF ANTITRUST ENFORCEMENT IN JAPAN

1. *The Position of the JFTC*

Competition policy has acquired a priority in Japan, particularly after the Structural Impediments Initiative (SII) talks with the government of the United States, which began in 1989 and continued to 1992.[24] A measure of this importance can be found in the statistics relating to the increase in the number of JFTC personnel. Since 1981, the JFTC has increased its authorized staff, while the size of the government as a whole has been cut. The number of the JFTC officials was 423 in 1981, 461 in 1989, and 564 in 2000.[25] By contrast, the size of the entire government fell from 716,261 in 1981 to 653,103 in 2000.[26] Given that the law requires that the size of each agency be allocated by Cabinet Order,[27] the increase in the JFTC and the decrease in the whole government is a definite signal of the priority given to the JFTC by Japan's government.

Although some may argue the JFTC is still too small,[28] the important point here is the relative increase in priority that the JFTC has enjoyed compared to the rest of the government of Japan. In addition to the number of employees, the rating of the JFTC's executive office was upgraded in 1996, from the simple "Secretariat" to the "General Secretariat" furnished with two bureaus, making the JFTC of equivalent grade to other agencies including METI (formerly MITI[29]) and the MPHPT.[30]

The size of any government agency is an important indication of its importance, because it shows that the agency's mission is sufficiently significant to enable it to compete successfully with other parts of the bureaucracy for resources. Indexes related to an agency's output may also be useful for assessing the importance of an agency's mission. For the JFTC this could be measured by looking at the number of cases brought, although the decision to bring cases can be influenced by many factors.[31]

2. *The JFTC and Other Agencies: From Industrial Policy to Competition Policy*

A significant recent legislative change has been the abolition of most statutory exemptions from antitrust, including the exemption for public utilities and the exemption for recession and rationalization cartels. Along with this increase in antitrust's domain has come an increase in the JFTC's assertion of jurisdiction over industries regulated by other ministries.

In dealing with other agencies the JFTC has in the past relied mainly on the tool of a study group, The Research Group for Competition Policy and Trade Regulations by the Government (Kiseiken), which consisted mostly of university scholars. The JFTC was able to make the case for deregulation through the vehicle of the Kiseiken's reports, using the Kiseiken as a cloak to avoid friction with other regulatory agencies.[32] Recently, however, the JFTC has moved into a more active phase, issuing joint guidelines with two agencies involved in important areas of the economy to which the JFTC seeks to bring more competition, electric power and telecommunications.

In 1999 the Electric Utilities Industry Act (EUIA) was amended, allowing for retail competition for sales to large purchasers of electric power. The act was to take effect in 2000. As a result of the introduction of more competition in the electric power industry, METI (then MITI) and the JFTC collaborated to issue the Electricity Fair Trade Guidelines in 1999.[33] METI invited the JFTC delegate, namely, the chief of the Coordination Division, to the Working Group for Fair Trade at the Electricity Industry Council (Denki Jigyō Shingikai), which consisted of antitrust law scholars and economists.[34] The purpose of the guidelines was to make sure that incumbent power companies did not engage in anticompetitive conduct that would disadvantage new entrants.

The critical point is that METI acknowledged the presence of the JFTC. To be sure, it is fair to say that METI took the leadership role. Above all else, the forum was the council led by METI. Taking a look at the contents of the guidelines, moreover, anticompetitive conduct which could be remedied by the tools articulated in the EUIA, including discriminatory transmission, were mentioned only in the context of the EUIA, even though that conduct could violate the Antimonopoly Act as well and thereby come under the jurisdiction of the JFTC. However, METI's jurisdiction under the EUIA does not extend to all types of anticompetitive behavior, such as exclusive dealing and primary line price discrimination, so it needed to work with the JFTC so that those problems would be dealt with effectively.

There continues to be shared interest between the JFTC and METI in competition issues in the electric power industry. For example, in 2001 and 2002 the JFTC investigated at least three incumbent electric power companies with regard to their conduct toward new entrants. Although the JFTC found no violation of the Antimonopoly Act in any of these cases, it did issue a "warning" to one company and "instructions" to the other two so that they might avoid future violations of the act.[35] On the other hand, METI would like to increase its influence in deregulating the economy, which means making use of competition principles. Although the Administrative Reform Act expressly states that competition policy would continue to be under the JFTC's jurisdiction, and not METI's,[36] METI has chosen the strategy of collaborating with the JFTC as a way of asserting competition policy competence over electric power companies. Indeed, the Electricity Guidelines were amended in exactly the same collaborative manner in 2002.[37]

A similar process has occurred in telecommunications. In 2001 the JFTC and the MPHPT collaborated to issue the Telecommunications Competition Promotion Guidelines.[38] In contrast to the Electricity Guidelines, it is fair to say that the JFTC led the telecommunications collaboration. According to the Secretary General of the JFTC, the JFTC had intended to issue antitrust guidelines on its own and had nearly finished their drafting, but decided to accept an offer from the MPHPT to prepare joint guidelines.[39] The guidelines that were issued refer to the Antimonopoly Act as well as the Telecommunications Industry Act, even when either statute can remedy the conduct, including discriminatory interconnections. Examining the byline of the joint guidelines, the JFTC appears first followed by the MPHPT, even though as a formal matter the JFTC was then an independent organ under the jurisdiction of the MPHPT.[40]

Another example of the improved position of the JFTC is the treatment of the Japan Airlines (JAL) / Japan Air System (JAS) merger. In 2002 the JFTC announced that the original plan submitted by the two airlines would violate the Antimonopoly Act.[41] The JFTC subsequently cleared a modified plan that included divestiture of nine "round-trip" slots at Haneda airport in Tokyo and other support to new entrants that, the JFTC believed, might enable them to act as "mavericks" in the industry.[42] The Ministry of Land, Infrastructure and Transport (MLIT) had reportedly approved the original plan. The action by the JFTC made the MLIT take some measures to require the incumbents to support new entrants.[43]

The consideration of competition by agencies involved in the regulation of electric power, telecommunications, and airlines shows that some agencies have now begun to shift from so-called industrial policy to competition policy. This fact in itself supports the view that competition policy has acquired priority in Japan. Indeed, the explicit statutory rejection of METI jurisdiction over competition policy may evidence METI's effort (in vain) to acquire power to enforce some parts of the Antimonopoly Act.[44]

3. *The JFTC's Monopoly on Enforcement*

Enforcement of the Antimonopoly Act has been centralized in the JFTC since the statute's enactment in 1947.

a. Private Enforcement

Private enforcement in civil courts has been limited. A number of sources have stressed that the obstacles to private enforcement are found in the courts' general approaches to civil law matters, particularly to the calculation of damages.[45] This critique, however, has been unduly influenced by cases that arose out of the kerosene cartel.[46] These cases involved the oil embargo of the early 1970s, in which calculation of damages was very difficult because the plaintiffs were indirect purchasers and proof of causation was a complicated task. In more recent cases involving municipal bid rigging, in contrast, plaintiffs have been successful in obtaining monetary relief; these cases are likely to involve direct purchasers and are far less complicated.[47] Further, commentators on antitrust damages in Japan have tended to focus on collusion cases, failing to pay adequate attention to the examples of cases in which plaintiffs have successfully recovered damages for exclusionary conduct.[48] Whatever the validity of the criticisms of the civil law's approach to damages, Article 248 of the Civil Procedure Code of 1998 attempted to clarify the law by prescribing, "When it is apparent that there existed damages and it is significantly difficult to prove the correct calculation, the court has discretion to adopt the appropriate amount of recovery taking account of all the trial and evidence."[49]

What may be more of a deterrent to plaintiffs bringing an antitrust lawsuit is the judges' meager knowledge of *antitrust* principles, more so than their allegedly wooden application of *civil law* doctrines.[50] There are a number of examples of judicial ignorance of antitrust. Some Supreme Court cases have established general rules by simply copying JFTC guidelines.[51] Another Supreme Court case neglected sixteen years' development of antitrust arguments since its former ruling.[52] An example in the lower courts is *Naigai v. Nisshō*, where the plaintiff argued that the defendant attempted to engage in unlawful exclusive dealing when it raised prices under a supply agreement in retaliation for the plaintiff's purchase of less expensive supplies from foreign importers. The district court avoided discussing the antitrust claim, merely holding that the defendant could not increase the price under the existing contract.[53] Finally, adding to the judges' lack of knowledge of antitrust principles is the shortage of judges.[54] Consequently, it is not surprising that private civil antitrust litigation has yet to become an important part of the antitrust enforcement system in Japan.

b. Insufficient Development of Legal Rules

The JFTC, as the centralized enforcer of antitrust, has been a cause of the inadequate development of legal doctrines. In other words, Japanese antitrust has been closer to the bureaucratic model of regulatory culture, rather than the legalistic model.[55]

The JFTC has less experience and sophistication in difficult categories such as exclusionary conduct. Most JFTC decisions have related to easy categories, which would be treated as per se illegal in the United States.[56] Some guidelines refer to more difficult areas, but with a high level of abstraction.[57] This leads the JFTC to a tendency to rely on informal enforcement to deal with hard areas. Thus, for example, the JFTC's IT and Public Utilities Task Force, which was begun in the fiscal year 2001, issued only one warning[58] and two announcements of informal guidance[59] during its first year.[60]

Another effect of the JFTC's operating in a bureaucratic framework is that the commission tends to make overbroad pronouncements regarding the rules for antitrust violations. An important example is the disregard of business justification. Being an administrative agency, the JFTC can announce rules without mentioning business justification claims (e.g., efficiency arguments). When there is conduct restricting competition but with solid business justification, the JFTC can simply keep silent. When it feels it must announce its approval of a transaction, it tends not to rely on business justification but simply to state its conclusion that the conduct is not anticompetitive at all. This behavior makes the JFTC's rulings unreliable.[61]

These factors lead to the conclusion that as a seldom-challenged monopolistic enforcer, the JFTC has not been forced to develop adequate legal explanations for its actions. It is true that since 1991 one administrative judge of the JFTC's three-judge hearing panels[62] has been a judge on loan from the courts to the JFTC, usually for three years,[63] and that this system has made after-hearing decisions relatively legalistic, both in substance and in procedure. Nevertheless, these decisions still stand in some contrast to the JFTC's other decisions. This lack of general legal justification has weakened the acceptance of JFTC decisions by lawyers and judges, a further cost of the way that the JFTC has chosen to protect its monopoly position.

III. DECONCENTRATED ANTITRUST ENFORCEMENT: UNITED STATES

A. THE BASIC STRUCTURE OF U.S. ANTITRUST ENFORCEMENT

There are four groups of enforcers of antitrust law in the United States: the Antitrust Division of the Department of Justice, the Federal Trade Commission, the states, and private litigants. There are also a wide variety of other government agencies, both federal and state, that have some responsibility for considering competition issues.

The two major federal antitrust enforcement agencies are the Antitrust Division of the Department of Justice and the Federal Trade Commission. The Justice Department, an executive branch cabinet-level agency, began enforcing federal antitrust law when the Sherman Act was passed in 1890. The Federal Trade Commission (FTC), an independent administrative agency, was organized in 1915, established as an agency to engage in "preventive regulation" by investigating and prosecuting business abuses.[64] It was charged with enforcing two new statutes, the Federal Trade Commission Act and the Clayton Act. Both statutes, however, covered practices included within the Sherman Act. In addition, the Clayton Act gave enforcement authority to the Justice Department as well as to the FTC. The result was a high degree of overlapping enforcement responsibility, without any clear direction on how that responsibility would be shared.[65]

Antitrust law is also enforced by the fifty states, the District of Columbia, and four U.S. territories. Most states have some form of state antitrust law that they can enforce in state courts; in fact, some of these state antitrust laws predate the Sherman Act.[66] In addition, since 1945 the courts have recognized that the states have jurisdiction to enforce federal antitrust law in federal court,[67] a power further confirmed by statute in 1976.[68] States can sue for damages incurred by their citizens, as well as for injunctive or structural relief to end anticompetitive practices.

The fourth set of enforcers is private parties. When Congress enacted the Sherman Act in 1890 it included a private right of action for those injured in their business or property by virtue of an antitrust violation. Indeed, the novelty of the Sherman Act was not the private right of action (contracts in unreasonable restraint of trade were unenforceable at common law) as much as it was the provision of public enforcement. An important aspect of the private right of action, of course, is that the successful plaintiff can be awarded treble damages and attorneys fees. This has been a significant inducement to plaintiffs to bring antitrust cases.

In addition to these four groups, competition issues are also considered by a wide array of federal and state regulatory agencies. It has often been the case that when Congress has enacted statutes establishing independent federal administrative agencies to regulate various sectors of the economy it has given these agencies either concurrent or exclusive jurisdiction over mergers and other competitive practices of the regulated industries. The Interstate Commerce Commission, for example, was given exclusive jurisdiction over railroad and trucking mergers under a broad "public interest" standard that was subsequently interpreted to include competitive considerations.[69] When Congress regulated the airlines it gave the Civil Aeronautics Board exclusive authority to review airline mergers, as well as unfair methods of competition.[70] Telecommunications and broadcasting mergers are reviewed by the Federal Communications Commission, which has also adopted a variety of market structure rules intended to maintain competition in broadcasting markets.[71] Banking mergers are reviewed under a competition standard by bank regulatory agencies.[72] Similarly, electric power company mergers are reviewed by the Federal Energy Regulatory Commission (FERC) for their competitive effects; the FERC also has jurisdiction over a variety of competitive practices in the electric power industry.[73] Some of these industries are also regulated on the state level (electric power and telecommunications, for example), with the result that state regulatory agencies may also consider competition-related issues.

In light of the importance of these sectors, the federal antitrust enforcement agencies, particularly the Department of Justice, have historically made a significant effort to force the regulatory agencies to take account of competitive considerations when applying the statutory "public interest" standard under which much federal regulation is judged. Although this effort has produced mixed results, it has at least forced regulatory agencies to take some account of competition principles when making regulatory decisions and helped widen the number of enforcers of these principles.[74]

B. DISTRIBUTED ANTITRUST ENFORCEMENT SYSTEM

1. *Cooperation and Competition*

The U.S. system of multiple antitrust enforcers stands in some contrast to Japan's system. The basic structure of Japan's enforcement system has fostered control over antitrust by the JFTC, control that the JFTC has tried to maintain. The basic structure of the U.S. enforcement system has kept any one agency from controlling antitrust, even if the federal agencies (and particularly the Justice Department) might have preferred otherwise. The United States has distributed its antitrust enforcement, rather than centralize it.

If the problem of a centralized system is excessive uniformity, the problem of a decentralized system is excessive diversity. Policy making can be chaotic, increasing compliance costs for business, and can lead to contradictory approaches if enforcers disagree. The U.S. system has not avoided these problems completely, but it has evolved in a way that allows different agencies to develop different competencies that reflect, in part, their different institutional and legal interests. The result is a complex system in which the four enforcement agencies act, at times, cooperatively and, at times, competitively.

The two federal antitrust enforcement agencies have most often operated in a cooperative manner, generally avoiding major confrontations.[75] Both agencies have handled antitrust prosecutions across the spectrum of possible violations, although with somewhat different statutory emphases. Prior to the 1950 amendment of Section 7 of the Clayton Act (the antimerger provision), the Justice Department played a "minor role" in the enforcement of that statute[76] (the commission filed approximately six times more cases than the Justice Department[77]). Even more pronounced was the attention paid by the FTC to Section 3 of the Clayton Act (exclusive dealing and tying) relative to the Justice Department; by 1940 the FTC had filed 154 proceedings under that section, while the Justice Department had filed only 7.[78] Even in the area of pricing conspiracies, the FTC was more active than the Justice Department, although by a small margin.[79] The only area in which one agency really "specialized" was criminal prosecutions under the Sherman Act, which are statutorily reserved to the Department of Justice.

It was not until 1938 that the first informal agreement was instituted between the commission and the Justice Department to determine which agency should handle a particular investigation. This agreement was formalized in 1948.[80] In recent years cooperation between the two agencies has become more complex, as both agencies have taken more aggressive enforcement stances. The need to cooperate in merger enforcement was codified in 1976 when Congress required that premerger notification be given to both agencies simultaneously, relying on the agencies themselves to determine which mergers each would investigate but providing no explicit statutory directives.[81] This required the agencies to improve their liaison procedures.[82] More recently, after the new Bush administration was elected in 2000, the heads of the Antitrust Division and the Federal Trade Commission made an agreement to redivide the industries for which each agency would have responsibility, in the hope of ending battles over particular cases to which both agencies had a plausible claim.[83] Although this agreement was subsequently abandoned in the face of congressional opposition,[84] the agencies continue to divide merger investigations, but presumably in line with past practices.[85]

Cooperation can also take the form of joint efforts. In the modern era the federal antitrust agencies have engaged with each other in a limited amount of this type of cooperation, generally limited to policy making rather than investigation or enforcement in particular cases. For example, prior to 1992 each agency had its own set of merger guidelines. The 1992 Horizontal Merger Guidelines, however, were issued jointly, as have been subsequent guidelines and policy statements in other areas.[86] This proliferation of joint guidelines reflects both the increasing bureaucratization of U.S. antitrust enforcement and a conscious effort to articulate a consistent federal approach to competition matters.[87]

A different form of cooperation occurs when the federal antitrust enforcement agencies become involved in competition issues that are statutorily within the jurisdiction of other federal agencies. The Justice Department, for example, has been an active participant in regulatory decisions involving the restructuring of the electric power industry[88] and in airline merger decisions when they were subject to Department of Transportation approval.[89] This type of participation has generally been in the form of publicly filed comments that the regulatory agencies then consider but are not required to accept.

More substantial cooperation in investigation and prosecution has taken place between the individual federal enforcement agencies and the states, and among the states themselves. These efforts are a relatively recent aspect of U.S. antitrust enforcement, beginning with cooperative efforts among the states in the 1980s and cooperative efforts between federal and state agencies in the 1990s.[90] This type of cooperation has several purposes. It extends enforcement resources in particular cases, by adding to the capacity that any single agency has to prosecute antitrust cases, and it helps to insure a common approach by different enforcement agencies. In addition to extending resources, such cooperation may also take advantage of different institutional competencies that the various antitrust enforcers might have. State antitrust enforcers, for example, may have a better understanding of local markets than federal enforcers, adding competence that can improve antitrust enforcement.[91]

A final form of cooperative effort involves the bringing of complementary cases. These are cases in which one enforcement agency makes use of the efforts of another. This can occur, for example, when private litigants sue for treble damages at the conclusion of a successful federal enforcement effort. Price-fixing cases are the clearest example of such complementary prosecution, where the Justice Department brings a successful criminal action and private parties then sue the cartel for treble damages.

Complementary cases are often derided as "free riding" on the government effort, but this label masks the extent to which private litigation can raise issues that are different from government litigation (e.g., proof of the damages caused by defendants' conduct) and can still require extensive litigation resources. The label also minimizes the extent to which private litigation furthers the goals of antitrust enforcement by ensuring redistribution of monopoly gains from offenders to victims.[92]

Antitrust enforcers also engage in competitive antitrust enforcement. "Competitive enforcement" occurs when one enforcer brings a case in which other enforcers have no interest. For example, private litigants have been quite concerned about distribution restraints, particularly dealer termination. When U.S. government enforcers were paying no attention to these restraints, private parties brought these suits.[93] Price discrimination cases are now rarely brought by government enforcers, but private litigants continue to enforce laws that restrict sales at discriminatory prices.[94]

Competition also occurs among government enforcers. One government agency either may be unable to follow through on an antitrust investigation[95] or may feel that a particular type of conduct should not be viewed as an antitrust problem.[96] The latter was particularly the case during the Reagan administration, when it took a consciously hands-off view of distribution restraints and mergers. State antitrust enforcers disagreed with this approach and became more active in the area, pursuing cases and issuing competing guidelines.[97]

2. *Networked Antitrust*

Recent U.S. antitrust enforcement has tended to become more cooperative, and the distinction between joint cooperative efforts and complementary litigation has become blurred. Indeed, it is becoming increasingly frequent for federal, private, and state enforcers to be investigating a particular practice at the same time. In such cases it may be difficult to determine which enforcer is following which, even when looking at the timing of case filings.[98] Government enforcers are able to obtain discovery prior to filing suit and are generally cautious about filing suit until after they have assembled such evidence.

Private parties cannot obtain prefiling discovery. They tend to file suit when they have sufficient evidence to file suit in good faith,[99] even if they do not have sufficient evidence to prove the full scope of their case, relying on pretrial discovery to obtain further information. Even in cases where private plaintiffs are first to investigate a possible antitrust violation, there are still substantial advantages to sharing information with the government enforcement agencies and to coordinating settlements with them.[100]

The increased cooperation among antitrust enforcers has led to the development of virtual networks of antitrust enforcers, as different antitrust enforcers deal with each other on a repeat basis. These networks help to coordinate the resources available for antitrust enforcement. Their nonhierarchical organization requires consensus for action, a process that may produce results that are different from what individual enforcers might have chosen. It also means that antitrust policy is less coordinated than if a single enforcer were making all the decisions. Enforcers are free to join the network or not, to operate cooperatively or competitively. Indeed, they are free to change from cooperation to competition in the course of litigation, for example, when some parties settle litigation and others choose not to do so.[101]

The U.S. system of multiple enforcers has often been criticized. The most frequently criticized aspect has been the sharing of jurisdiction between the Department of Justice and the FTC, although there seems little prospect of its being changed in any fundamental way.[102] Private enforcement has also been criticized, although court decisions limiting standing and damages have done much to narrow the ability of private plaintiffs to bring suit. State enforcement of antitrust law has similarly been criticized as duplicative of federal efforts or contradictory to the development of sound antitrust policy.[103] Various proposals have been made to manage better the diversity of enforcement efforts,[104] or to oust either private or state enforcement in some or all circumstances.[105]

At the least, having multiple antitrust enforcers likely increases the amount of antitrust enforcement. Although the total number of cases brought by the federal enforcement agencies has tended to be roughly constant since 1980 (except for dips in four of those years), the total number of cases brought by each agency has not necessarily moved in tandem (see figure 21.1).

More importantly, private enforcement has considerably increased the numbers of antitrust cases brought. Although the amount of private litigation has fluctuated over time, the number of private cases filed annually has exceeded U.S. government cases since the 1950s.[106] Between 1983 and 1990 there was a dramatic drop in private case filings, from approximately twelve

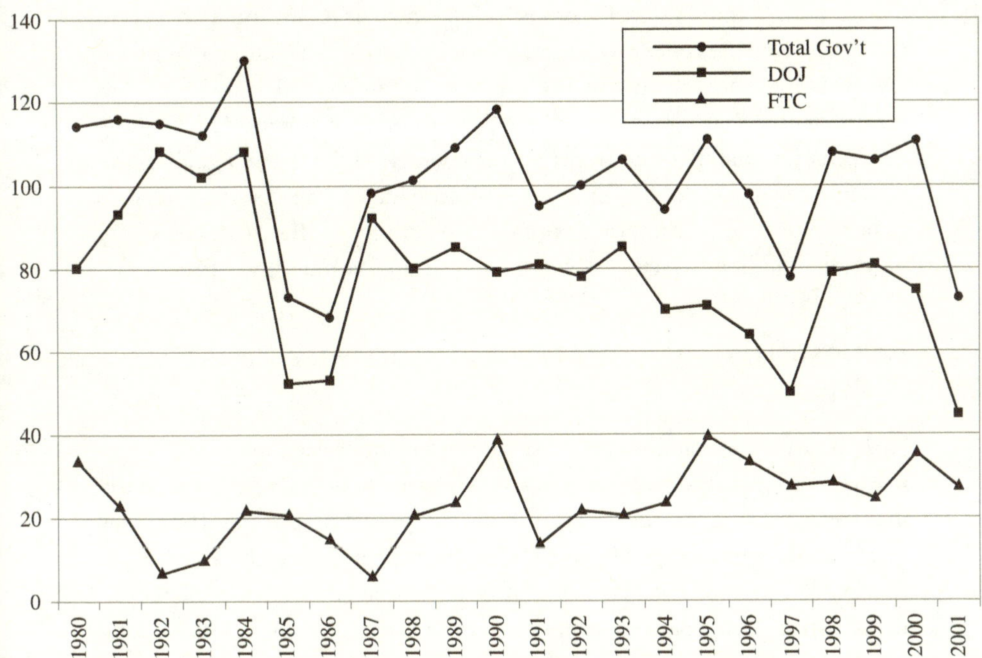

FIGURE 21.1. U.S. Government Antitrust Enforcement (DOJ and FTC), Cases Filed, 1980–2001

SOURCES: Dept. of Justice, Antitrust Div., Workload Statistics; FTC: 5 CCH Trade Reg. Rep.

hundred cases per year to approximately four hundred, but the numbers of filings in the 1990s have increased and they remain substantially higher than the number of cases brought by the federal enforcement agencies.[107]

The national system of networked antitrust, with multiple enforcers, is now being expanded to the international level. The European Commission is promoting the network idea for coordinating its efforts with those of the national authorities within the European Union, although the network in Europe is not as well "connected" as it is in the United States and raises different legal and institutional issues than national networking does in the United States.[108] In addition an "International Competition Network" (ICN) of antitrust enforcement agencies has been formed, the focus of which is on arriving at proposals for "procedural and substantive convergence in antitrust enforcement."[109] The ICN develops nonbinding recommendations on "best practices," which individual agencies then have the option to implement voluntarily.[110]

Criticism of the system of multiple enforcement has often come from commentators who are concerned about an overexpansive application of antitrust law. This does not prove that the multiple system actually produces such results, or even that it increases antitrust enforcement. It is, nevertheless, some confirmation that if robust antitrust enforcement is the desired goal, multiple enforcers make robust enforcement more likely. This certainly appears to be the judgment of national competition authorities that are increasingly working together on cases involving international competitive effects.[111]

IV. DESIGNING THE INSTITUTIONS OF ANTITRUST IN JAPAN

Japan is now in a period where it has chosen to emphasize the value of competition and markets over a regulatory industrial policy. This has led to the increased favoring of the JFTC within the government. The JFTC has increased its enforcement efforts to some extent, but these steps have not yet resulted in a marked increase in enforcement activity and there is still too little attention being paid to conduct outside the most obvious horizontal restraints.

Japan can learn from the decentralized system of enforcement that has been adopted in the United States and that is increasingly in use in Europe. Transposing institutions is, of course, a tricky business, as the United States itself learned when it proposed the original structure for the JFTC. Nevertheless, the U.S. experience does suggest at least three possible approaches that Japan could take.

The first is to increase the power of other government ministries to act on competition matters. In light of the past history of regulatory control in Japan, it might seem counterintuitive to urge an increase in the power of other ministries over competition matters. These ministries may very well be more institutionally prone to a regulatory approach to competition matters than to a market approach; indeed, the past history of these ministries would so indicate. Further, the most likely candidate for such concurrent jurisdiction, METI, is expressly restricted from handling competition matters under the Antimonopoly Act.[112] Nevertheless, an interim approach may be to network with these agencies and engage in cooperative enforcement on policy efforts, thereby enlightening these agencies on competition policy perspectives. As shown in the examples of the electricity and telecommunications sectors, other agencies have demonstrated a willingness to promote competition under certain circumstances and to work with the JFTC.

Cooperation and/or competition among government agencies might very well increase the vitality of competition policy. Mechanisms might need to be found to sort out problems if conflicts arise, but at least for the moment, the prospect of an increase in attention to competition matters could have very positive effects on the robustness of competition policy enforcement.

The second approach is to promote the greater power of the judiciary and the private bar in antitrust enforcement. For this to work satisfactorily, antitrust rules need to be more sophisticated and lawyers need to be better trained in antitrust tools and analysis. This means that the JFTC itself must make its articulation of antitrust rules more legally compelling. At the same time, antitrust education should play a greater role in the new law schools in Japan. With the increase in the number of candidates who will be passing the bar examination, more lawyers and judges will be entering the profession.[113] With a sufficient number of lawyers, the market mechanism should lead some of them to an antitrust specialty. With a sufficient number of judges, it would not be impossible for the judiciary to have a special tribunal for antitrust at the Tokyo District Court, at least as an interim step for advancing antitrust specialization in Japan.[114]

The third approach is to participate fully in the efforts of the ICN and to consider carefully its recommendations on best practices. The ICN may help provide a competitive spur that the JFTC needs to reexamine its internal operations and to engage in more effective enforcement in Japan. This network will bring a more open approach to antitrust enforcement generally and will give the JFTC an opportunity to articulate its policy approaches and the reasons supporting them. To the extent that these approaches are inadequate, the ICN can be instrumental in helping the JFTC improve.

V. CONCLUSION

Japan's antitrust enforcement system has been centralized in the Fair Trade Commission since the enactment of the Antimonopoly Act in 1947. The centralization of enforcement has produced a situation in which the JFTC has not adequately articulated antitrust rules and has preferred to rely on informal enforcement to deal with difficult problems. Although private litigation is possible under the Antimonopoly Act and under Civil Code Article 709, to date private litigation has not emerged as a significant aspect of the enforcement system. Indeed, the failure to provide adequate legal rules or seek judicial enforcement has in itself contributed to the weakness of private enforcement.

A distributed model of antitrust enforcement relies on cooperative networking among antitrust enforcers, and competition among antitrust enforcers, to increase the effectiveness of the antitrust enforcement system. This is the model that has been used in the United States with increasing effectiveness in the past decade and is the model that is being developed now on an international level to deal with the increasing internationalization of business. If Japan is to have an antitrust enforcement system that can help bring about the more competitive economy that government policy makers appear to want, it needs to distribute antitrust enforcement authority more widely among government agencies and private litigants and it needs to become a full participant in the international enforcement network now being put into place. Failure to take these steps will likely continue the paradox of a concentrated enforcement power that produces weak antitrust enforcement.

NOTES

The authors thank Nagashima Ohno & Tsunematsu for its kind support for the organization of the Seattle conference. Research support for Harry First was provided by a research grant from the Filomen D'Agostino and Max E. Greenberg Research Fund at New York University School of Law. Research support for Tadashi Shiraishi was provided by the Ministry of Education, Science, Sports and Culture, Grant-in-Aid for Encouragement of Young Scientists (B), 13720032, 2001–2.

1. Shiteki dokusen no kinshi oyobi kōsei torihiki no kakuho ni kansuru hōritsu [Act concerning Prohibition of Private Monopolization and Maintenance of Fair Trade] (Law No. 54 of 1947, as amended) (hereinafter "Antimonopoly Act"). Many sources abbreviate the act as "Antimonopoly Act," probably taking account of the fact that "Private Monopolization" appears first in the title. For a detailed analysis of the legislative history, see John O. Haley, *Antitrust in Germany and Japan: The First Half-Century, 1947–1998* (Seattle: University of Washington Press, 2001), 3–63; and Harry First, "Antitrust in Japan: The Original Intent," *Pacific Rim Law and Policy Journal* 9 (2000): 1.

2. Yoshio Kanazawa, "The Regulation of Corporate Enterprise: The Law of Unfair Competition and the Control of Monopoly Power," in Arthur Taylor von Mehren, ed., *Law in Japan: The Legal Order in a Changing Society* (Cambridge, MA: Harvard University Press, 1963), 480, 506. Makoto Yazawa, a commentator at the conference at which the chapter was discussed, stated that the Fair Trade Commission "has ceased active enforcement of the antimonopoly laws," although it

does publish "an annual report indicating the extent to which competition is restricted in certain industries" (491 n. *).

3. See ibid., 491.

4. Ibid., 496–505.

5. Ibid., 501.

6. Ibid.

7. In his first parliamentary policy speech on May 7, 2001, Prime Minister Koizumi said: "We will strengthen the structure of the Fair Trade Commission, which should serve as the guardian of the market, thereby establishing competition policies appropriate for the 21st century." *BNA Antitrust and Trade Regulation Report* 80 (May 18, 2001): 473.

8. Shogo Itoda, "Competition in Japan's Telecommunications Sector: Challenges for the Japan Fair Commission" (October 11, 2001), 1, available at (http://www.jftc.go.jp/e-page/policyupdates/speeches/011011speech.pdf).

9. For a fuller discussion of the Antimonopoly Act, see generally Tadashi Shiraishi, "Japan," in J. Basedow, ed., *Limits and Control of Competition with a View to International Harmonization* (The Hague: Kluwer Law International, 2002), 261–72. Note that this chapter describes the provisions of the Antimonopoly Act that were in effect as of January 2005. Various changes have subsequently been made to the act, effective in January 2006, including increases in the surcharge provision and changes in the statutory provisions relating to the JFTC's procedures for investigating and determining violations of the act.

10. For the JFTC's organization chart, see (http://www.jftc.go.jp/e-page/aboutjftc/role/role_all.pdf).

11. See Naikakufu setchi hō [Cabinet Office Organization Act], arts. 4(3) and 64.

12. See also arts. 7, 8-2, 17-2, 20 (power to issue cease and desist orders).

13. According to the JFTC (in its annual report of each year), the difference between warnings and cautions is that a warning needs "suspicion of violation," while a caution just indicates the "possibility of future violation."

14. See Gyōsei shidō ni kansuru dokusenkinshihō jō no kangaekata [JFTC Guidelines concerning Administrative Guidance under the Antimonopoly Act], June 30, 1994, available at (http://www.jftc.go.jp/e-page/legislation/ama/administrative.pdf).

15. This is according to public announcements by the JFTC. Some practitioners may disagree with this description.

16. Premerger notification is required for certain categories of mergers, corporate splits, and acquisitions of businesses (see arts. 15, 15-2, and 16); others must be notified ex post (see art. 10). The JFTC has jurisdiction over all mergers, whether

notified or not. In fact, it is extremely rare for the JFTC to take official measures in merger and acquisition cases. Rather, those cases are usually handled informally. For a detailed survey, see Yasuhide Watanabe and Yuko Tamai, "Japanese Merger Notification and Enforcement Policy," *Antitrust* 15 (2001): 49–54.

17. For details and exceptions, see arts. 7-2 and 8-3.

18. See "Dokusenkinshihō ihan ni taisuru keiji kokuhatsu ni kansuru kōseitorihiki iinkai no hōshin" [JFTC Policy of Filing Criminal Accusations against Violations of the Antimonopoly Act] (June 20, 1990). Prosecutors also have independent authority to prosecute price-fixing and bid rigging under the Criminal Code. For a description of the interaction between the JFTC and the public prosecutor, see David Boling, "The Role of the Prosecutors: Japanese Antimonopoly Law Criminal Cases," *Antitrust* 17 (2003): 90.

19. See art. 26(1).

20. See arts. 26, 84.

21. See, e.g., Nihon Keizai Shimbun (Nikkei) (April 27, 2002) (reporting lawsuit by allegedly excluded company, Hakodate Shimbun, against Hokkaidō Shimbun seeking damages pursuant to Civil Code in the Tokyo District Court, despite the fact that they could have relied on a previously entered JFTC decision, see Hokkaidō Shimbun (JFTC, February 28, 2000), Kōsei torihiki iinkai shinketsushū 46 (2000): 144. Note that the requirement that five judges be appointed to the Antitrust Tribunal of the Tokyo High Court is under criticism, even by a JFTC Research Group report, see "Dokusenkinshihō kenkyūkai hōkokusho" [Report by the Antimonopoly Act Research Group] (October 31, 2001). Indeed, it does not appear that the jurisdictional requirement has given the tribunal particular expertise in antitrust cases. An examination of the judges named in the decisions by the tribunal indicates that the Tokyo High Court cannot appoint judges to sit exclusively on antitrust cases, but, rather, appoints these judges on an ad hoc basis.

22. See "Dokusenkinshihō ihan kōi ni kakaru minjiteki kyūsaiseido ni kansuru kenkyūkai hōkokusho" [Report by Study Group on Civil Remedy System for Antimonopoly Act Violations] (October 22, 1999).

23. See, e.g., Fujiki Honten v. Shiseidō Keshōhin Hanbai (Sup. Ct., Dec. 18, 1998) (Shiseido case), *Minshū* 52 (1999): 1866 (assuming the point).

24. For details of the talks from an antitrust viewpoint, see Harry First, "Antitrust Enforcement in Japan," *Antitrust Law Journal* 64 (1996): 137, 163–73.

25. Kōsei torihiki iinkai jimusōkyoku [Fair Trade Commission General Secretariat], *Dokusenkinshi seisaku gojūnenshi* [Fifty Years of Antimonopoly Policy] (Tokyo: Kōsei torihiki iinkai jimusōkyoku, 1997), 2:98–102; "Kōsei torihiki iinkai nenji hōkoku heisei 12 nendo" [JFTC Annual Report of 2000], app., 1. There are 607 positions for 2002. JFTC announcement on December 22, 2001.

26. See (http: / /www.soumu.go.jp/english/gyoukan/img/001.gif).

27. See Gyōsei kikan no shokuin no teiin ni kansuru hōritsu [Act concerning Quantitative Capacity of Administrative Personnel] (Law No. 33 of 1969, as amended), art. 2.

28. The two U.S. federal antitrust enforcement agencies have an authorized staff of 1,355 "full-time equivalents" for 2002. See (http: / /www.usdoj.gov:80/jmd/ 2003summary/pdf/atr-bs.pdf) (851); and (http: / /www.ftc.gov/ftc/oed/fmo/bud getsum2002.htm#Personnel) (504 for competition mission). The U.S. economy, however, is about twice the size of Japan's, measured by gross domestic product. Adjusting for this difference by doubling the JFTC's size would give the JFTC an equivalent 1,214 positions, making it almost 90 percent the size of U.S. federal antitrust enforcement authorities. The U.S. figures do not include U.S. state government antitrust enforcement resources.

29. The Ministry of International Trade and Industry changed its name to the Ministry of Economy, Trade and Industry, in connection with the administrative reform in 2001.

30. See 1996 amendment to the Antimonopoly Act (Law No. 83 of 1996).

31. The number of JFTC decisions has fluctuated since 1981; e.g., thirteen in fiscal year 1981, five in fiscal year 1986, thirty-eight in fiscal year 1992, twenty in fiscal year 1995, and twenty-six in fiscal year 2000. The numbers exclude decisions on the amount of administrative surcharges. See "Kōsei torihiki iinkai nenji hōkoku heisei 12 nendo" [JFTC Annual Report of 2000], 32–33.

32. See Makoto Kurita, "Kisei kaikaku to kōsei torihiki iinkai no katsudō" [Regulatory Reforms and Activities by the JFTC], in Akinori Uesugi et al., eds., *21 seiki no kyōsō seisaku* [Competition Policy in the Twenty-first Century] (Tokyo: Nunoi Publishing Co., 2000). The author of this article was chief of the Coordination Division of the JFTC, which has been in charge of the Kiseiken.

33. Tekisei na denryoku torihiki ni tsuite no shishin [Ministry of International Trade and Industry and Fair Trade Commission, Guidelines for Fair Trade in Electricity] (December 20, 1999) (not available in English).

34. Professors Toshimasa Tsuruta, chairman (economics); Makoto Kojō (deregulation law); Toshihiro Matsumura (economics); Akira Negishi (antitrust law); and Tadashi Shiraishi (antitrust law).

35. See JFTC announcements on November 16, 2001 (Chūbu Electric Power Co.; instruction); March 26, 2002 (Kyūshū Electric Power Co.; instruction); and June 28, 2002 (Hokkaidō Electric Power Co.; warning).

36. See "Gyōsei kaikaku kaigi saishū hōkoku" [Final Report of Administrative Reform Council] (December 3, 1997). Chūō shōchō tō kaikaku kihonhō [Basic Act for Reforms of Central Government Agencies] (Law No. 103 of 1998, as

amended) (hereinafter "Administrative Reform Act"), art. 21(10) prescribes, "Competition policy, including antitrust law enforcement, shall be under the jurisdiction of the Fair Trade Commission, not of the Ministry of Economics, Trade and Industry."

37. Tekisei na denryoku torihiki ni tsuite no shishin [Fair Trade Commission and Ministry of International Trade and Industry, Guidelines for Fair Trade in Electricity] (July 25, 2002), available at (http://www.jftc.go.jp/e-page/legislation/ama/electric.pdf) (in English). The member list of the working group, set forth in note 34 above, was unchanged. The Electricity Industry Council is now a part of the Omnibus Natural Resource and Energy Council [Sōgō shigen enerugī chōsakai], due to the administrative reform in 2001.

38. Denki tsūshin bun'ya ni okeru kyōsō no sokushin ni kansuru shishin [Fair Trade Commission and Ministry of Public Management, Home Affairs, Posts and Telecommunications, Guidelines for Promotion of Competition in the Telecommunications Industry] (November 30, 2001), available at (http://www.jftc.go.jp/e-page/legislation/ama/telecom.pdf) (in English).

39. Press conference on June 27, 2001 (transcripts on file with the authors). Indeed, at the press conference the secretary general mentioned the headings of the draft, and the finalized guidelines contain the same headings.

40. This formal allocation was strongly criticized, mainly because it gave the appearance that the JFTC was dependent on the ministry in charge of the telecommunications and broadcasting industries. This allocation was abolished in 2003, as discussed earlier in section II.A.1.a.

41. JFTC announcement on March 15, 2002.

42. JFTC announcement on April 26, 2002. Other supports include airport facilities and aircraft servicing. With regard to "mavericks," see Jonathan B. Baker, "Mavericks, Mergers, and Exclusion: Proving Coordinated Competitive Effects under the Antitrust Laws," *New York University Law Review* 77 (2002): 135.

43. MLIT announcement on April 26, 2002.

44. See "Gyōsei kaikaku kaigi saishū hōkoku" [Final Report of Administrative Reform Council] (December 3, 1997); and Chūō shōchō tō kaikaku kihonhō [Basic Act for Reforms of Central Government Agencies] (Law No. 103 of 1998, as amended), art. 21(10) (discussed earlier).

45. Even the JFTC and its study group agreed with this analysis. See First, "Antitrust Enforcement in Japan," 168–169 (actions taken by the JFTC after SII).

46. Kai v. Nihon Sekiyū (Sup. Ct., July 2, 1987) (Tokyo Kerosene case), *Minshū* 41 (1987): 785; Nihon Sekiyū v. Satō (Sup. Ct., Dec. 8, 1989) (Tsuruoka Kerosene case), *Minshū* 43 (1990): 1259.

47. Earlier examples include Kawata v. Shimazu Seisakusho (Nara Dist. Ct.,

Oct. 20, 1999), *Hanrei taimuzu* 1041 (2000): 182, and Takahashi v. Tōshiba (Tottori Dist. Ct., Mar. 28, 2000), *Kōsei torihiki iinkai shinketsushū* 46 (2000): 673. Most of those cases were brought under the Chihō jichi hō [Municipal Autonomy Act] (Law No. 67 of 1947), which had permitted residents to sue on behalf of their municipal government; after an amendment in 2002, residents can sue the government to require it to sue the companies. The governments are usually direct purchasers from the bid riggers.

48. Examples include Tōshiba Elevator Technos v. Kōsei Denki (Osaka High Ct., July 30, 1993) (Toshiba Elevator case), *Hanrei jihō* 1479 (1993): 21 (¥110,000 for one plaintiff, ¥73,360 for the other), and Dejikon Denshi v. Nihon Yūgijū Kyōdō Kumiai (Tokyo Dist. Ct., Apr. 9, 1997) (Air Soft Gun case), *Hanrei jihō* 1629 (1997): 70 (¥18,461,634).

49. Civil law impediments have not been completely irrelevant, but the misperception itself may have contributed to the stagnation of private antitrust lawsuits by deceptively deterring private plaintiffs and even some lower court judges.

50. This complaint is not unique to Japan. See, e.g., Jeremy Lever, "Private Antitrust Enforcement in the European Community," in Clifford A. Jones and Mitsuo Matsushita, eds., *Competition Policy in the Global Trading System* (The Hague: Kluwer Law International, 2002), 225, 242 ("Most of Her Majesty's Judges have no knowledge of economic theory in general or competition and monopoly theory in particular").

51. See, e.g., Nihon Shokuhin v. Tokyo To (Sup. Ct., Dec. 14, 1989) (Shibaura Slaughterhouse case), *Minshū* 43 (1990): 2078 (Futō renbai ni kansuru dokusenkinshihō jō no kangaekata [JFTC Guidelines on Predatory Pricing] [Nov. 20, 1984] with regard to the factors for determining illegality); Fujiki Honten v. Shiseidō Keshōhin Hanbai, 1866 (Ryūtsū torihiki kankō ni kansuru dokusenkinshihō jō no shishin [JFTC Distribution Guidelines] [July 11, 1991]), with regard to the framework for analyzing requirements contracts between retailers and manufacturers).

52. Tokyo Ryōsuiki Kōgyōsho (Sup. Ct., Sept. 25, 2000) (Water Meter case), *Keishū* 54 (2000): 689, simply followed the doctrine of Idemitsu Kōsan (Sup. Ct., Feb. 24, 1984) (Oil Product Price-Fixing criminal case), *Keishū* 38 (1985): 1287, failing to consider the approach of the JFTC after-hearing decision, Osaka Basu Kyōkai (JFTC, July 10, 1995) (Osaka Bus Association case), *Kōsei torihiki iinkai shinketsushū*, 42 (1995): 3 (Narita, J.). In the Water Meter decision (and also in the Oil Product decision), the Supreme Court used the words "public interest" (art. 2[6]) to justify what it considers to be legitimate conduct. Art. 8(1), which prohibits similar conduct (i.e., horizontal restraints) initiated by trade associations, however, does not include the words "public interest." If "public interest" is the

critical phrase for considering justifications, then legitimate horizontal restraints by trade associations could never be justified, while those by companies could be. The Osaka Bus Association decision, an art. 8(1) case, made clear that it was the words "substantially restrict competition" rather than "public interest" that should be used for justification. Both arts. 2(6) and 8(1) include this phrase. The Water Meter decision completely neglects this approach (possibly without knowledge of the existence of the Osaka Bus Association decision).

53. See Naigai v. Nisshō, unreported case (Osaka Dist. Ct., No. 3884 [wa] 1996, March 29, 1999); Nipro v. Naigai, unreported case (Osaka High Ct., No. 1700 [ne] 1999 et al., Dec. 21, 2001). Naigai is a manufacturer of injection bottles based in Osaka, and Nisshō (now Nipro) is a sole provider of raw materials for injection bottles in West Japan. Nisshō tried to raise the price substantially immediately after Naigai began to import raw materials from Korea and Germany. Naigai sought certification that it only had to pay the original price, emphasizing that Nisshō's conduct was unlawful exclusive dealing. Although the courts ruled for Naigai, they did not find the conduct anticompetitive but relied on civil law for the proposition that there had not been an adequate conclusion of the contract to raise price. As a result, Nisshō can still try to negotiate a price increase. The decisions are not reported, probably because decisions without antitrust but only common civil law issues are not sufficiently unique for case journals. The JFTC had begun administrative hearings with Nisshō, see Nisshō (JFTC Decision of Commencing a Hearing, March 17, 2000), *Kōsei torihiki iinkai shinketsushū* 46 (2000): 466, which might have deterred the judges from discussing antitrust issues before a JFTC after-hearing decision was reached. For details of the parallel procedures, see Tadashi Shiraishi, "Hakodate shimbun to ampuru kijikan" [Hakodate Shimbun and Injection Bottle Materials], *Hōgaku kyōshitsu* 244 (2001): 87.

54. The quantitative shortage of judges in Japan has often been noted. See, e.g., J. Mark Ramseyer, "The Costs of the Consensual Myth: Antitrust Enforcement and Institutional Barriers to Litigation in Japan," *Yale Law Journal* 94 (1985): 604, 633–34.

55. For the bureaucratic and the legalistic models of regulatory culture, see First, "Antitrust Enforcement in Japan," 142, 176–79.

56. Seventy-nine out of 128 JFTC decisions from fiscal year 1995 to fiscal year 1999 involve "Unreasonable Restraints of Trade" (art. 2[6] and the latter part of art. 3), roughly equivalent to horizontal agreements. The total number of 128 is that of decisions on illegality, excluding decisions on amount of administrative surcharges. The other 49 decisions (out of the 128) include horizontal agreements led by trade associations. They are formally dealt with under another provision (art. 8), but are substantially the same as "unreasonable restraints of trade."

57. The landmarks are Ryūtsū torihiki kankō ni kansuru dokusenkinshihō jō

no shishin [JFTC Distribution Guidelines] (July 11, 1991) and Futō renbai ni kansuru dokusenkinshihō jō no kangaekata [JFTC Guidelines on Predatory Pricing] (November 20, 1984). Although a number of guidelines have appeared recently, most of them adopt the same rules as the classic landmarks. The newcomers are often industry-specific guidelines. See, e.g., Tokkyo nouhau raisensu keiyaku ni kansuru dokusenkinshihō jō no shishin [JFTC Guidelines on Patent and Know-How Licensing] (July 30, 1999); Shurui no ryūtsū ni okeru futō renbai sabetsu taika tō e no taiō ni tsuite [JFTC Alcohol Retailing Guidelines] (November 24, 2000, and April 2, 2001); Gasorin no ryūtsū ni okeru futō renbai sabetsu taika tō e no taiō ni tsuite [JFTC Gasoline Retailing Guidelines] (December 14, 2001); and also Electricity Guidelines and Telecommunication Guidelines. These are not intended to develop sophisticated rules, but are for enlightenment of those industries that have neglected antitrust. As far as exclusionary practices, the sophistication of the rules has not advanced since 1991.

58. NTT East and NTT West, issued on December 25, 2001.

59. See JFTC announcements on November 16, 2001 (Chūbu Electric Power Co.; instruction), and March 26, 2002 (Kyūshū Electric Power Co.; instruction). A second warning was issued in the 2002 fiscal year; see JFTC announcement on June 28, 2002 (Hokkaidō Electric Power Co.; warning).

60. We do not deny "the effect of education and adverse publicity" that can result from informal enforcement, see Haley, *Antitrust in Germany and Japan*, 168–70, although it is not clear how substantial that effect is. What is relevant here is the JFTC's lack of confidence in its legal doctrines involving exclusionary practices.

61. An example is the JAL/JAS integration, discussed in section II.B.2 above. When clearing the modified plan, the JFTC reasoned that there would not be a substantial restriction of competition, never mentioning the failing company doctrine. Reportedly, JAS would have gone bankrupt without the integration.

62. Hearings are usually held before three administrative judges. The commission approves proposed decisions submitted by the administrative judges, usually without any corrections.

63. Judges Tadahiko Mitsuda, 1991–94; Kitaru Narita, 1994–97; Toshifumi Shibata, 1997–2000; Jun'ichi Kaneko, 2000–2004; and Akihiro Nakayama, 2004–current (as of January 2005). The judge from the judiciary leads the hearing, with support from the other two, usually lifetime JFTC officials.

64. See Gerard C. Henderson, *The Federal Trade Commission: A Study in Administrative Law and Procedure* (New Haven, CT: Yale University Press, 1924), 86; and Richard S. Harvey and Ernest W. Bradford, *A Manual of the Federal Trade Commission* (Washington, DC: J. Byrne and Co., 1916), vii.

65. The lack of direction reflects the haste with which Congress changed the concept of the commission. The bill passed by the House would have established a purely investigative agency, "hardly more than an adjunct of the Department of Justice"; one week later the Senate reported a bill giving the commission the power to issue restraining orders. The bill was enacted into law barely three months later. See Henderson, *Federal Trade Commission*, 25–26. Early sources view the Department of Justice as the agency for litigation in court (an agency of "repression and punishment"), while the FTC was to be "a 'commercial police,' to maintain a constant guard over our vast and complex interstate commerce." Harvey and Bradford, *A Manual of the Federal Trade Commission*, vii, 132. But it was also recognized that "it is apparently contemplated that both the Attorney General and the Federal Trade Commission could if they were so minded bring simultaneous proceedings against the same party on the same charges." Henderson, *Federal Trade Commission*, 45. The lack of clarity in the division of antitrust statutes and enforcement responsibility in the United States was also confusing to Japan when the United States proposed an antimonopoly act that combined elements of the Sherman, Clayton, and Federal Trade Commission Acts into a single statute with a single enforcement agency. See First, "Antitrust in Japan," 50–53.

66. See James May, "Antitrust Practice and Procedure in the Formative Era: The Constitutional and Conceptual Reach of State Antitrust Law, 1880–1918," *University of Pennsylvania Law Review* 135 (1987): 495, 499. For a review of state antitrust law, see American Bar Association Section of Antitrust Law, *State Antitrust Practice and Statutes*, 2nd ed., 3 vols. (Chicago: Section of Antitrust Law, American Bar Association, 1999).

67. See Georgia v. Pennsylvania Railroad, 324 U.S. 439 (1945).

68. See 15 USC § 15c (parens patriae actions).

69. See, e.g., United States v. Interstate Commerce Commission (Northern Lines Merger Cases), 396 U.S. 491 (1970) (adequate consideration of competitive factors). Railroad mergers are still subject to regulatory approval under a public interest standard. See 49 U.S.C. § 11324 (Surface Transportation Board).

70. See 49 U.S.C. § 1378(b)(1). The Department of Transportation continues to have jurisdiction over "unfair methods of competition." See 49 U.S.C. § 41712; see also Department of Transportation, Enforcement Policy Statement on Unfair Exclusionary Conduct by Airlines (intended to prevent predatory pricing by major airlines in response to new entry; proposed April 6, 1998, but not adopted), available at (http://www.dot.gov/affairs/dkt3713.htm).

71. See 47 U.S.C. §§ 214(a), 310(d). For a discussion and critique of Federal Com-

munications Commission (FCC) merger reviews in the telecommunications sector, see William J. Kolasky, "The FCC's Review of the Bell Atlantic / NYNEX and SBC /Ameritech Mergers: Regulatory Overreach in the Name of Promoting Competition," *Antitrust Law Journal* 68 (2001): 771. These mergers are also subject to review by the antitrust enforcement agencies.

72. See Bank Merger Act of 1966, 12 U.S.C. § 1828(c).

73. See Federal Power Act, 16 U.S.C. §§ 824(b) (mergers), 824a-1, 824i–824k (wheeling and interconnection).

74. See, e.g., Gulf States Utilities Co. v. FPC, 411 U.S. 747 (1973) (requiring consideration of anticompetitive effects when determining whether to allow the utility to issue securities). Where the Department of Justice has concurrent jurisdiction, as in banking and energy, the regulatory agencies have often moved closer to antitrust standards in making their decisions on, e.g., mergers.

75. See Robert A. Katzmann, *Regulatory Bureaucracy: The Federal Trade Commission and Antitrust Policy* (Cambridge, MA: MIT Press, 1980), 193. Relations have not always been cordial, however, particularly in the early years when the commission attempted to use its investigative powers to prod the Justice Department to enforce previously entered antitrust decrees. See Thomas C. Blaisdell Jr., *The Federal Trade Commission: An Experiment in the Control of Business* (New York: Columbia University Press, 1932), 183–258 (investigations of meatpacking, steel, tobacco, oil, aluminum, and radio). These efforts "received slight consideration by the Department of Justice" (255).

76. David D. Martin, *Mergers and the Clayton Act* (Berkeley: University of California Press, 1959), 205.

77. See Gilbert H. Montague, "The Commission's Jurisdiction over Practices in Restraint of Trade: A Large-Scale Method of Mass Enforcement of the Antitrust Laws," *George Washington Law Review* 8 (1940): 365, 377–78 (sixty-four proceedings filed by FTC; ten by Department of Justice; 1915–39). Richard Posner lists eleven Justice Department cases brought for "acquisitions short of monopoly." See Richard A. Posner, "A Statistical Study of Antitrust Enforcement," *Journal of Law and Economics* 13 (1970): 365, 398 (table 23). The difference may represent a case brought only under the Sherman Act, which can also be used to prohibit mergers.

78. Montague, "The Commission's Jurisdiction over Practices in Restraint of Trade," 378–79.

79. Ibid., 388–99 (182 cases filed by FTC; 146 by Department of Justice) (1915–39).

80. See U.S. Department of Justice, Antitrust Division, *Antitrust Division Manual*, 3rd ed. (Washington, DC: Antitrust Division, U.S. Department of Justice,

1998), § 7.A.1, available at (http://www.usdoj.gov/atr/foia/divisionmanual/ch7.htm). The 1948 Memorandum of Agreement is described in *Report of the Attorney General's National Committee to Study the Antitrust Laws* (Washington, DC: U.S. Government Printing Office, 1955), 376.

81. See 15 U.S.C. § 18a(d) (concurrent jurisdiction).

82. The liaison process, as it operated by the 1970s, is described in Katzmann, *Regulatory Bureaucracy*, 193–94. The 1948 liaison procedure was formally modified in 1993; see *BNA Antitrust and Trade Regulation Report* 65 (1993): 746, and in 1995, see *BNA Antitrust and Trade Regulation Report* 68 (1995): 403.

83. See Memorandum of Agreement between the Federal Trade Commission and the Antitrust Division of the United States Department of Justice concerning Clearance Procedures for Investigations, available at (http://www.ftc.gov/opa/2002/02/clearance/ftcdojagree.pdf). According to information on clearance delays, on file with authors, in a 28-month period there were 136 matters to which both agencies asserted jurisdiction; the average delay in resolving case allocation was 17.8 business days.

84. See (http://www.usdoj.gov/atr/public/press_releases/2002/11178.htm) ("[I]n view of the opposition expressed by Senator Hollings, Chairman of the Commerce, Justice and State Appropriations Subcommittee, to the agreement and the prospect of budgetary consequences for the entire Justice Department if we stood by the agreement, the Department will no longer be adhering to the agreement") (statement by Charles James, assistant attorney general in charge of Antitrust Division) (May 20, 2002).

85. For a description of the current agreement, see U.S. Department of Justice, Antitrust Division, *Antitrust Division Manual*, § 7.A.

86. The agencies have issued joint guidelines for horizontal mergers, international operations, licensing of intellectual property, and competitor collaboration, along with a joint statement of enforcement policies in the health care sector, reproduced in John J. Flynn, Harry First, and Darren Bush, *Antitrust: Statutes, Treaties, Regulations, Guidelines, Policies 2001* (St. Paul, MN: West Publishing, 2001), 119–223, 256–87, 315–83. In 2002 the two agencies held joint hearings on "Competition and Intellectual Property Law and Policy in the Knowledge-Based Economy"; see (http://www.ftc.gov/opp/intellect/index.htm).

87. This contrasts with earlier conflicts in views between the two agencies. See Blaisdell, *The Federal Trade Commission*, 241 (with regard to 1920's FTC investigation of possible violations by Alcoa of a 1912 consent decree, "[t]he conflict between these two departments of government engaged in enforcing the law is striking").

88. See Federal Energy Regulatory Commission, Order No. 888, *Federal Energy Regulatory Commission Reports* 75 (1996): ¶ 61,080.

89. For example, the Northwest/Republic merger was opposed by the Department of Justice but approved by the Department of Transportation. See *BNA Antitrust and Trade Regulation Report* 51 (1986): 198.

90. See Robert Abrams and Lloyd Constantine, "Dual Antitrust Enforcement in the 1990s," in Harry First et al., eds., *Revitalizing Antitrust in Its Second Century: Essays on Legal, Economic, and Political Policy* (New York: Quorum Books, 1991), 484.

91. See Harry First, "Delivering Remedies: The Role of the States in Antitrust Enforcement," *George Washington Law Review* 69 (2001): 1004.

92. Government price-fixing prosecutions do not always lead to follow-on private treble damage litigation. For a study of follow-on litigation, which finds a lower percentage of follow-on cases than might otherwise be predicted, see Howard Marvel, Jeffry M. Netter, and Anthony Robinson, "Price Fixing and Civil Damages: An Economic Analysis," *Stanford Law Review* 40 (1988): 561, 572 (of 117 government criminal cases filed between 1972 and 1979, only about one-half resulted in follow-on civil suits, despite the fact that all but three of the cases resulted in convictions).

93. Note that private litigation in the distribution restraint area was not necessarily successful. See, e.g., Continental T.V., Inc. v. GTE Sylvania, Inc., 433 U.S. 36 (1977) (non-price vertical restraints subject to a rule of reason analysis; reversing jury award for plaintiff).

94. See, e.g., United Magazine Co. v. Murdoch Magazines Distrib., Inc., 2001 U.S. Dist. LEXIS 20878 (S.D.N.Y. 2001) (denying motion to dismiss claim of discriminatory pricing under Robinson-Patman Act); Intimate Bookshop, Inc. v. Barnes and Noble, Inc., 88 F. Supp. 2d 133 (S.D.N.Y. 2000) (granting motion to dismiss claim of discriminatory pricing under Robinson-Patman Act). For a critical government view of the Robinson-Patman Act and its underlying policy, see U.S. Department of Justice, "Report on the Robinson-Patman Act" (1977).

95. For a prominent example, see United States v. Microsoft Corp., 159 F.R.D. 318 (D.D.C. 1995) (Department of Justice brought suit brought after FTC deadlocked on whether to file an administrative complaint).

96. See, e.g., Edward T. Swaine, "The Local Law of Global Antitrust," *William and Mary Law Review* 43 (2001): 627, 762 (2001) (describing litigation involving collusion in restricting availability of pollution insurance coverage in the commercial general liability insurance market; case filed by private litigants and state enforcers after Justice Department declined to investigate); *BNA Antitrust and Trade*

Regulation Report 522 (July 20, 1971): A-16 (FTC issues complaint against Warner Lambert acquisition of Parke-Davis after Justice Department declines to bring suit).

97. The states, through the National Association of Attorneys General, issued guidelines dealing with merger cases and vertical restraints, reprinted in *Trade Regulation Reporter* (CCH), 4, ¶¶ 13,401, 13,405.

98. See In re Compact Disc Minimum Advertised Price Antitrust Litigation, 138 F. Supp. 2d 25 (D. Me. 2001) (complaint filed by states after concurrent FTC and state investigations; private class actions also filed; consolidated for pretrial proceedings).

99. See Federal Rules of Civil Procedure, Rule 11.

100. For an example of information sharing, see Arthur M. Kaplan, "Antitrust as a Public-Private Partnership: A Case Study of the NASDAQ Litigation," *Case Western Reserve Law Review* 52 (2001): 111 (describing sharing of information between private plaintiffs and Department of Justice) ($1.027 billion settlement).

101. The Microsoft litigation is a well-publicized example. The case was originally filed by twenty states (plus the District of Columbia) as well as by the Department of Justice. After the district court's major findings on liability were upheld by the court of appeals, the Justice Department announced a settlement with Microsoft, but not all the states agreed to join the settlement. Nine states (plus the District of Columbia) continued to litigate their relief claim separately from the other plaintiffs. Their different relief proposals, however, were eventually rejected by the courts. See Massachusetts v. Microsoft, 373 F.3d 1199 (D.C. Cir. 2004). See also Warren S. Grimes, "The Microsoft Litigation and Federalism in U.S. Antitrust Enforcement: Implications for International Competition Law," in Josef Drexl, ed., *The Future of Transnational Antitrust—from Comparative to Common Competition Law* (Berne: Staempfli Publishers; The Hague: Kluwer Law International, 2003), 237.

102. See, e.g., ABA Reports 1969, 1989 (case for abolishing the FTC 's antitrust jurisdiction "has not been made"), reprinted in *BNA Antitrust and Trade Regulation Report* 56, 1410 (special supp.) (April 6, 1989); and *Antitrust Law Journal*, 58 (1989): 42. See also Ernest Gellhorn, Charles James, Richard Pogue, and Joe Sims, "Has Antitrust Outgrown Dual Enforcement? A Proposal for Rationalization," *Antitrust Bulletin* 35 (1990): 695 (1990).

103. See, e.g., American Bar Association, Section of Antitrust Law, "Report of the Task Force on the Federal Antitrust Agencies—2001" (2001), 3 (describing current state and federal enforcement system as an "uncoordinated hodgepodge").

104. These include proposals to allow for more consolidation of litigation, see Andrew Gavil, "Federal Judicial Power and the Challenges of Multijurisdictional Direct and Indirect Purchaser Antitrust Litigation," *George Washington Law Review* 69 (2001): 860.

105. See Richard A. Posner, "Antitrust in the New Economy," *Antitrust Law Journal* 68 (2001): 925, 940–42 (2001) (urging repeal of state antitrust enforcement authority and allowing Department of Justice to sue for consumer damages, thereby ousting private litigants).

106. See Posner, "A Statistical Study of Antitrust Enforcement," 373 (fig. 2). Posner indicates that data for private litigation prior to 1938 are "very poor" and are only estimates. (370–71).

107. See B. Zorina Kahn, "Symposium on Antitrust," *Cornell Journal of Law and Public Policy* 9 (1999): 133, 137 (fig. 1). Data are lacking for the extent of antitrust enforcement by regulatory agencies, by private plaintiffs suing in state courts, and by state attorneys general. For a description of recent state enforcement, see First, "Delivering Remedies," 1017–18 (data for New York State).

108. See Alexander Schaub, "Developments of European Competition Law," Speech before Conference on Developments of Competition Law and Policy—European and National Perspective (April 19, 2002), 6 (describing the commission and member states as "network members"), available at (http://europa.eu.int/comm/competition/speeches/text/sp2002_014_en.pdf). The European Commission maintains greater legal control over the enforcement efforts of member states than do the U.S. federal agencies over the efforts of state antitrust enforcers.

109. See press release, U.S. Department of Justice, "U.S. and Foreign Antitrust Officials Launch International Competition Network" (October 25, 2001), 3, available at (http://www.usdoj.gov/atr/public/press_releases/2001/9400.htm). See also (http://www.internationalcompetitionnetwork.org/index.php/en/about-icn) ("The focus will be on improving world-wide cooperation and on enhancing convergence through focussed dialogue"). As of October 2002, the ICN had representatives from sixty-two countries (sixty-five competition authorities), with an interim steering committee representing fourteen jurisdictions including Japan. For current membership, see (http://www.internationalcompetitionnetwork.org/index.php/en/about-icn/steeringgroup).

110. For results of the ICN's initial meeting in September 2002, see (http://www.internationalcompetitionnetwork.org/index.php/en/library/conference/1).

111. For a description of these efforts, see Robert Pitofsky, "Antitrust Cooperation, Global Trade, and U.S. Competition Policy," in Jones and Matsushita, *Competition Policy in the Global Trading System*, 56.

112. See Chūō shōchō tō kaikaku kihonhō [Basic Act for Reforms of Central Government Agencies] (Law No. 103 of 1998, as amended), art. 21(10).

113. Cf. Curtis J. Milhaupt and Mark D. West, "Law's Dominion and the Market for Legal Elites in Japan," *Law and Policy in International Business* 34 (2003): 451

(presenting data indicating shift by elite university graduates away from civil service positions and into law practice; suggests that this may be due, in part, to an increased lifetime differential in earnings between the two careers).

114. This is in contrast to the current original antitrust jurisdiction of the Tokyo High Court, which presents procedural drawbacks to potential plaintiffs, as discussed in section II.A.2.a above. A special tribunal at the Tokyo District Court, by solving the procedural weaknesses of vesting original jurisdiction in the High Court, might prove more attractive to litigants and foster the growth of antitrust expertise (although plaintiffs could still go to another district court, of course). The Tokyo District Court currently has a tribunal accepting almost all antitrust private litigation, although the tribunal does not deal exclusively with antitrust matters. Reportedly, the tribunal is busily occupied with non-antitrust cases.

22 The Changing Roles of the Patent Office and the Courts after *Fujitsu/TI*

NAOKI KOIZUMI & TOSHIKO TAKENAKA

I. INTRODUCTION

Like many other areas of the Japanese legal system, intellectual property (IP) law has been undergoing major changes over the past decade.[1] These changes are a result of a strong U.S. influence on Japanese patent law and have led to the adoption of pro-patent policy.[2] A prime example of these trends is found in the patent enforcement process.

As originally designed, the Japanese patent system had the Japan Patent Office (JPO) playing a central role in the development of patent policy and also gave the JPO power to decide not only the validity of patents issued but also the protection scope of patents.[3] Although revisions of patent law codified in the Patent Act of 1959 had taken away the JPO's power to decide the protection scope,[4] JPO's exclusive power to decide patent validity remained intact until the Supreme Court handed down its *Fujitsu/TI* decision in 2000.[5] This decision gave Japanese courts the power to examine the validity of a patent and to refuse to enforce obviously invalid patents. The case signals a departure from German patent validity practice, which the Japanese patent system traditionally followed, and demonstrates movement toward the U.S. approach to patent validity.

Even though this new practice makes it possible to avoid multiple proceedings for validity challenges, as was done under the German approach, and for courts to provide quicker relief to Japanese patentees, it also brings with it some serious problems. This is attributable to the fact that the new practice does not also adopt other doctrines to remedy problems inherent in the U.S. approach. In order to have a better understanding of the current situation, this chapter will first examine the origins of and historical developments in the U.S. and Japanese systems for challenging patent validity. We will then turn to the *Fujitsu/TI* case and discuss the impact of that case.

II. U.S. AND JAPANESE PATENT ENFORCEMENT TRADITIONS

The U.S. patent system finds its origins in the United Kingdom's Statute of Monopoly.[6] The Statute of Monopoly was originally developed to limit Queen Elizabeth I's power to grant patents of monopoly. In *Darcy v. Allin*, a patent was granted to playing cards that were already extant in England and thus not novel.[7] Judges found the patent contrary to the common law, statutory law, and the freedom of people.[8] Moreover, they emphasized the limitation on the king's power to grant patents only to new inventions. Thus, the power of the courts to invalidate patents is inherent and essential to patent systems that follow the U.K. patent tradition.

The first U.S. patent statute followed the U.K. approach in viewing the power to invalidate a patent as being essential to a court's function.[9] United States courts monopolized the power to decide both patent infringement and validity until a reexamination system was introduced in 1980.[10] With the introduction of the U.S. patent system in 1790, courts held exclusive jurisdiction to decide the substantive requirements of patentability. This system continued until the creation in 1836 of the U.S. Patent and Trademark Office (USPTO), which started to examine applications before the issuance of a patent. The U.S. approach stands in stark contrast to the German approach, which provides exclusive jurisdiction over the examination of patentability requirements to the German Patent Office.

Another significant feature of the U.S. system is the low rate of validity findings in U.S. courts of U.S. Patent Office–issued patents. Although the rate was as high as 90 percent when the U.S. Patent Office started to examine substantive requirements in 1839, it gradually decreased to a mere 10 percent.[11] The rate then increased when courts of appeals were created to hear appeals from district courts, but decreased again in the 1930s as a result of the vigorous enforcement of antitrust laws and a general sentiment against monopolies. Even after the Patent Act of 1952 codified established case law that gave issued patents a presumption of validity, the rate did not exceed 50 percent.[12]

To address the uncertainty resulting from low validity rates, in 1982 Congress created the United States Court of Appeals for the Federal Circuit

(CAFC), which has exclusive jurisdiction over appeals arising from patents. The validity rate of U.S. patents rose above 50 percent only after creation of the CAFC, but nonetheless has still remained between 50 and 60 percent.[13] Under current U.S. patent practice, the CAFC plays a central role in developing patent policy in terms of patentability, patent validity, as well as infringement.

In contrast to the expansive power of U.K. and U.S. courts in determining patent validity, both German courts and Japanese courts following the German approach have refrained from exercising their power in deciding patent-related issues. In Germany, a great deal of importance is placed on the separation of powers between the judicial and administrative branches, and consequently Germany provides separate court systems for civil and administrative issues.[14] Demonstrating the significance of their separation of powers doctrine, without any express provision in the first German Patent Act, the Supreme Court of Germany gave the German patent office exclusive jurisdiction over the validity of patents issued by the office.[15] Reflecting these decisions, the 1892 Patent Act introduced a provision that further clarified the separation of powers between the civil courts and patent office.[16] Indeed, a leading patent law scholar justified the German Patent Office's exclusive power to decide patent validity by relying on the administrative nature of the patent-granting act and the separation of powers between the administrative branch (i.e., the patent office) and the judicial branch (i.e., the civil courts).[17] German courts still follow a well-established rule that establishes the binding effect of patent-granting authority. This rule deprives civil courts of authority to examine whether a patent was properly granted by the patent office and requires courts to treat a patent as being valid under any circumstance.[18]

In Japan, an early Patent Act adopted the German tradition of separation of powers between civil courts and the patent office and codified the requirement that those who wanted to invalidate a patent had to commence a trial at the JPO.[19] Early Supreme Court case law supported the view that civil courts should refrain from deciding patent validity in infringement proceedings.[20] However, unlike the German system, which followed a strict separation of powers between administrative and judicial branches, the Japanese system gave the JPO power to determine infringement related issues that were traditionally set aside for adjudication by the judicial branch. The Patent Act of 1899 introduced a trial to certify the protection scope of patented inventions (*kenri han'i kakunin shinpan*) and enabled the JPO to decide the scope of patents, which is the central issue when determining patent infringement.[21] Because Japanese courts developed a practice that required patentees to gain a decision from the JPO in a patent scope certification trial before commencing infringement proceedings, most disputes were resolved at JPO trials. As a result, this practice made it possible to centralize all patent-related authority in the JPO so that courts could take advantage of the JPO's technical expertise.[22]

After World War II, Japan adopted a U.S. court system and abolished special courts for dealing with administrative issues.[23] Although the German tradition of separation of powers is no longer enforced as strongly as it was prior to World War II, the Japanese patent system still afforded the JPO expansive power over patent matters. Only after extensive debate did the JPO relinquish its power to decide infringement issues; further, the Patent Act of 1959 abolished the protection scope certification trial.[24] However, the 1959 act did maintain JPO's exclusive jurisdiction over patent validity.[25] Until the Supreme Court handed down the *Fujitsu/TI* decision, Japanese courts interpreted the Patent Act to require them to follow the German rule of binding effect of patent-granting authority and refrained from deciding any issue resulting in a question of patent validity.[26]

III. THE ROLES OF THE PATENT OFFICE AND COURTS IN JAPAN

Expediting patent infringement trials was among the items on the Japanese Justice System Reform Council's agenda. The goal of speedier trials was also listed in the final report of the Strategic Council on Intellectual Property of the Cabinet, which was published in July 2002. Today, the average time for a first instance patent infringement trial at the Intellectual Property Chambers of the Tokyo District Court to reach a final decision is fifteen months. In 1990, it took thirty-two months. Though the time has been more than halved since 1990, the Supreme Court of Japan plans to reduce it even further, to one year. The Intellectual Property Strategic Task Force report proposes that the Tokyo and Osaka District Courts have exclusive first-instance jurisdiction for patent infringement cases and the Tokyo High Court have the second-instance (appellate) jurisdiction. In that scenario, the Tokyo High Court will effectively become a quasi "patent court," or a "Japanese CAFC."

However, sooner is not always better. We should not rush to achieve the laudable goal of speedier trials in the patent enforcement system without ensuring that invention claims are protected justly. "Justly" should mean that the dispute be heard by those competent to handle these issues. Patent infringement cases invariably involve complex technology and require judges to understand specialized scientific and technical knowledge. That is a difficult task for the average Japanese judge, who likely has no scientific or technical background. Also, because Japanese judges are transferred among courts every several years, they do not have enough time to gain specialized IP expertise.

For this reason, there has long existed a principle of distinct roles between the Japanese Patent Office and the civil courts: the JPO decides the validity of a patent and the courts interpret the scope of the valid patent claims. Claims for invalidation are decided before the special administrative board (*shinpan*) at a trial within the JPO. This trial system was introduced in 1888, modeled on German law, and the decision for invalidation applies in rem. In 1904, the prewar Japanese Supreme Court (*Daishin'in*, or Great Court of Judicature) affirmed this division of functions. Notwithstanding this bifurcation, even the first patent office commissioner in Japan envisioned courts eventually taking on a greater role in patent cases. Patent office commissioner Korekiyo Takahashi once wrote, as judges at that time were not familiar with patents and patent-related issues, that the board trial stage at the JPO should be taken advantage of and maintained until more IP professionals began to emerge.[27]

This divide forces the parties to run after two hares. In 2001, an average PTO trial lasted fifteen months. Parties were able to appeal adverse JPO decisions to the Tokyo High Court and finally to the Supreme Court. Infringement courts could stay their infringement proceedings and wait for the JPO to decide patent validity. But very few courts stayed their proceedings as the courts understandably aim to clear their backlogs, not add to them. More importantly, the focus should be on protecting the patentee as quickly as possible. In determining infringement, the most serious dilemma that judges confront is in a situation where patents at issue seem clearly to consist of technology that is already in the public domain, and therefore the patent should be invalid. In these cases, courts often dismiss the case, holding the patentee "misused (or abused)" his or her right. From a theoretical point of view, these holdings are odd, because the doctrine of abuse of right under general Japanese civil law requires the validity of the right involved as a prerequisite. To the contrary, in patent cases, this term has been used when a patent has not yet been invalidated but is very likely to be invalidated by the JPO trial board. In this context, interestingly, a judge in an infringement proceeding "anticipates" the outcome of a JPO decision and decides the case based on speculation.

How are judges able to predict the outcome of the JPO board? First, because the validity of a patent and its interpretation are closely related matters, judges must consider the prior art and its equivalents in interpreting the scope of a claim. Then, a situation where the patented invention is the same as the prior art as well as equivalent (obvious) to the prior art gives rise to a ground for invalidation.

IV. CHANGES BROUGHT ABOUT BY THE *FUJITSU/TI* CASE

In the *Fujitsu/TI* decision, the Supreme Court of Japan affirmed a recent practice developed by courts that deal with infringement issues.[28] When the patent at issue contains an obvious reason for invalidity and is expected with a high level of certainty to be invalidated at a JPO trial, requests for injunctive relief and damages are ruled an abuse of right. *Fujitsu/TI* was not an en banc decision, which means the decision by the Great Court of Judicature in 1904 is unchanged insofar as the infringement court still may not declare the validity of a patent.[29] In this connection, it is not theoretically correct to understand the holding in *Fujitsu/TI* as allowing the infringement court to declare a patent invalid in cases where the error of the JPO decision to issue the patent is "clear" under general administrative law theory.[30]

In handing down the *Fujitsu/TI* decision, the Supreme Court places a priority on affording fair and prompt relief to the patentee. More precisely, the court stresses that a dispute shall be resolved in one proceeding. This change in roles between the JPO and Japanese courts reflects the growing recognition of a patent as being personal property, not just a favor granted by the government. After the Supreme Court decision, more than a dozen lower courts have delivered decisions applying the new *Fujitsu/TI* abuse-of-right doctrine and have dismissed injunction claims before a final decision by the JPO trial board.

Therefore, after *Fujitsu/TI*, parties have an option between traditional two-track resolution (i.e., a JPO trial and court infringement proceeding) and the newly approved one-stop strategy (i.e., claiming obvious invalidity and infringement in a court infringement proceeding). An obvious risk of the one-stop option is a possible conflict between JPO and court decisions. For example, the JPO may affirm the validity of a patent after the infringement court holds the same patent "obviously" to be invalid. Under U.S. law, when a court declares a claim invalid, the effect of the decision applies to later cases brought by the same patentee as well as other parties through the operation of the collateral estoppel doctrine.[31] Because Japanese courts do not apply such a broad scope of the collateral estoppel doctrine, the patent that has already been found invalid in an earlier case will be unenforceable only as between the original parties. In practice, though, it is very likely that competitors will ignore patents once such patents are branded as invalid in an infringement procedure. Also, the business community expects the JPO will avoid this type of conflict between JPO and court decisions by "following" the judgment of the court. For those in the IP industry whose main concern is a fast resolution of disputes, the new track in the *Fujitsu/TI* decision is a welcome development.

V. CONCLUSION

Has the time come for us to abolish the JPO trial board, as Commissioner Takahashi predicted one hundred years ago? At least for the time being, the answer is no. Every year there are an increasing number of patent disputes. Likewise, each year the JPO trial board accepts more than two hundred claims for invalidation. Moreover, the courts are flooded by IP disputes. It would not be the wisest choice to let judges handle the entire caseload of IP disputes without first ensuring a sufficient number of judges capable of dealing with specialized IP issues. In fact, in order to cope with this situation, the JPO currently plans to expedite board procedure in order to maintain the viability of their invalidation trial system. Their goal is to resolve invalidation claims within one year.

In the long run, the institution more capable of ensuring efficient and accurate determinations of patent issues will survive. The critical factor is the competence of judges—that is, knowledge of both law and technology. The competition will be between judges and PTO examiners to see which of them will be able to achieve the necessary level of legal and technical background and expertise. The positive news is that the future may hold some promise in that more and more individuals with IP training may be adjudicating infringement and validity issues. This is attributable in large part to the recent reform of Japanese legal education, which has introduced a new system of graduate law schools, thereby opening up legal study to an increasing number of applicants whose undergraduate degrees are not only in law but also in science and technology.

NOTES

This chapter was prepared before the Japanese Patent Act was revised to merge opposition and invalidation proceedings and codify the holding of the Kilby decision. Chapters of Opposition and Trials in Japanese Patent Act were revised by the Act for Revising Part of Patent and Other Intellectual Property (Act No. 47 of 2003); and Article 104 added to the Japanese Patent Act by Act to Partially Revise the Court Organization Act and Other Laws] (Act No. 120 of 2004). For a discussion of recent patent and other intellectual property–related law revisions, see Toshiko Takenaka and Ichiro Nakayama, "Will Intellectual Property Save Japan from Recession? Japan's Basic Intellectual Property Law and Its Implementation through the Strategic Program," *International Review of Intellectual Property and Competition Law* 53 (2004): 877.

1. Toshiko Takenaka, "Recent Legislative Updates in Japan," *Center for Advanced Study and Research in Intellectual Property Newsletter* 6 (1) (1999): 11. This article is available online at the Web site for the Center for Advanced Study and Research in Intellectual Property, University of Washington School of Law (http://www.law.washington.edu/Casrip/newsletter/newsv6i1jp2.html).

2. Toshiko Takenaka, "Patent Infringement Damages in Japan and the United States: Will Enhanced Patent Infringement Damage Award Revive Japanese Economy?" in *Washington University Law and Policy Journal* 2 (2000): 309.

3. Toshiko Takenaka, "Interpreting Patent Claims: The United States, Germany and Japan," *IIC Studies* 17 (1995).

4. Tokkyohō [Patent Act], Act No. 121 of 1959.

5. Fujitsu v. Texas Instruments (Sup. Ct., Apr. 11, 2000), *Minshū* 54(4) (2000): 1368; English translation in Toshiko Takenaka, "A Major Change for Japanese Patent Enforcement," *Center for Advanced Study and Research in Intellectual Property Newsletter* 7(2) (2000). See also Naoki Koizumi and Institute of Intellectual Property, eds., *Tokkyo yūkōsei to shingai soshō* [Patent Validity and Infringement Procedure] (Tokyo: Keizai sangyō chōsakai , 2001).

6. The Statute of Monopoly, 1623, 21 Jam., c. 3, § 7, sched. 255.

7. Darcy v. Allin, 72 Eng. Rep. 839 (Moore, Rep. 671), 74 Eng. Rep. 1131 (Noy, Rep. 173).

8. 74 Eng. Rep. 1137–40.

9. Edward Waltersheid, "The Early Evolution of the United States Patent Law," *Journal of the Patent and Trademark Office Society* 76(11) (1994): 849–80.

10. 35 U.S.C. § 301.

11. Gloria Koenig, *Patent Invalidity: Statistical and Substantive Analysis*, 2nd ed. (New York: Clark Boardman Company, 1980).

12. 35 U.S.C. § 282.

13. John R. Allison and Mark A. Lemley, "Empirical Evidence on the Validity of Litigated Patents," *AIPLA Quarterly Journal* 26(3) (1998): 185.

14. For a general discussion on the German court system and German Patent Court, see Jim Patterson, "Übung Macht den Meister: How US District Courts Can Better Adjudicate Patents by Learning from Germany's Specialized Courts,"

Center for Advanced Study and Research in Intellectual Property 7(1) (2000): 27; available online at (http://www.law.washington.edu/Casrip/newsletter/newsv7i1Patterson.pdf). But see Christopher Heath, "The Connection between Infringement and Nullity Proceedings under German Law," in Koizumi and Institute of Intellectual Property, *Tokkyo yūkōsei to shingai soshō*, 289. Austria has a separate court system but gives civil courts power to determine patent validity.

15. Reichsgericht [Supreme Court], Judgment of January 7, 1882, RGSt (Entscheidungen des Rechsgerichts in Strafsachen) 5, 362; Reichsgericht, Judgment of October 24, 1887, RGSt 7, 146. For a general discussion on jurisdiction over patent validity in German civil courts and patent court, see Heath, "The Connection between Infringement and Nullity Proceedings under German Law," 285.

16. Tokkyohō, art. 28.

17. J. Kohler, *Handbuch des deutschen Patentrechts* [Handbook of German Patent Law] (Mannheim: J. Benscheimer, 1900), 362.

18. Georg Benkard, *Patentgesetz* [Patent Act], 8th ed. (Munich: C. H. Beck Verlag, 1998), 490.

19. Takenaka, "Interpreting Patent Claims," 41.

20. Koizumi and Institute of Intellectual Property, *Tokkyo yūkōsei to shingai soshō*, 5–7.

21. Takenaka, "Interpreting Patent Claims," 41.

22. See the discussion in section III on the roles of the patent office and courts in Japan.

23. Kenpō [Constitution], art. 76, ¶ 2.

24. Morifumi Uchida et al., *Hatsumei* [Inventions], pt. 2 (Tokyo: Yūhikaku, 1969), 843.

25. Tokkyohō, art. 123.

26. Japanese courts have, however, adopted a practice to examine the validity in determining the technical scope of a patented invention. See Takenaka, "Interpreting Patent Claims," 211.

27. Korekiyo Takahashi, "Wagakuni tokkyo seido no kigen" [The Origin of the Japanese Patent System], *Kōgyō shoyūken hō zasshi* [Journal of Industrial Property Rights Law], 32 (1908).

28. Fujitsu v. Texas Instruments, 1368.

29. Case comment by Judge Makiko Takabe in *Hōsō jihō* 54(5) (2002): 231.

30. A contrary view is set forth by Yoshiyuki Tamura, *Chizai—Kanri* 50(12) (2000): 1847.

31. Blonder-Tongue Lab. v. University of Illinois Found., 402 U.S. 313 (1971).

23 The Reform of the Japanese Tax System in the Latter Half of the Twentieth Century and into the Twenty-first Century

HIROSHI KANEKO

I. INTRODUCTION

The purpose of this chapter is to trace the development and reform of the Japanese tax system in the latter half of the twentieth century and to examine some important problems facing that system in the twenty-first century. In doing so, this chapter will address four major themes. First, it will reaffirm the importance and significance of the Shoup Mission Report as the starting point for the development of the Japanese tax system after World War II. Second, it will briefly describe the history of the modifications made to the Shoup tax system. Third, it will stress the importance of the tax reform of 1986–88 as the major turning point for the tax system in the period since World War II. Fourth, taking into account some important developments since the reform of 1986–88, it will examine the most important problems at present and offer a brief forecast of future developments.

For the Law in Japan conference held in 1961 at Harvard Law School, the essay on tax law was written by Morio Uematsu, an elite officer in charge of the formulation of the policy for individual and corporate income tax in the Tax Bureau of the Ministry of Finance.[1] After briefly describing the history of Japan's income tax system, Uematsu elaborately analyzed the income tax system at that time, based on various background theories and rationales. Though the approach of this chapter is different from that of Uematsu, the author of this chapter is very much inspired by the Uematsu essay and feels indebted to Uematsu and Rex Coleman (who ably translated the Uematsu essay).

II. THE SHOUP TAX REPORT OF 1949 AND THE SHOUP TAX REFORM OF 1950

The postwar reform of the Japanese tax system began in 1946. In 1940, Japan had adopted an income tax system that combined the schedular system and the global system. Under the schedular system, six types of income were subject to tax, each bearing a different rate. If the aggregate amount of income under the six schedules exceeded a certain amount, the excess amount was subject to a global, progressive income tax. Capital gains were not included in any schedule and were exempt from taxation.

The 1946 amendment adopted a few piecemeal reforms. Capital gains were made subject to tax and a new schedule for capital gains was added. In addition, a property tax was introduced as a one-time measure. This tax was imposed on the net assets of individuals in excess of one hundred thousand yen, utilizing progressive rates ranging from 25 percent to 90 percent. As a result of this tax, the economic inequalities and concentration of wealth in Japanese society decreased to a great extent. The following year, 1947, this hybrid system was replaced by a global, comprehensive, and progressive income tax system. In addition, the self-assessment system was adopted for direct national taxes.

Three years later, in 1950, this system was replaced yet again, pursuant to comprehensive tax reform based on the "Report on Japanese Taxation by the Shoup Mission" of 1949 (hereafter, "Shoup Mission Report" or "Shoup Report"). The Shoup Mission consisted of seven tax specialists, headed by Professor Carl Shoup of Columbia University. Among its members were such eminent scholars as Professors Stanley Surrey, William Warren, and William Vickrey. The Shoup Mission came to Japan in May 1949 on the invitation and request of General Douglas MacArthur, supreme commander for the Allied powers, to conduct thorough research on the Japanese tax system and to recommend comprehensive reform of that system. After intensive and extensive research spanning a period of almost two and a half months, the mission began drafting the report, which they completed in late August and submitted to General MacArthur on August 28, 1949. It is this report that is usually referred to as the Shoup Mission Report.[2]

The Shoup Report recommended comprehensive and long-term tax reform covering both national and local taxes and extending to both the tax system itself and the administration thereof. The report set forth three basic reform principles: (1) the establishment of an equitable tax system, (2) the improvement of tax administration, and (3) the promotion of local autonomy and strengthening of finances of local government. Based on these principles, the main recommendations were as follows:

First, the Shoup Mission recommended a tax system in which direct taxes occupied the central and dominant role. This was based on the rationale that direct taxes are superior to indirect taxes because taxpayers are conscious of a tax burden when they pay direct taxes and also because direct taxes better satisfy the principle of taxation according to ability to pay. For that reason, the report recommended that individual and corporate income taxes should be the main revenue source of the national government, and the main local taxes should be value-added type business tax, inhabitants tax, and real estate tax. Among direct taxes, the Shoup Mission recommended putting income tax at the center of the tax system. Concerning consumption taxes, the mission recommended a system of selective consumption taxes on liquor, tobacco, and other nonnecessities.

Second, the report strongly recommended promoting the idea of global, progressive taxation with a comprehensive tax base. They advised that the tax base should be as broad as possible. As a corollary to the principle of a comprehensive income tax, the mission strongly opposed preferential tax treatments and advised the elimination of such measures. Capital gains taxation was one of the most important subjects of the Shoup Report. According to the report, full taxation of capital gains was the most important element of modern progressive income taxation. To that end, the mission recommended that capital gains should be fully taxed and that capital losses should be fully deducted. The mission also recommended improving existing personal exemptions and introducing new deductions, such as a medical expense deduction and a deduction for the handicapped. These recommendations embodied the addition of a social policy element to income taxation to a great extent.

Third, the Shoup Report recommended simplifying the rate structure and cutting down the highest rate for the income tax from 85 percent to 55 percent. The reasons for this recommendation were that, if the rates were too high, the incentive to work or invest would be discouraged, and the fair and accurate enforcement of tax law would be rendered difficult because of tax evasion by those with high incomes. As a substitute for the 30 percent reduction in the highest rate, the Shoup Mission recommended introducing a net worth tax on wealthy people, utilizing four low progressive rates ranging from 0.5 percent to 3 percent. If it were assumed that the net return from a given asset would be 10 percent, then a 3 percent net worth tax would equal an income tax of 30 percent.

Fourth, the report deemed a corporation as an aggregate of shareholders and the corporate income tax as the advance payment of the income tax by the individual shareholders. Consequently, the Shoup Mission recommended repealing the withholding tax on dividends and adopting a dividend-received tax credit of 25 percent as a measure to avoid economic double taxation. To discourage corporations from retaining profits so as to protect shareholders from the high individual income tax rates, the report recommended that a low-rate interest surcharge be levied on corporations' accumulated retained profits at the end of each accounting year.

Fifth, the report recommended the revaluation of the assets of corporations as well as those of individuals. Since the postwar inflation had driven the book value of assets far below market value, it was difficult for enterprises to reserve funds for the reacquisition of assets by depreciation. Therefore, the report advised that the assets be revalued and that depreciation be based on this revaluation. This shows that the Shoup Mission gave due consideration to the restoration and stability of the Japanese economy.

Sixth, the report recommended that the inheritance tax and the gift tax be combined in a single "cumulative accession tax." Under this system, a person shall be taxed on the cumulative value of the properties that he or she acquires by inheritance or gift in his or her lifetime. Therefore, this is an equitable system from the viewpoint of the total amount of accession over one's lifetime. As is well known, this system was based on the idea of Vickrey, a member of the Shoup Mission and the author of the "Agenda for Progressive Taxation." The Shoup Mission conceived that this tax would be useful to eliminate the concentration of wealth (which is the major purpose of the inheritance tax). The mission recommended raising the highest rate of the cumulative accession tax to 90 percent, reasoning that, unlike the situation with the income tax, high tax rates on inheritance would not discourage people to work or invest.

Seventh, the report strongly recommended improving tax administration, increasing the severity and strictness of punishments for tax evasion, and stabilizing the self-assessment system. These recommendations were based on the view that, in order to realize equity in taxation, it is indispensable not only to enact statutes embodying an equitable tax system but also to enforce those statutes strictly and properly and to prevent tax evasion. At the same time, the mission recommended increased protection for taxpayers' rights, including the establishment of a conference group in the tax appeals procedure. The mission was especially concerned with the self-assessment system, which members thought was very important for democracy in taxation. Since its introduction in 1947, the self-assessment system had not worked well. Voluntary compliance by taxpayers had been very unsatisfactory. To improve taxpayer compliance, the mission recommended adoption of the so-called blue-return system, under which taxpayers who undertook accurate bookkeeping and filed honest returns based thereon, using the blue-return form, would be given various benefits.

Finally, the Shoup Mission recommended basic reform of the local tax system in various respects. First, before the end of the World War II, it was quite common for the national, prefectural, and local governments to share the same revenue sources. In fact, the prefectures and local communities were permitted to impose surtaxes on national taxes to a wide extent. This system was abolished in the reforms of 1947 and 1948. However, even after those reforms local communities were permitted to impose surtaxes on *prefectural* taxes. Moreover, a revenue transfer system, called the "local distribution tax," existed. Under this system, some portion of the revenue from the national income and corporation taxes was distributed to the local governments. The mission concluded that these systems were inappropriate; in the mission's view, sharing the same revenue sources among the different levels of governments would obscure the responsibility of each level. Accordingly, the mission recommended that any given revenue source should belong to just one level of government and that all surtaxes should be abolished as a matter of principle. However, there remained some exceptions in which the same revenue sources would be shared by the national and local governments, such as the income tax and the inhabitants tax.

Next, in order to promote local autonomy, which was guaranteed by the Constitution, the Shoup Report recommended strengthening the independent revenue sources of the local governments. In particular, the Shoup Mission stressed the importance of ensuring sufficient revenue for local communities to fulfill their role as the basic government body. From this viewpoint, the mission recommended (1) abolishing the prefectural inhabitants tax and making the inhabitants tax solely a revenue source for local communities; (2) imposing a new fixed assets tax on lands, houses, and depreciable assets, the revenue from which would go to the local communities (prior to that time, taxes on lands and houses were prefectural taxes); and (3) transforming the prefectural business tax from a net-income type to a value-added type, in order to supplement the revenue loss to prefectures caused by the transfer to local communities of the inhabitants tax and the taxes on lands and houses and to increase the revenue of prefectures.

The rationale for the value-added type business tax was that since business enterprises, regardless of the amount of their profits, benefit from public services provided by the prefectural governments regardless of the profits, they should bear the tax burden in accordance with the extent of the benefits so received. This shows that the mission adopted the philosophy of "taxation according to benefits" (benefit theory) as the principle for local taxation. At any rate, the proposal for the value-added type business tax was important, because, though it was a direct tax, it was the first attempt to introduce a value-added tax anywhere in the world.

As a general grant to local governments from the national government, the Shoup Mission Report recommended replacing the local distribution tax with a local equalization tax, designed so that every local government would be guaranteed revenue sufficient to offer inhabitants at least the minimum level of essential services. This objective was very important for the Shoup Mission. Unfortunately, time and space do not permit further exploration of the details in this chapter.

As mentioned earlier, the Shoup Mission submitted its report to General MacArthur on August 28, 1949. On September 15, less than three weeks later, MacArthur passed along the Shoup Report to Prime Minister Shigeru Yoshida with a letter advising him to adopt the recommendations as a whole. In his reply letter of September 17, Yoshida expressed his great appreciation for the report and promised to take necessary steps so that the recommendations thereof would be adopted as a whole.

The recommendations of the Shoup Mission Report were adopted in both basic structure and details by the tax reform legislation of 1950, albeit with some modifications. The legislation has usually been referred to as the "Shoup Tax Reform" and the resulting tax system as the "Shoup Tax System." In the 1950 reforms, the value-added type business tax was also adopted, but implementation of that system was "postponed" because of alleged difficulties in administration. During the period of "postponement," the existing net-income type business tax continued to be imposed. As it turned out, however, the value-added type business tax was repeatedly postponed and ultimately was abolished in 1954 without ever going into effect.

The Shoup Mission Report represented a grand reform plan for the tax system of an entire nation according to a coherent theoretical framework. In that sense, the Shoup tax reform was a magnificent experiment. The report was based on the latest tax theories of that time in the United States and reflected high academic standards. Moreover, the report was animated to a great extent by a spirit of reformism. The members of the mission were well aware of the problems of the tax system of the United States and had deep insight into how that system should be reformed. For that reason, they were able to design an ideal modern tax system from the viewpoint of equity.

To sum up, the Shoup Report contributed not only to the modernization of the Japanese tax system but also to the economic stability and growth of Japan, as exemplified by the recommendation for the revaluation of assets. Moreover, the mission encouraged Japanese scholars to pay attention to the importance of tax theory and tax law, and, in the long run, this constituted another of the Shoup Mission's major contributions.

III. THE PROCESS OF MODIFICATION (DETERIORATION?) OF THE SHOUP TAX SYSTEM

The basic structure of the Shoup Tax System was maintained intact for just three years. Since 1953, various modifications and amendments have been made to that system, and in the process the Japanese tax system has gradually taken a shape rather different from that envisioned by the Shoup Report.

The modifications to the Shoup Tax System can be divided into two major categories. One consists of revisions to, or the repeal of, the system adopted by the report. For instance, the net-worth, cumulative accession, and value-added type business taxes were abolished in 1953 and 1954. This was based on the reasoning that these taxes were too difficult to enforce or too complicated to be complied with.

The other consists of multiplication of the preferential tax treatments for both individual and corporate income taxes. As mentioned above, the Shoup Report took a strictly negative attitude toward preferential tax treatments. Since 1951, however, various preferential tax treatments have been introduced. The fact that a comprehensive revision of the Special Tax Treatments Act was deemed necessary as early as 1957 reflects just how rapidly such preferential tax treatments increased. The purpose of most of these treatments was to promote capital formation and development of the national economy by encouraging savings, the retention of profits, the modernization of equipment and machinery, the promotion of exports, and the like. The methods used for these purposes were varied, including (1) exclusions from income (e.g., interest from nontaxable savings, capital gains on the sale of securities); (2) separate taxation at a lower flat rate (e.g., interest from fixed-term savings); (3) special reserves (e.g., for the retention of profits, reserves against future fall in price for certain kinds of inventories, promotion of exports, and the development of foreign markets); (4) deferral (nonrecognition) (e.g., compulsory land transactions); and (5) special depreciation (for the modernization of equipment and machinery). One of the most notorious of these special treatment measures was a special expense deduction for doctors and dentists, which was introduced in 1954. Pursuant to this deduction, doctors and dentists were permitted to deduct, as expenses, 72 percent of the fees they received from social insurance funds, without providing any substantiation.

Since the mid-1960s, criticisms of the preferential tax treatments have become severe. As a result, some treatments have been abolished and others have been restricted in scope. At the same time, however, many new preferential tax treatments have been adopted; these include, for example, measures to protect small and medium-size enterprises, to promote regional development, to deal with pollution, to deal with land-use problems, and so on.

Thus, the Japanese tax system contains many and diverse preferential tax treatments. These preferential tax treatments have always been supported by some rationale or justification. Needless to say, however, they usually have been introduced and maintained under strong political pressure from business or professional organizations.

These treatments erode the tax base, undermine equity and neutrality in taxation, and cause distortion by interfering with decision making in the private sector. The preferential tax treatments have had another major adverse impact on the system as a whole: raising of tax rates. To recover the revenue loss resulting from the preferential tax treatments, the tax rates for both individual and corporate income tax were raised from time to time. In 1962, the top rate on the individual income tax reached its peak at 75 percent, and in 1984 the top rate on the corporate income tax reached 43.3 percent.

Turning attention to tax administration, the level of compliance has gradually improved owing to various measures, including the blue-return system. However, the income tax is very difficult to enforce accurately, especially with regard to business and property income. As a reflection of this difficulty, the so-called 9-6-4 phenomenon has been the subject of great controversy in Japan. According to the 9-6-4 phenomenon (or, more accurately, the 9-6-4 hypothesis), under the current system, on average 90 percent of salary income is caught, 60 percent of business income is caught, and only 40 percent of agricultural income is caught. Though it is not ascertainable whether the 9-6-4 hypothesis is true, it is the general consensus in Japan that, although difficult to quantify, there is a considerable difference and inequality in enforcement as between salary income and business-property income, because salary income is rather accurately caught and collected through the withholding system.

The perception of inequality is further exacerbated by the fact that almost all preferential tax treatments are for business and property income. In sum, salary income is more accurately caught than business and property income, and, at the same time, business and property income benefit from many more preferential treatment measures. Given these circumstances, it is hardly surprising to find that salary earners are inclined to believe that, as a matter of fact, they are more heavily taxed than those whose income consists mainly of business or property income. This has been the perennial cause of frustration and dissatisfaction toward the income tax system among salary earners, who constitute the majority of income taxpayers in Japan.

A lawsuit brought by Professor Tadashi Ōshima concerning his salary income of 1964 symbolizes this frustration and dissatisfaction. Ōshima asserted that the tax regime on salary income violated the equal protection clause of Article 14 of the Constitution, and therefore the taxation of his salary income was unconstitutional. Ōshima offered three reasons in support of his position: (1) the actual expense deduction is permitted for business income but not for salary income; (2) the tax burden on business income is reduced by various preferential tax treatments, but no preferential tax treatment exists for salary income; and (3) the business income is not accurately caught, whereas salary income is.

The Kyoto District Court and Osaka High Court did not accept Ōshima's contentions and dismissed the case. Ōshima filed a further appeal to the Supreme Court, which unanimously held that the income tax system on salary was not unconstitutional and dismissed the case.[3] The opinion of the Court was exceptionally long, and some justices wrote concurring opinions pointing out various problems with the Individual Income Tax Act and its enforcement. In response to the above frustration and dissatisfaction as well as the concurring opinions of the justices, the tax statutes have been amended from time to time to reduce the income tax and to increase indirect taxes.

In spite of these reductions in the income tax, the amount and the ratio of revenue from the income tax continued to increase as a result of Japan's high economic growth. In this sense, it could be said that the Shoup Report's recommendation that income tax should be the dominant revenue source was realized. However, the Shoup Report's basic ideal of keeping the tax base of the income tax comprehensive from the viewpoint of equity has been greatly damaged by the introduction of the various preferential tax treatments. Moreover, compliance still has not reached a satisfactory level.

The turning point for the next basic tax reform came with the first oil crisis of 1973, which will be described in the next section.

IV. THE BASIC TAX REFORM OF 1986–88—THE ADOPTION OF THE VALUE-ADDED TAX AND THE REFORM OF THE INCOME TAX

A. BACKGROUND TO THE REFORMS

As a result of the first and second oil crises of 1973 and 1974, the growth rate of the Japanese economy drastically declined. Consequently the revenue from income tax also drastically decreased. On the other hand, government expenditures steadily increased because of the increase in mandatory expenditures, such as expenses for education, social security, and so on. If no measures were taken, huge financial deficits would have resulted. To avoid deficits, both the national and local governments issued large amounts of bonds every year. Thus, the debts of both the national and local governments rapidly accumulated, and Japanese public finance fell into a vicious circle—issuing bonds to pay the interest on bonds.

In order to solve this problem and put Japanese public finance on a sound track, increasing tax revenue was indispensable. However, in view of the above-mentioned frustration and dissatisfaction of taxpayers, it was impossible to increase the income tax. Increasing the other taxes then in existence would not have generated much additional revenue, and thus that approach did not represent a viable solution to the problem. Therefore, the adoption of some new tax with large revenue potential was indispensable. The only tax that could satisfy this necessity was the general consumption tax, especially the value-added tax.

Prime Minister Masayoshi Ōhira was very concerned about the serious condition of public finance, especially the vast increase in accumulated debts. He requested the Tax Policy Committee to undertake research on ways to solve or mitigate the problem and submit their opinion to him. After comprehensive research, that committee reached the conclusion that only the turn-over tax or value-added tax had enough revenue potential to solve or mitigate the problem and that of these two alternatives the value-added tax would be preferable to avoid distortion in the national economy caused by the tax-on-tax problem under the turn-over tax.

However, opposition—amounting to an allergy—to the value-added tax was very strong among the taxpayers. Accordingly, instead of simply recommending a value-added tax, the Tax Policy Committee designed a new type of tax, which it labeled the "general consumption tax." Taxpayers of the general consumption tax consisted of all business enterprises, covering both corporations and individuals and extending to all levels of business from the production of materials to retail; the tax base was the amount of gross sales less the amount of gross purchases. The tax rate of 5 percent was to be applied to this tax base. In effect, the general consumption tax was similar to the value-added tax, though the method of calculation of the tax amount was different.

On the advice of the Tax Policy Committee, Ōhira's Cabinet formally decided in 1979 to prepare for implementation of the general consumption tax. However, Ōhira lost the stable majority in the general election held that year, in which the general consumption tax was one of the main issues, and he died soon thereafter. The succeeding Cabinet, aware of the strong opposition among taxpayers to any kind of general consumption tax, formally announced that it would give up the attempt to adopt a general consumption tax for the time being and instead promised to pursue the policy of reconstructing sound public finance without increasing taxes.

In 1985, however, inspired by the tax reform policy of the Reagan administration of the United States, Prime Minister Yasuhiro Nakasone, started to take actions for tax reform, and his successor as prime minister, Noboru Takeshita, followed Nakasone's policy. In the period of 1986–88, during which they served as prime ministers, very important tax reforms were realized. One was the introduction of the value-added tax, whose official name was the "consumption tax." Another reform was that of the income tax and other direct taxes.

B. INTRODUCTION OF THE VALUE-ADDED TAX

In 1985, Prime Minister Nakasone gave up the above-mentioned policy of reconstruction of sound public finance without a tax increase and announced that basic tax reform was necessary. He requested the Tax Policy Committee to study how the tax system should be reformed and to submit its opinion to him.

On the advice of the committee, Nakasone decided to adopt a value-added tax of the type used in the European Community (EC), under the official name "sales tax" and submitted a bill to that effect to the Diet. However, opposition was very strong. The most severe opponents were housewives and owners of small and medium-size businesses. Housewives were worried that the prices of goods and services would go up even more than the amount of tax. The businesspeople were worried that they could not shift the tax burden to the purchasers of their goods and services. They also expressed concern over the cost and other various burdens of compliance. An even greater, unstated reason for their opposition might have been that the invoice system would give the tax authorities the means to check the accuracy of their income tax returns.

Since the opposition was very strong, the sales tax bill was aborted and the Nakasone Cabinet resigned. The successor prime minister, Takeshita, took a somewhat different approach. Although what he planned to adopt was also an EC-type value-added tax, Takeshita inserted into the bill various devices to soothe and mitigate the opposition of the businesspeople, such as (1) the use of a bookkeeping method instead of an invoice method for the input tax credit; (2) the exemption of some enterprises from the tax, where the amount of the gross annual taxable sales was 30 million yen or less; (3) the tax rate of 3 percent (rather than 5 percent, as previously proposed); (4) a summary tax system, under which enterprises whose amount of gross annual taxable sales was 500 million yen or less could credit as input tax a fixed percentage of the gross annual taxable sales amount, and so on.

As a result of these measures and the tremendous efforts of Takeshita and his supporters, this time the bill passed the Diet late in 1988, and the value-added tax, renamed the "consumption tax," took effect from April 1, 1989. This tax was usually justified by the following four rationales:

First, as mentioned earlier, this general consumption tax, which was similar to a value-added tax, was the only tax that had sufficient revenue potential to finance the reduction of the tremendous amount of accumulated government debts and to cover the increase of expenditures for Japan's aging society.

Second, it was thought necessary to reduce the income tax in order to mitigate the frustrations and dissatisfactions of the working population. A value-added tax could raise a substitute fund that could help lower the income tax.

Third, the value-added tax was necessary to maintain equity between the aged generation and the working generation. A large part of the income tax revenue paid by people of the working generation is used as funds to take care of the aged and to pay their pensions. With the introduction of the value-added tax, the aged were also required to pay taxes when they used their pension income and their savings from past income for consumption. Thus, the value-added tax realizes, or helps to realize, equity between the aged and the working generation to a considerable extent. In a related point, it is sometimes stressed that income that may have evaded tax under the income tax system is taxed under the value-added tax system when used for consumption. In this sense, the value-added tax serves to recover equity—between salary earners and those with business or property income, for example—to some extent.

Fourth, the value-added tax renders the consumption tax system neutral; that is, a value-added tax can maintain tax neutrality between various goods and services. In contrast, under a selective consumption tax system (under which only specified types of products or services are taxed), the consumption is apt to flow to the nontaxed items, consequently causing distortion.

The Shoup Mission recommended a selective consumption tax on luxuries or quasi luxuries. Therefore, a value-added tax is apparently contrary to the basic idea of the mission with respect to the consumption tax. In this sense, the adoption of a value-added tax was a reform "going beyond Shoup." This means that in the forty years since the Shoup Report, the Japanese economy had developed and grown to an extent that the Shoup Mission could not predict.

C. REFORM OF DIRECT TAXES

In contrast to the value-added tax, which went beyond the Shoup Report, the reform of direct taxes undertaken between 1986 and 1988 was in line with the basic ideas of the Shoup Report. Therefore, it could be said that this was a reform "going back to Shoup."

As mentioned earlier, preferential tax treatments had proliferated over time, and, in part as a result, income tax rates had risen. The reforms to the direct taxes addressed each of these elements. In both the individual and corporate income taxes, many preferential tax treatments were abolished or reduced in scope, and the tax base was broadened. For instance, with respect to the individual income tax, the scope of nontaxable savings was substantially reduced and most interest income was brought back into the tax base. In addition, exclusions for capital gains on the sale of securities were also abolished, and these capital gains also were brought back into the tax base.

Concerning the tax rate, the highest individual income tax rate was reduced and the rate structure simplified. Prior to 1986, the highest rate was 70 percent and there were sixteen brackets. Through the reform, the highest rate was reduced to 50 percent and the number of brackets was reduced to six. The rate structure also was greatly simplified: the rates were set at 10 percent, 20 percent, 30 percent, 40 percent, and 50 percent. In addition, the width of the brackets was broadened. Most significantly, the first bracket was broadened from 0.5 million yen to 3 million yen. As a result, about 90 percent of working taxpayers fell into the 10 percent rate bracket, making it something like a flat tax for most people.

One serious remaining problem was that the interest income and the capital gains on the sale of securities, which were brought back to the tax base, were not aggregated with other kinds of income, but instead were separately taxed with lower flat rates. Therefore, the global, progressive income tax, which had been the ideal of the Shoup Report, was not fully realized. Nonetheless, the reforms of 1986–88 went a long way to restoring the Japanese income tax system to the Shoup ideal.

V. CONCLUDING REMARKS—SOME IMPORTANT PROBLEMS IN THE TWENTY-FIRST CENTURY

In the twenty-first century, Japan must continue to confront two serious problems that were carried over from the twentieth century and worsened by the unusually long and severe recession since the mid-1990s.

The first problem is how to reduce accumulated government debts and put public finance on a sound track. The accumulated government debts were reduced to a considerable extent by the adoption of the value-added tax and the increase of tax revenue as a result of the bubble economy for some years. However, during the recession years, both national and local governments have issued a tremendous amount of bonds. As of the end of the 2002 fiscal year (i.e., March 31, 2003), it was estimated that the amount of accumulated debts in the name of the national government would reach 528 trillion yen and that of local governments would reach 195 trillion yen. Together, this comes to a total of 693 trillion yen, which is equivalent to 139.6 percent of gross domestic product for the 2002 fiscal year. As this reflects, the huge accumulated debts represent a major problem for both national and local governments.

The second problem is how to finance the constantly increasing expenditures for the aged—an especially pressing problem for a society with a very low birthrate.

To solve these two problems, it is essential to cut unnecessary or less urgent expenditures. At the same time, however, increasing tax revenue is unavoidable.

Taking these two problems into consideration, the main issues facing the tax system of Japan in the first quarter of the twenty-first century are the following:

A. SHIFT IN THE TAX MIX

As a result of the introduction of the value-added tax in the late 1980s, the tax system of Japan moved from a tax system in which the income tax occupied the dominant position to a system of tax mix, in which each of the taxes on income, consumption, and property occupies an important role. In view of the two problems mentioned above, a tax increase will be unavoidable in the future, and the tax increase will mainly be accomplished through an increase in the value-added tax. As a result, the weight of the consumption tax will also increase in the tax mix in the future.

As mentioned earlier, one justification for the introduction of the value-added tax was the new idea of equity between the aged and the working generation. The increase in the value-added tax is also justified by the same equity principle: the view that it is fair to shift the relative tax burden from the working generation to the aged, who do not have much income, but many of whom have enough savings to engage in consumption.

The tax mix certainly has its own merits. Compared to the income-tax-dominant system or the consumption-tax-dominant system, under the tax-mix system, revenue would be relatively stable irrespective of business fluctuations, the dissatisfaction and frustration of people toward tax would be less serious, and enforcement would be improved through the possibility of cross-checking income tax returns and value-added tax returns. However, if the weight of the consumption tax becomes too great, then the tax system as a whole would lose progressivity and may become regressive. This is a crucial point of the tax mix.

B. REFORM OF THE INDIVIDUAL INCOME TAX

As mentioned above, in the reform of 1986–88, interest income and capital gains on the sale of securities were brought back into the tax base. However, since it was difficult to check accurately the personal attribution of these incomes (in connection with those reforms, it was seriously considered whether to adopt the taxpayers' accounting number system, but the system was not adopted), it was tentatively decided to tax these incomes separately with low, flat rates. How to treat these incomes is one of the most important policy issues at present.

Closely related to this issue is which type of income tax would be most appropriate in the future. There are three alternatives: (1) a comprehensive income tax, (2) an expenditure tax, and (3) a dual-income tax.

Under the influence of the Fisher-Kaldor-Andrews theory, since the late 1970s, some scholars have strongly asserted that in Japan, too, the income tax should have been transformed to an expenditure tax. However, this idea did not have much influence on actual tax policy and reform. In the 1986–88 reform, the comprehensive income tax alternative was the basic policy. Furthermore, since the value-added tax was adopted, the idea of the expenditure tax has been losing influence.

Recently, the dual-income tax system of the Nordic countries has been highly evaluated by some scholars. They assert that the present system should be replaced by a dual-income tax. At first glance, the dual-income tax looks attractive. However, this system has various problems in light of equity, neutrality, and simplicity. Therefore, at this moment, it is too early to make any prediction about whether Japan will adopt the dual-income tax system. It is likely that Japan will stay with the comprehensive income tax alternative for the time being, even if that system does have various flaws.

C. REFORM OF THE CORPORATE INCOME TAX

In corporate income tax, as well, broadening of the tax base has been realized to a considerable extent through the abolition of preferential treatments and reduction of the scope of the benefits from such treatments. However, many preferential treatments still exist, and the necessity of each should be strictly reexamined.

After several rate cuts, the corporate income tax rate stands at 30 percent at present. If prefectural and local communities' corporate income taxes and the prefectural business taxes are added together, the combined rate is about 41 percent (which is about the same as that for California-based U.S. corporations). The business society strongly asserts that further rate cuts are necessary for Japanese corporations to compete with corporations from the European Union and Asian countries, where rates are lower than in Japan. However, it is not certain at present whether the rate will be cut further in the near future. The two serious problems mentioned above relating to revenue shortfalls would only be aggravated by a tax reduction. What is certain, however, is that if the prefectural business tax were transformed from a net-income type to a value-added type (to be described in section F below), the combined corporate income tax rate would be lowered as a result.

D. REFORM OF THE INHERITANCE TAX

As mentioned above, Japan adopted the cumulative accession tax in 1950, following the Shoup Report, but abolished it soon thereafter. In recent years, however, the United States, the United Kingdom, Germany, and France have moved to a kind of cumulative system. Since the cumulative type better satisfies equity and may also produce beneficial economic effects by encouraging gifts, it is quite possible that Japan will adopt it again in some practical and workable way in the near future.

E. REFORM OF THE VALUE-ADDED TAX

The most important reform problem of the value-added tax at present is to eliminate or reduce so-called tax profits (profits that are equivalent to the value-added tax, but not paid to the government because they do not constitute tax). As mentioned earlier, in adopting the value-added tax, various measures were adopted to soothe or mitigate the impact so as to overcome bitter opposition by business. As a result, business enterprises are able to obtain tax-equivalent profits because of these measures. For instance, enterprises with gross taxable annual sales of 30 million yen or less are exempted from the value-added tax, but they can sell the commodities for the same price as the taxable enterprises. Needless to say, they have to recover the amount of the value-added tax included in the price of the commodities they bought (input tax), but they can sell the commodities at prices higher than would be necessary to recover the input tax and keep the excess amount as profit. Such tax profits are produced in various other ways, as well. The Consumption Tax Act has been amended to reduce tax profits a few times, and the government is preparing at present to amend the act to reduce tax profits more drastically. Nonetheless, this remains a shortcoming of the current value-added tax system.

Another important matter relates to raising the value-added tax rate. In 1997, the rate was raised from 3 percent to 4 percent, and a prefectural surtax was introduced at a rate of 25 percent of the amount of the value-added tax (resulting in an overall rate of 5 percent). In order to solve the two serious revenue-shortfall problems mentioned above, it is indispensable to raise the rate of the value-added tax further and to increase the revenue from that tax. However, since opposition is very strong, it is difficult to raise the rate to a high level in a short period. Consequently, the rate is likely to be raised gradually and is likely to reach 15 percent in the long run.

F. REFORM OF LOCAL TAXES

The most controversial problem in the field of local taxation at present is the reform of the prefectural business tax. As mentioned earlier, the Shoup Report recommended transforming the prefectural business tax from the net-income type to the value-added type. The value-added type business tax was adopted in the Shoup Tax Reform, but was abolished without implementation, and the net-income type business tax has continued to the present.

However, the net-income type business tax has two shortcomings. First, it does not meet the principle of "taxation according to benefit," which should be the basic principle of local taxes. Second, revenue from the net-income type business tax is not stable, but fluctuates with business fluctuations. For example, revenue from the business tax reached 42.2 percent of prefectural tax revenue in 1965, but dropped to just 27.3 percent in 2001.

To overcome these shortcomings, the government has been preparing to transform the business tax to the value-added type. However, opposition is very strong, especially because if the value-added type business tax were adopted, even business enterprises with deficits would be required to pay the tax. Therefore, the government has designed a less harsh amendment plan (a combination of the net-income and the value-added types), but it remains to be seen when it will be adopted.

G. IMPROVEMENT OF TAX ADMINISTRATION

Japan adopted the self-assessment system in 1947, even before the Shoup Mission arrived. The Shoup Mission strongly supported the self-assessment system from the viewpoint of democracy in taxation and recommended various measures, including the blue-return system, to strengthen and stabilize that system. As far as the author knows, the self-assessment system is followed only in the United States, Japan, South Korea, and the United Kingdom (in order of adoption). Despite the small number of nations following this system, it is useful not only to enhance the political consciousness of people but also to improve tax enforcement. Nonetheless, the self-assessment system is far from perfect. Since the taxpayers' accounting number system would be quite effective to improve taxpayer compliance and to make enforcement more effective, Japan will probably adopt it before long.

H. DEVELOPMENT OF TAX LAW AS A DISCIPLINE OF LAW

In closing, let me add a few words about the development of tax law as a discipline. Until around 1950, tax law was researched and taught in Japan, not as an independent subject, but rather as one part of administrative law. In its second report (issued in 1950), the Shoup Mission recommended that tax law should be taught as an independent field of law. Under the heading "University

Courses in Taxation," that mission stated: "The University Law Schools should institute courses in the legal aspects of income taxation, as distinguished from the fiscal policy and public finance aspects. Such courses would do much to interest attorneys in tax-matters and to increase informed criticism of the system. It would of course also bring about needed academic research into the legal phases of taxation. Sufficient funds should be provided in the budget to permit such courses to be given by the Law Schools."

Based on this recommendation, chairs in tax law were established at the law faculties of the University of Tokyo and the Kyoto University in 1951. Since that time, tax taw has been researched and taught as an independent field of law. The number of tax law professors has been steadily increasing, and the number of universities at which tax law is taught also has been steadily increasing. Nowadays, tax law is taught at almost all law faculties, and at some economics faculties as well. Tax law is also a standard subject at the new graduate-level law schools. Research on tax law has developed considerably, and many academic books and articles are published in the field every year. Perhaps it is symbolic of the development of tax law in Japan that this time a professor, and not a bureaucrat, wrote and submitted the tax law essay.

NOTES

1. Morio Uematsu (assisted by Rex Coleman), "Computation of Income in Japanese Income Taxation: A Study in the Adjustment of Theory to Reality," in Arthur Taylor von Mehren, ed., *Law in Japan: The Legal Order in a Changing Society* (Cambridge, MA: Harvard University Press, 1963), 567.

2. Some members of the mission returned to Japan in 1950 to undertake an update of the report. That group submitted a second report. Accordingly, the report of 1949 is often called the first report. In this essay, however, only the report of 1949 will be cited, and it will be referred to simply as the Shoup Mission Report.

3. Ōshima v. Sakyō zeimushochō [Ōshima v. Director, Sakyō District Tax Office] (Sup. Ct., Grand Bench, Mar. 27, 1985), *Minshū* 39(2) (1985): 247.

24 Some Observations on the Japanese Tax System at the Beginning of the Twenty-first Century

CHRISTOPHER H. HANNA

Professor Hiroshi Kaneko has written a detailed and fascinating chapter discussing the evolution of the Japanese tax system in the latter half of the twentieth century.[1] In his chapter, he identifies eight issues that will confront Japan with respect to its tax system as it moves into the twenty-first century.[2] In this brief comment, I wish to discuss a few high-profile tax issues that have arisen in Japan over the past few years and how these issues have been addressed and resolved.

The first tax issue involves consolidated tax returns.[3] In 1997, Japan enacted the Act for Partial Amendment of the Act concerning the Prohibition of Monopolization and Maintenance of Fair Trade permitting the use of holding companies, which had been prohibited in Japan since 1947.[4] From a tax standpoint, the immediate issue that came to mind was whether Japan would permit these holding company structures to file a consolidated tax return. Generally, filing a consolidated tax return is a government-permitted privilege in which all corporations that are members of the same corporate group may elect to be treated as one corporation. As a result, transactions between two corporations that are members of the same consolidated group are generally disregarded because the two corporations are treated as one. For example, if one corporation sells property to another corporation and both corporations are members of the same consolidated group, no gain or loss is recognized by the selling member. The group is taxed on its consolidated taxable income, representing primarily the group's dealings with the outside world.

One of the great advantages of filing a consolidated tax return is that the losses from one corporation can be used to offset the profits of another corporation in the same consolidated group.[5] The Japanese government was greatly concerned about the revenue loss if it permitted consolidated tax returns because the losses of one Japanese corporation would offset the profits of another Japanese corporation, thereby decreasing government revenue.[6] So the Japanese government studied the tax systems of other countries that permitted consolidated tax returns, including the United States and France. In 2002, Japan enacted consolidated tax return legislation but with a twist. It imposed an additional 2 percent tax if a corporate group files a consolidated tax return. This additional tax was designed to offset the revenue loss from allowing consolidated tax returns.[7] This was an idea that the Japanese government adopted from the United States. From 1942 until 1964, the United States imposed an additional 2 percent tax (on consolidated taxable income) when an affiliated group filed a consolidated tax return.[8]

A second issue is the increasing use of partnerships (i.e., flow-through entities) in Japan.[9] Traditionally, many businesses in Japan were conducted in corporate form, such as the *kabushiki kaisha*. But in more recent years, it appears there is an increasing use of partnerships as a business or investment form in Japan.[10] From a tax standpoint, the reason is fairly simple. Partnerships are generally treated as transparent entities, and therefore the income is only taxed at the partner level and not at the partnership level.[11] This single level of taxation provides partnerships a big tax advantage over corporations. But, unfortunately, the law of taxation of partnerships in Japan is not well developed, particularly with respect to foreign partners.[12] In other words, there are many unanswered questions involving the taxation of partnerships in Japan. What the United States experienced when the use of partnerships greatly increased in the 1960s and 1970s was taxpayers exploiting the use of partnerships, and, as a result, the United States had to issue a great deal of guidance on the taxation of partnerships throughout the 1980s and 1990s. Today, investors are exploiting the use of partnerships in Japan from a tax standpoint.[13] As a result, Japan, like the United States, may have to devote a lot of resources in developing well thought-out rules on the taxation of partnerships.

A recent interesting development is the new United States–Japan income tax treaty, which entered into force through the exchange of instruments of ratification at the end of March 2004.[14] The treaty becomes effective on January 1, 2005, although with respect to withholding taxes, it is generally applicable beginning on July 1, 2004. For a number of years, U.S. companies have pleaded with the U.S. government to negotiate a new tax treaty with Japan primarily focusing on the royalty withholding tax provision. The old United States–Japan Income Tax Treaty, dating back to 1971, had a 10 percent withholding tax on royalty payments. The 1996 U.S. Model Tax Treaty had a 0 percent withholding tax on royalty payments, and U.S. companies wanted to incorporate a 0 percent rate in a new tax treaty with Japan. The new treaty does that.[15] The new treaty also provides, in certain cases, a 0 percent withholding tax rate on dividends, which is a relatively recent phenomenon for the United States (having done this previously only with the United Kingdom, Australia, and Mexico).[16]

A final comment concerns the symmetry of tax rates and tax reform, whether intentional or not, between the United States and Japan. As Professor Kaneko notes in his chapter, in Japan, the top individual income tax rate was 75 percent in 1962, while the top corporate income tax rate reached 43.3 percent in the mid-1980s. In comparison, the United States had a top individual income tax rate in 1964 of 77 percent (which was lowered to 70 percent effective in 1965), not much different from Japan. And, in 1985, the United States had a top corporate income tax rate of 46 percent, less than a three-percentage point difference from Japan's top corporate income tax rate for the same year. In 1986, the United States passed the Tax Reform Act of 1986, substantially changing the U.S. tax laws.[17] Just two years later, Japan passed the Tax Reform of 1988, substantially changing its tax laws.[18]

At the present time, the top individual tax rate in Japan is 37 percent (national level), while the top individual tax rate in the United States is 35 percent. At the corporate level, the top rate in Japan is 30 percent, while the United States' top rate is 35 percent. The symmetry of the tax rates between the United States and Japan is still substantially present. Also, at the present time, Japan is considering fundamental tax reform to establish a "desirable tax system."[19] In the United States, President Bush has proposed, in September 2004, a bipartisan advisory panel on tax reform to report to the secretary of the Treasury "on options to fundamentally reform the tax code to make it simpler, fairer, and pro-growth."[20] It will be interesting to see if fundamental tax reform takes place in the next few years in both Japan and the United States.

NOTES

1. See Hiroshi Kaneko, "The Reform of the Japanese Tax System in the Latter Half of the Twentieth Century and into the Twenty-first Century" (this volume).

2. See ibid. (shift in the tax mix among income, consumption, and property taxes; reform of the individual income tax; reform of the corporate income tax;

reform of the inheritance tax; reform of the value-added tax; reform of local taxes; improvement of tax administration; and development of tax law as a discipline of law).

3. See, e.g., Andrew J. Dubroff et al., *Federal Income Taxation of Corporations Filing Consolidated Returns*, 2nd ed. (Newark, NJ: Matthew Bender, 1997); Kevin M. Hennessey et al., *The Consolidated Tax Return: Principles, Practice, Planning*, 6th ed. (Boston: Warren Gorham Lamont, 2003); Boris I. Bittker and James S. Eustice, *Federal Income Taxation of Corporations and Shareholders*, 7th ed. (Boston: Warren Gorham Lamont, 2000).

4. See, e.g., Andrew H. Thorson and Frank Siegfanz, "The 1997 Deregulation of Japan's Holding Companies," *Pacific Rim Law and Policy Journal* 8 (1999): 261.

5. See, e.g., Bittker and Eustice, *Federal Income Taxation of Corporations and Shareholders*, ¶ 13.42(1)(b) (principal advantage of consolidation includes "operating losses of one affiliate can be offset against profits of other members of the group"); Ichiro Suto, "Interaction between Japan's Consolidated Tax-Filing and Tax-Free Reorganization Regimes," *Tax Notes International* 30 (2003): 1157, 1158 ("Apparently, the main benefit of the consolidated filing is to offset the profits and losses of each corporation to reduce the tax burden").

6. See, e.g., Kohji Mori, "Diet Enacts Consolidated Corporate Tax Filing," *Tax Notes International* 27 (2002): 166; Mori, "Tax Panel Readies Consolidated Corporate Tax System," *Tax Notes International* 24 (2001): 453; and Torao Aoki, "Ongoing Tax Reform," *Asia-Pacific Tax Bulletin* 9 (October 2003): 321, 327 ("The Ministry of Finance estimated the revenue loss due to the institution of the consolidated tax regime to be about JPY 800 billion for FY 2002").

7. See Mori, "Diet Enacts Consolidated Corporate Tax Filing," 166 (revenue loss from consolidated tax filing "will be offset by, among other things, a temporary two percent surtax that will be valid for two years").

8. See, e.g., Dubroff et al., *Federal Income Taxation of Corporations Filing Consolidated Returns*, § 1.02 ("In 1934 and 1935, and again from 1942 until its repeal by the Revenue Act of 1964, this additional tax was generally imposed at a rate of 2 percent of consolidated taxable income"); Bittker and Eustice, *Federal Income Taxation of Corporations and Shareholders*, ¶ 13.40.

9. See, e.g., Christopher H. Hanna, "Initial Thoughts on Classifying the Major Japanese Business Entities under the Check-the-Box Regulations," *SMU Law Review* 51 (1997): 75 (suggesting an increase in use of the *tokumei kumiai* and *nin'i kumiai* because of the flow-through nature of the income earned by these entities).

10. See Hiroki Yamakawa, "The State of Japan's International Taxation," *Tax Notes International* 35 (2004): 807 (discussing increasing use of *tokumei kumiai* and *nin'i kumiai*).

11. Japan has four entities that are similar to American-style partnerships: *gōmei kaisha, gōshi kaisha, tokumei kumiai,* and *nin'i kumiai*. Both the *gōmei kaisha* and the *gōshi kaisha* are subject to the Japanese corporate income tax and, therefore, are not flow-through entities for tax purposes. The *tokumei kumiai* and *nin'i kumiai* are treated as flow-through entities (or the equivalent of flow-through entities) for Japanese tax purposes. See, e.g., Hanna, "Initial Thoughts on Classifying the Major Japanese Business Entities under the Check-the-Box Regulations"; 79, 81.

12. See, e.g., Hanna, "Initial Thoughts on Classifying the Major Japanese Business Entities under the Check-the-Box Regulations"; Yoshihiro Masui, "Taxation of Partnerships in Japan," *Bulletin for International Fiscal Documentation* 54 (April 2000): 150 ("Japan avoided the emergence of partnership tax issues by keeping the tax consequences unpredictable. There are only six circulars that cover the vast area of partnership taxation in Japan. Inevitably, it is almost impossible to find the predictable tax outcome if a person wants to form a partnership to conduct business"); Yamakawa, "The State of Japan's International Taxation," 819 ("The Tax Bureau of the Ministry of Finance is reviewing taxation of business entities, including pass-through entities such as *nin'i kumiai* . . . and a Japanese version of the LLC that is expected to be introduced. Necessary measures must be developed to address cases when nonresidents or foreign corporations receive income from that pass-through entity in Japan. . . . Authority will be needed to tax income from these entities when they move across the border, as well as when they are received within the country"); Ichiro Otsuka, "International Income Tax Problems of Partnerships: Japan," reprinted in International Fiscal Association, ed., *Cahiers de droit Fiscal International* (The Hague, Netherlands: Kluwer Law International, 1995), 317, 332 ("There are almost no laws, rulings or authoritative statements on most of the issues concerning [the] taxation of partnerships."); Yuri Matsubara, "International Tax Aspects of the *Tokumei Kumiai*," *Asia-Pacific Tax Bulletin*, 10 (January–February 2004): 76.

13. See Yamakawa, "The State of Japan's International Taxation," 815 ("It has been confirmed that foreign entities engaging in investment activities in Japan often use *tokumei kumiai* for tax avoidance, for example, by entering into nonperforming loan purchases").

14. For the full text of the treaty, protocol, and exchange of notes, see 2003 TNT 216-21 (November 7, 2003).

15. Convention between the Government of the United States of America and the Government of Japan for the Avoidance of Double Taxation and the Prevention of Fiscal Evasion with Respect to Taxes on Income (November 6, 2003), art. 12.

16. Ibid., art. 10. See generally Staff of the Joint Committee on Taxation, Expla-

nation of Proposed Income Tax Treaty between the United States and Japan, JCS-1-04, (February 19, 2004).

17. See, e.g., Michael J. Graetz and Deborah H. Schenk, *Federal Income Taxation: Principles and Policies*, rev. 4th ed. (New York: Foundation Press, 2002), 9 ("With considerable hyperbole, the Tax Reform Act of 1986 was widely heralded as the most significant tax change [in the United States] since the income tax was extended to the masses during the Second World War").

18. See Aoki, "Ongoing Tax Reform," 324 ("[T]he most recent major tax reform [in Japan] took place in 1988").

19. See Hiromitsu Ishi, "Thinking the Unthinkable: A Tax Rise for a Sustainable Future in Japan," *Asia-Pacific Tax Bulletin* 9 (January 2003): 26.

20. See (http://www.whitehouse.gov/news/releases/2004/09/20040902-7.html); Warren Rojas, "Bush Sets Tax Reform, Ownership Changes as Reelection Guideposts," *Tax Notes* 104 (September 6, 2004): 1017.

25 Insolvency Law for a New Century

Japan's Revised Framework for Economic Failures

KENT ANDERSON & MAKOTO ITŌ

I. INTRODUCTION

Insolvency was not covered in the original volume of *Law in Japan: The Legal Order in a Changing Society*. According to that book's index, the only reference to debtor-creditor law was a single notation that the Bankruptcy Act was adopted in 1922.[1] Perhaps this is not surprising given the focus of the original project on the "development and evolution" of Japanese law. For most of the postwar era, insolvency law[2] has not been at the cutting edge of law reform. Indeed, the initial citation to insolvency law in this review is to the same 1922 bankruptcy legislation.

The theme of this compendium, though, is "A Turning Point." This title in fact aptly describes the state of Japanese insolvency law at the beginning of the twenty-first century. Japan's continuing economic downturn through the 1990s and into this century has altered things significantly. To begin with, while the insolvency figures between the 1950s and early 1990s are relatively consistent, insolvency filings increased by over 1,000 percent in the ten years between 1992 and 2001. Included in these figures are some of Japan's largest and oldest blue chips that many had long predicted were too big to fail.[3] These bankruptcies have crushed the whole paradigmatic explanation for how businesses fold in Japan, as most will now agree that government bailouts, mainbank restructuring, and *keiretsu* injections are all things of the past, if they ever really existed at all.[4]

The huge swell in filings, and projections that it will continue, brought to the forefront a number of limitations in and problems with the insolvency system. This system had been tinkered with in 1936 and 1952, but remained largely based on the assumptions made at the adoption of the Bankruptcy and Composition Acts eighty years earlier. Thus, in response to this changed environment,[5] since 1996 the statutory framework for insolvencies has been under examination by the quasi-public Insolvency Law Deliberative Council.[6] This project has resulted in three major insolvency bills already enacted and likely will produce two additional bills that will be enacted, in whole or in part, after the writing of this chapter in 2002. Thus, we write this chapter largely based on a system that is still being drafted and has yet to be thoroughly tested by the courts or the various interested actors. Fortunately, Professor Itō is one of the central figures on the Insolvency Law Deliberative Council. Accordingly, we hope to be able to clarify the intent of, if not actual practice under, the revised framework.

In this chapter we seek to provide both a general overview of the revised formal insolvency regime and explore how that system functionally operates. Section II introduces the various proceedings that make up the comprehensive insolvency structure and reviews how that framework has been used over the past fifty years. In section III, we disassemble the comprehensive insolvency process and present a loose systems analysis of its various component stages.[7] For each of the six subsystems identified in section III, we highlight certain issues inherent in the subject matter and the policy determinations Japan has made regarding those issues. For context, we employ a partially comparative methodology referring particularly to the bankruptcy system in the United States. We conclude in section IV by arguing that the revisions produced by the Insolvency Law Deliberative Council are indeed a "turning point" in how Japan statutorily manages economic failure. However, we suggest that rather than a radical departure from past practice, the new system is best understood as a finetuning of the previous framework. The changes seek to make insolvency proceedings more systematic, pragmatic, and efficient. Yet, in a comparative context because the Japan system still maintains a more vigilant, individualized, and arguably creditor-friendly approach, we submit this does not result in a convergence with the U.S. insolvency system.

II. OVERVIEW OF JAPAN'S INSOLVENCY REGIME

A. ISSUE: UNIFIED OR DIVERSE APPROACH

Historically, the field of insolvency law has been organized on two axes—the corporate versus individual dichotomy and the liquidation versus reorganization dichotomy. One of the significant features of the United States system since 1978 is that it has largely (but not completely) done away with the distinction between corporate and individual insolvencies,[8] and some of the most advanced international research has further advocated abandoning the liquidation/reorganization diametric at least for the initial stages.[9] Despite these trends, the Japanese insolvency framework maintains both distinctions.[10] The Insolvency Law Deliberative Council considered a unified approach, but it was rejected for the pragmatic reason that the continuing economic downturn necessitated revisions, even partial, as soon as possible and for the substantive argument that debtors themselves were better positioned than the courts to decide whether liquidation or reorganization was more economically sound.

B. THE BASIC FRAMEWORK OF FORMAL INSOLVENCY

Reflecting this commitment to the diffused system, which arguably might be characterized positively as a menu-approach,[11] Japanese insolvency rules at present are found in three separate acts and two parts of the Commercial Code. Again, this contrasts, perhaps ironically, with the United States, which has sought to codify its insolvency law in a single statute—the Bankruptcy Code.[12] For individuals, the primary insolvency statutes in Japan are the Bankruptcy Act (*hasan hō*), which covers liquidations, and the Civil Rehabilitation Act (*minji saisei hō*), which covers reorganizations.[13]

Both of these statutes may also be used by corporate debtors.[14] Furthermore, the Diet has provided these debtors with three additional options. First, Japanese corporations (*kabushiki gaisha*) at present may also liquidate under proceedings in the Commercial Code known as Special Liquidation (*Tokubetsu seisan*).[15] However, there are indications that the Insolvency Law Deliberative Council will incorporate this procedure into special rules for consensual and expedited liquidations under the Bankruptcy Act. Second, the Commercial Code's corporate section currently further provides a streamlined reorganization process called Corporate Arrangement (*Kaisha seiri*).[16] But this proceeding too is under threat of elimination in the revisions, as it has become largely superfluous with the enactment of new rules for summary and consensual proceedings in the Civil Rehabilitation Act.[17] Finally, a third reorganization option for companies is contained in the independent statutory regime of the Corporate Reorganization Act (*Kaisha kōsei hō*).[18] Draft revisions for this law were published by the Deliberative Coun-

Informal	*Formal*		
	Type	*Liquidation*	*Rehabilitation*
1. Private Workouts (*cf. Guidelines on Private Arrangements [Shiteki seiri ni kansuru gaido-rain]*, 722 NBL 10 (2001))	Individual	Bankruptcy Act, Hasan hō, Law No. 71, 1922	Civil Rehabilitation Act, Minji saisei hō, Law No. 225, 1999, *as amended by* Law No. 128, 2000
2. Civil Conciliation Act, Minji chōtei hō, Law No. 222, 1951	Corporate	Bankruptcy Act, Hasan hō, Law No. 71, 1922	Civil Rehabilitation Act, Minji saisei hō, Law No. 225, 1999
3. Gray Market Ordering (*e.g., seiri-ya, etc.*)			Corporate Reorganization Act, Kaisha kōsei ho, Law No. 172, 1952
4. Write-offs/*yonige*			
		Commercial Code, Special Liquidation, Shōhō, tokubetsu seisan, arts. 431–55	Commercial Code, Arrangements, Shōhō, kaisha seiri, arts. 381–403
	Special Entities	Financial Institutions Reorganization Act, Law No. 95, 1996	Financial Institutions Reorganization Act, Law No. 95, 1996
		Foreign Insolvency Proceedings, Law No. 129, 2000	Foreign Insolvency Proceedings, Law No. 129, 2000

FIGURE 25.1. Formal and Informal Insolvency Procedures

cil in March 2002 and should have been enacted by late 2002 or early 2003.[19] Furthermore, it is important to remember that in addition to the substantive laws, each act is supplemented by Supreme Court Rules that provide a procedural context. For a graphical representation of this overview see figure 25.1.

C. THE CHOICE AMONG THE OPTIONS

Given all of these options, how do debtors and creditors choose among the possibilities? Surprisingly this question has not been deeply probed in the English or Japanese literature on Japanese insolvency.[20] For individuals, the decision is relatively straightforward. Either one liquidates under the Bankruptcy Act, taking advantage of its quick resolution and fresh start, or one reorganizes under the new, Chapter 13–inspired provisions for individual debtors in the Civil Rehabilitation Act.[21] Rehabilitation takes more time but provides advantages such as keeping the family home and the arguable benefit of avoiding the "bankrupt" label.[22]

Assuming the anticipated elimination of the two special proceedings found in the Commercial Code, corporate debtors will have the choice of liquidating under the Bankruptcy Act or reorganizing under either the Civil Rehabilitation Act or the Corporate Reorganization Act.[23] For a corporate debtor, the decision between liquidation and reorganization often turns on the self-interests of the debtors' owners and managers, because liquidated companies cannot benefit from a fresh start. Thus, the decision may be determined by, for example, whether the person controlling the company receives a salary from it, whether he or she might be liable for the company's obligations, and so forth. As a result, managers have a proclivity for rescue proceedings over liquidation.

Between the two rescue statutes available to companies, debtor-control and treatment of secured creditors arguably determine which proceeding is followed. Those debtors, such as small, owner-managed businesses, that place a priority on maintaining control of the debtor are likely to prefer Civil Rehabilitation proceedings where management is not automatically displaced. On the other hand, the drafters hoped that debtors who need to coordinate with secured creditors or a large number of unsecured creditors, such as large public corporations, will be drawn to Corporate Reorganization, the only proceeding automatically covering secured claims.

Some limits on these broad generalizations exist, though. For example, given the complexity inherent in dealing with secured creditors and automatically displacing management, Corporate Reorganization proceedings are comparatively more expensive, complicated, and time consuming than Civil Rehabilitation. Further, as noted above regarding corporate managers' determination between liquidation and rescue, often the decision of which proceeding to pursue is made based on not what is in the best interest of the company but rather what is in the best interest of the individual manager. In this regard, Corporate Reorganization's automatic replacement of management may arguably influence the decision.

Both of these corollaries would seem to encourage all but the most altruistic, secured-creditor-entangled, and pessimistic managers to choose Civil Rehabilitation before either Corporate Reorganization or Bankruptcy liquidation. In fact, a review of the largest filings since the Civil Rehabilitation Act's revision in 1999 would seem to confirm this. Most of Japan's recent and largest insolvencies, such as Sogo Department Stores and Mycal Supermarkets, have been Civil Rehabilitation proceedings rather than Corporate Reorganizations.[24] In response, large creditors such as financial institutions have tried to discourage this type of opportunistic behavior by forcing some debtors (e.g., Mycal) to convert to Corporate Reorganization proceedings.[25] Further, the courts have been able, both actively and passively, to prevent inappropriate Civil Rehabilitations by denying or threatening to deny debtors' applications for relief.[26] Nonetheless, as with all countries' systems, Japan continues to struggle with the classic challenge of trying to design a framework that can quickly distinguish between a rescuable company and a lost cause, and that will motivate managers to file for protection while there is still some hope of capturing going concern value. In sum, at least while the revisions are still taking place and the practitioners are becoming familiar with the differences, it would seem that it remains unclear whether Japan's diffused statutory insolvency framework has created an optimized menu scheme or a confusingly inefficient mélange.

D. SPECIAL INSOLVENCY PROCEEDINGS AND INFORMAL INSOLVENCY

In addition to the traditional branches of the insolvency tree, a number of special proceedings and informal options exist. For example, financial institutions and life insurers are subject to special rules under a new regime introduced in 1996, the Financial Institutions Reorganization Act.[27] Also, foreign insolvency proceedings seeking to extend into Japan may apply for protection and assistance under special rules enacted in 2000 covering cross-border cases.[28] Finally, as in the rest of the world, informal liquidations and workouts are where the largest number of troubled entities are managed.

Regarding informal insolvencies in Japan, others have argued that special consideration should be given to, among other things, the role of so-called main banks, Japan's notes and checks clearinghouse system, the mediation role provided by the Civil Conciliation Act, the role of informal gray market actors such as *seiri-ya* (fixers), and some sort of unique Japanese cultural aversion to bankruptcy.[29] This chapter, however, focuses on formal mainstream insolvency proceedings. We believe that the large and increasing number of insolvency filings, by itself, justifies the importance and vitality of the legal framework. Moreover, we submit (1) that informal resolutions are occurring in the legal shadow cast by the formal system;[30] (2) that the formal system is particularly important to those actors who do not have the connections, size, or reputations to resort to the informal proceedings;[31] and (3) that recent anecdotal evidence strongly suggests that informal resolutions are no longer as prevalent or desirable as they once might have been.[32]

E. INSOLVENCY TRENDS

So how do debtors and creditors actually employ all of these proceedings? Relying on Supreme Court of Japan data, a number of interesting trends may be detected in Japanese insolvency filings in the postwar and post-bubble eras.[33] First, as noted above, from 1952 until the early 1980s generally and the mid-1990s specifically, Japan had an extremely low rate of formal insolvency with an average of only 2,254 filings per year. This began to change in the decade between 1982 and 1991, but it is the explosion of petitions in the decade between 1992 and 2001 that has brought the annual total to over 150,000 filings per year. This is seen in figure 25.2.

This explosion, however, is not predominantly a change in business practice but rather an increase in consumer bankruptcies (i.e., personal liquidations). In fact, though the data show an increase in corporate insolvencies of 494 percent during the 1990s, the comprehensive rise is mostly due to the 1,314 percent increase in personal insolvencies. Further, total reorganization figures—almost exclusively a business practice until a law change in 2001—have been relatively consistent between 1952 and 2000 and have never exceeded 1,000 per year.

Most interesting regarding the reorganization statistics, and important to the current reform efforts, is that the balance among the use of the three rescue statutes was quite evenly distributed until the late 1970s, as seen in figure 25.3. This equal distribution challenges the received wisdom that Japan's divergent approach to statutory reorganization was due to the legislature's failure to amend, abandon, or consolidate the laws as new options were introduced[34] and supports the argument that the various reorganization alternatives allowed the parties to find the most efficient system for the specific facts of a case—an idea that is only recently gaining support in the United States.[35] Nonetheless, since the 1980s, reorganization has been dominated

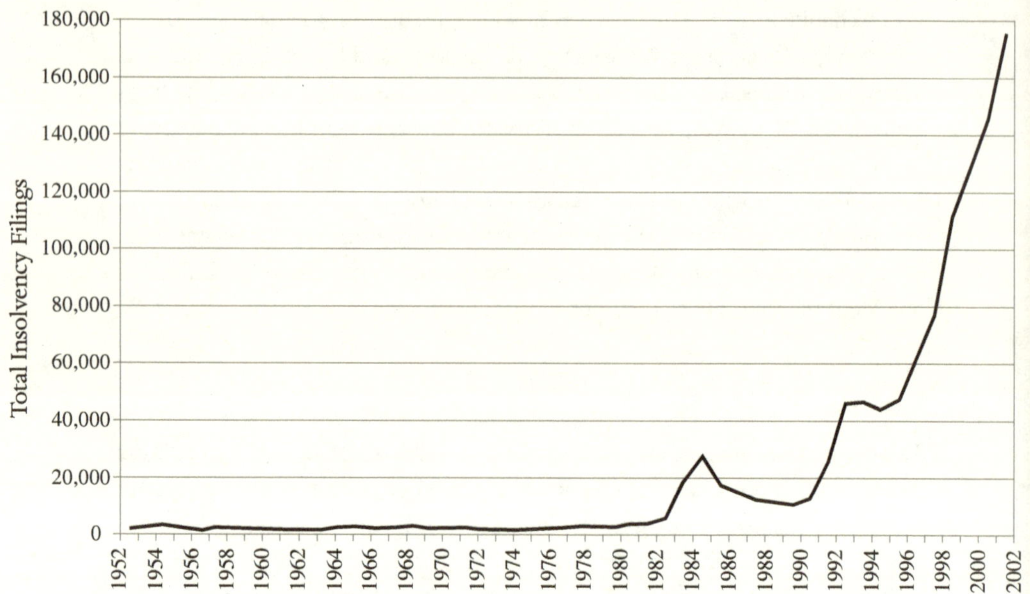

FIGURE 25.2. Fifty Years of Failures: Insolvency Filings, 1952–2001
SOURCE: See 1 General Secretariat, Supreme Court (Japan), *Shihō tōkei nenpō, Minji gyōsei hen* [Annual Report of Judicial Statistics, Civil and Administrative Cases Volume] (1952–2001).

by the small business–targeted Composition Act and its successor the Civil Rehabilitation Act. This may simply reflect the increases in personal and noncorporate business insolvencies, since Civil Rehabilitation is the only reorganization statute available for these debtors. On the other hand, it may indeed show a change in conditions or insolvency culture resulting in a preference for Civil Rehabilitation over Corporate Reorganization. However, because the data did not distinguish between corporate and noncorporate debtors until recently, no hard conclusions may be drawn.

Finally, when viewed comparatively with other countries of the Organization for Economic Cooperation and Development (OECD), Japan's insolvency rates are now consistent with many developed nations, though below the bankruptcy mecca of the United States. Total and business insolvency figures are largely illusory in a comparative context given the various insolvency regimes' different conceptions and definitions of proceedings, business debtors, and general incorporation rates.[36] However, using the basic building block of all insolvency systems—individual liquidations or consumer bankruptcies—

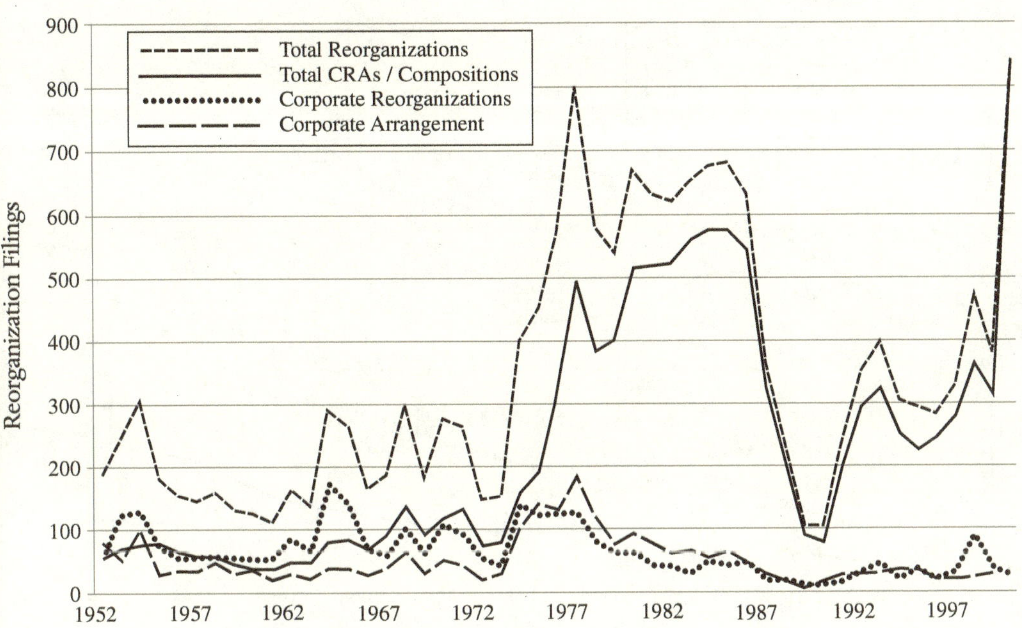

FIGURE 25.3. Japanese Reorganizations, 1952–2001
SOURCE: See 1 General Secretariat, Supreme Court (Japan), *Shihō tōkei nenpō, Minji gyōsei hen* [Annual Report of Judicial Statistics, Civil and Administrative Cases Volume] (1952–2001).

some comparisons may be made.[37] As summarized in figure 25.4, Japan's consumer bankruptcy rate over the late 1990s—in excess of 1 filing per thousand people—actually overtook the United Kingdom's rate and was quickly approaching Australia's. It was still well below that of the United States and Canada, but compared with the period prior to the 1980s, when Japan maintained a rate of less than 0.02 filings per thousand people, the gap has shrunk dramatically. Thus, the shift in the figures suggests the need to completely set aside the traditional socio-legal explanations of Japan's approach to insolvency.[38]

III. THE SYSTEMS WITHIN THE JAPANESE INSOLVENCY FRAMEWORK

In this section we shift the focus to look at the various subsystems that make up the comprehensive formal insolvency framework in Japan. The six specific stages considered include (1) initiation of proceedings, (2) control of proceedings, (3) protection of debtor, (4) priority and treatment of creditors'

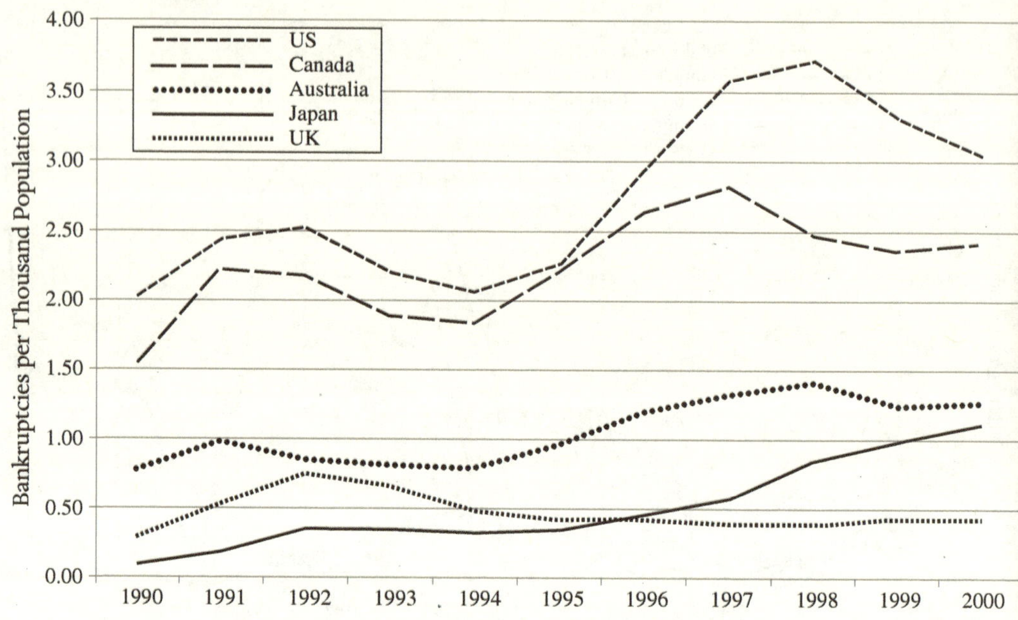

FIGURE 25.4. Comparative Individual Bankruptcy/ Liquidation Rates, 1990–2000
SOURCES: For population figures for each country, see U.S. Census Bureau, International Data Base, http://www.census.gov/ipc/www/idbprint.html. For the various countries' insolvency statistics, see: Insolvency and Trustee Service Australia, Bankruptcy Statistics, http://www.itsa.gov.au/aghome/commaff/itsa/frame_statistics.html; The Insolvency Service (United Kingdom), Our Statistics, http://www.insolvency.gov.uk/information/stats/statistics.htm; American Bankruptcy Institute, U.S. Bankruptcy Filing Statistics, http://www.abiworld.org/stats/newstasfront.html; Office of the Superintendent of Bankruptcy Canada, Bankruptcy Statistics, http://strategis.ic.gc.ca/SSG/br01011e.html. This information has been supplemented with specific inquiries with each of the offices, on file with the authors.

claims, (5) administering consumer insolvencies, and (6) rescuing corporate debtors. Each of these systems incorporates certain classical policy issues that we highlight and show how they have been resolved in Japan.

A. INITIATION OF PROCEEDINGS

Formal insolvency, which we focus on in this chapter, begins with the initiation of proceedings in the local district court of the debtor, whether corporate or natural.[39] Though all of the statutes now allow for creditors to file involuntary petitions, the overwhelming majority of cases in Japan, as well as the United States, are undertaken voluntarily by the debtor (colloquially the ubiquitous *jiko hasan*).[40] This is significant because, among other reasons, it means that debtors rather than creditors or courts decide initially whether to liquidate or reorganize and in what form. Despite this consistency with the United States, the standard procedure in Japan has historically departed from the North American model significantly by incorporating a court screening mechanism before a case is officially commenced.[41] Thus, in Japan the benefits and burdens of formal insolvency, such as stays on creditors and creation of the estate, have not been automatic but at the discretion of the court. In its revision, the Insolvency Law Deliberative Council has retained this approach for all proceedings.

As a practical matter the pre-commencement screening produces little to no difference in liquidations, because a court's denial or even delay in allowing an entity to liquidate is extremely unlikely.[42] Given the courts' failure to use affirmatively the discretion in liquidation proceedings, efficiency concerns strongly weigh in favor of completely dropping the test for voluntary petitions. This is in fact what has effectively been done by court rule in the consumer bankruptcy cases discussed below. The initial screening, however, is very important in rescue proceedings. Moreover, the temporal impact of the rule on reorganizations is compounded in certain districts by local practice that requires a pre-*filing* consultation with the court before that court will even accept an application.[43] Other courts, though—including the Tokyo District Court, which originally conceived the pre-filing consultation—have abandoned it for all but a one day pro forma notice.[44]

Whether under the general statutory requirement or under the enhanced version applied in some districts, Japan's pre-commencement screening mechanism produces a number of differences from an automatic acceptance regime, such as that in the United States. First, the screening requirement delays resolution of proceedings by anywhere from a week to six months.[45] Second, the court's gatekeeping creates comparative administrative inefficiencies, because in application it requires extra hearings to determine whether relief should be granted pending commencement and whether the case itself should be accepted. The third difference between discretionary and automatic commencement procedures is the primary justification for Japan's rule. By examining a debtor before commencement, a court may affirmatively direct cases into the most appropriate proceeding, whether liquidation or reorganization. This is one of the quintessential challenges in a rescue regime and is repaid by quicker and larger distributions in converted liquidations and more support and guidance in worthy rescues. Furthermore, the threat of the preliminary gauntlet strongly motivates debtors to file early and to self-select into the most appropriate regime.[46] In sum, Japan's traditional commencement approach, which has been reaffirmed by the Insolvency Law Deliberative Council, may be viewed as a reasoned choice in favor of a case-specific treatment at the cost of administrative efficiency. This is a tendency seen throughout Japan's traditional and revised statutory insolvency law.

B. CONTROL OF PROCEEDINGS

Once a case is initiated, the first question is who controls the matter and the debtor's estate. Ideally, selecting who controls the debtor's estate must balance concern over and prevention of possible debtor misconduct[47] with familiarity in the debtor's dealings allowing for their most economical handling. The two practical options are an outside, independent trustee, most often a licensed lawyer (*bengoshi*), or an insider such as a director or the debtor itself, the so-called debtor-in-possession ("DIP").[48] The former will possess skepticism but lack familiarity, while the latter possesses fluency but lacks objectivity.

As in the United States, bankruptcy—used in the overwhelming majority of personal and corporate liquidations—employs the outside trustee system.[49] This makes sense since bankruptcy is the most likely place for pre- and post-filing fraud. Further, for business debtors the appointment of an outside trustee is necessary because management losing their jobs have little motivation in carrying out an efficient liquidation. Notably there is no equivalent in Japan of the U.S. Trustees' Office to act as the default trustee in minor cases; therefore, most cases where a trustee is appointed proceed with a fully licensed private attorney. The bankruptcy law does not require trustees to be lawyers, but despite considering other alternatives including the British practice of using accountants, it appears the present custom will continue.[50] One interesting result is that most debtors are assigned trustee-lawyers with qualifications above the market demand and correspondingly the entire insolvency system is indirectly restricted by the cost and availability of the bankruptcy bar. As a result, the dynamics of "insolvency practice" in Japan differ considerably from the United States.[51]

The other proceeding in which an outside trustee is generally used is Corporate Reorganization.[52] In the current revision of this act there was a debate regarding whether to move toward a debtor-in-possession approach as used in U.S. reorganizations, but this lost to maintaining the outside trustee system already in place.[53] This decision probably is less significant than it appears since empirical research in the United States, which is acknowledged in Japan, suggests that almost all public companies in reorganization eventually undergo a management change.[54] Further, the revised law will allow for management to remain in power as an exception to the rule.[55] On the other hand, there is some concern that the rule will create a disincentive for management to file for Corporate Reorganization early and proactively.

In contrast to Corporate Reorganization, the small business-targeted Civil Rehabilitation Act, like Chapter 11 in the United States, employs a default rule pursuant to which management remains in power though a trustee may be appointed as an exception.[56] Despite this statutory principle, in practice courts have diverged from the American approach and have not left debtors solely in control. Instead, they have appointed "supervisors" (*kantoku in*) in almost all cases.[57] Supervisors are quasi trustees not given direct control of the debtor but charged with oversight duties.[58] Thus, despite the change in the law, the de facto approach is exactly what the rule was under the Composition Act before revision.[59] A variety of reasons for slipping back into this posture have been given, such as the failure of creditors' committees to take any initiative and the lack of a U.S. trustee-style outside supervising body.[60] Nevertheless, this predilection seems to be a matter of insolvency culture that instinctively does not trust debtors and historically has been overreliant on trustees' discretion.[61]

Viewed comprehensively, debtor control in Japan is actually a remarkably well-tuned and subtle mosaic. Liquidations, with the greatest risk of debtor fraud, are handled by outside trustees, though arguably overqualified ones. The de facto rule of large public reorganizations, where management control is soon displaced by outside experts, is formalized. And small- and medium-size firm management, which practically cannot be replaced since it is inevitably also the owner, is ostensibly left in control in rehabilitations, but with a passive supervisor to protect creditors' interests. The arguable problem with the system is that it is easy to manipulate, allowing for opportunism, especially since the debtor normally chooses which proceeding to pursue. For example, most large public insolvencies since 2000 have been filed as Civil Rehabilitations rather than Corporate Reorganizations. This potential problem, however, is minimized by the screening that the courts conduct before formally accepting a case. Thus, the courts' role as gatekeeper takes on an even greater significance, because it may direct a debtor from one type of proceeding to another and because it also determines at the same time whether to give control to an outside or inside trustee. The end result is that in resolving the perennial question of debtor control Japan again has maintained its balance in favor of precision and exacting scrutiny.

C. PROTECTION OF DEBTOR DURING PROCEEDINGS

After an insolvency proceeding has been initiated and someone placed in charge of it, the next fundamental subsystem to address is how a debtor and its assets can be protected during the liquidation or reorganization. The purpose of whatever system is used is to free the debtor from creditors' demands and self-interested behavior during the proceedings and, thereby, allow for the most equitable liquidation or enhance the likelihood of successful reform. In achieving this purpose, Japan, like most other countries, provides for both the protection of the debtor's existing assets and tools to recapture assets lost on the eve of insolvency.

1. *Preserving Existing Assets*

The first and primary tool for protection of a Japanese debtor during insolvency proceedings is the stay on creditors, otherwise called "preservation measures" (*hozen shobun*). Similar to the diverse choices Japan provides among available proceedings and debtor-control, the Japanese insolvency framework creates a wide variety of subtly different discretionary stays to protect a debtor's assets while it is liquidated or reorganized. This of course contrasts with the U.S. tendency for comprehensive and compulsory solutions, such as the automatic stay on all creditors. In practical terms, this means that U.S. debtors begin with a stay covering all assets, but courts will freely lift it where necessary; in comparison, Japanese debtors begin without any preservation protections, but courts will freely grant them in legitimate cases, even before official commencement.[62] That is, in functionality the two systems are much closer than a cursory review would suggest. Nonetheless, at a subtle level, the U.S. approach (1) is initially more cautious, which translates into more measured decisions at the chaotic start of proceedings, and (2) places the burden to prove the need for the stay on the party most able to bear it—the creditor. In contrast, the Japanese approach is more creditor friendly and is actually in line with U.S. law in most fields other than bankruptcy, where the party seeking a preliminary injunction must establish its necessity *before* the court will grant it. Though the difference in application is less than some would like to suggest, Japanese stay practice again reinforces the notion that in comparison with the United States, Japan is more cautious and specialized and, correspondingly, more costly.

One of the major differences between the U.S. and Japanese insolvency systems is the treatment of secured interests, including staying secured creditors during proceedings. In Japan, as in the majority of countries, secured claims are not included in insolvency proceedings, based on the so-called right of separation (*betsujo ken*). Limited exceptions to this general principle do exist, however. The new Civil Rehabilitation Act allows for a stay on secured debt foreclosure proceedings in the limited situation where the stay will not cause unreasonable harm considering the special interests of the secured creditor and the best interests of all creditors.[63] Combined with this, the Civil Rehabilitation Act also allows for a secured claim to be stripped down to the present value of the collateral.[64] The addition of these tools in 1999 was a serious departure for Japan, but to date they have not been widely relied on by debtors or courts.[65] On the other hand, practitioners suggest that the new powers have altered debtor-secured creditor dynamics, giving debtors more leverage in informal negotiations.

More significantly, Corporate Reorganization does not begin with the separation of secured claims principle and instead provides for discretionary stays at the preliminary stage and an automatic stay from official commencement of proceedings.[66] As discussed more fully below, this reflects the full inclusion of secured creditors in the handful of formal Corporate Reorganizations filed each year. Nonetheless, without an automatic stay bringing secured claims into most proceedings, Japanese legislators have placed the fulcrum between debtors and creditors farther to the creditors' side than in the United States.

2. *Recapturing Assets Lost prior to Insolvency*

The second aspect of protecting debtors during proceedings is providing rules to prevent opportunistic behavior by the debtor on the eve of filing. Left unregulated, debtors' pre-petition transfers would undermine any insolvency system. Therefore, most countries' frameworks provide a variety of "avoidance powers" (*hinin ken*) to allow a trustee or debtor to challenge and set aside pre-filing transfers that diminish the value of an insolvency estate. Though there are some minor differences among the acts, the three main Japanese avoidance powers cover (1) fraudulent transfers, (2) gratuitous or undervalued transactions within six months of petitioning, and (3) preferences to existing creditors within thirty days of petitioning.[67] The Japanese provisions roughly correspond with those in the U.S. Bankruptcy Code, though the arbitrarily determined time periods for application are slightly longer in the American model.[68]

One of the corollaries to avoidance powers is whether a creditor may set off (*sōsai ken*) mutual rights and obligations prior to proof of any claim in the insolvency proceeding. Both Japan and the United States answer this in the positive; that is, setoff is allowed.[69] In effect, where the creditor provides for setoff rights before insolvency, these powers will trump any claims of avoidance. One difference in practice that does arise between the regimes is that the U.S. creditor must get relief from the comprehensive automatic stay before setting off, while the specific, discretionary stays of Japan do not necessitate this. Thus, though there are some differences with regard to the details between the countries, the universal interest in preserving and rebuilding insolvency estates depleted on the eve of failure produces substantially similar rules in effect—if not terminology.

D. PRIORITY AND TREATMENT OF CLAIMS IN LIQUIDATION

The central tenet of modern insolvency law is equitable treatment of like creditors in the event of economic failure. The system that implements that policy is the priority rankings among creditors. As in the United States and most developed countries, Japan broadly prioritizes claims in bankruptcy as follows: (1) secured claims, (2) priority claims, (3) general claims, and (4) deferred claims. Within this scheme, the fundamental equality principle, or pari passu rule, is codified by providing that all general unsecured creditors will take equally to the proportional value of their claims.[70] Japan, like most other countries, diverges from this principle by recognizing the ex ante importance of respecting secured rights and allows secured creditors to take before all other creditors to the value of their collateral.[71] Thus, as explained above and discussed further below, secured claims are separated from and satisfied outside of all formal insolvency schemes except Corporate Reorganization.

A further difficulty in implementing the ideal of the pari passu doctrine is that all countries allow certain debts to come before general claims. By coming first in line, these "priority" creditors receive more than general creditors and are much more likely to be paid in full. Correspondingly, the categories and order of priority claims are a classic area for internal dispute and comparative divergence. Generally speaking, the Japanese insolvency statutes divide their priorities between, first, administrative costs and, subsequently, claims prioritized for public policy reasons. Administrative claims, also called

"Estate Claims" (*zaidan saiken*) or "Common Benefit Claims" (*kōeki saiken*),[72] are those expenses necessary for the running of the insolvency proceeding and are placed first to ensure that they are undertaken. The remainder of the priority claims are simply those things that Japanese legislators have decided should come before general unsecured claims as a matter of public policy, such as employees' wages and funeral expenses.[73]

The breakdown of the specific priorities between these two categories has been very contentious in the revision debate. Most significant is whether tax claims, namely, claims for taxes incurred before filing, should be treated to the first-priority status of administrative expenses, the second-priority status of public policy priorities, or as general claims. At present it is expected that the draft will give first-priority ranking to a set portion of tax claims and defer the balance of the claims to the general unsecured level. If this is implemented it will be an important addition to a slight global trend of treating at least a portion of government claims equal with general unsecured debts.[74]

The revisions also look set to modify the priority for workers' claims. As of this writing, despite theoretical inconsistencies, proposals seek to move workers' claims from the second-priority public policy category to the first-priority administrative claims class. Combined with this, though, the amount of the priority would be capped at two months' wages rather than the present six months and the balance of workers' claims would be treated as a general unsecured debt.

Comparative and international insolvency law commentators have noted and cautioned that public policy priority claims are one of the areas with the greatest potential for cross-border divergence and conflict.[75] The potential for conflict is evident even in the generally consistent approaches of Japan and the United States.[76] For example, Japan and the United States both give priority to workers' wages, but both Japan's present and proposed schemes of either six or two months of uncapped wages will likely exceed the United States' ninety days of wages capped at $4,000.[77] Similarly, one could readily conceive how the two countries' different tax schemes might produce significantly different amounts for tax priorities, especially if Japan restricts the tax priority. Even more glaring are the divergences produced by special interest. For example, Japan gives priority to funeral operators, while the United States prefers grain producers, commercial fishermen, and, more defendably, receivers of maintenance payments.[78] Considering these exceptions to the equality principle, Japan's priority rules appear much less parochial than those in the United States. There also appears, however, to be little hope in the near future for greater convergence between the United States and Japan on the subtle application of the priority rules.

E. ADMINISTERING CONSUMER INSOLVENCIES

Others have suggested that the paradigmatic division of insolvency is not corporate versus individual or liquidation versus rescue, but consumer versus business.[79] It is difficult empirically to make a clean separation between consumer and business cases, but the rough data available from Japan tend to support this dichotomy.[80] Japanese legislators and courts also seem to have responded to this split by creating a number of consumer-specific provisions and by optimizing the rescue rules for businesses. Stated differently, the insolvency scheme has been designed with subsystems that seek to systematize the procedures and enhance the social welfare aspects in consumer cases and to capture more going concern value in business cases.

Liquidation under the Bankruptcy Act is where most consumer proceedings occur. The Tokyo District Court, swamped with the huge increase in bankruptcy cases, has been at the forefront of developing special consumer-centered bankruptcy rules. These procedures both improve the efficient processing by the court and lessen the burdens of bankruptcy on debtors.[81] For example, pursuant to a local court rule implemented in April 1998, the court effectively made a formality of the initial screening process in simple consumer cases filed with the assistance of counsel (*kijitsu mensetsu*).[82] Now, when a lawyer files a case for a consumer, the court will immediately grant official commencement without requiring the debtor to be present or examined. A second expedited procedure for slightly more complex cases needing trustees (*shōgaku kanzai tetsuzuki*) is also available, though requiring the advanced payment of ¥200,000 (approximately US$2,000) in court costs.[83] Reflecting the success of these procedures and the simplicity of most straight consumer liquidation cases, fully 95 percent of the present Tokyo District Court bankruptcies proceed under one of the two expedited entries.[84]

Similarly, a statutory provision used affirmatively since the 1990s has greatly streamlined many consumer bankruptcy cases between commencement and discharge. Under the Simultaneous Bankruptcy Abolition rule (*dōji hasan haishi*), in no-asset consumer cases where it is clear that the debtor does not have unencumbered property sufficient to cover likely bankruptcy expenses, the court may avoid almost all of the intermediate procedures before discharge.[85] This includes assignment of a trustee, strict examination of pre-filing transactions, and so forth. Further, most courts now allow simultaneous filing of both commencement petitions and applications for discharge. The combined result is that, after allowing for notification of creditors and opportunity to dissent, many debtors are ready for discharge hearings only a few months after commencement.[86]

Finally, some courts have experimented with speeding up and simplifying the final step in consumer cases—the discretionary discharge. Discharge was introduced to Japan only in 1952 at the encouragement of the Occupation. It was never automatic as in the United States, and until the recent increase in cases, courts only cautiously exercised their discretion to grant it after an average of a year or two wait.[87] Between 1996 and 1998, however, the Tokyo District Court introduced collective discharge proceedings (*shūdan menseki shinjin*), where without examining each person individually, the court granted discharge to debtors as a group.[88] In other words, the process for most consumers became much like in the United States, where from filing to discharge debtors were not subjected to much, if any, direct public scrutiny by the bench or other administrator, and instead any questioning was left to private actors such as the debtor's counsel and creditors. The Tokyo court abandoned the collective discharge procedure, however, after determining that it was not expediting cases but merely shifting the burden from judges to the court registrars and officials and that some direct examination by the authority of the bench was desirable as a matter of public policy.[89]

The local courts' experimentation with processing consumer cases exemplifies the classic tension between trying to deal efficiently with small and no-asset cases, yet providing enough scrutiny to ensure that the system does not encourage spendthrift behavior or tolerate bankruptcy abuse. The movement to the expedited process for many cases suggests that Japan has become more willing to limit scrutiny. Yet, the reincorporation of individual discharge examinations and the general unwillingness to go to a completely automated system such as that in the United States reinforces the characterization of Japanese insolvency as relatively strict and specialized.

These local court rules for consumer cases also suggest some interesting trends. On the one hand, by doing away with the initial court examination and allowing Simultaneous Bankruptcy Abolition, control of economic failure is being shifted from administration by the courts to administration by private actors, namely, the lawyers representing the debtors and creditors. Both the court and the bar associations acknowledge this and assert that it is only possible given the trust that may be placed in lawyers as officers of the court.[90] On the other hand, the Tokyo District Court has reintroduced the individual discharge examination by a judge. This would seem to suggest that Japan is not willing to go as far as the United States in allowing private parties, including debtors' lawyers and creditors' committees, to act as the primary monitors in consumer cases. Therefore, one may summarize that, when contrasted with the United States, Japan's enhanced consumer system opts for a more prudent and tailored rule, though one that is more systematic than the original 1922 approach.

In addition to the special provisions in bankruptcy, since April 2001 the Civil Rehabilitation Act has included discrete rescue rules for consumer debtors.[91] Like Chapter 13 in the United States, the individual rehabilitation procedures (*kojin saisei tetsuzuki*) seek to allow debtors, with general debts of less than ¥30 million (approximately US$300,000), to negotiate a rehabilitation plan with creditors. By doing so, debtors may avoid going into bankruptcy and protect certain assets, such as the family home, that might otherwise be lost to creditors.[92] In the first nine months of the act, debtors filed 6,209 applications, suggesting that it indeed was filling a demand.[93] The data available cover only 78 completed cases, but suggest that only 14 percent of debtors were able to retain their homes through the proceedings.[94] Despite this small figure, of the plans that debtors have submitted to creditors, on average, small debtors (*shō kibo kojin saisei*) have proposed repayment of 73 percent of the value of claims, while wage-earning debtors (*kyōyo shotoku sha tō saisei*) have proposed repayment of 59 percent of the value of claims.[95] Both of these figures are much greater than what creditors historically have received in bankruptcy.[96] Again, this suggests that the new proceeding fills an important place in the insolvency framework, though whether this indeed proves to be a positive one will eventually depend on the success rate of these plans.[97]

F. RESCUING AND REHABILITATING CORPORATE DEBTORS

Given the comparatively high rate of incorporation in Japan, most business debtors are corporations. As reviewed above, managers of failing companies have little incentive to proceed directly into liquidation. Thus, it is crucial for the comprehensive insolvency system to develop subsystems that effectively manage corporate rescue and allow for the greatest capture of going concern value, whether that be through direct reorganization or eventual liquidation.

Two of the subsystems with special importance for rescue have already been reviewed above. The required screening mechanism at the outset of all formal insolvency proceedings is particularly important in corporate rescue because it allows the court, and to an extent creditors, to direct cases affirmatively and more objectively into the most appropriate proceedings, whether that be liquidation, Civil Rehabilitation, or Corporate Reorganization. Second, the partial inclusion of secured claims in Civil Rehabilitation and their complete incorporation in Corporate Reorganization limits the ability of secured creditors to manipulate opportunistically the crisis to their advantage and thereby prevent unsecured creditors from realizing going concern value.

The success of a reorganization in achieving the greatest going concern value is also directly related to the speed of proceedings. Thus, the Insolvency Law Deliberative Council introduced new rules that allow the quick transfer or sale of the whole or an important portion of a business. Codified in the Civil Rehabilitation Act and included in the Corporate Reorganization revisions, this procedure allows a debtor to sell its business with court approval but without shareholder or creditor approval.[98] Many commentators have hailed this system as an important aspect of developing merger and acquisition (M&A) and prepackaged reorganization markets in Japan.[99] In the first two years under the new program, though, only thirty-five cases have met the Civil Rehabilitation Act's "absolutely necessary for the debtor's successful rehabilitation" standard.[100]

The fourth subsystem particularly important to the success or failure of business rescues is the approval mechanism for reorganization plans. The Insolvency Law Deliberative Council significantly eased plan approval in both Civil Rehabilitation and Corporate Reorganization by reducing the percent of creditor consent needed to a simple majority of unsecured creditors.[101] Notably this is a lower standard than the two-thirds majority required in Chapter 11 in the United States.[102] The proposed Corporate Reorganization changes also seek to lower the approval rates for secured creditors, though at present it is unclear what the exact majority required will be.[103] By relaxing the requirements for plan endorsement to a simple majority of unsecured creditors and a diminished supermajority of secured creditors, more debtors will be able to confirm plans and return to trading. What is unclear is whether this means more businesses will survive and produce increased gains for creditors, or whether it simply means more businesses will fail to complete confirmed plans and thereby burn up debtor value and creditors' time.

IV. CONCLUSION

An enormous increase in the number of insolvencies over the late 1990s pushed insolvency law into the forefront at the turn of the twenty-first century. Japan's response, put forward by the Insolvency Law Deliberative Council, represents a turning point in insolvency procedure. Innovations such as streamlining the number of insolvency schemes, simplifying the screening process for commencement of consumer cases, and introducing rules for the quick transfer of businesses in reorganization all suggest that Japanese insolvency law is becoming more systematized and efficiency-focused. Japan has not, however, adopted an American approach of automatic and universal solutions. Rather, the revised Japanese model retains its diffuse and tailored approach pioneered over eighty years ago. For example, debtors may still choose among three insolvency acts, a variety of overseers, a host of discretionary stays, at least three avoidance powers, and a number of special procedures for consumer debtors and reorganizing companies. In short, the revised system is best understood and applied as a fine-tuned version of the original framework, not a new model.

As a result, despite all the talk of globalized and converging legal systems, and the corollaries regarding the Americanization of other countries' laws,[104] we assert these conclusions are mistaken, at least for Japanese insolvency law. It is our experience from the Insolvency Law Deliberative Council that the failure of Japan simply to adopt an American approach to insolvency regulation is not for lack of information, insight, imagination, inspiration, or political support. It is in fact the result of a conscious and considered decision that the competing interests of debtors, creditors, and the public are best balanced as the system stands, though with modifications based on past experience. Considering this, perhaps the United States—with its globally unparalleled number of formal insolvencies—has as much, if not more, to learn from Japanese law as it has to teach.

NOTES

We are indebted to Frank Bennett for his comments on an earlier draft, the attendees of the "Law in Japan: A Turning Point" conference for their questions and comments, and Professor Dan Fenno Henderson for his vision and guidance. As always, all remaining errors are our own.

1. Arthur Taylor von Mehren, ed., *Law in Japan: The Legal Order in a Changing Society* (Cambridge, MA: Harvard University Press, 1963), 31.

2. This chapter uses the term *insolvency* (*tōsan*) to describe all formal liquidation and reorganization proceedings, and *bankruptcy* (*hasan*) to describe those liquidation proceedings under the Bankruptcy Act. The United States appears to be the global exception, rather than the rule, in using the term *bankruptcy* to

describe both liquidation and reorganization proceedings and limiting the term insolvency to its financial definition.

3. Nineteen of the twenty largest insolvencies in Japan's history have occurred since 1993, including Mycal Supermarkets (debts of ¥1.6 trillion, 2001), Tokyo Life Insurance (debts of ¥980 billion, 2001), Kyōei Life Insurance (debts of ¥4.5 trillion, 2000), Chiyoda Life (debts of ¥2.9 trillion, 2000), Sogo Department Stores (debts of ¥689 billion, 2000), Long-Term Credit Bank and its subsidiary Japan Lease (debts of ¥2.2 trillion, 1998), Hokkaido Takushoku Bank (debts of ¥539 billion, 1997), and Yamaichi Securities (debts of ¥510 billion, 1997). A listing and description of every major insolvency in Japan from 1997 to the present is available at Tokyo Shoko Research (http://www.tsr-net.co.jp/topics/oogata/index.html).

4. For a typical summary of the classical explanation, see Ron W. Harmer, "Bankruptcy in the Global Village: The Pacific Rim," *Brooklyn Journal of International Law* 23 (1997): 139, 156:

> The first reason [for the comparatively low level of formal insolvency proceedings] has to do with Japanese society and culture. . . . That, coupled with a fairly high degree of protective intervention at both the government and financial industry levels (the latter involves the Japanese financing banks which, invariably, will have a stockholder stake in their customer enterprises), will often protect enterprises from a formal insolvency administration, even though they may be insolvent, and, indeed, may preclude the concerted initiation of a formal insolvency legal process.

5. Political pressure caused by the economic downturn alone did not trigger the review of insolvency law. Rather, it was brought about by a combination of catalysts including judicial concern over the administrative burden of handling the increase in cases and bureaucratic attention following the completion of the closely related Code of Civil Procedure reform in 1996. See Kent Anderson, "Small Business Reorganizations: An Examination of Japan's Civil Rehabilitation Act Considering U.S. Policy Implications and Foreign Creditors' Practical Interests," *American Bankruptcy Law Journal* 75 (2001): 355, 360–61. Whatever the reasons for reform in Japan, the situation seems to contrast with the contemporaneous bankruptcy reform in the United States, where consumer lenders' special interests apparently initiated the review. See, e.g., Donald L. Barlett and James B. Steele, "Soaked by Congress," *Time*, May 15, 2000.

6. Literally, this was the "Subcommittee on Insolvency Law" of the "Deliberative Council on the Legal System" (*Hōsei shingikai tōsan hō bukai*) and was attached to the Civil Affairs Bureau of the Ministry of Justice.

7. For the best explanation of a systems approach to insolvency in a comparative context, see Lynn M. LoPucki and George G. Triantis, "A Systems

Approach to Comparing U.S. and Canadian Reorganizations of Financially Distressed Companies," *Harvard International Law Journal* 35 (1994): 267, 269—74. See also Lynn M. LoPucki, "The Systems Approach to Law," *Cornell Law Review* 82 (1997): 479 (describing the methodology in general).

8. See 11 U.S.C. § 109; Toibb v. Radloft, 51 U.S. 157, 166 (1991) (holding individual not in business eligible for Chapter 11 protection).

9. See, e.g., United Nations, Commission on International Trade Law, *Possible Future Work on Insolvency*, U.N. Doc. A/CN.9/WG.V/WP.50 (New York: United Nations, 1999), ¶¶ 45–46 (advocating a unitary proceeding).

10. See notes 12–14 below and accompanying text. The Japanese system is at least more unified than the traditional British model that is still followed in Australia and New Zealand. Under the traditional British framework there is no overlap between corporate and individual insolvency statutes. See, e.g., Dennis Rose, *Lewis' Australian Bankruptcy Law*, 11th ed. (Pyrmont, N.S.W.: LBC Information Services, 1999), 37. But see New Zealand Law Commission, "Insolvency Law Reform Report" (2001), 116 (advocating creation of a unitary system in New Zealand).

11. See Robert K. Rasmussen, "A Debtor's Choice: A Menu Approach to Corporate Bankruptcy," *Texas Law Review* 71 (1992): 51 (advocating an insolvency system where debtor and creditors are allowed to select insolvency rules from various alternatives).

12. The irony would be that the Civil Law country of Japan seems to follow an ad hoc legislative approach to insolvency while the Common Law country of the United States tries to follow a systematic code approach.

13. Hasan hō [Bankruptcy Act], Act No. 71 of 1922; Minji saisei hō [Civil Rehabilitation Act], Act No. 225 of 1999.

14. See Hasan hō, art. 105; Minji saisei hō, art. 5.

15. Shōhō [Commercial Code], Act No. 48 of 1900, arts. 431–55.

16. Shōhō, arts. 381–403.

17. See Minji saisei hō, arts. 211–16 (Summary Proceedings, *kan'i saisei*); arts. 217–20 (Consensual Proceedings, *dōi saisei*).

18. Kaisha kōsei hō [Corporate Reorganization Act], Act No. 172 of 1952.

19. See Insolvency Law Deliberative Council, "Kaisha kōsei hō kaisei yō ami shian" [Draft Proposed Revisions to the Corporate Reorganization Act], *NBL* 733 (2002): 10.

20. In Japan, the question has mostly been addressed informally among the insolvency bar. See, e.g., Tōzai tōsan jitsumu kenkyūkai [East-West Insolvency Practice Study Group], eds., *Kaisha kōsei/kaisha seiri* [Corporate Reorganization/Corporate Arrangement] (Tokyo: Shōji hōmu kenkyū kai, 1989). The question

has received significant treatment in the United States. See, e.g., Elizabeth Warren and Jay L. Westbrook, *The Law of Debtors and Creditors: Text, Cases and Problems*, 2nd ed. (Boston: Little, Brown, 1991), 365–96 (reviewing the statutory incentives, strategic and systemic incentives, and debtor decision-maker variables in election among formal insolvency options); Lynn M. LoPucki, "The Demographics of Bankruptcy," *American Bankruptcy Law Journal* 63 (1989): 289 (providing empirical evidence of pervasive local influences on conduct of cases).

21. See Minji saisei hō, arts. 196–206, 221–45, as amended by Minji saisei hō tō no ichibu o kaisei suru hōritsu [Act to Revise a Portion of the Civil Rehabilitation Act], Act No. 128 of 2000.

22. If one were to believe all of the traditional rhetoric about a Japanese cultural aversion to bankruptcy, see, e.g., Harmer, "Bankruptcy in the Global Village," 156; Brooke Schumm III, "Comparison of Japanese and American Bankruptcy Law," *Michigan Yearbook of International Legal Studies* 1988 (1988): 291, 291, one would expect to see a huge shift to Civil Rehabilitation even among those not protecting homes. Over the first year of the individual Civil Rehabilitation Act, however, there still has been an overwhelming preference for individual bankruptcy. See Saikōsaibansho jimusōkyoku [General Secretariat, Supreme Court (of Japan)], *1 Shihō tōkei nenpō, Minji gyōsei hen* [Annual Report of Judicial Statistics, vol. 1, Civil and Administrative Cases Volume] (2001) (reporting a 13:1 preference for bankruptcy, with an average 13,400 individual Bankruptcy filings a month compared to 690 individual Civil Rehabilitation filings a month).

23. Some commentators argue for even more consolidation with the combination of the two rescue statutes. See Shinjirō Takagi, "Kaisha kōsei hō kaisei no mondaiten" [Problems in the Revision of the Corporate Reorganization Act], *NBL* 712 (2002): 6, 8 (arguing in favor of consolidation of the Civil Rehabilitation Act and Corporate Reorganization Act).

24. Of the four largest eligible insolvencies since the enactment of the Civil Rehabilitation Act, three have filed Civil Rehabilitation and only one has pursued Corporate Reorganization. See Tokyo Shoko Research, (http://www.tsr-net.co.jp/topics/oogata/index.html) (providing summaries of every major insolvency since 1997). For a review of the Mycal insolvency in English, see Eric Grouse, "Banks, Bonds and Risk: The Mycal Bankruptcy and Its Repercussions for the Japanese Bond Market," *Duke Journal of Comparative and International Law* 12 (2002): 571.

25. See, e.g., Hideki Matsushima, *Yoi tōsan to warui tōsan* [Good Insolvency and Bad Insolvency] (Tokyo: Kōdansha, 2002) (describing conversion of Mycal from Civil Rehabilitation to Corporate Reorganization based on pressure from its lead lender).

26. See, e.g., Theodore Eisenberg and Shoichi Tagashira, "Should We Abolish Chapter 11? The Evidence from Japan," *Journal of Legal Studies* 23 (1994): 111 (noting courts' reluctance to accept smaller entities for Corporate Reorganization).

27. Kin'yū kikan no kōsei tetsuzuki no tokurei tō ni kansuru hōritsu [Special Procedures for Reorganization of Financial Institutions Act], Act No. 95 of 1996, as amended by Kin'yū kikan tō no kōsei tetsuzuki no tokurei tō ni kansuru hōritsu no ichibu o kaisei suru hōritsu [Act to Amend a Portion of the Financial Institutions Reorganization Act], Act Nos. 92–93 of 2000.

28. Gaikoku tōsan shori tetsuzuki no shōnin enjo ni kansuru hōritu [Act regarding Recognition and Assistance to Foreign Insolvency Proceedings], Act No. 129 of 2000, translated at *Japanese Annual of International Law* 43 (2000): 331; available at (http://www.moj.go.jp/ENGLISH/CIAB/lrtr.pdf).

29. See Kent Anderson, "The Cross-Border Insolvency Paradigm: A Defense of the Modified Universal Approach Considering the Japanese Experience," *University of Pennsylvania Journal of International Economic Law* 21 (2000): 679, 721–27 (reviewing various informal insolvency systems in Japan).

30. See generally Robert H. Mnookin and Lewis Kornhauser, "Bargaining in the Shadow of the Law: The Case of Divorce," *Yale Law Journal* 88 (1979): 950 (discussing the impact of a legal system on negotiations and bargaining outside judicial proceedings).

31. See J. Mark Ramseyer, "Legal Rules in Repeated Deals: Banking in the Shadow of Defection in Japan," *Journal of Legal Studies* 20 (1991): 91, 96–97 (discussing parties who do not have the size or reputation to rely on informal resolution mechanisms); Paul Sheard, "Main Banks and the Governance of Financial Distress," in Masahiko Aoki and Hugh Patrick, eds., *The Japanese Main Bank System: Its Relevance for Developing and Transforming Economies* (Oxford: Oxford University Press, 1994), 188, 194 (noting debtors with weak or nonexisting ties to Japanese main banks as creditors are more likely to use formal insolvency measures rather than private, informal measures).

32. Following severe criticism and public outcry over the informal resolution of the Long-Term Credit Bank's insolvency, the government and creditors were unable or unwilling to provide an informal resolution for the insolvency of Sogo Department Stores in 2000. See, e.g., Michael Backman, "Gone Bust: Letting Sogo Sink," *Asian Wall Street Journal*, July 25, 2000, 12 (2000 WL-WSJA 23746044). Nonetheless, some might characterize the informal resolution of Daiei Supermarkets' economic troubles in 2001 as a return to an insidious preference for informal insolvency resolution. See, e.g., Osamu Nariai, "A Critical Moment for Economic Reform," *Japan Echo*, April 2002 (2002 WL 14842407). On the other hand, others might simply characterize it as a typical private restructuring common in the United

States. See, e.g., Robert W. Sawdey, "Out-of-Court Workouts," *Federal Lawyer* 45 (June 1998): 46 (reviewing private restructuring in the United States).

33. See Saikōsaibansho jimusōkyoku, *1 Shihō tōkei nenpō, Minji gyōsei hen* (1952–2001). Tokyo Shoko Research (Dun and Bradstreet Japan) and Teikoku Databank also provide statistics on insolvencies, but they focus only on businesses in both formal and informal insolvency. See Tokyo Shoko Research, "Tōsan no teigi" [Definition of "Insolvency"] (http://www.tsr-net.co.jp/topics/teigi/index.html); Teikoku Databank, "FAQ" (http://www.tdb.co.jp/qa/index.html).

34. See, e.g., Curtis Milhaupt and Mark West, "The Dark Side of Private Ordering: An Institutional and Empirical Analysis of Organized Crime," *University of Chicago Law Review* 67 (2000): 41, 54.

35. See, e.g., Rasmussen, "A Debtor's Choice"; Anderson, "Small Business Reorganizations," 404–6.

36. Nonetheless, the comparative trends seen in consumer bankruptcies are also reflected in a comparison of the comprehensive statistics. Thus, Japan's rate of total formal insolvencies per thousand population is between 0.10 in 1990 and 1.16 in 2000 and sandwiched above the United Kingdom's rates and below the United States' figures. Further, Miwa and Ramseyer provide data suggesting that the number of Japanese business insolvencies between 1976 and 1980 was equal to or greater than in France, Germany, and the United States. See Yoshiro Miwa and J. Mark Ramseyer, "The Myth of the Main Bank: Japan and Comparative Corporate Governance," *Law and Social Inquiry* 27 (2002): 401, 418.

37. For population figures for each country, see U.S. Census Bureau, "International Data Base," available at (http://www.census.gov/ipc/www/idbprint.html). For the various countries' insolvency statistics, see Insolvency and Trustee Service Australia, "Bankruptcy Statistics," available at (http://www.itsa.gov.au/aghome/commaff/itsa/frame_statistics.html); the Insolvency Service (United Kingdom), "Our Statistics," available at (http://www.insolvency.gov.uk/information/stats/statistics.htm); American Bankruptcy Institute, "U.S. Bankruptcy Filing Statistics," available at (http://www.abiworld.org/stats/newstatsfront.html); and Office of the Superintendent of Bankruptcy Canada, "Bankruptcy Statistics," available at (http://strategis.ic.gc.ca/SSG/br01011e.html). This information has been supplemented with specific inquiries with each of the offices, on file with the authors.

38. See, e.g., Schumm, "Comparison of Japanese and American Bankruptcy Law," 291 ("The Japanese martial and samurai traditions, and the consequent concern for family honor and pride, cause the Japanese to feel great shame and disgrace upon a failure such as a bankruptcy").

39. See, e.g., Hasan hō, art. 105; Minji saisei hō, art. 5. We readily admit this

is somewhat of an artificial place to begin a discussion of insolvency/bankruptcy. Of course, the insolvency process begins with economic failure or risk of failure, necessarily moves through informal negotiation between debtor and creditors, and only ends in the initiation of formal proceedings in the largest, or relatively wealthiest, of cases. Nonetheless, for the reasons discussed in section II.D. and simply for space concerns we limit our discussion accordingly.

40. For example, in 2000, 99.6 percent of Japanese bankruptcy filings were by debtors. See Saikōsaibansho jimusōkyoku, *1 Shihō tōkei nenpō, Minji gyōsei hen* (2000). In the United States, for fiscal year 1998 creditors filed only 809 of the 1,419,199 petitions in the United States (0.057 percent). Administrative Office of the U.S. Courts, U.S. Bankruptcy Court Statistical table F2B (1999).

41. See, e.g., Hasan hō, art. 1; Minji saisei hō, art. 33.

42. Of 147,016 debtor applications for bankruptcy in 2000, only 541 (0.37 percent) were denied. See Saikōsaibansho jimusōkyoku, *1 Shihō tōkei nenpō, Minji gyōsei hen* (2000).

43. See Makoto Ito, "Civil Procedure Law," *Law in Japan: An Annual* 26 (2000): 70, 73–74 (discussing the pre-filing consultation practice).

44. See Hiromasa Nakajima, "Minji saisei tetsuzuki ni yoru kigyō saikenjō no mondaiten" [Problem Areas with Corporate Restructuring under the Civil Rehabilitation Procedure], Address to Insolvency Study Committee of the Hokkaido District Court in Sapporo, Japan (March 22, 2001).

45. See Chieko Tsutsumi and Kazuhiro Kosuga, "Minji saisei jiken—shikō 1 nen han no gaikyō o furikaette" [Looking Back on the General Situation of the Civil Rehabilitation Cases a Year and a Half after Taking Effect (of the Law)], *NBL* 727 (2001): 6, 11 (establishing that 52 percent of the commencement decisions cases under the new Civil Rehabilitation Act are made within fifteen days of filing); Anderson, "Small Business Reorganizations," 368–69 (collecting figures).

It is important to note that this lag mostly just delays eventual conclusion; it does not usually place the debtor in an exposed limbo susceptible to creditors stripping assets pending determination. This is because upon filing courts freely grant "provisional" stays (*kari shobun*) protecting a debtor's assets and effective until they make a decision on commencement. See, e.g., Hasan hō, art. 155.

46. See Anderson, "Small Business Reorganizations," 403–4.

47. This is confusingly referred to in Japanese as the "moral hazard risk" (*moraru hazādo*). See, e.g., editorial, "Kaisha kōsei hō kaisei yōami shian no kōhyō" [Public Announcement of the Draft Proposal for Revision of the Corporate Reorganization Act], *Kin'yū hōmu jihō* 1637 (2002): 16.

48. In both the United States and Japan, the actual dynamics of debtor control are not as simple as this characterization suggests. For example, in the DIP

system most business debtors will be represented by lawyers who face an inherent conflict of interest by representing the debtor personally; representing the interested parties, particularly creditors, as DIP trustee; and representing the public's interest as an officer of the court. See, e.g., C. R. Bowles Jr. and Nancy B. Rapoport, "Has the DIP's Attorney Become the Ultimate Creditors' Lawyer in Bankruptcy Reorganization Cases?" *American Bankruptcy Institute Law Review* 5 (1997): 47, 49.

49. Hasan hō, art. 142.

50. For a discussion of the investigation of using certified public accountants as in the United Kingdom and Australia, see Minji saisei hō chōsa hōkokusho kentōkai [Investigation Committee for Presentation of Investigations in Civil Rehabilitation], "Minji saisei jiken no kantoku jimu ni okeru kōnin kaikeishi chōsa yōryō" [Significant Points in the Investigation of Certified Public Accountants for the Work of Supervisors in Civil Rehabilitation Cases], *NBL* 707 (2001): 17; Michiko Hara and Rieko Uchiyama, "Nagoya chisai ni okeru minji saisei tetsuzuki un'yo no kihon hoshin" [Basic Direction for the Use of the Civil Rehabilitation Act Procedure in the Nagoya District Court], *Ginkō hōmu* 575 (2000): 11, 12–13.

51. See Anderson, "Small Business Reorganizations," 374 (arguing, inter alia, that fewer attorneys in Japan translates to fewer debtors' lawyers actively soliciting clients, fewer lawyers committing to be creditor committee counsel, and so forth). In response to the shortage of debtors' counsel, "judicial scriveners" (*shihō shoshi*) are beginning to file insolvency cases for so-called self-filing debtors. See, e.g., Hiroyuki Kawai and Hiroshi Ida, "Ōsaka chisai ni okeru kojin saisei jiken shori no gaikyō" [The General Status of the Handling of Individual Civil Rehabilitation Cases in the Osaka District Court], *Kin'yū hōmu jijō* 1634 (2002): 24, 25 (noting that 7.2 percent of the individual Civil Rehabilitation cases filed in the first nine months after the act took effect were with the assistance of a judicial scrivener).

52. Kaisha kōsei hō, art. 46.

53. See Takagi, "Kaisha kōsei hō kaisei no mondaiten," 6, 7–8.

54. See Lynn M. LoPucki and William C. Whitford, "Corporate Governance in the Bankruptcy Reorganization of Large, Publicly Held Companies," *University of Pennsylvania Law Review* 141 (1993): 669, 729–37 (providing empirical evidence that 95 percent of chief executive officers in public U.S. companies are replaced during Chapter 11 reorganizations).

55. See Hōmushō minjikyoku sanjikan shitsu [Ministry of Justice, Civil Affairs Bureau, Councilors' Office], "Kaisha kōsei hō kaisei yōami shian hosoku setsumei" [Supplemental Explanation of the Proposed Draft Revisions to the Corporate Reorganization Act], *NBL* 733 (2002): 24, 37; Kaisha kōsei hō., art. 72.

56. Minji saisei hō, art. 38.

57. See Tsutsumi and Kosuga, "Minji saisei jiken," 6, 9 (noting a Supervisor was appointed in 92 percent of all cases in the first year and a half of the Civil Rehabilitation Act).

58. See Minji saisei hō, art. 54.

59. See Wagi hō [Composition Act], Act No. 72 of 1922, arts. 27, 32.

60. See Takagi, "Kaisha kōsei hō kaisei no mondaiten," 7.

61. Interview with Michiaki Nakano, attorney and frequent reorganization trustee, in Tokyo, Japan, July 24, 2000; Shin Ushijima, "The Internationalization of the Japanese Economy and Corporate Reorganization Procedures: The Iwazawa Group and Sapporo Toyopet Failures," trans. Scott Earnshaw, *Law in Japan: An Annual* 18 (1986): 27, 47; Hara and Uchiyama, "Nagoya chisai ni okeru minji saisei tetsuzuki un'yo no kihon hōshin," 11, 13.

62. See Ichirō Ōzawa, "Ōsaka chihō saibansho dai6minjibu ni okeru minji saisei hō no un'yo" [Use of Civil Rehabilitation in the Sixth Civil Department (which handles insolvency affairs) of the Osaka District Court], *Kin'yū shōji hanrei* 1091 (2000): 2 (stating that the Osaka bankruptcy court is freely granting stays); Ministry of Justice (Japan), "Minji saisei hō no gaiyō" [Outline of the Civil Rehabilitation Act] (December 15, 2000), available at (http://www.moj.go.jp/MINJI/minji19.htm) (promoting the ease of pre-commencement stays as an improvement over the Composition Act).

63. Minji saisei hō, art. 31.

64. Ibid., art. 148.

65. See Tsutsumi and Kosuga, "Minji saisei jiken," 14 (noting only ten cases in two years under the Civil Rehabilitation Act approved this kind of lien stripping).

66. Kaisha kōsei hō, arts. 37, 67.

67. See Hasan hō, art. 72; Minji saisei hō, art. 127.

68. See Bankruptcy Code, 11 U.S.C. §§ 547 (providing ninety-day and one-year periods for general and insider preferences), 548(a)(1)(A)–(B) (providing one-year period for fraudulent and undervalued transactions).

69. See, e.g., Hasan hō, art. 98; Minji saisei hō, art. 92; Bankruptcy Code, 11 U.S.C. § 553.

70. See Hasan hō, arts. 15, 40.

71. See ibid., arts. 92–97.

72. See ibid., art. 47 (*zaidan saiken*); Minji saisei hō, art. 119 (*kōeki saiken*). The breakdown between administrative and public policy priority claims does not align perfectly in all of the proceedings. For example, under the Bankruptcy Act an administrative claim for expenses for the common benefit is covered by the "priority claims" provision, while the public policy claim for taxes is covered by the

"estate claims" provision. See Hasan hō, arts. 39 (incorporating Minpō [Civil Code], Act No. 89 of 1899, art. 306[1]) (making expenses for the common benefit a priority claim rather than estate claim); 47(2) (treating pre-petition tax claims as estate claims).

73. See Hasan hō, art. 39.

74. See R. M. Goode, *Principles of Corporate Insolvency Law*, 2nd ed. (London: Sweet and Maxwell, 1997), 157 (summarizing the British position); Andrew Keay and Michael Murray, *Insolvency: Personal and Corporate Law and Practice*, 4th ed. (Rozelle, N.S.W.: Lawbook Co., 2002), 145 n.59 (summarizing the Australian position); New Zealand Law Commission, "Priority Debts in the Distribution of Insolvent Estates Report" (1999), 28–44 (summarizing the New Zealand position).

75. See, e.g., Jay Westbrook, "Universal Priorities," *Texas International Law Journal* 33 (1998): 27; Lynn M. LoPucki, "Cooperation in International Bankruptcy: A Post-Universalist Approach," *Cornell Law Review* 84 (1999): 696, 735.

76. See In re Kojima, 177 B.R. 696, 702 (Bankr. D. Colo. 1995) (holding Japanese priorities are substantially in accordance with those of the U.S. Bankruptcy Code).

77. Cf. Hasan hō, art. 39; Minpō, art. 308, *with* Bankruptcy Code, 11 U.S.C. § 507(a)(3).

78. Cf. Hasan hō, art. 39; Minpō, art. 309, *with* Bankruptcy Code, 11 U.S.C. § 507(a)(5), (7).

79. See, e.g., Warren and Westbrook, *The Law of Debtors and Creditors*, 195–97.

80. The data are discussed in section II.E. above.

81. See, e.g., "Debt-Saddled Japanese Get Break," *Nikkei Weekly*, April 9, 2001 (reviewing the interrelation between these two results).

82. See, e.g., Takashi Sonoo, "Tōkyō chisai ni okeru hasan jiken no jijō to kadai" [Data and Topics on Bankruptcy Cases in Tokyo District Court], *Kin'yū hōmu jihō* 1644 (2002): 6, 10.

83. See ibid., 10–12. This was originally designed for small consumer cases with low assets; but, as discussed by Sonoo, it has proved so popular that it has been opened to corporations and larger asset cases, leaving only extremely large corporate liquidations and creditor petitions under the standard rules.

84. See ibid., 10.

85. See Hasan hō, art. 145. Tokyo District Court requires at least assets to cover ¥200,000 (approx. US$2,000) in expenses while Sapporo and others require enough to cover ¥500,000 in expenses. See, e.g., Shūo Inoue, "Kojin hasan tetsuzuki (dōji hasan haishi) no jitsujō" [The Actual Situation of Personal Bankruptcy Proceedings (Simultaneous Bankruptcy Abolition)], address to Insolvency Law Study Committee of the Hokkaido District Court in Sapporo, Japan (June 16, 2000).

86. See Sonoo, "Tōkyō chisai ni okeru hasan jiken no jijō to kadai," 16 (noting the average processing time for Simultaneous Bankruptcy Abolition cases in Tokyo District Court in 2001 was four months); "Debt-Saddled Japanese Get Break" (noting discharge available in many cases one to two months after commencement).

87. See Act No. 173 of 1952 (amending Bankruptcy Act to include discharge); "Debt-Saddled Japanese Get Break" (noting pre-1995 practice).

88. See Sonoo, "Tōkyō chisai ni okeru hasan jiken no jijō to kadai," 17.

89. Ibid.

90. Ibid., 6, 10–11, 13.

91. See Minji saisei hō tō no ichibu o kaisei suru hōritsu, amending Civil Rehabilitation Act.

92. See generally "Shinpojiūmu, Tōsan hō no kaisei: Kojin saisei tetsuzuki no sōsetsu" [Symposium, Insolvency Law Reform: Establishment of the Individual Rehabilitation Procedure], *Jurisuto*, no. 1194 (2001): 2–40.

93. See Sonoo, "Tōkyō chisai ni okeru hasan jiken no jijō to kadai," 8.

94. See Yoshinori Naoi and Takeshi Hatano, "Kojin saisei jiken—Hō shikō go hannenkan no mōshitate no gaikyō tō" [Individual Rehabilitation Cases—the General Situation on Filings and Such a Half Year after Taking Effect of the Law], *NBL* 727 (2001): 19, 27–28.

95. Ibid., 25–27

96. For example, of the bankruptcy cases concluded in 2000, 55 percent of the cases paid 5 percent or less of the claims' value, 17 percent of the cases paid up to 10 percent, another 17 percent of the cases paid up to 25 percent, 7 percent of the cases paid up to 50 percent, 2 percent of the cases paid up to 75 percent, and less than 2 percent of cases paid over 75 percent. See Saikōsaibansho jimusōkyoku, *1 Shihō tōkei nenpō, Minji gyōsei hen* (2000), 62.

97. Comparable statistics on successful completion rates of reorganization are difficult to locate. The best comparative results, though dated, suggest that Japanese rates might be twice that of the United States. See Eisenberg and Tagashira, "Should We Abolish Chapter 11," 256–57.

98. Minji saisei hō, arts. 42–43.

99. See, e.g., Hiromasa Nakajima, "Minji saisei hō de kawaru tōsan tetsuzuki kōzō" [The Structure of Insolvency Proceedings as Changed by the Civil Rehabilitation Act], *Hōgaku seminā* 550 (2000): 20, 20–21; Haruhide Aikawa, "Minji saisei hō: Tekiyō shinsei kigyō tsugu" [The Civil Rehabilitation Act: Appropriate Businesses for Filing Are Following It], *Mainichi shinbun*, April 9, 2000; "Sōgō, kokyaku fushin osore ketsudan, minji saisei hō shinsei gurūpu kaitai manukarezu" [Sogo's Decisions regarding Its Fear of Customers' Distrust: a Civil Rehabilita-

tion Act Filing without Avoiding the Group's Dismantling], *Nikkei shinbun*, July 13, 2000, 3. The possibility of using the Civil Rehabilitation Act to facilitate M&A's has spawned a host of books, if not actual deals. See, e.g., Shōichirō Fujiwara, *Torihiki tōsan taisaku wa kō kawaru: Minji saisei tetsuzuki de* [By Civil Rehabilitation Proceedings the Strategy for Transactional Insolvency Will Change in This Way] (Tokyo: Chūō keizai sha, 2000).

100. In the first two years of the Civil Rehabilitation Act (i.e., from April 1, 2000, to March 31, 2002), a survey of the thirteen judicial centers found thirty-five transfers had been approved. See Tsutsumi and Kosuga, "Minji saisei jiken," 8, 14. One of Japan's largest lenders, the Mizuho Financial Group, has created a special team to facilitate this type of M&A expecting that it will profit from both the acquirer, by taking a fee for setting up the deal, and the merged debtor, by limiting the amount of its extended debt it must write off. See "Mizuho Financial Group Mulls Bigger M&A Role," *Nikkei Weekly*, March 19, 2001, available in LEXIS, News Library, News File.

101. See Minji saisei hō, art. 171(4); Insolvency Law Deliberative Council, "Kaisha kōsei hō kaisei yō ami shian," 10 (art. 50).

102. Bankruptcy Code, 11 U.S.C. § 1126(c).

103. If the reorganization plan postpones the term of a secured agreement it requires a two-thirds majority; if a plan diminishes the secured agreements amount it requires either three-fourths or four-fifths majority, still to be decided; if the plan liquidates the secured claim it requires nine-tenths or four-fifths majority, still to be determined. See Insolvency Law Deliberative Council, "Kaisha kōsei hō kaisei yō ami shian," 10 (art. 50).

104. See, e.g., R. Daniel Kelemen and Eric C. Sibbitt, "The Americanization of Japanese Law," *University of Pennsylvania Journal of International Economic Law* 23 (2002): 269.

Appendix A

Dan Fenno Henderson: A Tribute

DANIEL H. FOOTE

This volume is dedicated to the memory of Professor Dan Fenno Henderson, who passed away on March 14, 2001, at the age of seventy-nine. Henderson was a giant in the Japanese law field. His life profoundly affected all of us in the field of Japanese law today and played a vital role in shaping the field as we know it. To interject a personal note, one of the proudest days of my life was the day I was named the first Dan Fenno Henderson Professor of East Asian Legal Studies at the University of Washington School of Law; and one of my great regrets in moving from the University of Washington to the University of Tokyo was having to relinquish that title. To me, Henderson will always represent the epitome of what a scholar of Japanese law should strive to be.

Beginning with a thumbnail sketch of Henderson's life, he was born in Chelan, Washington, in 1921. In 1944, he graduated Phi Beta Kappa from Whitman College in Walla Walla, Washington, where he earned a BA in political science. It being the height of World War II, upon graduation he was promptly drafted by the U.S. Army; however, at the time, the army was giving all Phi Beta Kappa draftees the choice of learning either Chinese or Japanese. According to his wife of forty-three years, Carol Henderson, he later said that was "the hardest choice of his life." For those familiar with the breadth of his scholarship and academic pursuits, the reason for the difficulty in choosing is classically Henderson: "He was interested in both."[1] It goes without saying that he ultimately chose Japanese. He undertook his Japanese language studies at the army's Japanese Language School, which was located at the University of Michigan. While there, he earned a second BA degree, in Oriental studies (awarded in 1945).

By the time Henderson reached Japan, the war had ended. From 1946 through 1947, he served as Japanese language officer in the Occupation forces, handling censorship in Hokkaido and Kyushu. Upon completing military service, he entered Harvard Law School under the GI Bill, and, in 1949, earned his JD degree. Following graduation, he briefly practiced law in Seattle, but then decided to pursue further academic study of Japan and entered the PhD program in political science at the University of California, Berkeley. In 1955, he completed his dissertation, which was later published as a seminal two-volume study of conciliation under Tokugawa and modern Japanese law,[2] and received his doctorate. (In 1983 he was awarded a second doctorate, an Honorary LLD, by Whitman College.)

Henderson spent the next seven years in private practice with the law firm of Graham & James, in San Francisco and Tokyo. He was one of the last U.S. lawyers to be admitted to the Japanese bar in the mid-1950s, and he served as resident partner of the Tokyo office.

In 1962, the University of Washington (UW) School of Law, with the support of a grant from the Ford Foundation, established a new program in Asian and comparative law (commonly known as the Asian Law Program). The UW recruited Henderson to serve as the first director of that program and entrusted him with responsibility for constructing and shaping it. He served as director for nearly three decades—through his retirement in 1991 at the age of seventy—and throughout that time devoted extraordinary effort to the program. Following his retirement from the UW, he continued to teach regularly, first as a visiting professor at Washington University in St. Louis and then as a regular member of the faculty of the Hastings College of Law in San Francisco.

In addition to his heavy teaching and administrative responsibilities, Henderson somehow found time not only for his own prolific scholarship but also for numerous other endeavors. He taught widely, serving as visiting professor at ten leading universities in six nations and offering countless guest lectures around the world. He also continued to practice law. Not only did he consult; in 1972, together with two former students, he founded the law firm of Adachi, Henderson, Miyatake & Fujita in Tokyo. And he also pursued interests in book collecting, gardening, art, apples, horses, and tennis.

As the preceding thumbnail sketch reflects, Henderson's activities and interests were rich and varied. Yet a thumbnail sketch cannot possibly do justice to his influence. The following is an attempt to enumerate a few aspects of his impact.

Henderson was a prodigious scholar in his own right. As reflected in the attached bibliography of his works, he authored or coauthored ten major books on Japanese law, in addition to close to one hundred articles and other works. These works have had a tremendous impact on scholars and practitioners alike.

He also promoted and facilitated scholarship by others in countless ways. His vision was that the UW and its Asian Law Program should play a key role in propagating scholarship on and understanding of Japanese law (and, in later years, after the program had become more firmly established, other areas of Asian law). Among the many steps he took to achieve that end, he invited several young Japanese lawyers and scholars to the UW to teach or to work with resident faculty members in preparing comparative course materials, and he persuaded many of his American colleagues to undertake collaborative work with the visitors. These efforts led to important sets of materials, for example, an introduction to Japanese law (by Henderson himself with Kazuaki Sono); "U.S.-Japanese Contract and Sales Law" (Warren Shattuck with Zentarō Kitagawa); "U.S.-Japanese Taxation" (John Huston with Toshio Miyatake and Griffith Way); "U.S.-Japanese Administrative Law" (Yasuhiro Fujita); "U.S.-Japanese Corporate Law" (initially, Henderson himself, and later, Richard O. Kummert, with Misao Tatsuta); "Patent and Know-How Licensing in Japan and the United States" (Teruo Doi and Shattuck); and "Japanese Antitrust Law" (John O. Haley with Mitsuo Matsushita).[3]

Among Henderson's other efforts to promote scholarship on and understanding of Asian law, in the mid-1960s he organized a series of annual symposia on Asian law for the *Washington Law Review* and he persuaded the University of Washington Press to establish the Asian Law Series, dedicated to publishing important works on Asian law. He also viewed comprehensive library resources as crucial for fostering knowledge of Asian law; under his influence, the UW's Gallagher Law Library assembled (and to this day continues to maintain and expand) a superb collection of Asian law materials, staffed by research librarians knowledgeable about Asian law and fluent in Asian languages.

Above all, Henderson sought to promote knowledge of Asian law through his own teaching and the teaching efforts of others at the UW and, ultimately, through the scholarship and teaching of those who trained under him. He himself developed and taught the first regularly scheduled course on Japanese law offered outside Japan; under his guidance, the UW developed a wide array of comparative courses on U.S.-Japanese law, as well as courses on traditional and contemporary Chinese law and Korean law. Henderson was a demanding teacher, but one who cared very deeply about his students and who inspired dedication and outstanding scholarship. His former students include many scholars, American and non-American alike, teaching in the field of East Asian law, as well as scholars at leading universities throughout East Asia.

Henderson's efforts to promote knowledge of Japanese law extended well beyond the walls of the UW. In the late 1960s, he set aside the annual *Washington Law Review* symposia to begin serving as editor of the journal *Law in Japan: An Annual*, and for many years thereafter he kept a watchful eye over that journal as his former students assumed the primary editorial duties. His ties to the Japanese American Society for Legal Studies were just as close as his ties to *Law in Japan: An Annual*. From the time of the establishment of the society in 1964, Henderson was a member of the board of councilors; soon thereafter he became a member of the board of directors; and for the last seventeen years of his life he served as the American representative director of the society. He also taught and lectured widely.

One other feature of Henderson's vision for the Asian Law Program bears especial note: under his influence, the program has been highly integrative, in several respects. The program has provided Asian students with training in U.S. law; it has provided U.S. and foreign students alike with training in Japanese and Asian law; and, above all, it has sought to integrate the study of U.S. and Asian law.

The Asian Law Program also has sought to integrate theory and practice. Henderson was a true scholar, but he was also a practitioner; and he regarded it as very important that scholarship should inform, and should be informed by, the world of practice. From the outset, he invited practitioners, as well as academic scholars, to the program; he encouraged both groups to undertake collaborative research bridging theory and practice. In addition to practicing lawyers, the program has welcomed staff members of corporate legal departments, bureaucrats, judges, and prosecutors from Japan and other Asian nations and has sought to integrate the varied perspectives they bring.

Finally, the Asian Law Program has sought to integrate the study of law with the study of other disciplines. Henderson felt strongly that law could not be studied in isolation, but rather it must be considered as part of a much broader setting. His own passion was legal history, so it is natural that he viewed attention to law's historical context as vital. He also placed great weight on the importance of other contexts, including law's social, cultural, economic, and political contexts. Accordingly, Henderson regarded interdisciplinary study of law as essential. This view is reflected in the structure of the program. With respect to the major comparative research paper required of all LLM candidates, Henderson was flexible as to topic, but he had one firm stricture: the paper must not consist merely of "parallel exposition." In other words, no matter how long the paper or how much research it entailed, it was unacceptable simply to follow the formula: "U.S. law is A; Japanese law is B; the similarities are U, V, and W; the differences are X, Y, and Z." Rather, the paper must probe further, exploring, for example, the historical (or social, or economic, or political) settings that gave rise to the differences, and the implications of the respective systems in their existing context. It is not by chance, moreover, that the terminal degree in the program is the PhD, rather than the SJD. To Henderson, a fundamental aspect of the doctoral program was the need to place law in a broader context; to that end, he insisted that the program's doctoral track be an explicitly interdisciplinary PhD program.

Given the breadth of Henderson's scholarship, identifying all of its animating themes would be virtually impossible. The following quotation offers five themes that one might consider applying to Henderson's work:

> [First, it] is more academically concerned with law as a system or social science than with law as a professional discipline. This is not to imply, of course, that the organic understanding sought is not valuable to the practical lawyer. . . . [H]owever, . . . it is largely concerned with a discussion of the policy and function of modern Japanese law rather than with legal doctrine and nuances of its application—although there are many useful discussions of the latter. . . . A second feature . . . is the need for historical perspective in order to assess the progress of legal growth in Japan. A third and related emphasis . . . is the problem of the efficacy of legislation, foreign inspired or otherwise, to change and modernize Japan's highly refined and tenacious traditional social patterns. As Professor [Arthur T.] von Mehren [has] noted, there is a tendency to view all these problems as dichotomies—Anglo-American and Continental European law; modern and premodern Japanese law; Japanese and non-Japanese elements; and the legal and nonlegal—even though the underlying reality is a moving whole which comprehends all of these different facets in Japan's rather unique modernization process. Only acute attention to historical perspective as well as to underlying social behavior enables one to see the whole modernization process without the distortion of such dichotomies.

A fourth theme . . . is a desire to understand the fate of certain of the American legal ideas implanted in Japan during the basic reforms of the occupation period (1945–1952). A final and much related pervasive theme is the problem of Japan's earlier reception of German and French law and the adaptation of these foreign concepts to local needs since the Meiji Restoration (1868).[4]

As many readers undoubtedly inferred, the above words are Henderson's own. He did not write them in reference to his own work, however. Rather, they appeared in his book review of *Law in Japan: The Legal Order in a Changing Society*,[5] the 1963 predecessor to this volume. Yet all five of the above themes might equally be applied to Henderson's own work, with one notable exception. Henderson was intensely concerned "with law as a system or social science" and " with a discussion of the policy and function of modern Japanese law," but, as reflected in *Civil Procedure in Japan* and many other works, he *also* was intensely concerned "with law as a professional discipline" and "with legal doctrine and nuances of its application."

To offer my own one-word summation of the central theme I see animating Henderson's work, I would return to the adjective used earlier with regard to his vision for the Asian Law Program: integrative. Whether dealing with conciliation, civil procedure, contract law, corporate law, foreign investment regulation, constitutional law, or any one of numerous other topics, Henderson strove to integrate comparative perspectives, theoretical and practical perspectives, and historical and other interdisciplinary perspectives, so as to achieve a comprehensive and nuanced understanding of law in its overall context. Returning to Henderson's own words, by paying "acute attention to historical perspective as well as to underlying social behavior," he sought to capture "the underlying reality" of Japanese law, "a moving whole which comprehends all of [the] different facets in Japan's rather unique modernization process." That he succeeded so admirably in that goal is a testament to his thirst for knowledge and his fierce intellect. We are all the beneficiaries.

NOTES

1. Quoted in Eli Sanders, "Dan Henderson, UW Program Founder, Dies," *Seattle Times*, March 19, 2001.

2. Dan Fenno Henderson, *Conciliation and Japanese Law: Tokugawa and Modern*, 2 vols. (Seattle: Association for Asian Studies / University of Washington Press, 1965).

3. In addition, Henderson prepared a wide range of materials himself, including a guide to Japanese legal literature and research and materials for courses on transnational litigation and doing business in Japan. He also collaborated with Haley on the extensive set of materials "Law and the Legal Process in Japan." Under Henderson's influence, the UW also has encouraged faculty members, including Haley, Toshiko Takenaka, Veronica Taylor, and myself, in the preparation of materials for courses on specific fields of Japanese law, including administrative law, intellectual property, criminal justice, and labor law.

4. Dan Fenno Henderson, review of *Law in Japan: The Legal Order in a Changing Society*, edited by Arthur Taylor von Mehren, *Stanford Law Review* 16(4) (1964): 1129, 1130–31 (citation omitted).

5. Arthur Taylor von Mehren, ed., *Law in Japan: The Legal Order in a Changing Society* (Cambridge, MA: Harvard University Press, 1963).

Appendix B

Selected Writings of Dan Fenno Henderson

ROBERT BRITT

1952 "Some aspects of Tokugawa law." *Washington Law Review*, vol. 27, no. 1 (February): 85–109.

1954 Review of *Nihon seiji shisōshi kenkyū* [A Study in The History of Japanese Political Thought], by Masao Maruyama. *Far Eastern Quarterly*, vol. 14, no. 1 (November): 123–26.

1955 "The pattern and persistence of traditional procedures in Japanese law." (PhD thesis in Political Science, University of California, Berkeley).

1956 Review of *The Criminal Code of Japan*, by Thomas L. Blakemore. *Far Eastern Quarterly*, vol. 15, no. 2 (February): 302–4.

1957 "Japanese legal history of the Tokugawa period: Scholars and sources" In *Five Studies in Japanese Politics*, edited by Robert E. Ward, 101–21. Ann Arbor: University of Michigan Press.

1963 "Nichi-Beikan no jigyō katsudō ni okeru bengoshi no yakuwari" [The role of lawyers in U.S. / Japanese enterprise]. *Jurisuto*, no. 288 (December 15): 23–35.

1963 "The roles of lawyers in U.S.-Japanese business transactions." *Washington Law Review*, vol. 38, no. 1 (Spring): 1–21.

1964 "Contract problems in U.S.-Japanese joint ventures." *Washington Law Review*, vol. 39, no. 3 (August): 479–515.

1964 "Introduction to U.S.-Japanese investment." *Washington Law Review*, vol. 39, no. 3 (August): 405–11.

1964 Review of *Law in Japan: The Legal Order in a Changing Society*, by Arthur Taylor von Mehren. *Stanford Law Review*, vol. 16, no. 4 (July): 1129–42.

1964 "Settlement of homicide disputes in Sakya (Tibet)." *American Anthropologist*, vol. 66, no. 5 (October): 1099–1105.

1965 *Conciliation and Japanese Law: Tokugawa and Modern*. 2 vols. Seattle: Association for Asian Studies / University of Washington Press.

1965 "Kokusai keiyaku ni okeru funsō kaiketsu jōkō: Kokusai shihō gensoku no konran to chūsai" [Dispute settlement clauses in international contracts—Confusion in conflicts principles and arbitration]. *Kansai daigaku hōgaku ronshū*, vol. 14, nos. 4–6 (February): 745–65 (with Kazuaki Sono).

1965 Review of *American-Japanese Private International Law*, by Albert Armin Ehrenzweig, Sueo Ikehara, and Norman Jensen. *Law Library Journal*, vol. 58, no. 2 (May): 185–86.

1967 "Arbitration in U.S./Japanese sales disputes." *Washington Law Review*, vol. 42, no. 2 (March): 541–88 (with Tarō Kawakami).

1967 "Form of citation of Japanese legal materials." *Washington Law Review*, vol. 42, no. 2 (March): 589–99.

1967 "Introduction—U.S./Japanese trade: Its scope and legal framework." *Washington Law Review*, vol. 42, no. 2 (March): 333–45.

1967 "Promulgation of Tokugawa statutes." *Journal of Asian and African Studies*, vol. 2, no. 1: 9–25.

1967 Translation of *Meiji zenki ni okeru Minpōten hensan no keika to mondaiten* [Progress and Problems of Compiling the Civil Code in the Early Meiji Era], by Ken Mukai and Nobuyoshi Toshitani. *Law in Japan*, vol. 1: 25–59.

1968 "Abstract of Japanese lawyers: Types and roles in the legal profession." *Law and Society Review*, vol. 3, nos. 2–3 (November 1968–February 1969): 411–14.

1968 "The evolution of Tokugawa law." In *Studies in the Institutional History of Early Modern Japan*, edited by John W. Hall and Marius B. Jansen, 203–30. Princeton, NJ: Princeton University Press.

1968 "Japanese judicial review of legislation: The first twenty years." *Washington Law Review*, vol. 43, no. 5 (June): 1005–30.

1968 "Law and political modernization in Japan." In *Political Development in Modern Japan*, edited by Robert E. Ward, 387–456. Princeton, NJ: Princeton University Press.

1968 "Perspectives on the Japanese constitution after twenty years." *Washington Law Review*, vol. 43, no. 5 (June): 887–92.

1968 Translation of *Kaishahō ni okeru ultra vires no gensoku wa dono yō ni shite haiki subeki ka* [How Should We Abolish the Ultra Vires Doctrine in Corporation Law?], by Akio Takeuchi. *Law in Japan*, vol. 2: 140–63.

1969 *The Constitution of Japan: Its First Twenty Years, 1947–1967*. Seattle: University of Washington Press. (Copyright 1968.)

1969 Translation of *Shōhin baibai no keiyaku ni yoru songai baishō* [Damages in Contracts for the Sale of Goods], by Zentarō Kitagawa. *Law in Japan*, vol. 3: 43–89 (with L. Hurvitz and Kazuaki Sono).

1970 "Chinese legal studies in early 18th century Japan: Scholars and sources." *Journal of Asian Studies*, vol. 30, no. 1 (November): 21–56.

1970 "Japanese influences on communist Chinese legal language." In *Contemporary Chinese Law: Research Problems and Perspectives*, edited by Jerome Alan Cohen, 158–87. Cambridge, MA: Harvard University Press.

1970 Review of *Edo jidai ni okeru tosen mochiwatarisho no kenkyū* [A Study of Books Brought over by Chinese Ships during the Edo Period], by Osamu Oba. *Journal of Asian Studies*, vol. 29 no. 3 (May): 700–702.

1970 Review of *Japan's Managerial System: Tradition and Innovation*, by Michael Y. Yoshino. *Harvard International Law Journal*, vol. 11, no. 1 (Winter): 287–93.

1970 Translation of *Nakamura et al. v. Japan*. In *Comparative Judicial Politics*, edited by Theodore L. Becker, 280–97. Chicago: Rand McNally.

1973 "Eigo de kaku Nihon Minji soshōhō: Keika hōkoku" [Japanese Code of Civil Procedure in English: A progress report]. *Amerikahō*, no. 2: 218–23.

1973 *Foreign Enterprise in Japan: Laws and Policies*. Chapel Hill: University of North Carolina Press.

1973 "Modern China and Japan: History, politics and law." *Law Library Journal*, vol. 66, no. 4: 429–43 (Discussion Panelist).

1974 "'Contracts' in Tokugawa villages." *Journal of Japanese Studies*, no. 1 (Autumn): 51–90.

1974 "Japanese law: A profile." In *An Introduction to Japanese Civilization*, edited by Arthur Tiedemann, 570–91. New York: Columbia University Press (with James L. Anderson).

1974 "Japan's administration of foreign direct investment" In *Private*

Investments and International Transactions in Asian and South Pacific Countries, edited by Virginia Shook Cameron, 321–71. New York: Matthew Bender.

1975 *Foreign Enterprise in Japan: Laws and Policies*. Tokyo: C. E. Tuttle. (1st Tuttle edition; copyright 1973.)

1975 "The Japanese system for controlling art movement." In *Art Law: Domestic and International*, edited by Leonard D. Duboff, 263–67. Littleton, CO: Fred B. Rothman and Co.

1975 "Nihonhō to watakushi" [Japanese law and I]. *Jurisuto*, no. 600 (November 15): 51–52.

1975 Review of *Introduction to Japanese Law*, by Yoshiyuki Noda and Anthony H. Angelo. *Public Affairs*, vol. 50, no. 4 (Winter): 707–9.

1977 *Village Contracts in Tokugawa Japan: Fifty Specimens with English Translations and Comments*. Seattle: University of Washington Press.

1977 Review of *The Status System and Social Organization of Satsuma: A Translation of the Shumon Tefuda Aratame Jomoku*, by Torao Haraguchi et al. *Journal of Japanese Studies*, vol. 3, no. 2 (Summer): 438–40.

1977 "Trade with Japan." In *Law and Politics in China's Foreign Trade*, edited by Victor Li, 28–69. Seattle: University of Washington Press. (See also translations: 387–420; with Tasuku Matsuo.)

1978 Review of *Forces of Order: Police Behavior in Japan and the United States*, by David H. Bayley. *Journal of Asian Studies*, vol. 37, no. 3 (May): 542–44.

1978 Review of *Legal Reform in Occupied Japan: A Participant Looks Back*, by Alfred C. Oppler. *American Political Science Review*, vol. 72, no. 1 (March): 337–39.

1978 Review of *Patent and Know-How Licensing in Japan and the United States*, by Teruo Doi and Warren L. Shattuck. *American Journal of International Law*, vol. 69, no. 3 (April): 434–36.

1978 "Threshold advice to American businesses incorporating in Japan," In *Current Legal Aspects of Doing Business in Japan and East Asia*, edited by John O. Haley. [Chicago]: American Bar Association, 76–92.

1979 "Comments on civil dispute resolution in the U.S. and Japan." *Kokusai Bunka Kaikan Kaihō*, no. 36 (April): 35.

1980 "Chinese influence on 18th century Tokugawa codes." In *Essays on China's Legal Tradition*, edited by Jerome Alan Cohen, R. Randle Edwards, and Fu-mei Chang Chen, 170–302. Princeton, NJ: Princeton University Press.

1980 "Japanese law in English: Reflections on translation." *Journal of Japanese Studies*, vol. 6, no. 1 (Winter): 117–54.

1981 "Japan." In *Product Liability: A Manual of Practice in Selected Nations*, edited by Hans-Ulrich Stucki and Peter R. Altenburger. New York: Oceana (with Takeo Adachi, Toshio Miyatake, and Yasuhiro Fujita).

1981 "Japan: Economic aspects of national security and its impact on U.S. security." *Public Law Forum*, no. 1: 99–109.

1981 "Japanese regulation of recombinant DNA activities." *University of Toledo Law Review*, vol. 12, no. 4 (Summer): 891–902.

1981 "The role of law in Japan: Some issues." In *State and Law in East Asia: Festschrift Karl Bunger*, edited by Dieter Eikemeier and Herbert Franke, 204–6. Wiesbaden, Germany: Otto Harrassowitz.

1981 Translation of *Kinseihō* [Tokugawa Law], by Yoshirō Hiramatsu. *Law in Japan*, vol. 14: 1–48.

1983 *Civil Procedure in Japan*. New York: Matthew Bender (with Takaaki Hattori).

1983 "Code of Civil Procedure." In *Kodansha Encyclopedia of Japan*, vol. 1: 318–21. Tokyo: Kodansha.

1983 "Dispute resolution systems other than litigation" In *Kodansha Encyclopedia of Japan*, vol. 2: 117–19. Tokyo: Kodansha.

1983 "The Japanese law in English: Some thoughts on scope and method." *Vanderbilt Journal of Transnational Law*, vol. 16, no. 3 (Summer): 601–20.

1983 "The management of foreigners: Japan's new foreign exchange controls." In *Business Transactions with China, Japan, and South Korea*, edited by Parvis Saney and Hans Smit, chap. 7, sec. 7.01–7.06. New York: Matthew Bender.

1983 Review of *The Development of Kamakura Rule: A History with Documents*, by Jeffrey P. Mass. *Journal of Japanese Studies*, vol. 9, no. 2 (Summer): 367–73.

1983 Translation of *Arita v. Kojima* (app. B, "Sample Judgments"). In *Civil Procedure in Japan*, edited by Takaaki Hattori and Dan Fenno Henderson, app. B, 1–45. Dobbs Ferry, NY: Transnational Juris Publications.

1985 *A Japanese-English Legal Glossary*. Seattle: University of Washington School of Law (with John O. Haley and Frederick H. Rand).

1986 "Access to the Japanese market." In *Law and Trade Issues of the Japanese Economy*, edited by Gary Saxonhouse and Kozo Yamamura, 131 56. Seattle: University of Washington Press.

1987 "International economic law." In *Encyclopedia of the American Judicial System*, edited by Robert J. Janosik, vol. 1: 321–33. New York: Scribner.

1987 "Introduction to the Kujikata Osadamegaki (1742)." In *Hō to keibatsu no rekishiteki kōsatsu* [Historical Considerations on Law and Punishment], edited by Committee for Memorial Essays in Honor of Dr. Hiramatsu Yoshirō, 489–544. Nagoya: Nagoya daigaku shuppankai.

1987 "*Law and Justice in Tokugawa Japan*: The accomplishment of a century." *Japan Foundation Newsletter*, vol. 14, no. 6 (May): 1–3. (Concerns the history of the classic series *Law and Justice in Tokugawa Japan* by John Henry Wigmore.)

1987 "Nichi-Bei ni okeru chōtei/chūsai o tenbōshite" [The outlook for conciliation and arbitration in Japan and the United States]. *Hōritsu jihō*, no. 724 (July): 60–74.

1989 "Nichi-Bei ni okeru chōtei/chūsai o tenbōshite" [The outlook for conciliation and arbitration in Japan and the United States]. In *Chōtei to hō* [Conciliation and Law], by Takeshi Kojima, 189–216. Tokyo: Nihon hikakuhō kenkyūjo.

1990 "Comment." *Law and Contemporary Problems*, vol. 53, no. 1 (Winter–Spring): 89–96. (A response to the article appearing in the same issue titled "The Constitution of Japan: The fifth decade; Part 1, Understanding the Constitution" by Yasuhiro Okudaira et al.)

1990 "Mediation and arbitration in Japan and the U.S." In *Perspectives on Civil Justice and ADR: Japan and the U.S.A*, edited by Takeshi Kojima, 279–310. Tokyo: Institute of Comparative Law in Japan, Chuo University Press (with Ted L. Stein and Takeshi Kojima).

1990 "The trial process: Introduction." *In United States/Japan Commercial Law and Trade*, edited by Valerie Kusuda-Smick, 511. Dobbs Ferry, NY: Transnational Juris Publications.

1991 "Comparative law in the Japanese courts: Punitive damages," *Law in Japan: An Annual*, vol. 24 (1991): 98–104.

1991 "The interface between Japanese and American law (Lecture)" *Kantō Gakuin hōgaku*, vol. 1, no. 1 (December): 1–15.

1991 "Securities markets in the U.S. and Japan: Distinctive aspects molded by cultural, social, economic, and political differences." *Hastings International and Comparative Law Review*, vol. 14, no. 2 (Winter): 263–301.

1992 "Foreword." In *Order and Discipline in China: The Shanghai Mixed*

Court, 1911–27, edited by Thomas B. Stephens, vii–x. Seattle: University of Washington Press.

1992 "Rethinking the close corporation in Japan." In *Essays on Comparative Commercial and Consumer Law: Papers from the Fourth Biannual Conference of the International Academy of Commercial and Consumer Law, Melbourne, Australia, August 1988*, edited by Donald Barnett King. Littleton, CO: F. B. Rothman.

1992 Review of *The History of Law in Japan until 1868*, by Carl Steenstrup. *Japan Foundation Newsletter*, vol. 20, no. 3 (December): 16–18.

1992 "Traditional contract law in Japan and China." In *International Encyclopedia of Comparative Law*, vol. 7, chap. 6. Tübingen, Germany: J. C. B. Mohr (Paul Siebeck); New York: Oceana (with Preston M. Torbert).

1993 "Some developments in Japan's transnational law." In *Commercial and Consumer Law: National and International Dimensions*, edited by Ross Cranston and Roy Goode, 60–81. New York: Oxford University Press.

1994 "Foreign takeover of Japanese corporations." In *Japanese Commercial Law in an Era of Internationalization*, edited by Hiroshi Oda. Norwell, MA: Graham and Trotman.

1994 Review of *Japan's Public Sector: How the Government Is Financed*, by Tokue Shibata. *Japan Foundation Newsletter*, vol. 21, no. 5 (February): 17.

1995 "Foreign acquisitions and takeovers in Japan." *Saint Louis University Law Journal*, vol. 39, no. 3 (Spring): 897–915.

1995 Review of *Japanese Constitutional Law*, by Percy R. Luney Jr. and Kazuyuki Takahashi, *Japan Foundation Newsletter*, vol. 22, no. 5 (February): 23–25.

1997 "Role of lawyers in Japan." In *Japan, Economic Success and Legal System*, edited by Harald Baum. New York: Walter de Gruyter.

1998 "50 years of American contracting in Japan." In *Partnership, Prosperity, Potential: 50 Years of American Business in Japan*. Tokyo: American Chamber of Commerce in Japan.

1999 "Japanese and Asian philosophy of law." In *Philosophy of Law: An Encyclopedia*, edited by Christopher B. Gray, vol. 1: 443. New York: Garland.

2000 *Civil Procedure in Japan*. 2nd ed. Yonkers, NY: Juris Publishing, 2000 (with Takaaki Hattori).

Forthcoming	*Provisions concerning Suits: A Translation and Commentary on the Kujikata Osadamegaki* (Book 1).

EDITORIAL RESPONSIBILITIES OF DAN FENNO HENDERSON

1967	*Law in Japan: An Annual*. Seattle and Tokyo, Japanese American Society for Legal Studies. (Editorial Board.)
1968–70	*Law in Japan: An Annual* (Editorial Board Chairman).
1980–95	*Law in Japan: An Annual* (Editorial Advisory Committee).
1968–96	*Asian Law Series*. Seattle, University of Washington Press. (Editorial Committee Chairman for volumes 1–13.)
1974–78	*Journal of Japanese Studies*. Seattle, Society for Japanese Studies. (Associate Editor.)
1975–92	*American Journal of Comparative Law*. Berkeley, American Association for the Comparative Study of Law.

Contributors

KENT ANDERSON is Professor, The Australian National University, with a joint appointment in the ANU College of Law and the ANU College of Asian-Pacific Studies, and is Head of the Japan Centre in the Faculty of Asian Studies and Codirector, Australian Network for Japanese Law (ANJeL).

LAWRENCE W. BEER is the F. M. Kirby Professor of Civil Rights, Emeritus, Lafayette College.

ROBERT BRITT is the Japanese Legal Materials Specialist, East Asian Law Department, Marian Gould Gallagher Law Library, University of Washington School of Law.

ERIC A. FELDMAN is Professor of Law, University of Pennsylvania Law School.

HARRY FIRST is the Charles L. Denison Professor of Law and Director, Trade Regulation Program, New York University School of Law.

DANIEL H. FOOTE is Professor of Law, The University of Tokyo.

KŌICHIRŌ FUJIKURA is Professor of Law, Doshisha University Law School, and Professor Emeritus, The University of Tokyo.

TOM GINSBURG is Professor of Law and Political Science and Director, Program in Asian Law, Politics and Society, University of Illinois College of Law.

JOHN O. HALEY is the Wiley B. Rutledge Professor of Law and Director, Institute for Global Legal Studies, Washington University in St. Louis School of Law.

CHRISTOPHER H. HANNA is the Altshuler Distinguished Teaching Professor and Professor of Law, Southern Methodist University Dedman School of Law.

JOSEPH L. HOFFMANN is the Harry Pratter Professor of Law, Indiana University School of Law.

MAKOTO ITŌ is Professor of Law, Waseda University Law School, and Professor Emeritus, The University of Tokyo.

DAVID T. JOHNSON is Associate Professor of Sociology, University of Hawai'i.

HIDEKI KANDA is Professor of Law, The University of Tokyo.

HIROSHI KANEKO is Professor Emeritus, The University of Tokyo.

NOBUHIKO KASUMI is Professor of Law, Keio University.

NAOKI KOIZUMI is Professor of Law, Keio Law School.

ROBERT B LEFLAR is the Arkansas Bar Foundation Professor of Law, University of Arkansas School of Law, and Adjunct Professor, University of Arkansas for Medical Sciences.

KŌYA MATSUO is Professor Emeritus, The University of Tokyo, and Member, The Japan Academy.

CURTIS J. MILHAUPT is the Fuyo Professor of Law and Director, Center for Japanese Legal Studies, Columbia Law School.

YOSHIRŌ MIWA is Professor of Economics, The University of Tokyo.

YASUHARU NAGASHIMA is Advisor, Nagashima Ohno & Tsunematsu, Tokyo.

J. MARK RAMSEYER is the Mitsubishi Professor of Japanese Legal Studies, Harvard Law School.

KAHEI ROKUMOTO is Professor Emeritus, The University of Tokyo.

TADASHI SHIRAISHI is Professor of Law, The University of Tokyo.

CARL STEENSTRUP was Associate Professor at the Institute for Japanese Studies in Munich University, Germany, and after retirement taught at the Humboldt University in Berlin and at the Baikal University for Economics and Law in Irkutsk, Siberia.

KAZUYUKI TAKAHASHI is Professor of Law, The University of Meiji, and Professor Emeritus, The University of Tokyo.

TOSHIKO TAKENAKA is Washington Research Foundation / W. Hunter Simpson Professor of Technology Law; Director, Center for Advanced Study and Research on Intellectual Property, University of Washington School of Law; and Visiting Professor, Waseda University Law School.

YASUHEI TANIGUCHI is Professor of Law, Senshu University Law School; Professor Emeritus, Kyoto University; and of counsel, Matsuo & Kosugi, Tokyo.

VERONICA L. TAYLOR is the Dan Fenno Henderson Professor of Law and Director, Asian Law Center, University of Washington School of Law.

TAKASHI UCHIDA is Professor of Law, The University of Tokyo.

KATSUYA UGA is Professor of Law, The University of Tokyo.

RYŪICHI YAMAKAWA is Professor of Law, Keio University Law School.

E. ANTHONY ZALOOM is of counsel, Mori Hamada & Matsumoto, Tokyo.

Index

ASIAN LAW SERIES

1. *The Constitution of Japan: Its First Twenty Years, 1947–67,* edited by Dan Fenno Henderson
2. *Village "Contracts" in Tokugawa Japan,* by Dan Fenno Henderson
3. *Chinese Family Law and Social Change in Historic and Comparative Perspective,* edited by David C. Buxbaum
4. *Law and Politics in China's Foreign Trade,* edited by Victor H. Li
5. *Patent and Know-how Licensing in Japan and the United States,* edited by Teruo Doi and Warren L. Shattuck
6. *The Constitutional Case Law of Japan: Selected Supreme Court Decisions, 1961–70,* by Hiroshi Itoh and Lawrence Ward Beer
7. *Japan's Commission on the Constitution: The Final Report,* translated and edited by John M. Maki
8. *Service Regulations in Korea: Problems and Recommendations for Feasible Reforms,* by Young Moo Shin
9. *Order and Discipline in China: The Shanghai Mixed Court 1911–27,* by Thomas B. Stephens
10. *The Economic Contract Law of China: Legitimation and Contract Autonomy in the PRC,* by Pitman B. Potter
11. *Japanese Labor Law,* by Kazuo Sugeno, translated by Leo Kanowitz
12. *Constitutional Systems in Late Twentieth Century Asia,* edited by Lawrence W. Beer
13. *Constitutional Case Law of Japan, 1970 through 1990,* edited by Lawrence W. Beer and Hiroshi Itoh
14. *The Limits of the Rule of Law in China,* edited by Karen Turner, James V. Feinerman, and R. Kent Guy
15. *Legal Reform in Taiwan under Japanese Colonial Rule (1895–1945): The Reception of Western Law,* by Tay-sheng Wang
16. *Antitrust in Germany and Japan: The First Fifty Years, 1947–1998,* by John O. Haley
17. *The Great Ming Code / Da Ming lü,* translated and introduced by Jiang Yonglin
18. *Writing and Law in Late Imperial China: Crime, Conflict, and Judgment,* edited by Robert H. Hegel and Katherine Carlitz
19. *Law in Japan: A Turning Point,* edited by Daniel H. Foote

www.ingramcontent.com/pod-product-compliance
Lightning Source LLC
LaVergne TN
LVHW050145080826
844660LV00002B/86

* 9 7 8 0 2 9 5 9 8 7 3 1 6 *